SYSTEMATIC THEOLOGY

DR. NORMAN GEISLER

VOLUME ONE

INTRODUCTION

BIBLE

BETHANY HOUSE
Minneapolis, Minnesota

Systematic Theology, Volume One
Copyright © 2002
Norman L. Geisler

Senior Editor: Steven R. Laube
Managing Editor: Julie Smith
Content Editor: Christopher Soderstrom
Copy Editor: Nancy Renich
Editorial Assistant: Elizabeth Anderson
Art Director: Paul Higdon
Cover and Page Design: Eric Walljasper
Production Manager: LaVonne Downing
Indexing Services: Bruce Tracy

Published by Bethany House Publishers
11400 Hampshire Avenue South
Bloomington, Minnesota 55438
www.bethanyhouse.com

Bethany House Publishers is a Division of
Baker Book House Company, Grand Rapids, Michigan.

Printed in the United States of America
Volume One: Introduction, Bible ISBN 0-7642-2551-0 (Hardcover)
Volume Two: God, Creation ISBN 0-7642-2552-9 (Hardcover)
Volume Three: Sin, Salvation ISBN 0-7642-2553-7 (Hardcover)
Volume Four: Ecclesiology, Eschatology ISBN 0-7642-2554-5 (Hardcover)

Library of Congress Cataloging-in-Publication Data

Geisler, Norman L.
   Systematic theology : volume one : introduction, Bible / by Norman Geisler.
     p. cm.
Includes bibliographical references.
   ISBN 0-7642-2551-0 (alk. paper)
   1. Theology, Doctrinal 2. Bible—Introductions. I. Title.
   BT75.3 .G45 2002
   230'.04624—dc21

2002000913

NORMAN L. GEISLER has taught at the university and graduate level for forty-two years and has spoken, traveled, or debated in all fifty states and in twenty-five countries. He holds a B.A. and M.A. from Wheaton College, a Th.B. from William Tyndale College, and a Ph.D. in philosophy from Loyola University and now serves as President of Southern Evangelical Seminary in Charlotte, North Carolina. He is author or coauthor of more than fifty books and hundreds of articles. His books include:

Who Made God? (Zondervan, 2003)

Systematic Theology, Volume One (Bethany House, 2002)

Systematic Theology, Volume Two (Bethany House, 2003)

Systematic Theology, Volume Three (Bethany House, 2004)

Unshakable Foundations (Bethany House, 2001)

Baker Encyclopedia of Christian Apologetics (Baker, 1999)

Chosen But Free (Bethany House, 1999, 2001)

Legislating Morality (Bethany House, 1998)

Creating God in the Image of Man? (Bethany House, 1997)

When Cultists Ask (Baker, 1997)

Love Is Always Right (Thomas Nelson, 1996)

Roman Catholics and Evangelicals (Baker, 1995)

In Defense of the Resurrection (revised, Witness, Inc., 1993)

Answering Islam (Baker, 1993)

When Critics Ask (Baker, 1992)

Miracles and the Modern Mind (Baker, 1992)

Matters of Life and Death (Baker, 1991)

Thomas Aquinas: An Evangelical Appraisal (Baker, 1991)

In Defense of the Resurrection (Quest, 1991)

The Life and Death Debate (Greenwood, 1990)

When Skeptics Ask (Baker, 1990)

Gambling: A Bad Bet (Fleming H. Revell, 1990)

Come Let Us Reason (Baker, 1990)

Apologetics in the New Age (Baker, 1990)

The Battle for the Resurrection (Thomas Nelson, 1989)

Christian Ethics (Baker, 1989)

The Infiltration of the New Age (Tyndale, 1989)

Knowing the Truth About Creation (Servant, 1989)

Worlds Apart (Baker, 1989)

Christian Apologetics (Baker, 1988)

Signs and Wonders (Tyndale, 1988)

Philosophy of Religion (revised, Baker, 1988)

Introduction to Philosophy (Baker, 1987)

Origin Science (Baker, 1987)

The Reincarnation Sensation (Tyndale, 1986)

A General Introduction to the Bible (revised, Moody Press, 1986)

False Gods of Our Time (Harvest House, 1985)

To Drink or Not to Drink (Quest, 1984)

Explaining Hermeneutics (ICBI, 1983)

Is Man the Measure? (Baker, 1983)

Miracles and Modern Thought (Zondervan, 1982)

What Augustine Says (Baker, 1982)

Decide for Yourself (Zondervan, 1982)

The Creator in the Courtroom—Scopes II (Baker, 1982)

Biblical Errancy (Zondervan, 1981)

Options in Contemporary Christian Ethics (Baker, 1981)

Inerrancy (Zondervan, 1980)

To Understand the Bible, Look for Jesus (Baker, 1979)

The Roots of Evil (Zondervan, 1978)

A Popular Survey of the Old Testament (Baker, 1977)

From God to Us (Moody Press, 1974)

"The culmination and synthesis of decades of teaching and writing by Norm Geisler, this invaluable volume will interest those who enjoy philosophical, historical, and apologetic approaches to theology. Explanations and definitions of key terms make this an accessible text for a wide range of readers, beginning with introductory theology students. Amazing in its breadth and detail, the topics are logically presented in a manner that encourages both learning and dissemination to others. Here is an encyclopedic volume, containing countless gems hidden throughout its reader-friendly text, all available under one cover."

Gary R. Habermas
Professor, Liberty University

"Few modern-day Bible scholars have responded to the objections of critics and skeptics with the skill of Dr. Norman Geisler. Fortunately for us, he has presented the biblical evidence and logical analysis of the issues in a clear, precise way that will serve you well in your own study of biblical doctrines."

Dr. John F. Ankerberg
President, Ankerberg Theological Research Institute

"Great theologians are best when they are outstanding philosophers also. Then, of course, you often cannot fathom what they are saying. Norm Geisler has the unique ability as philosopher and theologian to deal with profound concepts in ways that the common man can easily grasp. Consequently, this systematic theology will not only sit on the desk of the scholar but also of the pastor, and on the coffee table of many a layman."

Dr. Paige Patterson
President, Southeastern Baptist Theological Seminary

"In an age when specialization abounds, Norman Geisler exemplifies that rare and precious ability to bring together the three areas necessary to do systematic theology: detailed philosophical training, facility in the categories of theology, and the ability to exegete the biblical text. I know of no one who brings these skills together better than Geisler, and Volume One, along with the ones to come, is the fruit of a lifetime of labor in these fields. When these skills are combined with Geisler's excellence as a communicator, the result is powerful indeed, and I am delighted that his *Systematic Theology* is finally available to the church."

J. P. Moreland
Distinguished Professor of Philosophy, Talbot School of Theology, Biola University

"Having greatly benefited from studying theology under Norman Geisler some twenty years ago, I have for a long time yearned to see his vast theological research compiled in a systematic theology. With the publication of this first volume, my wish is becoming reality! For those who value careful thinking, tight logic, fair evaluation, and keen theological insights, this systematic theology is 'must reading.'"

Dr. Ron Rhodes
President, Reasoning From the Scriptures Ministries

VOLUME ONE

PART ONE: INTRODUCTION

PART TWO: BIBLE

Three persons deserve special recognition for the final state of this volume.

First, my wife, Barbara, has provided detailed and meticulous proofing of the entire manuscript.

Likewise, my assistant, Jason Reed, has done voluminous research for citations from the great teachers of the church.

Finally, Christopher Soderstrom of Bethany House has performed dedicated, gracious, and extensive editing of every page.

To each, I express my sincere and heartfelt thanks.

TABLE OF CONTENTS

VOLUME ONE: INTRODUCTION AND BIBLE

Part One: Introduction (Prolegomena)

Part Two: Bible (Bibliology)

I. Section One: Biblical

II. Section Two: Historical

Appendices

PART ONE

INTRODUCTION (PROLEGOMENA)

CHAPTER ONE

INTRODUCTION

THEOLOGICAL DEFINITIONS

P*rolegomena* (lit.: *pro*, "before," and *lego*, "speak") is the introduction to theology. It deals with the necessary preconditions for doing systematic theology.

Theology (lit.: *theos*, "God," and *logos*, "reason" or "discourse") is a rational discourse about God.

Evangelical theology is defined here as a discourse about God that maintains that there are certain essential Christian beliefs.[1] These include, but are not necessarily limited to,[2] the infallibility and inerrancy of the Bible alone,[3] the tri-unity of God, the virgin birth of Christ, the deity of Christ, the all-sufficiency of Christ's atoning sacrifice for sin, the physical and miraculous resurrection of Christ, the necessity of salvation by faith alone through God's grace alone based on the work of Christ alone, the physical bodily return of Christ to earth, the eternal conscious bliss of the saved, and the eternal conscious punishment of the unsaved.[4]

Theology is divided into several categories:

---

[1]Not all of these are necessary for *traditional* orthodoxy, but they are necessary for a *consistent* orthodoxy. Inerrancy, for example, is not a test for evangelical *authenticity* but for evangelical *consistency*.

[2]The belief in a theistic God and miracles are also fundamental beliefs, as is creation *ex nihilo* ("out of nothing").

[3]Traditional Roman Catholics deny the "alone" in these statements.

[4]Recently a number of individuals and groups calling themselves "evangelicals" have denied eternal conscious punishment of the wicked in favor of annihilationism. Historically, however, eternal conscious punishment has been affirmed by orthodox theology, from the earliest time down through the Reformation into the modern era (see W. G. T. Shedd, *Eternal Punishment*).

(1) *Biblical Theology* is a study of the biblical basis for theology.

(2) *Historical Theology* is a discussion of the theology of the great theologians of the Christian church.

(3) *Systematic Theology* is an attempt to construct a comprehensive and consistent whole out of *all* revelation from God, whether special (biblical) or general (natural) revelation (see chapter 4).

Apologetics (Gk: *apologia*, "defense") deals with the protection of Christian theology from external attacks. *Polemics* defends orthodox Christianity from internal doctrinal threats such as heresy and aberrant teachings.

THE BASIC DIVISIONS OF SYSTEMATIC THEOLOGY

Systematic theology is generally divided into the following categories: (1) Prolegomena (Introduction); (2) Bibliology (Gk: *biblios*, "Bible"); (3) Theology Proper, the study of God; (4) Anthropology (Gk: pl. *anthropoi*, "human beings"); (5) Harmartiology (Gk: *harmartia*, "sin"); (6) Soteriology (Gk: *soterios*, "salvation"); (7) Ecclesiology (Gk: *ecclesia*, "[the] church"); (8) Eschatology (Gk: *eschatos*, "the last things").

In addition, the study of the Holy Spirit (a subdivision of Theology Proper) is titled Pneumatology (Gk: *pneuma*, "spirit"), and discourses about Christ are called Christology. Theological discussions about demons are designated Demonology, those about Satan are titled Satanology, and the study of angels is labeled Angelology.[5]

THE PRECONDITIONS OF EVANGELICAL THEOLOGY

Evangelical theologians believe the Bible is an infallible, absolutely true communication in human language that came from an infinite, personal, and morally perfect God. This belief presupposes that many things are true—most of which are challenged by our current culture. Evangelicalism presupposes that there is a theistic God (the metaphysical precondition—chapter 2) who created the world and can miraculously intervene in it (the supernatural precondition—chapter 3); a God who has revealed Himself in both general and special revelation (the revelational precondition—chapter 4); which revelation is subject to the laws of logic (the rational precondition—chapter 5) and which contains objectively meaningful statements (the semantical precondition—chapter 6) that are true objectively (the epistemological precondition—chapter 7) and true exclusively (the oppositional precondition—chapter 8); which statements can be properly understood in analogous language (the linguistic precondition—chapter 9), the meaning and truth of which can be understood objectively (the

---

[5]Subdivisions (3) through (8), as well as all corollary topics, will be published in subsequent volumes.

hermeneutical precondition—chapter 10), including those elements relating to historical events (the historical precondition—chapter 11); and which revelation can be systematized by a complete and comprehensive theological method (the methodological precondition—chapter 12).

Foreboding as this project may seem, these are the preconditions necessary to make evangelical theology a possibility. Each one will be treated successively in the following chapters.

THE IMPORTANCE OF PRECONDITIONS

A precondition makes possible what is based on it. For example, the preconditions for two human beings communicating with each other minimally include:

(1) There is a mind capable of sending a message.
(2) There is a mind capable of receiving a message.
(3) There is a common mode of communication (like a language) shared by both persons.

Without these necessary preconditions communication could not take place.

Likewise, without the above stated preconditions, evangelical systematic theology is not possible. One of the most important preconditions is the metaphysical one, theism, which is discussed in the next chapter.

CHAPTER TWO

GOD: THE METAPHYSICAL PRECONDITION

THE NATURE AND IMPORTANCE OF METAPHYSICS

The existence of a theistic God is the foundation of Christian theology. If the God of traditional Christian theism does not exist, then logically evangelical theology crumbles. Attempting to construct a systematic evangelical theology without the superstructure of traditional theism is like trying to put together a house without a frame.

The Significance of Metaphysics

Theism is the metaphysical precondition for evangelical theology. It is fundamental to all else, being the framework within which everything else has meaning. It makes no sense to speak about the Bible being the Word of God unless there is a God. Likewise, it is meaningless to talk about Christ as the Son of God unless there is a God who can have a Son. And miracles as special acts of God are not possible unless there is a God who can perform these special acts. In fact everything in evangelical theology is based on this metaphysical foundation of theism.

The Definition of Metaphysics

Metaphysics (lit.: *meta*, "beyond"; *physics*, "the physical") is the study of being or reality. It is the study of being as being, as opposed to studying being as physical (physics) or being as mathematical (mathematics). "Metaphysics" is often used interchangeably with "ontology" (lit.: *ontos*, "being"; *logos*, "study of").

Evangelical Theology Entails Metaphysical Theism

Evangelical theology implies a certain understanding of reality, and there are many views about the world that are incompatible with the claims of evangelical thought. For example, evangelicalism believes that God exists beyond this world ("world" in this case meaning "the whole created universe") and that He brought this world into existence. It also embraces the belief that this God is one eternal, infinite, absolutely perfect, personal Being. The name given for this view that God created everything else that exists is theism (God created all), as opposed to atheism (there is no God at all) and pantheism (God is all). All other worldviews (including pantheism, deism, finite godism, and polytheism) are incompatible with theism. If theism is true, all non-theisms are false, since the opposite of true is false (see chapter 8).

THEISM AND THE OPPOSING WORLDVIEWS

There are seven major worldviews, and each one is different from the others. With one exception (pantheism/polytheism), no one can consistently believe in more than one worldview because the central premises of each are opposed by those of the others. Logically, only one worldview can be true; the others must be false. The seven major worldviews are as follows: theism, atheism, pantheism, panentheism, deism, finite godism, and polytheism.[1]

Theism: An Infinite Personal God Exists Both Beyond and in the Universe

Theism is the worldview that says the physical universe is not all there is. There is an infinite, personal God beyond the universe who created it, sustains it, and can act within it in a supernatural way. He is both "out there" and "in here"; transcendent and immanent.[2] This is the view represented by traditional Judaism, Christianity, and Islam.

Atheism: No God Exists Beyond or in the Universe

Atheism claims that only the physical universe exists; there is no God *anywhere*. The universe (or cosmos) is all there is or ever will be, and it is self-sustaining. Some of the more famous atheists were Karl Marx, Friedrich Nietzsche, and Jean-Paul Sartre.

---

[1]For a further discussion of each worldview, see Norman Geisler, *Baker Encyclopedia of Christian Apologetics* (*BECA*).

[2]Transcendence is here defined as God's presence beyond the universe; immanence is here defined as the indwelling presence of God in the universe.

Pantheism: God Is the Universe (the All)

For the pantheist there is no Creator beyond the universe; rather, Creator and creation are two different ways of viewing one reality. God *is* the universe (or the All) and the universe is God; there is, ultimately, only one reality. Pantheism is represented by certain forms of Hinduism, Zen Buddhism, Christian Science, and most New Age religions.

Before describing the other worldviews, it will be profitable to contrast the three already mentioned: Pantheism affirms God is All, atheism claims there is no God at all, and theism declares that God created all. In pantheism, all is mind. According to atheism, all is matter. But theism asserts that both mind and matter exist. Indeed, while the atheist believes that matter produced mind, the theist believes that Mind (God) made matter.

Pan-en-theism: God Is in the Universe

Panentheism says God is in the universe as a mind is in a body; the universe is God's "body." But there is another "pole" to God other than the actual physical universe. (For this reason, panentheism is also called *bipolar theism.*) This other pole is God's eternal and infinite potential beyond the actual physical universe. And since panentheism holds that God is in the constant process of changing, it is also known as *process theology.* This view is represented by Alfred North Whitehead, Charles Hartshorne, and Schubert Ogden.

Deism: God Is Beyond the Universe, But Not in It

Deism is like theism minus miracles. It says God is transcendent over the universe but not immanent in the world, certainly not supernaturally. In common with atheism, it holds a naturalistic view of the operation of the world, yet in common with theism, it believes the origin of the world is a Creator. In brief, God made the world, but He does not involve Himself with it. The Creator wound up creation like a clock, and ever since it has run on its own. In contrast to pantheism, which negates God's transcendence in favor of His immanence, deism negates God's immanence in favor of His transcendence. Deism is represented by such thinkers as François Voltaire, Thomas Jefferson, and Thomas Paine.

Finite Godism: A Finite God Exists Beyond and in the Universe

Finite godism is like theism, only the god beyond the universe and active in it is not infinite but is limited in his nature and power. Like the deist, the finite godist generally accepts the creation of the universe but denies any miraculous intervention in it. Often, God's apparent inability to overcome evil is given as a reason for believing He is limited in power. John Stuart Mill, William James, and Peter Bertocci are examples of adherents to this worldview.

Polytheism: There Are Many Gods Beyond the World and in It

Polytheism is the belief that there are many finite gods. The polytheist denies any infinite God beyond the world, such as in theism; however, the gods are active in the world, in contrast to deism. And in contrast to finite godism, the polytheist believes in a plurality of finite gods, often each having its own domain. The belief that one finite god is chief over all the others (such as Jupiter for the Romans) is a subview of polytheism called *henotheism*. Chief representatives of polytheism are the ancient Greeks, the Mormons, and the neo-pagans (such as Wiccans).

Clearly, if theism is true, then all six forms of non-theism are false. God cannot be, for instance, both infinite and finite, or personal and impersonal, or beyond the universe and not beyond the universe, or able to perform miracles and not able to perform miracles, or unchanging and changing.

PLURALISM VS. MONISM

Pluralism,[3] as opposed to monism, holds that more than one being exists (e.g., God and creatures). While monism asserts that all reality is one—that there is only one being—pluralism, by contrast, believes that there are many beings in existence: God is an infinite Being, and He created many finite beings that are not identical to Him, though they are dependent on Him.

Thus, to be successful, evangelical theology must defend philosophical (or ontological) pluralism against monism. Since theism affirms there is at least one finite being that exists along with only one infinite Being, it follows that if theism is true then so is pluralism. However, it does not follow that theism is true simply because pluralism is true, since there are other forms of pluralism (e.g., deism, finite godism, and polytheism).

The Argument for Monism

If one is to defend pluralism, to say nothing of theism, there is a fundamental argument for monism that must be answered. This argument was stated by the early Greek philosopher Parmenides (b. 515 B.C.), who presented as follows (Parmenides, *P*): There cannot be more than one thing (absolute monism), for if there were two things, they would have to differ.

---

[3]Actually, there are two basic metaphysical preconditions entailed in evangelical theology: theism and pluralism.

For things to differ, they must differ either by being or by nonbeing. But since being is that which makes them identical, they cannot differ by being. Nor, on the other hand, can they differ by nonbeing, for nonbeing is nothing, and to differ by nothing is not to differ at all. Hence, there cannot be a plurality of beings but only one single indivisible being—a rigid monism.

The Alternatives to Monism

The alternatives to Parmenides are few and far between for pluralists who wish to escape the clutches of monism. Basically, there are four other options.

The first two forms of pluralism, which we will call atomism and platonism, affirm that the many beings differ *by nonbeing.* The last two views, called aristotelianism and thomism, hold that the many beings differ *in their being.*

Atomism: Things Differ by Absolute Nonbeing

The ancient atomists, such as Leucippus (fl. c. fifth century B.C.) and Democritus (c. 460–370 B.C.), contended that the principle separating one being (one atom) from another is absolutely nothing (i.e., nonbeing). They called this the Void. For them, being is full and nonbeing is empty. The atoms, which do not differ at all in their essence, are separated by the different space they occupy in the Void (empty space). This difference, then, is merely extrinsic; there is no intrinsic difference in the atoms (beings).[4]

In short, the atomists' response to Parmenides was that there are many beings (atoms) that differ by nonbeing. Each being occupies a different space in the Void that, in itself, is absolutely nothing (empty space).

Of course, this is scarcely an adequate answer to Parmenides, since he would simply point out that to differ by absolutely nothing is to have absolutely no difference at all. And to have absolutely no difference is to be absolutely the same. Monism appears to win the day over atomism.

Platonism: Things Differ by Relative Nonbeing

Plato (c. 427–347 B.C.), with the help of Parmenides, struggled with how "the Forms" could differ if they were absolutely simple.[5] Plato believed that all things had an ideal archetype behind them. This Idea (or Form) was the real world. All things in this world of our experience are only "shadows" of the real world by virtue of their participation in this true Form. For exam-

---

[4]For our purposes here, *extrinsic* means "lying outside, not properly belonging to" the nature of a thing, while *intrinsic* is defined as "belonging to the inmost constitution or essential nature of a thing" (*Webster's Third New International Dictionary*).

[5]On this whole question of Plato's later view of the Forms (Teske, *PLD*), his *Parmenides* and *Theaeteus* seem rather to represent a break away from his early theory. He apparently saw the fallacy of the atomistic position (with which his own earlier view of indivisible forms [ideas] behind all things was akin).

ple, each individual human being in this world participates in a universal form of humanness in the world of ideas. Plato later adopted the view that the Forms (or Ideas) are not indivisibly and unrelatedly separated by *absolute* nonbeing but are related by the principle of *relative* nonbeing.

By this principle of relative nonbeing, also called the "other," Plato believed he could have many different forms (beings) and thus avoid monism. Each form differed from other forms in that it was *not* that other form. All determination, in this case, is by negation.

For one example, the sculptor determines what the statue is in relation to the stone by chipping away (negating) what he does not want. Likewise, each form is differentiated from every other form by negation—what it is, is determined by what it is not. For another example, the chair is distinguished from everything else in the room in that it is *not* the table, it is *not* the floor, it is *not* the wall, etc. This does not mean that the chair is absolutely nothing. It is something in itself, but it is nothing in relation to other things. That is, it is not those other things.

Even so, Parmenides would not have been impressed by Plato's attempt to evade monism. He would simply have asked whether there were any differences in the beings themselves. If there were not, then he would have insisted that all these beings (forms) must be identical. For the monist there are not many beings but only one.

Aristotelianism: Things Differ as Simple Beings

Both Plato and the atomist took one horn (the same horn) of the parmenidean dilemma: They tried to differentiate things by nonbeing. But, as we have seen, to differ by nothing is not to differ at all. Aristotle (384–322 B.C.) and Thomas Aquinas (1225–1274) took the other horn of the dilemma: They sought to find a difference in the beings themselves. Both contend that there are many beings that are essentially different. Aristotle held that these beings are metaphysically simple, and Aquinas (see next page) viewed them as metaphysically composite, having an act/potency distinction on the level of pure forms or beings.

Aristotle argued that there is a plurality of forty-seven or fifty-five beings, or unmoved movers, that are separated from one another in their very being (Aristotle, *M*, XII). These beings (movers) caused all the motion in the world, each operating in its own separate cosmic domain. Each was a pure form (being) with no matter (which Aristotle used to differentiate things in this world). This plurality of totally separated substantial forms has no commonness or community of being whatsoever. They cannot be related to one another (Eslick, *RD*, 152–53), and they are completely diverse from one another.

Of course, Parmenides would ask Aristotle just how simple beings can differ in their very being. Things composed of form and matter can differ in that *this* particular matter is different from *that* matter, even though they have the same form. But how do pure forms (beings) differ from each other? They have no principle of differentiation. If there is no difference in their being, then their being is identical. Thus, neither does Aristotle's solution avoid monism.

Thomism: Things Differ As Complex Beings

The fourth pluralistic alternative to parmenidean monism is represented by Thomas Aquinas, who, in common with Aristotle, sought difference within the beings themselves. But unlike Aristotle, who had only simple beings, Aquinas believed that all finite beings are composed *in their very beings*. Only God is an absolutely simple Being, and there can be only one such Being (God). However, there can be other kinds of beings, namely, composed beings. Beings can differ in their very being because there can be *different* kinds of beings (Aquinas, *ST*, 1a.4.1, 3).

God, for example, is an infinite kind of Being; all creatures are finite kinds of beings. God is Pure Actuality (Act); all creatures are composed of actuality (act) and potentiality (potency). Hence, finite things differ from God in that they have a limiting potentiality; He does not. Finite things can differ from each other in whether their potentiality is completely actualized (as in angels) or whether it is being progressively actualized (as in humans).

In all creatures their essence (what-ness) is really distinct from their existence (is-ness). In God, on the other hand, His essence and existence are identical. Aquinas was not the first to make this distinction, but he was the first to make such extensive use of it.

Aquinas argues in his book *On Being and Essence* that existence is something other than essence, except in God, whose essence is His existence. Such a being must be one and unique, since *multiplication of anything is only possible where there is a difference.* But in such a being as God there is no difference. From this it follows necessarily that in everything else, except in this one unique existence, its existence must be one thing and its essence another.

In this way Aquinas provided an answer to the age-old predicament posed by monism. Things do differ in their being because there are different kinds of beings. Parmenides was wrong because he assumed that "being" is always understood univocally (the same way). Aquinas, on the other hand, saw that being is analogous (see chapter 9), being understood in similar but different ways. All beings are the same in that they are all actual; however, finite beings differ from an infinite Being in that they have differing potentialities that have been actualized.

THE SUPERIORITY OF THOMISTIC THEISM[6]

The value of Aquinas's view is made manifest by both its own rationality and the implausibility of its alternatives. Parmenides' position, by contrast,

---

[6]Thomistic theism is also called classical theism, a view shared among Augustine, Anselm, the Reformers, and many modern thinkers, including C. S. Lewis.

does violence to our experience of a differentiated yet interrelated multiplicity of beings. But again, if a rigid monism is unacceptable, it seems there are only four basic pluralistic alternatives.

The atomist attempts to explain multiplicity by affirming that *absolute nonbeing*—the Void—is that which separates one being from another. But surely this answer is insufficient, for as Parmenides painstakingly pointed out, to differ by that which is absolutely nonexistent is not to differ at all. And if there is no real distinction, then there is no distinction in reality at all. All is one.

The platonists tried to use *relative nonbeing* as the principle of differentiation. That is, while admitting that things differ by nonbeing, he argued that nonbeing in some way exists, even though it is "other" than being. That is, differentiation is by negation: One being is distinct from another not by what it is but by what it is not—different not by being but by nonbeing. In other words, the differentiating factor is not within being but is outside of being—it is not real or actual. But nothing that is external to being can be the principle of differentiation within being. And if there is no actual difference within the nature of things, then there is actually no difference between them at all—the old parmenidean dilemma in a different form.

The aristotelian multiplicity of simple, separated substances has no principle of individuation at all.[7] Aristotle calls on neither absolute nonbeing nor relative nonbeing to explain how there can be many *simple*, separate beings. Not only is this view without a principle of differentiation, but as Plotinus noted (*E*, VI.5.9), it is also without any principle of unification. That is, there is nothing to coordinate the separate operations of the many prime movers.

Finally, the thomistic (i.e., following Thomas Aquinas) position on plurality is that multiplicity is possible because there are different kinds of being. This is possible because beings have within them a real distinction in their being between their existence and their essence. That is to say, being is not a homogenous, undifferentiated whole. Rather, created being is a dynamic, *complex* composition of essence and existence. It has the correlative principles of potency and act. The question is not "to be" or "not to be," but "what *kind* of being?"

For Thomas Aquinas things differ from one another by the kind of being or actuality they are. Being is not predicated of things univocally,[8] for then all would be one. Nor is it predicated of things equivocally,[9] for then

---

[7]In the physical world Aristotle used matter as the principle of individuation, but these pure Forms have no matter. Hence, in the metaphysical realm Aristotle had no way to distinguish one being from another.

[8]In this case, *univocal* means "characteristic of or restricted to things of the same nature" (*Webster's Third New International Dictionary*).

[9]*Equivocal* here means "called by the same name but differing in nature or function" (*Webster's Third New International Dictionary*).

all would be totally different and isolated. Rather, being is predicated of things analogically—each essence has being in its own distinct way and is related to others only by analogy. Each thing has its one mode of be-ing. In other words, "essence," the principle of differentiation, is real. It is part of the very being of things; a co-constitutive principle.[10]

In brief, the real distinction within being (Lat. *ens*) between essence (*essentia*) and existence (*esse*) seems to be the only satisfactory answer to the parmenidean problem of unity and plurality. Without an analogy of being (see chapter 9) there is no way to account for multiplicity. In univocity of being, things are either unrelated or identical. As we have seen, if being is taken univocally (instead of analogically), then there can only be one being, for if wherever being is found it means entirely the same thing, then all being is identical (entire sameness leaves no room for any difference in being).

What is more, if being is taken equivocally (as entirely different), then there can be no more than one being, for if *this* is being and everything *else* is totally different from it, then everything else is nonbeing. (This is true because what is totally different from being would be nonbeing.) Seemingly, the only way to avoid the monistic conclusion that follows from either an equivocal or a univocal view of being is to take an analogical view. And the only way being can be analogical is if there is within being both the principle of unification and the principle of differentiation. Aquinas called these, respectively, esse and essentia: Existence (unification) is to essence (differentiation) what actuality is to potentiality. Since finite beings have different potentialities (essences), these finite beings can be differentiated in reality when these potentialities are actualized (or brought into existence) in different kinds of beings.

What is being? *Being is that which is.* How many beings are there? Being can be either simple (Pure Actuality—God) or complex (both actuality and potentiality). There cannot be two absolutely simple beings, since there is nothing in a pure Being by which it could differ from another pure Being.

Of course, a simple Being can (indeed, must) differ from complex beings, since it has no potentiality, as they do. Therefore, there can be only one Being purely and simply, but there are many beings with a mixture of act and potency. Only one *is* Being; everything else *has* being.

In this way Aquinas seemed to provide the only rational answer to monism. Plotinus did attempt to answer the problem by positing an absolute "One" that goes beyond reason and beyond being, but it is self-defeating to reason about what is beyond reason.

---

[10]This is not to say that essence is real prior to its connection to existence or independent of it (a position not held by Aquinas but by Giles of Rome). The reality of essence is in its correlation with existence. Thus an existing essence is real.

THE RATIONAL BASIS FOR THEISM:
THE ALTERNATIVE TO MONISM

Thomas Aquinas's answer for pluralism makes theism *possible*, but only sound arguments for God's existence make theism *viable*. Many such arguments have been offered, while four of them have dominated discussion over the centuries: the cosmological argument, the teleological argument, the ontological argument, and the moral argument.

The Cosmological Argument for God's Existence

The cosmological argument comes in two basic forms: horizontal and vertical. The horizontal argument, known as the kalam (Arabic for "eternal") argument, argues for a Beginner of the universe. The vertical argument reasons to a Sustainer of the universe. One posits an *original* Cause and the other a *current* Cause. The horizontal argument was embraced by Bonaventure (c. 1217–1274), who followed certain Arab philosophers. The vertical argument was championed by Thomas Aquinas.

The Horizontal Form of the Cosmological Argument

The essence of this argument is as follows:

(1) Everything that had a beginning had a cause.
(2) The universe had a beginning.
(3) Therefore, the universe had a Cause.

The first premise ("Everything that had a beginning had a cause") is often taken as self-evident, since to admit otherwise would amount to the ridiculous claim that nothing produces something. Even the infamous skeptic David Hume (1711–1776) confessed, "I never asserted so absurd a proposition as that anything might arise without a cause" (*LDH*, 1:187).

The second premise ("The universe had a beginning") is defended both philosophically and scientifically. Philosophically, it is argued that

(1) An infinite number of moments cannot be traversed.
(2) If there were an infinite number of moments before today, then today would never have come, since an infinite number of moments cannot be traversed.
(3) But today *has* come.
(4) Hence, there were only a finite number of moments before today (i.e., a beginning of time). And everything with a beginning had a Beginner. Therefore, the temporal world had a Beginner (Cause).

The scientific evidence for the world having a beginning comes from the so-called Big Bang view held by most contemporary astronomers. There are several converging lines of evidence that the space-time universe had a beginning. *First,* the universe is running out of usable energy (Second Law of Thermodynamics), and what is running down cannot be eternal (otherwise it would have run down by now). An entity cannot run out of an infinite amount of energy.

Second, the universe is said to be expanding. Thus, when the motion picture of the universe is put into reverse, logically and mathematically it reaches a point where it is nothing (i.e., no space, no time, and no matter). So the universe literally came into being out of nothing. But *nothing cannot produce something.*

Third, the radiation echo given off by the universe, discovered by two Nobel Prize–winning scientists, Arno Allan Penzias and Robert Woodrow Wilson (see Jastrow, *GA,* 14–15), has the identical wavelength of that which would be given off by a gigantic explosion.

Fourth, the large mass of energy resulting from such an explosion and predicted by Big Bang proponents was actually discovered by the Hubble Space Telescope in 1992.

Fifth, Einstein's own theory of general relativity demanded a beginning of time, a view he resisted for years and even defended by a fudge factor he introduced into his argument to avoid it and for which he was later embarrassed (see Heeren and Smoot, *SMG,* 109).

The cumulative philosophical and scientific evidence for an origin of the material universe provides a strong reason to conclude that there must have been a nonphysical originating Cause of the physical universe. Agnostic astronomer Robert Jastrow admits that this is a clearly theistic conclusion ("SCBTF" in *CT,* 17). After reviewing the evidence that the cosmos had a beginning, the British physicist Edmund Whittaker concurred: "It is simpler to postulate creation ex nihilo—divine will constituting nature from nothingness" (cited by Jastrow, *GA,* 111). Jastrow concludes, "That there are what I or anyone would call supernatural forces at work is now, I think, *a scientifically proven fact*" (Jastrow, "SCBTF" in *CT,* 15, 18, emphasis added).

The Vertical Form of the Cosmological Argument

The horizontal form of the cosmological argument argues from the *past* origin of the cosmos to an Original (First) Cause of it. By contrast, the vertical form of the cosmological argument begins with the *present* contingent existence of the cosmos and insists there must be a current Necessary Being causing it. Both are causal arguments and both begin with an existing cosmos. However, the horizontal argument starts with a universe that had a *beginning* (long ago), and the second with a universe that has *being* (right now). The former stresses originating causality, and the latter focuses on conserving causality. The first argues to a *First Cause* (back then), and the second argues to a *Necessary Cause* (at present).

The vertical cosmological argument was stated in several ways by

Thomas Aquinas (*ST*, 1.2.3). Two forms of it will illustrate the point: the argument from contingency and the argument from change.

The argument from contingency begins with the fact that at least one *contingent* being exists; that is, a being that exists but *can* not exist. A *Necessary* Being is one that exists but *cannot* not exist. The argument goes like this:

(1) Whatever exists but can/could not exist needs a cause for its existence, since the mere possibility of existence does not explain why something exists. The mere possibility for something is nothing (i.e., no-thing).
(2) But *nothing* cannot produce *something.*
(3) Therefore, something necessarily exists as the ground for everything that does exist but *can* not exist. In short, it is a violation of the principle of causality to say that a contingent being can account for its own existence.

Another way to put this form of the vertical argument is to note that if something contingent exists, then a Necessary Being must exist:

(1) If everything were contingent, then it would be possible that nothing existed.
(2) But something does exist (e.g., I do), and its existence is undeniable, for I have to exist in order to be able to affirm that I do not exist.
(3) Thus, if some contingent being now exists, a Necessary Being must now exist, otherwise there would be no ground for the existence of this contingent being.

The argument from change, another form of the vertical cosmological argument, begins with the fact that there are changing beings:

(1) Whatever changes passes from a state of potentiality (potency) for that change to a state of being actualized (act). That is, all changing beings have act(uality) and potency in their very being. If not, then all change would involve annihilation and re-creation, which is impossible without a Cause, since nothing cannot produce something.
(2) But no potentiality can actualize itself, any more than the potential for steel to become a skyscraper can actualize itself into a skyscraper.
(3) If no potency can actualize itself, and yet at least one being is actualized (e.g., me), then ultimately there must be something that is Pure Actuality (with no potentiality), otherwise there would be no ground for why something now exists that has the potential not to exist.

This form of the vertical cosmological argument addresses the impossibility of an infinite regress of beings that are composed of act and potency. It points out that the very first Being beneath a changing being (with act and potency) *cannot* be another being with act and potency, for what does not account for its own existence certainly cannot account for another's existence. To say it could is like arguing that one paratrooper whose chute did not open can hold up another whose chute did not open. And adding more paratroopers whose chutes do not open does not help the problem; it compounds it.

Another way to put the impossibility of an infinite regress of causes of the present existence of a changing being (with act and potency) is to point out that in an infinite regress of such causes at least one cause must *be causing*, since it is admitted that causing is occurring. Yet in an infinite series every cause *is being caused*, for if one were not being caused, then we have arrived at an *Uncaused Cause* (which scientists desire to avoid). One cause must be uncaused, for if every cause in an infinite series is being caused and at least one cause is causing, then that cause is *self-caused*. However, a self-caused being is impossible, since a cause is ontologically (see page 34), if not chronologically, prior to its effect, and something cannot be prior to itself.

Another form of the vertical cosmological argument begins with the *present dependence of every part of the universe*. Briefly stated:

(1) Every part of the universe is right now dependent for its existence.
(2) If every part is right now dependent for its existence, then the whole universe must also be right now dependent for its existence.
(3) Therefore, the whole universe is dependent right now for its existence on some Independent Being beyond itself.

In response, critics argue that the second premise commits the fallacy of composition. That every piece of a mosaic is square does not mean the whole mosaic is square. Also, putting two triangles together does not necessarily make another triangle; it may make a square. The whole may (and sometimes does) have a characteristic not possessed by the parts.

Defenders of the vertical form of the cosmological argument are quick to note that sometimes there is a necessary connection between the parts and the whole. For example, if every piece of a floor is oak, then the whole floor is oak. If every tile in the kitchen is yellow, then the whole floor is yellow. This is true because it is of *the very nature of* patches of yellow tile that when you put more like patches of yellow tile together, you still have a patch of yellow. And while putting two triangles together does not necessarily make another triangle, nevertheless, putting two triangles together will necessarily make another geometric figure. Why? Because it is of the very nature of geometric figures that when they are combined they still form a geometric figure.

Likewise, *it is of the very nature of dependent beings that when you put more of them together, you still have dependent beings.* If one thing is dependent for its being, then another dependent being can no more hold it up than adding more links to a chain will hold it up if there is no peg holding up the whole chain.

In response, some critics argue that the whole is greater than the parts. Therefore, while the parts are dependent, the whole universe is not. However, either the sum of the parts is *equal to* the whole or it is *more than* the whole. If the whole universe is equal to its parts, then the whole must be dependent just like the parts are.[11] If, on the other hand, the whole universe is more than the parts and would not vanish were the parts all destroyed, then the whole universe is the equivalent of God, for it is an uncaused, independent, eternal, and necessary Being on which everything in the entire universe depends for its existence.

The Teleological Argument for God's Existence

There are many forms of the teleological argument, the most famous of which derives from William Paley (1743–1805), who used the watchmaker analogy. Since every watch has a maker, and since the universe is exceedingly more complex in its operation than a watch, it follows that there must be a Universe Maker. In brief, the teleological argument reasons from design to an Intelligent Designer:

(1) All designs imply a designer.
(2) There is great design in the universe.
(3) Therefore, there must have been a Great Designer of the universe.

The first premise we know from experience; on any occasion that we see a complex design, we know by previous experience that it came from the mind of a designer. Watches imply watchmakers; buildings imply architects; paintings imply artists; and coded messages imply an intelligent sender. We know this to be true because we observe it happening over and over.

Also, the greater the design, the greater the designer.[12] A thousand monkeys sitting at typewriters for millions of years would never produce *Hamlet.* But Shakespeare did it on the first try. The more complex the design, the greater the intelligence required to produce it.

It is important to note here that by "complex design" is meant specified

---

[11]Proof of this is that if all the parts are taken away, the whole would vanish too. Thus, the whole universe must be contingent also.

[12]It begs the question to point out that beavers make dams, since this is taken by creationists as evidence that an intelligent Creator programmed this ability into beavers. Computers can produce amazing order and design but only because they were programmed by an intelligent being to do so.

complexity. A crystal, for example, has specificity but not complexity; like a snowflake, it has the same basic patterns repeated over and over. Random polymers,[13] on the other hand, have complexity but not specificity.[14] A living cell, however, has both specificity and complexity.

The kind of complexity found in a living cell is the same kind of complexity that is found in a human language; that is to say, the letter sequence in the four-letter genetic alphabet is identical to that in a written language. And the amount of specified complex information in a simple one-celled animal is greater than that found in *Webster's Unabridged Dictionary*. As a result, believing that life occurred without an intelligent cause is like believing that *Webster's Unabridged* resulted from an explosion in a print shop.

Michael Behe's excellent book *Darwin's Black Box* provides from the nature of a living cell strong evidence that it could not have originated by anything but intelligent design. The cell represents irreducible complexity, and it cannot be accounted for via the incremental changes called for by evolution (Behe, *DBB*, all). Even Charles Darwin (1809–1882) admitted, "If it could be demonstrated that any complex organ existed which could not possibly have been formed by numerous, successive, slight modifications, my theory would absolutely break down" (Darwin, *OOS*, 6th ed., 154). Even evolutionist Richard Dawkins agrees:

> Evolution is very possibly not, in actual fact, always gradual. But it must be gradual when it is being used to explain the coming into existence of complicated, apparently designed objects, like eyes. For if it is not gradual in these cases, it ceases to have any explanatory power at all. Without gradualness in these cases, we are back to miracle, which is a synonym for the total absence of [naturalistic] explanation. (Dawkins, *BW*, 83.)

But Behe provides numerous examples of irreducible complexity that cannot evolve in small steps. He concludes,

> No one at Harvard University, no one at the National Institutes of Health, no member of the National Academy of Sciences, no Nobel prize winner—no one at all can give a detailed account of how the cilium, or vision, or blood clotting, or any complex biochemical process might have developed in a Darwinian fashion. But we are here. All these things got here somehow; if not in a Darwinian fashion, then how? (Behe, *DBB*, 187.)
>
> Other examples of irreducible complexity abound, including aspects of DNA reduplication, electron transport, telomere synthesis, photosynthesis, transcription regulation, and more. . . . [Hence,] life on earth at

---

[13]Polymers are chemical compounds or mixtures of compounds that generally consist of repeating structural units.

[14]For something to have specificity is for it to have characteristics that are peculiar only to itself or to its group of organisms.

its most fundamental level, in its most critical components, is the product of intelligent activity (ibid., 160, 193).

Behe adds,

> The conclusion of intelligent design flows naturally from the data itself—not from sacred books or sectarian beliefs. Inferring that biochemical systems were designed by an intelligent agent is a humdrum process that requires no new principles of logic or science.... [Thus,] the result of these cumulative efforts to investigate the cell—to investigate life at the molecular level—is a loud, clear, piercing cry of "design!" The result is so unambiguous and so significant that it must be ranked as one of the greatest achievements in the history of science. The discovery rivals those of Newton and Einstein (ibid., 232–33).

The late agnostic astronomer Carl Sagan (1934–1996) unwittingly provided a powerful example of incredible design. He notes that the genetic information in the human brain expressed in bits is probably comparable to the total number of connections among neurons—about a hundred trillion, 10^{14} bits.

> If written out in English, say, that information would fill some twenty million volumes, as many as in the world's largest libraries. The equivalent of twenty million books is inside the head of every one of us. The brain is a very big place in a very small space.

Sagan went on to note that "the neurochemistry of the brain is astonishingly busy, the circuitry of a machine more wonderful than any devised by humans" (Sagan, *C*, 278). But if this is so, then why does the human brain not need an intelligent Creator, such as those wonderful machines (like computers) devised by humans?

Another support for the teleological argument comes from the *anthropic principle*, which states that from its very inception the universe was fine-tuned for the emergence of human life (see Barrow, *ACP*). That is, the universe intricately preadapted for the arrival of human life. If the delicate balance had been off in the least, then life would not have been possible.

For example, oxygen comprises 21 percent of the atmosphere. If it were 25 percent, fires would erupt, and if only 15 percent, humans would suffocate. If the gravitational force were altered by merely one part in ten to the fortieth power (ten followed by forty zeroes), the sun would not exist and the moon would crash into the earth or veer off into space (Heeren, *SMG*, 196). If the centrifugal force of planetary movement did not precisely balance the gravitational forces, nothing could be held in orbit around the sun. If the universe were expanding at a rate one-millionth more slowly than it is, the temperature on earth would be 10,000 degrees Celsius. If

Jupiter were not in its current order, the earth would be bombarded with space material. If the earth's crust were thicker, too much oxygen would be transmitted to it to support life. If it were thinner, volcanic and tectonic activity would make life untenable. And if the rotation of the earth took longer than twenty-four hours, temperature differences between night and day would be too great (see Ross, *FG*).

Again, Robert Jastrow sums up the implications: "The anthropic principle . . . seems to say that science itself has proven as a hard fact, that this universe was made, was designed, for man to live in. *It's a very theistic result*" (Jastrow, *SCBTF*, 17, emphasis added). Former atheistic astronomer Alan Sandage came to the same result:

> The world is too complicated in all of its parts to be due to chance alone. I am convinced that the existence of life on earth with all its order in each of its organisms is simply too well put together. . . . The more one learns of biochemistry, the more unbelievable it becomes unless there is some kind of organizing principle—an architect for believers. . . . (Sandage, "SRRB" in *T*, 54.)

The great Albert Einstein (1879–1955) likewise declared that "*the harmony of natural law . . . reveals an intelligence of such superiority that, compared with it, all systematic thinking and acting of human beings is an utterly insignificant reflection*" (Einstein, *IO—WISI*, 40, emphasis added).

The Ontological Argument for God's Existence

"Ontological" comes from the Greek word *ontos* ("being"). This is the argument from the *idea* of a Perfect or Necessary Being to the *actual existence* of such a Being. The first philosopher known to develop the ontological argument (though Immanuel Kant [1724–1804] was the first to call it this) was Anselm (1033–1109).

There are two forms of the argument. One derives from the idea of a Perfect Being and the other from the idea of a Necessary Being. These are sometimes called Anselm A and Anselm B, respectively.

The First Form of the Ontological Argument

According to this statement of the argument, the mere concept of God as an absolutely perfect Being demands that He exist. Briefly put:

(1) God is by definition an absolutely perfect Being.
(2) Existence is a perfection.
(3) Therefore, God must exist. If God did not exist, then he would be lacking one perfection, namely, existence. But if God lacked any perfection, then He would not be absolutely perfect. And God is *by definition* an absolutely perfect Being. Therefore, an absolutely perfect Being (God) must exist.

Since the time of Immanuel Kant it has been widely accepted that this form of the ontological argument is invalid because *existence is not a perfection.* It is argued that existence adds nothing to the concept of a thing; it merely gives a concrete instance of it. The dollar in my mind can have exactly the same properties or characteristics as the one in my wallet. The only difference is that I have a concrete example of the latter.

Kant's critique of the first form of the ontological argument is penetrating and widely embraced. There is, however, a second form that is not subject to this criticism.

The Second Form of the Ontological Argument

In his response to the monk Gaunilo (fl. c. eleventh century), who opposed the argument, Anselm insisted that the very concept of a Necessary Being demands His existence. It can be stated this way:

(1) If God exists, we must conceive of Him as a Necessary Being;
(2) but by definition, a Necessary Being cannot not exist;
(3) therefore, if a Necessary Being can exist, then it must exist.

Since there appears to be no contradiction to the idea of a Necessary Being, it would seem to follow that one must exist, for the very idea of a Necessary Being demands that it must exist—if it did not exist, then it would not be a necessary *existence.*

Critics point to a different problem with this form of the ontological syllogism.[15] It's like saying, "*If* there are triangles, then they must have three sides." Of course, there may not be any triangles. So the argument never really gets past that initial "if"; it never proves the big question that it claims to answer. It *assumes,* but does not *prove,* the existence of a Necessary Being, merely asserting that if a Necessary Being exists—and that is the open question—then it must exist necessarily, for this is the only way a Necessary Being can exist.

Some have further refined the argument by adding that a state of total nothingness is not logically possible, since our own existence is undeniable. And if something exists, then something else must exist (i.e., the Necessary Being). However, in this form it is no longer an ontological argument, since it begins with something that exists and reasons to something that must exist.

Most theists do not believe the ontological argument as such is sufficient in and of itself to prove the existence of God. This is not to say it cannot be useful. While the ontological argument cannot prove God's *existence,* it can prove certain things about His *nature,* if God does exist. For example, it

---

[15]Properly speaking, a syllogism is a deductive scheme (see chapter 5) of a formal arrangement consisting of a major and a minor premise and a conclusion (*Webster's Third New International Dictionary*).

shows that if God exists at all, then He must exist necessarily. He cannot cease to exist, and He cannot exist contingently.

The Moral Argument for God's Existence

The roots of the moral argument for God are found in Romans 2:12–15, where the apostle Paul speaks of humankind being without excuse because there is "a law written on their hearts." In the last 250 years this argument has been stated in various ways; the most popular form emanates from C. S. Lewis (1898–1963) in the first part of his popular book *Mere Christianity*. The heart of the argument follows this basic structure:

(1) Moral law implies a Moral Lawgiver.
(2) There is an objective moral law.
(3) Therefore, there is an objective Moral Lawgiver.

The first premise is self-evident. A moral law is a prescription, and *prescriptions come only from prescribers*. Unlike the laws of nature (which are only *descriptive*), moral laws are *prescriptive*: Moral laws don't describe what *is*; they prescribe what *ought to be*. They are not simply a description of the way people *do* behave but are imperatives as to how they *should* behave.

The weight of the moral argument for God's existence rests on the second premise—that there is an objective moral law. That is, there is a moral law not just prescribed *by* humans but also prescribed *for* humans. The question is whether there is evidence that there is a universal, objective prescription that is binding on *all* humans.

The evidence for an objective moral law is strong; it is implied in moral judgments that we make, such as, "The world is getting better (or worse)." How can we know this unless there is some standard beyond the world by which we can measure it? Likewise, statements like "Hitler was wrong" lose their intended significance if they are merely a matter of opinion or are culturally relative. But if Hitler was really (objectively) wrong, then there is a moral law beyond all of us by which we are all bound. And if there is such an objective moral law beyond all of us, then there is a Moral Lawgiver (God).

C. S. Lewis effectively answers typical objections to this moral argument as paraphrased in the following text (see Lewis, *MC*, part 1).

This Moral Law Is Not Herd Instinct

What we call the moral law cannot be the result of herd instinct[16] or else the stronger impulse in us would always win. It does not. Furthermore, we

---

[16]Herd instinct is "an inherent tendency to congregate or to react in unison; a theoretical human instinct toward gregariousness and conformity" (*Webster's Third New International Dictionary*).

would always act *from* our instinct rather than *for* it in order to bolster it (e.g., to help someone in trouble) as we only sometimes do. Finally, if the moral law were only herd instinct, then instincts would always be right, but they are not. Even love and patriotism are sometimes wrong.

This Moral Law Cannot Be Social Convention

Not everything learned *through* society is *based* on social convention (e.g., math or logic), so neither is the moral law merely a societal norm. Evidence of this is that the same basic moral laws can be found in virtually every society, past and present. Furthermore, judgments about social progress would not be possible if society were the basis of the judgments.

This Moral Law Is Different From the Laws of Nature

The moral law is not to be identified with the laws of nature because the latter are descriptive (are), not prescriptive (ought) as moral laws are. Indeed, factually convenient situations (the way it *is*) can be morally wrong and vice versa. For example, someone who tries to trip me and fails is in the wrong, while someone who accidentally trips me is not.

The Moral Law Is Not Human Fancy

Neither can the moral law be mere human fancy, because we cannot get rid of it even when we would sometimes like to do so. We did not create it; it is clearly impressed upon us from without. And if it were fancy, then all value judgments would be meaningless, including "Murder is wrong" and "Racism is wrong."

But if the moral law is neither a description nor a merely human prescription, then it must be a moral prescription from a Moral Prescriber who is beyond us. As Lewis notes, this Moral Lawgiver is more like mind than nature. He can no more be part of nature than an architect is part of the building he designs.

Injustice Does Not Disprove a Moral Lawgiver

The main objection to an absolutely perfect Moral Lawgiver is the argument from evil in the world. No serious person can fail to recognize that all the murders, rapes, hatred, and cruelty make the world far short of being absolutely perfect. But if the world is imperfect, how can there be an absolutely perfect God? Lewis's answer is simple and to the point: The only way the world could possibly be known to be imperfect is if there is an absolutely perfect standard by which it can be judged to be imperfect. Injustice makes sense only if there is a standard of justice by which something is known to be not just. And absolute injustice is possible only if there is an absolute standard of justice. In his own words Lewis clarifies:

My argument against God was that the universe seemed so cruel and unjust. But how had I got this idea of *just* and *unjust*? A man does not call a line crooked unless he has some idea of a straight line. . . . Thus in the very act of trying to prove that God did not exist—in other words, that the whole of reality was senseless—I found I was forced to assume that one part of reality—namely my idea of justice—was full of sense. Consequently atheism turns out to be too simple. (Lewis, *MC*, 45–46.)

Rather than disproving a morally perfect Being, then, the evil in the world presupposes an absolutely perfect standard. One could raise the question as to whether this Ultimate Lawgiver is all-powerful, but not as to whether He is perfect.

CONCLUSION ABOUT THE THEISTIC ARGUMENTS

Most theists do not rest their whole case for God on any one argument. Indeed, each argument seems to demonstrate a different attribute of God along with His existence. For example, the cosmological argument shows that an infinitely powerful Being exists; the teleological argument reveals that this Being is also super-intelligent; the moral argument establishes that He is morally perfect. And, granted that Something exists, the ontological argument demonstrates that He is a Necessary Being.

Some theists offer other arguments for the existence of God, such as the argument from religious need (see Geisler, "G, EF" in *BECA*) or the argument from religious experience (see Trueblood, *PR*). But the ones detailed above are the standard or classical arguments.

The objection is made that the cosmological argument does not prove a theistic God, such as evangelical Christianity holds. There *are* many other concepts of God besides theism, but these concepts cannot be identified with a theistic God.

Theism vs. Finite Godism

God must be infinite (in contrast with finite godism), since per the cosmological argument *every* finite thing needs a cause. Hence, the Cause of all finite things must not be finite.

Further, the finite universe is made of parts, yet there cannot be an infinite number of parts, since no matter how many parts there are, one more could always be added. And the First Uncaused Cause of the universe cannot be a part or have parts, otherwise He would be caused. Hence, He must be infinite, since only finite things have parts. Since nothing can be added to an infinite, but since all parts can be added to other parts, the Creator of the universe is infinite (and without parts).

Theism vs. Polytheism

The Uncaused Cause of theism is distinct from the many polytheistic gods, for there cannot be more than one unlimited existence as such. *More than the Most is not possible.* Such a Cause is Pure Actuality, and Actuality is unlimited and unique. Only act as conjoined with potency is limited, such as is found in contingent beings (which exist but have the possibility not to exist).

Further, in order to differ, one being would have to lack some characteristic that the other one had. But any being that lacked some characteristic of existence would not be an unlimited perfect existence. In other words, two infinite Beings cannot differ in their potentiality, since they have no potentiality; they are Pure Actuality. And they cannot differ in their actuality, since Actuality as such does not differ from Actuality as such. Hence, they must be identical. So, there is only one Unlimited Cause of all limited existence.

Theism vs. Pantheism

Further, the Uncaused Cause of Theism is not the God of *pantheism.* Pantheism affirms that an unlimited and necessary being exists but denies the reality of limited and finite beings. Theism begins with real, finite, contingent changing being(s), and from this it reasons to a real, infinite, necessary, unchanging being. So the theistic God is not the same as the god of pantheism.

The denial that a human being is finite and changing is self-defeating. A pantheist did not always believe this way; he *came to believe* this way by some process of "enlightenment." But if he went through some changing process, then he is not an unchanging being after all.

Theism vs. Atheism

Nor can the Uncaused Cause of theism be identical with the *material universe,* as many *atheists* believe. As ordinarily conceived, the cosmos or material universe is a limited and spatio-temporal system. It is, for example, subject to the Second Law of Thermodynamics and thus is running down. But an Uncaused Cause is unlimited and not running down.

Space and time imply limitations to a here-and-now kind of existence. But an Uncaused Cause is not limited, and so it cannot be identical to the space-time world. The theistic God is *in* the temporal world as its ground of continuing existence, but He is not *of* the world in that it is limited and He is not.

If, in response, one claimed that the whole of the material universe is not temporal and limited as are the parts, he would only demonstrate what theism claims, for his conclusion is that there exists beyond the contingent world of limited spatio-temporality a whole reality that is eternal, unlimited, and necessary. In other words, it agrees with theism that there is a God beyond the limited, changing world of experience. It is a substitute for God that admits that there is a whole reality that is more than the experienced part of reality and that has all the essential metaphysical attributes of the theistic God.

Theism vs. Panentheism

Neither can the Uncaused Cause of theism be identical with the God of *panentheism,* also known as bipolar theism or process theology. Again, panentheism affirms that God has two poles: an actual pole (which is identified with the changing temporal world) and a potential pole (which is eternal and unchanging). Such a conception of God must be rejected for the following reasons:

For one thing, the conclusion of the cosmological argument demonstrates the need for a God of pure actuality with no potentiality (pole) at all. Further, God cannot be subject to limitations, composition, or spatio-temporality, since He is unlimited in His being. Moreover, the theistic God cannot have poles or aspects, since He is absolutely simple (i.e., uncomposed) and has no duality at all. As Pure Actuality, He is a simple and unlimited existence as such, with no limited pole. A partly limited unlimited existence is a contradiction.

In addition, God cannot be subject to change, for anything that changes must be composed of actuality and potentiality for change. Change is a passing from potentiality to actuality, from what it can be to what it actually becomes. But since existence has no potentiality, it follows that it cannot change. If something changes, it proves thereby that it was not Pure Actuality but possessed some potentiality for the change it underwent. A pure and unlimited actuality cannot change.

Theism vs. Deism

Finally, the conclusion of the cosmological argument, at least the vertical form of it, cannot be a *deistic God,* for a deistic God is not the here-and-now Cause of the universe, as is the theistic God. Since the universe is dependent in its being, it needs something independent on which to depend—at all times. The universe never ceases to be dependent or contingent. Once contingent, always contingent; a contingent being cannot become a Necessary Being, for a Necessary Being cannot come to be or cease to be as a contingent being can. Hence, the God of theism is different from the deistic conception of God. This is to say nothing of the fact that the God of theism can and does perform miracles, and the God of deism does not (see chapter 3).

Further, deism denies that miracles can or do occur. But a God who has created the universe from nothing has already performed the greatest miracle. Hence, such a God cannot be the God of deism.

CONCLUSION

The God of theism can be established by sound reasoning. Further, He is distinct from all other views of God, since there can only be one indivisible, infinite, necessary, absolutely perfect Uncaused Cause of everything else that exists. And since metaphysical theism is a precondition of evangelical theology, the viability of this precondition of evangelicalism is well supported by numerous lines of evidence. To be sure, objections can and have been raised, but none have been successful (see appendix 1).

SOURCES

Anselm. *Basic Writings.*

Aristotle. *Metaphysics*, XII.

Barrow, J. D. *The Anthropic Cosmological Principle.*

Behe, Michael. *Darwin's Black Box.*

Craig, William. *The Kalam Cosmological Argument.*

Darwin, Charles. *On the Origin of Species.*

Dawkins, Richard. *The Blind Watchmaker.*

Einstein, Albert. *Ideals and Opinions—The World As I See It.*

Eslick, L. J. "The Real Distinction," *Modern Schoolman 38* (January 1961).

Findlay, J. N. "Can God's Existence Be Disproved?" in *The Ontological Argument*, Alvin Plantinga, ed.

Flint, Robert. *Agnosticism.*

Garrigou-LaGrange, Reginald. *God: His Existence and His Nature.*

Geisler, Norman. "Anthropic Principle, The" in *BECA.*

———. *Baker Encyclopedia of Christian Apologetics.*

———. "God, Evidence for" in *BECA.*

———. "Worldviews" in *BECA* (see also individual entries on each worldview).

Heeren, Fred, and George Smoot. *Show Me God.*

Hume, David. *Dialogues Concerning Natural Religion.*

———. *The Letters of David Hume.*

Hoyle, Fred, Sir, et al. *Evolution from Space.*

Jastrow, Robert. "A Scientist Caught Between Two Faiths: Interview with Robert Jastrow," *Christianity Today* (August 6, 1982).

———. *God and the Astronomers.*

Kant, Immanuel. *A Critique of Pure Reason.*

Kenny, Anthony. *Five Ways.*

Lewis, C. S. *Mere Christianity.*

Parmenides. *Proem.*

Plato. *Parmenides.*

———. *Sophists.*

———. *Theaeteus.*

Plotinus. *Enneads.*

Ross, Hugh. *The Fingerprints of God.*

Russell, Bertrand. *Why I Am Not a Christian.*

Sagan, Carl. *Cosmos.*

Sandage, Alan. "A Scientist Reflects on Religious Belief" in *Truth* (1985).
Sproul, R. C. *Not a Chance: The Myth of Chance in Modern Science and Cosmology.*
Teske, R. J. "Platos's Later Dialectic," *Modern Schoolman 38* (March 1961).
Thomas Aquinas. *On Being and Essence.*
——. *Summa Theologica.*
Trueblood, Elton. *Philosophy of Religion.*

CHAPTER THREE

MIRACLES:
THE SUPERNATURAL
PRECONDITION

INTRODUCTION TO MIRACLES

Evangelical theology is built on the supernatural. Christ's virgin birth, His miracle-filled ministry, His physical resurrection from the dead, and His bodily ascension into heaven are only some of the numerous miracles essential to biblical Christianity. So much is the supernatural a precondition of orthodox theology that without it historical Christianity would collapse. To quote the apostle Paul, "If Christ has not been raised, our preaching is useless and so is your faith. More than that, we are then found to be false witnesses about God. . . . And if Christ has not been raised, your faith is futile; you are still in your sins. Then those also who have fallen asleep in Christ are lost" (1 Cor. 15:14–18).

Before a miracle can be identified, to say nothing of verified, it must be defined; there is no way to find a miracle unless we know what we're looking for. Theologians have defined miracles in two different ways.

TWO DEFINITIONS OF MIRACLES

Historically, miracles have been defined in either a weak sense or a strong sense. Following Augustine (354–430), some describe a miracle as "a portent [that] is not contrary to nature, but contrary to our knowledge of nature" (*CG*, 21.8).

The problem with this weak view of miracles is that the event might not be supernatural at all; it could simply be a natural event for which the observer, as yet, has no natural explanation. This would mean that all natural anomalies, including meteors, earthquakes, volcanoes, and eclipses, were at one time miracles to everyone—and still are to many people. Certainly, these kinds of so-called miracles would have no apologetic value such as those in the Bible claim to have (Matt. 12:39–40; Mark 2:10–11; John 3:2; Acts 2:22; Heb. 2:3–4; 2 Cor. 12:12).

Others, following Thomas Aquinas, define a miracle in the strong sense of an event that is beyond nature's power to produce and that only a supernatural power (God) can do (*SCG*, Book 3). Again, only in this strong view can miracles be identifiable as acts of God, since in the weak sense they are indistinguishable from unusual natural events. Further, only in the strong sense do miracles have apologetic value, since they occur with direct supernatural intervention. In this sense, *a miracle is a divine intervention into the natural world.* As atheist Antony Flew put it, "A miracle is something which would never have happened had nature, as it were, been left to its own devices" (Flew, "M," in Edwards, ed., *EP*, 346). Natural law describes naturally caused *regularities;* a miracle is a supernaturally caused *singularity.*

DISTINGUISHING MIRACLES FROM NATURAL LAW

In order to explain what is meant by a supernatural act, we need an initial understanding of what is meant by natural law. Natural law is understood as the usual, orderly, and general way that the world operates. By contrast, a miracle is minimally an unusual, irregular, and specific way in which God acts within the world.

Miracles are supernatural but not anti-natural. As the famous physicist Sir George Stokes said, "It may be that the event which we call a miracle was brought about not by the suspension of the laws in ordinary operation, but by the super-addition of something not ordinarily in operation" (*ISBE,* 2063). In other words, if a miracle occurs, it is not a violation or contradiction of the ordinary laws of cause and effect, but rather a *new effect* produced by the introduction of a supernatural cause.

At this point, what we need is a biblical description of miracles. The Bible uses three basic words to describe them: *sign, wonder,* and *power.* A study of the usage of each will help in understanding what is meant by "miracle."

OLD TESTAMENT USAGE
OF THE WORDS *SIGN, WONDER,* AND *POWER*

Each of the words for "miracle" carries with it a connotation of its own. When the meanings of all three are combined, we gain a complete picture of biblical miracles.

Old Testament Usage of the Word *Sign*

Although the Hebrew word for "sign" (*oth*) is sometimes used to refer to natural things, such as stars (Gen. 1:14) or the Sabbath (Ex. 31:13), it usually carries a supernatural significance, namely, as something appointed by God with special assigned meaning.

The first usage of the word *sign* is in the divine prediction given to Moses that Israel would be delivered from Egypt and serve God at Horeb. God promised, "I will be with you. And this will be the sign to you that it is I who have sent you" (Ex. 3:12). When Moses asked God, "What if they do not believe me or listen to me?" (Ex. 4:1) the Lord gave Moses two "signs": His rod turned into a serpent (Ex. 4:3), and his hand became leprous (Ex. 4:6–7). These were given "that they may believe that the LORD, the God of their fathers . . . has appeared to you" (Ex. 4:5).

God said, "If they do not believe you or pay attention to the first miraculous sign, they may believe the second" (Ex. 4:8). Moses "performed the signs before the people, and they believed. And . . . they bowed down and worshiped" (Ex. 4:30–31). In fact, God assured Moses, "I will harden [strengthen] Pharaoh's heart, and . . . multiply my miraculous signs and wonders in Egypt. . . . And the Egyptians will know that I am the LORD when I stretch out my hand against Egypt and bring the Israelites out of it" (Ex. 7:3, 5; cf. 11:9).

Again and again it is repeated that the purpose of these signs is twofold: "By this you will know that I am the LORD" (Ex. 7:17; cf. 9:29–30; 10:1–2) and that these are "my people" (Ex. 3:10; cf. 5:1; 6:7; 11:7). The more the Lord multiplied the signs, the harder Pharaoh's heart became (Ex. 7:3, 9:35; cf. 11:9). But even through this stubborn unbelief God received "glory" (Num. 14:22).

Throughout the rest of the Old Testament there are repeated references to the miraculous "signs" God performed in delivering His people from Egypt. He complained to Moses in the wilderness, saying, "How long will they refuse to believe in me, in spite of all the miraculous signs I have performed among them?" (Num. 14:11; cf. v. 22). Moses challenged Israel, "Has any god ever tried to take for himself one nation out of another nation, by testings, by miraculous signs and wonders?" (Deut. 4:34). Later Moses reminded the people, "Before our eyes the LORD sent miraculous signs and wonders—great and terrible—upon Egypt and Pharaoh and his whole household" (Deut. 6:22). "So the LORD brought us out of Egypt with a mighty hand and an outstretched arm, with great terror and with miraculous signs and wonders" (Deut. 26:8; cf. Deut. 29:2–3; Josh. 24:17; Neh. 9:10; Ps. 105:27; Jer. 32:20–21).

Many times in the biblical record "signs" are given to prophets as confirmation of their divine call. Moses' miraculous credentials have already been mentioned (Ex. 3 and 4). Gideon asked of God, "Give me a sign that it is really you talking to me" (Judg. 6:17). God responded with miraculous fire that consumed Gideon's offering (v. 21). God confirmed Himself to Eli by miraculous predictions about his sons' deaths (1 Sam. 2:34). Likewise, predictive "signs" were made to confirm God's appointment of King Saul (1 Sam. 10:7, 9). Isaiah offered predictions as "signs" of his divine message (Isa. 7:14; 38:7–8).

Although the word *sign* is not used in these cases, God's miraculous confirmations of Moses over Korah (Num. 16) and Elijah over the false prophets of Baal (1 Kings 18) illustrate the same point. In short, miracles were used as signs to accredit the true prophet. Likewise, the lack of predictive powers (false prophecy) was an indication that the prophet was not of God (Deut. 18:22).

Other events in the Old Testament are called "signs" or "miracles" as well. These include the plagues on Egypt (Ex. 7:3), the provisions in the wilderness (spoken of in John 6:30–31), fire from a rock (Judg. 6:17–21), victory over enemies (1 Sam. 14:10), confirmation of healing (Isa. 38:7, 22), and judgments from the Lord (Jer. 44:29).

Old Testament Usage of the Word *Wonder*

Often the words *sign* and *wonder* are used of the same event(s) in the same verse (Ex. 7:3; cf. Deut. 4:34; 7:19; 13:1–2; 26:8; 28:46; 29:3; 34:11; Neh. 9:10; Ps. 135:9; Jer. 32:20–21). At other times the Bible describes as "wonders" (Heb: *mopheth*) the same events that are elsewhere called "signs" (Ex. 4:21; 11:9–10; Ps. 78:43; 105:27; Joel 2:30). Of course, sometimes the word *sign* is used of a natural "wonder," as of a prophet (Ezek. 24:24) or a unique thing a prophet did to get his message across (Isa. 20:3). But even here the word *wonder* has a special, supernatural (divine) significance.

Old Testament Usage of the Word *Power*

One Hebrew word for "power" (*koak*) is sometimes used of human power in the Old Testament (Gen. 31:6; Deut. 8:17; Nah. 2:1). However, very often it is used of divine power, sometimes of God's power to create: "God made the earth by his power; he founded the world by his wisdom and stretched out the heavens by his understanding" (Jer. 10:12; cf. Jer. 27:5; 32:17; 51:15). In other places the "power" of God overthrows His enemies (Ex. 15:6–7), delivers His people from Egypt (Num. 14:17; cf. v. 13), rules the universe (1 Chron. 29:12), gives the people of Israel their land (Ps. 111:6), and inspires His prophets to speak His Word (Mic. 3:8). "Power" is often in direct connection with events called "signs" or "wonders" or both (see Ex. 9:16; 32:11; Deut. 4:37; 2 Kings 17:36; Neh. 1:10). Sometimes other Hebrew words for "power" are used in the same verse with "signs and wonders"; Moses speaks of the deliverance of Israel "by miraculous signs and wonders . . . [and] by a mighty [*chazaq*] hand" (Deut. 4:34; cf. Deut. 7:19; 26:8; 34:12).

NEW TESTAMENT USAGE
OF THE WORDS *SIGN, WONDER,* AND *POWER*

The New Testament usage of the three basic words for miracles is directly parallel to that of the Old Testament.

New Testament Usage of the Word *Sign*

In the New Testament, "sign" (Gk: *semeion*) is used seventy-seven times (forty-eight times in the Gospels). It is occasionally used of ordinary events, such as circumcision (Rom. 4:11) or a baby wrapped in swaddling clothes (Luke 2:12). Here again these signs have special divine significance, but most often the word is reserved for what we would call a miracle. Many times it is used of Jesus' miracles, such as healing (John 6:2; 9:16), turning the water to wine (John 2:11), and raising the dead (John 11:43–44). Likewise, the apostles performed miracles of healing (Acts 4:16, 30), "great signs and miracles" (Acts 8:13), and "miraculous signs and wonders" (Acts 14:3; 15:12); "many wonders and miraculous signs were done by the apostles" (Acts 2:43). Even the Jewish authorities said, "What are we going to do with these men? . . . Everybody living in Jerusalem knows they have done an outstanding miracle, and we cannot deny it" (Acts 4:16).

The word *sign* is also used of the most significant miracle in the New Testament, the raising of Jesus Christ from the grave. Not only was the Resurrection a miracle, but it was also a miracle that Jesus predicted (John 2:19; Matt. 12:40; 16:21; 20:19). Jesus said to His unbelieving generation, "But none [no sign] will be given it except the sign of the prophet Jonah. . . . [T]he Son of Man will be three days and three nights in the heart of the earth" (Matt. 12:39–40). Jesus was also asked for a sign in Matthew 16, at which time He repeated this assurance of His resurrection.

New Testament Usage of the Word *Wonder*

The word *wonder* (Gk: *teras*) is used sixteen times in the New Testament and almost always refers to a miracle. In fact, in every occurrence it is used in combination with the word *sign*. It is used of the supernatural events before the second coming of Christ (Matt. 24:24; Mark 13:22; Acts 2:19), of Jesus' miracles (John 4:48; Acts 2:22), of the apostles' miracles (Acts 2:43; cf. Acts 4:30; 5:12; Heb. 2:3–4), of Stephen's miracles (Acts 6:8), of Moses' miracles in Egypt (Acts 7:36), and of Paul's miracles (Acts 14:3; 15:12; Rom. 15:19). *Teras* means "a miraculous sign, prodigy, portent, omen, wonder"

(Brown, *DNTH*, 2:633). It carries with it the idea of that which is amazing or astonishing (ibid., 623–25).

New Testament Usage of the Word *Power*

The word *power* (Gk: *dunamis*) is used on numerous occasions in the New Testament. It is occasionally used of human power (2 Cor. 1:8) or abilities (Matt. 25:15), and sometimes it is used of spiritual (satanic) powers (Luke 10:19; Rom. 8:38). Like its Old Testament parallel, the New Testament term for "power" is often translated "miracles." *Dunamis* is used in combination with "signs and wonders" (Heb. 2:4), of Christ's miracles (Matt. 13:58), of the power to raise the dead (Phil. 3:10), of the virgin birth of Christ (Luke 1:35), of the special gift of miracles (1 Cor. 12:10), of the outpouring of the Holy Spirit at Pentecost (Acts 1:8), and of the "power" of the gospel to save sinful people (Rom. 1:16). The emphasis of the word is on the *divine energizing* aspect of a miraculous event.

THE THEOLOGICAL NATURE OF A MIRACLE

Each of the three words for supernatural events (sign, wonder, power) delineates an aspect of a miracle. A miracle is an unusual event (wonder) that conveys and confirms an unusual message (sign) by means of unusual ability (power). From the divine vantage point a miracle is an act of God (power) that attracts the attention of the people of God (wonder) to the Word of God (by a sign). Respectively, these words designate the "source" (God's power), the "nature" (wonderful, unusual), and the "purpose" (to sign-ify something beyond itself) of a miracle. They are often used as a sign to confirm a sermon; a wonder to verify the prophet's words; a miracle to help establish his message (John 3:2; Acts 2:22; Heb. 2:3–4).

A miracle, then, is a divine intervention into, or an interruption of, the regular course of the world that produces a purposeful but unusual event that would not (or could not) have occurred otherwise. By this definition, natural laws are understood to be the normal, regular, and general way the world operates. But a miracle occurs as an unusual, irregular, and specific act of a God who is beyond the universe.

This does not mean that miracles are against natural laws; it simply means they find their source beyond nature. In other words, miracles don't violate natural laws of cause and effect, they simply have a cause that transcends nature.

THE PURPOSE OF MIRACLES

The Bible states at least three purposes of a miracle:

(1) to glorify the nature of God (John 2:11; 11:40);

(2) to accredit certain persons as the spokespeople for God (Acts 2:22; Heb. 2:3–4); and

(3) to provide evidence for belief in God (John 6:2, 14; 20:30–31).

Of course, not all people believe that the event is an act of God, even when they witness a miracle. But in this event, says the New Testament, the miracle is a witness against them. John grieved, "Even after Jesus had done all these miraculous signs in their presence, they still would not believe in him" (John 12:37). Jesus Himself said of some, "They will not be convinced even if someone rises from the dead" (Luke 16:31). So in this sense the result (not the purpose) of disbelieving in miracles is condemnation of the unbeliever (cf. John 12:31, 37).

THE VARIOUS DIMENSIONS OF MIRACLES

Miracles Have an Unusual Character

First, miracles have an *unusual character.* A miracle is an out-of-the-ordinary event in contrast to the regular pattern of events in the natural world. It is a "wonder" that attracts attention by its uniqueness. Fire from heaven, walking on water, and a burning bush that is not consumed are not normal occurrences. Hence, they will by their unusual character draw the interest of observers.

Miracles Have a Theological Context

Second, supernatural events have a *theological context.* A miracle is an act of God (Gk: *theos*); therefore, a miracle presupposes that there is a God who can act. The view that there is a God beyond the universe who created it, controls it, and can interfere in it is called theism. Miracles, then, imply a theistic view of the universe.

Miracles Have a Moral Dimension

Third, miracles have a *moral dimension.* They bring glory to God; that is, they manifest His moral character. Miracles are visible acts that reflect the invisible nature of God. Technically, there are no evil miracles, then, because God is good. All miracles by nature aim to produce and/or promote good.

Miracles Have Doctrinal Content

Fourth, miracles have *doctrinal content.* Miracles in the Bible are connected directly or indirectly with "truth claims," meaning that there is a message in the miracle. They are ways to tell a true prophet from a false prophet (Deut. 18:22); they confirm the truth of God through the servant of God (Heb. 2:3–4). A miracle is the sign that confirms the sermon; new revelation and divine confirmation go hand-in-hand (cf. John 3:2).

Miracles Have a Teleological Aspect

Finally, biblical miracles have a *teleological aspect.* Unlike magic, they are never performed to entertain (see Luke 23:8). Miracles have a distinctive purpose: To glorify the Creator and to provide evidence for people to believe by accrediting the message of God through the prophet of God. These five facets of a miracle form a theistic context for identifying a miracle.

There are two basic ways to know whether miracles are possible:

(1) to show that a supernatural God exists (which has already been done in chapter 2);
(2) to answer objections raised against the possibility and/or plausibility of miracles.

THEISM MAKES MIRACLES POSSIBLE

C. S. Lewis aptly put it,

> If we admit God, must we admit Miracles? Indeed, indeed, you have no security against it. That is the bargain.... Theology says to you in effect, "Admit God and with Him the risk of a few miracles, and I in return will ratify your faith in uniformity as regards the overwhelming majority of events" (Lewis, *M*, 109).

Miracles, in the strictest sense of the word, are possible only in a theistic world, for no other worldview admits there is an infinite, supernatural, personal Power beyond the natural world except deism, which denies that God can (or does) perform miracles. So not only does theism make miracles possible, but *only* theism does this.

Furthermore, theism demonstrates that the miraculous is actual, since theism affirms the Creation of the universe (see chapter 2), which is the greatest supernatural event of all. Some deists may admit that miracles are possible but not actual. Yet this is inconsistent, since they already admit that the biggest miracle—Creation—has actually happened.

If theism is true, not only are miracles possible, but the most astounding one has already occurred. The only question that remains is whether more have happened and how we can identify them. In short, philosophy can show that miracles are possible (by providing evidence that there was a

Creator of the universe), but only history can demonstrate that subsequent miracles have actually taken place. But if miracles *do* happen, then they *can* happen; the actual proves the possible (not the reverse).

ANSWERING OBJECTIONS AGAINST MIRACLES

Few philosophers have attempted to demonstrate that miracles are impossible. The pantheist Benedict Spinoza, the agnostic David Hume, and the atheist Antony Flew are notable exceptions.

Spinoza's Argument That Miracles Are Impossible

Benedict Spinoza (1632–1677) argued from a now-outdated closed view of the universe. He insisted on the universal, exceptionless essence of natural law, and from this he concluded that miracles are not possible.

A Statement of Spinoza's Argument

Spinoza declared that "nothing . . . comes to pass in nature in contravention to her universal laws, nay, everything agrees with them and follows from them, for . . . she keeps a fixed and immutable order." He insisted that "a miracle, whether in contravention to, or beyond, nature, is a mere absurdity." He was nothing short of dogmatic about the impossibility of miracles, unabashedly proclaiming, "We may, then, be absolutely certain that every event which is truly described in Scripture necessarily happened, like everything else, according to natural laws" (Spinoza, *T-PT*, 83, 87, 92).

When one reduces Spinoza's argument against miracles to its basic premises it goes something like this:

(1) Miracles are violations of natural laws.
(2) Natural laws are immutable.
(3) It is impossible to violate immutable laws.
(4) Therefore, miracles are impossible.

The second premise is the key to Spinoza's argument: Nature "keeps a fixed and *immutable* order." Everything "*necessarily* happened . . . according to natural laws." If it were true that nothing comes to pass in nature in contravention to nature's universal laws, then Spinoza would be right; to believe otherwise *would be* "a mere absurdity."

In order to appreciate what Spinoza meant, one must be aware that he was a rationalist who tried to construct his philosophy on the model of Euclid's geometry (Spinoza, *E*, Part One); that is, he believed that one should accept as true only what is self-evident or what is deducible from the self-evident. Like his French contemporary René Descartes, Spinoza argued in a geometric way from axioms to the conclusions contained in these axioms.[1] Spinoza lived in an age increasingly impressed with the orderliness of a physical universe, an era in which it was believed Newton's recently discovered law of gravitation was without exception. Because of this it seemed axiomatic to Spinoza that natural laws are immutable.

A Response to Spinoza's Argument

There are several serious problems with Spinoza's antisupernaturalism, all springing from his Euclidian (deductive) rationalism.

First of all, Spinoza's philosophy suffers from an acute case of *petitio principii* (Lat: "begging the question"),[2] for, as David Hume later noted, anything validly deducible from premises must have been present in those premises from the beginning. But if the antisupernatural is already presupposed in Spinoza's rationalistic premises, then it is no surprise to discover him denying all miracles, including those in the Bible. In other words, once one defines natural laws as "fixed," "immutable," and "unchangeable," then of course it is irrational to say a miracle occurred. How can anything break the unbreakable?

Further, Spinoza's concept of natural law views nature as a "closed system" and, hence, law describes the way things *must* behave. For most contemporary scientists, however, the universe is an "open system" in which natural laws are merely statistical averages or probabilities of the way things *do* behave. If so, then there is always, from the scientific perspective, the *possibility* that there may be exceptions to these "normal" patterns. In this way a miraculous event would only be viewed as an anomaly, not a violation of natural law. Consequently, in contemporary scientific discussion, miracles are not dismissed, like they were by Spinoza, as impossible *by definition*.

What is more, Spinoza's view of God is pantheistic—he believed that God and the universe were one and the same. Spinoza maintained that God is coterminous with nature; hence, a miracle as an act of a God beyond nature cannot occur, since nature is the whole show. (As we already noted, miracles as supernatural interventions are only possible in a theistic universe. Therefore, scientists will want good reason to believe that a theistic God exists before they are likely to believe there is any evidence for miracles. In Spinoza's monistically airtight concept of nature [as absolutely one], then, there is simply no room for the supernatural.)

Finally, the evidence has mounted for a unique beginning of the space-time universe (see chapter 2). If this is so, then the beginning of the universe would be a prime example of a miracle, for what else should we call something coming into existence from nothing? Additionally, concluding that the universe had a beginning provides a devastating blow to Spinoza's concept of God, calling into question the naturalistic view that no God

---

[1]For Spinoza, an axiom is a self-evident principle, proposition, or maxim from which other truths can be deduced. Hence, all truth is either self-evident or deducible from it.
[2]"Begging the question" occurs when an argument assumes what is to be proven.

exists beyond the world. So rather than arguing against miracles, science may be coming back (however reluctantly) to the supernatural. In any event, Spinoza's argument by no means demonstrated the impossibility of miraculous events; rather, it demonstrated the circularity of his mental processes.

Hume's Argument That Miracles Are Incredible

In Part X of his famous *Enquiry Concerning Human Understanding,* David Hume (1711–1776) introduces his argument with these words: "I flatter myself that I have discovered an argument . . . which, if just, will, with the wise and learned, be an everlasting check to all kinds of superstitious delusion, and consequently will be useful as long as the world endures" (Hume, *ECHU,* 10.1.18).

A Statement of Hume's Argument

Just what is this alleged argument of finality against miracles? In Hume's own words, the reasoning goes like this:

(1) "A wise man . . . proportions his belief to the evidence.

(2) "If such conclusions are founded on an infallible experience, he expects the event with the last [i.e., highest] degree of assurance and regards his past experience as a full *proof* of the future existence of that event.

(3) "As the evidence derived from witnesses and human testimony is founded on past experience, so it varies with the experience and is regarded either as a *proof* or a *probability,* according as the conjunction between any particular kind of report and any kind of object has been found to be constant or variable (ibid., 10.1.18–20).

(4) "There are a number of circumstances to be taken into consideration in all judgments of this kind; and the ultimate standard by which we determine all disputes that may arise concerning them is always derived from experience and observation.

(5) "Where this experience is not entirely uniform on any side, it is attended with an unavoidable contrariety in our judgments and with the same opposition and mutual destruction of argument as in every other kind of evidence.

(6) "We entertain a suspicion concerning any matter of fact when the witnesses contradict each other, when they are but few or of a doubtful character, when they have an interest in what they affirm, when they deliver their testimony with hesitation or . . . with too violent asseverations.

(7) "But when the fact attested is such a one as has seldom fallen under our observation, here is a contest of two opposite experiences; of which the one destroys the other as far as its force goes,

and the superior can only operate on the mind by the force which remains.

(8) "A miracle is a violation of the laws of nature; and . . . firm and unalterable experience has established these laws. . . .

(9) "[Therefore,] the proof against a miracle, from the very nature of the fact, is as entire as any argument from experience can possibly be imagined.

(10) "[Since] a uniform experience amounts to a proof, there is here a direct and full *proof*, from the nature of the fact, against the existence of any miracle" (ibid., 10.1.121–123).

Again using his own words, Hume's argument can be abbreviated in the following way:

(1) "A miracle is a violation of the laws of nature; firm and unalterable experience has established these laws.

(2) "A wise man proportions his belief to the evidence.

(3) "[Therefore,] the proof against a miracle . . . is as entire as any argument from experience can possibly be imagined."

Hume concludes, "There must, therefore, be a uniform experience against every miraculous event. Otherwise the event would not merit that appellation. [Consequently,] nothing is esteemed a miracle if it ever happened in the common course of nature" (ibid.).

The Two Interpretations of Hume's Argument

Hume's argument against miracles can be understood in two ways: hard and soft. According to the *hard interpretation,* Hume would be claiming that

(1) Miracles by definition are a violation of natural law.

(2) Natural laws are unalterably uniform.

(3) Therefore, miracles cannot occur.

Now, despite the fact that Hume's argument sometimes sounds like this, it isn't necessarily what he had in mind. If this is his argument, then it clearly begs the question by simply defining miracles as impossible, for if miracles are a violation of what cannot be altered, then miracles are *ipso facto* impossible—impossible by the facts themselves, as a result of their very nature. But a supernaturalist could easily avoid this dilemma by refusing to define a miracle as a "violation" of fixed law and simply call it an "exception" to a general rule. That is, he could define natural law as the regular (normal) pattern of events but not as a universal or unalterable pattern.

Actually, Hume's position contains an argument that is much more difficult to answer, one that utilizes a *soft interpretation* of natural law. It is not an argument for the *impossibility* of miracles, but for the *incredibility* of miracles. It can be stated this way:

(1) A miracle is by definition a rare occurrence.
(2) Natural law is by definition a description of regular occurrence.
(3) The evidence for the regular is always greater than that for the rare.
(4) A wise man always bases his belief on the greater evidence.
(5) Therefore, a wise man should never believe in miracles.

Notice that on this soft form of Hume's argument miracles are not ruled out entirely; they are simply held to be always incredible by the very nature of the evidence. The wise person does not claim that miracles cannot occur; he simply never believes they happen, because he never has enough evidence for that belief. One indication that Hume is stressing credibility (or believability) rather than viability (or possibility) is found in his use of such terms as "belief," "is esteemed," etc.

However, even in this soft interpretation of the argument, miracles are still eliminated, since by the *very nature of the case* no thoughtful person should ever hold that a miracle has indeed occurred. If this is so, Hume has seemingly avoided logical fallacy and yet has successfully eliminated the possibility of reasonable belief in miracles.

An Evaluation of Hume's Argument

Since the hard form of Hume's argument is easily answered by redefining the terms, we will concentrate primarily on the soft form.

First, a word of evaluation about Hume's claim for "uniform experience." On the one hand, it is begging the question if Hume presumes to know the experience is uniform *in advance* of looking at the evidence, for how can he know that all *possible* experience will confirm his naturalism unless he has access to all possible experiences, including those in the future? On the other hand, it is special pleading if by "uniform experience" Hume simply means the select experiences of *some* persons, namely, those who claim not to have encountered miracles, for there are other persons who *do* claim to have experienced miracles. As Stanley Jaki recognizes, "Insofar as [Hume] was a sensationist or empiricist philosopher he had to grant equal credibility to the recognition of any fact, usual or unusual" (Jaki, *MP*, 23).

In the final analysis, then, the debate over miracles cannot be settled by supposed "uniform experience," for this either begs the question in advance or else opens the door for a factual analysis of whether indeed there is sufficient evidence to believe that a miracle has occurred. As C. S. Lewis observed,

> Now, of course we must agree with Hume that if there absolutely is "uniform experience" against miracles, if in other words they have never happened, why then, they never have. Unfortunately we know the experience against them to be uniform only if we know that all the reports of them are false. And we can know all the reports to be false

only if we know already that miracles have never occurred. In fact, we are arguing in a circle. (Lewis, *M*, 105.)

The alternative to circular arguing on the question of the existence of miracles is to be open to the possibility that miracles have occurred.

Second, Hume does not truly *weigh* evidence for miracles; he really *adds* evidence against them. Since death occurs over and over and over again, and since resurrection occurs only on rare occasions (if ever), Hume simply adds up all the deaths against the very few alleged resurrections and then rejects the latter. In his own words,

> It is no miracle that a man, seemingly in good health, should die on a sudden, because such a kind of death has yet been frequently observed to happen. But it is a miracle that a dead man should come to life; because that has never been observed in any age or country. [Hence,] it is more probable that all men must die. (Hume, *ECHU*, 10.1.122.)

But Hume is not *weighing* evidence as to whether or not a given person, say, Jesus of Nazareth (see volume 3), has been raised from the dead; on what *evidence* is it postulated that resurrection has never been observed? Instead, Hume is simply *adding* the evidence of all other people who have died and have not been raised.

There is another problem with Hume's concept of adding up events to determine truth. Even if a few resurrections *have* actually occurred, according to Hume's principles one should not believe them, since the number of deaths will always outweigh them. However, *truth is not determined by majority vote.* Hume seems to commit a kind of *consensus gentium* here, which is an informal logical fallacy arguing that something is true because it is believed by most people.

This argument actually equates evidence and probability. It says in effect that one should always believe what is most probable, what has the highest odds. On these grounds I should never believe the three dice I just rolled show three sixes on the first try, since the odds against it are 216 to 1. Or, you should never believe it if you're dealt a perfect bridge hand (which has happened), since the odds against it are 1,635,013,559,600 to 1. What Hume seems to overlook is that wise people base their beliefs on *facts*, not on *odds*. Sometimes the odds against an event are very high, but the evidence for that event is very good.

Finally, Hume's concept of adding evidence would eliminate *any* unusual or unique event from the past, to say nothing of miracles. Richard Whateley satirized Hume's thesis in his famous pamphlet *Historical Doubts Concerning the Existence of Napoleon Bonaparte.* Since Napoleon's exploits were so fantastic, so extraordinary, so unprecedented, no intelligent person should believe that these events ever actually took place. After recounting the French leader's amazing and unparalleled military feats, Whateley wrote,

> Does anyone believe all this and yet refuse to believe a miracle? Or rather, what is this but a miracle? Is not this a violation of the laws of nature? ... [If skeptics do not deny the existence of Napoleon, they] must at least acknowledge that they do not apply to that question the same plan of reasoning which they have made use of in others. (Whateley, *HDCENB*, 274, 290.)

Third, Hume's argument seems to prove too much; it appears to demonstrate that a person should not believe in a miracle even if it happens! However, there is something patently absurd about claiming that an event should be disbelieved even if one knows it has occurred.

Fourth, it would seem that Hume wants the "wise" person always to *believe* in advance that miracles will never occur. Even before one examines the evidence for a miracle, he should come pre-armed with the "uniform" and "unalterable" testimony of the past against it *being* a miracle. Remember the second premise of Hume's argument:

> If such conclusions are founded on an infallible experience, he expects the event with the last [i.e., highest] degree of assurance and regards his past experience as a full *proof* of the future existence of that event. (Hume, *ECHU*, 10.1.118.)

But here again Hume's uniformitarian prejudice is evident. Only if one approaches the world with a kind of invincible bias that is believed in accordance with what has been supposedly perceived in the past, can he discount all claims for the miraculous. There are two important objections to this reasoning.

For one thing, Hume is inconsistent with his own epistemology.[3] Hume himself recognized the fallacy of this kind of reasoning when he argued that, based on past uniformity, we cannot even know for sure that the sun will rise tomorrow morning (Hume, *THN*, 14–16). Hence, for Hume to deny future miracles based on past experience is inconsistent with his own principles and is a violation of his own ideological system.

For another thing, if it were true that no present exception can overthrow laws that are based on our uniform experience in the past, then there would be no true progress in our scientific understanding of the world, for *established or repeatable exceptions to past patterns are precisely what prompt a change in scientific belief.* When an observed exception to a past law is established, that law (L^1) is revised, with a new law (L^2) replacing

---

[3]Epistemology is "the study of the methods and the grounds of knowledge, especially with reference to its limits and validity; broadly, the theory of knowledge" (*Webster's Third New International Dictionary*).

and/or amending it. This is what happened when certain outer-spatial exceptions to Newton's law of gravitation were found, and Einstein's relativity was considered broader and more adequate. In short, *Hume's objections to miracles seem to be unscientific.*

Exceptions to laws have a heuristic (discovery) value; they are goads to progress in our understanding of the universe. This does not necessarily mean that all exceptions to a known law call for another natural law to explain them. Since scientific understanding is based on regular and repeated events, one must be able to show how the exception is repeatable before he can claim it has a natural cause rather than a supernatural one. *No single exception to a known scientific law calls for another broader natural law to explain it; only repeatable exceptions call for natural causes.* An unrepeated exception may have a supernatural cause; indeed, if it has the earmarks of intelligent intervention from beyond the natural world (see chapter 2), then it may be held to have a supernatural cause, not a natural one.

Before leaving this point another observation is in order. Even though a rational or scientific understanding of the world is based on the observation of regular recurring events, it does not follow that the subject of this understanding must be a regular event. For instance, our general understanding of the paintings on the ceiling of the Sistine Chapel is based on the experience of seeing other painters do similar things over and over. Yet the particular object of this understanding (the Creation scene) on the Sistine Chapel ceiling is an unrepeated singularity.

In the same way, SETI[4] scientists will accept a single message from outer space via radio telescope as indication that there are intelligent beings out there, only because these scientists have repeatedly observed intelligent beings produce similar messages. *The basis for believing that an event has a supernatural cause is the observation of certain kinds of events being regularly connected with intelligent, not natural, causes.* Nevertheless, the object of this understanding can be an unrepeated singularity—namely, a miracle. After all, an archaeologist need only find one piece of pottery to know there was an intelligent cause of it, even though he no doubt must have seen many potters make pottery (or the like) in order to know that only intelligent beings make these kinds of things. To restate the point, *the basis of our understanding of whether an event has an intelligent supernatural cause is observing that intelligent beings regularly produce similar events within the natural world.* However, the *object* of this understanding may be a singular event, such as the resurrection of Christ.

Indeed, as we have suggested, if scientists, based on their observation of regular causal conjunctions in the present (as Hume himself argued), can conclude that the weight of the cosmological evidence points to a Big-Bang singularity, billions of years ago, in which the material space-time universe

---

[4]Search for Extra-Terrestrial Intelligence.

exploded into being out of nothing, then not only are miracles possible but the biggest one has already happened. It remains, then, only to look at human history to see if other singularities have also occurred. What is seldom appreciated is that the very basis of this argument for the possibility (and even actuality) of miracles is David Hume's principle of "constant conjunction" (the "repeatability principle").[5] So rather than eliminating miracles, Hume's own maxim is actually the grounds for identifying them.

Antony Flew's Restatement of Hume's Argument Against Miracles

Variations of Hume's argument against miracles are still held to be valid by some widely respected contemporary philosophers. In his article titled "Miracles" in the *Encyclopedia of Philosophy*, Antony Flew argues against miracles on the grounds that they are unrepeatable. As he sees it, Hume's argument really amounts to something like this:

(1) Every miracle is a violation of a law of nature.
(2) The evidence against any violation of nature is the strongest possible evidence.
(3) Therefore, the evidence against miracles is the strongest possible evidence (Edwards, *EP*, 346–53).

Flew insists that "Hume was primarily concerned not with the question of fact, but with that of evidence. The problem was how the occurrence of a miracle could be proved rather than whether any such events had ever occurred." However, adds Flew, "our sole ground for characterizing the reported occurrence as miraculous is at the same time a sufficient reason for calling it physically impossible." Why, we may ask, is this so? Because "the critical historian, confronted with some story of a miracle, will usually dismiss it out of hand" (ibid.).

On what grounds are miracles dismissed by the critical historian? Flew answers,

> To justify his procedure he will have to appeal to precisely the principle which Hume advanced: the "absolute impossibility or miraculous nature" of the events attested must, "in the eyes of all reasonable people . . . alone be regarded as a sufficient refutation" (ibid.).

In short, even though miracles are not logically impossible, they are scientifically impossible:

> For it is only and precisely by presuming that the laws that hold today held in the past . . . that we can rationally interpret the detritus [fragments] of the past as evidence and from it construct our account

---

[5]This is the principle stating that the evidence for what occurs over and over is always greater than for what does not.

of what actually happened (ibid.).

As to the charge that this uniformitarian approach to history is "irrationally dogmatic," Flew answers with what is really the heart of his amplification of Hume's argument. For one thing, "as Hume was insisting from first to last, the possibility of miracles is a matter of evidence and not of dogmatism." Further, "the proposition reporting the [alleged] occurrence of the miracle will be singular, particular, and in the past tense." Propositions of this sort "cannot any longer be tested directly. It is this that gives propositions of the first sort [i.e., the general and repeatable] the vastly greater logical strength" (ibid.). In view of this, Flew's argument can now be stated as follows:

(1) Miracles are by nature particular and unrepeatable.
(2) Natural events are by nature general and repeatable.
(3) Now, in practice, the evidence for the general and repeatable is always greater than that for the particular and unrepeatable.
(4) Therefore, in practice, the evidence will always be greater against miracles than for them.

With these statements it becomes clear that for Flew generality and repeatability (in the present) are what give natural events greater evidential value than miracles. And since, of course, it will continue to be this way in the future, the evidence against miracles will always be greater than the evidence for them.

An Evaluation of Flew's Restatement of Hume's Argument Against Miracles

There is a *central thread* to the Hume/Flew argument: Both are based on what may be called the repeatability principle, which posits that the evidence for what occurs over and over is always greater than for what does not. Since miracles by their very nature are singularities, the evidence against them is always greater. However, as there are some *distinctive features* in the two presentations, our evaluation of Flew's will be separate.

First, like Flew, most modern naturalists accept some unrepeated singularities of their own. Many contemporary astronomers believe in the singular origin of the universe by a Big Bang, and nearly all scientists believe that the origin of life on this planet is a singular event that has never been repeated here. Indeed, all naturalistic scientists believe that life arose from nonlife as a singularity, which is not now being repeated. But if Flew's argument against miracles is correct, then it is also wrong for scientists to believe in these singularities that many of them consider natural events. Thus Flew's argument against supernaturalism would eliminate some elemental naturalistic beliefs.

Second, Flew's view is subject to his own criticism of theists, namely, that it is an unfalsifiable position. No matter what state of affairs actually occurs (even a resurrection), Flew (contrary even to Hume's claims) would be obliged to believe it was not a miracle, for Flew argued,

> It often seems to people who are not religious as if there was no conceivable event or series of events the occurrence of which would be admitted by sophisticated religious people to be a sufficient reason for conceding "there wasn't a God after all" (Flew, "TF," in *NEPT*, 98).

In short, his accusation is that the belief of religious people is in actuality unfalsifiable. But in like manner we may ask Flew (rephrasing his own words), "What would have to occur or to have occurred to constitute for you a disproof of . . . your antisupernaturalism?" Flew's answer would be that no event in the world could falsify his naturalism, for he would respond that the evidence is always greater against miracles than for them.

Nor does it help for Flew to claim that his antisupernaturalism is falsifiable in principle but never in practice, on the grounds that in practice the evidence will always be greater for the repeatable. Surely he would then have to allow the theist to claim that, *in principle*, the existence of God is falsifiable but that, *in practice*, no event could disconfirm God's existence. The fact that Flew and other non-theists busy themselves to disprove God by arguing from the fact of evil in the world reveals their true interest; falsification in practice is what really concerns them.

It would appear that one cannot have it both ways. If naturalism is unfalsifiable in practice, then belief in God (or in miracles) can also be unfalsifiable in practice. On the other hand, if supernaturalism can never be established in practice, then neither can naturalism be so established. It is always possible for the theist to claim of every alleged natural event that "God is the ultimate cause of it." The theist may insist that all "natural" events (i.e., naturally repeatable ones) are the way God normally operates and that "miraculous" events are the way He works on special occasions. Now, on Flew's own grounds, there is no way, in practice, to falsify this theistic belief. Again, just as Flew claimed that naturalism is unfalsifiable in practice, so too the theist could claim the same for theism, for no matter what events (repeatable or unrepeatable) are produced in the natural world, the theist can still claim "God is the ultimate cause of it," and, on Flew's own grounds, no naturalist can disprove it.

Third, Flew's assumption that the repeatable always evidentially outweighs the unrepeatable is subject to serious challenge. If this were so, then, as Richard Whateley pointed out (see earlier comments on Napoleon), one could not believe in the historicity of any unusual events from the past (none of which are repeatable). In fact, if repeatability in practice is the true test of superior evidence, then one should not believe that observed births or deaths occurred, for a person's birth and death are both unrepeatable in practice. Likewise, even historical geology is unrepeatable in practice, as is the history of our planet. Hence, if Flew were correct, the science of geology should be eliminated.

The truth is, as noted professor Stanley Jaki has observed, scientists do not reject unrepeated singularities out of hand:

> Luckily for science, scientists relatively rarely brush aside reports about a really new case with the remark: "It cannot be really different from the thousand other cases we have already investigated." The brave reply of the young assistant, "But, Sir, what if this is the thousand and first case?" which . . . is precisely the rejoinder that is to be offered in connection with facts that fall under suspicion because of their miraculous character. (*MP*, 100.)

Plainly, then, if the naturalist pushes his arguments far enough to eliminate miracles, by implication he thereby eliminates the grounds for his own beliefs. If he qualifies them so as to include all the natural and scientific data he wishes, then he reopens the door for miracles.

However, that an event is unusual does not mean it is supernatural. It simply means that a miracle cannot be eliminated because it is unusual. As discussed above, in order for an unusual event to qualify as a supernatural act of God there must be

(1) a theistic God (see chapter 2);
(2) some supernatural earmarks of God on this event (such as of moral, theological, or teleological dimensions).

One cannot identify the fingerprints of God on an event unless he first knows what God's fingerprints are.

OTHER OBJECTIONS TO MIRACLES ARE UNSUCCESSFUL

There are, of course, other objections to miracles (see Geisler, "M, AA" in *BECA*). However, none of them is successful in eliminating the possibility of miracles. In point of fact, the only way to really disprove miracles is to disprove the existence of God—something anti-theists have found notoriously difficult. Indeed, each attempted argument is based on unjustified, unproven, or self-defeating premises (see Geisler, "G, AD" in *BECA*). But if a theistic God cannot be disproved, then miracles are possible. Consider the following logic:

(1) Theism makes miracles possible.
(2) Theism has not been shown to be impossible (it actually has been shown [in chapter 2] to be credible).
(3) Hence, miracles have not been shown to be impossible.

This being the case, the supernatural precondition of evangelical theology is secure.

SOURCES

Augustine. *City of God.*

Brown, Colin, ed. *Dictionary of New Testament Theology.*

Flew, Antony. "Miracles" in Paul Edwards, ed., *The Encyclopedia of Philosophy.*

———. "Theology and Falsification" in *New Essays in Philosophical Theology.*

Geisler, Norman. "God, Alleged Disproofs of" in *Baker Encylopedia of Christian Apologetics*

———. *Miracles and the Modern Mind.*

———. "Miracles, Arguments Against" in *Baker Encyclopedia of Christian Apologetics.*

Geivett, Douglas, and Gary Habermas. *In Defense of Miracles.*

Greenleaf, Simon. *The Testimony of the Evangelists.*

Hume, David. *An Enquiry Concerning Human Understanding.*

———. *A Treatise of Human Nature.*

Jaki, Stanley. *Miracles and Physics.*

Jastrow, Robert. *God and the Astronomers.*

Lewis, C. S. *Miracles.*

Spinoza, Benedict. *Ethics.*

———. *Theologico-Political Treatise and a Political Treatise.*

Stokes, George. *International Standard Bible Encyclopedia.*

Swinburne, Richard. *Miracles.*

Thomas Aquinas. *Summa Contra Gentiles* (Book 3).

Whateley, Richard. *Historical Doubts Concerning the Existence of Napoleon Bonaparte.*

CHAPTER FOUR

REVELATION:
THE REVELATIONAL
PRECONDITION

Another fundamental precondition of evangelical theology is revelation. If God has not unveiled Himself, then how can He be known? But God *has* chosen to disclose Himself, and His self-disclosure is called revelation. According to evangelical theology, God has revealed Himself in two ways: general revelation (in nature) and special revelation (in Scripture).

THE PREREQUISITES FOR DIVINE REVELATION

Divine revelation is not possible unless at least three basic things are in place:

(1) a Being capable of giving a revelation;
(2) a being capable of receiving a revelation;
(3) a medium through which a revelation can be given.

1. A Theistic God Is Capable of Giving a Revelation

Since there is good reason to believe a theistic God exists (see chapter 2), the first precondition for divine revelation exists. The theistic God is omniscient (all-knowing) and, hence, has truth to reveal. Further, He is omnipotent (all-powerful) and, thus, has the ability to create means of revealing this truth (see volume 2).

2. Human Beings Are Capable of Receiving a Revelation

According to the Bible, human beings are made in God's image (Gen. 1:27), and, therefore, they are like Him in that, among other things, they are *rational and moral beings* (see volume 2). Such beings are capable of receiving a *rational and moral revelation* from God. Evangelical theology affirms that this revelation can be found both in nature (Rom. 1:19–20) and in Scripture (2 Tim. 3:16–17). That it is found in nature has already been shown (in chapter 2) by virtue of the fact that we can discover through reason truths about both the existence and the nature of God. The special revelation that has been given by God in Scripture will be discussed later (in part 2). For now it will suffice to show that such a revelation between infinite God and finite man is possible.

3. The Medium Through Which Revelation Is Possible

In order for an infinite Mind to communicate with finite minds, certain things must be possible. To begin, there must be a common principle of reason that both possess. Since it can be shown that the basic laws of reason are based in the nature of God (who is the ultimate rational Being), they are common both to God and to finite rational creatures (see chapter 5). Thus, a necessary condition for divine revelation has been fulfilled.

Further, since both objective meaning (see chapter 6) and objective truth (see chapter 7) are possible, another necessary condition is in place. And the fact that there is an analogy between God and creation (see chapter 9) shows that communication between an infinite Mind and a finite mind is possible; it demonstrates that there can be a similarity between the understanding of God and that of humans made in His image. This being the case, the basic *necessary* conditions for divine revelation have been met.

The *sufficient* condition for divine revelation, of course, is the will of God. Philosophy shows divine revelation is possible; only reality manifests that it is actual. Since the reality of God's special revelation in Scripture will be discussed later (in part 2), attention here will center on general revelation and its relationship to special revelation.

GOD'S GENERAL REVELATION

General revelation refers to God's revelation in nature, as opposed to His revelation in Scripture. More specifically, general revelation is manifest in several areas: for example, physical nature, human nature, and history. In each case God has disclosed something specific about Himself and His relationship to His creation.

General revelation is integral to Christian apologetics, since it is the data with which theists construct arguments for the existence of God (see chapter 2). Without it there would be no basis for apologetics.

God's Revelation in Physical Nature

"The heavens declare the glory of God; the skies proclaim the work of his hands," the psalmist writes (Ps. 19:1). "The heavens proclaim his righteousness, and all the peoples see his glory" (Ps. 97:6). Job adds,

> Ask the animals, and they will teach you, or the birds of the air, and they will tell you; or speak to the earth, and it will teach you, or let the fish of the sea inform you. Which of all these does not know that the hand of the LORD has done this? (Job 12:7–9)

Paul told men to

> Turn . . . to the living God, who made heaven and earth and sea and everything in them. In the past, he let all nations go their own way. Yet he has not left himself without testimony: He has shown kindness by giving you rain from heaven and crops in their seasons; he provides you with plenty of food and fills your hearts with joy. (Acts 14:15–17)

He reminded the Greek philosophers,

> The God who made the world and everything in it is the Lord of heaven and earth and does not live in temples built by hands. And he is not served by human hands, as if he needed anything, because he himself gives all men life and breath and everything else. (Acts 17:24–25)

Paul declares that even the heathen stand guilty before God:

> What may be known about God is plain to them, because God has made it plain to them. For since the creation of the world God's invisible qualities—his eternal power and divine nature—have been clearly seen, being understood from what has been made, so that men are without excuse. (Rom. 1:19–20)

In view of this the psalmist concludes, "The fool says in his heart, 'There is no God'" (Ps. 14:1).

God is revealed in nature in two basic ways: as *Creator* and as *Sustainer* (see volume 2). He is the cause of the *origin* as well as the *operation* of the universe. The first speaks of God as the originator of all things: "By him all things *were created*" and "in him all things *hold together*" (Col. 1:16–17); God "*made* the universe" and He also "*sustains* all things by his powerful word" (Heb. 1:2–3); He "*created* all things" and by Him all things "*have their being*" (Rev. 4:11).

In addition to being their *originator*, God is also the *sustainer* of all things. He was active not only in the universe's *coming to be* but is also active in its *continuing to be*. The psalmist refers to this latter function when he says of God: "He makes springs pour water into ravines. . . . He makes grass grow for the cattle, and plants for man to cultivate—bringing forth food from the earth" (104:10, 14).

God's Revelation in Human Nature

God created human beings in His image and likeness (Gen. 1:27); consequently, something about God can be learned from studying human beings (cf. Ps. 8). Since humans are like God, it is wrong to murder them (Gen. 9:6) and even to curse them (James 3:9–10). The redeemed are "renewed in knowledge in the image of [their] Creator" (Col. 3:10). Paul affirms that

> God did this so that men would seek him and perhaps reach out for him and find him, though he is not far from each one of us. "For in him we live and move and have our being." As some of your own poets have said, "We are his offspring." Therefore since we are God's offspring, we should not think that the divine being is like gold or silver or stone—an image made by man's design and skill. (Acts 17:27–29)

By looking at the creature we can learn something about the Creator (see chapter 9), for "Does he who implanted the ear not hear? Does he who formed the eye not see? Does he who disciplines nations not punish? Does he who teaches man lack knowledge?" (Ps. 94:9–10). Even Christ in the flesh is said to be the "image" of the invisible God (John 1:14; Heb. 1:3).

God is manifested not only in the intellectual nature of human beings but also in their moral nature (see volume 3). God's moral law is written in human hearts:

> When Gentiles, who do not have the law, do by nature things required by the law, they are a law for themselves, even though they do not have the law . . . their consciences also bearing witness. (Rom. 2:14–15)

Since moral responsibility entails the ability to respond, man in God's image is also a free moral creature (Gen. 1:27; cf. 2:16–17).

God's Revelation in Human History

History has been called *His*-story. It is the footprints of God in the sands of time. Paul declared that God "determined the times set for them [the nations] and the exact places they should live" (Acts 17:26). God disclosed to Daniel, "The Most High is sovereign over the kingdoms of men and gives them to anyone he wishes and sets over them the lowliest of men" (Dan. 4:17). God also entrusted to Daniel that human history is moving toward the ultimate goal of the kingdom of God on earth (Dan. 2, 7). So a proper understanding of history informs us about the plan and purpose of God.

God's Revelation in Human Arts

The Bible declares that God is beautiful and so is His creation. The psalmist praises, "O LORD, our Lord, how majestic is your name in all the earth!" (Ps. 8:1). Isaiah beheld a marvelous display of God's beauty when he "saw the Lord seated on a throne, high and exalted, and the train of his robe filled the temple" (Isa. 6:1). The Scriptures encourage us to "worship the LORD in the beauty of holiness" (Ps. 29:2 NKJV; cf. Ps. 27:4).

Solomon points out that God "has made everything beautiful in its time" (Eccl. 3:11). The psalmist speaks of Zion, His city, as "perfect in beauty" (Ps. 50:2). What God created is good like Himself (Gen. 1:31; 1 Tim. 4:4), and the goodness of God is beautiful. Insofar as creation reflects God, it is also beautiful.

Not only is God beautiful and has made a beautiful world but He has also created beings who can appreciate beauty. Like Him, they can also make beautiful things. Human beings are, as it were, "sub-creators" (see Sayers, *MM*). God chooses to endow humans with special creative gifts that reveal something of His marvelous nature.

God's Revelation in Human Music

God apparently loves music, since He orchestrated the angelic choir at Creation when "the morning stars sang together and all the angels shouted for joy" (Job 38:7). Angels also continually chant the *tersanctus* in His presence: "Holy, holy, holy" (Isa. 6:3; Rev. 4:8). Furthermore, angels gather around God's throne and "in a loud voice they sing: 'Worthy is the Lamb, who was slain'" (Rev. 5:12).

Moses' sister, Miriam, led the triumphant Israelites in singing after God delivered them through the Red Sea (Ex. 15:20–21). David, the sweet psalmist of Israel, set up a choir for the temple and wrote many songs (psalms) to be sung in it. Paul admonished the church to "speak to one another with psalms, hymns and spiritual songs. Sing and make music in your heart to the Lord" (Eph. 5:19).

We learn something more about God's nature through the human voice, a God-ordained instrument of music. Even the Jewish high priest entered into the Holy of Holies with bells on his garment. And the psalmist commanded that God be praised with trumpet, harp, lyre, tambourine, and cymbals (Ps. 150:3–5). In heaven the angels play trumpets (Rev. 8:2), and others play harps (Rev. 14:2). Music, too, is a gift and manifestation of God. Like the rest of His creation, it is an expression of His glory.

Even apart from God's special revelation in Scripture, then, He has manifested Himself through general revelation in nature.

THE RELATIONSHIP BETWEEN
GENERAL AND SPECIAL REVELATION

While the Bible is God's only *written* revelation (see part 2), it is not God's *only* revelation; He has more to say to us than is in the Bible. His general revelation in nature, man, history, art, and music offers vast opportunities for continual exploration. The following chart summarizes this relationship:

General Revelation	Special Revelation
God As Creator	God As Redeemer
Norm for Society	Norm for Church
Means of Condemnation	Means of Salvation
in Nature	in Scripture

THE ROLE OF SPECIAL REVELATION

Special revelation contributes uniquely to Christian theology, for the Bible alone is infallible and inerrant (see part 2). Further, the Bible is the only source of both God's revelation as Redeemer and His plan of salvation (see volume 3). Thus, Scripture is normative for salvation (see part 2).

The Bible Alone Is Infallible and Inerrant

As a revelation of Jesus (Matt. 5:17; Luke 24:27, 44; John 5:39; Heb. 10:7), the Bible is normative for all Christian thought. The task of the Christian thinker, then, is "to bring every thought captive to Christ" (2 Cor. 10:5 NKJV) as revealed in Scripture. We must think, as well as live, Christocentrically (Phil. 1:21; Gal. 2:20).

The Bible Alone Reveals God As Redeemer

While general revelation manifests God as Creator, it does not reveal Him as Redeemer. The universe speaks of God's greatness (Ps. 8:1; Isa. 40:12–17), but only special revelation reveals His redemption (John 1:14). The heavens declare the glory of God (Ps. 19:1), but only Christ declared His saving grace (Titus 2:11–13). Nature may reveal the ages of the rocks, but only Scripture makes known the Rock of Ages.

The Bible Alone Has the Message of Salvation

In view of God's general revelation, all men are "without excuse" (Rom. 1:20), for "all who sin apart from the [written] law will also perish apart from the law" (Rom. 2:12). General revelation is sufficient ground for man's condemnation; however, it is not sufficient for his salvation. One can tell how the heavens go by studying general revelation, but he cannot discover from it how to go to heaven, for "there is no other name under heaven [except Christ's] given to men by which we must be saved" (Acts 4:12). In order to be saved people must confess, "Jesus is Lord" and believe in their hearts "that God has raised him from the dead" (Rom. 10:9). But they cannot call upon someone of whom they have not heard, "and how can they hear without someone preaching to them?" (Rom. 10:14). Thus preaching the gospel in all the world is the Christian's Great Commission (Matt. 28:18–20).

The Bible Is the Written Norm for Believers

Without the apostolic truth embedded in Scripture there would be no church, for the church is "built on the foundation of the apostles and prophets" (Eph. 2:20). The revealed Word of God is the norm for faith and practice. Paul says, "All Scripture is God-breathed and is useful for teaching, rebuking, correcting and training in righteousness" (2 Tim. 3:16). Of course, not all unbelievers have access to a Bible. Nonetheless, God holds them accountable to His general revelation. The reason there is justice in this is that "all who sin apart from the [written] law will also perish apart from the law," since *all people have God's law in their hearts* (Rom. 2:12, 14–15).

THE ROLE OF GENERAL REVELATION

While the Bible is all true, God has not revealed all truth in the Bible. Whereas the Bible is only truth, the Bible is not the only truth; some truth lies outside of it. Said another way, all truth is God's truth, but not all God's truth is in the Bible (see chapter 7). General revelation, then, plays an important role in God's plan, and as such it has several unique roles.

General Revelation Is Broader Than Special Revelation

General revelation encompasses much more than special revelation. Most of the truths of science, history, mathematics, and the arts are not in God's Word; the bulk of truth in all these areas is found only in God's general revelation. While the Bible is scientifically accurate, it is not a textbook on science. The mandate for doing science is not a *redemption* mandate but a *creation* mandate; right after God created Adam He commanded him to "fill the earth and subdue it" (Gen. 1:28). Likewise, there are no mathematical errors in God's inerrant Word, but then again there is very little geometry or algebra and no calculus in it either. Similarly, the Bible records accurately much of the history of Israel, but has little on the history of the world, except as it bears on Israel. The same is true of most every area of the arts and science. Whenever the Bible speaks in these areas, it speaks authoritatively, but God has largely left the discoveries of His truths in these areas to a study of general revelation.

General Revelation Is Essential to Human Thought

No one—even an unbeliever—thinks apart from God's general revelation in human reason (see chapter 5). God is a rational Being, and man is made in His image (Gen. 1:27). Since God thinks rationally, man was given the same capacity. Brute beasts, by contrast, are called "irrational" (Jude 10). Indeed, the highest use of human reason is to love the Lord with "all our mind" (Matt. 22:37).

The basic laws of human reason are common to believer and unbeliever (again, see chapter 5); without them, no writing, thinking, or rational inferences would be possible. But nowhere are these laws of thought spelled out in the Bible. Rather, they are part of God's general revelation and the special object of philosophical thought.

General Revelation Is Essential to Human Government

God has ordained that believers live by His written Law, but He has also written His law in the hearts of unbelievers (Rom. 2:12–15). Divine law in Scripture is the norm for Christians, but natural law is binding on all men. Nowhere in Scripture does God judge the nations by either the law of Moses He gave to Israel (Ex. 19–20) or by the law of Christ He enjoins on Christians; to think otherwise is the central error of theonomists (see House, *DT*).[1] That sojourners in Israel had to abide by Jewish law (see Lev. 25:10f.) no more proves Gentiles are bound by the law of Moses than does the reality that Christians visiting Saudia Arabia have to abide by Qur'anic law prove that Christians are under the Qur'an. Both of these simply mean that visitors must respect the law of the land they are visiting.

The law of Moses, for example, clearly was not given to the Gentiles (Rom. 2:14). The psalmist explains, "He has revealed his word to Jacob, his laws and decrees to Israel. He has done this for no other nation; they do

---

[1]Theonomy, literally "God's law," is the view that the Old Testament law is still binding today and is the divinely appointed basis for civil government (see Greg Bahnsen, *Theonomy in Christian Ethics*).

not know his laws" (Ps. 147:19–20). This is confirmed by the fact that, in spite of the many condemnations of the Gentiles' sins in the Old Testament, never once were they condemned for not worshiping on the Sabbath or not bringing sacrifices or tithes to Jerusalem. Nonbelievers *are* bound by the law "written in their hearts"; while they have no special revelation in Holy Scripture, they are responsible to general revelation in human nature.

General Revelation Is Essential to Christian Apologetics

As stated at the beginning of this chapter, without general revelation there would be no real basis for Christian apologetics, for if God had not revealed Himself in nature, there would be no way to argue from the design evident within it to the existence of a Designer (known as the teleological argument for God's existence, see chapter 2). Nor would there be any way to argue from the beginning or contingency of the world to the existence of a First Cause (known as the cosmological argument). Likewise, unless God had revealed Himself in the moral nature of human beings, it would not be possible to argue for a Moral Lawgiver. And, of course, without a God who can act in creating the world, there could be no special acts of God (miracles) in it (see chapter 3).

SOME OBJECTIONS TO GENERAL REVELATION

One of the most commonly heard Christian arguments against the objectivity of general revelation in natural law, as opposed to moral laws revealed in the Bible, is that natural law is not clear. Opponents claim that there is no place one can read of these natural laws. As the argument goes, they are vague, if not vacuous. Natural laws can be easily distorted by depraved minds.[2] On the other hand, these Christians insist that the Bible is clear and not lacking in content.

Rebuttal of the Idea That Natural Revelation Is Unclear and Without Content

In their evangelical zeal to exalt God's special revelation in the Bible, some have overstated their case. That the Bible is superior in content to natural revelation does not mean natural revelation is not perfectly adequate for its God-given task. True, sin impairs humankind's ability to apply natural revelation to life. Yet this is not a defect in the revelation but in people's refusal to accept it and order life according to it. According to Romans 1, natural revelation "is plain to them, because God has made it plain to them" (v. 19). The problem with such persons is not that they do

---

[2]Bahnsen, 399–400.

not apprehend the truth, but that "the man without the Spirit does not accept the things that come from the Spirit of God" (1 Cor. 2:14). It is not that they do not *perceive* it, but that they do not *receive* it.[3] The Greek word *dekomai* used in 1 Corinthians 2:14 means "to receive" or "to welcome." When there is no welcome of the truth, they cannot "know" (Gr: *ginosko*) it by experience (v. 14).

Rebuttal of the Idea That Natural Revelation Is Distorted by Sin

As was shown earlier, God has clearly revealed Himself in nature and in the conscience of humanity. So the problem with unbelievers is not that they do not *see* the truth of natural revelation but that they *shun* the truth it reveals to them (Rom. 1:18). Rejecting revealed truth is not unique to unbelievers in their response to God's *general* revelation; neither do believers always live according to the truth of God's *special* revelation.

To claim that general revelation is inadequate because unbelievers have distorted it is to reject special revelation for the same reason. Peter, for example, tells us, "People distort [Paul's writings], as they do the other Scriptures, to their own destruction" (2 Peter 3:15–16). There is practically nothing that God has revealed in Scripture that has not been subjected to the same kind of misrepresentation as those moral truths He has revealed to all people in His natural law. There is no defect with either of God's revelations; the problem is not with God's revelation but with humankind's rejection of it. The difficulty is not with God's disclosure but with humanity's distortion of it.

The existence of hundreds of religious sects and cults all claiming that the Bible is their revelation is ample testimony that even the teachings of supernatural revelation are not immune to misinterpretation or mutilation. In fact, the perversions of the teachings of the natural law (general revelation) among various human cultures are no greater than the perversions of the teachings of supernatural revelation among the various cults. Careful examination of both areas indicates that in spite of the clarity of both revelations, depraved human beings have found a way to deflect, divert, or distort God's commands; therefore, the teachings of God's Word have no more immunity from tortured contortion than does the reality of God's world.

Rebuttal of the Idea That Natural Revelation Isn't Identifiable

Others have argued that the Bible has an advantage over natural law in moral matters in that the Scriptures have a specifiable content. We know where to go to get a Bible, and we can read what it says, but where does

[3]Frederic R. Howe, *Challenge and Response.*

one go to read about natural law? The biblical response to this question is twofold: It is *"written on the hearts"* of all men, and it can be seen in what they *"do by nature"* (Rom. 2:14–15, emphasis added). The first of these two manifestations is the inner side of the natural law and the latter the outer side. There are two areas in which the natural law is revealed: both external and internal. Natural law is made manifest externally in nature (Rom. 1), and it is revealed internally in human nature (Rom. 2).

External Manifestations of Natural Revelation Are Identifiable

Since this point has been discussed earlier (chapter 2), only brief comments about it will be made here. There are several ways in which God has indirectly revealed Himself externally in nature. These include the mutability (changeability), temporality, and order of the world. From these facts of our experience the great arguments for the existence of God are built, for if the world is temporal, then it must have had a beginning. But since human reason naturally believes, even from special revelation, that every event has a cause, there must have been a Cause of this temporal world. Theists will recognize this as the *kalam* (horizontal) cosmological argument for God.[4] Likewise, if the world is contingent or dependent there must be a God, for what is dependent for its existence could not exist by itself. But nothing can actualize its own existence. Hence, there must be an Actuality outside of this changing world that actualizes the actual existence of all that exists but that could be nonexistent. In short, natural revelation involves the use of natural reason on the natural world.

Internal Manifestations of Natural Revelation Are Identifiable

What is written on perishable paper can be erased, but what is written on the heart of an imperishable person is not completely deletable. Virtually all theologians agree, no matter how Calvinistic they are, that the image of God is not completely destroyed in fallen humankind: It was effaced but not erased. This was true of Augustine and Calvin (1509–1564)[5] and it is also true of Luther (1483–1546).[6]

The Bible is very clear that *all* human beings bear God's image. As mentioned previously, it is wrong to kill (Gen. 9:6) or even to curse human beings (James 3:9) for this reason.

In the same way that we know God's external natural revelation, we also come to know God's natural revelation in our internal moral nature, the one "written on our hearts." The natural moral law is written in a way everyone can read. No lessons in language are necessary, and no books are needed. Natural law can be seen "instinctively" (Rom. 2:14 NASB). We

---

[4]See William Craig, *Apologetics: An Introduction.*
[5]See Calvin, *Institutes of the Christian Religion,* Part One.
[6]See Luther, *Bondage of the Will,* Section 94, 244.

know what is right and wrong by our own natural intuitions; our very nature predisposes us in that direction.

The most basic key to that natural moral law is found in human inclinations. Since we are made in God's moral image (Gen. 1:27; 9:6; James 3:9), it is understandable that we have in our very nature a natural inclination toward *knowing* what is morally right. To be sure, as fallen beings we do not always follow it (Rom. 7) and, thus, have a natural tendency toward *doing* what is wrong. However, we *know* what is right instinctively, even when we do not *do* it. We know it by way of *inclination*, even when we do not perform it by way of *action*. Further, we *know* what is wrong deep down inside, even when we do not *think* it is wrong, for we know things by *inclination* even when we sometimes reject them by *cognition*. This is because our cognition is influenced by our depraved condition. Our *choosing* obscures our *knowing*.

To put it hermeneutically,[7] we are inconsistent in our use of the proper principles of interpretation of these basic moral inclinations. This doesn't mean that human reason is unnecessary for knowing what is right and wrong by natural revelation, for the natural moral law, while not without content, is minimal: It only informs us to do good and to shun evil. Human reason is necessary for two things:

(1) It puts specificity on the general moral law.
(2) It aids us in knowing what it means to utilize in order to attain the good end.

Another clue to understanding natural revelation is our basic moral *inclinations*. This is why our best understanding of the natural law comes not from seeing our actions but from observing our reactions: *We know the moral law instinctively.* We don't have to read it in any book; we know it intuitively, written as it is on our own heart. So when interpreting the natural law, we must be careful to do so from reactions truly indicative of it. These are not necessarily the ones we *do to others*, but more often those that we *desire to be done to us*. Once again, Paul speaks to this point when he writes of the things we "do by nature" that "show" the moral law "written on our hearts" (Rom. 2:14–15).

Our moral inclinations are manifested in our reactions when others violate *our* rights; we don't see the moral law nearly as clearly when we violate *others'* rights. Herein is revealed our depravity. But again our sinfulness is not found in our inability to know what the moral duty is but in our unwillingness to do it to others.

---

[7]Specifically, hermeneutics is "the study of the general principles of biblical interpretation" (*Webster's Third New International Dictionary*).

The kind of reactions that manifest the natural moral law were brought home forcefully to me when a professor, after carefully reading a student's well-researched paper defending moral relativity, wrote: "*F. I do not like blue folders.*" After receiving his grade, the student stormed into his professor's office, protesting, "That's not fair. That's not just!" The student's reaction to the injustice done to him revealed, contrary to what he wrote, that deep down inside he really did believe in an objective moral principle of rightness. The real measure of his morals was not what he had written in his paper but what God had written on his heart. What he really believed was right manifested itself when he was wronged.

Natural Law Is Expressed in Writings

If there were a natural inclination toward what is right, one would expect to see some sort of expression of this in human culture. But as is widely known, moral conduct is diverse from culture to culture. However, what is not as well known is that while human *behavior* differs greatly, human *ethical creeds* are significantly alike. Since human beings are not perfect, one would anticipate that their conduct would not always measure up to their creeds. The latter, though, is a much better indicator of the moral law than the former.

Contrary to popular belief, the great moral writings of the world do not present a total diversity of perspectives; indeed, there is a striking similarity among them. In fact, the resemblance within writings expressing the natural law is just as great as that within writings on the divine law. That is, the great ethicists have read general revelation with as much agreement as the great theologians have read special revelation. Within both groups there are conservatives and liberals, rightists and leftists, strict constructionists and broad constructionists. The stark truth is that it matters little whether it is the Bible that is being viewed, general revelation, or the United States Constitution. A bad hermeneutic can distort one as well as the other. The problem is not with divine revelation but with human misinterpretation of it. No revelation is immune from distortion by fallible and fallen human beings who wish to make it fit their own depraved desires and actions.

In spite of human misrepresentations of God's general revelation, there nonetheless remains among non-Christian writers a general consensus on the nature of the natural law. C. S. Lewis has provided a noteworthy service in cataloging many of these expressions of the natural moral law (*AM*, appendix A). Of course, there also is diversity of ethical expression among the great cultures. But this diversity no more negates their essential unanimity regarding natural law than diversity of belief among evangelicals negates their unity on the essential Christian teachings.

INTERACTION BETWEEN
GENERAL AND SPECIAL REVELATION

Since it is the task of a systematic thinker to organize all truth about God and His relation to His creation, both general and special revelation are needed. However, since special revelation overlaps with general revelation, it is necessary to discuss the interaction between the two. God has revealed Himself in His Word and in His world. His truth is found both in Scripture and in science. The problem is what we do when they seem to conflict. It is much too simplistic to conclude that the Bible is always right and science is wrong. Of course, *the Bible is always right* (see Part 2), *but our interpretation of it is not.*

An Important Distinction

When dealing with conflicts between Christianity and culture, we must be careful to distinguish between *God's Word*, which is infallible, and *our interpretation* of it, which is not. Likewise, we must distinguish between *God's timeless revelation* in His world, which is always true, and *man's current understanding* of it, which is not always correct. The very progress of scientific understanding indicates that what was once believed to be true is no longer held to be so.

Two important things follow from these distinctions. *First,* God's revelations in His Word and His world never contradict each other. God is consistent; He never talks out of both sides of His mouth. *Second,* whenever there is a real conflict, it is between a human interpretation of God's Word and a human understanding of His world. Either one or both of these are wrong, but God has not erred.

Which Revelation Has Priority?

When conflicts in understanding God's general and special revelations occur, which one gets the priority? The temptation might be to give precedent to the biblical interpretation because the Bible is infallible, but this overlooks the crucial distinction just made. The Bible is inerrant, but not all of our interpretations of it are without error. The history of interpretation reveals that God's infallible Word is as subject to man's fallible misunderstandings as is anything else. Likewise, the history of the arts and science exposes human misunderstandings of God's general revelation that are as bad as the human history of misconstruing His special revelation.

This does not leave one in an impasse, for whenever there is a conflict between an interpretation of the Bible and a current understanding of God's general revelation, priority should generally be given to the interpretation that is more certain. Sometimes this is our understanding of special revelation, and sometimes it is our understanding of general revelation, depending on which one is more thoroughly proven. A few examples will help to illuminate the point.

Some interpreters have wrongly concluded on the basis of biblical references to "the four corners of the earth" (e.g., Rev. 7:1) that the earth is flat. However, science has proven with *certainty* that this is wrong. Therefore, in this case the certainty in interpreting God's general revelation takes precedence over whatever uncertainty there may be in interpreting these biblical references. "Four corners" can be understood as a figure of speech, and the Bible uses such literary devices (such as God having eyes, arms, and legs).

Others have claimed that the sun moves around the earth on the basis of Bible references to "sunrise" (Josh. 1:15) or to the sun's "standing still" (Josh. 10:13). However, this interpretation is not necessary; these expressions may be only the language of appearance from an on-the-face-of-the-earth observer's point of view (see part 2, chapter 15). Furthermore, since the time of Copernicus there is extremely good reason to believe that the sun does not move around the earth. Hence, we assign a higher probability to the heliocentric interpretation of God's world at this point than to a geocentric interpretation of His Word.

Unfortunately some are willing to believe in a given interpretation of God's Word, even if it involves a logical contradiction. But general revelation demands (by way of the law of noncontradiction) that opposites cannot both be true (see chapter 8). Therefore, we cannot believe that God is both one person and also three persons at the same time and in the same sense. Thus, monotheism so defined and trinitarianism (see volume 2) cannot both be true. We can, and do, believe that God is three *Persons* in one *Essence*, for even though this is a mystery, it is not a contradiction. Consequently, we can be *absolutely certain* that any interpretation of Scripture involving a contradiction is false.

However, there are times when an interpretation of Scripture should take precedence over even highly popular views in science. Macroevolution[8] is a good example (see volume 2). It is *virtually certain* that the Bible cannot be properly interpreted to accommodate macroevolution. Or to put it the other way, it is most evident that the Bible teaches that God brought the universe into existence out of nothing (Gen. 1:1), that He created every basic kind of animal and plant (Gen. 1:21), and that He specially and directly created man and woman in His image (Gen. 1:27). In spite of the prevailing and trendy evolutionary views to the contrary, then, the Christian must give priority to this highly probable interpretation of Scripture over the extremely improbable theory of macroevolution (see volume 2).

---

[8]*Macroevolution* means total (large-scale) evolution from one-celled animals to human beings; it insists upon the common ancestry of all living things. *Microevolution*, by contrast, means small-scale changes within a certain type of life that has a separate ancestry from other types.

Mutual Enrichment

Often there is no serious conflict between widely accepted biblical inter-pretation and the general understanding of the scientific world; rather, there is mutual enrichment. For example, knowledge of the content of the Bible is essential for much of Western art and literature. Furthermore, bib-lical history and world history overlap significantly, so much so that neither should ever be ignorant of the other. More neglected is the relationship between modern science and the biblical idea of Creation. In this connec-tion it is important to note that the biblical concept of Creation helped give rise to modern science (see Whitehead, *SMW*, 13, and Foster, "CDCRMNS"). Of course, in the study of origins there is a direct overlap of, and mutual enrichment between, the scientific and biblical data.

In theology the interaction between biblical studies and other disci-plines should always be a two-way street. No one provides a monologue for the other; all engage in a continual dialogue. Although the Bible is infalli-ble in whatever it addresses, it does not speak to every issue. Furthermore, as we have seen, while the Bible is infallible, our interpretations of it are not. Thus, those in biblical studies must listen to as well as speak to the other disciplines. Only in this way can a complete and correct systematic worldview be constructed (see chapter 11).

SUMMARY AND CONCLUSION

Evangelicals believe the Bible is essential both to systematic thinking and to apologetics. It is the only infallible writing we have (see part 2). It speaks with unerring authority on every topic it covers, whether spiritual or scientific, whether heavenly or earthly. However, the Bible is not God's only revelation to humanity. God has spoken in His world as well as in His Word. It is the task of the Christian theologian to appropriate the information from both and to form a worldview that includes a theocentric interpreta-tion of science, history, human beings, and the arts. However, without God's revelation (both general and special) as the basis, this task is as impossible as moving the world with no place to put one's fulcrum. Without question, in building a solid systematic theology both special revelation and general revelation are necessary.

SOURCES

Bahnsen, Greg. *Theonomy in Christian Ethics.*
Butler, Joseph. *The Analogy of Religion.*
Calvin, John. *Institutes of the Christian Religion.*
Craig, William. *Apologetics: An Introduction.*
Demerest, Bruce. *General Revelation.*

Foster, M. B. "The Christian Doctrine of Creation and the Rise of Modern Natural Science" in *Mind*, 43.

Geisler, Norman. "God's Revelation in Scripture and Nature" in David Beck, *The Opening of the American Mind*.

————. *Origin Science*.

Hodge, Charles. *Systematic Theology* (Vol. 1).

House, Wayne. *Dominion Theology*.

Howe, Frederic R. *Challenge and Response*.

Lewis, C. S. *The Abolition of Man*.

Locke, John. *The Reasonableness of Christianity*.

Luther, Martin. *The Bondage of the Will*.

Paley, William. *Natural Theology*.

Sayers, Dorothy. *The Mind of the Maker*.

Thomas Aquinas. *Summa Theologica*.

Whitehead, Alfred North. *Science and the Modern World*.

CHAPTER FIVE

LOGIC:
THE RATIONAL
PRECONDITION

Logic deals with the methods of valid thinking; it reveals how to draw proper conclusions from premises. It is a prerequisite of *all* thinking, including all theological thought. Logic is such an inescapable tool that even those who deny it cannot avoid using it, for it is built into the very fabric of the rational universe.[1]

THE FUNDAMENTAL LAWS OF THOUGHT

There are three elemental laws of all rational thinking:

(1) the law of noncontradiction (A is not non-A);
(2) the law of identity (A is A);
(3) the law of excluded middle (either A or non-A).

Each of these laws serves an indispensable function in theology.

The Law of Noncontradiction

Without the law of noncontradiction we could not say that God is not non-God (G is not non-G). Thus, God could be the devil or whatever is anti-God.

---

[1]For a more extensive treatment of logic, see Norman Geisler and Ronald Brooks, *Come, Let Us Reason: An Introduction to Logical Thinking.*

The Law of Identity

If the law of identity were not binding, we could not say that God is God (G is G). Without the law of identity, God would not be identical to Himself; He could be something other than Himself (e.g., the devil), which is plainly absurd.

The Law of Excluded Middle

Likewise, if the law of excluded middle didn't exist we could not affirm that it is either God or not God that we are speaking about. When we use the term "God," we could be referring to both God and not God. This clearly is meaningless.

Hence these three principles are necessary for all thinking, including all thought about God. Since theology is thinking about God, theology cannot escape the use of these three fundamental laws of all thought.

A DEFENSE OF THE LAWS OF THOUGHT

Why should anyone accept these three laws? Indeed, many reject them, at least when applied to the ultimate level. Zen Buddhism, for example, claims that the Tao (the Ultimate) goes beyond all categories, including true and false (see Suzuki, *IZB*). How can the primary standards of thought be defended against such criticism?

Actually, the laws of thought are self-evident and do not need any defense. As regards the law of identity, for instance, the predicate says the same thing as the subject (A is A); therefore, it neither needs nor admits direct proof. *Once one understands the terms, they speak for themselves.* For example, once one knows what "triangle" and "three-sided figure" mean, there is no need to prove that a triangle is a three-sided figure. It is simply seen (by rational intuition) to be true.

However, there is an indirect way of defending the basic laws of thought as self-evident. This can be shown in that they cannot be denied without using them; that is, any attempt to deny them is self-destructive. It is like saying, "I think that I cannot think," or "I know that I cannot know," or "I reason that I cannot reason." In each case, one is doing exactly what he claims he cannot do.

In the same manner, if the law of noncontradiction is not binding, then what is true can also be not true (false). But this is self-defeating, for that very sentence claims to be true and not false. If it does not claim to be true, then it is not even in the arena of truth and can be ignored by all who seek truth.

THE LAWS OF RATIONAL INFERENCE

In addition to the three fundamental laws of thought, there are laws of valid inference whereby a conclusion can be properly drawn from given premises. These fall into two broad categories: *deductive* logic and *inductive* logic.

The validity of these laws is dependent on the law of noncontradiction, for if these necessary rational inferences are not valid, then contradiction follows (see the following example).

DEDUCTIVE LOGIC

Deductive thinking is where one proposition is correctly deduced or drawn from others. For example, if:

(1) all A is inside of B, and

(2) all B is inside of C, then it follows that

(3) all A is inside of C.

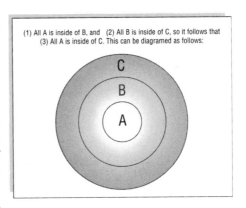

(1) All A is inside of B, and   (2) All B is inside of C, so it follows that (3) All A is inside of C. This can be diagramed as follows:

If all A is not inside (in the class of) C, then contradiction follows, for then B would both be inside C (according to the second premise) and not inside C. If B is inside C, then A must be inside C, too, since A is inside B. Without question it is contradictory to both have and not have A inside of B (as according to the first premise).

The device by which one proposition can be correctly drawn from others is called a syllogism.[2] Deductive logic comes in three forms:

(1) categorical syllogisms
(2) hypothetical syllogisms
(3) disjunctive syllogisms (see Aristotle, *PrA* and *PoA*).

Categorical Syllogisms

A categorical (unconditional) syllogism is one where a categorical (unconditional) proposition is deduced from two other categorical propositions. For example:

---

[2]As mentioned in chapter 2, a syllogism, formally, is a deductive scheme of a formal arrangement consisting of a major and a minor premise and a conclusion (*Webster's Third New International Dictionary*).

(1) All human beings are sinful.

(2) John is a human being.

(3) Therefore, John is sinful.

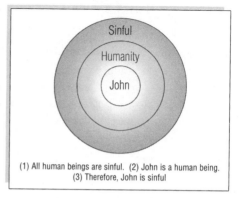

(1) All human beings are sinful. (2) John is a human being. (3) Therefore, John is sinful

There are rules for categorical syllogisms that must be followed if the conclusions are going to be correct, and if these are not followed, then the undeniable law of noncontradiction is violated. These syllogistic rules and the fallacies that violate them can be understood if some of the essential terms are defined first.

Propositions

A proposition is a declarative sentence that affirms or denies something. A proposition is composed of a *subject* (the subject of the affirmation/ denial, e.g., "John"), a *predicate* (what is affirmed/denied of the subject, e.g., "sinful"), and a *copula* (the connector of the subject and predicate, e.g., "is (are)" or "is (are) not"). Stated together: "John (subject) is (copula) sinful (predicate)."[3]

The subject can be *universal* (general, including all in its class) or *particular* (specific, including only some in its class). For instance, "*All* dogs (universal) are four-legged creatures"; "*some* dogs (particular) are brown." Universal propositions are said to be strong and particular ones weak. Propositions also can be either *affirmative* ("is" or "are") or *negative* ("is not" or "are not").

Combining universals and particulars with affirmatives and negatives yields four different kinds of propositions:

A Universal affirmative (*All* humans *are* sinners).

E Universal negative (*All* humans *are not* sinners) (or *no* humans *are* sinners).

I Particular affirmative (*Some* humans *are* sinners).

O Particular negative (*Some* humans *are not* sinners).

Distribution

In A-type propositions (universal affirmative) the subject is distributed and the predicate is not distributed.[4] Take, for instance, a proposition similar to what we have just seen: "All human beings are rational." The subject

---

[3]*Each* of the three statements of the syllogism is a proposition.

[4]That a subject or a predicate is "distributed" means all in its class are included.

is distributed because "all humans" includes all in its class, and the predicate is undistributed because "rational" means only some of its class—there are, after all, other rational beings, such as God and angels.

The distribution (D) or undistribution (U) of terms in all four kinds of propositions is as follows:

A All S(D) is P(U).
E No S(D) is P(D); or All S(D) is not P(D).
I Some S(U) is P(U).
O Some S(U) is not P(D).

For example:

A All human beings (D) are rational (U).
E No human being (D) is rational (D).
I Some human beings (U) are rational (U).
O Some human beings (U) are not rational (D).[5]

Again, a categorical syllogism contains two propositions from which a third is deduced. The syllogism as a whole contains three terms: a *subject term* (ST), a *predicate term* (PT), and a *middle term* (MT). The subject and the predicate are the subject and predicate of the *conclusion*, and the middle term occurs once in each premise, along with one occurrence each of the subject and predicate. For example:

All humans (middle term) are lost (predicate term). [A-type proposition]

John (subject term) is a human (middle term).

Therefore, John (subject term) is lost (predicate term).

The Rules of Categorical Syllogisms

Breaking any one of the seven rules of categorical syllogisms leads to an invalid conclusion, meaning that the conclusion does not follow (*non sequitur*) from the premises regardless of whether or not the conclusion happens to be true.

(1) There must be only three terms.
(2) The middle term must be distributed at least once.
(3) Terms distributed in the conclusion must be distributed in the premises.

---

[5]The subject of an *A-type* proposition is distributed because, for instance, "all human beings" means everything in that class; the predicate is undistributed because humans are only some of the rational beings that exist—others in that class include God and angels. The subject of an *E-type* proposition is distributed because "no" equals "all"; the predicate is likewise distributed, specifically, since no human being is in the class of any (all) rational beings. In an *I-type* proposition, both subject and predicate are undistributed because the statement means that some humans are in the class of some rational beings; again, there are others who fall into the class labeled "rational." The subject of an *O-type* proposition is undistributed because it refers only to some human beings; the predicate is distributed because it negates all in that class—that is, some human beings are not in the class of any (all) rational beings.

(4) The conclusion always follows the weaker premises (i.e., negative and particular ones).
(5) No conclusion follows from two negative premises.
(6) No conclusion follows from two particular premises.
(7) No negative conclusion follows from two affirmative premises.

The Fallacies of Categorical Syllogisms

Likewise, committing any one of the four fallacies of categorical syllogisms leads to an invalid conclusion.

(1) *Illicit major* is the fallacy where the major term is distributed in the conclusion but not in the premise.[6]
(2) *Illicit minor* is the fallacy where the minor term is distributed in the conclusion but not in the premise.[7]
(3) *Undistributed middle* is the fallacy where the middle term is not distributed at least once.
(4) *Four-term fallacy* is the fallacy where there are not three and only three terms in the syllogism (includes the fallacies of "ambiguous middle" and "equivocal middle").

Of course, the middle term must appear only once in each premise but never in the conclusion; else, a fallacy of form occurs. A more detailed explanation can be found elsewhere (see Geisler and Brooks, *CLUR*).

Hypothetical Syllogisms

Hypothetical syllogisms are an "If . . . then . . ." type of reasoning. If A, then B follows. For instance,

(1) If God is all-just, then He must punish all sin.
(2) God is all-just.
(3) Therefore, He must punish all sin.

There are only two ways to draw valid conclusions from a hypothetical syllogism:

(1) affirming the antecedent (the part of the sentence coming before "then");
(2) denying the consequent (the part of the sentence coming after "then").

The above example (regarding sin and God's justice) is one of affirming the antecedent (called *modus pollens*[8]), and the following is one of denying

---

[6]The "major term" comes from the major premise and contains the predicate of the conclusion.
[7]The "minor term" comes from the minor premise and contains the subject of the conclusion.
[8]Latin for "method of affirming."

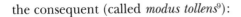

the consequent (called *modus tollens*[9]):

(1) If the Qur'an is God's Word, then it cannot err.
(2) The Qur'an has errors.
(3) Therefore, the Qur'an is not God's Word.

Disjunctive Syllogisms

A disjunctive syllogism is an either/or type of reasoning. It takes the following form:

(1) It is either A or not A (but not both).
(2) It is not non-A.
(3) Therefore, it is A.

To use a theological example:

(1) Either God is existent or He is nonexistent.
(2) God is not nonexistent.
(3) Therefore, God is existent.

There are two ways to draw a valid conclusion from a disjunctive syllogism: Either by denying one alternate or by denying the other alternate. An alternate is the statement on one side or the other of the "or."

These three types of logical thinking—categorical, hypothetical, and disjunctive—are used constantly in theology. Without them theology would not be possible, since they are the rules of rational thought, and systematic theology is a form of rational thinking.

INDUCTIVE LOGIC

Another type of logic is inductive reasoning. While Aristotle wrote on inductive reasoning (*T*), he is more famous for deductive logic. Inductive and experimental logic were most fully developed by Francis Bacon (see *NO*), the father of modern scientific thinking, and John Stuart Mill (see *SL*).

The Nature of Inductive Reasoning

Broadly speaking, while *deductive* reasoning is from the general to the particular, *inductive* reasoning is from the particular to the general. For example, *deductive* logic proceeds from the general statement that

(1) all human beings are rational beings, and notes that

---

[9]Latin for "method of denying."

(2) Mary is a human being, to the particular conclusion that

(3) Mary is a rational being.

Inductive logic begins with any number of particulars and makes a generalization about them. For instance, "Human beings such as Janna, John, Joan, Jim, and others have two legs and walk upright; therefore, all humans walk upright." Of course, unlike deductive logic, one cannot be absolutely sure of this conclusion, since all human beings have not been observed. Hence, the inductive conclusion is *generalizing*. It is a projection or *extrapolation* being made: "Since all humans we observe have two legs and walk upright, then even those we have not observed *probably* do the same."

There is, of course, such a thing as a *perfect induction*, where every particular instance has been examined. In this case, one can be certain about the conclusion. For example, "Every coin in my pocket is a penny" can be known for sure, since my pocket is a limited space and every coin in it can be scrutinized. Likewise, the Bible contains a limited amount of information, all of which can be examined. Hence, one can have a kind of certainty about what it teaches if every verse has been probed carefully.

The Rules of Inductive Logic

Several inductive reasoning guidelines must be followed. Put in question form:

How Many Cases Were Examined?

The degree of certainty about the conclusion will depend in part on how broad was the number of cases examined. The broader the sample, the better the chances are that the conclusion will be correct.

How Representative Was the Evidence?

Since it is usually not possible to examine all the cases, the quality of the samples examined is crucial to the validity of the conclusion. For example, the validity of a poll will depend on the representative nature of the sum of the people who were polled.

How Carefully Was the Evidence Examined?

Careful inductions are comprised of many factors. What were the similarities of the samples that were studied? What were the differences? Were all possible explanations accounted for? Were the results isolated from other factors? In short, how critically was the evidence examined?

How Does the Information Gained Correlate With Other Knowledge?

Finally, how well does the information that was gleaned match up with other things that are known to be true? Does it contradict other things known with certainty? Does it better explain things than other explanations do? Sometimes new evidence rocks foundations that were thought settled (such as Copernicus's view that the earth moved around the sun).

Kinds of Probability

There are two major kinds of probability in inductive reasoning: *a priori* (*ah* pree-*oh*-ree) and *a posteriori* (*ah* paw-ster-ee-*oh*-ree). A priori probability is probability prior to and independent of the facts; a posteriori probability is probability that arises after examining the facts. Both kinds have an application to theology and apologetics.

A Priori Probability

A priori probability is mathematical in nature, dealing with the advanced likelihood or odds of an event occurring. For example, the likelihood of getting three sixes on a roll of three dice before they are tossed is 1 in 216 ($\frac{1}{6} \times \frac{1}{6} \times \frac{1}{6}$). This does not mean that the dice must be thrown 216 times to get it; it simply means that these are the mathematical odds, for three dice with six sides numbered one through six offer that many combinations.

A priori probability has convinced even some former atheists to believe there must have been an Intelligent Designer of first life. After calculating that the odds for life to arise by only natural laws was 1 in 10 to the 40,000th power (one followed by 40,000 zeros), Sir Fred Hoyle (b. 1915) abandoned his God-denying beliefs. This chance, one in $10^{40,000}$, is less than that of finding one single particular atom while searching the entire universe (see *EFS*, 45–46).[10]

A Posteriori Probability

While a priori probability is probability before the fact, a posterior probability is probability after the fact. In science, it is *empirical* probability, also called scientific probability. A posteriori probability offers varying degrees of certainty that something is true based on an examination of the available evidence. This is generally done with the guidance of the principles listed above (under "The Rules of Inductive Logic").

Degrees of Probability

According to the inductive method, there are various degrees of probability, depending on the kind and extent of evidence available. These range from virtually impossible on the one end to virtually certain on the other

---

[10]Of course, there are factual observations used in this calculation, such as the age of the universe and the rate of mutations, etc.

end. Absolute certainty, at least of a *mathematical* type,[11] is possible only in deductive logic. A perfect induction, however, can provide *practical* certainty, since every one of the cases was examined.

LOGIC AND GOD

If logic is the basis of all thinking, and theology is thinking about God, then it follows that logic is the basis of all thinking about God. Nevertheless, some object to this conclusion, claiming that God is sovereign over all things, including logic, and that making logic the basis of thinking about God makes God subject to logic (see Dooyeweerd, *NCTT*).

Logic Is Subject to God Ontologically

It is true that in reality God is prior to everything else. In this sense, God is prior to logic in the order of being. Logic is a form of rational thought, and God is the ultimate rational Being. So ontologically,[12] logic is subject to God.

However, this does not mean that logic is arbitrary—God does not merely choose to be rational and consistent. *He is rational by His very nature.* The Scriptures inform us, for example, "It is impossible for God to lie" (Heb. 6:18) and that "He cannot deny Himself" (2 Tim. 2:13 NKJV). Likewise, God cannot be irrational. It is contrary to His nature as the ultimate, perfect, absolutely rational Being in the universe to violate the laws of logic.

God Is Subject to Logic Epistemologically

While God is prior to logic *in the order of being* (ontologically), nevertheless, logic is prior to God *in the order of knowing* (epistemologically). No knowledge is possible without the laws of thought; if this is not true, then nothing else follows. Even the statement "God is God" makes no sense unless the law of identity holds (A is A). Likewise, the affirmation that "God exists" cannot be true if the law of noncontradiction is not binding, otherwise God could exist and not exist at the same time and in the same sense.

Is God subject to something beyond Himself? No. When God is subject to good reason (logic), He is subject to *His own nature* (see Clark, *CVMT*), since He is the ultimate Reason or *Logos* (John 1:1). Likewise, when God is subject to the law of justice, He is not bound by something *beyond* Himself

---

[11]Moral certainty is possible, as it is not based on deductive logic but on moral, psychological, and/or spiritual factors. For example, God can grant moral (or spiritual) certainty of salvation (Rom. 8:16) where the actual evidence itself may justify only a probable conclusion (see volume 3).

[12]Ontology is the study of being.

but to something *within* Himself, namely, to His own unchangeable nature (see volume 2).

Technically speaking, in theology it is not God who is subject to logic; it is our *statements* about God that are subject to logic. Systematic theology is a series of statements about God that, if true, inform us about Him. No statement about God can make any sense, to say nothing of being true, unless it abides by the undeniable rules of reason.

Rationality or Rationalism?

Some object that making God subject to logic is a form of rationalism, since it makes truths about God subject to human reason. However, there is a difference between the use of good *reason*, which the Bible commends to *discover* truth (Isa. 1:18; Matt. 22:37; 1 Peter 3:15), and the use of *rationalism* to *determine* truth, which Scripture does not commend. Good reason does not subject God to finite minds but rather subjects our finite minds to His infinite Mind (2 Cor. 10:5; 1 Cor. 1:21).

Further, since we are created in the image of an infinitely intelligent God, it is not a form of rationalism to imitate His rationality. Rather, it is a way to express our love for Him (with all our minds) as Jesus commanded (Matt. 22:37).

Even special revelation cannot be known or communicated apart from logic. We could not distinguish between a revelation that is from God or one that is not from God without the law of noncontradiction. Nor could we determine which book was God's of the many that claim to be (e.g., the Bible, the Qur'an, the Book of Mormon) without using our reason to examine the evidence.

Finally, note that reason is a means of *discovering* truth, whereas rationalism is an attempt at *determining* truth. Christian theology falls into the former category. All truth is *revealed* by God, whether in special or general revelation (see chapter 4), but all truth is received by *reason*.

DID ARISTOTLE INVENT LOGIC?

Some critics object to the use of deductive logic, insisting that it was invented by Aristotle and that there is no reason we should accept "Western logic" over "Eastern logic," which does not accept the law of noncontradiction.

However, this criticism is misdirected for several reasons. *First*, Aristotle did not *invent* logic; at best, he simply *discovered* it. All rational creatures were using logic since the beginning; Aristotle was merely the first one known to put it down in written form (see *PrA* and *PoA*).

Second, this criticism implies that "Eastern thought" can somehow avoid using "Western logic." But this is impossible—logic does not have geographic boundaries. Inasmuch as logic is based on the law of noncontradiction, it is unavoidable, for it is impossible to deny this law without using it. Any statement to the effect that "truth claims do not have to be either true or false" is itself claiming to be true as opposed to false.

Third, no Eastern philosopher can even think without the law of noncontradiction; again, the very denial of noncontradiction employs it, and any statement to the effect that "ultimate reality [say, the Tao] goes beyond the law of noncontradiction" (see Suzuki, *IZB*) is itself a statement that uses the law of noncontradiction of ultimate reality, for it claims to be true, as opposed to false. If it is not a truth claim at all, then it is not even in the arena of truth and need not be considered by anyone in pursuit of truth.

Are There Different Logics?

Others object that there are many kinds of logic; why choose one and make it the norm over all others? In response, it should be pointed out that there are no kinds of logic that do not use the law of noncontradiction. *All* systems of valid thought—whether they are deductive logic, inductive logic, symbolic logic, modal logic, or whatever—employ the law of noncontradiction. Indeed, Alfred North Whitehead and Bertrand Russell demonstrated in *Principia Mathematica* that all mathematics is based on logic. It is literally impossible to think without logic.

Can't an Omnipotent God Break the Laws of Logic?

Some theologians argue that if God is omnipotent, then He can do anything, including breaking the laws of logic. The Bible says, "Nothing is impossible with God" (Matt. 19:26), and if this is so, it is suggested, it would seem to follow that God could violate the laws of thought if He wished.

However, this objection is based on a misconception. When the Bible declares that God can do anything, it does not mean that He can do what is impossible. It means that God can do anything that is *possible* to do. Indeed, the Scriptures declare that there are many things that are impossible for God. Hebrews 6:18 affirms, "It is impossible for God to lie"; 2 Timothy 2:13 NKJV adds, "He cannot deny Himself." It would be a denial of Himself for God to deny the laws of rational thought, since they are based on His rational nature.

Can't God Transcend Logic As He Does Natural Law?

Some have suggested that since God made natural law and can transcend it by supernatural intervention, it would seem to follow that He can do the same with the rational laws He has made. In short, if God can break His laws of physics, why can't He break His laws of rationality?

The response to this is that God did not *make* or *create* the laws of thought any more than He created Himself. *The laws of reason are based on God's uncreated nature.* That is the way He is, always has been, and always will be. God cannot change His nature and, hence, cannot break the laws that flow from His nature. The laws of physics are created, not uncreated, and can be transcended by God like everything else that is created. But as the laws of thought are based on God's uncreated nature, God can no more change them than He can cease to be God.

Are Not the Mysteries of the Faith Against Logic?

From inside Christian theology, several other objections have been set forth flowing from the great mysteries of the faith: The Trinity, the Incarnation, and the doctrine of predestination/free will.

The Trinity

The orthodox view of the Trinity posits that there is only one God and yet three different Persons make up that one God. This appears to some to violate the law of noncontradiction; how can God be only one and yet three at the same time and in the same sense?

Put in this way, the answer is that He cannot, but this misstates the doctrine of the Trinity. According to evangelical theology, God is not both three and only one *in the same sense.* He is only one *in nature* (essence) but three in a different sense—*in Persons.*

Three persons in one essence is no more a contradiction than are three corners on one triangle or three ones in one to the third power $(1 \times 1 \times 1 = 1)$. God has one *what* (nature) with three *whos* (persons). This is a mystery (cf. 1 Tim. 3:16) but not a contradiction. To be contradictory God would have to be both three and only one at the same time and in the same sense; that is, He would have to be three Persons and yet only one Person at the same time and in the same sense. Or, He would have to be three Natures and yet only one Nature at the same time and in the same sense. But this is not what orthodox theologians claim about the Trinity.

The Incarnation

Like the Trinity, the Incarnation is also a great mystery. Some even claim it is a contradiction, for it affirms that in Christ God became man, and this is impossible, since God is infinite and man is finite—an infinite cannot become finite. The Eternal cannot become temporal any more than the Uncreated can become a creature. How then can we claim that the Incarnation does not violate the law of noncontradiction?

The answer to this apparent contradiction lies in the misstatement of what the Incarnation really is. It was not God *becoming* man, but the second person of the Godhead *adding* humanity; in other words, the Son of God did not stop being divine in order to become human, but rather He embraced another nature—humanity—in addition to His divinity. In the Incarnation, the infinite nature of God did not become finite; the second person of the Godhead, who retained His infinite nature, also assumed another nature (a finite one). As we put it before, in God there is one *what* (nature) and three *whos* (persons).

In the Incarnation, Who[2] took on What[2], a human nature, in addition to the What[1] He retained (His divine nature). This is not a contradiction because the infinite did not become finite, nor the Uncreated become the created, which would be a contradiction.

In the Godhead there is one What and three Whos; in Christ, the second person of the Godhead, there is one Who and two Whats. In the Incarnation, one Who in God assumed another What, so that there were two Whats (natures) in one Who (person). Again, this is an amazing mystery but not a contradiction.

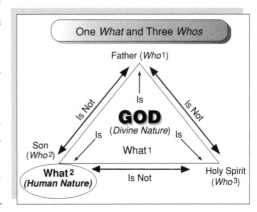

Predestination and Free Will

For everyone except extreme Calvinists (see volume 3), who deny free will in this matter, there is a seeming paradox between God's predetermination and human free choice. How can God determine the end from the beginning (Isa. 46:10), and how could He have chosen His elect before the foundation of the world (Eph. 1:4), when the Bible also affirms that human beings are free to accept or reject God's gift of salvation (John 1:12; Rom. 6:23; Matt. 23:37; 2 Peter 3:9)? If God determined in advance who will be saved and who will not be saved, then how can humans be free (see volume 3)?

The answer to this apparent dilemma resides in an understanding of how God predetermines events like these. God does not force them to happen *against our free will;* rather He predetermines that they will occur *through our free will.* Or, to put it minimally, God does not have to *make* these events occur; He can *see* them occur—from His eternal vantage point.[13]

A person standing on top of a building foreseeing a collision (between

---

[13]This does not mean God sees them in a passive sense. He sees them actively and chooses them eternally. Hence, His knowledge is causal, for the future preexists in God as the Cause of all things that have occurred, are occurring, or will occur.

two cars that cannot see each other around the corner) does not cause the crash. Likewise, God, who can by His omniscience foresee what we will freely do, need not cause us to do it. And even if He is the *ultimate* cause of all things, He is not the *immediate* cause of them. *Free moral agents* are the immediate cause of all free actions. God (the primary cause) produced the *fact* of freedom, and free agents (secondary causes), by God's grace, produce the *acts* of freedom (see volume 3).

Further, one and the same event can be both determined and yet free with no contradiction. For example, when one watches a recording of a televised game, it is already determined; nothing can be changed. It will turn out exactly the same, score and all, no matter how many times one watches it. Yet when the game was played, each and every person played according to his or her own free will. No one was forced to do anything. Thus, one and the same events were both determined and yet free (see Geisler, *CBF*, chapters 1–3).

To the objection that this is so because we are looking back on the game, the theist could reply, "God in His omniscience looks forward with an even greater certainty than we look backward." This leads to another point.

The God of orthodox theology is eternal, not temporal. Therefore, He does not really look *forward* to the future; He simply looks *downward* on it (see volume 2), since it is present to Him in His eternal now (as the great *I AM* of Ex. 3:14). To illustrate, a person in a cave can look out the tunnel and see only one train car going by at a time—the present one. He cannot see the one already past or the one yet to come. But the person on the top of that mountain can see all of them at the same time. Likewise, God can see past, present, and future all in His eternal present (the now). He sees the future, not because it has already occurred, but because it preexists in Him as the eternal Cause of all that was, is, and will be.

If God is eternal, there is no problem with an event being determined in advance (and, thus, not being free), for then God is actively seeing in His eternal present what we are freely doing. He is not passively seeing the future (as though He had to wait on it to occur). He is not literally *fore*seeing anything. It is only called foreseeing and predetermining from our standpoint in time, not from God's vantage point in eternity.

In point of fact, God knows the future not because He is looking *down* or *ahead*; He is simply looking *within* Himself, for all effects preexist in their cause,[14] and God is the Cause of all things, including the future.[15]

---

[14]Effects preexist in their cause because an efficient cause cannot give what it does not have. It cannot share with another what it does not have to share; it can only produce what it possesses (see chapter 9).

[15]God is the Cause of all that exists, but He causes it from eternity, where He alone exists. Even time—having had a beginning—is caused by the eternal God. All events in time caused by God were caused from eternity, even though the effect does not occur until a specific time. Of course, since evil is a privation or corruption of being, God is not the cause of evil. He is the cause of the good being in which the parasite of evil has taken residence.

Hence, God is seeing them in His eternal nature, before they ever occur, with the same certainty as if they had already occurred (see Aquinas, *ST*, 1a.14.6–9). There is no contradiction between God's predestination and our free will.

Finally, the harmony between predestination and free choice can be demonstrated from God's omniscience alone. Consider the following argument:

(1) God is all-knowing.
(2) An all-knowing Being knows everything, including the future.
(3) What an all-knowing Being knows will come to pass—must come to pass (if it did not, then God would have been wrong about what He foreknew. But an all-knowing God cannot be wrong about anything He knows).
(4) God knows all future free acts.
(5) Therefore, these free acts *must come to pass.* (If they didn't, then an all-knowing God would have been wrong.)
(6) But what must come to pass is determined.
(7) Therefore, our free acts are predetermined by God.

While the logic of this argument is tight, many believe that it proves we aren't free. This is not the case. What it demonstrates is that God can know for sure (has determined) what we will freely do. So one and the same event is *determined* from the standpoint of God's knowledge and *free* from the vantage point of our choice. Again, this may be a mystery, but the great mystery of predestination and free will, whatever else it is, is not a logical contradiction.

CONCLUSION

Systematic theology is dependent on logic in many ways. All of its claims are subject to the basic laws of thought. Contradictions cannot both be true and false. Likewise, as will be seen in chapter 12, the methods used in doing systematic theology are both deductive- and inductive-type logic. Systematic theology begins with an inductive study of both special revelation (in the Bible) and general revelation (in nature), it makes deductions from them, and these are put together in a unified and systematic whole. Without logic, this would not be possible; hence, philosophy (especially logic) is truly the handmaid of theology.

SOURCES

Aristotle. *Posterior Analytics.*
———. *Prior Analytics.*
———. *Topics.*

Bacon, Francis. *Novum Organum.*

Clark, Gordon. *A Christian View of Men and Things.*

Dooyeweerd, Herman. *New Critique of Theoretical Thought.*

Geisler, Norman. *Chosen But Free.*

Geisler, Norman, and Ronald Brooks. *Come, Let Us Reason: An Introduction to Logical Thinking.*

Hoyle, Sir Fred. *Evolution From Space.*

Mill, John Stuart. *System of Logic.*

Suzuki, D. T. *An Introduction to Zen Buddhism.*

Thomas Aquinas. *Summa Theologica.*

Whitehead, Alfred North, and Bertrand Russell. *Principia Mathematica.*

CHAPTER SIX

MEANING: THE SEMANTICAL PRECONDITION

Christianity makes truth claims. It asserts that a theistic God exists (see chapter 2), that Christ is the Son of God (see volume 2), and that the Bible is the Word of God (see part 2). These truths are held to be objectively (rather than merely subjectively) true; that is, they are true not only for me but for everyone (see chapter 7).

However, all true statements must be *meaningful*—they must make sense. Nonsensical statements are neither true nor false (e.g., "Zuplops cadlure gugemonts"). Likewise, emotive statements (like "Ouch!") have no cognitive meaning; they also are neither true nor false, but are simply an expression of our feelings.[1] Yet both true *and* false statements are meaningful statements. For example, "The capital of the United States is Canton, Ohio" is meaningful, but it is false. So, by definition, in order to be cognitively meaningful a statement must be either true or false.[2]

Now, if all true statements are meaningful, then all objectively true statements (as Christianity claims to possess) must be objectively meaningful. Thus the objectivity of truth is dependent on the objectivity of meaning. Unfortunately, the dominant view in the contemporary world is opposed to an objective embrace of meaning. This dominant view is called conventionalism.

---

[1]Of course, statements about our feelings (e.g., "I feel warm") are objectively true or false (see chapter 7). But strictly emotive statements are not statements *about* one's feeling but expressions *of* one's feelings.

[2]Questions and exclamations are meaningful, but in a noncognitive way, since they do not affirm or deny anything.

CONVENTIONALISM VS. ESSENTIALISM

Conventionalism is the theory that all *meaning* is relative. Since all truth claims are meaningful statements, conventionalism necessarily holds that all *truth* is relative. But this is contrary to the Christian claim that there is absolute truth—truths that are true at all times, in all places, and for all people (see chapter 7).

Conventionalism: A Reaction to Platonic Essentialism

Conventionalism is a reaction to essentialism, which (following Plato) claims that all language has an unchanging essence or form. By contrast, conventionalism maintains that all meaning is relative to changing situations; meaning is arbitrary and varies according to its context. According to conventionalism, there are no forms of meaning that transcend time and place (transcultural forms). Language (meaning) has no form or essence; linguistic meaning is therefore derived from the changing, relative experience on which language is based.

Essentialism: Plato's View of Absolute Meaning

Plato (c. 427–347 B.C.) defended a form of essentialism in his dialogue titled *Cratylus.* Augustine (A.D. 354–430) did also in his *Principia Dialtecticae* (384), *De Magistro* (389), and *De Trinitate* (394–419), although Augustine apparently did not hold to Plato's picture theory of meaning (the idea that language pictures meaning),[3] which Ludwig Wittgenstein critiqued in his famous *Tractatus.*

Simply stated, essentialism (also called naturalism)[4] insists that *there is a natural or essential relation between our statements and what they mean.* Language is not arbitrarily related to meaning; rather, there is a one-to-one correspondence between them.

Conventionalism: Challenging Platonic Essentialism

Three names loom large in the modern relativization of meaning: Ferdinand de Saussure (1857–1913), Gottlob Frege (1848–1925), and Ludwig Wittgenstein (1889–1951). Their presentation of conventionalism is widely accepted in current linguistic philosophy.

---

[3]The picture theory of meaning is the idea that language is a picture of reality, corresponding to it as does a photograph to its object. Many believe that the relevant passage in Augustine's *Confessions* (1.8), which Wittgenstein critiqued, was not embraced by Augustine but only offered for consideration, since he rejected it elsewhere (in *De Magistro*).

[4]"Naturalism" as used here, in a semantic sense, should not be confused with antisupernaturalistic naturalism, in a metaphysical sense.

Ferdinand Saussure

The forerunner of modern conventionalism was the famous Swiss linguist Ferdinand Saussure. His *Course in General Linguistics* is still a standard in the field.

Gottlob Frege

Although Frege wrote relatively little, his teachings, put together from the notes of his students, have had a strong influence on the adoption of conventionalism by modern linguists. These teachings are found in *Translations from the Philosophical Writings of Gottlob Frege.*

Ludwig Wittgenstein

Leaning on the works of his predecessors, Ludwig Wittgenstein is credited with making conventionalism the predominant view in philosophical and religious thought. His mature perspective is expressed in his *Philosophical Investigations*; section I presents a critique of "a particular picture of the essence of human language," which contains the following theses:

(1) The function of language is to state facts.
(2) All words are names (the referential theory of meaning).[5]
(3) The meaning of a name is the object denoted.
(4) Meaning is taught by ostensive definition.[6]

All of these theses are rejected by Wittgenstein as being either an oversimplification of language (theses 1 and 2), or, in the case of thesis 4, mistaken ("an ostensive definition can be variously interpreted in every case," *PI*, 1:28), or, as in thesis 3, shown to be absurd by giving examples (e.g., exclamations, *PI*, 1:27; *PI*, 1:39).

Other theses that are closely connected with the picture theory of meaning and that come in for criticism are the following:

(1) Meaning is a matter of producing mental images.
(2) Analysis of propositions = Clarification of propositions (*PI*, 1:60).
(3) Words have a determinate sense.[7]

Wittgenstein offers an alternative view of meaning that employs:

(1) family resemblances (*PI* 1:67);
(2) language games (*PI* 1:7);[8]
(3) forms of life (*PI*, 1:19, 23, 241; II, 194, 226).

---

[5]The referential theory of meaning is the idea that meaningful statements have objects to which they refer.
[6]Meaning that is ostensive is meaning that is readily apparent or easily demonstrated.
[7]That is, words have a definite meaning.
[8]That is, language is like a game that is played with a certain set of rules. Meaning is based in life experiences and has no essence, but merely family resemblance to other experiences.

Since Wittgenstein rejected both univocal[9] and analogical language[10] (see chapter 9), he held an *equivocal* view[11] reflected in family resemblances and based on changing experience. As such he is one of the strongest proponents of conventionalism.

Wittgenstein and Religious Language

In Wittgenstein's earlier work *Tractatus*, religious language was placed in the realm of the inexpressible. He ended *Tractatus* with the famous line, "That of which you cannot speak, speak not thereof." It is alleged that religious discourse has no factual meaning, and there is an unbridgeable gulf between fact and value.[12] Thus, according to consistent conventionalism, God-talk is nonsense.

It is clear from Wittgenstein's *Notebooks* that such feelings as dependence, as well as the recognition that "to believe in a God means to see that the facts of the world are not the end of the matter" (*T*, 11), are elements that Wittgenstein "knows" but that are not expressible in language. They are supposedly outside the limits of language and thought.

That the higher and transcendent are inexpressible does not say they are totally incommunicable, for they can be shown yet not said. This is called the doctrine of "showing and saying."[13] An apparent contradiction in the *Tractatus* is found in that although propositions about language are employed, nevertheless they are, strictly speaking, nonsensical because they are not propositions of natural science. Wittgenstein acknowledges that they are nonsensical and thus can only serve as elucidations (*T*, 6:45). The fairest interpretation to put on this is to treat the *Tractatus* as an example of the doctrine of showing and saying. Otherwise, it is inconsistent.

Later, in *Philosophical Investigations*, Wittgenstein does not directly speak about religious discourse, but seems to indicate that praying and theology are legitimate and meaningful linguistic activities. (Praying, in particular, is mentioned as a language game.) Since stating facts is only one of a multiplicity of meaningful linguistic activities, there is no a priori bar against the meaningfulness of religious language. This also means that since language games have an intrinsic (internal) criterion of meaning, and since religious language is a language game, religious language must be judged by its own standards and not by standards imposed upon it, which is a form of fideism.[14]

---

[9]Univocal language can have only one meaning.

[10]Analogical language is based on similarity or analogy.

[11]Equivocal language is ambiguous, having two or more meanings.

[12]Ethics and religion are matters of value, while science deals with facts.

[13]The doctrine of showing and saying holds that language can point to the higher and transcendent but cannot describe it.

[14]Fideism is "exclusive or basic reliance upon faith alone accompanied by a consequent disparagement of reason" (*Webster's Third New International Dictionary*).

In Wittgenstein's *Lectures and Conversations* religious language is portrayed as having the possibility of being meaningful (as a language game). But it is clear from this work that Wittgenstein is a religious acognostic,[15] meaning that he rejects any cognitive knowledge in religious language. He recognizes the legitimacy of a form of life that could "culminate in an utterance of belief in a last judgment" (Wittgenstein, *LC* 58). He believes that it would be impossible to contradict such a belief or even say that it is possibly true.

The only sense in which such a belief might be a blunder is if it is a blunder in its particular system (ibid., 59), that is, inside of a given language game. Such beliefs are not based on evidence—they are purely a matter of (blind) faith. However, Wittgenstein would not ridicule those who have such a belief—only those who claim it is based on evidence, e.g., historical apologetics. Belief in these cases is used in an extraordinary way (not in an ordinary way). He wrote,

> It has been said that Christianity rests on an historical basis. It has [also] been said a thousand times by intelligent people that indubitability is not enough in this case. Even if there is as much evidence [for Christianity] as for Napoleon. Because the indubitability wouldn't be enough to make me change my whole life (ibid., 57).

Religious beliefs have commissive force; that is, they orient our lives. However, says Wittgenstein, they are not informative about reality. We are allegedly locked in a linguistic bubble, and while religious language is meaningful as a language game, it tells us nothing about God or ultimate reality. God-talk is experientially meaningful, but God-talk is not *real* talk about God; God is still the inexpressible. Human language is not capable of making any objectively meaningful statements about God, whether these statements are univocal or analogical (see chapter 9). All meaning is culturally and experientially relative—thus says conventionalism.

Distinction Between Conventional Symbols and Conventional Meaning

There is an important difference between a conventionalist theory of *symbols* and a conventionalist theory of *meaning*. Other than natural symbols (like smoke to fire) and onomatopoeic terms (like crash, bang, and boom),[16] whose sound *is* their meaning, virtually all linguists acknowledge that symbols are conventionally relative. That is to say, the word *bark* has no intrinsic relation to the sound of the canine mammal to which it may refer;

---

[15]An acognostic is one who believes there is no cognitive meaning.

[16]"Onomatopoeia" is "a formation of words in imitation of natural sounds: the naming of a thing or action by a more or less exact reproduction of the sound associated with it" (*Webster's Third New International Dictionary*).

it can also mean the outer coating of a tree. Indeed, different languages have different names for the same referents. And this is true of most such words.

However, admitting that most words in a sentence are conventional or relative is not the same as claiming that the *meaning* of a sentence is culturally relative; it means only that the *words* used to convey meaning are relative. That is, individual symbols change in meaning, but the meaning of a *sentence* (a unit of thought composed of words) does not change.

Critique of Conventionalism's Theory of Meaning

As a theory of meaning, conventionalism suffers from some serious faults. Several can be briefly noted.

First, conventionalism is self-falsifying. If the statement "All linguistic meaning is conventional" were true, then this statement itself would be relative, for it claims to be an objectively meaningful statement affirming that there are no such objectively meaningful statements. It offers itself as a nonrelative statement affirming that the meaning of all statements is relative.

Second, if conventionalism were correct, then universal statements would not necessarily translate into all languages as universal statements, but they do. For example, "All triangles have three sides" translates as universally true, everywhere, all the time. So does "All wives are married women." If meaning were only culturally relative, then no such universal, transcultural statements would be possible.

Third, if conventionalism were true there would not be any universal truths in any language, but there are. For instance, mathematical statements, such as 4+3=7, are universally true. So also are the basic laws of logic, such as the law of noncontradiction (see chapter 5). In fact, no conventionalist can even deny these first principles of thought without using them. The very statement "The meaning of all statements is relative to a culture" is dependent for its meaning on the fact that there are laws of logic that are not relative to a culture but that transcend all cultures and languages.

Fourth, if conventionalism were true, we would not know any truth independent of and/or prior to knowing the conventions of that truth in that language. But we know 2+1=3 before we know the conventions of a language. Mathematics may depend on relative symbols to express itself, but the truths of mathematics are not dependent on any culture.

Fifth, the laws of logic are not based on human conventions; they are true apart from *all* linguistic conventions. Logic is not arbitrary. We do not *choose* its laws; rather, we are *ruled* by them. We do not *create* them but merely *discover* them. They are logically prior to and independent of the culture in which they are expressed; cultures do not think them up or even think them up differently. *Without them, people in a culture could not even think.* People in every culture must use them before they think about them.

Sixth, conventionalism confuses the immediate *source* of meaning with its ultimate *grounds.* The *source* of learning that "all bachelors are unmarried" may be social; for example, one may have learned it from his parents or teachers. But the *grounds* for knowing this are not social but logical, for, like other first principles, the predicate is reducible to the subject. It is true by definition, not by acculturation.

Seventh, if conventionalism were correct, then no meaning would be possible. If all meaning is based on changing experience, which in turn gets its meaning from changing experience, etc., then there is actually no basis for the meaning. An infinite series is no more possible in meaning than it is in causes. Forever putting off the basis for meaning is not the same as finding the basis for it. And a statement without any basis for its meaning is a baseless affirmation.

Eighth, conventionalism has only an internal criterion for meaning, such as coherence. But internal criteria cannot adjudicate conflicts in meaning regarding the same statements from different worldview vantage points. For example, the statement "God is a Necessary Being" can be interpreted either pantheistically or theistically. Mere internal criteria, such as coherence or logical consistency, cannot determine which of these is correct.

Ninth, conventionalism involves a circular argument. It does not *justify* its claims; it simply *asserts* them. When a conventionalist is asked for the basis of his belief that all meaning is conventional, he cannot give a non-conventional basis, for then he would no longer be a conventionalist. But if he gives merely a conventional basis for his conventionalism, i.e., a relative basis for his relativism, then he argues in a circle.

Tenth, conventionalists often distinguish between surface and depth grammar[17] to avoid certain problems, such as those just given. But such a distinction assumes they have a vantage point independent of language and experience in order to make such a distinction, and conventionalism by its very nature does not allow such a vantage point outside of one's culture. Hence, the very distinction they make is not possible on the theory they espouse.

Eleventh, no truly descriptive knowledge of God is possible in a conventionalist view of language, since in conventionalism, language is simply based on our experience. It tells us only what God *seems to be* (to us) in our experience but not what He *really is* (in Himself). This reduces to self-defeating agnosticism (the claim that we know that we cannot know anything about the nature of God). Thus conventionalism reduces the

---

[17]Surface grammar is here defined as one that is obvious in the linguistic structure, while depth grammar is defined as one that is hidden beneath it.

meaning of "God" to a mere interpretive framework rather than an extra-cosmic Being beyond the world, which theism shows Him to be (see chapter 2).

REALISM: AN ALTERNATIVE TO ESSENTIALISM AND CONVENTIONALISM

The conventionalist's view of meaning is clearly an overreaction against platonic essentialism. There is a third alternative that avoids the rigidity of essentialism and the relativism of conventionalism: realism. Realism contends that meaning is objective, even though symbols are culturally relative, for meaning transcends our symbols and linguistic means of expressing it. Meaning is objective and absolute, not because a given linguistic expression of it is, but because there is an absolute Mind, God (see chapter 2), who has communicated it to finite minds (human beings) through a common but analogous means of human language (see chapter 9) that utilizes transcendent principles of logic common to both God and humans (see chapter 5).

A Framework for Understanding the Meaning of Meaning

The traditional six causes will help explain the point. Following Aristotle, scholastic philosophers distinguished six different causes:

(1) efficient cause—that *by which* something comes to be;
(2) final cause—that *for which* something comes to be;
(3) formal cause—that *of which* something comes to be;
(4) material cause—that *out of* which something comes to be;
(5) exemplar cause—that *after which* something comes to be;
(6) instrumental cause—that *through which* something comes to be.

For example, a wooden chair has a carpenter as an efficient cause, to provide something to sit on as a final cause, its structure as a chair as its formal cause, wood as its material cause, its blueprint as its exemplar cause, and the carpenter's tools as its instrumental cause.

Meaning Is Found in the Formal Cause

Applying these six causes to the meaning of a written text yields the following analysis:

(1) The writer is the *efficient* cause of the meaning of a text.
(2) The writer's purpose is the *final* cause of its meaning.
(3) The writing is the *formal* cause of its meaning.
(4) The words are the *material* cause of its meaning.

(5) The writer's ideas are the *exemplar* cause of its meaning.

(6) The laws of thought are the *instrumental* cause of its meaning.

The meaning (formal cause) of an intelligible expression, such as a writing, is not found in the "meaner"; he is the efficient cause of the meaning. The formal cause of meaning is in *the writing itself*. What is signified is found in the signs that signify it; verbal meaning is found in the very structure and grammar of the sentences, *in* the literary text itself (formal cause), not in its purpose (final cause). Note that meaning is *not* found in the individual words (material cause).

Words in themselves have no actual meaning; they have only potential meaning. Words have usage in a sentence, which is the smallest unity of meaning. To go back to an earlier example, the word *bark* has no inherent meaning, but it has several different usages (in sentences) that do have meaning, such as in the example below for the word *board*:

(1) The board came from an oak tree.

(2) The board member came from New York.

Words are only the parts of a whole (the whole sentence), which does have meaning. Likewise, pigments have no beauty but are the parts of a whole that does have beauty in a painting. Meaning, then, is found in the text as a whole, not in the parts independently.

The Locus of Meaning

A text's meaning is not found *beyond* the text (in the author's mind), *beneath* the text (in the mystic's mind), or *behind* the text (in the author's unexpressed intention); rather, it is found *in* the text (in the author's expressed meaning). In the same way, the beauty of a painting is not found behind, beneath, or beyond the painting; rather, it is expressed in the painting.

All textual meaning is *in* the text. The sentences (in the context of their paragraphs in the context of the whole piece of literature) are the formal cause of meaning. They are the form that gives meaning to all the parts (words, punctuation, etc.).

The Unity of Meaning

Since the meaning of Scripture comes ultimately from an objective Mind (God) and is found in an objective text that uses terms with the same meaning for both God and human beings (see chapter 9), it follows that there is only *one meaning* in a biblical text—the one given to it by the author. Of course, there can be *many implications and applications*—indeed, it can be expressed in different ways in the same language. This is made possible because there is an objective meaner, an objective means of meaning (logic), and a common medium (language) between meaner and meanee that is capable of expressing this meaning (see chapter 9). This objective meaning is found in the formal cause (language), which provides the structure or form of meaning. Thus the meaning of God's revelation, whether in Scripture or nature (see chapter 4) is found in an objective expression of the meaner. Thus, while the *sensus unum* (one sense) view is correct when it affirms only one meaning to a text, there is, however, a *sensus plenum* (full sense) in terms of implications and applications. For example, Einstein (1879–1955) knew that e=mc² (energy equals mass times the speed of light [constant] squared) and so does an average high school science student. However, Einstein knew many more implications and applications of this than the average high school student.

Likewise, God, inasmuch as He inspired the text (2 Tim. 3:16), knows infinitely more about the topic and sees more implications and applications in a biblical affirmation than does the human author (1 Pet. 1:10–12). *But He does not affirm any more meaning in the text than the human author does,* for whatever the Bible says, God says; whatever the Bible affirms is true, God affirms is true. Both the divine and human authors of Scripture affirm one and the same meaning in one and the same text. There are not two texts, and there are not two meanings of the text.

The Objectivity of Meaning

Human languages vary, but meaning does not. The same objective meaning can be expressed in widely diverse language.

Unlike essentialism, which insists on a one-to-one correlation between the meaning and the expression, and unlike conventionalism, which contends there is a many-to-one correlation between the meaning and the expression, realism affirms that there is a one-to-many correlation. That is, one meaning can be expressed in many different ways in many languages and even in the same language. Thus *language can and does change, but the meaning it expresses does not.* The usage of a word changes from time to time, but the meaning of that word in a sentence does not change. For example, in the King James Version of 1611 the word *let* (cf. 2 Thess. 2:7) meant to "hinder." (Today it means the opposite.) But the *meaning expressed* by the *New King James Version* (1982) when it renders it "restrain" is the same as that of the old King James Version (1611). Usage of words change, but meaning does not.

Another example of the same point is mathematical meaning. Whether one writes "Two plus two equals four" or "2+2=4" the meaning is the same, even though the mode of expression is different. Further, the meaning is objective, even though the mode of expression is relative.

CONCLUSION

The objectivity of truth that Christianity embraces is based on the premise that meaning is objective. This objectivity in meaning is rejected by much of contemporary linguistics; the prevailing conventionalist theory of meaning is a form of semantical relativism. However, in addition to being an overreaction to platonic essentialism, conventionalism is self-defeating, for, as we have seen, the very theory of conventionalism that "all meaning is relative" is itself a nonrelative statement. "All meaning is relative" is a meaningful statement intended to apply to *all* meaningful statements; it is a nonconventional statement claiming that all statements are conventional. As such, it self-destructs, for in the very process of expressing itself it implies a theory of meaning that is contrary to the one it claims is true of all meaningful statements. The usages of symbols and words do change, but the meaning properly expressed by them does not.

SOURCES

Augustine. *De Magistro* [*The Teacher*].
———. *De Trinitate* [*On the Trinity*].
———. *Principia Dialtecticae* [*Principles of Dialectics*].
Frege, Gottlob. *Uber Sinn und Bedeutung* ("On Sense and Reference" by Peter Geach in *Translations From the Philosophical Writings of Gottlob Frege*).
Gilson, Étienne. *Linguistics and Philosophy.*
Howe, Thomas. *Objectivity in Hermeneutics.* Dissertation; Southeastern Baptist Theological Seminary. May 1998.
Plato. *Cratylus.*
Saussure, Ferdinand. *Cours de Linguistique Generale* [*Course in General Linguistics*].
Thomas Aquinas. *Summa Theologica.*
Wittgenstein, Ludwig. *Lectures and Conversations.*
———. *Notebooks.*
———. *Philosophical Investigations.*
———. *Tractatus.*

CHAPTER SEVEN

TRUTH: THE EPISTEMOLOGICAL PRECONDITION

Another important precondition of evangelical theology is the nature of truth. Up to modernity, orthodox theology has held that truth is what corresponds to the objects of its affirmations—this is called a correspondence view of truth. This paradigm, however, has been seriously challenged in more recent times. It is necessary, therefore, to discuss and defend the biblical and theological basis for the correspondence view of truth.[1]

THE IMPORTANCE OF THE DEFINITION OF TRUTH

The Bible claims to be true. The psalmist declared, "Your law is truth" (Ps. 119:142 NKJV), and Jesus prayed, "Sanctify them by Your truth. Your word is truth" (John 17:17 NKJV). Yet Pilate's question remains: "What is truth?"

The nature of truth is crucial to the Christian faith. Not only does Christianity claim there is absolute truth (which is true for everyone, everywhere, always) but it also insists that truth is that which corresponds to the way things really are. For example, the statement "God exists" means that there truly is a God outside the universe, an extra-cosmic Being. Likewise, the claim that "God raised Christ from the dead" means that the dead corpse of Jesus of Nazareth supernaturally vacated its tomb—alive—after its

---

[1]Epistemology is "the study of the methods and the grounds of knowledge, especially with reference to its limits and validity; broadly, [epistemology is] the theory of knowledge" (*Webster's Third New International Dictionary*).

burial. Christian truth claims actually correspond to the state of affairs about which they claim to inform us.

The nature of truth will determine what is meant by the claim that the Bible is true. Also, it will seriously affect an important discussion about whether the Bible is without error and precisely what is meant by inerrancy (see part 2, chapter 27), for if truth is not what corresponds to the facts, but rather merely what the author intends, then the Bible can be wholly true and yet contain factual errors—as strange as this may seem.

THE DEFINITION OF TRUTH

Truth can be understood both from what it is and from what it is not. Before we can know what truth is, we must examine what truth is not.

What Truth Is Not

There are many inadequate views of the nature of truth. Most of these result from confusion between the nature (definition) of truth and a test (defense) of truth, or from not distinguishing the result from the rule. (This will be clarified below, in the examples of what truth isn't.)

Truth Is Not "That Which Works"

One popular theory of truth is the pragmatism of William James (1842–1910) and his followers. According to the pragmatic view (see James, *P*), truth is what works; truth is found in the "cash value" of a statement. In William James's own words, "Truth is the expedient in the way of knowing." This means that a statement is known to be true if it brings the right results. It is present expedience as confirmed by future experience.

The inadequacy of this view of truth is evident from several considerations. *First*, the proponents of it do not expect us to understand their expression of their view of truth for pragmatism but for correspondence. That is, they do not want us to accept a pragmatic view of truth because it seems to be effective but because it corresponds with the way they believe things really are.

Second, the pragmatic view confuses cause and effect. If something is true it will work, at least in the long run. But that something *works* does not make it *true*. Lies often work, but their effectiveness doesn't make them true; they remain false, regardless of their result.

Third, the concept of truth as "what works" is a narrow and restrictive view of truth. At best it refers only to practical truths, not to theoretical or mathematical truths ($5+5=10$ not because it works but because it is correct), or to metaphysical truths (see chapter 2).

Fourth, pragmatism's presentation of "truth" is not how truth is understood in everyday life, or in court, where knowing and telling the truth can

be a matter of life and death. No judge would accept the testimony of anyone who says, "I swear to tell the expedient, the whole expedient, and nothing but the expedient, so help me future experience."

Fifth, results do not settle the question of truth, for even when the
results are already in, one can still ask whether or not the initial statement
corresponded to the facts. If it did not, then it isn't true, no matter what
the results were.

Truth Is Not "That Which Coheres"

Some thinkers have suggested that truth is what is internally consistent;
what coheres within; what is self-consistent. However, this also is an inadequate definition of truth for two basic reasons:

First, the very statement "Truth is that which coheres" is offered by the
coherentist as a statement that corresponds to reality. Hence, the coherence theory depends on the opposing correspondence view of truth even
to express itself. No coherentist wants us to accept his view simply because
he believes it coheres but because he believes it is true (i.e., because he says
it correctly represents the state of affairs to which it refers).

Second, empty statements can cohere or stand together even though
they are devoid of content (meaning that they do not refer to anything).
For example, "All wives are married women" is internally consistent, but
it's empty—it tells us nothing about the real world. The statement would
be true even if there were no wives; it really means, "*If* there is a wife, then
she must be married," but it does not inform us that there is a wife anywhere in the universe. Also, a set of false statements can be internally consistent; such is the case in a conspiracy to lie under oath. In addition, coherence is at best only a negative test of truth—that is, statements are wrong if
they are inconsistent, but not necessarily true if they are consistent.

Truth Is Not "That Which Was Intended"

Others have suggested that truth is found in intentions, not necessarily
in affirmations. That is, a statement is true if the author intends it to be
true, and a statement is false if he does not intend it to be true (see Rogers,
BAI). But there are likewise serious problems with this position.

First, as with coherence, a proponent of the intentionalist view of truth
has to use a correspondence view of truth to express his view, for the very
statement "The intentionalist view of truth is *true*" is true not because he
intended to say it but only if it *corresponds* to its referent. The word *true* in
that sentence means "correct" or "corresponds," otherwise the claim
makes no sense.

Second, many statements do not agree with the intention of the author,
but they are mistaken nonetheless. Slips of the tongue do occur, and they
are false. But if a statement was true because it was intended to be true,
even if it was mistaken, then all such errors would be true.

Third, if something is true because someone intended it to be true, then all sincere statements ever uttered would be true—even those that were patently absurd. But many sincere people have been sincerely wrong. Hence, the intentionalist view of truth is inadequate.

Truth Is Not "That Which is Comprehensive"

Others claim that truth is found in what is most comprehensive. That is to say, the view that explains the most data is true, and those that are not as comprehensive are not true—at least not *as* true. This theory of truth falls far short of being a comprehensive definition of truth for several reasons.

First, as we have seen with the other examples, the claim that "the comprehensiveness view of truth is *true*" depends for its truth on the correspondence view of truth. The word *true* in that sentence means what corresponds to reality, to what is correct.

Second, comprehensiveness is at best only a *test* for truth, not the *definition* of truth. Certainly a good theory will explain all the relevant data, and a true worldview will be comprehensive. However, this is only a *negative* test of whether or not it is true—the *affirmations* of that view must still correspond with the alleged state of affairs in order to be true.

Third, if a view were true simply because it is more encyclopedic, then a comprehensive view of error would be true and a brief presentation of truth would be in error; automatically, long-winded presentations would be true and concise ones false. But this is plainly ridiculous—clearly one can have an exhaustive view of what is false and an incomplete view of what is true.

Truth Is Not "That Which Is Existentially Relevant"

Following Søren Kierkegaard (1813–1855), other existentialist philosophers have insisted that what is relevant to our existence or life is true, and what is not relevant to our existence or life is false. Truth is subjectivity, as Kierkegaard put it; truth is what is livable.[2] As another existentialist (Martin Buber, 1878–1965) stated, truth is found in persons not in propositions (*IAT*). There are a number of problems with the existential definition of truth.

First, the very statement "Truth is not found in propositions" is itself a propositional truth claim. In other words, it is self-defeating.

Second, the existentialist confuses the *nature* of truth and the *application* of truth. Of course, all applicable truth should be applied to one's life; that is, all objective truth should be appropriated subjectively where possible. But this does not mean that truth itself is subjective.

---

[2]Kierkegaard did not deny factual truth, but he affirmed that in religious matters it had to be subjectively appropriated to be true.

Third, existentialism presents too narrow a definition of all truth. Even if truth is existential in some sense, not all truth fits into this category—there are many other kinds of truth, including physical, mathematical, historical, and theoretical truths. If truth by its very nature were found only in existential relevance, then none of these could be true. *Existential relevance fails as a complete definition of truth.*

Fourth, what is true will always be relevant, but not everything that is relevant is true. A pen is relevant to an atheistic writer, and a gun is relevant to a murderer. But relevance makes neither the former true nor the latter good. A truth about life will be relevant to one's life, but not everything relevant to one's life will be true.

Fifth, many existentialists make a false dichotomy between fact and value, relegating religious truth to the nonfactual domain. This, however, is not possible because one cannot separate the spiritual significance of Christ's death and resurrection from the objective facts of His literal death, empty tomb, and physical appearances (1 Cor. 15:1–19).

Truth Is Not "That Which Feels Good"

The popular subjectivist view is that truth is what provides a satisfying feeling, while error is what feels bad. Accordingly, truth is found in our subjective feelings. Many mystics and New Agers hold to versions of this model (Shirley MacLaine, *Out On a Limb*); however, this view is faulty for many reasons.

First, this view is self-defeating, for the claim that "What feels good is *true*" is so only if it corresponds to the way things *are*. Thus it depends on a correspondence view of truth to make sense out of its claim to be true in a factual or objective sense. Subjectivism is actually claiming that its view of truth is correct only if it corresponds to the facts of the matter, not simply because it feels good.

Second, it is evident that bad news (which makes us feel bad) can be true. But if what feels good is always true, then this would not be possible. Poor report cards do not make a student feel good, even though they are true. The truth is, the truth often hurts.

Third, feelings are relative to individuals, and thus what feels good to one may feel bad to another. If this were because of truth, then truth would be relative. But all truth cannot be relative, for the truth claim that "all truth is relative" is itself offered as an absolute statement and therefore as an absolute truth (see page 119, "A Response to Arguments for a Relative View of Truth").

Fourth, even if truth makes us feel good, we cannot be convinced that what feels good is necessarily true—there is a confusion here of the cart and the horse. The nature of truth is not the same as the result of truth.

What Truth Is: Truth Is That Which Corresponds to Its Object

Now that the inadequate views of the nature of truth have been examined, it remains to state the positive view. *Truth is found in correspondence.* Truth is what corresponds to its object (referent), whether this object is abstract or concrete. As applied to the world, truth is the way things really are. Truth is "telling it like it is."

Of course, there can be truth about abstract realities as well as tangible realities. For example, there are mathematical truths, and there are also truths about ideas, such as the ideas in one's mind. Truth is what accurately expresses these states of affairs, whatever they may be.

By contrast, falsehood is that which does not correspond to its referent (object). Falsehood does not tell it like it is, but like it is not; it is a misrepresentation of the way things are. Statements are false if they are mistaken, even if the speaker intended to say the correct things.

Philosophical Arguments for a Correspondence View of Truth

There are many reasons that support a correspondence view of the nature of truth—the view that truth is what accurately describes its referent. Several are enumerated as follows:

First, noncorrespondence views of truth are self-defeating. As we have seen again and again, all noncorrespondence views of truth imply a correspondence view of truth in their very attempt to deny the correspondence model. For example, the claim that "the noncorrespondence view is true" implies that noncorrespondence corresponds to reality; therefore, the noncorrespondence view cannot even express itself without using the correspondence view of truth.

Second, even lies are impossible without a correspondence view of truth. If one's statements need not correspond to the facts in order to be true, then any factually incorrect statement could be true. And if this is the case, then lies become impossible because any statement is compatible with any given state of affairs.

Third, without correspondence there could be no such thing as truth or falsity. In order to know that something is true as opposed to knowing that something is false, there must be a real difference between things and the statements about the things. But this real difference between thought and things is precisely what is entailed in a correspondence view of *truth.*

Fourth, factual communication would break down without a correspondence view of truth. Factual communication depends on informative statements, but informative statements must be factually true (that is, they must correspond to the facts) in order to inform one correctly. Further, all communication seems to depend ultimately on something being literally or factually true, for we cannot know something (like a metaphor) is not literally true unless we understand what is literal. This being the case, it follows that all communication depends in the final analysis on a correspondence view of truth.

Fifth, even the intentionalist theory depends on the correspondence view of truth. The intentionalist theory claims something is true only if the accomplishments correspond to the intentions. Consequently, within the intentionalist system, without correspondence of intentions and accomplished facts there is no truth.

Biblical Arguments for a Correspondence View of Truth

From a theological point of view, it is important to know whether the biblical authors employed a correspondence view of truth. There are many lines of evidence to confirm that they did (see Preus, *IS*, 24).

First, the ninth commandment is predicated on a correspondence view of truth. "You shall not give false testimony against your neighbor" (Ex. 20:16) depends for its very meaning and effectiveness on correspondence, implying that a statement is false if it does not correspond to reality.

Indeed, this is precisely how the term "lie" is used in Scripture. Satan is called a liar (John 8:44); his statement to Eve, "You will not surely die" (Gen. 3:4), did not correspond to what God *really* said, namely, "You will surely die" (Gen. 2:17). Ananias and Sapphira lied to the apostles by misrepresenting the factual state of affairs concerning their finances (Acts 5:1–4).

Second, the Bible gives numerous examples of the correspondence view of truth. Joseph said to his brothers, "Send one of your number to get your brother; the rest of you will be kept in prison, so that your words may be tested to see if you are telling the truth" (Gen. 42:16).

Moses commanded that false prophets be tested on the grounds that "if what a prophet proclaims . . . does not take place or come true, that is a message the LORD has not spoken" (Deut. 18:22).

Solomon prayed at the dedication of the temple, "And now, O God of Israel, let your word that you promised your servant David my father [that there would be a temple] come true" (1 Kings 8:26).

The prophecies of Micaiah were considered "true" and the false prophets' false words "lies" because the former corresponded with the facts of reality (1 Kings 22:16–22).

Something was considered a "falsehood" if it did not correspond to God's law—truth (Ps. 119:163).

Proverbs states, "A truthful witness saves lives, but a false witness is deceitful" (Prov. 14:25), which implies that truth is factually correct. In court, intentions alone will not save innocent lives when they have been accused. Only "the truth, the whole truth, and nothing but the truth" will do it.

Nebuchadnezzar demanded of his wise men to know the *facts*; he considered anything else "misleading" (Dan. 2:9).

Jesus' statement in John 5:33 entails a correspondence view of truth: "You have sent to John and he has testified to the truth."

In Acts 24 there is an unmistakable usage of the correspondence view. The Jews said to the governor about Paul, "By examining him yourself you will be able to learn the truth about all these charges we are bringing against him" (v. 8). They continued, "You can easily verify [the facts]" (v. 11).

Paul clearly implied a correspondence view of truth when he wrote, "Each of you must put off falsehood and speak truthfully to his neighbor" (Eph. 4:25).

Third, the biblical use of the word *err* does not support the intentionalist theory of truth, since it is used of unintentional "errors" (cf. Lev. 4:2, 27, etc.). Certain acts were wrong, whether the trespassers intended to commit them or not, and hence a guilt offering was called for to atone for their error. Of the five times *shagag* ("to err") is used in the Old Testament (Gen. 6:3; Lev. 5:18; Num. 15:28; Job 12:16; Ps. 119:67), the Leviticus and Numbers references plainly refer to erring unintentionally.

Further, the noun *shegagah* ("error") is used nineteen times, and all but two are of unintentional errors (Lev. 4:2, 22, 27; 5:15, 18; 22:14; Num. 15:25 [twice], 26, 27, 28, 29 [twice]; 35:11 [twice]; Josh. 20:3, 9.) Only Ecclesiastes 5:6 and 10:5 could be understood as using *shegagah* to refer to intentional errors.

To summarize, the Bible consistently employs a correspondence view of truth. A statement is true if it corresponds to the facts and false if it does not. Rarely are there even apparent exceptions to this usage. John 5:31 appears to be an exception. Jesus said, "If I testify about myself, my testimony is not valid." This would seem to imply that Jesus' factually correct statements about Himself were not "true."

However, this would not make sense even by an intentionalist's definition of truth, for surely Jesus *intended* truth about Himself. What is meant here is that a self-testimony was not *established* as true. Or, as the NIV puts it, such "testimony of two or three [other] witnesses" is needed that every word might be *established* (Matt. 18:16; cf. John 8:17) and not by one's own word. Elsewhere Jesus clearly said, "Even if I testify on my own behalf, my testimony is valid" (John 8:14), meaning that it is factually correct, even if they did not accept it.

If the biblical arguments are this strong for a correspondence view of truth, why is it that many Christians—even some who believe in inerrancy— claim to hold a noncorrespondence (intentionalist) view of truth? Actually the reason is often quite simple: There is a confusion between *theory* of truth and *test* of truth. That is, often both parties hold the correspondence theory of truth but differ in their claims as to how truth is tested. In short, truth should be *defined* as correspondence but may be *defended* in some other way.

Answering Objections to Truth as Correspondence

Objections to the correspondence view of truth come from within as well as without; they emanate from both Christian and non-Christian sources. The major objections from both sides include the following:

Objection One

When Jesus said "I am the truth" (John 14:6), He demonstrated that truth is personal, not propositional. This falsifies the correspondence view of truth in which truth is a characteristic of propositions (or expressions) about reality.

Reply One

What Jesus said does not refute the correspondence view of truth. A person can be "true" in the sense that he is the reality of which true statements are made. Further, a person can correspond to reality as well as a proposition can. As the "exact image" of the invisible God (Heb. 1:3), Jesus perfectly corresponds to the Father (John 1:18); He said to Philip, "Anyone who has seen me has seen the Father" (John 14:9). So a person can correspond to another in his character and actions, and in this sense, persons can be said to be true, or express the truth.

Objection Two

God is truth, yet there is nothing outside of Himself to which He corresponds. But according to the correspondence view, all truth is that which correctly represents reality. And since there is nothing outside God to which He can correspond, it would follow that He is not true as the Bible says He is (Rom. 3:4).

Reply Two

Truth as correspondence relates to God in several ways. *First*, God's words correspond to His thoughts, so God is said to be true in the sense that His Word can be trusted.

Second, God's thoughts are identical to themselves, which is a kind of perfect "correspondence." In this sense, God is "true" to Himself.

Third, if truth is understood as what corresponds to another, then in this sense God would not be true; he would simply be the ultimate reality to which something else corresponds.

Fourth, the basic fallacy in this objection is an equivocal use of the definition. If correspondence means to something *outside* oneself, then of course God cannot be truth but only that ultimate reality to which all truth must correspond. If, on the other hand, correspondence can also be *inside*, then God can correspond to Himself in the most perfect way. In this sense, God is truth in a perfect way by self-identity.

Consider the following fallacious thinking:

(1) All who submit to the authority of the Pope are Roman Catholic.
(2) The Pope cannot submit to himself.
(3) Therefore, the Pope is not Roman Catholic.

The mistake is in the second premise. Contrary to the claim, the Pope *can* submit to himself; he simply has to follow the standards he lays down for every Roman Catholic, including himself. Likewise, God can and does live in accord with His own authority, and in this sense He is true to Himself and, thus, cannot lie (Heb. 6:18).

SUMMARY OF TRUTH'S DEFINITION

Truth may be tested in many ways, but it should be understood in only one way, namely, as correspondence. There may be many different ways to *defend* different truth claims, but there is only one proper way to *define* truth. The confusion between the nature of truth and the verification of truth is at the heart of the rejection of a correspondence view of truth.

Likewise, there is a difference between what truth *is* and what truth *does*. Truth is *correspondence*, but truth has certain *consequences*. Truth itself should not be confused with its results or with its application. The failure to make this distinction leads to wrong views of the nature of truth. *Truth is that which corresponds to its referent, i.e., to the state of affairs it purports to describe.* Falsehood is what does not correspond.

THE NATURE OF TRUTH AS ABSOLUTE

Not only is truth correspondence, truth is also absolute. Evangelical theology is predicated on the premise that the Bible is *the* truth (John 17:17), not just *a* truth; it is God's Word (John 10:34–35), and God cannot lie (Heb. 6:18; Titus 1:2). Thus Christianity is not just true for me, it is true for everyone (see chapter 8). It is not only true subjectively, but it is also true objectively.

This view, of course, runs headlong into the mainstream of our present relativistic culture. Hence, it calls for a discussion and defense of the absolute nature of truth.

The Relative View of Truth

By "relative" is meant any one of several things. For one, some things are true only for some people but not for all. For another, some things are true only for some times but not for all times. Or maybe some things are only true in some places but not in all places. By an absolute truth, then, is meant something that would be true for all people, at all times, and in all places.

A Response to Arguments for a Relative View of Truth

Contemporarily, the idea of the relativity of truth is popular. However, truth is not determined by majority vote. Let's take a look at the reasons people give for the belief that truth is relative.

Are Some Things True Only at Some Times?

First, relativists argue that some things are true at some times and not at others. For example, people once believed the world was square; now we know this is wrong. It would seem that this truth changed with the times. Or did it? Did the truth change, or did *beliefs* about what is true change? Certainly the world did not morph from a box to a sphere. What was altered is our belief, not our earth. The change was from a false affirmation to a true one.

Are Some Things True Only for Some People?

Second, other things appear to be true only for some people but not for others. For example, "I feel warm" may be true for me but not for you; you may feel cold. Isn't this an example of a relative truth? Not really. Actually, the statement "I (Norman Geisler) feel warm" (said May 1, 2001) is true for everyone in the universe. Why? Because it is not true for anyone that Norman Geisler did not feel warm on May 1, 2001. In fact, it is not only true for every*one* but it is also true every*where* that Norman Geisler felt warm on May 1, 2001. And it will be true in all places—in Moscow, Peking, Washington, and even in outer space—that Norman Geisler felt warm on May 1, 2001. But if it is true for all people in all places for all time, then it is an absolute truth. So what at first looked relative turned out to be unchanging.

Let's take another example of a supposed relative truth. If a teacher, facing her class, says, "The door to this room is on my right," when it is on the left for the class, then this truth would seem to be relative to the teacher since it is false for the class. However, this is not so, since the referent in the statement is the place from where the professor stands, not from where the class sits. That the door is on the professor's right is really an absolute truth, for it will never be true for anyone, anywhere, at any time, that the door was on the professor's left. It will always, everywhere, and for everyone be true that the door was on her right. Likewise, the other truth—that the door was on the students' left—will always be true for everyone everywhere.

Are Some Things True Only in Some Places?

Third, it seems obvious enough that it is hot in Mexico but cold at the North Pole. So some things appear to be true for some places but not for other places. This is true, but it misses the point, since those are two different statements (both of which are true) about two different places. It is not affirming that it is both cool and hot at the North Pole (or Mexico) at the same time.

Each statement is absolutely true with regard to its referent. The statement "It is cold at the North Pole" is true in Mexico, even in the summertime. It is true everywhere that "It is cold at the North Pole." Likewise, the statement "It is hot in Mexico" is true at the North Pole and everywhere else. Truth is what corresponds to the facts, and the fact is that it is cold at the North Pole. And this truth (that it is cold at the North Pole) is true everywhere, for there is nowhere that this statement does not correspond to the facts at the North Pole.

The truth of the matter is that *all truth is absolute—there are no relative truths.* If something really is true, then it really is true everywhere and for everyone. After all, 7+3=10, and it's not just true for mathematics majors. It's true everywhere, not just in math class but in your workplace and at home as well.

Like an old apple, relativism may look good on the surface but it is rotten at the core. Let's take a look at some of the problems.

Relativism Is Self-Defeating

Most relativists really believe relativism is true for everybody, not just for them. But that is the one thing they cannot believe if they are truly relativists, for a relative truth is true for me but not necessarily for everyone. So if the relativist thinks relativism is true for everyone, then he really believes that it is an absolute truth. Of course, this being the case, he is no longer truly a relativist, since he believes in at least one absolute truth.

Here is the dilemma: A consistent relativist cannot say, "It is an absolute truth for everyone that truth is only relatively true for me." If he says it is absolutely true that relativism is true, then he is not a relativist but an absolutist. If, on the other hand, he says, "It is only relatively true that relativism is true," then we cannot know if relativism is really true, for if it is only relatively true for him (but not for all), then relativism may be false for me. Why then should it be accepted as true?

Furthermore, for the relativist it can only be relatively true that it is relatively true for him, and so on infinitely. Either the claim that truth is relative is an absolute claim, which would falsify the relativist position, or it is an assertion that can never be made, because every time you make it you have to add another "relatively." It is just the beginning of an infinite regress that will never pay off in a real statement.

The only way the relativist can avoid the painful dilemma of relativism is to admit that there is absolute truth. Indeed, as already noted, most relativists really believe that relativism is absolutely true, for they really believe that everyone should be a relativist. Therein is the basic self-destructive nature of the relativist: He stands on the pinnacle of his own absolute truth to relativize everything else. But as the mythological Hercules understood, one needs a firm place to put a fulcrum before he can move the world. The sinking sand of relativism is not a firm place to set anything.

Relativism Entails a World Filled With Contradictions

If relativism were true, then the world would be full of contradictory conditions, for if something is true for one but false for another, then opposite conditions exist. If one person says, "There is milk in the refrigerator," and another insists, "There is no milk in the refrigerator"—and they are both right—then there must both be and not be milk in the refrigerator at the same time and in the same sense. This is impossible, since it violates the law of noncontradiction (see chapter 5). So if truth were relative, the impossible would be actual. But that is not possible.

In the religious realm it would mean that Billy Graham was telling the truth when he said "God exists," and Madalyn Murray O'Hair was also right when she claimed "God does not exist." But, as even a child knows, these two statements cannot both be true. If one is true, then the other is false. And since they exhaust the only possibilities, one of them must be true.

Relativism Means No One Has Ever Been Wrong About Anything

If truth is relative, then no one is ever wrong—even when he is. As long as something is true to him, then he is right even when he is wrong. The drawback to this is that I could never learn anything, either, because learning is moving from a false belief to a true one—that is, from an absolutely false belief to an absolutely true one.

Answering Some Objections to a View of Truth As Absolute

Relativists have leveled several objections to the view of truth as absolute. The following are the most important ones:

Objection One: Absolute Knowledge Is Not Possible
It is objected that truth cannot be absolute since we do not have an absolute knowledge of truth. Even most absolutists admit that most things

are known only in terms of degrees of probability. How then can all truth be absolute?

Reply One

This objection is misdirected, for absolute certainty is possible of some things. One can be absolutely sure that he exists. In fact, one's own existence is undeniable, for one would have to exist in order to make the statement "I do not exist." One can also be absolutely sure that he cannot both exist and not exist at the same time. Just as he can be certain, for example, that there are no square circles.

Of course, there are many more things of which absolute certainty is not possible. But even here relativists miss the mark in rejecting absolute truth simply because of the lack of absolute evidence that some things are true, for they fail to recognize that the truth can be absolute no matter what our grounds for believing it are. For instance, if it is true that Sydney, Australia, is next to the ocean, then it is absolutely true no matter what my evidence or lack of evidence may be. An absolute truth is absolutely true in and of itself no matter what evidence there is for it. *Evidence (or the lack thereof) does not change the facts.* And truth is what corresponds to the facts. The truth doesn't change simply because we learn something more about it.

Objection Two: Some Things Are In Between

Another objection is that many things are in between—like relative sizes, such as shorter and taller. As such, they cannot be absolute truths, since they change depending on the object to which they are relative. For example, some people behave nicely compared to Hitler but poorly compared to Mother Teresa.

Reply Two

Contrary to the claim of relativists, in between things do not disprove absolutism. For the facts that "John is short in relation to most NBA players" and "John is tall compared to most jockeys" are absolutely true for all times and all people. John is in between in size, and determining whether he is short or tall depends on to whom he is being compared. Nonetheless, it is absolutely true that John (being 5'10") is short compared to Shaquille O'Neal and tall compared to a Pygmy. The same thing is true of other in-between things, such as warmer or colder, and better or worse.

Objection Three: New Truth (or Progress) Is Not Possible

Relativists claim that if truth never changes, then there can't be any new truth. This would mean that no progress is possible.

Reply Three

In response to this, "new truth" can be understood in two ways. It might mean "new to us," like a new discovery in science. But that is only a matter of our discovering an "old" truth. After all, the law of gravity was there long before Newton discovered it. Many truths have always been there, but we are just finding out about them. In this sense we do come to know new truths—that's what scientific discovery is all about.

The other way we might understand "new truth" is that something new has come into existence that makes it possible to make a new statement about it that is only then true for the first time. This is not a problem. When January 1, 2020, arrives, a new truth will be born, because it will not be true until that day to say, "This is January 1, 2020." But when that happens, it will be true for all people and places forevermore that that day was January 1, 2020. So "old" truths don't change and neither do "new" truths when they come to pass. Once it is true, it is always true—for everyone.

Objection Four: Truth Changes With Our Growth in Knowledge

It is also objected that knowledge of truth is not absolute, since we grow in truth. What is true today may be false tomorrow. The progress of science is proof that truth is constantly changing.

Reply Four

This objection fails to note that it is not the truth that is changing but our *understanding* of what is true. When science truly progresses it does not move from an old truth to a new truth but from error to truth. When Nicolaus Copernicus (1473–1543) argued that the earth moves around the sun and not the reverse, truth did not change. What changed was the scientific understanding about what moves around what.

Objection Five: Absolute Truth Is Too Narrow

Relativists often complain that absolute truth is narrow.

Reply Five

This objection is common but without substantive basis. *Of course truth is narrow.* There is only one answer for what is 4+4. It is not 1. It is not 2. It is not 3. It is not 4, 5, 6, 7, or any other number from 9 on to infinity. It is only 8 and nothing else. That's narrow! But it's correct. Non-Christians often claim that Christians are narrow-minded because Christians claim that Christianity is true and all non-Christian systems are false (see chapter 8). However, the same is true of non-Christians, who claim that their view is true and all opposing beliefs are false.

The truth of the matter is that if C (Christianity) is true, then it follows that all non-C is false. Likewise, if H (Humanism) were true, then all non-H would be false. Both views are equally narrow. That's the way truth is.

Whenever anyone makes a truth claim, he has thereby claimed that whatever opposes it is false. Christianity is not narrower than anything else that claims to be true, whether it is atheism, agnosticism, skepticism, or pantheism.

Objection Six: Belief in Absolute Truth Is Dogmatic

Relativists also claim that those who believe in absolute truth are dogmatic. And, besides being untenable, dogmatism is obnoxious.

Reply Six

This objection misses the point. All truth is absolute, for, as we have seen, if something is really true, then it is true for all people, times, and places. So in this sense everyone who claims anything is true is "dogmatic." (And, as has been demonstrated, there isn't anyone who doesn't claim that something is true.)

Even the relativist who claims that relativism is true is dogmatic. Indeed, the relativist who claims that relativism is absolutely true is particularly dogmatic, for he is claiming that he has the only absolute truth that can be uttered, namely, that everything else is relative.

Further, something important is overlooked in this charge of dogmatism. There is a big difference between the pejorative charge that belief in absolute truth is dogmatic and the manner in which someone may hold to this belief. No doubt the way many absolutists have held to and conveyed their belief in what truth is has been less than humble. However, no agnostic would consider it a telling argument against agnosticism that some agnostics have held to and communicated their agnosticism in a very dogmatic manner. What we have here is an entirely different issue, and while it is one that certainly is worthy of our examination, it has nothing to do with truth being absolute.

SUMMARY AND CONCLUSION

Expressed truth is what corresponds to its object. To deny this is self-defeating, since to deny assumes that one's denial corresponds to the facts.

Likewise, the noncorrespondence view, like the relative view of truth, is self-defeating. The relativism of truth cannot be affirmed as truth unless relativism is false; it is absurd to affirm that it is objectively true for all that truth is not objectively true for all. Absolute truth is literally undeniable, and therefore it is not illegitimate to make absolute truth claims about the Bible or Christianity, such as evangelical theology does.

There is an important distinction to keep in mind, nonetheless: Truth is absolute, but our grasp of it is not; that there is absolute truth does not mean our understanding of it is absolute. This fact in itself should cause absolutists to temper their convictions with humility. As finite creatures, we grow in our understanding of truth; indeed, our knowledge of divine truth is not univocal but analogical (see chapter 9). In the words of Scripture, "For now we see in a mirror dimly, but then face to face" (1 Cor. 13:12).

SOURCES

Adler, Mortimer J. *Truth in Religion.*

Anselm. *Truth, Freedom, and Evil.*

Aristotle. *Posterior Analytics.*

Augustine. *Against the Academics.*

Buber, Martin. *I and Thou.*

Bultmann, Rudolph. *"Aleithia" [Truth]* in *The Theological Dictionary of the New Testament.*

Childs, Brevard. *Introduction to the Old Testament As Scripture.*

Copan, Paul. *True for You, But Not for Me.*

Geisler, Norman L. *Thomas Aquinas: An Evangelical Appraisal.*

———. "Truth, Nature of" in *Baker Encyclopedia of Christian Apologetics.*

James, William. *Pragmatism: A New Name for Some Old Ways of Thinking.*

MacLaine, Shirley. *Out On a Limb.*

Plato. *Theaetetus.*

Preus, Robert. *The Inspiration of Scripture.*

Rogers, Jack. *Biblical Authority and Interpretation.*

Thiselton, A. C. "Truth" in *The New International Dictionary of New Testament Theology.*

Thomas Aquinas. *On Truth.*

CHAPTER EIGHT

EXCLUSIVISM:
THE OPPOSITIONAL
PRECONDITION

SOME IMPORTANT DEFINITIONS

Several terms related to religions need to be distinguished: pluralism, relativism, inclusivism, and exclusivism.

Pluralism is the belief that every religion is true, that each provides a genuine encounter with the Ultimate. One may be better than the others, but all are adequate.

Relativism is similar to pluralism, claiming each religion is true to the individual who holds it. Relativists believe that since there is no objective truth in religion, there are no criteria by which one can tell which religion is true or which religions are false.

Inclusivism claims that one religion is explicitly true, and all others are implicitly true.

Exclusivism is the belief that only one religion is true, and all others opposed to it are false.

Since Christianity claims to be *the* true religion, it is at odds with the dominant trend in modern comparative religions. Alister McGrath set the stage properly: "How can Christianity's claims to truth be taken seriously when there are so many rival alternatives and when 'truth' itself has become a devalued notion?" He adds that according to current popular belief "no one can lay claim to possession of the truth. It is all a question of perspective. All claims to truth are equally valid. There is no universal or privileged vantage point that allows anyone to decide what is right and what is wrong" (McGrath, "CPCCC" in *JETS* 365).

THE ALLEGED MORAL AND SPIRITUAL EQUALITY OF ALL WORLD RELIGIONS

A Statement of the Argument for Pluralism

Pluralist John Hick argues, "I have not found that the people of the other world religions are, in general, on a different moral and spiritual level from Christians," for "the basic ideal of love and concern for others and of treating them as you would wish them to treat you is, in fact, taught by all the great religious traditions" ("PV," 39). Hick offers as proof that statements similar to Christianity's Golden Rule can be found in other religions (ibid., 39–40).

A Response to the Argument for Pluralism

Hick's conclusion can be challenged at several levels. *First*, it is debatable whether "the fruit of the Spirit" (Gal. 5:22–23) can be found in non-Christian religions. While no one denies there are good people in other religions, this is not to say they are manifesting the widely recognized highest moral standard, *agape* love. One can lead a philanthropic life and even die for his beliefs without having true love (see 1 Cor. 13:3). While God's common grace enables even evil men to do good (see Matt. 7:11), nonetheless, only the supernatural love of God can motivate a person to express *agape* (cf. John 15:13; Rom. 5:6–8; 1 John 4:7).

Before people too quickly conclude that William James (1842–1910) demonstrated the equality of all forms of saintliness in his famous *Varieties of Religious Experience*, they should read carefully Jonathan Edwards' *Religious Affections*. Edwards (1703–1758) argues forcefully that there are unique manifestations of Christian godliness. A careful half-century study of the matter confirms to this writer that there is a difference in the highest level of Christian and non-Christian piety in favor of the former.

Second, even if one could demonstrate a kind of moral equality of practice among most adherents of the great religions, this would not in itself prove there was no moral superiority in the teachings of Christianity over the other religions. There are several reasons for this.

For one thing, a person perfectly practicing a lesser moral code may appear to be better than a person imperfectly living according to a higher ethical standard. In order to make a fair comparison one must do two things: Compare the highest moral teachings of the various religions, and compare the best examples of the adherents to each. A close comparison between Mother Teresa and Mahatma Gandhi demonstrates the superiority of Christian compassion for the needy.

What is more, one must sort out what was inherent to another religion before the advent of Christian influence and what was incorporated into it as the result of Christian missionary activity. For example, Hinduism as a system did not generate social compassion. *The social compassion found in some forms of current Hinduism is not indigenous; it is a foreign import from Christianity.* Indeed, the degree to which Gandhi manifested such compassion comes from his training in Christianity and his self-confessed admiration for the teaching of Jesus in the Sermon on the Mount.

Finally, finding a moral principle akin to the Golden Rule of Judeo-Christian belief (cf. Matt. 7:12) would not be enough to show equality of all religions. This is a manifestation of general revelation—the law written in the hearts of *all* men (Rom. 2:12–15) by God. This is not the same as the supernatural manifestations of love, joy, and peace (Gal. 5:22–23). Indeed, while applied Christian morality has produced dynamic social compassion, Eastern religions have produced stagnant societies and Islam intolerant ones (Pinnock, *WGM*, 61).

Third, Hick's analysis begs the question, for only by assuming that the moral common denominator of all religions is the standard by which they should all be judged does he arrive at the not too surprising conclusion that they are all equal. One has to negate the superior aspects of Christian morality or teaching in order to show that Christianity is not superior. Hick seems to acknowledge this tacitly in confessing that the "acceptance of some form of the pluralistic view prompts each to de-emphasize and eventually winnow out that aspect of its self-understanding that entails a claim to unique superiority among the religions of the world" (Hick, "PV" in Okholm, *MTOW*, 51).

Fourth, the moral manifestation of a belief does not settle the truth question. For example, that there are good Mormons does not prove that Joseph Smith (1805–1844) was a true prophet. In fact, there is strong evidence that he was not a true prophet, since he gave demonstrably false prophecies (see Tanner, *CWM*, chapters 5, 11, 14). In addition, there is evidence for whether something is true apart from the way its adherents live. Truth is what corresponds to reality (see chapter 7) and, hence, a religion is true if its central tenets correspond to the real world, not merely whether its followers live a good life or even a better one than adherents of another religion.

Fifth, in the final analysis, the moral superiority of Christianity does not rest on our imperfection as Christians but on Christ's unique perfection (see volume 2, part 1). It is not based on our fallible moral character but on His impeccable moral character (John 8:46; 2 Cor. 5:21; Heb. 4:15; 1 John 3:3). In this context, Christianity is clearly morally superior to all other religions.

THE ALLEGED REDEMPTIVE EQUALITY OF ALL RELIGIONS

The Statement of the Argument for Redemptive Equality

As for the Christian claim to a superior mode of salvation, Hick believes this either begs the question or is not evident in practice:

> If we define salvation as being forgiven and accepted by God because of Jesus' death on the cross, then it becomes a tautology[1] that Christianity alone knows and is able to preach the source of salvation.

And,

> If we define salvation as an actual human change, a gradual transformation from natural self-centeredness (with all the human evils that flow from this) to a radically new orientation centered in God and manifest in the "fruit of the Spirit," then it seems clear that salvation is taking place within all of the world religions—and taking place, so far as we can tell, to more or less the same extent. (Hick, "PV" in Okholm, *MTOW*, 43.)

Further, what is common to all world religions is for Hick an adequate response to the Ultimate: "But they seem to constitute more or less equally authentic human awareness of and response to the Ultimate, the Real, the final ground and source of everything" (ibid., 45). There are, of course, "a plurality of religious traditions constituting different, but apparently more or less equally salvific, human responses to the Ultimate. These are the great world faiths" (ibid., 47).

A Response to the Argument for Redemptive Equality

There appear to be a net of problems in this analysis. *First,* it's based on the assumption that all religions have a proper relation to what is truly Ultimate. This begs the question; maybe some are not connected at all to what is *truly Ultimate.* Or, perhaps they are not *rightly related* to what is truly Ultimate. After all, as Sigmund Freud (1856–1939) pointed out in his famous *Future of an Illusion,* deception is possible.

Second, Hick wrongly assumes that all religions are merely a human response to the Ultimate. But this begs the question in favor of antisupernatural views of religion (see chapter 3). In fact, it assumes a pantheistic view of the Ultimate as what transcends all particular cultural manifestations of the Ultimate in the various world religions.

Third, this denial of the truth of any particular religion is itself a form of exclusivism, for it favors the worldview known as pantheism in order to deny the particularity of the worldview known as Christian theism. That is to say, even the pantheist is making a particular truth claim, one that is opposed to all nonpantheistic views. But to assume a pantheistic position as a basis for one's analysis of all religions, including nonpantheistic ones, again begs the question. Or, to put it another way, when the pluralist denies any particular religion is true as opposed to others, he thereby makes a particular truth claim.

---

[1] "A *tautology* is a contentless statement, something true by definition and uninformative of the real world" (Geisler, *BECA*, "*Tautology*").

Fourth, the pluralist view often degenerates to the position that whatever is sincerely believed is true. But this would mean that it matters not whether one is a passionate Nazi, Satanist, or Flat-Earth adherent, for in any event the holder's view would be truth. This is patently incorrect; *sincerity is clearly not a test of truth.* The road to destruction is paved with good intentions, and many sincere people have been sincerely wrong about many things.

Fifth, the argument for redemptive equality implies that all truth claims are a matter of both/and and not either/or. But on this ground, there could be touted such absurdities as triangular squares and educated illiterates. Whether we like it or not, *opposites cannot both be true,* for the opposite of true is false. Hence, opposing truth claims of various religions cannot be mutually inclusive. For example, Hindu pantheism and Christian theism cannot both be true, since they affirm mutually exclusive worldviews. Likewise, Islam, which denies that Jesus died on the cross and rose from the dead three days later, and Christianity, which affirms this fact about Jesus, cannot both be true.

THE ALLEGATION THAT CHRIST IS NOT UNIQUE

A Statement of the Argument Against Christ's Uniqueness

As for the Christian dogma about the uniqueness of Christ (see volume 2, part 1) as God incarnate in human flesh, John Hick contends that there are two main problems. He is misinformed on both points.

A Statement of the First Allegation

The first problem is that the historical Jesus did not teach this doctrine.... Among mainline New Testament scholars today there is a general consensus that these are not pronouncements of the historical Jesus but words put in his mouth some sixty or seventy years later by a Christian writer expressing the theology that had developed in his part of the expanding church. (Hick, "PV" in Okholm, *MTOW,* 52–53.)

Hick then cites a list of biblical scholars who allegedly agreed that "Jesus did not claim deity for himself" (ibid.).

A Response to the First Allegation

The New Testament documents are historically reliable, and their historicity has been abundantly attested (see part 2). The New Testament books that are crucial to this issue were not written after the eyewitnesses were dead, but while they were still alive. Indeed, the gospel of John claims to have been written by an eyewitness apostle (John 21:24), and Luke was written by a contemporary disciple who knew the eyewitnesses (Luke 1:1–4). First Corinthians, which even biblical critics admit was written about A.D. 55–56, speaks of five hundred eyewitnesses (1 Cor. 15:5–7), most of whom were still alive when Paul wrote it only twenty-two years after Jesus' death. Even the late Bishop John A. T. Robinson, a liberal New Testament scholar, dated Gospels as early as A.D. 40–60, much too early to support Hick's view of books written by a later generation who had already formulated a view contrary to that of the historical Jesus. Therefore, since the Gospels are reporting, not creating, the words and deeds of Jesus, they are firm support for His unique claims to be God incarnate (see volume 2, part 1).

A Statement of the Second Allegation

The second problem is that it has not proved possible, after some fifteen centuries of intermittent effort, to give any clear meaning to the idea that Jesus had two complete natures, one human and the other divine. . . . Is it really possible for infinite knowledge to be housed in a finite human brain? . . . Do we really want to claim that Jesus was literally omnipotent but pretended not to be, as in Mark 6:5? . . . While he was good, loving, wise, just, and merciful, there is an obvious problem about how a finite human being could have these qualities in an *infinite* degree. . . . A finite being cannot have *infinite* attributes (ibid., 55–56).

A Response to the Second Allegation

First, Hick falls short of claiming that the Incarnation involves an outright logical contradiction, though his language could be taken to imply the same. If the Incarnation is not, however, a logical contradiction, then there is no demonstrated incoherence in the view. Indeed, Hick himself admits, "It is logically permissible to believe anything that is not self-contradictory" (*MGI,* 104). As for the claim that it is difficult to show just how the Incarnation is true, on the same grounds one would have to reject much of our common experience as well as modern science (which, for instance, has difficulty explaining how light can be both waves and particles).

Second, Hick appears to be misinformed about the view of the two natures of Christ. Indeed, his objections assume the unorthodox Monophysite view, which confuses Christ's two natures. His question as to whether it's "really possible for infinite knowledge to be housed in a finite human brain" reveals such a confusion, for the orthodox view does not claim that there was infinite knowledge in the finite brain of Christ. Rather, it affirms that Christ had two distinct natures, one infinite and the other finite. So the person of Christ did not have infinite knowledge in his finite brain, but infinite knowledge in His infinite nature. As God, He knew all things; as man, Jesus grew in knowledge (Luke 2:52). The same thing applies to Jesus' other attributes—as God, He was omnipotent; as man, He was not (see volume 2, part 1).

THE ALLEGATION OF INTOLERANCE

A Statement of the Objection From Intolerance

Another charge laid at the feet of exclusivism is that of intolerance, which is directed at the exclusivist's view that one religious view is true and those opposed to it are false. This, to pluralists, seems to be bigotry; after all, why should only one view have a franchise on the truth and all the others be disenfranchised?

A Response to the Objection From Intolerance

A number of observations are relevant in this connection. *First*, if holding an exclusivist view makes one intolerant, then pluralists are also intolerant, for they claim their view is true to the exclusion of opposing views (like exclusivism); they certainly would not tolerate the position that their pluralistic view and the opposing nonpluralistic views were both true.

Second, if the charge of intolerance is leveled because of the manner in which one holds his view, then nonpluralists have no monopoly on the market, for if consistent with the nature of his position against nonpluralism, a pluralist is as "intolerant" as anyone else.

Third, the very concept of tolerance implies a real disagreement. One does not *tolerate* that with which he agrees, he *embraces* it. Hence, the concept of tolerance presupposes a nonpluralist view of truth.

THE ALLEGATION OF NARROW-MINDEDNESS

One of the favorite allegations of pluralists is that nonpluralists are narrow-minded, for nonpluralists claim that their view is true while everyone else is in error. This seems utterly presumptuous on the face of it. Why should only exclusivists be in possession of the truth?

The response to this is clear: *Both* the pluralists (P) and the exclusivists (E) make an equal claim to truth and error. *Both* claim that their view is true and that whatever opposes it is false. For example, if E is true, then all non-E is false. Likewise, if P is true, then all non-P is false. What the facts reveal is that exclusivism and pluralism are equally "narrow." In point of fact, all truth is narrow. Remember what we saw in the last chapter—2 plus 3 is not 1, 2, 3, 4, 6, 7, 8, 9, 10 or any other number on to infinity. There is only one true answer, and while this is narrow, that is the very nature of truth.

THE ALLEGATION OF INTELLECTUAL IMPERIALISM

Another charge against exclusivism is that of intellectual imperialism; pluralists claim exclusivists are totalitarian with regard to truth, and that they should be more open to input from many sources, not just to one. Indeed, some postmodern pluralists go so far as to claim that not only *truth* but the very idea of *meaning* smacks of fascism (cited by Alister McGrath, "RJH" in Okholm, *MTOW*, 364).

While this allegation has a certain appeal, especially to those of a particular political mindset, it is without merit in determining what is true and what is false with regard to religions. *First*, the frequent intention of this allegation is a form of the *ad hominem* logical fallacy—it attacks the person rather than the position.

Second, this objection has an unjustified presumption, namely, that truth should be more democratic. But truth does not hinge on the percentage of its adherents. Truth is what corresponds to reality (see chapter 7), whether the majority believes it or not.

Third, do pluralists really believe that all views are equally true and good? Is fascism or communism as good as democracy? Was Nazism as good as any other form of government? Should one have tolerated the burning of widows in the Hindu funerals of their husbands? No, we see thereby that pluralists don't truly believe in pluralism.

SOME CHALLENGEABLE PRESUPPOSITIONS OF PLURALISM

The Claim That There Are Universally Agreed-Upon Trans-Religious Moral Criteria

In order to make effective the argument for moral equality, one must assume a set of moral criteria not unique to any particular religion by which all can be evaluated. But pluralists generally deny any universally binding moral law. If there were such absolute moral laws, then there would need to be an absolute Moral Lawgiver. At best, however, only broadly theistic-type religions accept these criteria, and even then some reject the absolute perfect nature of God, e.g., some finite godists. Further, if there is a moral law common to all religions, then it is not unique to one, and by the tenets of pluralism no religion can be judged inferior for lacking it. Finally, if there are no such universal moral laws, then there is no way to morally judge all religions from any standard beyond them, and it is not fair to take the standards of one religion and apply them to another, claiming that the other falls short.

The Claim That All Religious Phenomena Can Be Explained Naturalistically

Beneath the pluralist's attack on exclusivism is a naturalistic pre-supposition: All religious phenomena can be explained naturalistically; no supernatural explanations are allowed. But this presumptive naturalism is without justification; miracles cannot be ruled out a priori (see chapter 3). Neither, as David Hume claimed, are miracles incredible, nor are miracles without evidence. Indeed, there is substantial support for the greatest miracle of all, the ex nihilo ("out of nothing") creation of the world (see chapter 3). Also, there is abundant evidence that the miracle of the resurrection of Christ has occurred (see volume 2, part 1).

The Claim That the World Is "Religiously Ambiguous"

Hick believes "the universe, as presently accessible to us, is capable of being interpreted intellectually and experientially in both religious and naturalistic ways" (Hick, *IR*, 129). Meaning, "The Real is perfectly undifferentiated; that is, it has no properties to which our concepts veridically [truly] apply" (Geivett, in *MTOW*, 77).

In response, some important observations should be made. *First*, it is self-defeating to claim that we know that we cannot know the Real (see Geisler, *BECA*, "Agnosticism").

Second, that we do not know reality exhaustively does not mean we cannot know it truly. As Geivett notes, "To the extent that God is known at all, he is known truly" (ibid.).

Third, the very notion of an undifferentiated Real is implausible, if not self-defeating. Hick's claim that the Real can be symbolized by the concept of Sunyata in Buddhism is a case in point, for if the Real is so undifferentiated, then how can any symbol represent it?

Fourth, neither can the Real be manifested in various traditions, as Hick claims. In order for something to be manifested, at least some of its characteristics must be revealed (ibid.). But the Real as totally undifferentiated has no discernible characteristics. Hence, it could not be manifested in our experience in any meaningful way.

Fifth, there is a kind of mystical epistemology presumed in this "God is unknowable" approach. It has a rather imperialist degree on how God can and cannot reveal Himself. But one wonders what pipeline to metaphysical truth could have supplied this absolute information (ibid.).

The Claim That Pluralistic Dialogue Is the Only Way to Truth

Another seriously flawed presupposition is the position that pluralistic interreligious dialogue is the only valid way to discover truth. No genuine religious dialogue, supposedly, is possible if one assumes his religion is true in advance of the dialogue. This is sure proof that he is not open to truth. True dialogue assumes one is tolerant, open, humble, willing to listen and learn, engage in a shared search for truth in a self-sacrificing, other-oriented love (ibid., 239).

In response, a number of things are necessary to point out. *First,* true dialogue is possible without adopting a pluralistic position on truth. One can have the attitude of humility, openness, and willingness to listen and learn without sacrificing his convictions about truth.

Second, the pluralist is not willing to relinquish his commitment to pluralism as a condition for such dialogue; hence, he violates his own imperative.

Third, the very idea of tolerance implies that some views are in error, for it makes no more sense to say one tolerates truth than one tolerates good. It is error and evil that are tolerated, not truth and good.

The Claim That Hick's View Is Religiously Neutral

John Hick feigns religious neutrality, but no such thing exists. His alleged pluralism is not religiously neutral at all; it is patterned after Hinduism's conception of the Ultimate, and it is antagonistic to the core principles of Christianity.

Furthermore, it does not truly encourage genuine dialogue between the traditions; indeed, it renders vacuous the concept of being "in a given religious tradition." After all, according to pluralists, every tradition is essentially the same. So to accept pluralism is to reject one's own tradition for another—the pluralist's tradition.

The Claim That a Relativistic View of Truth Is Correct

Beneath the pluralist's assertion that all major religions have equal claim to the truth is a relativistic view of truth. But as we have seen (in chapter 7), the denial of absolute truth is self-defeating. It claims that relativism is true for everyone, everywhere, always. But what is true for everyone, everywhere, and always is an absolute truth. Therefore, it claims that relativism is absolutely true. The relativist is well advised to exercise a healthy hermeneutic of suspicion with regard to his own platform.

CONCLUSION

As a challenge to the evangelical claim to truth, pluralism is impotent. In fact, it is self-defeating, since the claim that pluralism is true as opposed to nonpluralism is itself exclusivistic—the view that insists it is inherently wrong to make exclusive truth claims is filled with exclusive truth claims of its own. So the evangelical claim to objective truth (see chapter 7) as opposed to all views that are contradictory is left standing.

SOURCES

Clark, David, and Norman Geisler. *Apologetics in the New Age.*

Clarke, Andrew D., and Bruce Hunter, eds. *One God, One Lord: Christianity in a World of Religious Pluralism.*

Freud, Sigmund. *The Future of an Illusion.*

Geisler, Norman. *Baker Encyclopedia of Christian Apologetics.*

Geivett, Doug, et al., in Dennis Okholm, et al. *More Than One Way: Four Views on Salvation in a Pluralistic World.*

Gnanakan, Ken. *The Pluralistic Predicament.*

Hick, John. *An Interpretation of Religion.*

———. *The Metaphor of God Incarnate: Christology in a Pluralistic Age.*

———. "A Pluralist's View" in Dennis Okholm, *MTOW.*

James, William. *Varieties of Religious Experience.*

McGrath, Alister. "The Challenge of Pluralism for the Contemporary Christian Church" in *The Journal of the Evangelical Theological Society* (September 1992).

———. "Response to John Hick" in Okholm, *MTOW.*

Nash, Ronald. *Is Jesus the Only Savior?*

Netland, Harold. *Dissonant Voices: Religious Pluralism and the Question of Truth.*

Okholm, Dennis, et al. *More than One Way: Four Views on Salvation in a Pluralistic World.*

Pinnock, Clark. *"Response to John Hick"* in Okholm, *MTOW.*

———. *A Wideness in God's Mercy.*

Tanner, Jerald, and Sandra Tanner. *The Changing World of Mormonism.*

CHAPTER NINE

LANGUAGE: THE LINGUISTIC PRECONDITION

E vangelicals believe that the Bible is God's Word in human words; therefore, another precondition for doing evangelical theology is the belief that finite human language is capable of meaningfully expressing the nature of the infinite God of Christian theism, which is displayed in both general and special revelation.

THREE BASIC ALTERNATIVES

Evangelicals reject any alternative that denies it is possible to speak meaningfully about God. This includes views such as are embraced by many atheists, agnostics, skeptics, and even religious mystics and existentialists.

Logically, there are only three possible views with regard to God-talk:

(1) It is equivocal (totally different from the way God actually is).
(2) It is univocal (totally the same as God actually is).
(3) It is analogous (similar to the way God actually is).

Evangelicals have defended versions of both univocal and analogical religious language; some have combined the two views. But, as we shall see, both equivocal and univocal God-talk have serious problems: the former leads to self-defeating skepticism, and the latter to an unacceptable dogmatism. We are left, then, with some form of analogy by which God communicates with us.

Equivocal God-Talk

Equivocal God-talk leaves us in total ignorance about God. At best, one can only feel, intuit, or sense God in some experiential way, but no human expressions can describe what it is that is being experienced. Evangelical theology rejects this alternative for several reasons.

First, it is self-defeating, since it affirms with human language about God that we cannot affirm anything about God. Religious mystics certainly write books about God. In brief, any attempt to express the equivocal view about God implies that some non-equivocal language about God is possible.

Second, the Bible declares that God can be described in human language. Indeed, Scripture as a whole is an attempt to inform us about God and to evoke a response from us. Even the colorful, figurative, and metaphorical language of the Bible implies a literal understanding beneath the nonliteral expressions, for one cannot even understand that a figure of speech (e.g., God has arms) is not literal unless he knows what is literally true (viz., that He is pure Spirit [John 4:24]).

Third, there is a continual and consistent tradition in orthodox theology from the earliest centuries to the present that assumes human language can express truth about the transcendent God. This is manifest in the great confessions, creeds, and councils of the Christian church (see Schaff, *CC*), to say nothing of all the theological treatises of the great Fathers of the church from the second century to the present.

Univocal God-Talk

Some Christian thinkers like John Duns Scotus (1266–1308), following Plato and Augustine, have argued that God-talk is univocal. While there is an important element of truth in this view (see below), it was severely criticized by Thomas Aquinas and has come in for hard times in contemporary thought—with good reason.

A more detailed discussion is found later, but here the two most basic problems are noted. *First*, how can our understanding of God be entirely the same as God's (i.e., univocal)? Our understanding and expressions are finite, and God's are infinite, and there is an infinite gulf between finite and infinite. As transcendent, God is not only beyond our limited understanding, but He is also beyond our finite expressions.

Second, the Bible makes it clear that God is far above our thoughts and words. As the prophet Isaiah aptly put it, " 'For my thoughts are not your thoughts, neither are your ways my ways,' " declares the LORD. " 'As the heavens are higher than the earth, so are my ways higher than your ways and my thoughts than your thoughts' " (Isa. 55:8–9). For a mortal human being to know as God knows, he would have to be God, since only God knows infinitely.

Analogous God-Talk

It appears, then, that the only viable alternative to avoid self-defeating skepticism on the one hand and self-deifying dogmatism on the other is to demonstrate that legitimate God-talk is analogous to the way God actually is. That is to say, language about God is neither equivocal (totally different) nor univocal (totally the same), but is similar (analogous) to the way God truly exists.

TWO ATTEMPTS TO DEVELOP A POSITIVE GOD-TALK

There are two basic attempts to develop a positive God-talk. One is by way of univocal language and the other by way of analogical language. The former was expounded by John Duns Scotus, and the latter by Thomas Aquinas. Although the positions seem to be mutually exclusive, their complementarity provides a crucial insight into the nature of religious language.

The Scotistic Insistence on Univocal *Concepts*

John Duns Scotus made one point unmistakably clear: There can be no meaningful positive talk about God unless at the basis of it univocal concepts are involved, for equivocal or analogical concepts leave one in skepticism. Scotus's argument may be summarized in two parts: first, the impossibility of analogous concepts; and second, the necessity of univocal concepts.

The Impossibility of Analogous Concepts of God
Henry of Ghent (c. 1217–1293), a contemporary of Scotus, defended what he called an "analogous concept of being." According to Henry, God is known in terms of a universal concept, which while conceived of as though it were only one notion (because of its close resemblance to the concepts within it), in reality the concepts (of God and humans) are diverse. Therefore, the concept of being common to both God and creatures is really not one concept but two, yet because of the similarities in these two concepts, the mind fails to distinguish between them, as two distant objects tend to fuse before the eye. This dual concept is what Henry calls *analogous* (Scotus, *PW*, 20–21, 180–81).

Scotus strongly objected to Henry's analogous concept. *First,* Scotus reminded Henry that if God and creatures are distinguished only by a negation (that is, by what we don't know about God), then there is no distinction at all, for "there is no need to make the distinction that we cannot know what God is; we can only know what He is not. For every denial is intelligible only in terms of some affirmation."

Second, Scotus noted that since an analogous concept is really two different concepts, it is actually equivocal, for either there is at the base of these two concepts one univocal concept from which they draw their common meaning or else they are two entirely different concepts. If the *former,* then there must be a univocal concept at the basis of the so-called analogous concept, as whatever is predicated of God and creatures by way of an equivocal concept must mean two entirely different things. Therefore, if concepts of God truly were analogous, they would be equivocal (ibid., 18, 22–23). If the *latter,* then they are equivocal, at any rate. According to Scotus, in either event, then, an analogous concept tells us nothing about God.

The Necessity of Univocal Concepts of God

In the outlook of Scotus, language about God is not equivocal or analogical; it is univocal, and hence it evades the alternative of skepticism. By univocal Scotus means that which "possesses sufficient unity in itself, so that to affirm and deny it of one and the same thing would be a contradiction. It also has sufficient unity to serve as the middle terms of a syllogism." Scotus gives four arguments to support his contention that concepts must be univocally understood of both God and man (ibid., 23).

First, "every intellect that is certain about one concept, but dubious about others, has . . . another concept of which it is certain." Scotus offered proof of this premise as follows: "One and the same concept cannot be both certain and dubious, or [else] there is no concept at all, and consequently no certitude about any concept." The other premise is this: "Every philosopher was certain that what he postulated as a first principle was a being. . . . Yet he was not certain whether it was created or an uncreated being, whether it was first or not first." The reason for this is, "Someone perceiving the disagreement among philosophers can still be certain that any of the things that they have acclaimed as the first principle has being [e.g., fire, water]."

Scotus dismissed the possibility that the different philosophers had different concepts of *being.* He said,

> By such an evasion all possibility of proving the unity of any concept would be destroyed. The fact of great similarity plus the irreducible simplicity of all the concepts argue that ultimately they are one. Further, if there were two different formal concepts, one would have to conclude that there were two formally opposed first principles of being (ibid., 23–25).

In summation, if the intellect can be certain about the concept of being without knowing whether it refers to created or uncreated being, and if it is necessary to have a univocal concept in order to be certain about anything, then we must have a univocal concept of God's being. Otherwise, we would have no knowledge at all of God, which is contrary to both faith and philosophy.

Second, the concepts used of God must be univocally understood because:

> No object will produce a simple and proper concept of itself and a simple and proper concept of another object, unless it contains this second object essentially or virtually. No created object, however, contains Uncreated essentially or virtually. . . . Therefore, it produces no simple and proper concept of the "uncreated" at all. But no concept could arise in virtue of the active intellect and the sense image [which are the way all created objects are understood in this life] that is not univocal but only analogous with, or wholly other than, what is revealed in the sense image. Hence, it would be impossible to have any natural knowledge of God unless it is known via univocal concepts. But we do have natural knowledge of God. Therefore, this knowledge must come by way of univocal concepts (ibid., 25–26).

Third, our concept of God must be univocal, since *it is wrong to argue as follows*:

> The proper concept of any subject provides sufficient ground for concluding to everything conceivable which necessarily inheres in that subject. But we have no concept of God . . . that enables us to know every necessary attribute which we conceive of Him, as is evident from the fact of the Trinity, and other necessary attributes that we know by faith.

Therefore, we have no proper concept of God.

Scotus insists that this is patently false, as revelation teaches us much about God. Hence, we must have at least some concept that is properly (i.e., univocally) applicable to Him (ibid., 26).

Fourth,

> Either some pure perfection has a common meaning as applied to God and creatures or not. If not, it is either because its meaning does not apply formally to God at all (which is inadmissible), or else it has a meaning that is wholly proper to God [and not to creatures]. . . . But this latter alternative is contrary to the truth affirmed by Anselm that "we first know something to be a pure perfection and secondly we attribute this perfection to God" (Anselm, *M*, appendix).

Furthermore, if pure perfections were found only in God, there would be no such perfections among creatures. The proper metaphysical approach is to begin with a concept (such as will or intellect) and, finding that it contains no imperfection, "attribute [it] to God—but in a most perfect degree." Finally,

If you maintain that this is not true, but that the formal concept of what pertains to God is another notion of anything found in creatures, nothing at all can be inferred about God, for the notion of what is in each is wholly different (ibid., 27–28).

Beneath these four arguments for univocity is one fundamental contention: If there is no univocity in our concepts about God, then there is no certainty in our knowledge about God, for again, "one and the same concept cannot be both certain and dubious. Therefore, either there is another concept [which is certain], or there is no concept at all, and consequently no certitude about any concept." In other words, if there is no univocal basis for meaning, then one is forced to an infinite regress of non-univocal concepts in search for the one elusive univocal concept by which the non-univocal ambiguity can be resolved. "For every intellect that is certain about one concept, but dubious about others has, in addition to the concept about which it is in doubt, another concept about which it is certain." Hence, Scotus concluded, "I say that God is conceived . . . in some concept univocal to Himself and to a creature" (ibid., 23).

In summation, there are only three alternatives in our concepts about God. Either the concepts of God are understood equivocally (i.e., in a totally different sense), in which case we know nothing about God; or they are understood analogically (i.e., with partly the same but partly different meaning), in which case, at any rate, we must have some univocal concept of God enabling us to know which part of the analogous concept applies to God and which does not apply to Him; or they are understood univocally (i.e., having totally the same meaning) in the first place. Therefore, either there are univocal concepts about God or else we know nothing about God. There must be either univocity or skepticism.

It would appear that Scotus made his point. Equivocal God-talk says nothing about God, and analogical God-talk seems to work only if there is in the analogy an identifiable univocal element. If there is no such identifiable univocal element, the concept is at best ambiguous and at worst equivocal. If it is ambiguous, it can be clarified only in terms of a non-ambiguous univocal concept. But if there is an identifiable univocal element in the analogy, then analogy is actually a form of univocal understanding of God, for it involves an identifiable univocal concept that can be applied to Him without change, along with the other elements of the combined analogous statement that cannot be applied to God. In brief, analogy either has a univocal element in it or it does not. If it does not, it is ultimately equivocal talk, which leaves us in skepticism about God. On the other hand, if analogy does have a univocal element in it, then it really contains a univocal concept after all, which proves some true knowledge about God.

This same argument for the necessity of a univocal concept has been repeated by many evangelicals. See, for example, W. G. T. Shedd, *Dogmatic Theology* (1:89ff.), and Stuart Hackett, *The Resurrection of Theism* (127–30).

The Thomistic Defense of Analogous *Predication* (Affirmation)

Thomas Aquinas was familiar with and flatly rejected the insistence on univocal God-talk. He wrote, "It is impossible for anything to be predicated univocally of God and a creature" (Aquinas, *OPG*, 7.7, body).

Rejection of Univocal Predication

Aquinas's rejection of univocal predication of God involves two important facts: *First*, there cannot be a one-to-one understanding between the finite minds of humanity and the infinite Mind of God. *Second*, it is necessary to admit that there is a negative element in our knowledge of God—that is, we know what God is not (e.g., He is not finite).

Arguments Against Univocal Predication

In the *Summa Contra Gentiles* Aquinas offered six arguments against univocal predication of God and creatures. Several crucial ones are noted (*SCG*, 1.32).

First, only those effects that receive from their cause the specific form of that cause can receive a univocal predication of that form of them and of God. But "the forms of the things God has made do not measure up to a specific likeness of the divine power." All creatures are "in a divided and particular way that which in Him is found in a simple and universal way." So "it is evident that nothing can be said univocally of God and other things." [Arguments 2 and 3 are omitted here.]

Fourth, "What is predicated of many things univocally is simpler than both of them, at least in concept. Now, there can be nothing simpler than God either in reality or in concept. Nothing, therefore, is predicated univocally of God and other things." Since the one thing in common is always simpler than the many things having it in common, any univocal predication of God and others would have to be simpler than God, which is impossible.

Fifth, "Everything that is predicated univocally of many things belongs through participation to each of the things of which it is predicated. . . . But nothing is said of God by participation. . . . Nothing, therefore, can be predicated of God and other things" in a univocal way. In short, God does not participate in anything; rather, all things participate in Him. If there were a common univocal predication in which God participated, then this something would be more ultimate than God.

Sixth, "Nothing is predicated of God and creatures as though they were in the same order, but rather, according to priority and posteriority." This is true because God is Being *essentially*, and all other things have being only by participation in God. However, "what is predicated of some things according to priority and posteriority is certainly not predicated univocally," for the prior possesses the characteristic essentially and the posterior possesses it only by participation in the prior. "It is impossible, therefore, that anything be predicated univocally of God and other things."

In the *Summa Theologica* (1.13.5) Aquinas rests his case against univocal predication on the first argument from *Summa Contra Gentiles*: "All perfections existing in creatures dividedly and multiply preexist in God unitedly." Therefore, any perfection applied to God signifies God's very essence; for example, creatures *have* wisdom but God *is* wisdom. "Hence it is evident that the term wise is not applied in the same way to God and to man. The same applies to other terms. Hence, no name is predicated univocally of God and other creatures."

Implied in Aquinas's objection to univocal predication is another argument, one with which he did agree:

> God is more distant from creatures than any creatures are from each other. But the difference of some creatures [from each other makes any univocal predication of them impossible], as in the case of those things which are not in the same genus. Therefore, much less can anything be predicated univocally of God and creatures.

In essence, then, the argument for analogous God-talk is this: Between an infinitely perfect Being and finitely perfect beings there is an infinite difference in perfection (certainly an infinite differs from a finite in more than a finite way). Also, where there is an infinite difference in perfection there cannot be a univocal predication. A given perfection cannot mean totally the same thing as applied to God and creatures, for God and creatures are separated by an infinite degree of perfection. As Aquinas put it elsewhere, "Every effect of a univocal agent is adequate to the agent's power: and no creature being finite, can be adequate to the power of the first agent which is infinite" (*OPG*, 7.7).

What is true of power is likewise true of any other perfection. An infinitely perfect Cause produced finitely perfect effects, and the perfections found in these effects cannot be predicated in exactly the same manner (i.e., univocally) as God.

The Need for the Via Negativa

At this point the need for the *via negativa* (the way of negation) becomes apparent. As Plotinus correctly observed, God cannot possess perfections the way created things possess them; in this sense God does "produce what he does not possess" (see Plotinus, *E*, 5.3.14–15), because God doesn't really possess the finite characteristics found in His creation. God does not *have* being and wisdom; God *is* being and wisdom. Hence, whatever limitations are found in creaturely perfections must be completely negated of God, since He is unlimited (infinite) in His being.

It is for this reason that univocal predication must be rejected, for it destroys the distance between God and creatures necessitated by the different kinds of beings that they are. God is an infinitely perfect Being, and all other beings are only finitely perfect. If any attribute were predicated in the same way (i.e., univocally) of both God and creatures, then it would either imply the finitude of God or else the infinitude of creatures. As long as God is viewed as infinitely perfect, nothing that is finitely perfect can be applied to God without qualifications. The proponents of negative theology appreciated the necessity for these qualifications in order to preserve God's transcendence. When a perfection taken from the finite world is applied to God, it must be applied to God infinitely, since He is an infinite Being. Unless the finite conditions of perfection can be negated, there is no way it can be appropriately applied to an infinite Being.

The Rejection of Equivocal Predication

However, the *via negativa* alone will not suffice, for if all meaning is negated when one removes the finite connotations of a term, he is speaking mere equivocations. Unless there is some common meaning that applies to both God and creatures, the meaning it has as applied to creatures is totally different from the meaning it has as applied to God. And a totally different meaning is an equivocation that leaves us in a state of skepticism about God.

Aquinas agrees with Scotus that equivocal language deprives one of any knowledge of God. Although Aquinas refers to God as an "equivocal Cause" (i.e., of a different order than finite causes), he offers several arguments against equivocal prediction of that Cause (*SCG*, 1.33).

First, in equivocals, "it is entirely accidental that one name is applied to diverse things: The application of the name to one of them does not signify that it has an order to the other." But "this is not the situation with names said of God and creatures, since we note in the community of such names the order of cause and effect. . . . It is not, therefore, in the manner of pure equivocation that something is predicated of God and other things." That is, terms with the same spelling but different meaning [as we have seen with "bark," of a tree or a dog] are equivocals by chance. Yet where one thing is the cause of the other, there is no mere chance connection between the terms expressing these things, but there is an order of reference that signifies that one is related to the other.

Second, "Where there is pure equivocation, there is not likeness in things themselves; there is only a unity of a name. But . . . there is a certain mode of likeness of things to God. It remains, then, that names are not said of God in a purely equivocal way." The minor premise was supported by a preceding article (*SCG* 1.29), where Aquinas argued, "Some likeness must be found between them [cause and effect], since it belongs to the nature of action that an agent produce its like, since each thing acts according as it is in act." The similarity of Creator and creature is supported, too, by Holy Scripture, which says that God made man in His image and likeness (Gen. 1:27).

Third, "When one name is predicated of several things in a purely equivocal way, we cannot from one of them be led to the knowledge of another. . . ." But "from what we find in other things, we do arrive at a knowledge of divine things, as is evident from what we have said." Therefore, "such names are not said of God and other things in a purely equivocal way." That is to say, unless there is some likeness between creatures and God, we could never rise, as we do, from a knowledge of created things to a knowledge of God.

Fourth, "Equivocation in a name impedes the progress of reasoning," and "if nothing was said of God and creatures except in a purely equivocal way, no reasoning proceeding from creatures to God would take place. But the contrary is evident from all those who have spoken about God." That is to say, not only would equivocation make knowledge of God impossible (as the third argument contends) but it would also impede any reasoning about God built on knowledge gained from the world, in which reasoning all theologians engage.

Fifth, "It is also a fact that a name is predicated of some being uselessly, unless through that name we understand something of the being. But if names are said of God and creatures in a purely equivocal way, we understand nothing of God through those names," for "the meanings of those names are known to us solely to the extent that they are said of creatures. In vain, therefore, would it be said or proved of God that He is a being, good, or the like."

Sixth, even if non-equivocal names tell us only what God is not, at least they agree in what they deny of God. A totally equivocal denial of God would be the same as affirming the same thing that is being denied of God. Hence, even negations of God cannot be equivocal.

In a later work, Aquinas rests the case against equivocal predication on one central argument: Equivocal predication is impossible "because if that were so, it follows that from creatures nothing at all could be known or demonstrated about God" (*ST,* 1.13.5). It is patently false that we know nothing about God; hence, there must be some non-equivocal predications about God. For instance, we know things about Him from both special revelation in the Bible and general revelation in nature (Rom. 1:19–20).

Analogical Predication: The Only Alternative
If terms can be applied to God neither univocally nor equivocally, then they must be predicated of Him analogically. In Aquinas's own words,

This name God . . . is taken neither univocally nor equivocally, but analogically. This is apparent from this reason—univocal names have absolutely the same meaning, while equivocal names have absolutely diverse meanings; whereas analogicals, a name taken in one signification must be placed in the definition of the same name taken in other significations. (*ST*, 1.13.10.)

Therefore, terms denoting perfections taken from creatures can be applied to God only in an analogous way:

We can name God only from creatures. Hence, whatever is said of God and creatures is said according as there is some relation of the creature to God as to its principal cause, wherein all the perfections preexist excellently.

Further,

This mode of communication [i.e., analogy] is a means between pure equivocation and simple univocation. For in analogies the idea is not, as in univocals, one and the same [in its application]; yet it is not totally diverse as in equivocals; but the name which is used in a multiple sense signifies various proportions to some one thing. (*ST*, 1.13.5.)

For example, God is named Good because He is the Cause of goodness. The Cause is Good and hence when it causes goodness in something else it communicates of what it is to what its creature has by created participation. The causal connection between Creator and creature cannot be totally unlike its Creator, since every perfection it possesses it has acquired from Him.

There is another fundamental argument for analogy that takes us back to the dilemma of Parmenides the monist[1] (see chapter 2): If there is more than one being in the universe, these beings must differ by either being or nonbeing. But they cannot differ by nonbeing for that is nothing, and to differ by nothing is not to differ at all. Neither can things differ by being, for that is the very respect in which they are identical, and they cannot differ in the very respect in which they are identical. Hence, there cannot be more than one being in the universe. Thus there is only one being— that is, monism. Now there are only two horns to this dilemma.

Either one's principle of differentiation is inside of being or it is outside of being. If outside, then things do not differ in being; they are identical in being, and monism is true. The only way to maintain a pluralism essential to theism is to insist that things differ in their very being. Yet how can they differ by what they have in common? The answer is that they cannot, if being is univocal. But it isn't.

---

[1] Monism holds that all reality is one.

Since being is used analogously between God and creatures, being can be predicated of God and creatures only in an analogous way. Otherwise, we end in monism. In short, analogy of being (and predication) is the only salvation from monism and from skepticism. It is the only alternative to monism, since if beings cannot differ there can be only one being. It is the salvation from skepticism, because unless there is a similarity in being, there can be no knowledge of infinite Being derived from finite beings.

A POSITIVE SYNTHESIS OF UNIVOCAL CONCEPTS AND ANALOGICAL PREDICATION

One apparent contradiction has not yet been resolved. Scotus demonstrated that analogous *concepts* would not save one from skepticism; only univocal concepts can guarantee knowledge of God. But if Aquinas rejects univocal *predication*, how then can he avoid skepticism, for God possesses the common perfection infinitely, and creatures possess it only finitely.

Univocal Concepts But Analogical Predication

The answer and reconciliation between scotism and thomism lies in the distinction between a *concept* and a *predication*. Scotus was right that the concept applied to both God and man must be univocally *understood*, but Aquinas was correct in arguing that this concept must be analogically *affirmed* of God and creatures.[2] That is, the *definition* of the attribute *applicable* to both God and creatures must be the same, but the *application* of it differs, for in the one case (God's) it is applied without limits, while in the other (humankind's) it is predicated with limitations.

God, for instance, is good infinitely; man is good only finitely. Good may be defined in the same way for both, for example, as "that which is desired for its own sake." But God is to be desired for His own sake absolutely, whereas creatures are to be desired for their own sakes only relatively. Likewise, being may be defined univocally as "that which is," but this univocal concept is predicated of God and creatures in an analogous way. God is "that which is" infinitely; a creature is "that which is" only finitely. Or, more properly, God *is* Existence and creatures merely *have* existence.

This distinction has not always been fully appreciated by thomists, but in more recent works on analogy they have come to recognize its validity. Armand Maurer stated the difference clearly: "It is not generally realized that St. Thomas's doctrine of analogy is above all a doctrine of the *judgment* of analogy, and not of the analogy of concept. . . ." ("STAG" in *NS*, 143). Generic concepts are univocal when abstracted, but analogical when

---

[2]This difference between apprehension and judgment is what Aquinas, following Aristotle, referred to as the first and second act of the intellect, respectively.

asserted of different things, as man and dog are equally animal but are not equal animals. *Animal* is defined the same way (say, as "a sentient being"), but *animality* is predicated differently of Fido and of Socrates (c. 470–399 B.C.). (Socrates possesses animality in a higher sense than Fido does.) Likewise, both the flower and God are said to be beautiful, but God is beautiful in an infinitely higher sense than flowers are.[3]

While this tells us nothing directly about the similarity between God and creation, it does inform us about the difference between an infinite being and a finite being. For if beauty means "that which, being seen, pleases," then the pleasure of the beatific vision of God is infinitely greater than the pleasure of viewing a flower. In brief, Scotus was correct in insisting that our concepts must be univocally understood and defined. But Aquinas was right in insisting that any concept drawn from the finite world must be predicated of God in an analogous way.

Finite Concepts and Predication About the Infinite

Aquinas recognized that all concepts are finite; they are limited by the very finite circumstances in which they arise (*ST*, 1.84.1–8). People never derive infinite concepts from sensory experience:

> Since God infinitely exceeds the power of our intellect, any form we conceive cannot completely represent the divine essence, but merely has in some small measure an imitation of it. (*OT*, 2.1, body.)

This is why Aquinas said God "is one in reality and many things logically" (*OPG*, 7.6, body), for the simple essence of God is not known by any concept of it but only by way of many predications about it.

No concept taken from creation is adequate to express the essence of divinity, yet many things can be affirmed of the essence of God. We cannot know the substance of God, but we can predicate many substantive things about God (*ST*, 1.12.4; 1.13.2).

The Mode of Signification Differs From What Is Signified

How can univocally understood finite concepts be predicated analogously of God without losing their meaning? Does not a limited concept lose all of its meaning when it is applied without limits to an infinite Being? Aquinas answered this question by making a distinction between the (unlimited) thing signified and the (limited) mode of signification. The mode in which concepts are conceived is always finite for human beings,

---

[3]Aquinas explains the relationship between God and creatures by the analogy of proper proportionality. In this analogy there is a proper relationship between the attribute each thing possesses and their own respective natures. Applied to God, this analogy declares,

$$\frac{\text{Infinite good}}{\text{Infinite Being}} \quad \text{what} \quad \frac{\text{Finite good}}{\text{Finite Being}}$$

but what these concepts signify is not necessarily finite (Aquinas, *SCG*, 1.29).

In fact,

> Since every perfection of creatures is to be found in God, albeit in another and more eminent way, whatever terms denote perfections absolutely and without any defect whatever, are predicated of God and other things; for instance, goodness, wisdom, and so forth.

On the other hand,

> Any term that denotes such like perfections together with a mode proper to creatures, cannot be said of God except by similitude and metaphor (ibid., 1.29).

Some terms by their very denotation cannot be applied to an unlimited Being. Other terms, however, do not necessarily denote what is limited, even though they are conceived in finite concepts. For instance, there is nothing essentially limited about the term "being" (that which is) or "goodness" (that which is desired for its own sake) or "beauty" (that which, being seen, pleases). Hence, these terms may be predicated of God metaphysically (i.e., actually) and not merely metaphorically (i.e., symbolically). Such terms do not lose their content, because they retain the same univocal definition. Neither do these terms carry with them the necessary implications of finitude, because they are not applied to God univocally (i.e., in the same way they are applied to creatures). They are predicated analogically, meaning neither identically nor in a totally different way.

The Need for Intrinsic Analogy Based on Causality

How is it known that God must be (in an infinitely perfect way) what these terms denote? Because God is the cause of these perfections in a mode appropriate to the effects they cause. An infinitely perfect God communicated perfections to His creatures in a finitely perfect manner. Hence, even though there is an infinite difference in perfection between God and creatures, there is nevertheless not a total lack of similarity. The created sequents are similar to their creative Source, because the creature must bear some similarity to its Creator.

It could be argued that metaphysics, let alone natural theology, is impossible apart from having first established the analogical nature of religious language. After all, such terms as "First Cause" or "Creator of the Universe" must be understood analogically. But then it would appear that we are caught in a vicious circle, since, as we shall see, analogy is dependent on the reality of the metaphysical relationship between God and the world. Thus natural theology works because of analogy, and analogy works because of natural theology. Each grounds the other, which means that neither is grounded.

Can this progression be avoided? Yes, because even though both sides are dependent on each other, the dependencies are of two different kinds. Thus, there is no vicious circularity. In natural theology we establish certain conclusions by using religious language, which then turns out to be analogical. But we did not have to know that analogy was at work. The language was analogical, whether we were ever cognizant of that fact or not. When we're dealing with analogy, we are in a sense merely discovering what has been true of the nature of our language all along. It is only in explaining how this language works that we need to make reference to metaphysical truths. Niels C. Nielsen Jr. has elaborated the ontological requisites for analogy, particularly in theological contexts (Nielsen, *AKG*).

The Causal Basis for Analogy Between God and Creatures

Aquinas rested the case for a similarity between God and creatures in the causal relation. Each of the first four ways of proving God's existence is clearly based on causality. (Causality is also implied in the fifth way.) Even the very platonic appearance of the fourth way imports causality to complete the argument (*ST*, 1.2.3), and once it is shown by causality *that* God is, then Aquinas can demonstrate *what* God is from the analogy implied in this causal relation. Just how often Aquinas makes explicit reference to causality as the basis for analogy will become apparent in the following quotations. The important question here is, "What kind of causality is the basis for the similarity between God and creatures?" The most helpful work on Aquinas's doctrine at this point is the classic by Battista Mondin, *The Principle of Analogy in Protestant and Catholic Theology*. The analysis here follows his.

(1) *Analogy is based in intrinsic causality.* Unlike Maimonides (1135–1204) and the neoplatonists, Aquinas held to an intrinsic causal relationship between God and creation. An extrinsic causal relationship is such that only one thing possesses the characteristic properly—the other thing possesses the characteristic improperly, by virtue of a causal relation to it. To illustrate, food is called healthy only because it *causes* health in a body, but, properly speaking, only organisms *are* healthy. And God is called good because He *causes* goodness, not because He *is* good. Not so with the causal relation between God and the world; this is an intrinsic relation where both God and creatures possess the perfections properly, only each according to its own mode of being. God must *be* good because He *causes* goodness; He must *be* Existence because He *causes* things to exist, and so on. There is an intrinsic causal connection and, therefore, analogy between the Cause and its effects (Aquinas, *ST*, 1.13.5; *SCG*, 1.29–30).

(2) *Analogy is based on efficient causality.* God is the producing Cause of all that exists, not merely the purposing (final) Cause of neoplatonic philosophy. For Aquinas, God brought the world into being from nothing. The world did not come about by a creation flowing from it. The theistic God is

the Cause of the world's *being*, not merely of its *form*. God created the world; He did not simply make it out of matter that was already there. In brief, creation is ex nihilo, not ex materia. God is the efficient cause of the very *be*ing of the world, for, wrote Aquinas,

> Everything that, in any way whatever *is*, must needs be from that to which nothing else is the cause of being.... Therefore, from Him is everything that in any way whatever *is*. (*ST*, 2.15.2.)

Elsewhere he wrote,

> It belongs to a thing to have an efficient cause according as it has being ... the reason why an efficient cause is required is not merely because the effect cannot be, but because the effect would not be if the cause were not. (*ST*, 1.44.1, 2, and 3.)

(3) *Analogy is based on essential causality.* It is clear from the foregoing that God is the essential (*per se*) Cause of creation and not merely an accidental (*per accidens*) cause of it; that is, God causes the very *being* of the world and not merely its *becoming*. Further, essential causes generate their own kind. For instance, musicians give birth to non-musicians (*per accidens*), but humans generate only humans (*per se*). Hence, when beings are created, it is by virtue of an essential causal relationship with their Creator. Only Being gives rise to being. Aquinas wrote,

> Some likeness must be found between them [i.e., between effects and their cause], since it belongs to the nature of action that an agent produces its like, since each thing acts according as it is in act. The form of the effect, therefore, is certainly found in some measure in a transcending cause, but according to another mode and in another way. (*SCG*, 1.29.2.)

Only that which exists can communicate existence to another. *Nothing* cannot cause *something*, and since all caused existence is communicated to it by its cause, there must be some essential similarity in existence between this existing effect and its cause.

(4) *Analogy is based on principal, not instrumental, causality.* Effects resemble their primary causes but not necessarily their instrumental causes. To illustrate, the pen is the instrumental cause of the exam, and the student is the principal cause of it. Only the student's mind resembles the exam; the pen does not. The exam does reflect the thoughts of the student, even though it is not like the pen. In like manner, the perfections of the world resemble their principal Cause (God) but not necessarily their instrumental causes.

In summation, the analogy between creature and Creator, based on causality, is secured only because God is the principal, intrinsic, essential, efficient Cause of the being and perfections of the world. In any other kind of causal relationship an analogical similarity would not necessarily follow, but in an analogy of being similarity must follow, for Being communicates only being, and perfections or kinds of being do not arise from an imperfect being. Existence produces only after its kind, namely, other existences.

ANALOGOUS LANGUAGE IN GOD'S REVELATION

Evangelical theology affirms that God has two great revelations: special revelation in the Bible and general revelation in nature. Both involve an analogous understanding of God.

Analogous Language and Special Revelation (Scripture)

The Bible is emphatic about two things in this connection. *First,* God is beyond our thoughts and concepts, even the best of them (cf. Rom. 11:33). God is infinite and our concepts are finite, and no finite concept can capture the infinite. It is also clear in Scripture that God goes infinitely beyond the puny ability of human concepts to convey His ineffable essence. Paul said, "Now we see as in a mirror, dimly" (1 Cor. 13:12 NKJV). John said of mortal man in this life, "No one has seen God at any time" (John 1:18 NKJV).

Second, human language is adequate for expressing the attributes of God, for in spite of the infinite difference between God and creatures, there is not a total lack of similarity, since the effect always resembles its efficient Cause in some way.

But if God is both adequately expressed in and yet infinitely more than human language—even inspired language—can express, then at best the language of Scripture is only analogous; i.e., no term taken from human experience—and that is where all biblical terms come from—can do any more than tell us what God is like. None of them can express comprehensively what God really is. Religious language at best can make valid predications of God's essence, but it can never express His essence fully.

Analogous Language and General Revelation (Nature)

There are two basic reasons that statements made about God on the basis of general revelation are merely analogous. *First,* we return to the matter of causality already mentioned. The arguments for God's existence are arguments from effect to the efficient Cause of their being (Aquinas, *ST,* 1a.2.3). Since the effects get their actuality from God (who is Pure Actuality), they must be similar to Him, for Act communicates act; Actuality produces actualities (see Mondin, *PAPCT,* all).

Second, Pure Act (God) cannot create another Pure Act. Pure Act is uncreated, and it is impossible to create an uncreated Being. But if un-created Act cannot create another Pure Actuality, then it must create an actuality with potentiality (Aquinas, *OBE*, all). Thus, every created being must be composed of actuality and potentiality. All created beings have actuality because they actually exist, and they have potentiality because they have the potential not to exist.

Anything that comes into existence can pass out of existence. But if all created beings have a potential that limits their existence, then they are limited kinds of existences, and their uncreated Cause is an unlimited kind of existence. Thus, there must be a difference between creatures and their Creator. They have limitations (potency), and He does not. It follows, then, that when making statements about God based on what He has revealed of Himself in His creation, there is one big proviso—God is not like His crea-tion in its potentialities but only in its actuality. This is called the way of negation (via negativa). All adequate God-talk must have this negative ele-ment in it, a conclusion that emerges from the very nature of the proofs for His existence.

First, it was demonstrated that He is a Cause. This is the positive element of similarity in the analogy between God and creatures. Whatever actuality (not potentiality) there is in the creatures, is actually like the Actuality that gave it to them.

Second, it was concluded that He was an uncaused kind of Cause (the negative element in the analogy). Uncaused means not-caused; it is a neg-ative term. The same is true of the other attributes of God that emerged from the argument for His existence, for, as Aquinas said, "No creature, being finite, can be adequate to the first agent which is infinite" (*SCG*, 7.7).

God is the infinite cause of all finite existence. But in-finite means not-finite; it too is a negation. God is the eternal, that is, the not-terminal or not-temporal Cause. Some of the negations are not immediately obvious from the etymology of the term, but they are negative nonetheless. God is the simple Source of all complex being; simple here really means non-complex.

The same is true of the attribute of necessity. We know creatures are contingent, but by "necessary" we simply mean that God is not contingent. We have no positive concepts in our experience that can express the tran-scendent dimension of God's unlimited metaphysical characteristics. Therefore, the analogy with which we speak of God will always contain an element of negation. The creature is like God because Act communicates act, but it is unlike God because it has a limiting potentiality that God does not have; He is Pure Actuality.

A RESPONSE TO
OBJECTIONS AGAINST ANALOGOUS GOD-TALK

Now that we have expounded analogy more completely, we can respond to those objections that are relevant here. Most of these are listed in the works of David Burrell (see *APL*) and Frederick Ferre (see "A" in Edwards, *EP*).

(1) *Why select some but not all qualities drawn from the world and apply only these to God?* Because only some things flow from God's efficient, essential, principal, and intrinsic causality. As noted above, only these are the perfections found in finite creation that do not necessarily denote what is finite. Hence, since only these concepts do not necessitate a limited application of their meaning, they alone may be appropriately applied to an unlimited Being.

(2) *Words divorced from their finite mode or conditions are vacuous or devoid of meaning.* This critique ignores the distinction between a concept and its predication. The univocal concept of the words remains the same; only the way in which they are predicated changes. And even in the predication there is a similarity based on the efficient causal relation to God: The meanings of the words *goodness, being,* and *beauty* are not *emptied* when applied to God; the words are merely *extended without limits.* That is, the perfection indicated by an analogous predication is not negated; rather, it is released from any limiting mode of signification and applied essentially to God. Since the perfection denoted by some terms does not necessarily imply any limitations, there is no reason why perfection cannot be predicated of an unlimited Being.

(3) *Analogy rests on the assumption that causality provides a similarity.* This is true, but the assumption is justifiable in terms of intrinsic, essential, principal, efficient causality, *not* in terms of just any kind of causality. Mondin, whose work was not mentioned in Ferre's criticism of analogy, successfully defends analogy against this charge. Being communicates only being. The Cause of existence cannot produce perfections that it does not "possess." If God causes goodness, then He must be good. If He causes existence, then He must exist. Otherwise the absurd consequence ensues that God gives what He does not have to give.

Of course, God causes finitude, contingency, and potency, which He does not have. However, these are not perfections, but only the limited conditions under which a creature receives these perfections. After all, an infinite, necessary Being of Pure Actuality cannot make another such Being. Hence, the only kind of beings He can make are finite, contingent beings with potency, and all the actuality and perfections they have, they received from God's hand—He cannot give any perfection He does not have to give. Hence, there is a solid ontological basis for the similarity between God and creatures in the principle of causality.

(4) *Any analogous predication of God as a First Cause involves an infinite regress of meaning to identify the univocal element.* This objection holds true for non-univocal concepts, but it is not true of univocal concepts that have analogical predication. It is true that one must have a univocal understanding of what is being predicated of the First Cause, but it does not follow

from this that how it is predicated of different kinds of beings must be identical (i.e., univocal). Indeed, if it is known that one Being is infinite and another being is finite, then how a quality is predicated must differ from what is being predicated, for to predicate a perfection in the same way of an infinite Being as it is predicated of a finite being (viz., finitely) is really to predicate it equivocally, since an infinite Being does not have qualities in a finite way. The only way to avoid equivocation when predicating the same perfection of both finite beings and infinite Being is to predicate it differently (i.e., analogously) according to the mode of being that each is.

(5) *Even accepting the challengeable metaphysical assumption that there is a similarity among beings, this ontology is not univocally expressible. First,* this is not a mere assumption for a theist; it is the only alternative to monism. If there are many beings, there must be an analogical similarity among beings; were this not so, there could be only one being in the universe, for if being means entirely the same thing wherever it is found (univocity), there can be only one being. And if being means something entirely different (equivocality), then once one being is identified, everything else must be totally different, which is nonbeing.

Only if beings are similar but neither totally identical nor totally different, can there be more than one being in the universe. But God is, and I am (and you are); we are all different beings. Hence, there must be an analogy of being that permits all of us to exist (the similarity) and yet allows each of us to exist differently; each of us has being (existence) but each is a different kind of being (essence). In God, existence and essence are identical. Hence, creatures, like God, exist, but the existence of creatures is only analogous to that of God, for God exists essentially, and all else exists dependently.

Second, being is univocally conceived, but it is analogically predicated of God and finite beings. The concept is understood to mean the same thing, namely, being is "that which is or exists." God exists and a man exists—this they have in common—but God exists infinitely and independently, whereas a man exists only finitely and dependently—this they have in difference. In short, *that* they both exist is *univocally conceived; how* they each exist is *analogically predicated,* for God exists necessarily and creatures exist only contingently; there is a distinct difference in the mode of existence, even though the fact of their existence is the same (i.e., they both exist).

(6) *Since Ludwig Wittgenstein (1889–1951), the distinction between univocal and equivocal is obsolete, and consequently the notion of analogy is obsolete.* To understand this objection we need to remind ourselves of Wittgenstein's proposal for understanding language. Expressions receive their meaning from their use in the context of language games, wherein the chosen rules are used to judge consistency. Each language game is autonomous insofar as there are no universal criteria for meaning. Words that carry over from

game to game or words with similar meanings bear family resemblances, but they have no essence, and we can never isolate a core meaning they must share. Thus the rigid designations of language, being univocal or equivocal, break down before this dynamic understanding based on usage.

David Burrell responds to this idea by insisting on equivalence between language in ordinary use on the one hand and univocal language on the other. There may not be any obligatory standard for univocal language, but this fact is irrelevant, since all we mean by "univocal meaning" is language in its ordinary context of meaning. Burrell says, "We can, then, speak of an ordinary or univocal usage so long as we neither insist on its fixity nor count on it as our final norm" (*APL*, 221). He observes that in this sense even terms such as "disc jockey" or "Girl Friday" may take on a univocal role. Thus the distinction between univocal and equivocal still holds, and analogy is still called for.

(7) *A general theory of analogy does not work.* Even though Burrell defends a theory of analogy, he is wary of making it too rigid. In particular, he objects to the theory of analogy of proper proportionality as expounded by noted thomistic scholar Cardinal Cajetan (1468–1534). Burrell contends that it simply does not work, no matter how hard we try to fill in all of our parameters. Any formula we try to set up will still leave us with ambiguity and equivocation (ibid., 9–20). The same problem applies to other theories of analogy as well.

First, in response to Burrell, we need to note that the present account does not provide a specific formula for univocal language meaning. Critics of analogy, including Frederick Ferre, usually bring their criticisms down to the conclusion that models of analogy do not ultimately yield only univocal meaning for language as applied to God. Burrell recognizes the nonsense of this, for if correct, there would be no need for analogy at all. Still he faults traditional understandings of analogy for getting involved in complicated systems that do not resolve equivocation.

Second, we can point out that the present account gives no formula for meaning at all. We have stayed away from picking one or more of Cajetan's categories and locking ourselves into it. One could conceivably argue that what we have in our understanding of Aquinas is the analogy of intrinsic attribution combined with proper proportionality.[4] But these are not Aquinas's categories, and it is well not to be tied to one formal understanding of language mechanisms. Instead, we have presented a primarily metaphysical scheme into which language fits, and this scheme is rooted in reality. As long as analogy is tied to the metaphysics of intrinsic causality, it must work, even if a theoretical language formula does not do the trick. This response should not be far from Burrell's intentions, either.

---

[4]In other words, the similarity is based on the relation between a cause and its effect, while the difference is depicted by a similarity in relationship.

The objections to analogous God-talk based on existential causality appear insufficient. Analogy seems to be the only adequate answer to the question of religious language.

All negative God-talk implies some positive knowledge of God. But positive affirmations of God are possible only if there are some univocally understood concepts that can be applied to both creatures and Creator (as Scotus argues). Conversely, since God is infinitely perfect, and creatures are only finitely perfect, no perfection found in the finite world can be applied univocally to both God and creatures (as Aquinas argues). But to apply them equivocally would leave us in skepticism. Hence, whatever perfections found in creation that can be applied to God without limits are predicated analogically. This perfection is understood univocally (in the same manner), but it is predicated analogously (in a similar manner), because to affirm it univocally in a finite way of an infinite Being would not truly be descriptive of the way He is, and to affirm it equivocally in an infinite way would not be descriptive of Him at all. Therefore, a univocal concept drawn from the finite world can be predicated of God only analogically.

SUMMARY AND CONCLUSION

The linguistic precondition of evangelical theology is that we do have some positive knowledge of God. Human language, however limited, is capable of making true statements about God and His relation to the world. However, as we have seen, these predications cannot be univocal, since all human concepts (even if univocally understood) cannot apply to an infinite Being without qualification.

With the help of the via negativa, all limitations must be stripped before they are applied to God. Hence, they are affirmed of God in a different (though similar) way from which they are of finite things. John Duns Scotus was right in insisting on univocal *concepts*, but Thomas Aquinas was correct in insisting that these univocally defined terms must be *applied* to the transcendent God in an analogical way. In this manner, univocally understood concepts, sans their finite connotations, can be applied to (predicated of) God analogically and yield a positive knowledge of God.

SOURCES

Anselm. *Monologium.*
Burrell, David. *Analogy and Philosophical Language.*
Ferre, Frederick. "Analogy" in Paul Edwards, ed., *Encyclopedia of Philosophy.*
Geisler, Norman. *Thomas Aquinas: An Evangelical Appraisal.*
Geisler, Norman, and W. Corduan. *Philosophy of Religion.*
Hackett, Stuart. *The Resurrection of Theism.*
Maurer, Armand. "St. Thomas and the Analogy of Genus," *New Scholasticism* 29 (April 1955).

McInerny, Ralph. *The Logic of Analogy.*

Mondin, Battista. *The Principle of Analogy in Protestant and Catholic Theology.*

Nielsen, Niels C. Jr., "Analogy and the Knowledge of God: An Ecumenical Appraisal," *Rice University Studies* 60 (1974).

Plotinus. *Enneads.*

Schaff, Philip. *The Creeds of Christendom.*

Scotus, John Duns. *Philosophical Writings.*

Shedd, W. G. T. *Dogmatic Theology.*

Thomas Aquinas. *On Being and Essence.*

———. *On the Power of God.*

———. *On Truth.*

———. *Summa Contra Gentiles.*

———. *Summa Theologica.*

CHAPTER TEN

INTERPRETATION: THE HERMENEUTICAL PRECONDITION

Another important precondition to evangelical theology is the belief that it is possible to obtain an objective interpretation of God's revelation in both Scripture and nature. Since these two revelations are the bases of all that we know about God, it is necessary that we understand them correctly, for if an objective understanding of the truth God has revealed through them is not possible, then discourse about God is not possible, let alone a comprehensive discourse about God (which is known as systematic theology).[1]

SUBJECTIVITY IN HERMENEUTICS

The primary challenge to the hermeneutical precondition of systematic theology is the subjective interpretation of God. According to this view, it is not possible to have an objective understanding of a disclosure from God for several reasons.

Subjectivity in Meaning (Conventionalism)

First of all, it is argued that there is no such thing as objective meaning in a text. The prevailing view in modern linguistics is conventionalism, which insists that all meaning is culturally relative. This model springs from such modern writers as Ferdinand de Saussure (1857–1913), Gottlob Frege (1848–1925), and Ludwig Wittgenstein (1889–1951).

---

[1]Hermeneutics is the study of the general principles of biblical interpretation.

This argument was examined earlier (in chapter 6) and found wanting for many reasons. For one thing, it is self-defeating to claim, "All meaning is culturally relative"; this very proposition is offered as a nonrelative, meaningful statement. One cannot claim to have an objective view that all meaning is subjective—not without self-contradiction. In order to make a meaningful statement about all meaning, one must take an objective stance *outside* the culture. But if all statements are culturally dependent, then this is not possible. Thus, the first pillar of subjectivism crumbles under close scrutiny.

Subjectivity in the Mode of Communication

Another argument offered in favor of subjectivism in interpretation is that no objective grounds exist for communicating a revelation from God to us. Since God is an infinite Mind, while human beings have finite minds, and since there is an infinite difference between an infinite and a finite, no common ground of meaning is possible between the two.

This objection was handled in two earlier chapters (6 and 7) in which it was demonstrated that there are undeniable principles of rational thought that are common to both God and man. Since logic is based in the very rational nature of God, it is neither arbitrary nor relative. God is subject to the law of noncontradiction just as we are. He is a self-consistent rational being, and as such He cannot hold logically opposite propositions to be true.

Likewise, the infinite difference between God and man does not mean there is a total lack of similarity, for the Creator must resemble its creature. A cause cannot give what it does not have to give; God cannot produce what He does not possess. He who brought other things into existence must exist Himself, and He who gave goodness must be good. The principle of analogy between God and creatures is firmly rooted in the intrinsic relation between an efficient cause and its effect. Thus, another premise of subjectivism is unsuccessful.

SUBJECTIVITY IN INTERPRETATION

So far it has been shown that there is objective meaning, and that it can be objectively expressed, even by an infinite, rational God to finite, rational beings. The remaining question is whether or not finite beings are capable of deriving the objective meaning that is objectively expressed in a divine revelation. Many modern and contemporary scholars have argued that this is not possible. A few crucial names will illustrate the point.

Heidegger's Existentialism

Martin Heidegger (1889–1976) developed an existential hermeneutic that denied objective meaning was possible. He was influenced by the phenomenological method[2] of Edmund Husserl (1859–1938), the nihilistic concerns of Friedrich Nietzsche (1844–1900), the historical approach of G. W. F. Hegel (1770–1831), the personal subjectivity of Søren Kierkegaard (1813–1855), and the mystical metaphysics of Plotinus (205–270 A.D.).

The earlier and later Heidegger are a study in contrasting emphases:

Early Period	Late Period
Anthropological	Hermeneutical
Heavy Style	Freer and Lighter
(*Being and Time*)	(*Intro to Metaphysics*)
DREAD	JOY
Phenomenological	Mystical

The later Heidegger gave rise to a subjective hermeneutic, but the groundwork of this was laid in his earlier existentialism of *Being and Time*. In this work he stressed man's inauthentic everyday existence, which has three fundamental aspects:

(1) *Facticity*, in which man finds himself cast into a world not of his own willing;

(2) *Existentiality*, which is the act of appropriating or making my world mine. Through this, man, by self-projection and self-transcendence, understands the world and becomes himself;

(3) *Forfeiture*, meaning that unfortunately we not only shape our world but we also forfeit to it. We forget "Being" in our quest for particular beings. So man is determined (put here), yet man is free to make of the world what he will. But the all essential "I" is hidden throughout most of life by daily routines in the tension of the historical (e.g., the call of my situation, family, country).

Nonetheless, against this scattering inauthenticity, Heidegger singles out an authentic being, called Dasein,[3] and develops his concept of existential time, which involves three things.

---

[2]Phenomenology is "a method for the description and analysis of consciousness through which philosophy attempts to gain the character of a strict science. A 20th-century philosophical movement, the primary objective of which is the direct investigation and description of phenomena as consciously experienced, without theories about their causal explanation and as free as possible from unexamined preconceptions and presuppositions. The word itself is much older, however, going back at least to the 18th century, when the Swiss-German mathematician and philosopher Johann Heinrich Lambert applied it to that part of his theory of knowledge that distinguishes truth from illusion and error. In the 19th century the word became associated chiefly with the Phänomenologie des Geistes (1807; Phenomenology of Mind, 2nd ed., 1931), by G. W. F. Hegel, who traced the development of the human spirit from mere sense experience to 'absolute knowledge.' The so-called Phenomenological movement did not get under way, however, until early in the 20th century. But even this new Phenomenology includes so many varieties that a comprehensive characterization of the subject requires their consideration" (*Encyclopedia Britannica Online*).

[3]Lit. "the being there," i.e., man.

The first is *dread*, which is a momentary state of mind in which we turn back in the flight from ourselves with honesty. Dread is an objectless fear, a sense of nothingness that grasps me when I face the whole of it as ending in death. Hence, I dread my life as a whole, because it is bounded and grounded in death (nothingness). Dread, then, reveals that we are a "being-unto-death." This sets us free from the illusion of the "they."[4]

The second is *conscience*, which is the voice that expresses itself through dread. It is the voice of the self to itself, calling it from forgetfulness to the responsibility of being itself. It is the call from inauthenticity. We must recognize that we are "thrown" into the world not of our own choosing, and yet it is precisely this condition that I must choose.

The third is *destiny*, which is found in death. Existential time is my time, namely, from birth to death. Only by choosing my time and the role into which I have been cast am I properly "historical," that is, in possession of a destiny.

In brief, *Being and Time* pictures the lonely will, driven by dread, to face the prospect of its own nothingness and in retrospect its own guilt, and yet also to realize in this the terror of its own freedom.

Building on this existential basis, the later Heidegger turns his attention to hermeneutics (in *Introduction to Metaphysics*). Here four emphases are found.

The first emphasis is *history*, in which the intellectual history of the West is found. Being, as distinct from particular things, is almost nothing—a haze, as Nietzsche said. We have "fallen out of Being" and betrayed our true vocation by running foolishly after this thing and that. So it is the history of our being that we should be forgetful about Being.

The second emphasis is *the darkening of the world*, a world in which we live in our forgetfulness of Being. We are more concerned with *beings*, from genes to spaceships, than with our true calling, which is to be shepherds and watchers of *Being*. Inventiveness, not understanding, has been our occupation. We are more concerned with proliferation of technical skills than with metaphysical unity. So we have lost Being; it has become haze, an error—nothing.

The third emphasis is *Greek philosophy*, the key to overcoming this forgetfulness of Being. In fact, according to Heidegger, philosophy can only be done properly in Greek and German; the Latinization of Greek philosophy has been the source of error. Between Parmenides (b. 515 B.C.) and Aristotle (384–322 B.C.), the error began by making a dichotomy between Being and Thought. For Parmenides these were one, but by the time of Aristotle, Being had broken loose from its first great anchorage and floated out in that tide of nihilism on which we are still adrift. Thus, we have lost

---

[4]That is, the anonymous crowd.

the presocratic *aletheia* (Gr: "truth"), the unhiddenness of being, and truth has become a characteristic of propositions (a mere "correspondence" with "facts"). It is this loosening of truth from Being that has lead to nihilism.

The fourth emphasis is *poetry and language*, the means through which Heidegger wishes to recall humankind from nihilism to Being. It is by language that man stands open to Being, and unlike the pseudo-terminology of science, which has lost its hold on Being, the true origin of language is in poetry. Poetry is the primal language of a historical people in which it founds Being; hence, the great poets are the ones who can restore language to its essential power—as a revealer of Being. Thus language is the foundation and house of being, especially the poetic language of Friedrich Hölderlin (1770–1843) (who had a keen tie with classical antiquity). Through him we may hope to get some "mittances"[5] of truth, some illumination of Being, some relevation of the Holy. We are, as it were, "waiting for god" (cf. *Waiting for Godot*)—a god remote from theology or piety, a god who presides over the long-lost Being of which we are in quest.

In his later works, Heidegger discarded Kierkegaard as a mere religious writer, refuted Jean-Paul Sartre's (1905–1980) humanistic existentialism, and opted more for Nietzsche, Holderlin, and Rainer Maria Rilke (1875–1926, "pathological poetry"). In his early work, Heidegger affirmed that man speaks through language; in his later work, he affirmed that Being speaks through language. Since the presocratics let Being speak through language, etymology of Greek works is the key to the true meaning of words. This became the basis of Kittels's massive *Theological Dictionary of the New Testament*, which traces the origin and history of Greek words in a quest to find their real meaning.

An Evaluation of Heidegger's Existential Hermeneutic

Heidegger is commendable in displaying a quest for being, expressing an openness to being, seeing language as a key to reality, preserving the evocative value of poetry and metaphor, and even asking the right question: "Why is there something rather than nothing at all?"

Nonetheless, there are serious flaws in his subjective existential hermeneutic. A few can be briefly spelled out.

First, Heidegger's subjective existential hermeneutic involves the unfounded assumption that Being is unintelligible in itself. But how could Heidegger know this about Being unless Being were intelligible?

Second, it is self-defeating to attempt to express the inexpressible. If Being is beyond description, how is it that Heidegger succeeds in describing it for us?

---

[5]Pieces, or sparks.

Third, language does not establish being but expresses it. It does not found Being but reveals it to us, that is, if it is truly descriptive of it.

Fourth, Heidegger's assertion against a correspondence view of truth is self-destructive, for he assumes that his denial of a correspondence view of truth corresponds with reality. But correspondence with reality is precisely what is meant by a correspondence view of truth.

Fifth, he purports an openness to Being but rejects God, who *is* Being—Pure Actuality (see volume 2, part 1). Every contingent being (which Heidegger admits man is) needs a Necessary Being to ground its existence.

Sixth, Heidegger neglects the analogical ability of language to speak meaningfully of God (see chapter 9), and he rejects the descriptive ability of language for its evocative dimension.

Seventh, Heidegger asks the right question but rules out an adequate answer. He responds to "Why something, not nothing?" by saying it can be asked about God too. But it cannot—at least not meaningfully. God is an Uncaused Being, and of such a Being it is not meaningful to ask what caused the Uncaused. One may as well ask, "Who is the bachelor's wife?"

Eighth, Heidegger expects all readers of his books to use the standard hermeneutic of searching for the author's meaning. But this is directly contrary to the subjective hermeneutic he taught to be used on other writings.

Ninth, etymology is not the key to the meaning of a term. This position was thoroughly critiqued by a noted liberal scholar, James Barr, in his *Biblical Semantics*. The fact that the word *board* originally meant a wooden plank is not helpful in determining its meaning in the term "Chairman of the Board."

Tenth, Heidegger's hermeneutic reduces to an unverifiable mysticism. How does one know that the "mittances" of light obtained through the "pathological" poets are not from the angel of light (2 Cor. 11:14)?

In spite of the defects in his view, Heidegger had a significant influence on the work of others, including the metaphysics of Paul Tillich (1886–1965), the *sitz-im-leben* (real-life situation) ground for demythology of Rudolf (Karl) Bultmann (1884–1976), the unprotectedness (or openness to Being's voice) of Karl Barth (1886–1968), and the "new hermeneutic" of Gerhard Ebeling and Hans Gadimer.

Derrida's Deconstructionism

Like most thinkers, even innovators, Jacque Derrida (b. 1930) stands on the shoulders of great minds who have gone before him. From Plato he received his negationism—the idea that all determination is by negation. From Immanuel Kant (1724–1804) he learned his agnosticism, and Søren Kierkegaard taught him fideism. From G. W. F. Hegel he borrowed his progressivism (see definition on page 167), albeit applied to hermeneutics; Friedrich Nietzsche taught him atheism, and Sigmund Freud (1856–1939) modeled psychologism for him. Ludwig Wittgenstein is the source of his linguistical solipsism, and Ferdinand de Saussure instructed him in conventionalism. Edmund Husserl is his model for perspectivalism, or relativity in truth (see chapter 7); William James (1842–1910) taught him pragmatism and the will to believe, while Martin Heidegger is the one whose existentialism he emulates.

Derrida is responsible for writing many influential books, among which are *Speech and Phenomena* (1973); *Of Grammatology* (1976); *Writing and Differance* (1978); *Positions* (1981); *Ear of the Other* (1985); *Limited, Inc.* (1988); *Edmund Husserl's Origin of Geometry: An Introduction* (1989); and *Spectors of Marx* (1994).

Derrida was an atheist regarding the existence of God and an agnostic concerning the possibility of knowing absolute truth. He was also anti-metaphysical, claiming that no metaphysics is possible. He believed we are locked in our own linguistic bubble, yet he recognized that using language to deny metaphysics is a form of metaphysics itself. This incoherence points to the need for archi-writing (a new poetic protest against metaphysics).

Derrida realized that archi-writing may be a use of signs without signification, that is, a writing that risks meaning nothing—it may be words facing the infinity of a white page. Nonetheless, he pressed his deconstructional objection.

What Deconstructionism Is Not

Deconstructionism, at least for Derrida, is not a destruction of a text but a reconstruction of it. As such, it is not negation but criticism; it is not a dismantling of a text but a remodeling of it. Deconstructionism does not annihilate, but rather recreates the text; it is not against analysis but against all fixed analyses, and accordingly it claims not to be angry with the text but in love with it. It is not opposed to reading the text but opposed to not rereading it constantly for new meanings.

What Deconstructionism Is

Deconstructionism involves many beliefs that challenge an evangelical understanding. Some of the more important ones are the following:

Conventionalism. Following Saussure, Frege, and Wittgenstein, Derrida was a conventionalist, holding that all meaning is relative. There is no objective or absolute meaning, at least not for finite minds (and he rejected an infinite Mind—God).

Nonreferentialism. Derrida believed that there is no perfect reference—all one-to-one correspondence is impossible. My concepts are uniquely mine; hence, meaning is never perfectly transferable.

Contextualism. Further, Derrida held a form of contextualism, which means that all texts have different context, and the meaning of a text is determined by the context in which it is read. We can constantly change a given context, but we cannot escape having a limited context—we cannot know from an infinite perspective.

Differentialism. According to Derrida, "difference" or the unknown in a text is the most important part of it. All rational structures leave something out, and, therefore, we must bring everything under suspicion.

Linguistical Solipsism. Derrida embraced a form of linguistical solipsism, namely, that we cannot escape the limits of language. We can broaden our linguistic concepts, but we cannot transcend linguistic boundaries.

Semantical Progressivism. Derrida also held to semantic progressivism—that possible meanings never end. Thus, philosophy never ends, for we never exhaust all possible meanings of a text; the text can always be further deconstructed.

Fideism. Derrida has also insisted that faith is always necessary. Since absolute meaning is impossible, indecision is inescapable. We are always between absolute certainty and absolute doubt, between skepticism and dogmatism. As a result, faith is always essential.

An Evaluation of Deconstructionism

First, deconstructionism is a form of linguisticalism, which affirms that all meaning is limited by language. However, this very statement—that all meaning is limited by language—places itself outside the limits of language.

Second, deconstructionism also embraces conventionalism, contending that all meaning is relative to our situation. But once again, how can it make these nonconventional statements? If "All meaning is culturally relative," then so is that statement. If the statement is not culturally relative, then it destroys itself.

Third, deconstructionism believes that the laws of logic are dependent on language, which is culturally relative. But the reverse is true: Language is based on logic. Without logic language would not be possible; indeed, the laws of logic are undeniable (see chapter 5).

Fourth, deconstructionism's linguisticalism is self-defeating, for if there were no meaning prior to language, then language could not be learned. One must have the rational ability to understand language in order to learn a language.

Fifth, deconstructionism is also a form of perspectivalism—holding that all truth is conditioned by one's perspective. But if "all truth is perspectival," what about that statement? It is a nonperspectival statement, and it claims that there can be no such statements.

Sixth, there is the self-defeating nature of Derrida's hermeneutic. He expects his texts to be interpreted according to what he meant by them, which is directly contrary to how he says texts should be interpreted.

Seventh, recall the self-defeating nature of agnosticism about truth and meaning. Derrida's view amounts to saying that "it is an ultimate truth that there is no ultimate truth." Or, "No meaning is fixed, even the meaning of this statement." Or, "All truth is perspectival, including this truth." Or, "Meaning is never perfectly transferable, including the meaning of this sentence."

Eighth, Derrida's implicit defense of fideism is self-defeating. It is tantamount to making a case for not making a case.

Ninth, as Derrida seems at least partially aware, it is self-defeating to attempt to deny metaphysics without making metaphysical statements. His effort to resist it (by poetic language) is futile, for he knows he cannot avoid the use of metaphysical language to deny metaphysics. Such an absurdity does not point to the need for poetic language; it shows the self-destructive nature of denying metaphysics.

Tenth, it is fruitless to turn to poetry to avoid metaphysics. Metaphysical questions still exist, and they cannot be answered in anything but metaphysical language. Any so-called poetical protest is nothing more than an exercise in ventilating one's tonsils.

Eleventh, Derrida's view is a form of reader imperialism. The birth of the reader spells the death of the author; the author's meaning dies once a reader takes over. But no deconstructionist really wants his books read in this manner; clearly he expects the reader to understand his (the author's) meaning and not to read his (the reader's) own meaning into it.

Twelfth, there is the failure to see that the lack of one-to-one correspondence does not eliminate all true correspondence. True correspondence can be one to many, i.e., one and the same meaning can be expressed in many ways.

Thirteenth, in deconstructionism there is a subtle dogmatism of attempting to eliminate the dogmatic. Nothing is more dogmatic than the dogmatic claim that nothing can be known for sure. There is nothing of which we should be more suspicious than the view that demands that we be suspicious of everything else. Deconstructionists do not blush to ask us to accept as a fixed meaning the claim that no meaning can be fixed.

Bultmann's Demythology

Rudolf Bultmann (1884–1976) applied Heidegger's existentialism to the New Testament by his demythological subjectivism.

Bultmann's Argument for Demythological Naturalism
Rudolf Bultmann built his case on several lines of thought. At the basis of it is his concept of a three-storied universe with the earth in the center, the heaven above (where God and angels are), and the underworld beneath. Supernatural forces intervene in the course of nature and in all that we think and will and do (Bultmann, *KM*, 1).

We need to strip the New Testament documents of this mythological structure. For all this is the language of mythology and is incredible to modern man, for he is convinced that the mythical view of the world is obsolete. For all our thinking today is shaped by modern science. So "a blind acceptance of the New Testament would involve a sacrifice of the intellect. It would mean accepting a view of the world in our faith and religion, which we should deny in our everyday life" (ibid., 3–4).

Bultmann pronounces the biblical picture of miracles as impossible to modern man, for "man's knowledge and mastery of the world have advanced to such an extent through science and technology that it is no longer possible for anyone seriously to hold the New Testament view of the world—in fact, there is hardly anyone who does." Therefore, the only honest way of reciting the creeds is to strip the mythological framework from the truth they enshrine. Bultmann concludes confidently that the Resurrection is not an event of history, "for an historical fact which involves a resurrection from the dead is utterly inconceivable" (ibid., 38–39).

Bultmann offers several reasons for this antisupernatural conclusion. *First,* there is the incredibility of a mythical event like the resuscitation of a corpse. *Second,* there is the difficulty of establishing the objective historicity of the Resurrection no matter how many witnesses are cited. *Third,* the Resurrection is an article of faith, which, as such, cannot be a miraculous proof. *Fourth,* there are other like events known to mythology (ibid., 39–40).

Therefore, according to Bultmann, since the Resurrection is not an event of objective, space-time history, it is an event of subjective history; that is, it is an event of faith in the hearts of the early disciples. Consequently, it is not subject to objective historical verification or falsification, for it is not really an event in the space-time world. Christ did not rise from Joseph's tomb; He arose only by faith in the disciples' hearts.

Bultmann's argument can be summarized like this:

(1) Myths are by nature more than objective truths; they are transcendent truths of faith.
(2) But what is not objective cannot be part of a verifiable space-time world.
(3) Therefore, miracles (myths) are not part of the objective space-time world.

An Evaluation of Bultmann's Argument That the New Testament Contains Myths

Several objections have been offered to Bultmann's mythological naturalism. *First,* it is built on at least two unproven assumptions:

(1) Miracles are less than historical because they are more than historical.

(2) Miracles cannot occur in the world without being of the world.

Both of these assumptions are wrong. Miracles can be more than historical without being less than historical, and miracles can originate from beyond the world and still be acts within the world (see chapter 3).

Second, Bultmann's view is without foundation, having no evidential basis. Mythological events are unverifiable; that is, they have no evidential value.

Third, Bultmann's view is unbiblical, being contrary to the overwhelming evidence for the authenticity of the New Testament documents and the reliability of the witnesses. Indeed, it is contrary to the New Testament claim for itself not to be "cunningly devised fables" (2 Peter 1:16 NKJV) but an eyewitness account (cf. John 21: 24; 1 John 1:1–3).

Fourth, the New Testament is not the literary genre of mythology. One great Oxford scholar, himself a writer of myths (fairy tales), keenly noted, "Dr. Bultmann never wrote a gospel." He asks, therefore, "Has the experience of his learned . . . life really given him any power of seeing into the minds of those long dead [who *have* written one]?" As a living author of myth, C. S. Lewis (1898–1963) found the critics usually wrong when they attempted to read his mind rather than his words. However, he adds, "the 'assured results of modern scholarship,' as to the way in which an old book was written, are 'assured,' we may conclude, only because the men who knew the facts are dead and can't blow the gaff." In brief, Bultmannian biblical critiques are unfalsifiable because, as Lewis wryly remarks, "St. Mark is dead. When they meet St. Peter, there will be more pressing matters to discuss" (Lewis, *CR*, 161–63).

Finally, the claim that the New Testament miracles are myths, not history, is refuted by numerous lines of evidence (see part 2, chapter 26).[6]

---

[6]The evidence that the New Testament is not a myth is based upon sound evidence. *First*, it was written by contemporaries and eyewitnesses of the events (cf. Luke 1:1–4). *Second*, insufficient time exists for a legend to develop while the eyewitnesses were still alive to refute the story (see Craig, *KTAR*, 96); It takes two full generations for a myth to develop, time not available between the New Testament events (primarily c. A.D. 29–33) and the earliest documents (c. A.D. 50–55). *Third*, the work of noted Roman historian Colin Hemer overwhelmingly confirms the historicity of the New Testament (see Hemer, *ASHH*). *Fourth*, the Virgin Birth accounts do not show any signs of being mythological. One great twentieth-century myth writer himself noted, "I have been reading poems, romances, vision-literature, legends, myths all my life. I know what they are like. I know that not one of them [the Gospels] is like this" (Lewis, *GD*, 154–55). *Fifth*, the surrounding persons, places, and events of Christ's birth were all historical. Luke goes to great pains to note that it was in the days of "Caesar Augustus" (Luke 2:1) that Jesus was born and later baptized in "the fifteenth year of the reign of Tiberius Caesar, Pontius Pilate being governor of Judea, Herod being tetrarch of Galilee . . . Annas and Caiaphas were high priests" (Luke 3:1–2 NKJV). *Sixth*, no Greek myth spoke of the literal incarnation of a monotheistic God into human form (cf. John 1:1–3, 14) by way of a literal virgin birth (Matt. 1:18–25). The Greeks were polytheists, not monotheists. *Seventh*, the *stories* of Greek gods becoming human via miraculous events like a virgin birth were not prior to but after the time of Christ (Edwin Yamauchi, "Easter—Myth, Hallucination, or History" in *Christianity Today*, 2 parts; 3/15/74; 3/29/74).

OBJECTIVITY IN HERMENEUTICS

There are, of course, many other forms of subjectivism in hermeneutics. They too fail, since all involve self-defeating statements, and any attempt to deny an objective interpretation implies that one is possible, namely, the one by which the subjectivist's view is expected to be understood. That is, every subjectivist expects that readers can and should come to an objective understanding of his subjectivistic views.

The Basis of an Objective Hermeneutic

The foundation for objectivism in hermeneutics is not simply found in the self-destructive nature of subjectivism; it is based also in the solid arguments in favor of all the major elements necessary to have an objective interpretation of a revelation. These include:

(1) the existence of an absolute Mind (God);
(2) the absolute nature of meaning;
(3) the analogy between infinite understanding and finite understanding; and
(4) the ability of finite minds (made in God's image) to understand truths revealed by God.

The Existence of an Absolute Mind

The existence of an absolute Mind was established earlier (in chapter 2). To refresh:

(1) At least one finite mind exists (me), for without thinking I cannot deny I think. And I am limited in my thought, or I would not doubt or discover new thoughts, which I do.
(2) The principle of causality demands that every finite thing needs a cause (see chapter 2).
(3) Hence, it follows that there must be an infinite Mind that caused my finite mind. This is true for two reasons: One, a cause can't give what it doesn't have (analogy—see chapter 9). Two, the effect cannot be greater than its cause; water cannot rise higher than its source. So, if the effect is intelligent, the Cause must be intelligent. An infinite Mind must exist.

Absolute Meaning

If there is an absolute Mind, then there can be absolute meaning. The objective basis for meaning is found in the Mind of God. Whatever an infinite Mind means by something is what it means objectively, infinitely, and absolutely. Therefore, the existence of objective and absolute meaning is grounded in the existence of an absolute Meaner (God).

Analogy and Meaning

Not only is the theistic God (see chapter 2) of Christianity infinitely knowledgeable (omniscient), but He is also omnipotent (infinitely powerful). An infinitely powerful God can do whatever is not contradictory, and it is not contradictory for an infinite Mind to convey meaning to finite creatures, since there is a common ground between them in both the undeniable laws of thought (see chapter 5) and in the similarity (analogy) between Creator and creature (see chapter 9).

To be sure, an infinite Mind knows things in a much higher way than finite minds do. But while *how* God knows things is different than how man knows, nevertheless, *what* He knows is the same as what He reveals to humankind. That is, the *thing signified* is the same, but the *mode of signification* is different for God and for us.

The Image of God in Man

If an absolute Meaner exists, then there can be absolute meaning. An all-powerful God can do whatever is not impossible to do. It is not impossible for an infinite Mind to communicate with finite minds, since there is common (analogous) ground between them.

However, there remains one question: Can a finite mind *discover* the objective truth that has been objectively *disclosed* to it? It's one thing for an author to disclose his thoughts in a book, and quite another for a reader to *understand* what he has *revealed.*

The answer to this question is in two parts. *First,* it is *possible* to know, since all the necessary conditions for knowing the objective meaning expressed by God have been met. *Second,* whether one will *actually* know the objective meaning that has been objectively expressed will depend on meeting the necessary conditions for understanding this objective meaning.

THE PRINCIPLES OF OBJECTIVE HERMENEUTICS

The Principles of Understanding God's Special Revelation Objectively

Since God has given revelation, and since it is possible for us to understand its meaning, we need to understand what guidelines to use in the process of interpreting it. The following are the principles we must bring with us as we approach God's special revelation, Scripture.

Look for the Author's Meaning, Not the Reader's

The objective meaning of a text is the one given to it by the author, not the one attributed to it by the reader. Readers should ask what was meant by the author, not what it means to the reader. Once a reader discovers what the author meant by the text, he has obtained its *objective* meaning. Thus, asking, "What does it mean to *me*?" is the wrong question, and it will almost certainly lead to a subjective interpretation. Asking of the author, "What did *he* mean?" will almost certainly lead the reader in the right direction, that is, toward the objective meaning.

Look for the Author's Meaning (What), Not His Purpose (Why)

Another road to hermeneutical subjectivity leads to the author's purpose rather than to his meaning. Meaning is found in what the author has affirmed, not in why he affirmed it. Purpose does not determine meaning. One can know *what* the author said without knowing *why* he said it. Two examples will suffice to elucidate this point.

First, if one says, "Come over to my house tonight," there is no difficulty in understanding what is meant, even though the purpose for the invitation is not known. *What* is understood apart from *why*. The meaning is apprehended, even though the purpose is not known.

Of course, if the purpose is known, then the statement may take on a whole new *significance*. But meaning and significance are not the same. Meaning deals with *what?* and significance deals with *so what?* For example, if the purpose of the invitation is to inform you that you lost a loved one, as opposed to that you won ten million dollars, then the significance is quite variant. However, the meaning of the statement, "Come over to my house," is identical in either case.

Second, to offer a biblical illustration, Exodus 23:19 commanded the Israelites: "Do not cook a young goat in its mother's milk." The meaning of this sentence is very clear, and every Israelite knew exactly what they were not supposed to do. However, the purpose of this command is not clear at all. A survey of a few commentators yields a variety of different hypotheses as to the purpose of this command:

(1) It profaned the Feast of Ingathering.
(2) It would cause indigestion.
(3) It was cruel to cook a goat in the milk that nourished it.
(4) It was a form of idolatry.
(5) It violated the parent/child relationship.

In other words, nobody seems to know for sure what the purpose was. Yet everyone knows for sure what the meaning is. If purpose determined meaning, then no one would know what the meaning is. Thankfully, it doesn't. What is said is clear apart from why it was said.

Look for Meaning in the Text, Not Beyond It

The meaning is not found *beyond* the text (in God's mind), *beneath* the text (in the mystic's mind), or *behind* the text (in the author's unexpressed intention); it is found *in* the text (in the author's expressed meaning). For instance, the beauty of a sculpture is not found behind, beneath, or beyond the sculpture. Rather, it is expressed in the sculpture.

All textual meaning is in the text. The sentences (in the context of their paragraphs in the context of the whole piece of literature) are the formal cause of meaning. They are the form that gives meaning to all the parts (words, punctuation, etc.).

Applying the six causes to meaning will help explain the point. Following Aristotle, scholastic philosophers distinguished six different causes:

(1) efficient cause—that *by which* something comes to be;
(2) final cause—that *for which* something comes to be;
(3) formal cause—that *of which* something comes to be;
(4) material cause—that *out of which* something comes to be;
(5) exemplar cause—that *after which* something comes to be;
(6) instrumental cause—that *through which* something comes to be.

Remember the example of the chair? A wooden chair has a carpenter as its efficient cause, to provide something to sit on as its final cause, its structure as a chair as its formal cause, wood as its material cause, the blueprint as its exemplar cause, and the carpenter's tools as its instrumental cause.

As we have seen, applying these six causes to meaning yields the following analysis:

(1) The writer is the efficient cause of the meaning of a text.
(2) The writer's purpose is the final cause of its meaning.
(3) The writing is the formal cause of its meaning.
(4) The words are the material cause of its meaning.
(5) The writer's ideas are the exemplar cause of its meaning.
(6) The laws of thought are the instrumental cause of its meaning.

The meaning of the writing is not found in the meaner; he is the efficient cause of the meaning. *The formal cause of meaning is in the writing itself;* what is signified is found in the signs that signify it. Verbal meaning is found in the very structure and grammar of the sentences themselves. Meaning is found *in* the literary text itself—not in its author (efficient cause) or purpose (final cause), but in its literary form (formal cause). Again, meaning is not in individual words (which are the material cause).[7]

Look for Meaning in Affirmation, Not Implication

Another guideline in discovering the objective meaning of a text is to look for its affirmation, not its implication. Ask what the test affirms (or denies), not what it implies. This is not to say that implications are not possible or important, but only that the basic meaning is not found there. *Meaning* is in what the text affirms, not in how it can be applied.

There is only *one meaning* in a text, but there are *many implications and applications.* In terms of meaning, the *sensus unum* (one sense) view is correct; however, there is a *sensus plenum* (full sense) in terms of implication.[8]

The Principles of Understanding God's General Revelation Objectively

God has not only revealed Himself in Scripture (special revelation) but in nature (general revelation) as well. And, like Scripture, general revelation must be interpreted—there are right and wrong ways to do so. In the same way, there are good and bad guidelines for interpreting general revelation.

The Biblical Basis for the Intelligibility of General Revelation

General revelation is found both in creation (Ps. 19:1f) and in conscience (Rom. 2:12–15). The latter, called natural law, is described in the Bible as that which human beings "do by nature" (Rom. 2:14). It is the law "written on the hearts" of all men (ibid.). Those who disobey it go "contrary to nature" (Rom. 1:27).

The general revelation in nature is objectively clear and evident to all men, even in their fallen state. Psalm 19:1–4 affirms,

> The heavens *declare* the glory of God; the skies *proclaim* the work of his hands. Day after day they pour forth *speech*; night after night they

---

[7]As has been demonstrated, words have no meaning in themselves; they have only usage in a sentence, which is the smallest unity of meaning. Words are only the parts of a whole (the sentence), and it is the whole that has meaning.

[8]Recall this example: Einstein knew that $e=mc^2$ (Energy equals mass times the speed of light [constant] squared), and so does an average high school science student. However, Einstein knew many more implications of this than the average high school student.

Inasmuch as God inspired the text, He sees more implications in a biblical affirmation than does the human author (1 Pet. 1:10–12; 2 Tim. 3:16). But He does not affirm any more meaning in the text than the human author does, for whatever the Bible says, God says. That is, whatever the Bible affirms is true, God affirms is true. They both mean exactly the same thing by the text. There are not two texts, and there are not two meanings of the text. So both the divine and human authors of Scripture affirm one and the same meaning in one and the same text.

display knowledge. There is no *speech or language* where their *voice* is not *heard.* Their voice goes out into *all the earth,* their *words* to *the ends of the world.* (emphasis added)

The use of terms like "declare," "proclaim," "speech," "knowledge," "words," and "voice" demonstrate that it is an intelligible, objective revelation of God. Phrases like "all the earth," and "to the ends of the world," and the fact that it covers all language groups, show beyond question that this natural revelation is universal.

In Acts 14, where Paul is speaking to the heathen at Lystra, he appeals to a common "nature" (v. 15 NKJV) and that "He [God] did not leave Himself without witness" (v. 17 NKJV) as the grounds for their believing that there was a "living God, who made the heaven, the earth, the sea, and all things that are in them" (v. 15 NKJV). Unless this natural revelation to pagans was intelligible, such an appeal would be meaningless.

Likewise, while speaking to the Greek philosophers on Mars Hill, the apostle appealed to natural revelation as the basis for belief that there is a "God, who made the world and everything in it" (Acts 17:24). Indeed, he even argues from the nature of human beings as "the offspring of God" (v. 29 NKJV) to the spiritual essence of the "Divine Nature."

Using this same reasoning in Romans 1, Paul declared that "since the creation of the world His [God's] invisible attributes are clearly seen, being understood by the things that are made" (Rom. 1:20 NKJV). Noteworthy here is the assertion that this natural revelation is absolutely clear to all human beings, even those without the aid of special revelation. The use of the words "clearly seen" (Rom. 1:20), "manifest in them" (v. 19), "is revealed" (v. 17–18), and "God has shown it to them" (v. 19) demonstrate unquestionably that this objective revelation is not only knowable (v. 19), but it is actually known by unbelievers. Indeed, it is so clear that "they are without excuse" and condemned to their eternal destiny because they "repress" (v. 18) this truth they possess.

The same is true of God's natural revelation in the human heart. In Romans 2:12–15 (NIV) Paul affirms,

All who sin apart from the law will also perish apart from the law [of Moses], and all who sin under the law will be judged by the law.... (Indeed, when Gentiles, who do not have the law, do *by nature* things required by the law, they are a law for themselves, even though they do not have the law [of Moses], since they show that the requirements of the law are *written on their hearts,* their consciences also bearing witness, and their thoughts now accusing, now even defending them.) (Emphasis added)

In fact, Paul deems the natural revelation so clearly "written on their hearts" that even the heathen, who do not have special revelation, will "perish." In brief, Scripture teaches that God's objective revelation in nature is intelligible and all human beings are accountable before God in view of it.

Objections to the Intelligibility of General Revelation

Many arguments have been offered against the objectivity of general revelation. However, all of them fall short of the mark. For detailed responses to these objections see chapter 4.

Hermeneutical Principles for Interpreting Natural (General) Revelation

Once natural revelation has been located, it remains to be seen how it should be interpreted. Like the correct principles of understanding God's special revelation in Scriptures, the truth expressed in nature and the law "written on our hearts" can be readily understood as well.

As we have seen, according to Scripture, God's revelation expressed in nature is clear and evident to all rational beings (Rom. 1:19–20). Why, then, is the validity of God's natural revelation so hotly disputed?

The Principle of Causality

Famous atheist Friedrich Nietzsche revealed the reason when he said, "We receive, but we do not ask where it came from." In short, he rejected one of the principles of human reason that would lead naturally to God if he had applied it. *It is natural to conclude that the gifts of life come from the Giver of life*—unless, of course, one rejects the fundamental guideline of reason that every gift (effect) has a giver (cause). In short, the *principle of causality* is an essential hermeneutical principle in interpreting natural revelation.

In his BBC debate with Frederick Copleston, renowned agnostic Bertrand Russell (1872–1970) gave the same maneuver as Nietzsche. When asked what caused the universe, Russell responded that it did not need a cause: "I should say that the universe is just there, and that's all" (cited in John Hick, *EG*, 175). But every other thing that could not be—yet is— needs a cause, so why does the universe not need one? As Richard Taylor showed long ago, if all would agree that a small glass ball found in the woods needs a cause, then making it bigger does not eliminate the need for a cause—even if one makes it as big as the whole universe (Taylor, *M*, 87–88). The fact is, the reason non-theists do not come to the reasonable conclusion that the world needs a cause is that they fail to apply consistently a fundamental principle of reason—that *every* finite thing needs a cause. In other words, they are not using the correct hermeneutical approach to natural revelation. This is evident also in the failure to interpret properly God's revelation in human nature.

The Principle of Consistency

Another fundamental principle of interpreting the law written on our own nature can be called the *principle of consistency*, which is a practical application of the law of noncontradiction. Being selfish creatures, we do not always desire to do what is right. However inconsistently, we do, nonetheless, desire that it be done to us. So by *reason* we conclude that consistency demands that we should also do the same to others; this is why Jesus summarized the moral law by declaring, "In everything do to others what you would have them do to you" (Matt. 7:12). Confucius (551–479 B.C.) recognized the same basic truth by general revelation when he said, "Never do to others what you would not like them to do to you" (Confucius, *AC* 25.23; cf. 12:2). Human reason, then, is necessary to determine the proper means to the good end that we intuitively know is right.

The Principle of Uniformity

While we intuitively know that we should do no harm to another, nevertheless we must use our reason to tell us that shooting a gun at someone will do them harm. This we know because of the *principle of uniformity*. All past experience tells us that a gun can kill someone (which is severe harm). Just like the *principle of causality* is needed to understand God's natural revelation in nature, the law of uniformity is necessary to understand that it is wrong to intentionally take the life of another person.

The Principle of Teleology

Briefly stated, the *principle of teleology* says that every rational agent acts for an end. This principle is behind all rational communication, whether in special revelation or in general revelation. Purpose (design) can be seen in nature and, hence, we posit a Designer of nature. Intelligent beings act for an end, and so when we see nature act for an end, we naturally come to the conclusion that there is an intelligent Being behind nature.

The principle of teleology is also assumed in all ethical acts, for if there were no purpose (or intent) to perform an act, then a person is not responsible for the act. Personal moral responsibility implies the ability of the person to respond. Moral culpability implies intentionality. Thus to know if an act is morally wrong we must look for evidence of moral intention. Here, too, reason is necessary to interpret properly what is morally right or wrong.

Other Principles of Interpreting Natural Revelation

In addition to the four principles just mentioned as necessary for a proper hermeneutic of natural revelation—causality, consistency, uniformity, and teleology—there are also four general laws of logic:

(1) the principle of noncontradiction;

(2) the principle of identity;

(3) the principle of excluded middle; and

(4) the principle(s) of rational inference (see chapter 5).

Without these principles, valid reasoning about anything is not possible, to say nothing of reasoning about natural revelation. When these principles are applied correctly and consistently to natural revelation, the result is a valid natural theology (Rom. 1:1–20) and natural ethic (Rom. 2:12–15), the very areas in which God holds all persons responsible.

SUMMARY AND CONCLUSION

God has two great revelations: general and special, natural and supernatural. Both are objective and clear. Both are capable of distortion by depraved human beings. There are proper and improper ways to interpret each. The correct way in each case is to follow the basic principles inherent to each. These include the basic laws of logic as well as the principles of causality, consistency, uniformity, and teleology. When these principles are applied correctly and consistently to general revelation, they will yield a proper understanding of it. But like the interpreting of special revelation, a correct understanding of natural revelation depends on using the right principles and using them consistently. In the final analysis, the natural law is not hard to understand; like God's supernatural law, it is simply hard to practice.

SOURCES

Barr, James. *Biblical Semantics.*

Blackstone, Sir William. *Commentaries on the Laws of England.*

Bultmann, Rudolph. *Kerygma and Myth: A Theological Debate.*

Calvin, John. *Institutes,* Book I, Chapters 2, 10.

Carson, Donald. *Gagging God.*

Confucius. *Analects of Confucius.*

Craig, William. *Knowing the Truth About the Resurrection.*

Derrida, Jacque. *Of Grammatology.*

———. *Limited, Inc.*

———. *Speech and Phenomena.*

———. *Writing and Differance.*

Evans, Stephen. *Christian Perspectives on Religious Knowledge.*

Geisler, Norman L. *Miracles and the Modern Mind* (chapter 6).

Hemer, Colin J. *Acts in the Setting of Hellenistic History.*

Hick, John. *The Existence of God.*

Hooker, Richard. *Of the Laws of Ecclesiastical Polity.*

Howe, Thomas. *Objectivity in Hermeneutics* (unpublished doctoral dissertation for Southeastern Baptist Seminary, 1998).

Jefferson, Thomas. *Declaration of Independence.*
Lewis, C. S. *The Abolition of Man.*
———. *Christian Reflections.*
———. *The Great Divorce.*
Locke, John. *The Second Treatise on Government.*
Lundin, Roger. *The Culture of Interpretation.*
Luther, Martin. *Bondage of the Will.*
Lyotard, Jean-Francois. *The Postmodern Condition: A Report on Knowledge.*
Madison, Gary B. *Working Through Derrida.*
McCallum, Dennis. *The Death of Truth.*
Philips, Timothy. *Christian Apologetics in the Postmodern World.*
Sherwin-White, A. N. *Roman Society and Roman Law in the New Testament.*
Taylor, Richard. *Metaphysics.*
Thomas Aquinas. *Summa Theologica.*
Wells, David. *No Place for Truth.*
Wolterstofff, Nicholas. *Divine Discourse.*
Yamauchi, Edwin. "Easter—Myth, Hallucination, or History" in *Christianity Today* (2 parts; 3/15/74; 3/29/74).

CHAPTER ELEVEN

HISTORIOGRAPHY: THE HISTORICAL PRECONDITION

U nlike some religions, historical Christianity is inseparably tied to historical events, including the lives of Adam, Abraham, Moses, David, and Jesus. These events, especially those of the life, death, and resurrection of Christ, are crucial to the truth of evangelical Christianity (cf. 1 Cor. 15:12–19); without them, it would cease to exist. Thus, the existence and knowability of certain historical events are essential to maintaining biblical Christianity.

The knowability of history is important not only theologically but also apologetically, for the overall argument in defense of Christianity is based on the historicity of the New Testament documents (see chapter 26). Hence, since the objective knowability of history is strongly challenged by many contemporary historians, it is necessary to counter this claim in order to secure the defense of Christianity.

OBJECTIONS TO THE OBJECTIVITY OF HISTORY

Many arguments have been advanced against the position that history is objectively knowable (see Craig, *NH*),[1] and several will now be examined (see Beard, "TND" in Stern, *VH*, 323–25). If these disputations are valid, they make the essential historical basis of Christianity both unknowable and unverifiable. These arguments fall into six broad categories: epistemologi-

---

[1]Much of the discussion here follows an excellent summary found in an unpublished master's thesis by William L. Craig, *The Nature of History* (Trinity Evangelical Divinity School, Deerfield, Ill., 1976).

cal, axiological, methodological, metaphysical, psychological, and hermeneutical.

The Epistemological Objections

Epistemology deals with how one *knows*, and relativists believe that
objective truth is unknowable. Since this position has earlier been examined and found wanting (see chapter 7), the focus here will be on the historical relativists, who contend that the very conditions by which one knows
history are so subjective that one cannot have an objective knowledge of it.
Three main challenges are offered.

The Unobservability of History

Historical subjectivists argue that history, unlike science, is not directly
observable; in other words, that the historian does not deal with past events
but with statements about past events. This enables the historian to deal
with facts in an imaginative way, attempting to reconstruct events he did
not observe as they occurred. Historical facts, they insist, exist only within
the creative mind of the historian, and historical documents do not contain
facts, but are without the historian's understanding mere ink lines on the
paper. Further, once the event is over it can never be fully recreated.
Hence, the historian must impose meaning on his fragmentary and secondhand record (see Becker, "DWH," in Snyder, *DWH*, 131).

There are two reasons offered as to why the historian has only indirect
access to the past. *First*, it is claimed that, unlike a scientist, the historian's
world is composed of records and not events. This is why the historian must
contribute a "reconstructed picture" of the past, and in this sense the past
is really a product of the present.

Second, historical relativists assert that the scientist can test his view,
whereas the historian cannot—experimentation is not possible with historical events. The scientist has the advantage of repeatability; he may subject
his views to falsification. However, the unobservable historical event is no
longer verifiable; it is part of the forever departed past. Therefore, what
one believes about the past is no more than a reflection of his own imagination, a subjective construction in the minds of present historians that
cannot hope to be an objective representation of what really happened.

The Fragmentary Nature of Historical Accounts

The second objection to the objectivity of history relates to its fragmentary nature. At best historians can hope for completeness of documentation, but completeness of the events themselves is never possible. Optimally,
documents cover only a small fraction of the events themselves (Beard,
"TND" in Stern, *VH* , 323), and from only fragmentary documents one
cannot validly draw full and final conclusions.

Furthermore, the documents do not present the events, but only an interpretation of the events mediated through the one who recorded them. The best-case scenario, then, is that we have only a fragmentary record of what someone else thought happened: "What really happened would still have to be reconstructed in the mind of the historian" (Carr, *WIH*, 20). Because the documents are so fragmentary and the events so distant, objectivity becomes a will-o'-the-wisp for the historian. He not only has too few pieces of the puzzle, but the partial pictures on the few pieces he does have were merely painted from the mind of the one who passed the pieces down to us.

The Historical Conditioning of the Historian

Historical relativists insist that the historian is a product of his time, and as such he is subject to the unconscious programming of his era. It is impossible, allegedly, for the historian to stand back and view history objectively because he too is part of the historical process. Hence, historical synthesis depends on the personality of the writer as well as the social and religious milieu in which he lives (Pirenne, "WAHTD" in Meyerhoff, *P*, 97). In this sense one must study the historian before one can understand his history.

Since the historian is part of the historical process, objectivity, it is said, can never be attained. The history of one generation will be rewritten by the next, and so on; no historian can transcend his historical relativity and view the world process from the outside (Collingwood, *IH*, 248). At best there can be successive but less than final historical interpretations, each viewing history from the vantage point of its own generation of historians. Therefore, there is no such person as a neutral historian; each remains a child of his own day.

The Axiological (Value) Objection

The historian cannot avoid making value judgments. This, argue historical relativists, renders objectivity unobtainable, for even in the selection and arrangement of materials, value judgments are made. Titles of chapters and sections are not without implied value judgments, and such judgments are relative to the one making them.

As one historian put it, the very subject matter of history is "value-charged" (Dray, *PH*, 23). The facts of history consist of murders, oppression, and so forth, and these cannot be described in morally neutral words. By his use of ordinary language, then, the historian is forced to make value judgments.

Further, by the very fact that history deals with flesh-and-blood human beings with motives and purposes, an analysis of history must of necessity comment on these. Whether, for instance, one is called a "dictator" or a "benevolent ruler" is a statement of value; how can one describe Josef

Stalin without making such statements? And if one were to attempt a kind of scientifically neutral description of past events without any stated or implied interpretation of human purposes, it would not be history but mere raw-boned chronicle without historical meaning.

Once the historian admits what he cannot avoid, namely, that he must make some value judgments about past events, then his history has lost objectivity. In short, so the objection goes, there is no way for the historian to keep himself out of his history.

The Methodological Objections

Methodological objections relate to the procedure by which history is done. There are several methodological objections to the belief in objective history necessary to establish the truth of Christianity.

The Selective Nature of Historical Methodology

As was suggested by the epistemological objections, the historian does not have direct access to the events of the past, but merely to fragmentary interpretations of those events contained in historical documents. Now, what makes objectivity even more hopeless is the fact that the historian makes a selection from these fragmentary reports and builds his interpretation of the past events on a select number of partial reports of the past events. There are volumes in archives that most historians do not even touch (Beard, "TND" in Stern, *VH*, 324).

The actual selection among the fragmentary accounts, so the argument goes, is influenced by many subjective and relative factors, including personal prejudice, availability of materials, knowledge of the languages, personal beliefs, social conditions, and so on. Hence, the historian himself is inextricably involved with the history he writes, and what is included versus what is excluded in his interpretation will always be a matter of subjective choice. No matter how objective an historian may attempt to be, it is practically impossible for him to present what really happened. His "history" is no more than his own interpretation based on his own subjective selection of fragmentary interpretations of past and unrepeatable events.

It is argued, consequently, that the facts of history do not speak for themselves: "The facts speak only when the historian calls on them; it is he who decides to which facts to give the floor, and in what order or context" (Carr, *WIH*, 32). To summarize, when the "facts" speak, it is not the original events that are speaking but later fragmentary opinions about those events. The original facts or events have long since perished, and so, according to historical relativism, by the very nature of the endeavor the historian can never hope for objectivity.

The Need to Select and Arrange Historical Materials

Once the historian takes his fragmentary documents that he must view indirectly through the interpretation of the original source, and once he takes his selected amount of material from the available archives and begins to provide an interpretive structure to it, by the use of his own value-laden language, and within the overall worldview that he presupposes, he not only understands it from the relative vantage point of his own generation but he also must select and arrange the topic of history in accordance with his own subjective preferences. In short, the dice are loaded against objectivity before he picks up his pen. That is, in the actual writing of the fragmentary, secondhand accounts from his philosophical and personal point of view, there is a further subjective choice of arrangement of the material (Collingwood, *IH*, 285–90).

The selection and arrangement of material will be determined by personal and social factors already discussed. The final written product will be prejudiced by what is included in and what is excluded from the material. It will lack objectivity by how it is arranged and by the emphasis given to it in the overall presentation. The selection made in terms of the framework will either be narrow or broad, clear or confused. Whatever its nature, the framework is necessarily reflective of the mind of the historian (Beard, "TND" in Stern, *VH*, 150–51), and this moves one still further away from objectively knowing what really happened. It is concluded by the subjectivists, then, that the hopes of objectivity are finally dashed.

The Metaphysical (Worldview) Objections

Several metaphysical objections have been leveled against the belief in objective history. Each one is predicated, either theoretically or practically, on the premise that one's worldview colors the study of history.

The Need to Structure the Facts of History

This objection is stated along these lines: Partial knowledge of the past makes it necessary for the historian to "fill in" gaping holes out of his own imagination. As a child draws the lines between the dots on a picture, so the historian supplies the connections between events. Without the historian the dots are not numbered, nor are they arranged in an obvious manner. The historian must use his imagination in order to provide continuity to the disconnected and fragmentary facts provided him.

Furthermore, the historian is not content to tell us simply *what* happened; he feels compelled to explain *why* it happened (Walsh, *PH*, 32). In this way history is made fully coherent and intelligible—good history has both theme and unity, which are provided by the historian. Facts alone do not make history any more than disconnected dots make a picture, and herein, according to the subjectivist, lies the difference between chronicle and history: The former is merely the unrefined material used by the historian to construct history. Without the structure provided by the historian, the mere "stuff" of history would be meaningless.

In addition, the study of history is a study of causes. The historian wants to know *why*; he wishes to weave a web of interconnected events into a unified whole. Because of this he cannot avoid interjecting his own subjectivity into history; hence, even if there is some semblance of objectivity in chronicle, nonetheless there is no hope for objectivity in history. History is in principle nonobjective, since the very thing that makes it history (as opposed to mere chronicle) is the interpretive structure or framework given to it from the subjective vantage point of the historian. Therefore, it is concluded that the necessity of structure inevitably makes historical objectivity impossible.

The Unavoidability of Worldviews

Every historian interprets the past within the overall framework of his own *Weltanschauung*, that is, his world-and-life-view. Basically, there are three different philosophies of history within which historians operate: the chaotic, the cyclical, and the linear views of history (Beard, "TND" in Stern, *VH*, 151). Which one of these the historian adopts will be a matter of faith or philosophy and not a matter of mere fact.

Unless one view or another is presupposed, no overall interpretation is possible; the *Weltanschauung* will determine whether the historian sees the events of the world as a meaningless maze (chaotic), as a series of endless repetitions (cyclical), or as moving in a purposeful way toward a goal (linear). These worldviews inevitably are both necessary and value-oriented. So, it is argued by the subjectivists, without one of these worldviews, the historian cannot interpret the events of the past. However, through a worldview objectivity becomes impossible.

Further, subjectivists insist that a worldview is not generated from the facts; facts do not speak for themselves, but gain their meaning only within the overall context of the worldview. Without the *structure* of the worldview framework, the stuff of history has no meaning. Augustine (354–430), for example, viewed history as a great theodicy,[2] but Hegel (1770–1831) saw it as an unfolding of the divine. Supposedly, then, it is not any archaeological or factual find but the religious or philosophical presuppositions that prompted each man to develop his view. Eastern philosophies of history are even more diverse, as they involve a cyclical rather than a linear pattern.

Once one admits the relativity or perspectivity of his worldview as opposed to another, the historical relativists insist that he has thereby given up all right to claim objectivity. If there are several different ways to

---

[2]Theodicy is "vindication of the justice of God, especially in ordaining or permitting natural or moral evil" (*Webster's Third New International Dictionary*).

interpret the same facts, depending on the overall perspective one takes, then there is no single objective interpretation of history.

Miracles Are by Nature Superhistorical

Even if one grants that secular history could be known objectively, there still remains the problem of the subjectivity of religious history. Some writers make a strong distinction between *Historie* and *Geschichte* (Kahler, *SCHJ*, 63): The former is empirical and objectively knowable to some degree, but the latter is spiritual and unknowable, historically speaking—as spiritual or superhistorical, there is no objective way to verify it.

Spiritual history, allegedly, has no necessary connection with the spatio-temporal continuum of empirical events. It is a myth with subjective religious significance to the believer but with no objective grounding. Like the story of George Washington and the cherry tree, *Geschichte* is a story made up of events that probably never happened, but that inspire men to some moral or religious good.

If this distinction is applied to the New Testament, then even if the life and central teachings of Jesus of Nazareth could be objectively established, there is no historical way to confirm the New Testament's miraculous dimension. Miracles do not happen as part of *Historie* and, therefore, are not subject to objective analysis; they are *Geschichte* events and as such cannot be analyzed by historical methodology.

Many theologians have accepted this distinction. Paul Tillich (1886–1965) claimed that it is "a disastrous distortion of the meaning of faith to identify it with the belief in the historical validity of the biblical stories" (*DF*, 87). He believed, with Søren Kierkegaard, that the important thing is whether or not it evokes an appropriate religious response. With this Rudolf Bultmann and Schubert Ogden would also concur, along with much of recent theological thought.

Even those like Karl Jaspers (1883–1969), who opposed Bultmann's more radical demythologization view, accepted, nevertheless, the distinction between the spiritual and empirical dimensions of miracles (Jaspers, *MC*, 16–17). On the more conservative end of those maintaining this distinction is Ian Ramsey (d. 1972), who insisted, "It is not enough to think of the facts of the Bible as 'brute historical facts' to which the evangelists give distinctive 'interpretation.' " For Ramsey, the Bible is historical only if " 'history' refers to situations as odd as those which are referred to by that paradigm of the Fourth Gospel: 'the Word became flesh.' " Ramsey concludes, "No attempt to make the language of the Bible conform to a precise, straightforward public language—whether that language be scientific of historical—has ever succeeded" (*RL*, 118–19).

According to the historical subjectivists, there is always something "more" than the empirical in every religious or miraculous situation. The purely empirical situation is "odd" and thereby evocative of a discernment that calls for a commitment of religious significance (Ramsey, *RL*, chapter 1).

Miracles Are in Principle Historically Unknowable

On the basis of Ernst Troeltsch's principle of analogy (see quotation below), some historians have come to object to the possibility of ever establishing a miracle based on testimony about the past. Troeltsch (1865–1923) stated the problem this way:

> On the analogy of the events known to us we seek by conjecture and sympathetic understanding to explain and reconstruct the past. . . . [And] since we discern the same process of phenomena in operation in the past as in the present, we see, there as here, the various historical cycles of human life influencing and intersecting one another. (Troeltsch, "H" in Hastings, *ERE*.)

Without uniformity, so the argument goes, we could know nothing about the past, for without an analogy from the present we could know nothing about what happened previously. In accord with this principle, some have insisted, "No amount of testimony is ever permitted to establish as past reality a thing that cannot be found in present reality. . . . In every other case the witness may have a perfect character—all that goes for nothing" (Becker, "DWH" in Snyder, *DWH*, 12–13). In other words, unless one can identify miracles in the present, he has no experience on which to base his understanding of alleged miracles in the past.

The historian, like the scientist, must adopt a methodological skepticism toward alleged events in the past for which he has no parallel in the present—the present is the foundation of our knowledge of the past. As F. H. Bradley put it:

> We have seen that history rests in the last resort upon an inference from our experience, a judgment based upon our own present state of things. . . . [So] when we are asked to affirm the existence in past time of events, the effects of causes which confessedly are without analogy in the world in which we live, and which we know—we are at a loss for any answer but this, that . . . we are asked to build a house without a foundation. . . . How can we attempt this without contradicting ourselves? (Bradley, *PCH*, 100.)

The Psychological Objection

It is argued, especially by those opposed to the New Testament, that history recorded by persons with religious motives cannot be trusted—their religious passion is said to obscure their historical objectivity, and thus they tend to reinterpret history in the light of their religious beliefs.

A similar criticism is at the basis of traditional form and redactional criticism, by which the New Testament writers are said to be *creating* or *recreating* the words of Jesus rather than strictly *reporting* them (see part 2, chapters 19 and 26). That is, the Gospels as we now have them more reflect the religious experience of the subsequent Christian church than they do the pure words of Jesus.

The Hermeneutical Objection

Perhaps the most radical form of historical relativism is deconstructionism, which treats history as literature. One of the foremost proponents of this view is Hayden White, who claims in his book *Metahistory* that history is poetry. White insists that no history can be written without bringing the material into a "coordinated whole" under some "unifying concept" (*M*, 89), and he believes these concepts are chosen from poetry: "I have identified four different archetypal plot structures by which historians can figure historical processes in their narratives as stories of a particular kind: Romance, Tragedy, Comedy, and Satire" (*M*, 41). No one of these is better than the others or correct as opposed to incorrect; they are simply different. This has "permitted me to view the various debates over how history ought to be written ... as essentially matters of stylistic variation within a single universe of discourse" (*M*, 42).

A RESPONSE TO HISTORICAL RELATIVISM

Despite these many strong objections to the possibility of historical objectivity, the case is by no means closed, for there are many flaws in the historical relativists' position. First, a direct response will be offered to each objection. Then, some overall arguments against historical subjectivism will be given.

The direct responses given are in the order of the above objections.

A Response to the Epistemological Objections

Response to the Problem of the Unobservability of Historical Events
The first and most fundamental response to the historical subjectivists is to point out that whatever is meant by the "objective" knowledge of history they deny, it must be possible, since in their very denial they imply that they have it. How could they know that everyone's knowledge of history was not objective unless they had an objective knowledge of it by which they could determine that these other views were not objective? One cannot know *not that* unless he knows *that*.

Further, if by "objective" the subjectivists mean absolute knowledge, then of course no human historian can be objective. On the other hand, if "objective" means an *accurate and adequate*[3] presentation that reasonable people should accept, then the door is open to the possibility of objectivity.

Assuming this latter sense, it should be argued that history can be just as objective as some sciences (Block, *HC*, 50). For example, paleontology (historical geology) is considered to be an objective science, and it deals with physical facts and processes of the past. However, the events represented by the fossil finds are no more directly accessible or *repeatable* to the scientists than are historical events to the historian.

True, there are some differences. The fossil is a mechanically accurate imprint of the original event, and the eyewitness of history may be less precise in his report. But the historian may rejoin by pointing out that the natural processes that mar the fossil imprint parallel the potential personal filtering of events through the testimony of the eyewitness. At least it may be argued that if one can determine the integrity and reliability of the eyewitness, one cannot slam the door on the possibility of objectivity in history any more than on objectivity in geology.

The scientist might contend that he can repeat the processes of the past by present experimentation, whereas the historian cannot. But even here the situations are similar, for in this sense history too can be "repeated." Similar patterns of events, by which comparisons can be made, recur today as they occurred in the past. Limited social experiments can be performed to see if human history repeats itself, so to speak, and widespread experiments can be observed naturally in the differing conditions throughout the ongoing history of the world. In short, the historian, no less than the scientist, has the tools for determining what really happened in the past. The lack of direct access to the original facts or events does not hinder the one more than the other.

Some have suggested that there is yet a crucial difference between history and science of past events. They insist that scientific facts "speak for themselves," while historical facts do not. However, even here the analogy is close for several reasons.

If "fact" means the original event, then neither geology nor history is in possession of any facts. "Fact" must be taken by both to mean information about the original event, and in this latter sense facts do not exist merely subjectively in the mind of the historian. Facts are objective data whether anyone reads them or not.

What one does with data, that is, what meaning or interpretation he gives to them, can in no way eliminate the data. There remains for both science and history a solid core of objective facts, and the door is thereby left open for objectivity in both fields. In this way one may draw a valid

---

[3]To be more accurate, a historical presentation does not have to be either totally comprehensive or unrevisable. One can always learn more and improve a limited but accurate account.

distinction between propaganda and history: the former lacks sufficient basis in objective fact, but the latter does not. Indeed, without objective facts, no protest can be raised either against poor history *or* propaganda.

If history is entirely in the mind of the beholder, there is no reason one cannot decide to behold it any way he desires. In this case there would be no difference between good history and trashy propaganda. But historians, even historical subjectivists, recognize the difference. Hence, even they assume an objective knowledge of history.

Response to the Problem of Fragmentary Accounts

The fact that accounts of history are fragmentary does not destroy historical objectivity any more than the existence of only a limited amount of fossils destroys the objectivity of geology. The fossil remains represent only a very tiny percentage of the living beings of the past; this does not hinder scientists from attempting to reconstruct an objective picture of what really happened in geological history. Scientists sometimes reconstruct a whole man on the basis of only partial skeletal remains—even a single jawbone. While this procedure is perhaps rightly suspect, nonetheless one does not need every bone in order to fill in the probable picture of the whole animal. Like a puzzle, as long as one has the key pieces he can reconstruct the rest with a measurable degree of probability. For example, by the principle of bilateral similarity one can assume that the left side of a partial skull would look like the right side that was found.

Of course, the finite reconstruction of both science and history is subject to revision. Subsequent finds may provide new facts that call for new interpretations. But at least there is an objective basis in fact for the meaning attributed to the find. Interpretations can neither create the facts nor ignore them if they wish to approach objectivity. We may conclude, then, that history need be no less objective than geology for depending on fragmentary accounts. The history of human beings is transmitted to us by partial record; scientific knowledge is also partial, and it depends on assumptions and an overall framework that may prove to be partially inadequate upon the discovery of more facts.

Whatever difficulty there may be from a strictly scientific point of view in filling in the gaps between the facts, once one has assumed a philosophical stance toward the world, the problem of objectivity in general is resolved. If there is a God, and good evidence says there is (see chapter 2), then the overall picture is already drawn; the facts of history will merely fill in the details of its meaning. If this is a theistic universe, then the artist's sketch is already known in advance; the detail and coloring will come only as all the facts of history are fit into the overall sketch known to be true from the theistic framework. In this sense, historical objectivity is most certainly possible within a given framework—such as a theistic worldview.

Objectivity resides in the view that best fits all the facts into the overall system, that is, into systematic consistency.

A Response to the Axiological (Value) Objection

One may grant the point that ordinary language is value-laden and that value judgments are inevitable. This by no means makes historical objectivity impossible (Butterfield, "MJH" in Meyerhoff, *P*, 244). Objectivity means to be fair in dealing with the facts; it means to present what happened as accurately as possible.

Further, objectivity means that when one interprets why these events occurred, the language of the historian should ascribe to these events the value they really had in their original context. If this is accomplished, then an objective account of history is achieved. In this way objectivity is seen to be *demanding* value judgments rather than *avoiding* them.

The question is not whether value language can be objective but rather whether value statements objectively portray the events the way they really were. Once the worldview has been determined, value judgments are not undesirable or merely subjective; they are, in fact, essential and objectively required. If this is a theistic world, then it is not objective to place anything but a proper theistic value on the facts of history.

A Response to the Methodological Objections

Every historian employs a methodology—this in itself does not demonstrate the inadequacy of his history. *The question is whether his methodology is good or bad.* In response to this objection, several dimensions of the problem need discussion.

Response to the Problem of Historical Conditioning

It is true that every historian is a product of his time; each person does occupy a relative place in the changing events of the spatio-temporal world. However, it does not follow that because the historian is a product of his time, his history is also purely a product of the time. That a person cannot avoid a relative place in history does not mean his perspective cannot attain a meaningful degree of objectivity. This criticism confuses the content of knowledge and the process of attaining it (Mandelbaum, *PHK*, 94), as well as incorrectly joining the formation of a view with its verification. Where one derives a hypothesis is not essentially related to how its truth can be established.

Further, if relativity is unavoidable, then the position of the historical relativists is self-refuting, for either their view is historically conditioned and therefore unobjective, or else it is not relative but objective. If the latter, it thereby admits that it is possible to be objective in viewing history.

On the contrary, if the position of historical relativism is itself relative, then it cannot be taken as objectively true—it is simply a subjective opinion that has no immovable basis. In short, if it is a subjective opinion it cannot eliminate the possibility that history is objectively knowable, and if it is an objective fact about history, then objective facts can be known about history. In the first case objectivity is not eliminated, and in the second relativity is self-defeated; in either case, objectivity is possible.

Finally, the constant rewriting of history is based on the assumption that objectivity is possible: Why strive for accuracy unless it is believed that the revision is more objectively true than the previous view? Why critically analyze unless improvement toward a more accurate view is the assumed goal? Perfect objectivity may be practically unattainable within the limited resources of the historian on most if not all topics, but be this as it may, the inability to attain 100 percent objectivity is a long way from relativity. Reaching a degree of objectivity that is subject to criticism and revision is a more realistic conclusion than the relativist's arguments. There is no reason to eliminate the possibility of a sufficient degree of historical objectivity.

Response to the Problem of the Selectivity of Materials

That the historian must select his materials does not automatically make history purely subjective. Jurors make judgments "beyond reasonable doubt" without having *all* the evidence. If the historian has the relevant and crucial evidence, it will be sufficient to attain objectivity; one need not know everything in order to know something. No scientist knows all the facts, and yet objectivity is claimed for his discipline. As long as no important fact is overlooked, there is no reason to eliminate the possibility of objectivity in history any more than in science.

The selection of facts can be objective to the degree that the facts are selected and reconstructed in the context in which the events represented actually occurred. Since it is impossible for any historian to pack into his account everything available on a subject, it is important for him to select the points representative of the period of which he writes (Collingwood, *IH*, 100). Condensation need not imply distortion; the minimum can be an objective summary of the maximum.

What is more, the evidence for the historicity of the New Testament, from which Christian apologetics draws its primary evidence, is greater than for that of any other document from the ancient world (see part 2, chapter 26). Thus, if the events behind it cannot be known objectively, then it is impossible to know anything else from that time period.

A Response to the Metaphysical (Worldview) Objections

Admittedly, each historian has a worldview, and the events are interpreted through this grid. But this in itself does not make objectivity impossible, since there are objective ways to treat the question of worldviews.

Response to the Problem of Arranging Materials

There is no reason why the historian cannot arrange materials without distorting the past (Nagel, "LHA" in Meyerhoff, *P*, 208). Since the original construction of events is available to neither the historian nor the geologist, it is necessary to reconstruct the past on the basis of the available evidence. Yet *reconstruction* does not necessitate *revision*; selecting material may occur without neglecting significant matters. Every historian must arrange his material. The important thing is whether or not it is arranged or rearranged in accordance with the original arrangement of events as they really occurred. As long as the historian incorporated consistently and comprehensively all the significant events in accordance with the way things really were, he was being objective. It is neglecting or twisting important facts that distorts objectivity.

The historian may desire to be selective in the compass of his study; he may wish to study only the political, economic, or religious dimensions of a specific period. But such specialization does not demand total subjectivity, for one can be particular without losing the overall context in which he operates. It is one thing to focus on specifics within an overall field and quite another to totally ignore or deliberately distort the big picture in which the intensified interest is occurring. As long as the specialist stays in touch with reality rather than reflecting the pure subjectivity of his own fancy, there is no reason why a measurable degree of objectivity cannot be maintained.

Response to the Problem of the Structuring of the Materials

Those who argue against the objectivity of history apart from an overall worldview must be granted the point, for without a worldview it makes no sense to talk about objective meaning (Popper, *PH*, 150f). Meaning is system-dependent within a given meaning, but within another system it may have a very different meaning. Without a context meaning cannot be determined, and the context is provided by the worldview and not by the bare facts themselves.

Assuming the correctness of this criticism, as we do, does not eliminate the possibility of an objective understanding of history. Rather, it points to the necessity of establishing a worldview in order to attain objectivity. This has already been done earlier (chapter 2) in establishing the evidence for a theistic worldview. Once this is clear, the metaphysical framework for an objective view of history is in place.

Without such a metaphysical structure, one is simply arguing in a circle with regard to the assumed causal connection and the attributed importance of events. To affirm that facts have "internal arrangement" begs the question; the real question is, "How does one know the correct arrangement?" Since the facts are arrangeable in at least three different ways (chaotic, cyclical, and linear), it is logically fallacious to assume that one of these is the way the facts were actually arranged. The same set of dots can have the lines drawn in many ways.

The assumption that the historian is simply discovering (and not drawing) the lines is gratuitous. The fact is that the lines are not known to be there apart from an interpretive framework through which one views them. Therefore, the problem of the objective meaning of history cannot be resolved apart from appeal to worldview. Once the skeletal sketch is known, then one can know the objective placing (meaning) of the facts. However, apart from a structure the mere grist of history means nothing.

Without a metaphysical framework there is no way to know which events in history are the most significant and, hence, there is no way to know the true significance of these and other events in their overall context. The argument that importance is determined by which events influence the most people is inadequate for several reasons. This is a form of historical utilitarianism, and as such it is subject to the same criticisms as any utilitarian test for truth (see chapter 7). The most does not determine the best; all that is proved by great influence is great influence, not great importance or great value. Even after most people have been influenced, one can still ask the question as to the truth or value of the event that influenced them. Significance is not determined by ultimate outcome but by overall framework. Of course, if one assumes as an overall framework that the events that influence the most people in the long run are most significant, then that utilitarian framework will indeed determine the significance of an event. But what right does one have to assume a utilitarian framework any more than a non-utilitarian one? Here again, it is a matter of justifying one's overall framework or worldview.

The argument advanced by some objectivists is that past events must be structured or they are unknowable and faulty. However, all this argument proves is that it is necessary to understand facts through some structure, otherwise it makes no sense to speak of facts. The question of which structure is correct must be determined on some basis other than the mere facts themselves. Further, even if there were an objectivity of bare facts, it would provide at best only the mere *what* of history. But objective meaning deals with the *why* of these events; this is impossible apart from a structure of meaning in which the facts may find their placement of significance. Objective meaning apart from a worldview is impossible.

Nevertheless, granted that there is justification for adopting a theistic worldview, the objective meaning of history becomes possible, for within the theistic context each fact of history becomes a theistic fact. Given the factual order of events and the known causal connection of events, the possibility of objective meaning surfaces. The chaotic and the cyclical frameworks are eliminated in favor of the linear, and within the linear view of events causal connections emerge as the result of their context in a theistic universe. Theism provides the sketch on which history paints the complete picture. The pigments of mere fact take on real meaning as they are blended together on the theistic sketch. In this context, objectivity means systematic consistency; that is, the most meaningful way all of the facts of history can be blended together into the whole theistic sketch is what really happened—historical facts.

Response to the Alleged Unknowability of Miracles

Even if the objectivity of history is accepted, many historians object to any history that contains miracles, which poses a further metaphysical problem for Christianity. This secular rejection of miracle-history is often based on Troeltsch's principle of analogy, and this argument turns out to be similar to Hume's objection to miracles built on the uniformity of nature (see chapter 3). David Hume argued that no testimony about alleged miracles should be accepted if it contradicts the uniform testimony of nature; in like manner, Troeltsch would reject any particular event in the past for which there is no analogue in the uniform experience of the present.

Now, there are at least two reasons for rejecting Troeltsch's argument from analogy. *First*, as C. S. Lewis insightfully commented,

> If we admit God, must we admit Miracles? Indeed, indeed, you have no security against it. That is the bargain. Theology says to you in effect, "Admit God and with Him the risk of a few miracles, and I in return will ratify your faith in uniformity as regards the overwhelming majority of events" (Lewis, *M*, 109).

A miracle is a special act of God. If God exists, then acts of God are possible; hence, any alleged historical procedure that eliminates miracles is bogus.

Second, Troeltsch's principle begs the question in favor of a naturalistic interpretation of all historical events (see chapter 3)—it is a methodological exclusion of the possibility of accepting the miraculous in history. The testimony for regularity in general is in no way a testimony against an unusual event in particular; the cases are different and should not be evaluated in the same way. As we demonstrated, empirical generalizations (e.g., "Men do not rise from the dead") should not be used as counter-testimony to good eyewitness accounts that in a particular case someone *did* rise from the dead. The historical evidence for any particular historical event must be assessed on its own merits, completely aside from generalizations about other events.

There is another objection to the Troeltsch analogy-type argument: It proves too much. Again, as Richard Whateley (1787–1863) convincingly argued, on this uniformitarian assumption not only would miracles be excluded but so would many unusual events of the past, including those surrounding Napoleon Bonaparte (1769–1821) (Whateley, *HDCENB*, all).

No one can deny that the probability against Napoleon's successes was great. His prodigious army was destroyed in Russia, and a few months later he led a different army in Germany that likewise was ruined at Leipzig. However, the French supplied him with yet another army sufficient to make a formidable stand in France—this was repeated five times until at last he was confined to an island. Without question, the particular events of his career were highly improbable, but there is no reason on these grounds that we should doubt the historicity of the Napoleonic adventures. History, contrary to scientific hypothesis, does not depend on the universal and repeatable; rather, it stands on the sufficiency of good testimony for particular and unrepeatable events. Were this not so, nothing could be learned from history.

It is clearly a mistake to import uniformitarian methods from scientific experimentation into historical research. Repeatability and generality are needed to establish scientific laws or general patterns (of which miracles would be particular exceptions), but what is needed to establish historical events is credible testimony that these particular events did indeed occur (see part 2, chapter 26). So it is with miracles—it is an unjustifiable mistake in historical methodology to assume that no unusual and particular event can be believed no matter how great the evidence for it. Troeltsch's principle of analogy would destroy genuine historical thinking. The honest historian must be open to the possibility of unique and particular events of the past, whether they are miraculous or not. He must not exclude a priori the possibility of establishing events like the resurrection of Christ without a careful examination of the testimony and evidence concerning them.

It is incorrect to assume that the same principles by which *empirical* science works can be used in *forensic* science. Since the latter deals with unrepeated and unobserved events in the past, it operates on the principles of *origin science*, not on those of *operation science* (see Geisler, "O, S" in *BECA*, 567f.). These principles do not eliminate, but establish, the possibility of objective knowledge of the past—whether in science or history.

Observations on the Nature of Miracles and History

In response to these analyses of the historical objectivity of miracles, it is important to make several observations.

First, surely the Christian apologist does not want to contend that miracles are a mere product of the historical process. The supernatural occurs *in* the historical but it is not a product *of* the natural process. What makes it miraculous is the fact that the natural process alone does not account for it; there must be an injection from the realm of the supernatural into the natural, or else there is no miracle. This is especially true of a New Testament miracle (see chapter 3), where the means by which God performed the miracle is unknown.

Second, in accordance with the objectivity of history just discussed, there is no good reason why the Christian should yield to the radical existential theologians on the question of the objective and historical dimensions of a miracle. Again, miracles are not of the natural historical process, but they do occur in it. Even Karl Barth (1886–1968) made a similar distinction when he wrote,

> The resurrection of Christ, or his second coming . . . is not a historical event; the historians may reassure themselves . . . that our concern here is with the event which, though it is the only real happening in, is not a real happening of, history. (*WGWM*, 90.)

But unlike many existential theologians, we must also preserve the historical context in which a miracle occurs, for without it there is no way to verify the objectivity of the miraculous. Miracles do have a historical dimension without which no objectivity of religious history is possible, and, as was argued above, historical methodology can identify this objectivity (just as surely as scientific objectivity can be established) within an accepted framework of a theistic world. In short, miracles may be more than historical but they cannot be less than historical. It is only if miracles do have historical dimensions that they are both objectively meaningful and apologetically valuable.

Third, a miracle can be identified within an empirical or historical context both directly and indirectly, both objectively and subjectively. A miracle is both scientifically unusual as well as theologically and morally relevant. The first characteristic is knowable in a directly empirical way; the second is knowable only indirectly through the empirical in that it is "odd" and evocative of something more than the mere empirical data of the event. For example, a virgin birth is scientifically odd, but in the case of Christ it is represented as a sign that was used to draw attention to Him as something more than human. *The theological and moral characteristics of a miracle are not empirically objective*, in this sense they are experienced subjectively.

This does not mean, however, that there is no objective basis for the moral dimensions of a miracle. Since this is a theistic universe (see chapter 2), morality is objectively grounded in God. Therefore, the nature and will of God are the objective grounds by which one can test whether or not the event is subjectively evocative of what is objectively in accord with what is already known of God; if not, one shouldn't believe the event is a miracle. It is axiomatic that acts of a theistic God would not be used to confirm what is not the truth of God.

To sum up, miracles happen *in* history but are not completely *of* history. Miracles, nonetheless, are historically grounded—they are more than historical but are not less than historical. There are both empirical and superempirical dimensions to supernatural events. The former are knowable in an objective way, and the latter have a subjective appeal to the believer. But even here there is an objective ground in the known truth and goodness of God by which the believer can judge whether or not the empirically odd situations that appeal to him for a response are really acts of this true and good God.

A Response to the Psychological Objection

Another charge that is often heard is that the religious purposes of the Gospel writers, which are evident to all, negate their ability to present an objective historical report. Both A. N. Sherwin-White and Michael Grant have responded to this complaint.[4] Indeed, a form of this criticism is implied in both form criticism and redactional criticism, by which the Gospel writers are said to be *creating* the words of Jesus in terms of their own religious setting rather than strictly *reporting* them. This objection is without grounds for several reasons.[5]

First, there is no logical connection between one's purpose and the accuracy of the history he writes. People with no religious motives can write bad history, and people with religious motives can write good history.

Second, other important writers from the ancient world wrote with motives similar to the Gospel authors. Plutarch (b. A.D. 46), for example, declared, "My design was not to write histories, but lives."[6]

Third, complete religious propaganda literature, such as some critics see the New Testament, was actually unknown in the ancient world. Sherwin-White declared, "We are not acquainted with this type of writing in ancient historiography" (*RSRLNT,* 189).

Fourth, unlike other early accounts, the Gospels were written, at a maximum, only decades after the events. Many other secular writings, such as those of Livy (59/64 B.C.–A.D. 17) and Plutarch, were recorded centuries after the events.

Fifth, as shown above, the historical confirmation of New Testament writings is overwhelming (see part 2, chapter 23). So the argument that their religious purpose destroyed their ability to write good history is simply contrary to the facts.

Sixth, the New Testament writers take great care to distinguish their words from the words of Jesus, as any red-letter edition of the Bible clearly indicates (see also John 2:20–22; 1 Cor. 7:10, 12; 11:24–25; Acts 20:35). This act of distinguishing reveals their honest attempt to separate what Jesus actually said from their own thoughts and feelings on the matter.

Seventh, in spite of the religious purpose of Luke's gospel (Luke 1:4; cf. Acts 1:1), he states a clear interest for historical accuracy, which has been

[4]See A. N. Sherwin-White, *Roman Society and Roman Law in the New Testament* and Michael Grant, *Jesus: An Historian's Review of the Gospels.*
[5]Our objections here are based largely on those given by Gary Habermas, "Why I Believe the New Testament Is Historically Reliable" in Norman Geisler, ed., *Why I Am a Christian,* 155–56.
[6]Plutarch, *The Lives of the Noble Grecians and Romans* in *Great Books of the Western World,* Robert Maynard, ed., 541–76.

overwhelmingly corroborated by archaeology (see part 2, chapter 26). In his own words,

> Many have undertaken to draw up an account of the things that have been fulfilled among us, just as *they were handed down to us by those who from the first were eyewitnesses* and servants of the word. [Therefore,] *since I myself have carefully investigated everything from the beginning, it seemed good also to me to write an orderly account for you, most excellent Theophilus, so that you may know the certainty of the things you have been taught.* (Luke 1:1–4, emphasis mine)

Eighth, the existence of religious bias is no guarantee of historical inaccuracy. A writer can recognize his own bias and avoid its crippling effects. If this were not so, then even people with nonreligious (or anti-religious) biases could not write accurate history either. Yet many claim to be able to do so.

Ninth, the New Testament is confirmed to be historical by the same criteria applied to other ancient writings. Thus, this criticism either misses the mark or else it destroys all ancient histories.

Tenth, if the historicity of an event must be denied because of the strong motivation of the person giving it, then virtually all eyewitness testimony from survivors of the holocaust must be discounted. But this is absurd, since these people provide the best evidence of all. Likewise, a physician's passion to save his patient's life does not negate his ability to make an objective diagnosis of his disease, nor do an author's religious motives nullify his ability to record accurate history.

A Response to the Hermeneutical Objection

The hermeneutical objection utterly fails to show that all history is relativistic. There are several basic reasons sufficient to demonstrate why the possibility of objectivity in history has not—and cannot—be systematically eliminated.

The Relativity Argument Presupposes Some Objective Knowledge

A careful look at the arguments of the relativists reveals that they presuppose objective knowledge about history, and this is seen in at least two ways. *First,* they speak of the need to select and arrange the "facts" of history. But if they are really "facts," then they, as facts, represent some objective knowledge in themselves. After all, it is one thing to argue about the *interpretation* of the facts, but quite another to deny that there are any facts of history to argue about. For example, it is understandable that one's worldview will color how he understands the fact that Christ died on a cross in the early first century; it is quite another to deny that this is an historical reality (see volume 2, chapter 26).

Second, the very fact that relativists believe one's worldview can distort how one views history implies that there is a correct way to view it. Otherwise, how would one know that some views are distorted? That some views are incorrect (not correct) implies that there is a correct view. This leads to the next criticism.

Total Historical Relativity Is Self-Defeating

As a matter of fact, total relativity (whether historical, philosophical, or moral) is self-defeating. How could one know that history was completely unknowable unless he knew something about it? How could he know all historical knowledge was subjective unless he had some objective knowledge of it? In truth, the total relativist must stand on the pinnacle of his own absolutism in order to relativize everything else. The claim that all history is subjective turns out to be an objective claim about history. Total historical relativism cuts its own throat.

Ironically, one of history's most noted relativists later gave one of the best critiques of it. Charles Beard (1874–1948) wrote,

> Contemporary criticism shows that the apostle of relativity is destined to be destroyed by the child of his own brain. [For] if all historical conceptions are merely relative to passing events . . . then the conception of relativity is itself relative. . . . [In short,] *the apostle of relativity will surely be executed by his own logic.* (In Meyerhoff, ed., *PH*, 138, emphasis added.)

Of course, some might claim that historical knowledge is not totally but only partially relative. To this, objectivists note two things. *First,* it is an admission that history, at least some history, is objectively knowable, and thus it cannot claim to have eliminated in principle the possibility that the Christian claims are historically knowable.

Second, since the historical evidence for the central truths of Christianity is more amply supported by historical evidence than for almost any other event from the ancient world, it is also clear that a partial relativity view does not eliminate the historical verifiability of Christianity. In brief, total historical relativism is self-defeating, and partial historical relativism admits historically verifiable truths.

Historical Relativists Attempt Objective History Themselves

Another inconsistency in historical relativism is that the heralders of this view sometimes attempt to write objective history themselves. For example, while Beard was the apostle of historical relativism, he nevertheless attempted to write his own "scientific work" on the "essence of history" (see Meyerhoff, *PH*, 200–01). Beard believed his own understanding of the Constitution "was objective and factual" (ibid., 190–96; 200–01).

Ability to Recognize Bad History Implies Objective Knowledge

Another overlooked point is that the ability to detect bad history is itself a tacit admission that objectivity is possible. Ernest Nagel (1901–1985) pointed out that "the very fact that biased thinking may be detected and its sources investigated shows that the case of objective explanations in history is not necessarily hopeless" (in Meyerhoff, ibid., 213). In other words, the very fact that one can know that some histories are better than others reveals that there must be some objective understanding of the events by which this judgment is made.

Historians Employ Normal Objective Standards

Like science, history employs normal inductive measures that render the facts knowable. As W. H. Walsh observed, "Historical conclusions must be backed by evidence just as scientific conclusions must" (in Gardiner, *TH*, 301). Thus, Beard adds, "The historian . . . sees the doctrine of relativity crumble in the cold light of historical knowledge" (in Meyerhoff, *PH*, 148). Even Karl Manheim, whom Patrick Gardiner called "the most forthright proponent of historical relativism in recent times," observes, "The presence of subjective concerns does not imply renunciation of the postulate of objectivity and the possibility of arriving at decisions in factual disputes" (see Habermas, "PHHRHE" in Bauman, *EA*, 105).

SOME GENERAL REMARKS CONCERNING THE OBJECTIVITY OF HISTORY

There are several general conclusions to be drawn from the foregoing analysis of the subjectivity/objectivity controversy. *First*, absolute objectivity is possible only for an infinite Mind. Finite minds must be content with systematic consistency, that is, fair but revisable attempts to reconstruct the past based on an established framework of reference that comprehensively and consistently incorporates all the facts into the overall sketch provided by the worldview. Of course, if there is good reason to believe this infinite Mind exists (and there is—see chapter 2), and if this infinite Mind (God) has revealed Himself (see chapter 4), then an interpretation of history from an absolute perspective is available (see part 2) in His Word (the Bible).

Second, even without this absolute perspective, an adequately objective, finite interpretation of history is possible, for, as was shown above, the historian can be as objective as the scientist. Neither geologists nor historians have direct access to complete data on repeatable events. Further, both must use value judgments in selecting and structuring the partial material available to them.

Third, in reality, neither the scientist nor the historian can attain objective meaning without the use of some worldview by which he understands the facts. Bare facts cannot even be known apart from some interpretive framework; hence, the need for structure or a meaning-framework is crucial to the question of objectivity. Unless one can settle the question as to whether this is a theistic or non-theistic world on grounds independent of the mere facts themselves, there is no way to determine the objective meaning of history. If, on the other hand, there are good reasons to believe that this is a theistic universe, then objectivity in history is a possibility, for once the overall viewpoint is established, it is simply a matter of finding the view of history that is most consistent with that overall system. That is, systematic consistency is the test for objectivity in matters historical as well as scientific.

SUMMARY AND CONCLUSION

Some historians contend that there is no objective basis for determining the past, and that even if there were an objective basis, miracles are not a part of objective history. These arguments, however, fail. History can be as objective as science. Once again, the geologist likewise has only second-hand, fragmentary, and unrepeatable evidence viewed from his own vantage point and in terms of his own values and interpretive framework. Although it is true that interpretive frameworks are necessary for objectivity, it is not true that every worldview must be totally relative and subjective. Indeed, this argument is self-defeating, for it assumes that it is an objective statement about history that all statements about history are necessarily not objective.

As to the objection that miracle-history is not objectively verifiable, two points are important. *First,* miracles can occur *in* the historical process without being *of* that natural process (see chapter 3). *Second,* the moral and theological dimensions of miracles are not totally subjective. They call for a subjective response, but there are objective standards of truth and goodness (in accordance with the theistic God) by which the miracle can be objectively assessed. It can be concluded, then, that the door for the objectivity of history and thus the objective historicity for miracles is open. No mere question-begging uniformitarian principle of analogy can slam the door a priori. Evidence that supports the general nature of scientific law may not be legitimately used to rule out good historical evidence for unusual but particular events of history. This kind of argument is not only invincibly naturalistic in its bias but if applied consistently it would rule out much of known and accepted secular history. The only truly honest approach is to examine carefully the evidence for an alleged event in order to determine its authenticity (see part 2, chapter 26).

SOURCES

Barth, Karl. *The Word of God and the Word of Man.*
Bauman, Michael, ed. *Evangelical Apologetics.*

Beard, Charles. "That Noble Dream," in Fritz Stern, *The Varieties of History.*

Becker, Carl L. "Detachment and the Writing of History," in *Detachment and the Writing of History*, Phil L. Snyder, ed.

———. "What are Historical Facts?" in *The Philosophy of History in Our Time.*

Block, Marc. *The Historian's Craft.*

Bradley, F. H. *The Presuppositions of Critical History.*

Butterfield, Herbert. "Moral Judgments in History," in *Philosophy*, Hans Meyerhoff, ed.

Carr, E. H. *What Is History?*

Clark, Gordon. *Historiography: Secular and Religious.*

Collingwood, R. G. *The Idea of History.*

———. "The Limits of Historical Knowledge," in *Essays in the Philosophy of History*, William Debbins, ed.

Craig, William L. *The Nature of History* (unpublished master's thesis for Trinity Evangelical Divinity School, Deerfield, Ill., 1976).

Dray, W. H., ed. *Philosophy of History.*

Gardiner, Patrick, ed. *Theories of History.*

Geisler, Norman. *Christian Apologetics* (chapter 15).

———. "Origins, Science of" in *Baker Encyclopedia of Christian Apologetics.*

———, ed. *Why I Am a Christian.*

Grant, Michael. *Jesus: An Historian's Review of the Gospels.*

Habermas, Gary. "Philosophy of History, Historical Relativism and History as Evidence" in *Evangelical Apologetics*, Michael Bauman, et al., eds.

Harvey, Van A. *The Historian and the Believer.*

Jaspers, Karl, et al. *Myth and Christianity.*

Kahler, Martin. *The So-Called Historical Jesus.*

Lewis, C. S. *Miracles.*

Mandelbaum, Maurice. *The Problem of Historical Knowledge.*

Meyerhoff, Hans, ed. *The Philosophy of History.*

Montgomery, John W. *The Shape of the Past.*

Nagel, Ernest. "The Logic of Historical Analysis," in *Philosophy*, Hans Meyerhoff, ed.

Pirenne, Henri. "What Are Historians Trying to Do?" in *Philosophy*, Hans Meyerhoff, ed.

Plutarch. *The Lives of the Noble Grecians and Romans* in *Great Books of the Western World*, Robert Maynard, ed.

Popper, Karl. *The Poverty of Historicism.*

Ramsey, Ian. *Religious Language.*

Sherwin-White, A. N. *Roman Society and Roman Law in the New Testament.*

Stern, Fritz, ed. *The Varieties of History.*

Tillich, Paul. *Dynamics of Faith.*

Troeltsch, Ernst. "Historiography," in *Encyclopedia of Religion and Ethics*, James Hastings, ed.

Walsh, W. H. *Philosophy of History.*

Whateley, Richard. *Historical Doubts Concerning the Existence of Napoleon Bonaparte.*

White, Hayden. *Metahistory: The Historical Imagination in Nineteenth-Century Europe.*

CHAPTER TWELVE

METHOD: THE METHODOLOGICAL PRECONDITION

L ike other theological topics, the method of doing theology is widely debated. Nonetheless, methodology is of vital importance, because in a very real sense methodology determines theology. That is to say, *how* theology is done will determine *what* the theological conclusion will be. For example, if theology is done with a naturalistic method, inevitably the conclusions will be naturalistic. Likewise, if one begins with a theistic God (see chapter 2) and a method open to the supernatural (see chapter 3), the conclusions will not be unfavorable to the supernatural.

THE NATURE AND KINDS OF METHODS

There are many kinds of methods, the most widely known being the scientific method as set forth by Francis Bacon (see page 207 on the inductive method). This, of course, was the inductive and experimental logic (method) of modern science, as opposed to the deductive logic formulated by Aristotle (see page 206 on the deductive method).

In actual practice there are many methods that have been employed in the discipline of theology, including the inductive, deductive, abductive, retroductive, systematic, and pragmatic methods, as well as several others. First, each method will be defined; then, the question will be asked whether and how it is applicable to the construction of a systematic theology. One particular doctrine—the doctrine of Scripture—will be used as an example. This will serve as an introduction to part 2.

VARIOUS KINDS OF THEOLOGICAL METHODS

Since theological methods have been borrowed from other disciplines, it will be helpful to survey the major methods of discovering truth from the earliest times to the present. While not all these methods will make a positive contribution to the theological enterprise, still they are illuminating.

The *Reductio Absurdum* Method

The presocratic philosopher Zeno (c. 495–c. 430 B.C.) was a disciple of Parmenides (b. 515 B.C.), the monist who argued that nothing existed except one solitary Being (see chapter 2). In order to demonstrate this thesis, Zeno, the disciple, would reduce the opposing view to the absurd by showing how it ended in paradox. For example, assume that time, space, or motion is composed of real parts (as pluralism does); Zeno insisted that consequently we would end up in hopeless contradictions. Nothing, he argued, could move from point A to point B, since there are an infinite number of points between them, and it is impossible to traverse the infinite. Therefore, by reducing pluralism of being to the absurd, he believed he had proven monism (that all is one).

Even though Zeno's application of the *reductio absurdum* argument is rejected by theists (see chapter 2), nonetheless, the method itself does not necessitate any view contrary to Christian belief. Indeed, it is simply an application of a valid disjunctive syllogism later developed by Aristotle (see chapter 5).

The Socratic Method

This method, named after its fourth century B.C. founder, could better be called the dialogical method or the method of interrogation, for it is based on the simple technique of discovering truth by asking the right questions. Socrates (c. 470–399 B.C.) illustrates this method in his dialogue, *Meno* (recorded by Plato), a text named after an untutored slave boy who is taught geometry by Socrates' thoughtful, logical, and systematic questioning of him.

Of course, in the socratic context the method was based on the belief in reincarnation, where allegedly Meno had known these geometric truths in their pure form in a previous life. However, others have abstracted this methodology from the belief in reincarnation and used it to lead a mind down the path of truth by asking the right questions.

The Deductive Method

Aristotle (384–322 B.C.) is credited with being the first to record the canons of deductive logic (*Prior Analytics*), whereby a person can validly infer one truth from other truths. These deductions are done by way of logical syllogisms, which take on either a categorical, hypothetical, or disjunctive form (see chapter 5). An illustration of each will suffice to sketch the method.

A *categorical (unconditional) deduction (syllogism)* is as follows:

(1) If the whole Bible is true, then so is John 14:6.
(2) The whole Bible is true.
(3) Consequently, John 14:6 is true—Jesus is the only way to God.

If the first two premises are true, then the conclusion must be true, since it follows necessarily from them. The seven rules of the categorical syllogism and all valid forms resulting from them are spelled out elsewhere (see chapter 5).

A *hypothetical (conditional) deduction (syllogism)* is:

(1) If all men are sinners, then John is a sinner.
(2) John is a man.
(3) Hence, John is a sinner.

In this case the second premise has met the condition stated in the first premise, and thus if the conditional is correct, the conclusion must be true. In this logical form the conclusion follows validly only if the second premise either affirms the antecedent (the "if" part of the first premise) or else denies the consequent (the "then" part of the first premise).

A *disjunctive syllogism* is an either/or reasoning process. For example:

(1) Either a person is saved or else he is lost (not saved).
(2) John is not lost.
(3) Therefore, John is saved.

A conclusion follows logically from a disjunctive syllogism only if one of the two disjuncts (statements on either side of the "or") is negated.

Although Aristotle also spoke of inductions, his deductive method of logic dominated major philosophies of the ancient, medieval, and even more recent times.

The Inductive Method

The monopolistic spell of deductive logic was broken when Francis Bacon (1561–1626) published his new logic, *The Novum Organum* ("The New Organ"). In it he developed inductive logic and experimental logic, known popularly as the scientific method. Later, John Stuart Mill (1806–1873) put these into their current form.

There are two broad categories of induction: imperfect and perfect. Most inductions fall into the former, since it is practically impossible to examine every particular thing in its class to see if they all have the same characteristics that the observed ones have. For high probability, it is sufficient to examine a large number of them.

On the other hand, a perfect induction is where every one of the particulars in that class can be and has been examined. For instance, I can easily examine every object in the bag and affirm with certainty that (for instance) all are apples. Perfect inductions are also possible with regard to biblical teaching, since the Bible contains a finite and manageable amount of material. Hence, a high degree of certainty is obtainable in a perfect induction.

The Cartesian Method

The French philosopher René Descartes (1596–1650) developed a method for discovering truth that began in systematic and methodical doubt. Its steps include the following:

(1) I doubt, therefore, I think.
(2) I think, therefore, I am.
(3) I am, therefore, God is (because I am an imperfect being—namely, a doubter), and the imperfect implies the Perfect (God) by which I know that
(4) God is, and therefore the world is (for a perfect God would not deceive me about the strong, steady impression I am getting of an external world outside myself).
(5) Consequently, I exist, God exists, and the world exists (see Descartes, *M*).

If there is doubt about any of these conclusions, Descartes outlined a method by which one could obtain certainty. The steps are as follows:

(1) The rule of certainty: Only indubitably clear and distinct ideas should be accepted as true.
(2) The rule of division: All problems should be reduced to their simplest parts.
(3) The rule of order: All reasoning should proceed from simple to complex.
(4) The rule of enumeration: One should review and recheck each step of the argument (see Descartes, *DM*).

In this way Descartes believed we could not only arrive at truth but that we could know it with certainty. While we need not accept all of Descartes' conclusions, his method of using self-refuting statements and his rules for being more certain are helpful to the theologian.

The Euclidian Method

Euclid (fl. 300 B.C.) developed a system of geometry that began with certain basic definitions and axioms held to be self-evident (e.g., parallel lines never meet). From these all other postulates and theorems were deduced logically and systematically; for example, the Pythagorean theorem—the square of the hypotenuse of a right triangle is equal to the sum of the squares of the other two sides ($A^2 + B^2 = C^2$). This can be deduced by noting that an example of a right triangle, having two sides of 3 and 4 inches and a third side (hypotenuse) of five inches, would yield $3 \times 3 = 9$ + $4 \times 4 = 16$ (which added together equals 25) and a hypotenuse of $5 \times 5 = 25$. This ability to deduce such things not only provided certainty but also invaluable knowledge for architecture and engineering.

This Euclidian deductive method was used in modern times by the great rationalist and philosopher Benedict Spinoza. Spinoza developed an entire philosophical system, including proofs for God as well as descriptions of the creation and nature of human beings, free will, and ethics (see Spinoza, *E*).

From deductive rationalism Spinoza also deduced the impossibility of miracles, and he began the first systematic effort at negative higher criticism of the Bible (*TPT*). This method applied to Scripture dramatically illustrates that not all methods can be fruitfully utilized in evangelical theology, particularly those with antisupernatural implications (see chapter 3). Nonetheless, once one has universal premises from either general or special revelation (see chapter 4), deductive logic is helpful in coming to other conclusions.

The Transcendental Method

The agnostic philosopher Immanuel Kant (1724–1804) is credited with the development of a transcendental method (Kant, *CPR*). A transcendental argument is neither deductive nor inductive; it is more reductive, arguing back to the necessary preconditions of something being the case. The transcendental method seeks for necessary conditions of a given state of affairs, not an actual cause of them.

Evangelical thinkers have used this methodology in both minimal and maximal ways. In the maximal category, it has been utilized by Cornelius Van Til and his followers as an apologetic method (*IDF*, 100–101). As such they affirm that in order to make sense out of the world, it is necessary to postulate the existence of the triune God as revealed in the Bible as the necessary (though not sufficient) condition to make sense out of our world.[1]

---

[1] As an illustration, the necessary condition for leaves burning is that they be dry, but the sufficient condition is a fire that can ignite them.

Some Christian apologists have also made minimal usage of a transcendental argument. John Carnell, for example, used it to defend the principle of noncontradiction, insisting that one had to posit it as an absolute condition for all thought, otherwise, no thought would be possible (Carnell, *ICA*, 159).

The Abductive Method

Charles Sanders Pierce (1839–1914) is credited with developing the abductive method (see *PSM*). It is neither deductive (which argues from general to particular) nor inductive (which argues from particular to general). Rather, an abduction is more like an insight or intuitive flash that provides one with a model for doing science or theology, as the case may be.

Sometimes this abduction comes as an intelligent guess and other times in a dream or vision. The father of modern rational philosophy, René Descartes, received his insight from dreams of a man selling watermelons. The scientist Nikola Tesla (1856–1943) got his idea for the internal workings of an alternating current motor from a vision he had while reading the poet Goethe. Friedrich August Kekulé (1829–1896) received the idea for the scientific model of the benzine molecule while having a vision of a snake biting its tail. Often, an abduction comes from applying the model derived from one discipline of study to another (see Ramsey, *MM*). Sometimes the model is abduced from concentrating on the particular problem at hand.

Whatever the source of the model, it is neither deduced from prior premises nor induced from previous data; it is simply intelligent insight into the situation. Theology, like other disciplines, fruitfully uses abductions to derive models by which Scripture can be correctly interpreted.

The Retroductive Method

The retroductive method is the method of enrichment. As a snowball gathers more snow on each turn downhill, so a retroduction in theology is where additional insight is gained from further knowledge. In this way, the more one knows, the more one knows what he knows better. For example, each time one reads through the Bible, it enables him to understand more clearly what he already knew about the Bible. Likewise, the more one learns, the better one comprehends what he already comprehends, no matter what the subject.

Sometimes this movement is described as a circle. But it is considered a benign circle, not a vicious circle;[2] in the discipline of interpretation it is

---

[2]A vicious circle is the fallacy of begging the question. A benign circle is more of a spiral by which one's understanding is continually enriched by subsequent understanding.

called "the hermeneutical circle." This is the process by which one understands the whole in the light of the parts and the parts in the light of the whole. Of course, each time one goes through the parts, he experiences a retroductive increase in his knowledge of the whole.

The Analogical Method

Joseph Butler (1692–1752) is best known for his famous *Analogy of Religion* (c. 1736), in which he defends Christianity against deism, particularly that of Anthony Ashley Cooper (1671–1713), third Earl of Shaftesbury, who wrote *Characteristics of Men, Manners, Opinions, Times* (1711), and Matthew Tindal (c. 1655–1733), who penned *Christianity As Old As the Creation* (1730).

Butler was influenced by an older contemporary, Samuel Clarke (1675–1729), who was a disciple of Sir Isaac Newton (1642–1727) and a defender of the Christian faith. Butler's famous *Analogy of Religion* is a presentation of the plausibility of Christianity in terms of the analogy between revealed and natural religion.

The Use of Probability

In accordance with the empirical basis of our knowledge and the limited nature of science, Butler argued that our knowledge of nature is only probable. From this he concluded two things in the defense of Christianity. *First*, since this is the case, "one is always in the position of a potential learner, and so one never can posit what one knows of nature as *the standard* to judge what is natural" (Rurak, "BA" in the *ATR*). *Second*, probability, which is the guide to life, supports the belief in a supernatural revelation from God in the Bible and the miracles of Christ.

The Objection to Deism

Butler directed his attack against the deist Tindal, who argued, "There's a religion of nature and reason written in the hearts of every one of us from the first creation by which mankind must judge the truth of any instituted religion whatever . . ." that may come after it (*AR*, 50).

For deists who reject Scripture as a supernatural revelation because of its difficulties, Butler responds,

> He who believes the Scriptures to have proceeded from him who is the Author of nature, may well expect to find the same sort of difficulties in it as are found in the constitution of nature. [Hence,] he who denies Scripture to have been from God, upon account of these difficulties, may for the very same reason deny the world to have been formed by him. (*AR*, 9–10.)

Since deists admit the latter, they should not deny the former. As James

Rurak notes, "Both natural and revealed religion will be assessed by the same standard, the constitution and course of nature. Natural religion cannot be used as a standard to judge revelation" ("BA" in *ATR*, 367). There is analogy between them.

A Religion Should Be Judged As a Whole

Another result of Butler's analogous argument is that a system of religion must be judged as a whole, not simply from attacks leveled against specific parts, as the deists were prone to do. When this standard was applied to Christianity, Butler believed it revealed that there is an "Intelligent Author and Governor of nature, [and] mankind is appointed to live in a future state; that everyone shall be rewarded or punished" (*AR*, 16–17).

The Relation of Natural and Supernatural Revelation

With the deists Butler agrees that God is the Author of nature and that Christianity contains a republication of this original revelation in creation. However, Christianity, while being a supernatural revelation, is also *more*. Butler explains,

> [T]he essence of natural religion may be said to consist in the religious regards to "God the Father Almighty": and the essence of revealed religion, as distinguished from natural, to consist in religious regard to "the Son," and to "the Holy Ghost."

The Defense of Miracles

Butler devoted his second chapter to the subject "of the supposed Presumption against a Revelation, considered as miraculous." In his own summary of the argument (in the margin) he insists that there is

> I. No presumption, from analogy, against the general Christian Scheme; for (1) although undiscoverable by reason or experience, we only know a small part of a vast whole; (2) even if it be unlike the known course of nature, (a) the unknown may not *everywhere* resemble the known; (b) we observe unlikeness sometimes in nature; (c) the alleged unlikeness is not complete. Thus no presumption lies against the general Christian scheme, whether we call it miraculous or not.

Further,

> II. [There is] no presumption against a primitive revelation, for (1) *miracle* is relative to a *course* of nature. (2) Revelation may well have followed Creation, which is an admitted fact. (3) The further miracle [is] no additional difficulty. (4) Tradition declares that religion was revealed at the first. III. [There is] no presumption from analogy against miracles in historical times, for (1) we have no parallel case of a second

fallen world; (2) in particular, (a) there is a presumption against all alleged facts before testimony, not after testimony. [And] (b) reasons for miraculous intervention may have arisen in 5,000 years. (c) Man's need of supernatural guidance is such a reason. (d) Miracles [are] comparable to *extraordinary* events, against which some presumption always lies. Thus (i) miracles [are] not incredible. [In fact,] (ii) in some cases, [they are] *a priori* probable. (iii) In no case is there a peculiar presumption against them. (*AR*, 155–61.)

Butler adds,

Upon all this I conclude; that there certainly is no such presumption against miracles, as to render them in any way incredible; that on the contrary, our being able to discern reasons for them, gives a positive credibility to the history of them, in cases where those reasons hold; and that is by no means certain, that there is any peculiar presumption at all, from analogy, even in the lowest degree, against miracles, as distinguished from other extraordinary [natural] phenomena. (*AR*)

In short, by analogy with nature, miracles are both credible and even a priori probable.

An Evaluation of Butler's View of Miracles

Space does not permit a complete evaluation of Butler's apologetic; however, a few things call for comment.

On the positive side, given the context, Butler made a significant defense of Christianity against deism. Arguing from deistic premises of natural revelation, he showed that there was no probable presumption against Christianity. Further, by reducing the test for truth from absolute certainty to reasonable probability, he made the apologetic task easier. Regardless of how one evaluates his results, Butler should be commended for his rational attempt to defend Christianity against the attacks of its naturalistic critics.

On the negative side, Butler has been criticized from both the left and the right. From the standpoint of a classical apologist, Butler unnecessarily weakened the stronger cosmological argument (see chapter 2) in favor of a weaker probability argument from analogy.

Further, some naturalists insist that Butler's argument for miracles is based on a false analogy for two reasons. *First,* "The presumption against miracles is not merely a presumption against a specific event, but against that *kind* of event taking place." *Second,* the comparison with extraordinary events in nature is said not to be valid, "for in the case of these forces, given the same physical antecedents, the same consequents will always follow; and the truth of this can be verified by experiment" (Mossner, *BBAR*, 161–162).

While this critique appears sound for some of the illustrations that Butler provides (e.g., electricity and magnetism), it does not work with all singularities in nature. In particular, it would not apply to the Big Bang theory (see chapter 2) held by many naturalistic scientists, since the antecedent conditions (conditions before the Big Bang) were nothing or nonbeing, from which no prediction can be made or be verified by further experiment. Further, Butler appears to be correct in the negative side of his argument that there is no a priori probability against miracles; indeed, he makes a prima facie case *for* their a priori probability (in chapter 3).

Finally, it should be noted that some who have used an analogical method (like John Stuart Mill) concluded that God must be finite (*TER*). This is directly contrary to the evangelical claim that God is infinite in power and perfection (see volume 2, part 1). So analogicals have been used to conclude opposing systems, and, hence, as helpful as it may be as a defense or illustration of truth, analogy does not appear to be a definitive method as a sole test for the truth of a worldview. Even so, analogies are helpful supportive arguments that assist in illustrating truths grounded elsewhere.

The Dialectical Method

The dialectical method was developed by Karl Marx (1818–1883) out of what was believed to be the dialectic of his professor G. W. F. Hegel (1770–1831); as noted previously, it was actually that of Johann Gottlieb Fichte (1762–1814), Hegel's contemporary (see Meuller, "HLTAS" in *JHI*, 19). The dialectical method consists in opposing a thesis with an antithesis and making a synthesis of them. For example, Marx held that the thesis of capitalism is opposed by the antithesis of socialism and will eventually emerge into the utopian synthesis of communism.

Following Hegel's time, there was an attempt to use a version of this method on Christianity by F. C. Baur (1792–1860) and his Tubingen school, which claimed that the first century's supposed tension between Peter's Judaistic form of Christianity (thesis) and Paul's anti-Judaistic form of Christianity (antithesis) found its reconciliation (synthesis) in John's second-century gospel. The tragedy has been that this dialectic tended to determine the facts rather than discover them, and it has led to an overlooking if not rejecting of the evidence that points to a much earlier date for John (see part 2).

Others, like Karl Barth (1886–1968), have employed a dialectical method in their theology. In Barth's case it was the thesis of orthodoxy opposed by the antithesis of liberalism that he synthesized into neo-orthodoxy. Here again the dialectical method had significantly less than biblical and evangelical results, for while Barth accepted an orthodox view of the Virgin Birth, Trinity, and Resurrection (bodily), he retained a liberal view of universalism and a denial of the infallibility and inerrancy of Scripture.

The Pragmatic Method

Although Charles Sanders Pierce used the term "pragmatic" for the clarification of ideas, William James (1842–1910) is credited with developing a pragmatic methodology for discovering truth. James said,

> Truth *happens* to an idea. It *becomes* true, is *made* true by events.... *"The true," to put it very briefly, is only the expedient in the way of our thinking, just as "the right" is only the expedient in the way of our believing.* (*P*, 201–202.)

In brief, according to pragmatism, we know what is true by whether or not it works.

Although few acknowledge the pragmatic method to be their test for theological truth, on a popular level it is widely used. The same is true of the next method, that of experimentation.

The Experimental Method

Along with James, the "instrumentalism" of John Dewey (1859–1952), more popularly known as experimentalism, is an American contribution to the discipline of methodology. From Dewey's perspective one discovers the truth by doing, and the final vote is cast by whether or not our experimentation produces progress. In this sense it is a melioristic methodology in that progress determines whether or not our beliefs are true, that is, whether they have heuristic value in prompting further achievement (*LTI*).

Stated in popular language, Dewey was asking us to "try before you buy"—something that can have devastating effects in one's life (as manifested in our culture's subsequent sexual and chemical experimentation). The result can be no less devastating when applied to theology, as Dewey's humanistic and antisupernatural religiosity showed (*CF*).

THE LIMITATION AND NEGATION
OF CERTAIN METHODOLOGIES

It has become apparent from even the brief survey of various methods of discovering truth that not all of them are compatible with evangelical theology. A few related observations are in order.

Methodological Category Mistakes

One of the greatest books ever written on philosophical methodology, much of which applies to theological method, is *The Unity of Philosophical Experience* by Étienne Gilson (1884–1978). In it he demonstrates with penetrating insight the fruitless cul-de-sacs caused in the history of philosophy by thinkers taking a methodology appropriate to one discipline and mistakenly applying it to another. This is a classic methodological category mistake.

Perhaps the most pervasive of all such errors in our time is that of evolutionism. Now, it's well established that microevolution occurs—survival of the fittest is a fact. Specific types of animals can and do adapt to their changing environment in order to survive—these small (micro) changes are observable in nature.

However, all naturalistic evolutionists and many others take a big leap from there to macroevolution—the hypothesis of common ancestry. That evolution works on a small scale within specific kinds of animals does not mean that this method can be imposed on large-scale changes between different kinds of animals.[3]

What's worse is taking the evolutionary method, which is based on small-scale biological changes, and imposing this method of understanding on entirely different disciplines, such as ethics and religion. Sir James George Frazer's flawed but widely touted *The Golden Bough* is an example of this serious methodological error. Frazer (1854–1941) assumed that religions evolved from animism through polytheism and henotheism to monotheism. This assumption, however, has careless disregard for the evidence that monotheism is earlier than these other forms (see Mbiti, *ARP;* Schmidt, *HGNA*).

Antisupernaturalistic Methods

Clearly, any method that necessitates a naturalistic conclusion should not be used in evangelical theology. Benedict Spinoza is a classic example. His form of deductive rationalism entailed naturalism (see chapter 3), but evangelical theology is based on theism (see chapter 2), and it goes without saying that if natural law is defined as unbreakable, and a miracle as what breaks a natural law, then miracles are impossible.

However, since theism entails supernaturalism, and since the theistic belief in the creation of the universe from nothing is the biggest supernatural event of all, then miracles are automatically possible.

Some forms of antisupernaturalism are more subtle than Spinoza's question-begging definition of natural law as unbreakable. Ernst Troeltsch's historiography is a case in point (see chapter 11); his principle of analogy is a much more hidden and implicit form of naturalism. As we saw previously, he argued,

(1) The past can only be reconstructed based on the analogy of events known to us in the present.

---

[3] See Norman Geisler and Peter Bocchino, *Unshakable Foundations;* Michael Behe, *Darwin's Black Box;* and Philip Johnson, *Darwin on Trial.*

(2) Present historical events do not provide us with any miraculous events.

(3) Hence, miraculous events cannot be part of any reconstruction (history) of past events.

In response, it need only be pointed out that Troeltsch's understanding of the principle of historical analogy is a form of historical uniformitarianism. It assumes that all history must be understood without miraculous events. Further, since it admittedly is not an argument against the possibility of miracles (but only against their being part of legitimate reconstruction of the past we call "history"), it entails a counterintuitive claim. Like David Hume, historical uniformitarianism assumes that we should disbelieve in miracles even if they occur. But it's clearly absurd to lay down a method that refuses to believe in an event even if it occurs (see chapter 3). Such methods must be soundly rejected by a biblically based theology.

Incompatible Methods

Other methodologies, while not being antisupernatural, are still incompatible with evangelical beliefs. For example, pragmatism and experimentalism are incompatible with belief in absolute truth; according to pragmatism and experimentalism, one and the same thing can work for one person but not for another. If so, then truth would be relative, but truth is not relative. Whatever is true is true for all persons, at all times, and in all places, which is what is meant by absolute truth (see chapter 7). Any pragmatic-type method that implies the relativity of truth should not be employed in evangelical theology.

This does not mean, of course, that theological truth is not practical and does not apply to one's life; it simply means that the pragmatic method is not a legitimate means of obtaining truth. If something is true, it will be practical, but simply that it is practical (workable) does not make it true.

Inappropriate Methods

Other methods must be rejected because they are inappropriate to the subject at hand, even if they are not antisupernatual or incompatible with evangelical belief. This point is made evident by Gilson's analysis (*UPE*). Taking, for example, a mathematical method and trying to do metaphysics with it (as Spinoza did), is clearly wrongheaded. Math is perfectly capable of dealing with abstract entities but not necessarily with all concrete ones.

For example, mathematically there are an infinite number of abstract points between the two ends of my bookshelf. However, I cannot get an infinite number of books on it, no matter how small they are. Nor can one get an infinite number of sheets of paper between them, no matter how thinly the paper is sliced. A mathematical series of points (that are abstract and dimensionless) does not equate with actual, concrete objects.

Traditional logic is another case in point (see chapter 5)—it is a perfectly appropriate tool for discovering truth when dealing with known truths from which it can derive others. But as a method of discovering truth on its own, it is useless. It is not geared to inform us about reality; it can deal with only the reality that is provided to it. Failing to recognize this is the basic flaw of the ontological argument (see chapter 2). No reality, not even divine reality, can be proven by logic alone. To make the argument work one must start with something that exists; then it is no longer an ontological argument but a form of the cosmological argument (see chapter 2). A triangle is a good example: Logically, a triangle must have three sides, three angles, and they must total 180°. However, mere logic does not demand that any triangular thing actually exists. Only if an actual triangular shaped object exists does logic inform us that it must have three sides, etc.

Likewise, modern symbolic logic is not designed to handle *what* questions but only *how* questions; unlike traditional logic, it cannot deal with substances but only relationships (see Veath, *TL*).

TOWARD DEVELOPING AN APPROPRIATE THEOLOGICAL METHODOLOGY

Two things should be apparent from the foregoing discussion:

(1) The method should fit its object.
(2) The method should not be contrary to the results it is supposed to produce.

A third can be added:

(3) No one method can suffice for the many steps involved in developing an evangelical theology. (This will become obvious from the following discussion.)

Step 1: An Inductive Basis in Scripture

Evangelical theology is based on a belief that the Bible and the Bible alone is the only written, infallible and inerrant revelation from God (general revelation is not written); as a result, any adequate methodology must be based on a sound exposition of Scripture. Broadly speaking, an inductive approach to understanding the text must be taken; that is, all the particular parts of the text of Scripture must be examined carefully in context before one can safely assume he has the proper interpretation (see chapter 10). Each part must be seen as a part of the whole. Likewise, the whole must be viewed as what makes sense of each part.

The *socratic method* of interrogation can be used effectively in discovering the meaning of the text, for one of the best ways to derive the meaning from a piece of literature is to ask questions like:

(1) Who wrote it?
(2) When did he write it?
(3) Where were they located?
(4) To whom was he speaking?
(5) What was said (or done) according to the text?[4]

By asking these crucial inductive questions, one may more effectively assess the author's expressed meaning in the text.

This broadly *inductive* method involves an *abductive* step, for once all the parts are studied, one may receive intuitive insight into how they all fit together to make up that whole. This is true whether we speak of a sentence (the smallest unit of meaning), a paragraph, a whole book, or even the Bible as a whole (since evangelicals believe there is one Mind behind all of Scripture).

Of course, there is more to systematic theology than exegesis of the biblical text. For one thing, the teaching of each text must be correlated with that of every other teaching in the Bible. For another thing, all the teachings of Scripture must be correlated with all the teachings of God's other revelation (general revelation), with all this entails, including the systematic correlation of all human knowledge (see step 7 on page 223). This is not only a massive but also a progressive and always less-than-perfect process. Nonetheless, it is the task systematic theology has staked out for itself and to which the four volumes of this work are dedicated.

Step 2: A Deduction of Truths From Scripture

One thing systematic theology does that isn't done by exegesis alone is to draw certain logical conclusions from the premises provided by a biblical analysis. For example, the Bible teaches,

(1) God is one.
(2) There are three Persons who are God—the Father, the Son (Jesus), and the Holy Spirit.

From this it follows by logical deduction that

(3) There are three persons in the one God (God is a Tri-unity or Trinity) (see volume 2).

Also, the Bible teaches,

---

[4]Some would add: (6) What were the purposes for which it was said (or done)? While especially stated (not surmised), purpose is illustrative of meaning; it is not determinative of meaning (see chapter 10).

(1) God cannot err (Heb. 6:18).

(2) The Bible is the Word of God (2 Tim. 3:16–17; John 10:34–35).

From this we can deduce:

(3) Therefore, the Bible cannot err.

Many other teachings of Scripture can also be derived by logical deduction.

Step 3: The Use of Analogies

In addition to an induction of the biblical text and also deductions from it, the method of analogy can be used to derive and refine an understanding of God's revealed truth. Since God has revealed Himself in both special and general revelation, systematic theology can make use of analogies from either to help explain and expound truth.

One good analogy can be used to explain how the Bible can be both the Word of God and yet the words of men. A parallel theological truth is found in the two natures of Christ found in one Person, called the hypostatic union (see volume 2, part 1). Jesus had both a divine and a human nature in one person who was without sin (Heb. 4:15). Likewise, the Bible has both a divine and human nature in one book, yet without error (Matt. 22:39; John 17:17; John 10:35). In other words, the Bible is a theanthropic book just as Christ is a theanthropic person.[5]

Of course, no analogy is perfect, and there are differences here too. For instance, Christ, the theanthropic person, can be worshiped, since He is God. However, even though the Bible is a theanthropic book, it is not God and should not be worshiped.

Sometimes analogies can come from nature. Jesus and other biblical writers used them, and theology can avail itself of them as well. Read again these words from Joseph Butler:

> He who believes the Scriptures to have proceeded from him who is the Author of nature, may well expect to find the same sort of difficulties in it as are found in the constitution of nature. [Hence,] he who denies Scripture to have been from God, upon account of these difficulties, may for the very same reason deny the world to have been formed by him. (*AR*, 9–10.)

Analogies for other doctrines are also helpful. For instance, there are tri-unities in nature that are illustrative of the Tri-unity in God. Love has a "threeness" within its oneness, for love involves a Lover (the Father), a loved One (the Son), and a Spirit of love between them (the Holy Spirit).

---

[5]Theanthropic means "partaking of the natures of God and man" (*Webster's Third New International Dictionary*).

Likewise, our mind, our ideas, and our words are one, yet all three are distinctly different. Even though these are not perfect illustrations, the two illustrations of the Trinity (love and mind) are three and one at the same time.

Of course, not all analogies from nature are helpful, even if they involve a distinction involving three and one. For example, water has three states: liquid, solid, and gas. But normally these three states do not exist in the same water at the same time. Thus, the illustration lends to a heresy about God called modalism.[6]

It should be remembered that analogies do not *prove* a doctrine. Doctrine must be taught scripturally and only *illustrated* or *supported* by good analogies.

Step 4: The Use of General Revelation

Another important step in the overall theological method is the use of general revelation. God has revealed Himself in all of nature (Ps. 19:1; Acts 14:17), including human nature (Rom. 2:12–15). Indeed, every perfection in creation, wherever it is found, is similar (analogous) to God, since He cannot produce what He does not possess; He cannot give to creation what He does not have to give (see chapters 4 and 9).

Now, there are many things known from general revelation that are not found in Scripture, but that do cast light on what is found in Scripture. For example, as we have noted, the Bible speaks of the "four corners of the earth" (Rev. 7:1; Rev. 20:8), which, were it not for His general revelation that the earth is round, could lead one to conclude that Scripture teaches that the earth is square. Thus, the clear teaching of general revelation can be used to correct any possible misinterpretation in special revelation. Another example, though disputable, is whether the earth moves around the sun or the sun around the earth. As we stated earlier, without the knowledge gained by modern astronomy since the work of Nicolaus Copernicus (1473–1543), it wasn't difficult to interpret Joshua 10:13 ("the sun stood still") as supporting a geocentric (earth-centered) solar system. Since that time, however, it seems wiser to take Joshua's reference as an observational comment no different than "the sunrise" (cf. Josh. 1:15), that is, as a statement made from the biblical writer's geographical perspective.

Sometimes the reverse is true. A widely held scientific misinterpretation of general revelation says that macroevolution is true. However, the clear teaching of special revelation affirms that God supernaturally created certain specific kinds of life that did not evolve from each other by natural processes (Gen. 1:1–27). Thus, the plain meaning of special revelation can

---

[6]Modalism is "the theological doctrine that the members of the Trinity are not three distinct persons but rather three modes or forms of activity (the Father, Son, and Holy Spirit) under which God manifests himself" (*Webster's Third New International Dictionary*).

be used to correct a misinterpretation of general revelation. Included in "general revelation" are also facts yielded by observation and the various sciences. These would include archaeological, chronological, historical, and other factual materials. For instance, with regard to the doctrine of Scripture it is relevant to know:

(1) We do not possess the original manuscripts of Scripture.
(2) There are some errors in the manuscript copies.
(3) We must include as a part of the facts known from outside the Bible the so-called data (or phenomena) of Scripture.

The above list of things known from outside of what the Bible teaches is important because any nuanced and sophisticated doctrine of Scripture must take these concepts into consideration, as will be done in our next step, retroduction.

It is also worth noting that the information derived from general revelation comes via the normal scientific method, which broadly includes induction (see above). Of course, science can also involve experimentation, intuition, and even deductions.

Step 5: The Retroductive Method

The next step in an adequate theological method involves the use of all the information gained in step 4 in order to help refine, nuance, and fill out our understanding of what is meant in the teachings of steps 1 through 3. To be specific, let's use the doctrine of Scripture as the illustration. Here is what we learn about the full theological doctrine of the inerrancy of Scripture in each step:

1. The Inductive Basis:
   (a) God cannot err.
   (b) The Bible is God's Word.
2. The Deductive Conclusion:
   (c) The Bible cannot err.
3. The Use of Analogies:
   (d) Just as Christ was divine and human yet without sin, even so the Bible is divine and human yet without error.
   (e) Just as nature (God's general revelation) presents difficulties with possessing errors, so does the Bible (God's special revelation).
4. The Use of General Revelation:
   (f) The earth is not square.
   (g) The sun does not move around the earth.
5. The Retroductive Method:
   (h) The biblical teaching is fleshed out in view of facts known from general revelation and the data (phenomena) of Scripture.

(i) There are errors in the manuscript copies.

(j) The Bible uses figures of speech and other literary devices, round numbers, everyday (nontechnical) language, paraphrases, etc.

(k) The deductive conclusion (point c) is understood in the light of the retroductive enhancement. For example:

(1) The Bible is without error only in the original text, not in all the copies.

(2) Round numbers, observational language, figures of speech, and paraphrased citations are not errors.

Step 6: Systematic Correlation (of all information into a fully orbed doctrine through use of the laws of logic that insist all truth must be noncontradictory)

The Bible is the infallible and inerrant Word of God in the original text (not in all copies). In accord with a good analogy, it is like Christ (the Word of God) in that both have a divine and human dimension, yet without error. However, the Bible should be understood in terms of the literary forms in which it is expressed, its own phenomena (data), and in accord with other revelation from God in nature.

It is important to point out that when step 2 affirms, "The Bible cannot err," we have the logically deduced and formal doctrine of inerrancy, but only in step 5 do we know specifically what this means—what the Bible *says* (steps 1 and 2) in the light of what it *shows*. The *doctrine* of Scripture must be understood in view of the *data* of Scripture.

Step 7: Each Doctrine Is Correlated With All Other Doctrines

The word *systematic* in systematic theology implies that all the teachings of both general and special revelation are comprehensive and consistent. This entails the use of another methodology—logic. Remember, the fundamental law of all thought is the law of noncontradiction, which affirms that A is not non-A. No two or more truths can be contradictory, which is why all biblical and extrabiblical truth can and must be brought into a consistent whole.

Consistency must be both internal and external. Internally, each biblical teaching must be logically consistent with every other biblical teaching. Externally, no teaching of Scripture can be inconsistent with any truth from general revelation. God is the author of both revelations, and He cannot contradict Himself. Hence, all contradictions must be between our *interpretation* of one revelation or the other. In principle, all conflicts between the two are resolvable, and the systematic theologian must attempt to harmonize them.

Step 8: Each Doctrine Is Expressed in View of the Orthodox Teachings of the Church Fathers.

Systematic theology is a fallible discipline; only the Bible is an infallible guide for faith and practice. However, theology should not be done in a vacuum—just as we can see farther spatially if we stand on the shoulders of giants, we likewise can see further theologically if we stand on the shoulders of the church fathers. One ignores the works of these great teachers at his own peril. As with other disciplines, he who ignores the past is condemned to repeat its errors.

Considering seriously the enduring teachings of the orthodox Fathers of the past is essential in constructing a viable evangelical systematic theology for the present. The church has struggled long and hard with understanding God's revelations to us, and as a result the historic orthodox expressions of Christian truth have stood the test of time. To summarize, an adequate evangelical theology must be molded in the context of the ecumenical truth of the historic orthodox Christian church.

While not everything that every orthodox Father said on every theological topic is binding on contemporary evangelical theology, nonetheless, no one has any right to claim orthodoxy for any teaching that has been condemned by any of the ecumenical creeds, confessions, or councils of the church. Likewise, any teaching not addressed in the ecumenical creeds and councils that is contrary to the universal consent of the Fathers should be considered highly suspect. The burden of proof rests on anyone who wishes to hold to any such precepts; he must have overwhelmingly clear and convincing evidence from infallible Scripture.

These tests for orthodoxy can be summarized as follows: (1) What is contrary to ecumenical creeds, councils, and confessions is certainly unorthodox; (2) What is not addressed in the ecumenical creeds, councils, and confessions but is contrary to the universal consent of the Fathers is almost certainly unorthodox; and (3) What is contrary to the general consent of the Fathers is highly suspect. It is within these parameters that we employ the use of the teachings of the great theologians of the historic Christian church.

Step 9: Livability Is the Final Test for Systematic Theology

True Christianity is not merely metaphysics; it is also ethics. It is not simply theoretical; it is practical. Its goal is not only to satisfy the mind but also to shape the life. Therefore, it must be livable; its truths must be effective in a pragmatic way. Of course, not all that works is true, but what is true will work. Systematic theology must lead to practical theology; as it does, a proper view of God and the relation of His creation to Him will change one's life (see volume 2).

SUMMARY AND CONCLUSION

Methodology is crucial to theology. An unorthodox method leads logically to unorthodox conclusions. An inadequate methodology will lead to an inadequate theology. Many of the methods developed to study other disciplines are not suited for theology—at least not an evangelical theology. Those that are adaptable must be stripped of their antisupernatural and unorthodox presuppositions.

An adequate method for evangelical theology includes many steps that employ various parts of other methodologies. This is not an eclectic method; rather, it is a comprehensive methodology consistent with the corpus of evangelical theology. Used as individual methods they are inadequate, but employed as part of a total methodology, they serve an important function. For example, assuming that all truth comes from the inductive method is fruitless; nevertheless, induction (step 1) is an important element in discovering the truth of God's revelation both in nature and in Scripture.

SOURCES

Aristotle. *Posterior Analytics.*
———. *Prior Analytics.*
———. *Topics.*
Behe, Michael. *Darwin's Black Box.*
Butler, Joseph. *Analogy in Religion.*
Carnell, Edward J. *An Introduction to Christian Apologetics.*
Dewey, John. *A Common Faith.*
———. *Logic: The Theory of Inquiry.*
Descartes, René. *Discourse on Method.*
———. *Meditations.*
Frazer, James. *The Golden Bough.*
Geisler, Norman, and Peter Bocchino. *Unshakable Foundations.*
Gilson, Étienne. *The Unity of Philosophical Experience.*
James, William. *Pragmatism.*
Johnson, Philip. *Darwin on Trial.*
Kant, Immanuel. *The Critique of Pure Reason.*
Mbiti, J. S. *African Religion and Philosophy.*
Meuller, G. E. "The Hegel Legend of Thesis, Antithesis-Synthesis" in *Journal of History of Ideas* 19, no. 3 (1958).
Mill, John Stuart. *Three Essays on Religion.*
Mossner, E. C. *Bishop Butler and the Age of Reason.*
Pierce, Charles Sanders. *Popular Science Monthly* (1878).
Plato. *Meno.*
Ramsey, Ian. *Models and Metaphors.*
Rurak, James. "Butler's Analogy: A Still Interesting Synthesis of Reason and Revelation" in *Anglican Theological Review* (October 1980).

Schmidt, W. *High Gods in North America.*
Spinoza, Benedict. *Ethics.*
———. *A Theological-Political Treatise.*
Van Til, Cornelius. *In Defense of the Faith.*
Veath, Henry. *Two Logics.*

PART TWO

BIBLE
(BIBLIOLOGY)

BIBLICAL

CHAPTER THIRTEEN

THE ORIGIN AND INSPIRATION OF THE BIBLE

THE NATURE OF BIBLICAL INSPIRATION

The Bible claims to be a book from God, a message with divine authority. Indeed, the biblical writers say they were moved by the Holy Spirit to utter His very words—that their message came by revelation so that what they wrote was breathed out (inspired) by God Himself.

Two Basic Texts on Revelation and Inspiration

A summary of what the Bible claims about itself is found in two crucial texts. Peter said the writers were moved by the Holy Spirit, and Paul claimed their writings were breathed out by God. Hence the Bible's claim that Spirit-moved writers uttered God-breathed writings.

2 Peter 1:20–21 declares:

> Above all, you must understand that no prophecy of Scripture came about by the prophet's own interpretation. For prophecy never had its

origin in the will of man, but men spoke from God as they were carried along by the Holy Spirit.

In short, the prophetic Scriptures (of the Old Testament) did not originate with man but with God moving on men called prophets of God (see next page).

2 Timothy 3:16, the other classic New Testament text, reads:

> All Scripture is God-breathed and is useful for teaching, rebuking, correcting and training in righteousness, so that the man of God may be thoroughly equipped for every good work.

While Peter speaks of the message originating with God, Paul says it becomes the written Word of God. God is the ultimate Cause, and the Scriptures are the authoritative result.

There are numerous passages in the Bible supporting the claim that the message of the Bible came from God through men of God and was inscripturated in the Word of God. Let's first examine those passages that speak of the inspiration of the Old Testament, and then we'll look at those pertaining to the New Testament.

Descriptions About the Inspiration of the Old Testament

In Deuteronomy 18:18 God said to Moses: "I will put my words in his mouth, and he will tell them everything I command him." On his deathbed David testified, "*The Spirit of the LORD spoke through me; his word was on my tongue*" (2 Sam. 23:2).[1] God spoke to Isaiah of "*my words that I have put in your mouth*" (Isa. 59:21). Second Chronicles 34:14 tells of "*the Book of the Law of the LORD that had been given through Moses.*" The prophet Zechariah wrote of "*the words* that *the LORD Almighty had sent by his Spirit through the earlier prophets*" (Zech. 7:12).

Likewise, in Matthew 22:43 Jesus questioned, "How is it then that *David, speaking by the Spirit,* calls Him 'Lord'?" (Ps. 110:1). Peter referred to "*God . . . who spoke by the Holy Spirit through the mouth of your servant, our father David . . .*" (Acts 4:24–25). The writer of Hebrews adds, "*He [God] . . . spoke through David as was said before*" (Heb. 4:7).

Descriptions About the Inspiration of the New Testament

The New Testament writers considered their writings to be inspired Scripture. Peter, speaking of Paul's epistles, said they too were "Scripture" (cf. 2 Tim. 3:16) just as the Old Testament was. He wrote,

> Our dear brother Paul also wrote you with the wisdom that God gave

---

[1]Emphasis in all scriptural citations is added.

him. He writes the same way *in all his letters,* speaking in them of these matters. His letters contain some things that are hard to understand, which ignorant and unstable people distort, as they do the *other Scriptures,* to their own destruction. (2 Peter 3:15–16)

Paul cites the gospel of Matthew as Scripture along with the Old Testament book of Deuteronomy, asserting, *"For the Scripture says* [in Deut. 25:4], 'Do not muzzle the ox while it is treading out the grain,' and, [in Matt. 10:10] 'The worker deserves his wages' " (1 Tim. 5:18).

Paul declared in 1 Corinthians that his *"words"* are *"taught by the Spirit"* (2:13), for *"God has revealed it to us by his Spirit"* (v. 10). The apostle concludes his exhortation by saying, "If anyone thinks himself to be a prophet or spiritual, let him acknowledge that *the things which I write to you are the commandments of the Lord"* (1 Cor. 14:37). He also begins his epistle to the Galatians by reminding them that what he preached came from God: *"I did not receive it from any man, nor was I taught it; rather, I received it by revelation from Jesus Christ"* (Gal. 1:12).

John the apostle opens the book of Revelation with *"The revelation of Jesus Christ, which God gave him"* (Rev. 1:1), and he concludes the book with the declaration that he is a prophet (alongside the Old Testament prophets): "I [the angel speaking to John] am a fellow servant, with you and with *your brothers the prophets* and of all who keep the words of this book" (Rev. 22:9).

The Nature of a Prophet

The biblical authors were prophets and apostles of God. There are many designations of a prophet that are informative about his role in producing Scripture. A prophet is called

(1) a man of God (1 Kings 12:22), meaning that he was *chosen* by God;
(2) a servant of the Lord (1 Kings 14:18), indicating that he was *faithful* to God;
(3) a messenger of the Lord (Isa. 42:19), showing that he was *sent* by God;
(4) a seer (*Ro'eh*) or beholder (*Hozeh*) (Isa.30:9–10), revealing that his *insight* was from God;
(5) a man of the Spirit (Hos. 9:7 RSV; cf. Mic. 3:8), telling that he spoke by the *Spirit of the Lord*;
(6) a watchman (Ezek. 3:17), reflecting his *alertness* for God; and
(7) a prophet (by which he is most commonly called), marking him as a *spokesperson* for God.[2]

The prophets received their messages from God in various ways. Some

---

[2]From Norman Geisler and William Nix, *A General Introduction to the Bible,* chapter 4.

got it by dreams (Gen. 37); others by visions (Dan. 7); some by an audible voice (1 Sam. 3) or an inner voice (Hos. 1; Joel 1). Others received revelations from angels (Gen. 19), and some by miracles (Ex. 3, Judg. 6) or the lot (Prov. 16:33). The high priest used jewels known as the Urim and Thummim (Ex. 28:30). God spoke to still others as they meditated on His revelation in nature (Ps. 19). Whatever the means, as Hebrews puts it, "In the past God spoke to our forefathers through the prophets at many times and in various ways" (Heb. 1:1).

The nature of a biblical prophet is described in these vivid terms: "The Sovereign LORD has spoken—who can but prophesy?" (Amos 3:8). He is one who speaks "everything the LORD had said" (Ex. 4:30). Again, God said, "I will put my words in his mouth, and he will tell them everything I command him" (Deut. 18:18). He added, "Do not add to what I command you and do not subtract from it" (Deut. 4:2). Jeremiah was commanded: "This is what the LORD says: Stand in the courtyard of the Lord's house and speak to all the people. . . . Tell them everything I command you; do not omit a word" (Jer. 26:2). In brief, a prophet was someone who said what God told him to say, no more and no less.

As a mouthpiece for God bound neither to add to nor take away from His words, the very nature of a prophet guarantees that a prophetic writing is exactly what God wants to say to humankind. Since the Bible is presented as a prophetic writing from beginning to end (Matt. 5:17–18; 2 Peter 1:20–21; Rev. 22:9), it follows that the written record of the prophets was considered inspired of God. This is what the prophet Zechariah meant when he wrote,

> They made their hearts as hard as flint and would not listen to the law or to the words that the LORD Almighty had sent by his Spirit through the earlier prophets. So the LORD Almighty was very angry. (Zech. 7:12)

To be sure, not all prophets were known by that name. Some were kings, like David; yet he was also a mouthpiece of God, nonetheless—he is even called a "prophet" (in Acts 2:29–39). Others were lawgivers, like Moses; but he too was a prophet or spokesman for God (Deut. 18:18). Some biblical writers even disclaimed the term "prophet" (Amos 7:14), meaning they were not a professional prophet, like Samuel and his "group of prophets" (1 Sam. 19:20). Nonetheless, even if Amos was not a prophet by office, he was certainly a prophet by gift (cf. Amos 7:15), for he was being used as a mouthpiece of God.

Nor did all who were prophets always speak in the first-person style of an explicit "Thus *saith* the LORD." Those who wrote historical books—like the prophet Jeremiah, who wrote Kings—spoke in an implied "Thus *did* the Lord." Theirs, in such instances, was a message more about the *acts* of God on behalf of His people than the words of God *to* His people. Nonetheless, all the biblical writers were channels through which God conveyed His message to humankind.

What the Bible Says, God Says

Another way the Bible claims to be the Word of God is expressed in the formula "What the Bible says, God says." This is manifested in that often an Old Testament passage will claim God said it, yet when this same text is cited in the New Testament it asserts that the Scriptures said it. Sometimes the reverse is true—in the Old Testament it is the Bible that records it, while the New Testament declares that it was God who said it.

Consider this comparison:

What God Says	The Bible Says
Genesis 12:3	Galatians 3:8
Exodus 9:16	Romans 9:17
Genesis 2:24	Matthew 19:4–5
Psalm 2:1	Acts 4:24–25
Isaiah 55:3	Acts 13:34
Psalm 16:10	Acts 13:35
Psalm 2:7	Hebrews 1:5
Psalm 97:7	Hebrews 1:6
Psalm 104:4	Hebrews 1:7
Psalm 95.7	Hebrews 3:7

A couple of passages make the point. Consider Genesis 12:1–3:

> The LORD *had said* to Abram, "Leave your country, your people and your father's household and go to the land I will show you. . . . I will bless those who bless you, and whoever curses you I will curse; and all peoples on earth will be blessed through you."

But when this passage is cited in Galatians 3:8, we read, "*The scripture . . . announced . . .* , 'All the nations will be blessed through you' " (emphasis added).

Likewise, in Exodus 9:13–16:

> And *the LORD said* to Moses, "Get up early in the morning, confront Pharaoh and say to him, 'This is what the LORD, the God of the Hebrews, says: Let my people go, so that they may worship me. . . . But *I [the LORD]* have raised you up for this very purpose, that I might show you my power and that my name might be proclaimed in all the earth.' "

However, when the New Testament quotes this passage it says, "For *the*

Scripture says to Pharaoh: 'I raised you up for this very purpose, that I might display my power in you and that my name might be proclaimed in all the earth' " (Rom. 9:17, emphasis added).

Again, often the order is reversed; for example, in Genesis 2:24 *the author of the book* says, "For this reason a man will leave his father and mother and be united to his wife, and they will become one flesh." Yet when this is cited by Jesus in the New Testament, He says, "Haven't you read that at the beginning *the Creator* 'made them male and female,' and *said*, 'For this reason a man will leave his father and mother and be united to his wife, and the two will become one flesh'?" (Matt. 19:4–5).

The same is true with Psalm 2:1 (NKJV), where it is David who said, "Why do the nations rage, And the people plot a vain thing?" but when this is cited in Acts 4:24–25 (NKJV) we read: "So when they heard that, they raised their voice to God with one accord and said: 'Lord, You are *God, who . . . said*: "Why did the nations rage, and the people plot vain things?" ' "

Commenting on this scriptural phenomenon, B. B. Warfield keenly observed:

> It would be difficult to invent methods of showing profound reverence for the text of Scripture as the very Word of God, which will not be found to be characteristic of the writers of the New Testament in dealing with the Old.

Warfield spent a whole chapter dealing with the above kinds of citations, noting,

> In one of these classes of passages the Scriptures are spoken of as if they were God; in the other, God is spoken of as if He were the Scriptures. [Thus] in the two taken together, God and Scriptures are brought into such conjunction as to show that in point of directness of authority no distinction was made between them. (*IAB*, 299.)

The Biblical Writers Claim: "Thus Says the Lord"

Phrases such as "thus says the Lord" (Isa. 1:11, 18; Jer. 2:3, 5, etc.), "God said" (Gen. 1:3, 6, etc.), "the Word of the LORD came to me" (Jer. 34:1; Eze. 30:1, etc.) or the like are found hundreds of times in Scripture. These reveal beyond question that the writer is claiming to give the very Word of God. In the book of Leviticus alone there are some sixty-six occurrences of phrases like "the LORD spoke unto Moses" (cf. 1:1; 4:1; 5:14; 6:1, 8, 19; 7:22).

Countless times Ezekiel records phrases such as "I saw visions" or "the word of the LORD came to me." In one short section (chapter 12) there are eleven such examples (vv. 8, 10, 17, 19, 21, 23, 25–26, 28 twice), and sometimes there are two in the same verse (Ezek 20:3). The same is true of Jeremiah (cf. 1:2, 4, 11, 13; 2:1, 3, 5, etc.), Isaiah (cf. 1:1, 11, 18, 24; 2:1, etc.), and other prophets. The overall impression leaves no doubt as to the confessed source of their messages.

The Bible Claims to Be the "Word of God"

Many times the Bible claims to be "the Word of God" in these very terms. Jesus told the Jews of His day, "You nullify *the word of God* for the sake of your tradition" (Matt. 15:6). Paul speaks of the Scriptures as "*the oracles of God*" (Rom. 3:2 NKJV), and Peter declares, "For you have been born again, not of perishable seed, but of imperishable, through *the living and enduring word of God*" (1 Peter 1:23). And the writer of Hebrews affirms, "For *the word of God* is living and active. Sharper than any double-edged sword" (4:12).

The Bible Claims to Have Divine Authority

There are many other words or phrases the Bible uses to describe itself that entail the claim to divine authority. Jesus said the Bible has indestructibility in that it will never pass away (Matt. 5:17–18); it is infallible or "cannot be broken" (John 10:35); it has final authority (Matt. 4:4, 7, 10); and it is sufficient for faith and practice (Luke 16:31; cf. 2 Tim. 3:16–17).

The extent of divine authority in Scripture includes:

(1) all that is written—2 Tim. 3:16;
(2) even the very words—Matt. 22:43; 1 Cor. 2:13;
(3) and tenses of verbs—Matt. 22:32; Gal. 3:16;
(4) even the smallest parts of words—Matt. 5:17–18.

That is, even though the Bible was *not mechanically dictated* by God to man, nonetheless, the result is just as perfect as if it had been. The biblical authors claimed that God is the source of the very words of Scripture, since He supernaturally superintended the process by which they wrote, using their own vocabulary and style message to record His message (2 Peter 1:20–21).

THE LOCUS OF BIBLICAL INSPIRATION—VERBAL

Numerous passages make it evident that the locus of revelation and inspiration is the written Word, the Scriptures (Gk: *grapha*), not simply the idea or even the writer. Notice that in the texts just cited the reference is to revealed or divinely inspired "Scriptures" (2 Tim. 3:16; 2 Peter 3:16), "words" (1 Cor. 2:10–13), "the book" (2 Chron. 34:14), "his [God's] word" (2 Sam. 23:2), "my [God's] words" (Isa. 59:21), and "the words" (Zech. 7:12).

When referring to the Old Testament as the authoritative Word of God, the New Testament most often (over ninety times) uses the phrase "it is *written*" (cf. Matt. 4:4, 7, 10). Jesus described this written word as that which "comes out of the mouth of God" (Matt. 4:4). So important were the exact words of God that Jeremiah was told:

> This is what the LORD says: "Stand in the courtyard of the Lord's house and speak to all the people of the towns of Judah who come to worship in the house of the LORD. Tell them everything I command you; *do not omit a word*" (26:2).

So it wasn't simply God's message that men were free to state in their words; the very choice of words was from God. Exodus 24:4 records that "Moses then wrote down *everything the LORD had said. . . .*" Again, Deuteronomy adds, "I [God] will raise up for them a prophet like you from among their brothers; I will put *my words* in his mouth, and *he will tell them everything I command him*" (Deut. 18:18).

Sometimes we are reminded that even the tenses of verbs are stressed by God. Jesus said, "But about the resurrection of the dead—have you not read what God said to you, 'I *am* [not *was*] the God of Abraham, the God of Isaac, and the God of Jacob'? He is not the God of the dead but of the living" (Matt. 22:31–32). Paul based his argument on a singular noun versus a plural in Galatians 3:16, insisting "The Scripture does not say 'and to *seeds*,' meaning many people, but 'and to your *seed*,' meaning one person, who is Christ." Even one letter ("s") can make a big difference. Recall that Jesus went so far as to declare that *parts* of letters are inspired: "I tell you the truth, until heaven and earth disappear, not the smallest letter, not the least stroke of a pen, will by any means disappear from the Law until everything is accomplished" (Matt. 5:18).[3]

THE EXTENT OF BIBLICAL INSPIRATION—PLENARY

Biblical inspiration is not only verbal (located in the words), but it is also plenary, meaning that it *extends to every part of the words and all they teach or imply.*

What Inspiration Guarantees

Inspiration does guarantee the truth of all the Bible teaches, implies, or entails (spiritually or factually). Paul said "all," not some, Scripture is God-

---

[3]Of course, neither letters nor words are inspired in and of themselves but only as part of a whole sentence, which alone bears meaning (and truth). This was shown earlier, in chapter 6.

breathed (2 Tim. 3:16), and Peter declared that "no prophecy of Scripture" came from man but that all came from God (2 Peter 1:20–21).

Jesus told His disciples that "the Counselor, [which is] the Holy Spirit, whom the Father will send in my name, will teach you *all things* and will remind you of *everything* I have said to you" (John 14:26). He added, "But when he, the Spirit of truth, comes, he will guide you into *all truth*" (John 16:13). As a matter of fact, the church is "built on the foundation of the apostles and prophets, with Christ Jesus himself as the chief cornerstone" (Eph. 2:20). And the early church "devoted themselves to the *apostles' teaching*" (Acts 2:42), which was recorded for us in the pages of the New Testament and was considered "Scripture" along with the Old Testament (cf. 2 Peter 3:15–16; 1 Tim. 5:18).

The inspiration of God, then, extends to every part of Scripture, including everything God affirmed (or denied) about any topic. It is inclusive of not only what the Bible *teaches* but what it *touches*; that is to say, it includes not only what the Bible teaches explicitly but also what it teaches implicitly, covering not only spiritual matters but factual ones as well. The omniscient God cannot be wrong about anything He teaches or implies (see volume 2).

What Inspiration Does Not Guarantee

There are, however, many things that inspiration does not guarantee.

(1) It does not guarantee that *every part* of a parable is conveying a truth (as opposed to the truthfulness of *the point* the parable is illustrating—Luke 18:2);

(2) nor that everything *recorded* in the Bible is true (as opposed to only what is *taught* or implied—Gen. 3:4);

(3) nor that no exaggerations (hyperboles) can be used (Col. 1:23);

(4) nor that all statements about God and creation are purely literal (Heb. 4:13; Job 38:7);

(5) nor that all factual assertions are technically precise by modern standards (as opposed to accurate by ancient standards—2 Chron. 4:2);

(6) nor that all statements about the universe must be from a modern astronomical perspective (as opposed to a common observational standpoint—Josh. 10:12);

(7) nor that all citations of Scripture must be verbatim (as opposed to faithful);

(8) nor that all citations of Scripture must have the same *application* as the original (cf. Hos. 11:1; Matt. 2:15), rather than having the same *interpretation* (meaning);

(9) nor that the same truth can be said in only one way (as opposed to many ways, such as in the Gospels);

(10) nor that whatever a writer personally believed (as opposed to merely what he actually affirmed in Scripture) is true (Matt. 15:26);

(11) nor that truth is exhaustively revealed or treated (as opposed to adequately presented) in the Bible (1 Cor. 13:12);

(12) nor that quotations imply the truth of everything in the source it is citing, rather than only the part cited (Titus 1:12);

(13) nor that the grammatical construction will always be the customary one (rather than an adequate one to convey the truth).

How do we know that these are not included in what inspiration covers? The answer is called "the phenomena of Scripture"; that is, what the Bible *says* must be understood in view of what the Bible *shows*. What it *preaches* must be read in view of what it *practices*. The *doctrine* of Scripture is to be understood in the light of the *data* of Scripture.

All thirteen things listed above are part of the data of Scripture. For instance, the Bible uses round numbers; thus, when the Bible claims to be true it does not mean to exclude the use of round numbers. The same is true of hyperboles, figures of speech, observational language, and literary genre (poetry, parable, etc.). In short, everything the Bible affirms is true, but what is meant by truth must be understood in the light of the phenomena or data of Scripture (see chapter 12).

THE DEGREE OF BIBLICAL INSPIRATION—EQUAL

Are there different degrees of inspiration in the Bible? That is, are some things more inspired than others? The answer to this is best understood in terms of what is meant by inspiration, namely, that whatever the Bible affirms (or implies) is true, God affirms (or implies) is true. This being the case, there can be no degrees of inspiration any more than there can be degrees of truth: Something is either true or false. One thing is not more or less true than another any more than a woman can be more or less pregnant.

Thus, the affirmation that "Jezebel died" is as inspired as "Jesus died." However, while everything in the Bible is equally true, not everything is equally important. The death of the perfect Christ is much more important than the death of the wicked queen. Likewise, the resurrection of Christ is more important than the raising of Lazarus (John 11). In short, there are no degrees of truth, but there are degrees of importance of one truth over another.

A BIBLICAL DEFINITION OF INSPIRATION

In view of what the Bible says and shows about itself, a definition of divine inspiration can be formulated. First, the elements of a definition will be set forth; then, the definition will be derived from them. There appear to be six basic elements stated or implied in the Bible.

The Bible Has a Divine Origin

The ultimate source of a divinely inspired Bible is God Himself, for the Scriptures are "breathed" (inspired) by Him (2 Tim. 3:16): "Every word that comes from the mouth of God" (Matt. 4:4). Scripture did not originate from human impulse, "for prophecy never had its origin in the will of man, but men spoke from God as they were carried along by the Holy Spirit" (2 Peter 1:20–21).

The Bible Came Though Human Agency

With the exception of a few occasions, like the giving of the Ten Commandments—which were "inscribed by the finger of God" (Deut. 9:10)—the Bible did not come directly from God but only indirectly from Him through the instrumentality of His prophets. Hebrews 1:1 declares: "In the past God spoke to our forefathers *through the prophets* at many times and in various ways. . . ." The Holy Spirit "moved" on "holy men of God" (2 Peter 1:21 NKJV). David said it well: "The Spirit of the LORD spoke *through me,* his word was *on my tongue*" (2 Sam. 23:2; see also Deut. 18:18; Isa. 59:21; Zech. 7:12; Acts 4:24–25; Heb. 4:7).

Furthermore, judging by the various vocabulary, grammar, styles, figures of speech, and human interests of the various authors, God did not disregard the personality and culture of the biblical writers when He providentially guided them to be the vehicles through which He revealed His written Word to humankind. On the contrary, the Bible is a thoroughly human book in every respect, except that it is without error (see chapter 15).

Regardless of the mystery surrounding how God was able to make His word certain without destroying the freedom and personality of the authors (see chapter 15), several things are clear. The human authors of Scripture were not mere secretaries taking dictation; their freedom was not suspended or negated, and they were not automatons. What they wrote is what they desired to write in the style that they were accustomed to using. God in His providence engaged in a divine concurrence between their words and His so that what they said, He said (see above).

The Bible Is a Written Authority

Inspiration deals with the written text of Scripture; it is the *grapha* (writings) of the prophets that are inspired (2 Tim. 3:16). The phrase "It is written" (cf. Matt. 4:4, 7, 10) reveals that the focus of God's authority for His people was in His written Word. Nowhere does the Bible speak of inspired ideas or of inspired persons. To be sure, God moved on the writers (2 Peter 1:20–21), but this was to insure that their writings were inspired. The repeated references to the very "words" of the prophets being from God stresses this point (cf. Ex. 24:4; Deut. 18:18; Jer. 26:2).

The Bible's Divine Authority Is Located in the Autographic Text

This important fact of the divine inspiration of the Bible is implied from two facts. *First*, all the biblical references to the God-given authority of Scripture are to what God gave or "breathed-out," which was the original text. *Second*, not all *copies* of the original text are perfect; there are minor errors in them, and these can be seen by comparing parallel passages (cf. 2 Kings 8:26; 2 Chron. 22:2). But *God* cannot lie (Heb. 6:18; Titus 1:2); His law is "perfect" or flawless (Ps. 19:7). Hence, whatever errors there are in copies of the Bible could not have been in the original text. This leads to another characteristic of an inspired text—its inerrancy.

The Bible's Original Text Is Inerrant

If God cannot err, and the original text was breathed out by God, then it follows that the original text of the Bible is without error. Hence, any real errors found in biblical manuscripts or in translations of them were not in the original. Copies of the original are only inspired insofar as they are accurate copies of the original. As Augustine aptly put it,

> If we are perplexed by any apparent contradiction in Scripture, it is not allowable to say, "The author of this book is mistaken"; but either the manuscript is faulty, or the translation is wrong, or you have not understood. (*AF*, 11.5.)

The Bible Has Final Authority

When speaking of its divine authority, the Bible makes it clear that this is a final authority, the court of last appeal in everything it affirms (or implies). The psalmist said, "*For you have exalted above all things your name and your word*" (Ps. 138:2). He added, "*Your word, O LORD, is eternal; it stands firm in the heavens*" (Ps. 119:89).

Again, Jesus declared, "I tell you the truth, until heaven and earth disappear, *not the smallest letter, not the least stroke of a pen, will by any means disappear from the Law* until everything is accomplished" (Matt. 5:18). He rebuked the religious leaders of His day for exalting their teaching above the Word of God (Matt. 15:3–6). Again, the manner in which Jesus and the New Testament writers use the phrase "it is written" in the Scriptures manifests their belief that it was the final court of appeal in all disputes on which it speaks.

The Sixty-Six Canonical Books of the Bible Alone Have This Divine Authority[4]

One other element of the evangelical view of the inspiration of Scripture should be added here, though it is discussed elsewhere (see chapter 28). This element is one of the distinguishing factors between the evangelical and Roman Catholic views of Scripture: The sixty-six canonical books of the Protestant canon alone are invested with divine authority. No other source equals or surpasses that of Scripture; the Bible, and the Bible alone, is a supremely authoritative book in matters of faith and practice.

SUGGESTED DEFINITION OF INSPIRATION

Inspiration is the supernatural operation of the Holy Spirit, who through the different personalities and literary styles of the chosen human authors invested the very words of the original books of Holy Scripture, alone and in their entirety, as the very Word of God without error in all that they teach or imply (including history and science), and the Bible is thereby the infallible rule and final authority for faith and practice of all believers.

THE MODUS OPERANDI OF INSPIRATION

The mode of operation by which the Holy Spirit worked with the authors in order to assure an infallible and inerrant product is a matter of much speculation among theologians. The mystery remains inscrutable, but the process is intelligible and the parameters are definable.

The Parameters of the Modus Operandi

Two factors define the limits within which legitimate speculation may occur:

(1) The product is infallible and inerrant.
(2) Whatever means is used, different personalities, different styles, and the freedom of the authors manifested in their books must be accounted for.

The first point is known from the *doctrine* of Scripture supported above by numerous references. The second is known from the *data* of Scripture, clearly manifested in its human characteristics (see chapter 15).

---

[4]For a comprehensive treatment of the Protestant principle of *Sola Scriptura* (the Bible alone), see Keith A. Mathison, *The Shape of Sola Scriptura* (Moscow, Ida.: Canon Press, 2001).

Problematic Explanations

Like illustrations of the Trinity, no analogies of scriptural inspiration are perfect, some are better than others, and still others are misleading. Several fall into this latter category.

In particular, two illustrations should be avoided: that of a *secretary* and that of a *musical instrument.* Early church fathers were particularly known to use the latter (see chapter 17). The problem with these illustrations is that they lend to the false charge that evangelicals believe in mechanical dictation.

The *musical instrument* illustration is unhelpful because a musical instrument has no free will, no personality, and no literary style—it is an inanimate object, and not an efficient cause of the writing but only an instrumental cause.

The *secretary* illustration is not much better, because faithful secretaries take dictation. While they are not inanimate or nonfree instruments, nevertheless, by the very nature of their occupation they are not creating the material but merely recording it. The words written are not theirs, nor is their personality expressed. This is not true of biblical inspiration, which, as we have seen, employs the freedom, style, vocabulary, and personalities of the various biblical authors to convey God's Word to humankind.

In his noted *Theopneustia,* Louis Gaussen (1790–1863) uses the illustration of an *orchestra conductor.* This is somewhat better, since all members of the orchestra are freely participating and expressing their distinctive sounds while the master brings them together in unity and harmony, as does God with the Scriptures. Even here the analogy breaks down, however, since the whole sound is not really the result of each member playing his own solo. Further, instrumentalists make mistakes, while the Bible does not.

Many evangelicals have been content to rely on the *providentially pre-planned personalities* model, whereby God preplanned the lives, styles, and vocabularies of the various biblical authors so that they would freely choose to write the correct thing in the right way at the right time, which God, by preordained divine concurrence, has determined would be their part of His Word. While this is no doubt true, even this does not account for the whole story. For one thing, it does not explain how free will fits into the picture. Were the free choices of the various authors causally predetermined? If so, were they really free? Further, how could God guarantee that the results would be infallible and inerrant if the authors were really free to do otherwise?

While some models are better than others, no matter how good the model is there always seems to be some mystery left at the very point where there is a divine/human encounter. This is true of the doctrines of predestination and free will (see volume 2) as well as the doctrines of how the two natures of Christ relate and the mode of inspiration.

Without attempting to solve the mystery, there are meaningful ways to describe it. Thomas Aquinas offered one of these in his *teacher/student analogy*, arguing that the relationship between God and the human authors of Scripture is more like that of a teacher to his pupil. The value of this analogy is that it preserves the personality of the human authors while at the same time explaining the commonality between what the teacher conveyed and what the student expressed (see *ST*, 2a2ae 171, 6; 172, 6).

This analogy also makes a distinction between primary (God) and secondary (man) causality, thus avoiding reducing the human authors to mere instrumental causes. A primary cause is an efficient cause whose power to cause comes from the primary cause, but the exercise of the power of causality rests in its own free expression. But here too there is a difference, since the secondary cause (the student) can and sometimes does deviate from the primary cause (God). Not so when God (the primary cause) worked in and through the human authors of Scripture (the secondary causes).

CONCLUSION

One final comment is in order: The ultimate process, however illustrated, retains an element of mystery. Nonetheless, it is correct to say that while the Bible was not dictated by God to secretaries, the final product is as infallible and inerrant *as though it were dictated*.

SOURCES

Archer, Gleason. *Old Testament Quotations in the New Testament.*
Augustine. *Against Faustus.*
Gaussen, Louis. *Theopneustia.*
Geisler, Norman, ed. *Inerrancy.*
Geisler, Norman, and William E. Nix. *A General Introduction to the Bible.*
Henry, Carl F. H., ed. *Revelation and the Bible.*
Hodge, Charles, and B. B. Warfield. *Inspiration.*
Johnson, S. Lewis. *The Old Testament in the New.*
Lindsell, Harold. *The Battle for the Bible.*
Nash, Ronald. *The Word of God and the Mind of Man.*
Packer, J. I. *"Fundamentalism" and the Word of God.*
Pasche, Rene. *The Inspiration and Authority of the Bible.*
Thomas Aquinas. *Summa Theologica.*
Turretin, Francis. *The Doctrine of Scripture.*
Warfield, B. B. *The Inspiration and Authority of the Bible.*
———. *Limited Inspiration.*

CHAPTER FOURTEEN

THE DIVINE NATURE
OF THE BIBLE

Since the Bible is divine in origin (see chapter 13), it is understandable that it manifests some divine characteristics. These earmarks of the divine set the Bible apart from all purely human books.

THE SANCTITY OF THE BIBLE

The Hebrew (*qodesh*) and Greek (*hagios*) words for holy or sacred mean "to be set apart." As an attribute of God, holiness means to be totally and utterly set apart from all creation and from evil.

The Holiness of God

As applied to God, holiness is associated with His jealousy (Josh. 24:19), His exaltation (Ps. 99:9), His righteousness (Isa. 5:16), His almightiness (Rev. 4:8), His absolute uniqueness (Ex. 15:11), His moral purity (2 Cor. 7:1), His being vexed by evil (Ps. 78:41), and that which should inspire a deep sense of awe (Isa. 29:23) and perpetual worship in His creatures (1 Chron. 16:29; Rev. 4:8).

Consider what the Bible says of God: "Who among the gods is like you, O LORD? Who is like you—majestic in holiness, awesome in glory, working wonders?" (Ex. 15:11); "I am the LORD your God; consecrate yourselves and be holy, because *I am holy*. Do not make yourselves unclean by any creature that moves about on the ground" (Lev. 11:44); "Joshua said to the people, 'You are not able to serve the LORD. *He is a holy God*; He is a jealous God. He will not forgive your rebellion and your sins' " (Josh. 24:19); "*There is no one holy like the LORD;* there is no one besides you; there is no Rock like our God" (1 Sam. 2:2); "*Who can stand in the presence of the LORD, this holy God?* To whom will the ark go up from here?" (1 Sam. 6:20); "Ascribe to the LORD the glory due to his name. Bring an offering and come before him; *worship the LORD in the splendor of his holiness*" (1 Chron. 16:29); "Again and again they put God to the test; *they vexed the Holy One of Israel*" (Ps. 78:41); "Exalt the LORD our God and worship at his footstool; *he is holy*" (Ps. 99:5); "Exalt the LORD our God and worship at his holy mountain, for *the LORD our God is holy*" (Ps. 99:9); "But the LORD Almighty will be exalted by his justice, and the holy *God will show himself holy by his righteousness*" (Isa. 5:16); "When they see among them their children, the work of my hands, they will keep my name holy; *they will acknowledge the holiness of the Holy One of Jacob, and will stand in awe of the God of Israel*" (Isa. 29:23); "For I am the LORD, your God, the *Holy One* of Israel, your Savior" (Isa. 43:3; cf. "Holy One" in Ps. 71:22; 78:41; Isa. 5:19; 29:23; 48:17; 54:5; 55:5; 60:9; Jer. 51:5; Hos. 11:9, 12; Hab. 1:12; 3:3; Mark 1:24; Luke 1:35; 4:34; John 6:69); "Since we have these promises, dear friends, let us *purify ourselves from everything that contaminates body and spirit, perfecting holiness out of reverence for God*" (2 Cor. 7:1); "Each of the four living creatures had six wings and was covered with eyes all around, even under his wings. Day and night they never stop saying: '*Holy, holy, holy is the Lord God Almighty, who was, and is, and is to come*' " (Rev. 4:8).

The Holiness of God's Word

Holiness is used of God's Word similarly to the way it is used of God, namely, to be set apart from other things, to be sacred, to be exalted. Paul told Timothy, "From infancy you have known the *holy* Scriptures, which are able to make you wise for salvation through faith in Christ Jesus" (2 Tim. 3:15).

From the very beginning the Scriptures were considered sacred. When Moses wrote, his words were placed alongside the ark of the covenant in the most holy and sacred place in ancient Israel (Deut. 31:24–26).

God's Word is not only holy itself, but it is able to make us holy. Jesus prayed, "*Sanctify them by the truth; your word is truth*" (John 17:17). Timothy was told the Holy Scriptures were "able to make you wise for salvation" (2 Tim. 3:15). The Bible is set apart above all other books in the world, since it alone is able to save (Rom. 1:16; 1 Peter 1:23) and sanctify. Paul spoke of Christ's desire to "*make her* [the church] *holy, cleansing her by the washing with water through the word, and to present her to himself as a radiant church, without stain or wrinkle or any other blemish, but holy and blameless*" (Eph. 5:26–27).

The Divine Authority of the Bible

As the Word of God, the Bible has divine authority. This is manifested in several ways. *First,* it is the final authority for faith and practice (2 Tim. 3:16–17).

Second, Jesus said God's Word is exalted above all human teaching (Matt. 15:3–6).

Third, because the Bible is the Word of God it speaks with the authority of God. Jesus described it in these words: "Is it not written in your *Law,* 'I have said you are gods'? If he called them 'gods,' to whom the *word of God came*—and the Scripture *cannot be broken . . .*"(John 10:34–35). In these two verses "Scripture" is called three things:

(1) the Torah (law) of God,
(2) the Word of God, and
(3) unbreakable.

Fourth, remember that "Scripture" is sometimes used interchangeably with God Himself, which reveals that it speaks with His authority (see chapter 13).

Fifth, Jesus spoke of the Bible as coming from God's mouth (Matt. 4:4).

Sixth, we have seen that Jesus declared, "I tell you the truth, until heaven and earth disappear, *not the smallest letter, not the least stroke of a pen, will by any means disappear from the Law until everything is accomplished*" (Matt. 5:18). This can be said only of that which has divine authority, such as the Bible does.

THE INFALLIBILITY OF THE BIBLE

The word *infallible* is not used in Scripture of itself; however, other statements are used of the Bible that imply its infallibility (unfailingness). Jesus said, "The Scripture cannot be broken" (John 10:35). Matthew 5:17–18 also reveals that the Bible is imperishable (see above). Further, God affirmed through Isaiah, "My word that goes out from my mouth: *It will not return to me empty, but will accomplish what I desire and achieve the purpose for which I sent it*" (Isa. 55:11; cf. Matt. 15:3–6; Matt. 4:4, 7, 10). Indeed, Paul speaks of God's Word as "*the oracles of God*" (Rom. 3:2 NKJV).

THE INDESTRUCTIBILITY OF THE BIBLE

As we have seen, Jesus declared that the Bible is indestructible, saying,

> Do not think that I have come to abolish the Law or the Prophets; I have not come to abolish them but to fulfill them. I tell you the truth, until heaven and earth disappear, *not the smallest letter, not the least stroke*

of a pen, will by any means disappear from the Law until everything is accomplished. (Matt. 5:17–18)

Isaiah confirmed the same when he wrote, "The grass withers and the flowers fall, but *the word of our God stands forever*" (Isa. 40:8). The psalmist added, *"Your word, O LORD, is eternal; it stands firm in the heavens"* (Ps. 119:89).

History is a testimony to the Bible's durability. It has been banned, burned, and banished, but in spite of it all, it stands as the world's all-time bestseller.

THE INDEFATIGABILITY OF THE BIBLE

What is more, the Bible has indefatigable power—it cannot be worn out; it is tireless and inexhaustible. Hebrews declares that *"the word of God is living and active. Sharper than any double-edged sword,* it penetrates even to dividing soul and spirit, joints and marrow; it judges the thoughts and attitudes of the heart"* (4:12). God asked Jeremiah, *"Is not my word like fire . . . and like a hammer that breaks a rock in pieces?"* (Jer. 23:29). Paul said, "The weapons we fight with are not the weapons of the world. On the contrary, *they have divine power to demolish strongholds"* (2 Cor. 10:4). One such weapon is the *"sword of the Spirit which is the word of God"* (Eph. 6:17).

This tireless power of Scripture comes from the infinite God whose inexhaustible power is manifest in his infallible Word. Paul reminded the Thessalonians: "When you received the word of God, which you heard from us, you accepted it not as the word of men, but as it actually is, *the word of God, which is at work in you who believe"* (1 Thess. 2:13). Indeed, Peter affirmed, "For you have been born again, *not of perishable seed, but of imperishable, through the living and enduring word of God"* (1 Peter 1:23).

THE INDEFEASIBILITY OF THE BIBLE

In addition, the Bible has the quality of being indefeasible; that is, it cannot be overcome, made void or ineffective—it always accomplishes its purpose. Recall that God announced through Isaiah, "So is my word that goes out from my mouth: *It will not return to me empty, but will accomplish what I desire and achieve the purpose for which I sent it"* (Isa. 55:11). This is true of those who receive its message as well as those who reject it. As Paul, who preached it, said, *"For we are to God the aroma of Christ among those who are being saved and those who are perishing"* (2 Cor. 2:15–16). Those who accept it magnify God's mercy, and those who reject it manifest His wrath (cf. Rom. 9:21–22). But it *always* accomplishes God's purpose.

THE INERRANCY OF THE BIBLE

As the Bible is firmly rooted in the God whose Word it is, each member of the Trinity is involved in its inerrancy. Thus, three arguments can be stated, one in terms of each member of the Godhead. That the Bible is without error is clear from these three arguments.

The Argument From God the Father

The logic is simple and irrefutable:

(1) God cannot err.
(2) The Bible is the Word of God.
(3) Hence, the Bible cannot err.

Since chapters 13 has demonstrated the second premise, only the first needs support here.

Hebrews declares emphatically: "God did this so that, by two unchangeable things in which *it is impossible for God to lie*, we who have fled to take hold of the hope offered to us may be greatly encouraged" (Heb. 6:18). Paul spoke of "a faith and knowledge resting on the hope of eternal life, which *God, who does not lie*, promised before the beginning of time" (Titus 1:2). Romans asserts: "*Let God be true*, and every man a liar" (3:4). Jesus said to the Father, "Sanctify them by the truth; *your word is truth*" (John 17:17). And the psalmist declared to God: "*All your words are true*" (Ps. 119:160).

If God cannot err and the Bible is the Word of God, then it follows necessarily that the Bible cannot err.

The Argument From God the Son

The argument from the divine authority of Christ is powerful. Basically, it is this: If Jesus is the Son of God, then the Bible is the Word of God (which cannot err). Hence, to deny the Bible is the Word of God is to deny that Jesus is the Son of God (see chapter 16). The Scriptures teach that Jesus *is* the Son of God (Matt. 16:16–17; Mark 14:61–62; John 1:1; 8:58; Col. 2:9; Heb. 1:8). Therefore, the Bible is the Word of God, which cannot err.

The Argument From God the Holy Spirit

The third person of the Trinity is called "the Spirit of truth" (John 16:13), who cannot err (cf. 1 John 4:6).

(1) He who is the Source of truth cannot be in error.
(2) The Bible is an utterance of the Spirit of truth.
(3) Therefore, the Bible cannot be in error.

The authors of Scripture were moved by the Holy Spirit (2 Peter 1:20–21), and they uttered God-breathed writings (2 Tim. 3:16) that are said to have come "from the mouth of God" (Matt. 4:4). Remember what David said: "The Spirit of the LORD spoke through me; his word was on my tongue" (2 Sam. 23:2). But if this is the case, then the Bible can no more utter an untruth than can the Spirit of truth Himself.

THE OBJECTION FROM THE HUMAN NATURE OF THE BIBLE[1]

Some critics have offered a rebuttal to the above logic by noting:

(1) The Bible contains the words of humans.
(2) Humans err.
(3) Therefore, the Bible errs.

However, this does not follow, since (2a) humans do not *always* err.

Even without special divine aid, humans can avoid making errors—most anyone can write an inerrant book. Furthermore, the human authors of Scripture had divine aid (John 14:26; 2 Peter 1:20–21). As to how God can produce a perfect product through an imperfect instrument, we need only remember that it is possible to draw a straight line with a crooked stick.

Another form of the objection goes like this:

(1) The Bible is a human book.
(2) Humans can err.
(3) Therefore, the Bible can err.

In this form it would seem that both premises are true and that the conclusion follows logically from them. This notwithstanding, there is a flaw in the argument if it is intended to deny the inerrancy of the Bible.

At best, this argument only shows that the Bible *can* err, not that it actually *does* err. One could still affirm that the Bible does not err (a weaker sense of inerrancy), even if he could not conclude that the Bible cannot err (a stronger sense of inerrancy).

However, even the stronger sense of inerrancy can be preserved by making an important distinction brought out by the following argument:

(1) Insofar as the Bible is the Word of God, it cannot err.
(2) The Bible is the Word of God.
(3) Therefore, the Word of God cannot err.

Likewise, since the Bible is also the words of men it can err (but doesn't). This is no more a contradiction than to say of Christ, insofar as He was a human being, He did not know everything (Luke 2:52; Matt. 24:36). But

---

[1]For a discussion of other objections to inerrancy see chapter 27.

insofar as Christ is God, He does know everything (Job 11:7–9; Ps. 147:5). Both Christ and Scripture have two natures, and what is true of one is not necessarily true of the other. So one and the same words of Scripture can be inerrant in the strong sense (that they *cannot* err) insofar as they are the Word of God, and errorless in the weaker sense (that they *do not* err) insofar as they are the words of human beings.

OTHER CHARACTERISTICS OF THE BIBLE

The Bible contains many powerful metaphors and figures of speech about itself that help us in visualizing one or more of the above characteristics.

The Bible Is Like a Seed That Saves Us (1 Peter 1:23)

Peter wrote: "For you have been born again, not of perishable seed, but of imperishable, through the living and enduring word of God."

The Bible Is Like Milk That Nourishes Us (1 Peter 2:2)

Peter adds, "Like newborn babies, crave pure spiritual milk, so that by it you may grow up in your salvation."

The Bible Is Like Meat (Solid Food) That Satisfies Us (Hebrews 5:14)

The author of Hebrews notes about Scripture: "But solid food is for the mature, who by constant use have trained themselves to distinguish good from evil."

The Bible Is Like Water That Washes Us (Psalm 119:9; Ephesians 5:25–26)

The psalmist asks, "How can a young man keep his way pure?" He answered: "By living according to your word." Paul added, "Husbands, love your wives, just as Christ loved the church and gave himself up for her to make her holy, cleansing her by the washing with water through the word."

The Bible Is Like a Fire That Cleanses Us (Jeremiah 23:29)

Through the prophet Jeremiah: " 'Is not my word like fire,' declares the LORD."

The Bible Is Like a Hammer That Shatters Us (Jeremiah 23:29)

In the same passage, Jeremiah adds for God, "Is not my word . . . like a hammer that breaks a rock in pieces?"

The Bible Is Like a Sword That Cuts Deeply Into Us (Hebrews 4:13)

The writer of Hebrews affirms, "Nothing in all creation is hidden from God's sight. Everything is uncovered and laid bare before the eyes of him to whom we must give account."

The Bible Is Like Medicine to Keep Us From the Sickness of Sin (Psalm 119:11)

David asserts, "I have hidden your word in my heart that I might not sin against you."

The Bible Is Like a Mirror to Reflect Ourselves to Us (James 1:23–25)

James admonishes, "Anyone who listens to the word but does not do what it says is like a man who looks at his face in a mirror and, after looking at himself, goes away and immediately forgets what he looks like. But the man who looks intently into the perfect law that gives freedom, and continues to do this, not forgetting what he has heard, but doing it—he will be blessed in what he does."

The Bible Is Like a Lamp to Our Feet (Psalm 119:105)

David wrote, "Your word is a lamp to my feet and a light for my path."

The Bible Is Like a Counselor That Comforts Us (Romans 15:4)

Paul assures, "For everything that was written in the past was written to teach us, so that through endurance and the encouragement of the Scriptures we might have hope."

The Bible Is Like a Forecaster That Never Fails Us (2 Peter 1:19)

Peter observes, "We have the word of the prophets made more certain, and you will do well to pay attention to it, as to a light shining in a dark place, until the day dawns and the morning star rises in your hearts."

CONCLUSION

The internal evidence that the Bible is of divine origin is very strong. Unlike any other book in the world, the Bible bears the fingerprints of God. It has sanctity, divine authority, infallibility, indestructibility, indefatigability, indefeasibility, and inerrancy. Indeed, as we have shown, the denial of the inerrancy of the Bible is an attack on the authenticity of God the Father, the authority of God the Son, and the ministry of God the Holy Spirit. The infallibility of the Bible is as firm as the character of God, who cannot lie. The Word is like a seed that saves, milk that nourishes, meat that satisfies, water that washes, fire that cleanses, a hammer that breaks, a sword that cuts, medicine that heals, a mirror that reflects, a lamp that lights, a counselor that comforts, and a forecaster that never fails. Once again,

The grass withers and the flowers fall, but the word of our God stands forever. (Isa. 40:8)

SOURCES

Archer, Gleason. *Old Testament Quotations in the New Testament.*
Clark, Gordon. *God's Hammer: The Bible and Its Critics.*
Gaussen, Louis. *Theopneustia.*
Geisler, Norman, and William Nix. *A General Introduction to the Bible.*
Geisler, Norman, ed. *Inerrancy.*
Henry, Carl F. H., ed. *Revelation and the Bible.*
Hodge, Charles, and B. B. Warfield. *Inspiration.*
Johnson, S. Lewis. *The Old Testament in the New.*
Lindsell, Harold. *The Battle for the Bible.*
Nash, Ronald. *The Word of God and the Mind of Man.*
Packer, J. I. *"Fundamentalism" and the Word of God.*
Pasche, Rene. *The Inspiration and Authority of Scripture.*
Turretin, Francis. *The Doctrine of Scripture.*
Warfield, B. B. *The Inspiration and Authority of the Bible.*
———. *Limited Inspiration.*

CHAPTER FIFTEEN

THE HUMAN NATURE
OF THE BIBLE

The Bible is not only of divine origin (see chapters 13–14); it also has human authors, and therefore it is a human book. Indeed, it is a theanthropic book (Gk: *theos*, "God"; *anthropos*, "man"). Its primary Cause is God, but its secondary causes are human beings, and although the Bible is the Word of God, it is also the words of men.

AVOIDING TWO EXTREMES

Two extremes are to be avoided when describing the Bible: Either denying or diminishing its divine characteristics while affirming its human traits, or else affirming its divine properties while denying or diminishing its human elements. Most liberals do the former (see DeWolf, *CTLP*, 58–66) and many fundamentalists fall into the latter (Rice, *OGBBB*, 265, 285–87).[1] These two errors are the bibliological equivalents of arianism and docetism, respectively (see F. L. Cross, *ODCC*, 87, 413).

Many on the conservative end of the theological spectrum tend to forget that it is as heretical to deny Christ's humanity as it is to deny His deity; conservatives tend to neglect, if not deny in practice, the humanity of Scripture. Biblical docetism, however, is a serious doctrinal deviation, for the Bible is truly a human book, and to deny this is no less a doctrinal deviation than to deny the humanity of Christ.

---

[1]Few, if any, fundamentalist scholars would admit to denying the humanity of the Bible, but John Rice came close to it by affirming that the Scriptures are "verbally dictated" (Rice, ibid.).

THE HUMAN CHARACTERISTICS OF THE BIBLE

There are numerous human characteristics of the Bible, including its human writers, literary styles, perspectives, thought patterns, emotions, interests, and sources.

The Bible Has Human Authors

Every book in the Bible is the composition of a *human writer*, nearly forty persons in all. This includes Moses, Joshua, Samuel, Ezra, Nehemiah, David, Solomon, Agur (Prov. 30), Lemuel (Prov. 31), Asaph (various psalms), the Sons of Korah (various psalms), Isaiah, Jeremiah, Ezra, Nehemiah, Ezekiel, Daniel, Hosea, Joel, Amos, Obadiah, Jonah, Micah, Nahum, Habakkuk, Zephaniah, Haggai, Zechariah, Malachi, Matthew, Mark, Luke, John, Paul, James, Peter, and Jude. Other than these traditional authors, there are the unknown human authors of Job, Esther, and Hebrews. Like all other books in the world, the Bible had human composers.

The Bible Was Written in Human Languages

The languages of the Bible are *human languages*. Some have ventured to speak of "Holy Ghost Greek," believing God created some special language to convey His truth. However, this speculation was put to rest with the discovery of the Greek papyri manuscripts (see Deissman, *LAE*) and a better understanding of Koine Greek, the common trade language of the first century (in which the New Testament was written).

The Old Testament was also written in a human language known as Hebrew, with some small sections of Aramaic. Hebrew and Aramaic were common Semitic languages, and there is nothing nonhuman or super-human about them. God simply deemed them particularly fitting to be the vehicle by which He originally conveyed His truth to humankind (see Geisler and Nix, *GIB*, chapter 18).

The Bible Has Human Literary Styles

The Bible also utilizes different literary styles. Even readers not familiar with the original languages can detect a distinct difference in the literary ability and forms of biblical authors. Amos, a farmer from southern Israel (Judah), reflects his earthy roots in his style of speech, while Dr. Luke's use of specialized and technical terms reveals a more sophisticated training in the Greek culture (as does the wording used by the author of Hebrews).

For an exalted poetic style, the book of Isaiah stands out. By contrast, the mournful tone of Jeremiah in Lamentations is distinctive by its differences. All first-year Greek students appreciate the simple grammar and vocabulary of John the fisherman in contrast to the complex Greek of Luke. The simple fact of the matter is that not only is the Bible a human book, but it also reflects different degrees of human ability and training in the various languages in which it was written.

The Bible Uses Different Human Literary Forms

The Bible not only reflects different literary styles but it also employs various *human literary forms of speech.* These include *narrative* form, as in Samuel and Kings; *poetry,* as in Job and Psalms; *parables,* as in the Synoptic Gospels; some *allegory,* as in Galatians 4; the use of *symbols,* as in the Revelation; and *metaphors* and *similes* abound in Scripture (cf. James 1–2). Even *satire* (Matt. 19:24) and *hyperbole* are found (Col. 1:23). Like other human writings, the Bible uses a wide range of literary forms to convey its meaning.

The Bible Reflects Different Human Perspectives

The human finitude of the Bible is seen in the variety of *human perspectives* it manifests. David spoke in Psalm 23 from a shepherd's view. Kings is written from a prophetic vantage point, and Chronicles from a priestly perspective. Acts manifests a historical interest (cf. Luke 1:1–4 and Acts 1:1), and 2 Timothy reflects a pastor's heart. Unlike a modern book on astronomy, biblical writers speak from an observer's perspective when they write of the sun rising or setting (Josh. 1:15; cf. 10:13), and remember that even round numbers are used (Josh. 3:4; 4:13; 2 Chron. 4:2).

The Bible Reflects Different Human Thought Patterns

The Bible reveals *human thought patterns and processes,* including human reasoning. The book of Romans, for example, is a tightly knit logical treatise that has been used to demonstrate the principles and processes of rational thought. Acts 17:2 says, "As his custom was, Paul went into the synagogue, and on three Sabbath days he *reasoned* with them from the Scriptures."

Nothing is more human than forgetfulness. In 1 Corinthians Paul reveals this very trait, writing, "I am thankful that I did not baptize any of you except Crispus and Gaius, so no one can say that you were baptized into my name. (Yes, I also baptized the household of Stephanas; beyond that, I don't remember if I baptized anyone else)" (1 Cor. 1:14–16).[2]

---

[2]There is no error affirmed here. Paul affirms the truth about what he could remember when he could remember it. And what he remembered was true.

The Bible Reveals Human Emotions

The Bible does not hide the *emotions* of the authors. The apostle Paul, for example, expresses great anguish over Israel, saying, "I have great sorrow and unceasing anguish in my heart" (Rom. 9:2). He also reveals great anger over the Galatian error, declaring, "You foolish Galatians! Who has bewitched you? Before your very eyes Jesus Christ was clearly portrayed as crucified" (Gal. 3:1). Melancholy and loneliness are manifest in his last prison days (2 Tim. 4:9–16). Of course, joy is expressed in various passages like the following: "In all my prayers for all of you, I always pray with joy" (Phil. 1:4).

The writers of Scripture were not passive androids; they were real human beings, and their emotion is expressed in their books.

The Bible Manifests Specific Human Interests

The human interests of the Bible are revealed in the choice of topics as well as the selections of images to convey them. Luke had a medical interest, as indicated by his use of medical terms (see Ramsay, *LP*). Hosea had a distinctive rural interest, as did Amos, the herdsman from Tekoa (Amos 1:1). James's many images from the natural world betray an interest in nature (cf. James 1–2). David's years of shepherding are clear in his writing, and so on. The presentation of the material in each biblical book is colored by the experiences and interests of its author.

The Bible Expresses Human Culture

Being basically a Semitic book, the Bible is filled with expressions and practices of its Hebrew culture. The common means of greeting by "kissing" is one example: "Greet all the brothers with a holy kiss," Paul exhorted (1 Thess. 5:26). Likewise, a woman's veil as a sign of her respect for her husband is a manifestation of human culture, for "every woman who prays or prophesies with her head uncovered dishonors her head—it is just as though her head were shaved" (1 Cor. 11:5).

Numerous other Near-Eastern cultural practices are indicated in Scripture, including washing feet upon entering a home (cf. John 13), shaking off the dust of one's feet as a sign of condemnation (Luke 10:11), and reclining (not sitting) at meals (John 13:23).

The Bible Utilizes Other Written Human Sources

While many elements in the Bible came by direct revelation from God, like the Ten Commandments (Ex. 20) and messages to the prophets (cf. Dan. 2:28–30), nonetheless, sometimes God revealed Himself indirectly.

Since all truth is God's truth, sometimes the biblical author found God's truth embedded in *human sources*. The Old Testament often used non-canonical writings as sources; the Book of Jashar (Josh. 10:13) and the Book of the Wars of the LORD (Num. 21:14) are examples. "The records of Samuel the seer . . . Nathan the prophet . . . and Gad the seer" may also fit in this category (1 Chron. 29:29).

In the New Testament, Luke is believed to have referred to written sources about Christ available to him (Luke 1:1–4).[3] Paul quoted non-Christian poets three times (Acts 17:28; 1 Cor. 15:33; Titus 1:12); Jude cited material from the noncanonical sources of the Assumption of Moses and the Book of Enoch (Jude 9, 14). These citations do not guarantee the truthfulness of everything in the source but only what is cited. Of course, ultimately all truth comes from God, whatever the immediate source may be.

THE BIBLE IS WITHOUT ERROR

There is one human characteristic the Bible does not have: errors. Although a more extended discussion of the inerrancy of the Bible is found later (see chapter 27), the basic outline of its errorlessness will be stated here.

The Original Text Is Without Error

The logic of inerrancy is straightforward:

(1) God cannot err.
(2) The Bible is God's Word.
(3) Therefore, the Bible cannot err.

Since the Scriptures are breathed out by God (2 Tim. 3:16–17), and since God cannot breathe out falsehood, it follows that the Bible cannot contain any falsehood.

The Copies Are Not Without Error

Christians only claim that God breathed out everything in the original text, not everything in the copies. Divine inspiration and inerrancy, therefore, applies to the original text, not to every detail of every copy. The copies are without error only insofar as they are copied correctly, and they *were* copied with great care and a very high degree of accuracy.

Christians believe that God in His providence preserved the copies from all substantial error; in fact, the degree of accuracy is greater than that of

---

[3]However, these could be the canonical gospels of Matthew and Mark, which may have been written earlier than Luke's gospel.

any other book from the ancient world, exceeding 99 percent (see Geisler and Nix, *GIB*, chapter 22). The reasons for this amazing accuracy are: (1) we have many more manuscripts of the Bible than for other books from the ancient world, (2) the manuscripts date more closely to the originals, and (3) they were copied accurately.

There are, however, some minor copyists' errors in the biblical manuscripts—two examples will suffice: Second Chronicles 22:2 says Ahaziah was forty-two, yet 2 Kings 8:26 asserts that Ahaziah was twenty-two. He could not have been forty-two (a copyist error), or he would have been older than his father (see NIV and NKJV). Also, 2 Chronicles 9:25 affirms that Solomon had four thousand horse stalls, but 1 Kings 4:26 says there were forty thousand horse stalls, which would have been far more than needed for the twelve thousand horsemen he had (see NIV and NKJV).

It is important to note of these copyist errors that:

(1) No original manuscript has ever been found with an error in it.
(2) Errors are relatively rare in the copies.
(3) In most cases we know which wording is wrong from the context or parallel passages.
(4) In no case does an error affect any doctrine of Scripture;
(5) Errors vouch for the accuracy of the copying process, since the scribes who copied them knew there were errors in the manuscripts but were duty-bound to copy what the text before them said.
(6) Errors don't affect the central message of the Bible.

In fact, one can get a message with errors in it, yet 100 percent of the message comes through clearly. For example, suppose you received a message from Western Union that read as follows:

Y#u have won ten million dollars!

No doubt you would gladly pick up your money. And if the telegram read in the following way, you would have no doubt at all:

Yo# have won ten million dollars!
You #ave won ten million dollars!
You h#ve won ten million dollars!

Why are we *more* sure if there are *more* errors? Because each error is in a different place, and with it we get another confirmation of every other letter in the original.

Three things are important to note. *First*, even with one line, error and all, 100 percent of the message comes through. *Second*, the more lines, the more errors. But the more errors, the more sure we are of what the intended message really is. *Third*, there are hundreds of times more biblical manuscripts than there are lines in the above example. And there is a greater percentage of error in this telegram than in the collated biblical manuscripts.

Christ and the Bible: A Good Analogy

No analogy is perfect. Good ones, however, have crucial similarities. Of course, all analogies have differences, or they would not be analogies.

Some Strong Similarities

Both Christ and Scripture are theanthropic. They involve three major factors:

(1) *Both are called the Word of God.* Christ is the Living Word (John 1:1), and the Bible is the written Word (John 10:34–35).

(2) *Each has two natures,* one divine and one human.

(3) *The two natures of each are united by one medium.* To borrow a term from Christology (see volume 2), both have a kind of "hypostatic union." The two natures of Christ are united in one *person.* And the two natures of Christ are united in one set of *propositions* (i.e., sentences). Likewise,

(4) *Both Christ and Scripture are without flaw.* Christ is without sin (Heb. 4:15; 2 Cor. 5:21), and the Bible is without error (Matt. 22:29; Heb. 6:18; cf. John 17:17).

Some Significant Differences

The strong similarities between God's living and written Words notwithstanding, some significant differences must be noted lest one fall into bibliolatry. Unlike Christ who is God,

(1) *The Bible is not God.*

(2) Hence, *the Bible should not be worshiped.*

The difference is that the unifying medium of Christ's two natures is God, the Second Person of the Godhead, whereas the unifying factor in the Bible is the human words. While in Scripture there is a divine and human concurrence, this is not God, and in Christ the unity is found in the one Person who is both God and man. Hence, God is to be revered (worshiped) but the Bible should only be respected, not revered.

ANSWERING SEVERAL CRITICAL OBJECTIONS

Building on the clear biblical teaching that it is a human book, critics sometimes argue that the Bible is an errant book; that is, they claim the Bible has errors.

The Objection That Human Books Err

This objection is based on the old adage "to err is human" and takes two forms, strong and weak. The first form contains a false premise, and the second form a non sequitur.

Statement of the Strong Form

Some opponents of biblical inerrancy insist that if the Bible is a human book, then it must have errors in it, since humans make errors. More formally put,

(1) The Bible is a human book.
(2) Human books always contain errors.
(3) Therefore, the Bible contains errors.

Response to the Strong Form

Put in the strong form, the minor (second) premise is false. It wrongly states, "Human books *always* contain errors." They don't; virtually anyone can write a book without error, and if mere humans can write errorless books, then how much more can humans do so who are under the special providential care of God to preserve them from all error, as were the writers of Holy Scripture (2 Tim. 3:16–17; 2 Peter 1:20–21)?

Statement of the Weak Form

The weaker form of the argument goes as follows:

(1) The Bible is a human book.
(2) Human books sometimes contain errors.
(3) Hence, the Bible contains errors.

Response to the Weak Form

As is plain to see, the conclusion does not follow, since the Bible could be an exception—the conclusion overdraws the premises. That books sometimes, even often, err does not mean there are errors in the Bible. Again, the fact that the Bible was penned by humans who came under the special providential care of God to preserve them from all error is sufficient to explain why it is an exception to the rule.

The Objection That Human Books Can Err

A more sophisticated criticism of inerrancy argues from the nature of human free will. This can best be understood by contrasting it with a typical statement of the logic of inerrancy, which goes like this:

(1) God cannot err.
(2) The Bible is God's Word.
(3) Therefore, the Bible cannot err.

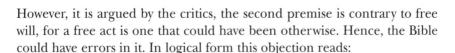

However, it is argued by the critics, the second premise is contrary to free will, for a free act is one that could have been otherwise. Hence, the Bible could have errors in it. In logical form this objection reads:

(1) Human beings can err.
(2) The Bible is a human book.
(3) Therefore, the Bible can err.

Response to the Objection That Human Books Can Err

There are three possible responses that inerrantists can give to this objection. The first accepts this definition of free will and holds to the weak form of inerrancy; the second rejects this definition of free will and holds to the strong form of inerrancy; and the third accepts this definition of free will but retains a strong form of inerrancy by making a crucial distinction.

Response One: Accept the Weak Form of Inerrancy
This response accepts that

(1) humans can err.
(2) The Bible is a human book.
(3) Therefore, the Bible *can* err.

However, this response simply denies that the Bible *does* err.
This response restates the logic of inerrancy this way:

(1) The Bible is a human book.
(2) It is possible that humans are always telling the truth.
(3) Hence, it is possible that the Bible is always telling the truth.

Therefore, even in this weaker form one may hold to this strong view of free will and hold a weaker view of inerrancy.

Response Two: Accept the Strong Form of Inerrancy
Another possible response is to accept the strong form of inerrancy, meaning to believe that the Bible *cannot* err (not merely *does not* err) and deny this strong form of free will. Strong Calvinists (see volume 3) hold this view (Arminians hold the former view, acceptance of free will and weaker inerrancy). On this second model one need only insist that when the biblical authors wrote their books (if not at all other times) they were not free to write error, since God was moving on them in an irresistible way to preserve them from it.

Response Three: Accept Both a Strong View of Free Will and a Strong View of Inerrancy
There is one more option open to a strong inerrantist. He may hold both that

(1) the Bible cannot err, and that

(2) the human authors of Scripture were *free* to err when they wrote their biblical books.

This is possible by making an important distinction between the divine and human natures of Scripture. Let's apply it first to God's Living Word (who also has two natures) and then also to God's written Word.

As God, Christ could not get tired; as man, He could. As God, Christ could not get hungry; as man, He could. As God, He could not die; as man, He could. Also, as God, Christ could not sin; as man, He could (since He was free), but He did not (Heb. 4:15; 2 Cor. 5:21). While some evangelicals (usually extreme Calvinists) deny that Christ could have sinned (see volume 2), many moderate Calvinists and all consistent Arminians hold that Christ could have sinned but did not.

How is this possible? Because Christ has two natures, and, thus, a distinction must be made between them. Hence, sin is impossible insofar as Christ is God, and it is possible insofar as He is man. Likewise, the same reasoning applies to God's written Word, which also has two natures, namely,

(1) insofar as it is the Word of God, the Bible cannot err, but

(2) insofar as it is the words of men, the Bible can err (but did not).

Since one and the same words of the Bible are both God's and man's, one must distinguish which relationship is in view. This is not a violation of the law of noncontradiction (see chapter 5), since to be a contradiction one must both affirm and deny the same thing at the same time *in the same relationship.*[4]

Adaptation to Finitude Without Accommodation to Error

There is a mysterious theanthropic union between the two natures of Scripture, just as there is between the two natures of Christ. In both cases one must ask two questions of each, since both have two distinct natures. One cannot simply ask, "Could Christ sin?" He must ask:

(1) "Could Christ sin *as God?*" (No) and

(2) "Could He sin *as man?*" (Yes, but He did not)

Likewise, two questions, not one, must be asked of the Bible:

(1) "Could it err as God's Word?" (No, God cannot err), and

(2) "Could it err as man's word?" (Yes, but it did not.)

---

[4]There is a direct parallel here between the question of God's predestination and human free will. Both are possible without contradiction, provided that we distinguish between the same action being determined from the standpoint of the foreknowledge of God and yet being free from the vantage point of human free choice (see volume 2, part 2).

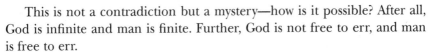

This is not a contradiction but a mystery—how is it possible? After all, God is infinite and man is finite. Further, God is not free to err, and man is free to err.

The answer to this question lies in what orthodox theologians have often called divine "accommodations," but which we (because of misuse of this term) prefer to label divine *adaptation*.

Obviously, if there is to be union between God and man at any level, it is the infinite God who must adapt to finite man. This is possible because there is an analogy between the two (see chapters 4 and 9); without similarity, unity would not be possible. This is true no less in God's Living Word than in His written Word. God had to condescend to take on humanity in the Incarnation (see volume 2), and He had to condescend to make possible a unity of His Word and man's words in Scripture. Indeed, the concurrence between each affirmation (or denial) in Scripture is a divinely initiated one. It can be summarized in this contrast between the orthodox view of divine adaptation to finitude and the unorthodox view of divine accommodation to error (see Geisler, *BECA*, 1–3).

Adaptation	Accommodation
• Adaptation to Finite Understanding	• Accommodation to Finite Error
• Finitude of Man	• Sinfulness of Man
• Partial Truths	• Actual Errors
• Truth *Disclosed* in Human Language	• Truth *Disguised* in Human Language
• Condescension of God's Truth	• Compromise of God's Truth
• Anthropomorphisms Necessary	• Myths Necessary
• We Can Know God's *Nature*	• We Can Know God's *Activity*
• We Know What *Really* Is	• We Know What *Seems* to Be

The Objection That Human Books Are Fallen

This objection, springing from the neo-orthodox theology of Karl Barth, insists that the Bible, like all human books, is a fallen book. Reasoning from a strong view of human depravity, this position can be summarized as follows:

(1) Total depravity extends to all human activity, including human language.
(2) The Bible is written in human language.
(3) Hence, human depravity extends to the Bible.

This would mean that the Bible, being the human book that it is, is a depraved book. As such, it would be infected by both error and sin.

Of course, scholars from the Barthian school hasten to add that in spite of its fallenness the Bible is both a record of divine revelation (fallible as it may be) and an instrument through which God speaks to us, just as the original voice is still heard through a broken record. So in spite of the fact that the Bible is a human, fallen, and errant book, says this view, nonetheless, it is the instrument through which God speaks to us today.

In response to this neo-orthodox presentation of Scripture, we must point out a number of crucial errors.

First, this view is contrary to what the Bible claims for itself, namely, to be an infallible revelation from God, not a mere fallible record of God's revelation (see chapters 13 and 27).

Second, this position is contrary to the virtually unanimous and continuous view of the great Fathers and teachers of the Christian church up to modern times (see chapters 17–18).

Third, this view is based on a self-defeating disjunction of fact and value that springs from Immanuel Kant (see Geisler, "K" in *BECA*).

Fourth, this teaching is contrary to the biblical assertion that even fallen human beings are made in the image of God (Gen. 9:6; James 3:9), which, although effaced by sin, is not erased by sin.

Fifth, this perspective is grounded in the faulty logic that God's revelation can be in acts but not in words. It affirms that even though God is not dead, He is mute. But surely a God who can create beings that can speak, can speak Himself (see chapter 9).

Sixth, Barth believed that Christ was God incarnated in human flesh. If so, then when Jesus spoke on earth He was speaking the words of God. But if Barth is right about the fallenness of all human language, then when Jesus spoke in human language His words were fallen, errant, and sinful. As the apostle Paul would say, "Perish the thought!"

Seventh, Barth's view denies the validity of general revelation (see chapter 4), which the Bible affirms (Ps. 19:1f; Rom. 1:19–20; Rom. 2:12–15; Acts 14:15–17; 17:24–27), for God's general revelation is available and "clearly" seen even by fallen human beings who refuse it only at their eternal peril (Rom. 1:20; 2:12).

CONCLUSION

The Bible is a thoroughly human book. It has human authors, is written in human languages, and shows virtually every human characteristic of any other book—except that it is without error. But its errorlessness does not make it any less human than Jesus Christ, who was completely human, yet without sin. In fact, if anything, *it is not the lack of error and sinfulness that diminishes one's humanity; it is the presence of them.* Adam before the Fall as well as the saints in heaven lacked sin but was not less human for it. Among all books known to humankind, the Bible is as human as people are, but without error. How is this possible? By adaptation to finitude without accommodation to error.

SOURCES

Barth, Karl. *Church Dogmatics,* Volume I.
Brunner, Emil. *Revelation and Reason.*
Clark, Gordon. *God's Hammer: The Bible and Its Critics.*
Cross, F. L., ed. *The Oxford Dictionary of the Christian Church.*
Deissman, Adolph. *Light From the Ancient East.*
DeWolf, Harold. *The Case for Theology in Liberal Perspective.*
Geisler, Norman. *Baker Encyclopedia of Christian Apologetics.*
———. *Inerrancy.*
———. "Kant" in *Baker Encyclopedia of Christian Apologetics.*
Geisler, Norman, and Thomas Howe. *When Critics Ask.*
Geisler, Norman, and William Nix. *A General Introduction to the Bible.*
Henry, Carl. *God, Revelation, and Authority.*
Ramsay, Sir William. *Luke the Physician.*
Rice, John R. *Our God-Breathed Book—The Bible.*
Warfield, B. B. *Limited Inspiration.*

CHAPTER SIXTEEN

JESUS AND THE BIBLE

J esus' view of the Bible is of particular interest to evangelicals, since He is held to be God Incarnate (see volume 2), and, hence, whatever He affirms has divine authority. Thus whatever Jesus taught about the Bible is the last word on the topic.

Granting that God exists (see chapter 2) and that miracles are possible (see chapter 3), even non-evangelicals are hard-pressed to avoid the conclusion that Jesus speaks with divine authority—at least if one accepts the authenticity of the Gospel accounts (see chapter 26). If the Gospels present accurately what Jesus taught, and if what He taught was confirmed by miracles to have divine authority (cf. John 3:2; Acts 2:22; Heb. 2:3–4), then what Jesus taught about the origin and nature of Scripture is divinely authoritative.

WHAT JESUS TAUGHT ABOUT THE OLD TESTAMENT

Since the New Testament was not yet written, Jesus' words apply directly only to the Old Testament. However, since Jesus made certain promises to the apostles about New Testament truth, and since the apostolic writings were considered on a par with the Old Testament, then what Jesus taught about the divine authority of the Old Testament applies indirectly to the New Testament as well (see below).

Jesus Affirmed Its Divine Authority

Over and over Jesus declared, "*It is written*" (Matt. 4:4, 7, 10). He instructed, "Man does not live on bread alone, but on every word that comes from the mouth of God" (Matt. 4:4). Jesus even appealed to Scripture as the highest authority by which Satan can be rebuked: "Away from me, Satan! For *it is written*: Worship the Lord thy God, and serve him only" (Matt. 4:10).

Jesus Affirmed Its Imperishability

"Do not think that I have come to abolish the Law or the Prophets; I have not come to abolish them but to fulfill them. I tell you the truth, until heaven and earth disappear, not the smallest letter, not the least stroke of a pen, will by any means disappear from the Law until everything is accomplished" (Matt. 5:17–18).

Jesus Asserted Its Unbreakability

"If he called them 'gods,' to whom the word of God came—and *the Scripture cannot be broken* . . ." (John 10:35). (This is the equivalent of claiming that the Bible is infallible.)

Jesus Declared Its Ultimate Supremacy

The Bible is exalted above all human instruction. Jesus said to the Jewish leaders, "Why do you break the command of God for the sake of your tradition? . . . Thus you nullify the word of God for the sake of your tradition" (Matt. 15:3, 6).

Jesus Affirmed Its Factual Inerrancy

"Jesus replied, 'You are in error because you do not know the Scriptures or the power of God' " (Matt. 22:29). Again, Jesus said to the Father, "Sanctify them by the truth; your word is truth" (John 17:17). In brief, the Bible is wholly true, without any error.

Jesus Insisted on Its Historical Reliability

Jesus even affirmed highly disputed passages, such as the Flood of Noah's time and Jonah and the great fish, as historically true. "*For [just] as Jonah was three days and three nights in the belly of a huge fish,* so the Son of Man will be three days and three nights in the heart of the earth" (Matt. 12:40; cf. 16:4). Further, "as it was in the days of Noah, so it will be at the coming of the Son of Man. For in the days before the flood, people were eating and drinking, marrying and giving in marriage, up to the day Noah entered the ark" (Matt. 24:37–38; cf. 10:15; 12:42; 19:4–6).

Jesus Affirmed Its Scientific Accuracy

Even on the highly disputed matter of the origin of the world and of humankind, Jesus insisted on the truthfulness of Scripture. He referred to the creation of the universe, saying, "Those will be days of distress unequaled from *the beginning, when God created the world,* until now—and never to be equaled again" (Mark 13:19).

Jesus also affirmed the creation of Adam and Eve, saying, "Haven't you read . . . that *at the beginning the Creator 'made them male and female,'* and said, 'For this reason a man will leave his father and mother and be united to his wife, and the two will become one flesh'?" (Matt. 19:4–5). He added elsewhere, "I have spoken to you of *earthly things* and you do not believe; how then will you believe if I speak of heavenly things?" (John 3:12).

The authority of the Bible is confirmed by the authority of Jesus; if He is the Son of God, then the Bible is the Word of God. Indeed, even if Jesus is only a prophet of God, the Bible is the Word of God. Only if one rejects the divine authority of Christ can he consistently reject the divine authority of the Scriptures, for if Jesus is telling the truth, then it is true that the Bible is God's Word.

JESUS AND THE NEW TESTAMENT AUTHORS AFFIRMED THE SCOPE OF THE OLD TESTAMENT

Jesus affirmed the authority of the whole Jewish Old Testament, which is the same as the Protestant Old Testament (of thirty-nine books), although the books are numbered and ordered differently (see chapter 28). This affirmation is evident from several truths.

Jesus Used Phrases That Encompass the Whole Old Testament

Jesus employed several terms that refer to the Old Testament as a whole; three in particular come to mind. *First,* "*law and the prophets*" or its equivalent (e.g., "Moses and all the Prophets") is employed about a dozen times in the New Testament. Jesus' use of it clearly refers to the whole Old Testament (Luke 24:27; cf. 24:44).

Second, the term "the Scriptures" is utilized by Jesus and other New Testament writers to refer to the whole Old Testament. Two cases in point are found in John (5:39; 10:35).

Third, Jesus used a phrase equivalent to our "from Genesis to Revelation" to refer to the entire Old Testament: "And so upon you will come all the righteous blood that has been shed on earth, *from the blood of righteous Abel to the blood of Zechariah* son of Berekiah, whom you murdered between the temple and the altar" (Matt. 23:35).

Jesus Referred to Most of the Individual Books of the Old Testament

According to the Jewish numbering of the Old Testament there were twenty-two (or twenty-four) books, depending on whether Ruth was considered part of Judges and Lamentations part of Jeremiah. Of the twenty-two books, Jesus and His disciples, who wrote the New Testament, referred to eighteen (see Geisler and Nix, *GIB*, chapter 4).

Jesus Referred to the Old Testament as a Whole

Jesus indicated that the whole Old Testament is the Word of God in phrases like "the Law and the Prophets" (the entire Old Testament canon): "Do not think that I have come to abolish the Law and the Prophets; I have not come to abolish them but to fulfill them" (Matt. 5:17). Also, "beginning with Moses and all the Prophets, he explained to them what was said in *all the Scriptures* concerning himself" (Luke 24:27). Once He referred to all the books from Genesis to 2 Chronicles (the last book in the Jewish listing of the Old Testament): "And so upon you will come all the righteous blood that has been shed on earth, from the blood of righteous Abel to the blood of Zechariah son of Berekiah" (Matt. 23:35). This is the equivalent of our phrase, "from Genesis to Malachi."

Jesus Promised the Divine Authority of the New Testament

Not only did Jesus confirm the Old Testament to be the Word of God, He also promised the same for the New Testament, affirming that the Holy Spirit would teach the apostles "all things" and lead them into "all truth." He announced, "The Counselor, the Holy Spirit, whom the Father will send in my name, will teach you all things and will remind you of everything I have said to you" (John 14:26). He added, "But when he, the Spirit of truth, comes, he will guide you into all truth" (John 16:13).

The Apostles Claimed This Divine Authority for Their Words

Jesus' handpicked apostles understood His claims and their role in fulfilling them, for they too claimed to speak with the authority of God, as is evident from the claims made in their books. Paul declared, "The gospel I preached is not something that man made up. *I did not receive it from any man, nor was I taught it; rather, I received it by revelation from Jesus Christ*" (Gal. 1:11–12). In 1 Corinthians he added, "*What I am writing to you is the Lord's command*" (1 Cor. 14:37).

John claimed, "That which was from the beginning, *which we have heard, which we have seen with our eyes*, which we have looked at and our hands have touched—this we proclaim concerning the Word of life" (1 John 1:1). Hence, he insisted, *"We are from God, and whoever knows God listens to us;* but whoever is not from God does not listen to us. This is how we recognize the Spirit of truth and the spirit of falsehood" (1 John 4:6).

Peter insisted that what he wrote was from God, just like the Old Testament prophets: "Above all, you must understand that no prophecy of Scripture came about by the prophet's own interpretation. For prophecy never had its origin in the will of man, *but men spoke from God as they were carried along by the Holy Spirit"* (2 Peter 1:20–21). He added, "We did not follow cleverly invented stories when we told you about the power and coming of our Lord Jesus Christ, but *we were eyewitnesses of his majesty. . . . We ourselves heard this voice that came from heaven when we were with him on the sacred mountain"* (2 Peter 1:16, 18).

Paul Cited the Gospels

Paul cited the words of Jesus from the Gospel of Luke (10:7; cf. Matt. 10:10), calling them "Scripture" right alongside the Old Testament: "The Scripture says, 'Do not muzzle the ox while it is treading out the grain,' and 'The worker deserves his wages' " (1 Tim. 5:18).

Peter Acknowledged Paul's Letters As Scripture

Peter wrote, "Bear in mind that our Lord's patience means salvation, just as our dear brother Paul also wrote you with the wisdom that God gave him. He writes the same way in all his letters, speaking in them of these matters. *His letters* contain some things that are hard to understand, which ignorant and unstable people distort, as they do the *other Scriptures,* to their own destruction" (2 Peter 3:15–16, emphasis added).

The New Testament Is the Only Authentic Record of Apostolic Teaching

There are few other sources that even claim to record apostolic teaching not found in the New Testament, and these are apocryphal (see chapter 28), being composed by non-apostles a century or more after the time of Christ. The only historically reliable (see chapter 25) first-century record of what Jesus and His apostles taught is found in the New Testament.

So *the New Testament too is confirmed to be the Word of God.* Therefore, the Old Testament was directly confirmed by Jesus to have divine authority, and the New Testament was indirectly confirmed to have the same. Thus, the whole Bible, Old and New Testaments, is confirmed by Christ to be the Word of the Living God.

CHRIST AND THE CRITICS

To the everlasting embarrassment of Bible critics, at least those who claim to be followers of Christ, Jesus affirmed exactly the opposite of what much of negative "higher criticism" teaches. The following are a crucial sampling of the topics on which there is a clash between Christ and His detractors.

Jesus Affirmed that Daniel Was a Prophet, Not a Mere Historian

Many critics insist that Daniel was a historian, not a predictive prophet, who wrote around 165 B.C.—*after* the events he announced about Babylon, Medo-Persia, Greece, and Rome (Dan. 2, 7). Jesus, however, claimed that Daniel was a prophet who predicted things in advance, saying, "So when you see standing in the holy place 'the abomination that causes desolation,' spoken of through *the prophet Daniel*—let the reader understand—then let those who are in Judea flee to the mountains" (Matt. 24:15–16). Jesus went on to give a detailed prediction about the destruction of Jerusalem almost four decades in advance.

Jesus Confirmed That God Created Adam and Eve

Most Bible critics believe that the first human being evolved from lower forms of life. But in response to a question on the relationship between a husband and a wife, Jesus established the basis for the marriage of the first couple, whom He said were created by God: "Haven't you read . . . that at the beginning the Creator 'made them male and female,' and said, 'For this reason a man will leave his father and mother and be united to his wife, and the two will become one flesh'?" (Matt. 19:4–5).

Jesus Affirmed That Jonah Was Swallowed by a Great Fish

Many critics deny the story of Jonah and the fish, calling it a myth. Jesus, however, took it as literally true, comparing it with His own literal death and resurrection: "For *as Jonah was* three days and three nights in the belly of a huge fish, so the Son of Man will be three days and three nights in the heart of the earth" (Matt. 12:40).

Jesus Verified That the World Was Drowned by a Flood

Old Testament critics have long denied the historicity of the first eleven chapters of Genesis, especially that of Noah's Flood. However, Jesus affirmed it as true, comparing it with His own literal second coming: "*As it was* in the days of Noah, so it will be at the coming of the Son of Man. For in the days before the flood, people were eating and drinking, marrying and giving in marriage, up to the day Noah entered the ark; and they knew nothing about what would happen until the flood came and took them all away. That is how it will be at the coming of the Son of Man" (Matt. 24:37–39).

Jesus Maintained That There Was One Isaiah, Not Two

Old Testament critics have long held that there were at least two prophets named Isaiah, the first who wrote chapters 1–39 and the second who wrote chapters 40–66. One reason prompting this is the disbelief the critics have regarding miracles (see chapter 3). Since Isaiah refers to King Cyrus, who was not born until long after the first section of Isaiah was written, skeptics, on purely natural grounds, feel it necessary to postdate the second section after the time of Cyrus to account for the mention of his name.

However, Jesus quoted from both sections of Isaiah, referring them to one prophet. In Luke 4:17–20 Jesus cites Isaiah 61:1–2 and in Mark 7:6 He quotes Isaiah 29:13. What is more, one disciple whom Jesus taught cites from both sections of Isaiah in the same passage, referring both quotes to one and the same prophet named Isaiah (John 12:37–41; cf. Isa. 6:10; 53:1).

Jesus Confirmed David Wrote Psalms Ascribed to Him

Most Old Testament critics deny that David wrote the seventy-plus psalms attributed to him, claiming that he wrote few, if any. Yet Jesus cites one of the disputed psalms (Ps. 110:1) and attributes it to King David, asking the Jewish leaders, "How is it then that David, speaking by the Spirit, calls him 'Lord'? For he says, " 'The Lord said to my Lord: "Sit at my right hand until I put your enemies under your feet.' " If then David calls him 'Lord,' how then can he be his son?" (Matt. 22:43–45).

Jesus and His Disciples Affirmed Many Other Old Testament Persons and Events

The most disputed sections of the Old Testament were personally validated by Christ and His disciples—whom He taught. Of these sections, some of which are mentioned above, they affirmed something in every one of the most disputed chapters in the Old Testament (Gen. 1–22):

1. Creation of the universe (Gen. 1 →John 1:3; Col. 1:16).
2. Creation of Adam and Eve (Gen. 1–2 →1 Tim. 2:13–14).
3. Marriage of Adam and Eve (Gen. 2 →1 Tim. 2:13).
4. Temptation of the woman (Gen. 3 →1 Tim. 2:14).

5. Disobedience of Adam (Gen. 3 →Rom. 5:12; 1 Cor. 15:22).
6. Sacrifices of Abel and Cain (Gen. 4 →Heb. 11:4).
7. Murder of Abel by Cain (Gen. 4 →1 John 3:12).
8. Birth of Seth (Gen. 4 →Luke 3:38).
9. Translation of Enoch (Gen. 5 →Heb. 11:5).
10. Marriage before the Flood (Gen. 6 →Luke 17:27).
11. The Flood and destruction of man (Gen. 7 →Matt. 24:39).
12. Preservation of Noah and his family (Gen. 8–9 →2 Peter 2:5).
13. Genealogy of Shem (Gen. 10 →Luke 3:35–36).
14. Birth of Abraham (Gen. 11 →Luke 3:34).
15. Call of Abraham (Gen. 12–13 →Heb. 11:8).
16. Tithes to Melchizedek (Gen. 14 →Heb. 7:1–3).
17. Justification of Abraham (Gen. 15 →Rom. 4:3).
18. Ishmael (Gen. 16 →Gal. 4:21–26).
19. Promise of Isaac (Gen. 17 →Heb. 11:18).
20. Lot and Sodom (Gen. 18–19 →Luke 17:29).
21. Abraham's sojourn in the Land (Gen 20 →Heb. 11:9).
22. Birth of Isaac (Gen. 21 →Acts 7:8).
23. Offering of Isaac (Gen. 22 →Heb. 11:17).[1]
24. The burning bush (Ex. 3:2–6 →Luke 20:37).
25. Exodus through the Red Sea (Ex. 14:22 →1 Cor. 10:1–2).
26. Provision of water and manna (Ex. 16:4; 17:6 →1 Cor. 10:3–5).
27. Lifting up the serpent in the wilderness (Num. 21:9 →John 3:14).
28. Fall of Jericho (Joshua 6:12–25 →Heb. 11:30).
29. Miracles of Elijah (1 Kings 17:1, 18:1 →James 5:17–18).
30. Jonah in the great fish (Jonah 2 →Matt. 12:40).
31. Three Hebrew youths in the furnace (Dan. 3 →Heb. 11:34).
32. Daniel in the lion's den (Dan. 6 →Heb. 11:33).
33. Slaying of Zechariah (2 Chron. 24:20–22 →Matt. 23:35).

In light of the evidence, the choice is clear: Christ or the critics? What Jesus affirms, they deny. But if Jesus is the Son of God, then the Bible is the Word of God, including what it says about these authors and events. And if the Bible is not the Word of God, then Christ is not the Son of God. The two Words of God, the Living and the written, are tied together.

A RESPONSE TO THE CRITICAL THEORIES

In addition to denying the historicity of the Gospel accounts (see chapter 26), critics have proposed two basic ways to avoid the logic of the above argument. Some embrace the accommodation theory and others hold to the limitation theory.

---

[1]The following are a representative sample of major events in the rest of the Old Testament that are cited as authentic by Jesus or His disciples in the New Testament.

Arguments for the Accommodation Theory

As shown above, Jesus expressed a high view of Scripture in the New Testament, including its divine authority (Matt. 4:4, 7, 10), imperishability (Matt. 5:17–18), inspiration (Matt. 22:43), unbreakability (John 10:35), status as the Word of God (John 10:34–35), supremacy (Matt. 15:3, 6), inerrancy (Matt. 22:29; John 17:17), historical reliability (Matt. 24:37–38; Matt. 12:40), and scientific accuracy (Matt. 19:4–5).

In order to avoid the conclusion that Jesus was actually affirming all this to be true, some negative critics insist that He was merely accommodating Himself to the accepted Jewish belief of the day. Allegedly, since His primary concern was spiritual, Jesus avoided any attempt to debunk their false views; rather, He merely overlooked them and used them as a starting point to convey His own spiritual and moral message. This "accommodation theory," stemming from Johann Semler (see chapter 19), is seriously flawed for several reasons.

Accommodation to Error Is Contrary to the Pattern of Jesus' Life

Everything that is known about Jesus' life and teaching reveals that He never accommodated what He knew to be true to the false teaching of the day. Indeed, He did just the opposite.

First, Jesus rebuked those who accepted Jewish teaching that contradicted the Bible, declaring, "And why do you break the command of God for the sake of your tradition? . . . Thus *you nullify the word of God for the sake of your tradition*" (Matt. 15:3, 6).

Second, Jesus often set His word against false views about the Bible. For instance, in His Sermon on the Mount, Jesus affirmed emphatically, "*You have heard* that it was said to the people long ago, 'Do not murder, and anyone who murders will be subject to judgment.' *But I tell you* that anyone who is angry with his brother will be subject to judgment" (Matt. 5:21–22). This, or the similar formula of "It has been said. . . . But I say unto you . . ." is repeated over and over in subsequent verses (cf. Matt. 5:23–48).

Third, Jesus rebuked Nicodemus, saying, "*You are Israel's teacher . . . and do you not understand these things?*" (John 3:10). This is far from accommodation to his false views.

Fourth, speaking specifically about their erroneous view of Scripture, Jesus told the Sadducees bluntly that they were mistaken: "*You are in error* because you do not know the Scriptures or the power of God" (Matt. 22:29).

Fifth, Jesus' words of denunciation to the Pharisees were scarcely accommodating: "*Woe to you, blind guides! . . .* Woe to you, teachers of the law and Pharisees, you hypocrites! . . . You blind guides! You strain out a gnat but swallow a camel. Woe to you, teachers of the law and Pharisees, you hypocrites! . . . Woe to you, teachers of the law and Pharisees, you hypocrites! . . . You snakes! You brood of vipers! How will you escape being condemned to hell?" (Matt. 23:16–33).

Sixth, Jesus did not accommodate false beliefs and practices in the temple. The Bible says, "So he made a whip out of cords, and drove all from the temple area, both sheep and cattle; he scattered the coins of the money-changers and overturned their tables. To those who sold doves he said, '*Get these out of here! How dare you turn my Father's house into a market!'* " (John 2:15–16).

Seventh, Jesus often spoke specifically about the authorship of portions of the Old Testament. Again, He attributed Psalm 110 to David (Matt. 22:43), and He ascribed Deuteronomy to Moses (Matt. 19:8). He even made specific reference to the origin of circumcision, correcting a false belief: "Moses gave you circumcision (*though actually it did not come from Moses, but from the patriarchs*)." As William Caven observed, "This is not the style of one who does not wish his words to be taken strictly!" ("TCOT" in *TF*, 225).

Eighth, even Jesus' enemies recognized that He did not compromise. Testing Him, the Pharisees said to Him, "*Teacher, we know you are a man of integrity and that you teach the way of God in accordance with the truth. You aren't swayed by men, because you pay no attention to who they are*" (Matt. 22:16).

The facts are that there is nothing in the Gospel record to indicate that Jesus was an accommodator to accepted error on any topic. He even rebuked Nicodemus for not understanding empirical things, saying, "*I have spoken to you of earthly things and you do not believe; how then will you believe if I speak of heavenly things?*" (John 3:12).

Accommodation to Error Is Contrary to Jesus' Character

Even from a purely human standpoint, Jesus was known as a man of high moral character. His closest friends found Him impeccable (1 John 3:3, 4:17; 1 Peter 1:19), and the crowds were amazed at His teaching "because he taught as one who had authority, and not as their teachers of the law" (Matt. 7:29).

Pilate examined Jesus and declared, "I find no basis for a charge against this man" (Luke 23:4). The Roman soldier crucifying Jesus exclaimed, "Surely this was a righteous man" (Luke 23:47). Even unbelievers have paid high tribute to Christ. Ernest Renan (1823–1892), the famous French infidel, declared about Jesus: "His perfect idealism is the highest rule of the unblemished and virtuous life" (*LJ*, 383). He also wrote, "Let us place, then, the person of Jesus at the highest summit of human greatness" (ibid., 386) and "Jesus remains an inexhaustible principle of moral regeneration for humanity" (ibid., 388).

From a biblical point of view, Jesus was the Son of God (see "C, DO" in Geisler, *BECA*) and, as such, He could not deceive, for "God . . . does not lie" (Titus 1:2). Indeed, "it is impossible for God to lie" (Heb. 6:18); His "word is truth" (John 17:17); God is true "and every man a liar" (Rom. 3:4). So whatever divine self-limitation is necessary in order to communicate with human beings, there is no error involved. Error is contrary to His very nature.

An Objection Answered

Admittedly, God adapted to human limitations in order to communicate with us. Indeed, Jesus, who was God, was also a human being (see volume 2), and as a human being He was limited in His knowledge. This is borne out by several passages of Scripture; for instance, as a child "he grew in wisdom" (Luke 2:52). Even as an adult He had certain limitations on His knowledge. According to Matthew, Jesus did not know what was on the fig tree before He got to it (Matt. 21:19). Jesus Himself said He did not know the time of His second coming: "No one knows about that day or hour, not even the angels in heaven, *nor the Son*, but only the Father" (Matt. 24:36, emphasis added).

However, despite the limitations on Jesus' human knowledge, we know that He never erred for two basic reasons. *First*, limits on understanding are different from misunderstanding. The fact that He did not know some things does not mean He was wrong in what He did know. It is one thing to say Jesus did not know as a man the JEPD theory[2] of the authorship of the law (see chapter 19). But it is quite another to say Jesus was wrong when He affirmed that David wrote Psalm 110 (Matt. 22:43) or that Moses wrote the law (Luke 24:27; John 7:19, 23) or that Daniel wrote the prophecy attributed to him in Matthew 24:15. In short, Jesus' limitations on things He did not know as a man did not hinder Him from affirming truly the things He did know.

Second, what Jesus did know and teach He affirmed with divine authority. This is evident for many reasons. For one thing, Jesus said to His disciples: "*All authority in heaven and on earth has been given to me.* Therefore go and make disciples of all nations, baptizing them in the name of the Father and of the Son and of the Holy Spirit, and teaching them to obey everything I have commanded you. And surely I am with you always, to the very end of the age" (Matt. 28:18–20). Further, He affirmed many things He taught with emphasis. In the gospel of John, Jesus said twenty-five times "*Truly, truly . . .*" (John 3:3, 5, 11 RSV). Indeed, He claimed His words were on the level of God's, declaring, "*Heaven and earth will pass away, but my words will never pass away*" (Matt. 24:35). What is more, Jesus taught only

---

[2]J (Jehovah), E (Elohim), P (Priestly), D (Deuteronomy) is the abbreviation given for the view, springing from Julius Welhaussen (1844–1918) and other OT critics, that claims Moses did not write the first five books of the Bible but at least four different authors did, each being characterized by the name of God (J and E) or the kind of literature, whether priestly (P) or legal (D).

what the Father told Him to teach: "*I do nothing on my own but speak just what the Father has taught me*" (John 8:28). He added, "By myself I can do nothing; I judge only as I hear, and my judgment is just, for I seek not to please myself but him who sent me" (John 5:30). So to charge Jesus with error is to charge God the Father with error, since He spoke only what the Father told Him.

Conclusion Regarding the Accommodation Theory

There is no evidence that Jesus ever accommodated Himself to human error in anything He taught. Nor is there any indication that His self-limitation in the Incarnation necessitated any error. He never taught anything false in the areas in which the Incarnation limited Him as a man, and what He did teach, He affirmed with the authority of the Father, having all authority in heaven and earth. Hence, there was no error in anything He taught about Scripture or anything else.

Arguments for the Limitation Theory

Another critical hypothesis aimed at undermining the above argument that Jesus affirmed the Bible to be the Word of God is the limitation theory. According to this view, Jesus was so limited in His human knowledge that it did not extend to matters such as the authority and authenticity of the Old Testament, and thus He was not really affirming these issues. Rather, His ministry was limited only to spiritual or moral matters, and He affirmed nothing about historical, scientific, or critical matters.

There are two main pillars in the argument for the limitation theory: the humanity of Christ and the kenosis theory. Both will be addressed briefly.

The Argument That the Humanity of Christ Reveals His Knowledge Was Limited

Jesus was clearly human. The Bible reveals this in many ways (see "Christ, Humanity of" in Geisler, *BECA*): Jesus had a human ancestry (Matt. 1:20–25; Luke 2:1–7); a human conception (Matt. 1:20); a human birth (Luke 2:4–7; cf. Luke 1:26–27; Gal. 4:4); a human childhood (Luke 2:21–22, 40); normal human growth (Luke 2:52); human hunger (Luke 4:2); human thirst (John 4:6–7); human fatigue (Mark 6:31); human emotions (John 11:33, 35; John 2:15); human sense of humor (Matt. 23:24); human language, culture, and national origin (Matt. 1:1; John 4:5–9); human flesh and blood (Heb. 2:14); human death (1 Cor. 15:3; Matt. 16:21; Rom. 5:8); human pain (Matt. 27:34, 46; Matt. 26:38; Luke 22:44; Heb. 5:7); and human temptation (Matt. 4:1f.; cf. Heb. 4:15). But if Jesus was truly human in every respect, then why could He not experience human error?

Why could not Jesus have been wrong about many of the things He believed, so long as they did not hinder His overall redemptive mission?

The Argument That in the Incarnation Christ Emptied Himself of Omniscience

Further, some critics have argued that in His incarnation Jesus "emptied himself" of omniscience. He was ignorant, allegedly, of the time of His second coming, for He Himself said, "No one knows about that day or hour, not even the angels in heaven, nor the Son, but only the Father" (Mark 13:32). Again, neither did He know whether there were figs on the tree (Mark 11:13). Luke informs us that Jesus "increased in wisdom" as other humans do (Luke 2:52), and asked many questions that revealed His ignorance of the answers (Mark 5:9, 30; 6:38; John 14:9). This being the case, perhaps Jesus was ignorant of the origin of the Old Testament and of the historical truth of the events in it.

Response to the Arguments for the Limitation View

The limitation theory is faulty at the core. Both arguments in favor of it are mistaken, and each ignores a very important point about Christ.

Jesus Was Also God

While it is true that Jesus was God (see volume 2), it is also true that He was man. That is, one and the same person was both God and man at the same time. This means that if the human person Christ had sinned or erred, then the one and the same person that was God would have sinned or erred as well. This is why the Bible is careful to say "we have one who has been tempted in every way, just as we are—*yet was without sin*" (Heb. 4:15). He was human enough to be tired and tempted but not to be sinful (cf. 2 Cor. 5:21; 1 Peter 3:18; 1 John 3:3).

Likewise, if a sin attributed to Christ must also be attributed to God who cannot sin (Hab. 1:13; Heb. 6:18), then an error attributed to Him would have to be attributed to God as well—one and the same person who is Christ is also God. Thus, it is not possible that error can be attributed to Christ, whether as man or as God, since there is only one and the same person in Christ, who is both God and man.

Jesus Never Emptied Himself of Deity

The so-called kenosis theory (that Jesus emptied Himself of deity when He became man) is biblically and theologically unfounded, for many reasons.

First, this is not what the text affirms in Philippians 2, which claims only that He emptied Himself of His divine prerogatives (not of His deity) by humbling Himself to become a human being (Phil. 2:5–8).

Second, when He emptied Himself He was still in the "form" (essence) of God, for if the same word "form" as applied to a servant means He was a servant (Phil. 2:7), then when applied to God it means He was God (Phil. 2:6). Indeed, this is precisely what John 1:1 declares, viz., "the Word was God" (cf. Col. 2:9).

Third, while on earth in human form Jesus claimed to be God (Mark 2:10; John 8:58; 10:35–36; John 17:1–6).

Fourth, Jesus accepted the attribution of deity given Him by others (Matt. 16:16; John 20:28), as well as worship due only to God (Matt. 28:17; John 9:38).

When Christ became man He never ceased being God. *The Incarnation was not the subtraction of deity; it was the addition of humanity.* Thus, had Jesus sinned or erred when on earth as a man, He would have simultaneously sinned or erred as God, for Jesus was one and the same person with the Second Person of the Godhead (see volume 2, part 1).

Criticism of the Limitation Theory

The limitation theory is much more plausible and potentially damaging to the case for the authority of the Old Testament than is the accommodation theory discussed above. Let us examine the evidence carefully.

Since the orthodox doctrine of Christ acknowledges that He was fully human, there is no problem in admitting that Jesus was ignorant of many things as a man. As God, of course, Jesus was infinite in knowledge and knew all things (Ps. 147:5). But *Christ has two natures*: one infinite or unlimited in knowledge, the other finite or limited in knowledge. Could it be that Jesus did not really err in what He taught about the Old Testament but that He simply was so limited as a human being that His knowledge and authority did not extend into those areas? The evidence in the New Testament records demands an emphatically negative answer to this question for many reasons.

Jesus Had a Supernormal Knowledge Even in His Human State

Even in His human state, Christ possessed supernormal if not supernatural knowledge of many things. He saw Nathaniel under the fig tree, although He was not within visual distance (John 1:48). Jesus amazed the woman of Samaria with the information He knew about her private life (John 4:18–19). He knew who would betray Him in advance (John 6:64) and "all that would befall him" in Jerusalem (John 18:4). He knew about Lazarus's death before He was told (John 11:14) and of His crucifixion and resurrection before it occurred (Mark 8:31; 9:31). He likewise had superhuman knowledge of the location of fish (Luke 5:4–9).

There is no indication from the Gospel record that Jesus' finitude deterred His ministry or teaching. Whatever the limitations to His knowledge, it was still vastly beyond that of normal men and completely adequate for His mission and doctrinal teaching.

Christ Possessed Complete and Final Authority for Whatever He Taught

One thing is crystal clear: Christ claimed that whatever He taught came from God with absolute and final authority: "Heaven and earth will pass away, but my words will never pass away" (Matt. 24:35). Jesus believed and proclaimed, "All things have been committed to me by my Father" (Matt. 11:27). When Jesus commissioned His disciples, He claimed, "All authority in heaven and on earth has been given me. Therefore go and make disciples . . . teaching them to obey everything I have commanded you" (Matt. 28:18–20).

Elsewhere Jesus claimed that the very destiny of humanity hinged on His words (Matt. 7:24–27) and that His words would judge us in the last day (John 12:48). The emphatic "truly, truly" is found more than two dozen times in John alone (RSV), and in Matthew Jesus declared that not an iota, not a dot, will pass from the law He came to fulfill (Matt. 5:18). Jesus then placed His own words on the level of the law (Matt. 5:21f.) and claimed that His words bring eternal life (John 5:24), vowing that all His teaching came from the Father (John 8:26–28). Furthermore, as we have seen, despite the fact that He was a man on earth, Christ accepted the acclaims of deity and allowed men to worship Him on many occasions (cf. Matt. 28:17; John 9:38).

Conclusion Regarding the Limitation Theory

In view of the foregoing evidence, the only reasonable conclusion is that Jesus' teachings are possessed of divine authority. Despite the necessary limitations involved in a human incarnation, there is no error or misunderstanding in what Christ taught. Whatever limits there were in the extent of Jesus' knowledge, there were no limits to the truthfulness of His teachings. Just as Jesus was fully human and yet His *moral* character was without flaw (Heb. 4:15), likewise, He was finite in human knowledge and yet without *factual* error in His teaching (John 8:40, 46). In summation, whatever Jesus taught came from God. Hence, if Jesus taught the divine authority and historical authenticity of the Old Testament, then His teaching is the truth of God.

SOURCES

Bromley, Geoffry, ed. "Accommodation" in the *International Encyclopedia of Bible and Ethics* (*ISBE*), rev. ed.

Caven, William B. "The Testimony of Christ to the Old Testament" in *The Fundamentals* (volume 1, chapter 10).

Geisler, Norman. "The Bible, Jesus' View of" in *Baker Encyclopedia of Christian Apologetics*.

———. "Christ, Deity of" in *Baker Encyclopedia of Christian Apologetics*.

———. *Christian Apologetics* (chapter 18).

Geisler, Norman, and William Nix. *A General Introduction to the Bible*.

Lightner, Robert. *The Savior and the Scriptures*.

Renan, Ernest. *The Life of Jesus*.

Saphir, A. *Christ and the Scriptures*.

Wenham, John. *Christ and the Bible*.

———. "Christ's View of Scripture" in Norman Geisler, *Inerrancy*.

HISTORICAL

CHAPTER SEVENTEEN

CHURCH FATHERS ON
THE BIBLE

Threa history of the Christian church is in overwhelming support of what the Bible claims for itself, namely, to be the divinely inspired, infallible, and inerrant word of God (see chapters 13 and 27). This is true of the earliest Fathers after the time of Christ, as well as down through the centuries following them up to modern times. Just as the New Testament writers assumed the inspiration of the Old, the Fathers assumed the inspiration of the New. This fact is observable in the two major periods of the development of the Christian church prior to about A.D. 350.

THE APOSTOLIC AND SUB-APOSTOLIC FATHERS' VIEW OF SCRIPTURE (C. A.D. 70–C. 150)

These writers are important because they overlap with the time of the apostles. An examination of their writings indicates an early and widespread acceptance of the New Testament claim for inspiration.

The Testimony of the *Epistle of Pseudo-Barnabas* (c. 70–130)[1]

The title of the *Epistle of Pseudo-Barnabas* indicates that it was later wrongly ascribed to Paul's first associate. This work cites the gospel of Matthew (26:3) after stating that it is what "God saith" (5:12). The same writer refers to the gospel of Matthew (22:14) by the New Testament title "Scripture" in 4:14, which the New Testament says is "inspired" or "breathed out" by God (2 Tim. 3:16).

Clement of Rome's *Epistle to the Corinthians* (c. 95–97)

Clement of Rome, also a contemporary of the apostles, wrote his epistle after the pattern of Paul. In it he quotes the Synoptic Gospels (Matt. 9:13; Mark 2:17; Luke 5:32) after calling them "Scripture" (chapter 2). He urges his readers to "act according to that which is written" ("for the Holy Spirit saith, 'Let not the wise man glory in his wisdom,' " chapter 1, quoting Jer. 9:23). He further appeals to "the Holy Scriptures, which are true, given by the Holy Spirit" (chapter 45). The New Testament is included as Scripture by the formula "It is written" (chapter 36), and as being written by the apostle Paul "with true inspiration" (chapter 47).

Polycarp's *Epistle to the Philippians* (c. 110–135)

Polycarp was a disciple of the apostle John. He referred to the New Testament several times in his epistle, introducing Galatians 4:26 as "the word of truth" (chapter 3) and presenting citations of Philippians 2:16 and 2 Timothy 4:10 as "the word of righteousness" (chapter 9). In chapter 12, Polycarp cites numerous Old and New Testament passages as "the Scriptures."

Papias (c. 130–140)

Papias wrote five books titled *Exposition of the Oracles of the Lord*, which is the same title given to the Old Testament by the apostle Paul in Romans 3:2, revealing Papias's high regard for the New Testament as the very Word of God. (In the *Exposition of the Oracles of the Lord* he included the New Testament.)

Other Early Writings

In addition to these early books that cite the New Testament, there are several others that allude to it as Scripture. These include the writings of

---

[1]Unless otherwise noted, all citations are from Philip Schaff, *Nicene and Post-Nicene Fathers of the Christian Church.*

Ignatius of Antioch (d. 110), *The Shepherd of Hermas* (c. 115–140), *The Didache* (c. 100–120), and the *Epistle to Diognetus* (c. 150).

Taken together, this important early material demonstrates that by about A.D. 150 the early church, both East and West, accepted the New Testament claim for divine inspiration. The Fathers looked upon those books with the same high regard as the New Testament writers did the Old Testament Scriptures, namely, as the inspired, authoritative, and absolutely true Word of God.

THE ANTE-NICENE AND NICENE FATHERS' VIEW OF SCRIPTURE (c. 150–c. 350)

After the sub-apostolic Fathers, those of the later second century and following provided strong testimony for the divine origin of Scripture. These include noted Fathers like Justin Martyr, Tatian, Irenaeus, Clement of Alexandria, Tertullian, and others.

Justin Martyr (d. 165)

In his first *Apology* (c. 150–155), Justin Martyr spoke of the Gospels as the "Voice of God" (chapter 65). He added, "We must not suppose that the language proceeds from men who were inspired, but from the Divine Word which moves them" (1.36). Elsewhere, he declared that Moses wrote in the Hebrew character by the "divine inspiration" and that "the Holy Spirit of prophecy taught us this, telling us by Moses that God spoke thus" (*JHOG*, 12, 44).

Tatian (c. 110–180)

A disciple of Justin, Tatian called John 1:5 "Scripture" in his *Apology* (chapter 13). In this work Tatian made a passionate defense of Christianity and regarded it as so pure that it was incompatible with Greek civilization. He also wrote a harmony of the Gospels, *Diatessaron* (c. 150–160), which reveals his high regard for their divine authority.

Irenaeus (c. 130–202)

Irenaeus is reported to have actually heard the teachings of Polycarp, disciple of the apostle John. In his treatise *Against Heresies* (3.1.1), Irenaeus referred to the divine authority of the New Testament, declaring,

> For the Lord of all gave the power of the Gospel to his apostles, through whom we have come to know the truth, that is, the teaching of the Son of God. . . . This Gospel they first preached. Afterwards, by the

will of God, they handed it down to us in the Scriptures, to be "the pillar and ground" of our faith. (*AH*, 3:67.)

In fact, Irenaeus affirmed his belief in the inerrancy of Scripture, proclaiming "the Faith in Scripture and Tradition," in which he acknowledged the apostles to be "above all falsehood" (3.5.1). He called the Bible "Scriptures of truth," and he was "most properly assured that the Scriptures are indeed perfect, since they are spoken by the Word of God and His Spirit" (ibid., 2:28.2; 2.35).

Clement of Alexandria (c. 150–215)

Clement became head of the Church School at Alexandria in 190 but was compelled to flee in the face of persecution in 202. He held to a strict doctrine of inspiration, which can be seen in his *Stromata*:

> There is no discord between the Law and the Gospel, but harmony, for they both proceed from the same Author . . . differing in name and time to suit the age and culture of their hearers . . . by a wise economy, but potentially one . . . since faith in Christ and the knowledge . . . of the Gospel is the explanation . . . and the fulfillment of the Law. (Westcott, *AISG*, 439.)

Clement of Alexandria also called the gospel "Scripture" in the same sense as the Law and the Prophets, as he writes of "the Scriptures . . . in the Law, in the Prophets, and besides by the blessed Gospel . . . [which] are valid from their omnipotent authority." He went so far as to condemn those who rejected Scripture because "they are not pleased with the divine commands, that is, with the Holy Spirit" (Geisler, *DFY*, 31–32).

Tertullian (c. 160–220)

Tertullian, the "Father of Latin Theology," never wavered in his support of the doctrine of inspiration of both the Old and the New Testaments. In fact, he maintained that the four Gospels "are reared on the certain basis of Apostolic authority, and so are inspired in a far different sense from the writings of the spiritual Christian; all the faithful, it is true, have the Spirit of God, but all are not Apostles" (Westcott, *AISG*, 434). For Tertullian,

> [T]he apostles have the Holy Spirit properly, who have Him fully, in the operations of prophecy, and the efficacy of [healing] virtues, and the evidences of tongues; not particularly, as all others have. Thus he attached the Holy Spirit's authority to that form [of advice] to which he willed us rather to attend; and forthwith it became not an *advice* of the Holy Spirit, but, in consideration of His majesty, a precept. ("OEC" in Schaff, *NPNFCC*, 4)

Hippolytus (c. 170–236)

Hippolytus, a disciple of Irenaeus, exhibited the same deep sense of reverence toward Scripture. Speaking of the inspiration of the Old Testament, he said,

> The Law and the Prophets were from God, who in giving them compelled his messenger to speak by the Holy Spirit, that receiving the inspiration of the Father's power they may announce the Father's counsel and will. In these men therefore the Word found a fitting abode and spoke of Himself; for even then He came as His own herald, showing the Word who was about to appear in the world. (Westcott, *AISG*, 431–32.)

Of the New Testament writers, Hippolytus declared,

> These blessed men . . . having been perfected by the Spirit of Prophecy, and worthily honoured by the Word Himself, were brought to an inner harmony like instruments, and having the Word within them, as it were to strike the notes, by Him they were moved, and announced that which God wished. . . . [For] they did not speak of their own power (be well assured), nor proclaim that which they wished themselves, but first they were rightly endowed with wisdom by the Word, and afterwards well foretaught of the future by visions, and then, when thus assured, they spake that which was [revealed] to them alone by God. (Westcott, *AISG*, 432.)

Origen (c. 185–c. 254)

Origen, a successor of Clement at the Alexandrian School, held that God "gave the law, and the prophets, and the Gospels, being also the God of the apostles and of the Old and New Testaments." He wrote, "This Spirit inspired each one of the saints, whether prophets or apostles; and there was not one Spirit in the men of the old dispensation, and another in those who were inspired at the advent of Christ" (Schaff, *NPNFCC* 4:240).

Origen's view of the authority of the Scriptures is "that the Scriptures were written by the Spirit of God, and have a meaning . . . not known to all, but to those only on whom the grace of the Holy Spirit is bestowed in the words of wisdom and knowledge" (ibid., 241). He went on to assert that there is a supernatural element of thought "throughout all of Scripture even where it is not apparent to the uninstructed" (Geisler, *DFY*, 28–30).

Cyprian (c. 200–258)

Cyprian was an important bishop in the Western church during the time of Roman emperor Decius (249–251). In his treatise *The Unity of the*

Catholic Church, Cyprian appeals to the Gospels as authoritative, referring to them as the "commandments of Christ." He also adds the Corinthian letters of Paul to his list of authorities and appeals to Paul's Ephesian letter (4:4–6). In the same location, he reaffirms the inspiration of the New Testament as he writes, "When the Holy Spirit says, in the person of the Lord. . . ." Again, he adds, "The Holy Spirit warns us through the apostle" as he cites 1 Corinthians 11:19 (*TUCC*, 5:126). These and several other examples in his writings lead to the conclusion that Cyprian held that both the Old and New Testaments are "Divine Scriptures" (*EACN*, 5:328).

Eusebius of Caesarea (c. 263 or 265–340)

As the great early-church historian, Eusebius is an important witness to the views of Scripture in the nascent Christian church. He held to the inspiration of the Old and New Testaments and wrote much about God's Word in his *Ecclesiastical History*. It was Eusebius who was commissioned to make fifty copies of the Scriptures following the Council of Nicea (325).

Eusebius was a tremendous defender of Scripture, writing extensively on the topic. Related works include *Against Hierocles* (a pagan governor of Bithynia), *The Preparation for the Gospel*, and *Demonstration of the Gospel*. On top of these he wrote a work on the Incarnation titled *The Theophany*, and he penned another book (*Against Marcellus, Bishop of Ancyra*) that is a collection of Old Testament passages foretelling the coming of Christ. Also, *Problems of the Gospels* (Schaff, 2nd series, volume 1, 36) and *On the Theology of the Church, a Refutation of Marcellus*. Add to these his treatise on *Easter* and his *On the Names of Places in the Holy Scriptures* (*Onomastica Sacra*) to round out his massive defense of the Bible as the divinely inspired Word of God.

Athanasius of Alexandria (c. 295–373)

Known as the "Father of Orthodoxy" because of his successful stand against arianism (the heresy denying Christ's deity) at Nicea (325), Athanasius was the first to use the term "canon" in reference to the New Testament books, which he called "the fountains of salvation" (Westcott, *AGSHCNT*, 456). Athanasius cites the Scriptures repeatedly as having divine authority with final say in resolving all doctrinal issues.

Cyril of Jerusalem (c. 315–386)

Cyril offered what he called a summary of "the whole doctrine of the Faith" that "has been built up strongly out of all the Scriptures." Then he proceeded to warn others not to change or contradict his teachings because of the Scripture's injunction as found in Galatians 1:8–9 (Cyril of

Jerusalem in Schaff, 7:32). In his treatise *Of the Divine Scriptures*, he speaks of "the divinely-inspired Scriptures of both the Old and the New Testaments" (ibid., 26–27). He then proceeds to list all the books of the Hebrew Old Testament (twenty-two) and all of the books of the Christian New Testament except Revelation (twenty-six), saying, "Learn also diligently, and from the Church, what are the books of the Old Testament, and what are those of the New. And, pray, read none of the apocryphal writings." For Cyril the matter was drawn clearly when he wrote,

> With regard to the divine and saving mysteries of faith no doctrine, however trivial, may be taught without the backing of the divine Scriptures. . . . For our saving faith derives its force, not from capricious reasoning, but from what may be proved out of the Bible (ibid., as cited in J. N. D. Kelly's *ECD*, 4).

Summary of the Early Fathers on Scripture

Virtually every early church Father enthusiastically adhered to the doctrine of the inspiration of the Old and New Testaments alike. J. N. D. Kelly, noted authority on the doctrine of the early church, affirmed,

> There is little need to dwell on the absolute authority accorded to the Scripture as a doctrinal norm. It was the Bible, declared Clement of Alexandria about A.D. 200, which as interpreted by the Church, was the source of Christian teaching. His greater disciple Origen was a thorough-going Biblicist who appealed again and again to Scripture as the decisive criterion of dogma. . . . "The holy inspired Scriptures," wrote Athanasius a century later, "are fully sufficient for the proclamation of the truth." Later in the same century John Chrysostom bade his congregation seek no other teacher than the oracles of God. . . . In the West Augustine . . . [and] a little while later Vincent of Lerins (c. 450) took it as an axiom [that] "the Scriptural canon was sufficient, and more sufficient, for all purposes" (*ECD*, 42–43).

In short, the Fathers of the early church believed that both the Old and New Testaments were the inspired writings of the Holy Spirit through the instrumentality of the prophets and apostles. They also believed the Scriptures were completely true and without error because they were the very Word of God given for the faith and practice of all believers.

THE GREAT MEDIEVAL CHURCH TEACHERS' VIEW OF SCRIPTURE (C. 350–C. 1350)

The medieval church is represented by several great theologians who represent wide segments of Christianity and had a vast influence on the later centuries of the Christian church. They too held to the orthodox view of Scripture as the divinely inspired and inerrant Word of God. These include Jerome, Augustine, Anselm, and Thomas Aquinas, to say nothing of Ambrose, the teacher of Augustine.

Ambrose of Milan (340–397)

Ambrose, bishop of Milan, had the distinction of mentoring the great Father of the medieval church, Augustine. In his *Letters* Ambrose cites Matthew 22:21 by using the familiar introductory statement for a divinely inspired writing ("It is written," 20.19) as he proceeds to quote loosely John 6:15 and 2 Corinthians 12:10 (*L*, 20, 5:209–17). Ambrose also appeals to "The Divine Scriptures" (10.7) in his letter to the Emperor Gratian (375–83), where he presents his disputation with the followers of arianism (ibid., 10, 184–89).

Jerome (c. 340–420)

Next to Origen, Jerome was the greatest biblical scholar of the early church, and his writings include many references to the "Holy Scriptures" and to their authority. Much of his life work centered around translating the Bible and disputing with others over the canon of the Old Testament. In addition, he assumed the inspiration, canonicity, and authority of the New Testament as it has come down to the modern world.

In a letter to Nepotian in A.D. 394, Jerome wrote, "Read the divine scriptures constantly; never, indeed, let the sacred volume out of your hand" (Schaff, Letter 52.7, v.6). In the same year he enumerates the books of the New Testament as he writes,

> I beg you, my dear brother, to live among these books, to meditate upon them, to know nothing else, to seek nothing else. Does not such a life seem to you a foretaste of heaven here on earth? Let not the simplicity of the Scriptures offend you; for these are due either to faults of translators or else to deliberate purpose: for in this way it is better fitted for instruction (ibid., Letter 53.10, 102).

In his discussion of the difference between righteous ignorance and instructed righteousness, Jerome answers the question "Why is the apostle Paul called a chosen vessel?" His response is "Assuredly because he is a repertory of the Law and of the holy scriptures" (ibid., Letter 53.3, 97–98).

The Syrian School at Antioch

John Chrysostom (c. 347–407) and Theodore of Mopsuestia (c. 350–428) are representative exegetes and theologians of the Syrian School at Antioch, the city in which the disciples were first called Christians (Acts

11:26). During the early centuries of the Christian church, Antioch was the chief rival to Alexandria in the struggle for theological leadership in the East. Theodore and his contemporaries held that the primary author of all Scripture was the Holy Spirit. They viewed the Holy Spirit as providing the content of revelation and the prophet (in cooperation with the Holy Spirit) as giving it the appropriate expression and form (Wiles, "TMRAS", 1, in Ackroyd and Evans, *CHB*). However, unlike virtually all of their predecessors and successors, they allowed for minor discrepancies in this human form (see Ackroyd and Evans, *CHB*, 493–494).

Augustine of Hippo (354–430)

Augustine was not only the greatest theologian of the early Middle Ages but one of the greatest of all time. He completely endorsed the claims of the New Testament for its inspiration; an example of this view may be seen in his *Confessions* (8.29), where the reading of Romans 13:13–14 was sufficient for him to be converted. His monumental work *The City of God* contains much Scripture, and therein he indicates the authority of Scripture in contrast to all other writings (see 11.3; 18.41). All through his letters and other treatises, he asserted the truth, authority, and divine origin of Scripture.

In *The City of God* Augustine used such expressions as "Sacred Scripture" (9.5), "the words of God" (10.1), "Infallible Scripture" (11.6), "divine revelation" (13.2), and "Holy Scripture" (15.8). Elsewhere he referred to the Bible as the "oracles of God," "God's word," "divine oracles," and "divine Scripture." With his widespread influence throughout the centuries, such a testimony has stood as an outstanding witness to the high regard given to the Scriptures in the church. Speaking of the gospel writers, Augustine said,

> When they write what He has taught and said, it should not be asserted that he did not write it, since the members only put down what they had come to know at the dictation [dictis] of the Head. Therefore, whatever He wanted us to read concerning His words and deeds, He commanded His disciples, His hands, to write. Hence, one cannot but receive what he reads in the Gospels, though written by the disciples, as though it were written by the very hand of the Lord Himself. (Geisler, *DFY*, 34.)

Consequently, he added,

> I have learned to yield this respect and honour only to the canonical books of Scripture: of these alone do I most firmly believe that the authors were completely free from error (ibid., 40). . . . If we are perplexed by any apparent contradiction in Scripture, it is not allowable to

say, the author of this book is mistaken: but either the manuscript is faulty, or the translation is wrong, or you have misunderstood. (*Against Faustus*, 11.5.)

Gregory I ("The Great," 540–604)

Gregory the Great wrote *Commentary on Job*, in which he refers to Hebrews 12:6 as "Scripture" (*CJ*, 9:189), the term used for divinely inspired writings in the New Testament (2 Tim. 3:16). He, being the first medieval pope, set the tone for the succeeding centuries just as he epitomized the preceding ones.

Louis Gaussen summarized the view of Scripture in the early Middle Ages well:

> With the single exception of Theodore of Mopsuestia, (c. A.D. 400), that philosophical divine whose numerous writings were condemned for their Nestorianism in the fifth ecumenical council . . . it has been found impossible to produce, in the long course of the *eight first centuries of Christianity*, a single doctor who has disowned the plenary inspiration of the Scriptures, unless it be in the bosom of the most violent heresies that have tormented the Christian Church; that is to say, among the Gnostics, the Manicheans, the Anomeans, and the Mahometans [Muslims]. (Gaussen, *T*, 139–40.)

Anselm of Canterbury (1033–1109)

In his famous *Cur Deus Homo?* (chapter 22), Anselm continued to state the orthodox view of inspiration when he wrote, "And the God-man himself originates the New Testament and approves the Old. And, as we must acknowledge him to be true, so no one can dissent from anything contained in these books" (*SABW*, 287–88). As Archbishop of Canterbury, Anselm addressed the question of authority in another treatise, where he said, "What is said in Scripture . . . I believe without doubting, of course" (*TFE*, 185).

The Victorines (Twelfth Century)

The Victorines were noted Christian teachers in the Abbey of St. Victor in Paris; they followed the historical and literal approach to biblical interpretation. Victorine representatives included Hugh (d. 1142), Richard (d. 1173), and Andrew (d. 1175), and their respect for Scripture was based on the belief of their predecessors—that the Bible is the divinely inspired Word of God (Ramm, *PBI*, 51).

Thomas Aquinas (c. 1225–1274)

The foundations for late medieval theology were laid by such outstanding scholars as the categorizer Peter Lombard (c. 1100–c. 1160) and the encyclopedist Albert the Great (c. 1193 or 1206–1280). But the greatest spokesman of scholasticism was Thomas Aquinas, who clearly set forth the orthodox doctrine of inspiration. In his *Summa Theologica* Aquinas states, "The Author of Holy Scripture is God." Although he asks the question of "senses" of Scripture, he *assumes* the "inspiration" of both the Old and New Testaments. He concurred with the traditional view that the Scriptures are "divine revelation" (*ST* 1.1.1,8; 2) and "without error" (*ST* 2.1.6.1).

God Is the Author of Scripture

Aquinas insisted "that God is the author of Holy Scripture." Again, "the Author of Holy Scripture is God" (*ST*, 1a, 1, 10). Thus, "revelation is the basis of sacred Scripture or doctrine" (ibid., 1a. 1, 2 ad 2), for "holy Scripture looks at things in that they are divinely revealed" (ibid., 1a. 1, 2 ad 2), and it is "in Holy Scripture [that] the divine will is declared to us" (ibid., 1a. 1, 2 ad 2). Citing Paul's words to Timothy ("All Scripture is inspired of God," 2 Tim. 3:16), Aquinas referred to the Bible as "divinely inspired Scripture" (ibid., 1a 1, 1) and said we stood in need of an errorless "divine revelation," otherwise the "rational truth about God would have appeared only to a few, and even so after a long time and mixed with many mistakes" (ibid., 1a. 1, 1).

God Spoke Through Prophets

"Prophecy implies a certain vision of some supernatural truth beyond our reach" (ibid., 2a2ae. 174, 5). Thus "a true prophet is always inspired by the spirit of truth" (ibid., 2a2ae. 172, 6, ad 2). Again, "prophecy is a knowledge which divine revelation engraves in the mind of a prophet, in the form of a teaching" (ibid., 2a2ae. 171, 6).

The Relation of the Divine and Human in Scripture

Like the Fathers before him, Aquinas sometimes spoke of the human authors of Scripture as being the "instruments of divine operation" (ibid., 2a2ae. 172, 4, ad 1), for "in prophetic revelation the prophet's mind is moved by the Holy Spirit as a defective instrument by its principal cause." Aquinas cites 2 Samuel 23:2 in support of his view: David said, "The Spirit of the Lord spoke by me" (ibid., 2a2ae. 173, 4). When God moves upon a human writer, an imperfect instrument can utter a perfect message, even to the very "words" (ibid). This is possible because of the perfection of the principal or primary Cause (God) working on the imperfect secondary cause.

However, unlike many of his predecessors, Aquinas did not view the human authors as *mere* instruments of God's causality; rather, they were secondary causes under the direct providential action of God, the primary Cause. Aquinas argued that "the proper disposition is a necessary requirement for the correct use of prophecy, since the use of prophecy proceeds from the created power of the prophet. Therefore, a determinate disposition is also required" (*OT*, 12, 4).[2]

This disposition is provided by the Divine Architect of salvation history: God disposes men and events so that they will communicate His Word precisely as they did (*ST*, 2a2ae. 172, 3). In this way the personal characteristics of the prophets in no way deprecate the message they convey; rather, the message "proceeds in harmony with such dispositions" (*OT*, 12, 4 ad 1).[3]

Aquinas illustrated the divine-human relation in prophecy by the model of teacher-learner:

> Prophecy is a type of knowledge impressed on the prophet's intellect from a divine revelation; this happens after the manner of education. Now the truth of knowledge is the same in both the student and the teacher since the student's knowledge is a likeness of the teacher's knowledge. (*ST*, 2a2ae. 171, 6)[4]

Unlike the mechanical illustrations used by many of his predecessors (such as God playing on a musical instrument), Aquinas provided new insight into the process of inspiration. Just as a teacher activates the potential of the student for knowledge, so God (the Primary Cause) activates the potential of man (the secondary cause) to know what He desires to reveal to him. Thus, the prophet is not a puppet or even a secretary but a human learner. And, like a human teacher, God only activates in the prophet what he has the potentiality to receive in terms of his own capacities, culture, language, and literary forms.

The Inerrancy of Scripture

While many in modern times have denied the inerrancy of Scripture, there is no question where Aquinas stood on the matter. In his *Commentary on the Book of Job* he declared, "It is heretical to say that any falsehood whatsoever is contained either in the gospels or in any canonical Scripture" (13, lecture 1). Elsewhere he insists, "A true prophet is always inspired by the spirit of truth in whom there is no trace of falsehood, and so he never utters untruths" (*ST*, 2a2ae. 172, 6, ad 2). Pointedly, he declares that "nothing false can underlie the literal sense of Scripture" (ibid., 1a. 1, 10, ad 3). Therefore, "the truth of prophetic proclamations must needs be the same as that of divine knowledge. And falsity . . . cannot creep into prophecy" (ibid., 1a. 14, 3). Agreeing with Augustine, Aquinas confesses of Holy

---

[2]cf. *Summa Theologica*, 2a2ae. 174, 3 ad 3.
[3]cf. *Summa Theologica*, 2a2ae. 172, 3 ad 1 and 171, 6.
[4]cf. *Summa Theologica*, 172, 6 ad.

Scripture, "I firmly believe that none of their authors have erred in composing them" (ibid., 1a. 1, 8). In this same passage Aquinas refers to Scripture as "unfailing truth." The Bible, then, is the inerrant Word of God.

In his *Commentary on John*, Aquinas claimed,

> Those who wrote the Scriptural canon, such as the Evangelists, Apostles and others like them, so firmly asserted the truth that they left nothing to be doubted. Thus it stresses: "And we know his testimony is true" and "If anyone preach to you a gospel, besides that which you have received, let him be anathema" (21, lecture 6).

In short, the Bible is so completely without error that nothing is to be doubted.

Contrary to some today who believe that only what is essential to faith is without error,[5] Aquinas believed that the Bible is not only true in all it *teaches* but also in all it *touches*, for things "incidentally or secondarily related to the object of faith are all the contents of Scripture handed down by God" (*ST*, 2a2ae. 2, 5). As examples of things in the Bible not essential to faith, but nevertheless without error, Aquinas lists examples such as that Abraham had two sons, or that a dead man rose when Elijah's bones touched him (ibid., 2a2ae. 1, 6 ad 1).

The Superiority of Scripture

Aquinas agreed with the later Protestant principle of *Sola Scriptura*, the Bible alone as the Word of God, the totally sufficient norm for our faith. He said clearly,

> We believe the prophets and apostles because the Lord has been their witness by performing miracles. . . . And we believe the successors of the apostles and the prophets *only in so far as they tell us those things which the apostles and prophets have left in their writings.* (*OT*, XIV, 10, ad 11, emphasis added.)

Elsewhere he added, "The truth of faith is contained in sacred Scripture" (*ST*, 2a2ae. 1, 9). Hence, "one is held to explicit belief in such matters *only when it is clear to him that they are in truth contained in the teaching of faith*" (ibid., 2a2ae. 2, 6, emphasis added). The context of this statement makes it clear that "the teaching of faith" refers to the Scriptures.

After insisting that the biblical writers "so firmly asserted the truth that they left nothing to be doubted" and that anyone who rejects it should be "anathema," Aquinas added:

> The reason for this is that *only the canonical Scriptures are normative for faith.* . . . Others who write about the truth do so in such a way that they

---

[5]See Jack Rogers, *The Authority and Interpretation of the Bible: An Historical Approach.*

do not want to be believed unless what they affirm is true. (TCJ, 21, lecture 6, emphasis added.)

While believing that the Bible alone was God's written revelation,[6] Aquinas did not mean to imply that it needed no interpretation (*ST*, 2a2ae. 1, 9 ad 1; 10 ad 1); he meant that the Scriptures have no peer. "So, sacred Scripture, which has no superior science over it, disputes the denial of its principles; it argues on the basis of those truths held by revelation" (ibid., *ST*, 1a. 1, 8). The Bible is superior to any other book or person, and all else must be subject to its divine authority.

SUMMARY AND CONCLUSION

While there were minor differences with regard to the mode of inspiration, there was essential unity in the great Fathers of the early and medieval church on the nature of inspiration. Virtually all agreed that the Old and New Testaments were the divinely authoritative and verbally inspired Word of God, having final authority for the faith and practice of the church. While none actually believed in mechanical word-for-word dictation, their language supporting the plenary (full) verbal divine inspiration was so strong at times that they were convinced that it was just as inspired *as if it has been* dictated (see, for example, the above quotation by Augustine).

While there were deviations on the manner of interpretation (particularly from the allegorical school of Origen) that undermined the authority of certain sections of Scripture, there was unanimity that the Bible itself was the Word of God written. Again, many used such strong illustrations of the writers as the mouthpieces of God that they opened themselves up to the unjustified charge of verbal dictation. One thing is certain: While the fact that speaking of the authors of Scripture as the instruments through whom God spoke may have tended to diminish their humanity (see chapter 15), it certainly exalted the divinity of their writings—the Holy Scriptures.

SOURCES

Ackroyd, P. R., and C. F. Evans, eds. *The Cambridge History of the Bible.*

Ambrose. *Letters*, in *The Library of Christian Classics.*

---

[6]Some have challenged the conclusion that Aquinas believed the Bible was God's only revelation to the Church appealing to his comments on 2 Thess. 2:15 that "much has not been written by the apostles and which, therefore, must be observed." However, this overlooks the context and the rest of his quotation (from 1 Cor. 11:34) in which Paul says, "The rest I will set in order when I come" (NKJV). In the context of the living apostles, yes, there was still unwritten apostolic authority. However, after their deaths Aquinas never seems to refer to any apostolic or revelatory authority outside of the Bible. His one isolated reference (in Job) to the fall of the devil as the "tradition of the church" can easily be understood as "teaching" of the church based on Holy Scripture. After all, Aquinas believed that many Scriptures clearly teach the fall of Satan both before (cf. Gen. 3) and after Job (cf. Rev. 12), and he cites them himself.

Anselm. *Saint Anselm's Basic Writings.*

———. *Truth, Freedom, and Evil.*

Cyprian. *Epistle About Cornelius and Novation,* in *The Ante-Nicene Fathers.*

———. *The Unity of the Catholic Church,* in *The Library of Christian Classics.*

Cyril. *Catechetical Lectures,* in *Nicene and Post-Nicene Fathers.*

Gaussen, Louis. *Theopneustia.*

Geisler, Norman. *Decide for Yourself: How History Views the Bible.*

Geisler, Norman, and William Nix. *A General Introduction to the Bible.*

Gregory the Great. *The Commentary on Job,* in *The Library of Christian Classics.*

Hannah, John, ed. *Inerrancy and the Church.*

Irenaeus. *Against Heresies* in *The Library of Christian Classics.*

Jerome. *St. Jerome: Letters and Selected Works.*

Justin Martyr. *Justin's Hortatory Oration to the Greeks.*

Kelly, J. N. D. *Early Christian Doctrine.*

Ramm, Bernard. *Protestant Biblical Interpretation.*

Rogers, Jack. *The Authority and Interpretation of the Bible: A Historical Approach*

Schaff, Philip. *The Nicene and Post-Nicene Fathers of the Christian Church.*

Tertullian. *On Exhortation to Chastity* in Philip Schaff, *The Nicene and Post-Nicene Fathers of the Christian Church.*

Thomas Aquinas. *Commentary on John 21,* lecture 6.

———. *The Commentary on the Book of Job,* 13, lecture 1.

———. *On Truth.*

———. *Summa Theologica.*

Westcott, Brooke Foss. *A General Survey of the History of the Canon of the New Testament.*

———. *An Introduction to the Study of the Gospels.*

Wiles, M. F. "Theodore of Mopsuestia as Representative of the Antiochene School," in P. R. Ackroyd and C. F. Evans, eds., *The Cambridge History of the Bible.*

Woodbridge, John. *Biblical Authority: A Critique of the Roger/McKim Proposal.*

CHAPTER EIGHTEEN

THE HISTORICAL CHURCH ON THE BIBLE

O n the nature of Scripture, there are no substantial differences between the views of the Reformers and the great early and medieval Fathers of the church. They all held that the Old and New Testaments were the verbally inspired, divinely authoritative, written Word of God. The first serious deviations within the church were not to come for several centuries after the Reformation, in modern times (see chapter 19).

MARTIN LUTHER ON SCRIPTURE

As an Augustinian monk, Martin Luther (1483–1546) did not depart from the doctrine of Scripture held by his great mentor, Augustine (see chapter 17). He firmly adhered to the divine authority, infallibility, and inerrancy of Scripture, as the following citations demonstrate.

The Origin of Scripture

Like many early and medieval Fathers before him, Luther believed the Bible came from God through the instrumentality of the men God used. In this he did not deviate from the standard orthodox view of Scripture.

The Bible Is the Word of God

Luther wrote: "This is exactly as it is with God. His word is so much like himself, that the godhead is wholly in it, and he who has the word has the whole godhead" (*LW*, 52:46). He added, "It must be observed, however, that another one is the author of this book [Genesis], namely the Holy Ghost. . . . The Holy Spirit wanted to write this [Gen. 26:19–21] to teach us." In his exposition of 2 Peter is the statement: "Says Peter, what has been written and proclaimed in the Prophets has not been imagined nor invented by men, but holy and devout men have spoken it *through the Holy Ghost*" (Reu, *LS*, 35, 33, italics original).

Luther stated emphatically,

> He is called a prophet who has received his understanding directly from God without further intervention, *into whose mouth the Holy Ghost has given the words.* For He (the Spirit) is the source, and they have no other authority than God. . . . Here (2 Sam. 23:2, "The Spirit of the Lord spake by me, and His word was in my tongue") it becomes too marvelous and soars too high for me. . . . It is these and similar statements to which St. Peter refers in the II Epistle 1:21, "For the prophecy came not in old time by the will of men, etc. . . ." Therefore we sing in the Creed, concerning the Holy Ghost, "Who spake by the Prophets." So *we refer all of Scripture to the Holy Ghost.* (*LW*, 36–37, italics original.)

He exhorted, "We must know what we believe, namely, what God's Word says, not what the pope or the saintly fathers believe or say. For you must not rely on a person. No, you must rely on the Word of God alone" (ibid., 30:105).

> Would to God that my exposition and that of all doctors might perish and each Christian himself make the Scriptures and God's pure word his norm. You can tell by my verbosity how immeasurably different God's words are in comparison with any human word, how no single man is able to fathom sufficiently any one word of God and expound it with many words (ibid., 52:286).

The Bible Is Words From God

Luther declared, "The Scriptures, although they too are written by men, are neither of men nor from men but from God. Now since Scriptures and the doctrines of men are contrary one to the other, the one must lie and the other be true" (ibid., 35:153):

> They do not believe they are God's words. *For if they believed they were God's words they would not call them poor, miserable words but would regard such words and titles as greater than the whole world and would fear and tremble before them as before God himself. For whoever despises a single word of God does not regard any as important.* (Reu, *LS*, 32, italics original.)

Luther added, "I see that Scripture is consonant in all and through all and agrees with itself in such a measure that it is impossible to doubt the truth and certainty of such a weighty matter in any detail" (ibid., 37).

The Divinely Authoritative Nature of Scripture

Having come from God, the Scriptures have divine authority. Luther expressed this in no uncertain terms:

> We hope that everyone will agree with the decisions that the doctrines of men must be forsaken and the Scriptures retained. For they will neither desire nor be able to keep both, since the two cannot be reconciled and are by nature necessarily opposed to one another, like fire and water, like heaven and earth. . . . We do not condemn the doctrines of men just because they are the doctrines of men, for we would gladly put up with them. But we condemn them because they are contrary to the gospel and the Scriptures. (*LW*, 35:153.)

Thus, "I have learned to ascribe this honor only to books which are termed canonical, so that I confidently believe that not one of their authors erred" (Reu, *LS*, 17). Hence,

> Nothing but God's Word alone should be preached in Christendom. The reason for this is no other, as we have said, than this, that a Word must be proclaimed that remains eternally a Word through which souls may be saved and may live forever. (*LW*, 30:167.)

The Infallibility and Inerrancy of Scripture

Luther proclaimed,

> Neither does it help them to assert that at all other points they have a high and noble regard for God's words and the entire gospel, except in this matter. My friend, God's Word is God's Word; this point does not require much haggling! When one blasphemously gives the lie to God in a single word, or says it is a minor matter if God is blasphemed or called a liar, one blasphemes the entire God and makes light of all blasphemy. (*LW*, 37:26.)

He went on,

> So the Holy Ghost has had to bear the blame of not being able to speak correctly but that like a drunkard or a fool He jumbles the whole and uses wild, strange words and phrases. But it is our fault that we have not understood the language nor the style of the prophets. It cannot be otherwise, because the Holy Ghost is wise and also makes the prophets wise. But one who is wise must be able to speak correctly; that never fails. But because whoever does not hear well or does not know the

language well may think he speaks ill because he hears or understands scarcely half the words. (Reu, *LS,* 44.)

In addition,

Whoever is so bold that he ventures to accuse God of fraud and deception *in a single word* and does so willfully again and again after he has been warned and instructed once or twice will likewise certainly venture to accuse God of fraud and deception in all His words. Therefore it is true absolutely and without exception, *that everything is believed or nothing is believed.* The Holy Ghost does not suffer Himself to be separated or divided so that He should teach and cause to be believed one doctrine rightly and another falsely (ibid., 33, italics original).

Further,

This is a rather unimportant story, therefore we shall not devote much time to its explanation; indeed, I do not know how to say much about it. But since it is *written by the Holy Spirit,* we cannot well pass by this text but will treat it to some extent. (Rue, *LS,* 35, italics original.)

The Scriptures Are a Revelation of Christ

According to Luther, you should

dismiss your own opinions and feelings, and think of the Scriptures as the loftiest and noblest of holy things, as the richest of mines which can never be sufficiently explored, in order that you may find that divine wisdom which God here lays before you in such simple guise as to quench all pride. Here you will find the swaddling clothes and the manger in which Christ lies, and to which the angel points the shepherds [Luke 2:11–12]. Simple and lowly are these swaddling clothes,[1] but dear is the treasure, Christ, who lies in them. (*LW,* 35:236.)

The Bible Is Scientifically Accurate

Luther was so convinced of the scientific accuracy of the Bible that he is even cited as believing that the sun actually moves around the earth.

There was mention of a certain new astronomer who wanted to prove that the earth moves and not the sky, the sun, and the moon. This would be as if somebody were riding on a cart or in a ship and imagined that he was standing still while the earth and the trees were moving. . . . [Luther remarked,] so it goes now. Whoever wants to be clever must agree with nothing that others esteem. He must do something of his

---

[1]By the phrase "simple and lowly" Luther obviously (in view of the earlier quotes) did not mean that the Bible was fallible and errant but rather simply human.

own. This is what that fellow does who wishes to turn the whole of astronomy upside down. Even in these things that are thrown into disorder I believe the Holy Scriptures, for Joshua commanded the sun to stand still and not the earth [Josh. 10:12]. (Luther, *TT*, June 4, 1539.)

Luther added,

> Because we are not sufficiently able to understand how these days occurred nor why God wished to observe such distinctions of times, *we shall rather admit our ignorance than attempt to twist the words unnecessarily into an unnatural meaning*. As far, therefore, as St. Augustine's opinion is concerned, we hold that Moses spoke literally not allegorically or figuratively, that is, the world and all its creatures was created within the six days as the words declare. Because we are not able to comprehend we shall remain disciples and leave the instructorship to the Holy Ghost. (Reu, *LS*, 51, italics original.)[2]

The Bible Is Self-Consistent

Luther's difficulty with the book of James was not due to his disbelief in inerrancy but rather his strong belief in it. He was so convinced that the Bible could not err that he found it difficult to accept James, since James appeared to him to contradict other Scripture.

> Though this Epistle of St. James was rejected by the ancients, I praise it and regard it as a good book, because it sets up no doctrine of men and lays great stress upon God's law. But to state my own opinion about it, though without injury to anyone, I consider that it is not the writing of any apostle. My reasons are as follows: First: Flatly in contradiction to St. Paul and all the rest of Scripture it ascribes righteousness to works and says that Abraham was justified by his works in that he offered his son Isaac, though St. Paul, on the contrary, teaches, in Romans 4, that Abraham was justified without works, by faith alone, before he offered his son and proves it by Moses in Genesis 15. . . . Second: Its purpose is to teach Christians, and in all its teaching it does not once mention the Passion, the Resurrection, or the Spirit of Christ. (Reu, *LS*, 24.)[3]

Summary of Luther's View on Scripture

Some have launched a misdirected attack on Luther's view of the *nature* of Scripture because of his questions about the *extent* of Scripture (Luther having had doubts about James, Revelation, Esther, and Hebrews). But, as

---

[2]While one can question Luther's interpretation of the text, there is no question as to his belief that its inspiration extends to scientific as well as to spiritual matters.

[3]Once again, Luther's interpretation of James is questioned by most evangelicals; nonetheless, the fact that he would not allow for any contradiction in Scripture indicates how strongly he believed in its inerrancy.

James Orr notes, "These judgments affected canonicity rather than inspiration."

In his landmark study *Luther and the Scriptures*, M. Reu noted that Luther himself regarded the Bible to be "so much like himself [God], that the Godhead is wholly in it, and he who has the word has the whole Godhead." As for the words of the Bible, Luther writes, "And the Scriptures, although they too are written by men, are neither of men nor from men but from God." Again, elsewhere he says, "Nothing but God's Word alone should be preached in Christendom" (*LS*, 30.167).

Luther believed that the Bible is God's Word, not mere human words. Since God is the author of every word of Scripture, even the smallest part of Scripture (including references to history and science) possesses absolute divine authority. So, to deny anything in the Bible is to deny God Himself.

After Luther, the *Book of Concord* (1580) compiled the nine creeds and confessions of the Lutheran faith. It affirms, "Lutherans believe, confess, and teach that the only rule and norm, according to which all doctrines ought to be esteemed and judged, is not other than the prophetic and apostolic writings both of the Old and of the New Testaments." It adds,

> And indeed, as long as the divine authority of the Bible is maintained, and as long as it is conceded that it is the product of a unique cooperation of the Holy Spirit and the human writers and, therefore, as a whole and in all its details the Word of God without contradiction and error, so long as the question after the mode of inspiration is of an entirely secondary nature, and so long as one is in harmony with the best Lutheran theologians from Luther up to the year 1570.

JOHN CALVIN ON SCRIPTURE

John Calvin (1509–1564), the founder of the Reformed tradition, was just as repeatedly emphatic about the divine inspiration and inerrancy of Scripture as were Augustine, Aquinas, and Luther.

The Origin of Scripture

Calvin believed the Bible found its ultimate source in God; the very words of the Bible came from the mouth of God, albeit through the instrumentality of men of God.

The Words of the Bible Are From God

Calvin believed that "the Bible has come down to us from the mouth of God" (*ICR*, 1.18.4). Thus,

We owe to Scripture the same reverence which we owe to God; because it has proceeded from Him alone, and has nothing belonging to man mixed with it. . . . The Law and the prophets are not a doctrine delivered according to the will and pleasure of men, but dictated by the Holy Spirit. (Urquhart, *IAHS*, 129–30.)

Hence,

Our faith in doctrine is not established until we have a perfect conviction that God is its author. Hence, the highest proof of Scripture is uniformly taken from the character of him whose word it is. . . . If, then, we would consult most effectually for our consciences, and save them from being driven about in a whirl of uncertainty, from wavering, and even stumbling at the smallest obstacle, our conviction of the truth of Scripture must be derived from a higher source than human conjectures, judgments, or reasons; namely, the secret testimony of the Spirit.

Thus,

If they are not possessed of shameless effrontery, they will be compelled to confess that the Scripture exhibits clear evidence of its being spoken by God, and, consequently, of its containing his heavenly doctrine. We shall see a little farther on that the volume of sacred Scripture very far surpasses all other writings. Nay, if we look at it with clear eyes and unbiased judgment, it will forthwith present itself with a divine majesty which will subdue our presumptuous opposition, and force us to do it homage. (Calvin, *ICR*, 1.7.4.)

Further,

The Scriptures are the only records in which God has been pleased to consign his truth to perpetual remembrance, the full authority which they ought to possess with the faithful is not recognized unless they are believed to have come from heaven, as directly as if God had been heard giving utterance to them (ibid., 1.7.1).

Calvin concluded,

But as the Lord was pleased that doctrine should exist in a clearer and more ample form, the better to satisfy weak consciences, he commanded the prophecies also to be committed to writing, and to be held part of his word. To these at the same time were added historical details, which are the composition of prophets, but dictated by the Holy Spirit (ibid., 4.8.6).

The Bible Is Conveyed Through Humans

"As I have observed," said Calvin,

There is this difference between the apostles and their successors, they were sure and authentic amanuenses of the Holy Spirit; and, therefore, their writings are to be regarded as the oracles of God, whereas others have no other office than to teach what is delivered and sealed in the holy Scriptures (ibid., 4.8.9).

Scripture Has Divine Authority

Having come from God, the Bible has both divine authority and inerrancy in the original manuscripts. It is the certain and unerring rule of the Christian faith. Calvin wrote, "For our wisdom ought to consist in embracing with gentle docility, and without any exceptions, all that is delivered in the sacred Scriptures" (ibid., 1.18.4).

The Bible Is Inerrant in the Original Manuscripts

Calvin said plainly, "[Scripture is] the certain and unerring rule" (*CC*, Ps. 5:11).

> For if we reflect how prone the human mind is to lapse into forgetfulness of God, how readily inclined to every kind of error, how bent every now and then on devising new and fictitious religions, it will be easy to understand how necessary it was to make such a depository of doctrine as would secure it from either perishing by the neglect, vanishing away amid the errors, or being corrupted by the presumptuous audacity of men. (*ICR*, 1.6.3.)

He concluded,

> So long as your mind entertains any misgivings as to the certainty of the word of God, its authority will be weak and dubious, or rather will have no authority at all. Nor is it sufficient to believe that God is true, and cannot lie or deceive, unless you feel firmly persuaded that every word which proceeds from him is sacred, inviolable truth (ibid., 3.2.6).

There Are Copyist Errors in the Manuscripts

Calvin believed that only the original text of Scripture was without any error. Speaking of what he believed to be an error in a copy, he wrote,

> How the name of Jeremiah crept in [the manuscripts at Matt. 27:9], I confess that I do not know, nor do I give myself much trouble to inquire. The passage itself plainly shows that the name of Jeremiah has been put down by mistake, instead of Zechariah. (*CC*, Matt. 27:9.)

Calvin held that the sacred Scriptures are the unerring norm for the Christian faith, having originated from the very mouth of God by the dictates of the Holy Spirit. The only errors were copyists' errors in some manuscripts, not in the originals.

EVANGELICAL TRADITION AFTER CALVIN
(c. 1536–c. 1918)

Ulrich Zwingli (1484–1531) differed from the other Reformers on some points concerning the *interpretation* of the Scripture, but there was unanimity among them on the *inspiration* and *authority* of Scripture. Zwingli affirmed his view of Scripture in the *Sixty-seven Articles* (1523) by writing,

> The articles and opinions below I, Ulrich Zwingli, confess to having preached in the worthy city of Zurich as based upon the Scriptures which are called inspired by God, and I offer to protect and conquer with the said articles, and where I have not now correctly understood said Scriptures I shall allow myself to be taught better, but only from said Scripture.

John Knox (c. 1513–1572), who established Calvinism as the official affiliation of Scotland, believed in the inspiration and authority of Scripture, as did his mentor. It was Knox's disciples who trained King James I of England, during whose reign the famous King James (Authorized) Version of the Bible was produced (in 1611).

The Reformed position was expressed in Switzerland through *The Sixty-Seven Articles (or Conclusions) of Ulrich Zwingli* (1523), *The Ten Conclusions of Berne* (1528), *The First Helvetic Confession* (1536), and *The Second Helvetic Confession* (1566).

Francis Turretin (1623–1687) was raised in this tradition and, alongside his son Johann Alfons (1671–1737), taught at Geneva. In France the work of Calvin was perpetuated in the *Gallican Confession* (1559), which asserts, "We believe that the Word contained in these [canonical] books has proceeded from God, and receives its authority from him alone, and not from men." This confession was published in a somewhat modified and abridged form and used by the Waldenses as *A Brief Confession of Faith of the Reformed Churches of the Piedmont* (1655).

Elsewhere, the Reformed view of Scripture was set forth in three basic treatises: *The Belgic Confession* (1561), *The Heidelberg (Palatinate) Catechism* (1563), and *The Canons of Dort* (1618–1619). *The Belgic Confession* was the basic confessional statement of the Netherlands during the period when Jacob Arminius (1560–1609), a Dutch theologian, promulgated the doctrines now known as Arminianism. His immediate followers were called "the Remonstrants," after their anti-Calvinistic *Remonstrance*, or "Five Articles," published in 1610.

Arminius devoted six of his seventy-nine private disputations to the nature, authority, and adequacy of Scripture. In them he asserted that in the transmission of His Word, God "first employed *oral enunciation* in its delivery, and afterwards, *writing*, as a more certain means against corruption and oblivion . . . so that we now have the infallible word of God in no other place than in the Scriptures . . . the instrument of religion." He continued his argument by stating that the "authority of the word of God, which is comprised of the Old and New Testaments, lies both in the veracity of the whole narration, and of all the declarations, whether they be those about things past, about things present, or about those which are to come, and in the power of the commands and prohibitions, which are contained in the divine word."

The Synod at Dort (1618–19) contains five articles devoted to the Scriptures, including this statement from Article V:

> This Word of God was not sent nor delivered by the will of man, but *holy men of God spake as they were moved by the Holy Ghost*, as the apostle Peter saith. . . . Afterwards God, from a special care which he has for us and for our salvation, commanded his servants, the Prophets and Apostles, to commit his revealed Word to writing; and he himself wrote with his own finger the two tables of the law. Therefore we call such writings holy and divine Scriptures.

Following its presentation of the canonical books and their sufficiency, *The Belgic Confession* ends its statement on Scripture by concluding,

> Therefore we reject with all our hearts whatsoever doth not agree with this infallible rule, which the apostles have taught us, saying, *Try the spirits whether they are of God*. Likewise, *If there come any unto you, and bring not this doctrine, receive him not into your house*.

The Belgic Confession was adopted as the official doctrinal standard for the Reformed churches following its revision at the Synod of Dort. The Reformed Church settled on the Calvinistic position as it pertained to the doctrine of the inspiration and authority of Scripture and held to that position into the twentieth century.

The Westminster Tradition (c. 1538–c. 1918)

The Thirty-Nine Articles of Religion of the Church of England became the official view of the Church of England (1571) and Ireland (1615). The *Thirty-Nine Articles* combined features both of the Swiss (or Reformed) and Lutheran confessions. The Article "Of the Sufficiency of the Holy Scriptures for Salvation" affirms,

> Holy Scripture containeth all things necessary to salvation: so that whatsoever is not read therein, nor may be proved thereby, is not to be required of any man, that should be believed as an article of the Faith, *or* be thought requisite or necessary for salvation.

The Westminster Assembly of Divines was called in 1642 to legislate for Christian doctrine, worship, and discipline in the state church. Its work stands at the forefront of Protestant councils. The Assembly produced *A Confession of Faith* (1647) and two "Catechisms" that were written in English and used throughout Anglo-Presbyterian churches into the twentieth century. The first article of *The Westminster Confession of Faith* affirms:

> Because of the insufficiency of mankind's knowledge of God, His will, and His salvation, it pleased the Lord, at sundry times, and in diverse manners, to reveal himself, and to declare that his will unto his Church; and afterwards for the better preserving and propagating of the truth, and for the more sure establishment and comfort of the church against corruption of the flesh, and the malice of Satan and of the world, to commit the same wholly unto writing; which maketh the holy Scripture to be most necessary; those former ways of God's revealing his will unto his people being now ceased.

The *Confession* adds,

> The authority of Scripture, for which it ought to be believed and obeyed, dependeth not upon the testimony of any man or church, but wholly upon God (who is truth itself), the Author thereof; and therefore it is to be received, because it is the word of God . . . yet notwithstanding, our full persuasion and assurance of the infallible truth, and divine authority thereof, is from the inward work of the Holy Spirit, bearing witness by and with the Word in our hearts. . . .
>
> VI. The whole counsel of God, concerning all things necessary for his own glory, man's salvation, faith, and life, is either expressly set down in Scripture, or by good and necessary consequence may be deduced from Scripture: unto which nothing at any time is to be added, whether by new revelations of the Spirit, or traditions of men. . . .
>
> IX. The infallible rule and interpretation of Scripture is the Scripture itself. . . .
>
> X. The Supreme Judge, by which all controversies of religion are to be determined, and all decrees of councils, opinions of ancient writers, doctrines of men, and private spirits, are to be examined, and in whose sentence we are to rest, can be no other but the Holy Spirit speaking in the Scripture.

The Wesleyan Tradition

After the American Revolution John Wesley (1703–1791) drew up *The Twenty-Five Articles of Religion,* which were adopted by the American Methodists in 1784. These *Articles* were a liberal and judicious abridgment of *The Thirty-Nine Articles,* with Calvinistic and other features omitted. Nevertheless, in Article II, "The Sufficiency of the Holy Scriptures for Salvation," Wesley set forth:

The Holy Scriptures contain all things necessary to salvation; so that whatsoever is not read therein, nor may be proved thereby, is not to be required of any man that it should be believed as an article of faith, or be thought requisite or necessary to salvation. In the name of the Holy Scripture we do understand those canonical books of the Old and New Testaments of whose authority was never any doubt in the Church. (Wesley, cited in Schaff, *CC*, 3.808.)

Wesley frequently affirmed his belief in the inspiration and authority of Scripture as "the oracles of God," written by "men divinely inspired." He attested to their truthfulness by saying, " 'All Scripture is given by inspiration of God,' consequently, all Scripture is infallibly true," and "If there be any mistakes in the Bible, there may as well be a thousand. If there be one falsehood in that book, it did not come from the God of truth" (*WJW*, 5.193; 6.117; 8.45–46; 10.80).

Wesley's followers continued in the same high view of the inspiration and authority of Scripture. As Wesleyan scholar Wilber T. Dayton stated,

The absolute authority and total reliability of the Bible was taken for granted in early Wesleyanism as emphatically as motherhood has been assumed to be the principle for the survival of the human race. Nothing would have been more repugnant to original Methodism than to cast doubt on the Word of God, the very source of life. ("IWBW" in Hannah, *IC*, 223.)

Irish Wesleyan Adam Clarke (c. 1760–1832) affirmed his belief in the plenary inspiration and infallibility of Scripture as "the only complete directory of the faith and practice of man" (*MW*, 12.80, 83, 122; cf. 6.420). Richard Watson (1781–1833), the first systematic theologian of the Wesleyan movement, declared in his two-volume *Theological Institutes* (1823),

The sacred writers composed their works under so plenary and immediate an influence of the Holy Spirit, that God may be said to speak by them to man, and not merely that they spoke to men in the name of God, and by his authority. (*TI*, 6.11.)

It was not until the opening years of the twentieth century that Methodism moved from its moorings in this high view of Scripture. Even then, the shift was based on tendencies other than the objective and historical record of Scripture, tendencies resulting from the impact of subjectivism and secularism, and from when the methodology of modern science as the basis of authority in social matters was transferred to theology.

The Anabaptist and Baptist Tradition (c. 1524–c. 1918)

Early figures associated with this movement include John Wycliffe (c. 1324–1384), John Hus (c. 1372–1415), Balthasar Hubmaier (c. 1480–

1528), Martin Bucer (1491–1551), and Menno Simons (1496–1561). Hubmaier's influence is evident in one of the earliest Anabaptist statements of their beliefs, *The Schleitheim Confession* (1527). In the introduction to his *Treatise Against the Anabaptists,* John Calvin acknowledged that "this sect receives the Holy Scripture, as we do" (*TAA*, 39).

Martin Bucer and Menno Simons' position on Scripture exerted influence on John Calvin during the time that the Genevan Reformer was in Strassburg. Simons became the leader of the peaceful Anabaptists in the Netherlands, and his view of Scripture is set forth in *The Foundation of Christian Doctrine* (1539–1540).

In general, Baptists have tended to avoid creedal statements; in particular, they have built their confessional statements on earlier models within their particular tradition. An example of Baptist statements is the *Confession of Faith* (1644) of the seven Baptist churches in London, which was reissued in 1688 and 1689 as *A Confession Put Forth by the Elders and Brethren of Many Congregations of Christians (Baptized Upon Profession of Their Faith) in London and the Country.* This was a slight modification of the *Westminster Confession* of the Church of England and the *Savoy Declaration* (1658) of the Congregational churches in order to suit the distinctives of Baptist polity and baptism.

The *Second London Confession* was "adopted by the Baptist Association [that] met at Philadelphia, Sept. 25, 1742," and called *The Philadelphia Confession.* It followed the model of the *Westminster Confession* by placing the doctrine of Scripture in Article I (paragraphs 1–10), where it states,

> (1) The Holy Scripture is the only sufficient, certain and infallible rule of all-saving knowledge, faith, and obedience. . . . (4) The authority of the Holy Scriptures, for which it ought to be believed, dependeth not upon the testimony of any man or church, but wholly upon God (Who is truth itself), the author thereof; therefore it is to be received, because it is the Word of God. (*The Philadelphia Confession of Faith*, 6th ed.)

In the area of North Carolina, Separate Baptists joined their efforts with the Sandy Creek Church, and in 1758 the Sandy Creek Association was formed, with the Sandy Creek Church as its nucleus. Separate Baptists from Virginia and the Carolinas cooperated in their outreach for more than a dozen years; Article II of their brief doctrinal statement says, "The Scriptures of the Old and New Testaments are the word of God, and only rule of faith and practice" (Lumpkin, *BCF*, 358).

During the nineteenth century, Baptists in both the northern and southern United States came to use the shorter, moderately Calvinistic statement, *The New Hampshire Declaration of Faith* (1833). The same statement was adopted, with some additions, deletions, and other changes, as *A Statement of the Baptist Faith and Message* of the Southern Baptist Convention in 1925. *The New Hampshire Declaration of Faith* (9–12) asserts,

We believe that the Holy Bible was written by men divinely inspired, and is a perfect treasure of heavenly instruction;*[4] that it has God as its author, salvation for its end,* and truth without any mixture of error for its matter;* that it reveals the principles by which God will judge us;* and therefore is, and shall remain to the end of the world, the true center of Christian union,* and the supreme standard by which all human conduct, creeds, and opinions shall be tried* (Article I, *Of the Scriptures*).

In the meantime the Southern Baptist Convention reaffirmed and even strengthened this particular article in its adoption of *The Baptist Faith and Message* (1963).

The Roman Catholic View on Scripture (c. 1545–c. 1918)

The traditional teaching on the doctrine of the inspiration and inerrancy of Scripture is based in the teachings of the church fathers (see chapter 17), such as Augustine and Aquinas. Even the great Protestant Reformers never changed the Roman Catholic view on the *origin* and *nature* of Scripture; their differences with the Catholic Church were over the *extent* of the canon (see chapter 28) and the *interpretation* of it.

The official Roman Catholic position in *The Canons and Dogmatic Decrees of the Council of Trent* (1563) says,

> The Council clearly perceives that this truth and rule are contained in the written books and unwritten traditions which have come down to us, *having been received by the apostles from the mouth of Christ Himself or from the apostles by the dictation of the Holy Spirit*, and have been transmitted as it were from hand to hand. . . . [Following, then,] the example of the orthodox Fathers, *it receives and venerates with the same sense of loyalty and reverence all the books of the Old and New Testaments—for God alone is the author of both.* (Neuner and Dupuis, *CF*, 77, emphasis added.)

The Council of Vatican I proclaimed the inerrancy of Scripture, saying, "They contain revelation without error*[5] because having been written by the inspiration of the Holy Spirit they have God as their author*" (Denzinger, 1787, 444). Pope Leo XIII affirmed that "it would be entirely wrong either to confine inspiration only to some parts of Scripture, or to concede that the sacred author himself has erred" (Denzinger, 1950, Encyclical, *Providentissimus Deus*, 1893).

Vatican II added,

> Since, therefore, all that the inspired authors, or sacred writers,

---

[4]An asterisk indicates the omission of scriptural citations contained in the Declaration.
[5]Again, an asterisk indicates the omission of scriptural citations contained in the text.

affirm should be regarded as affirmed by the Holy Spirit, we must acknowledge that the books of Scripture, firmly, faithfully and without error, teach that the truth which God, for the sake of our salvation, wished to see confided to the sacred Scriptures. (*Documents of Vatican II*, "On Revelation," chapter 3, 757.)

More liberal Catholic theologians see a caveat in the phrase "for the sake of our salvation," arguing that inerrancy covers only salvific truths, but this is contrary to the whole of the Catholic tradition up to modern times. All agree, however, that inspiration and inerrancy are limited to the meaning the sacred authors "intended to express and did in fact express, through the medium of contemporary literary forms."

To rightly understand what the sacred author wanted to affirm in his work, due attention must be paid both to the customary and characteristic patterns of perception, speech and narrative which prevailed at the age of the sacred writer, and to the conventions which the people of his time followed in their dealings with one another (ibid., 757–58).

During the nineteenth century, Pope Pius IX issued *The Papal Syllabus of Errors* (1864), in which he attacked the positions of "Pantheism, Naturalism, and Absolute Rationalism" by listing among their errors the views:

Divine revelation is imperfect, and therefore, subject to continual and definite progress of human reason. . . . The prophecies and miracles set forth and narrated in the Sacred Scriptures are fictions of poets . . . mythical inventions, and Jesus Christ is himself a mythical fiction. (In Schaff, *CC*, 2.214–215.)

The position of the papacy has not deviated concerning the doctrine of the inspiration and authority of Scripture.

The same view is reflected in *The Dogmatic Decrees of the Vatican Council concerning the Catholic Faith and the Church of Christ* (1870), which addressed the question of Scripture as

divine revelation that can be known by every one with facility, with firm assurance, and with no mixture of error. . . . Further, this supernatural revelation, according to the universal belief of the Church, declared by the sacred Synod of Trent, is contained in the written books and unwritten traditions which have come down to us. (Schaff, *CC*, 2.240–241.)

As James T. Burtchaell has suggested, "The Catholic Church has displayed little spontaneous desire to refine, revise, and improve her doctrinal formulations. Only when she is goaded and provoked from without does she bestir herself to this apparently disagreeable task" (*CTI*, 1). Justo L. Gonzalez speaks similarly in referring to the papal response to the development of higher criticism during the late nineteenth and early twentieth centuries:

> When modern forms of critical research were developed, Rome condemned those who tried to relate them to religious questions . . . [which] provides some justification for the commonly held view among Protestants that the Catholic Church was one of the most reactionary forces in the world. (*HCT*, vol. 3, 373.)

As Carl F. H. Henry correctly notes:

> Throughout its long medieval influence, the Roman church therefore promoted the doctrine of scriptural inerrancy and opposed notions of a limited inerrancy restricted to faith and morals. The effort by Henry Holden (1596–1662) in *Divinae Fidei Analysis* to promote limited inerrancy garnered no enthusiasm.

He continues,

> But in the late-nineteenth and early-twentieth century, Roman and Protestant clergy alike shared in the flight from inerrancy. *The New Catholic Encyclopedia* indicates the Roman church's traditional support for inerrancy but then goes on to indicate the contemporary mood: "It is nonetheless obvious that many biblical statements are simply not true when judged according to modern knowledge of science and history. . . ." Even the Vatican II declaration that Scripture teaches "without error that truth which God wanted put into the Sacred Writings for the sake of our salvation" is interpreted descriptively by some priests. . . . Others interpret it restrictively. (*RA*, 374.)

Contrary to the historic view, this ambiguous phrase left the door open for Roman Catholics who deny the doctrine of inerrancy.

The Eastern Orthodox View on Scripture (c. 1643–c. 1918)

Putting aside differences about the role of authority, the Eastern Church has maintained a high view of the authority of Scripture, in line with both Roman Catholic and Protestant views. As recently as 1839, for example, *The Longer Catechism of the Orthodox Catholic Eastern Church* contained a lengthy presentation in its "Introduction to the Orthodox Catechism" for use of *The Orthodox Confession of the Eastern Church* (1643). In that introduction the discussion "On Divine Revelation" asks, "Why are not all men capable of receiving a revelation immediately from God?" and answers that it is "owing to their sinful impurity, and weakness both in soul and body." After naming the prophets, our Lord Jesus Christ, and the apostles as the heralds of divine revelation, the introduction addresses the question "Can not man, then, have any knowledge of God without a special revelation from him?" and answers by stating that "this knowledge is imperfect and insufficient, and can serve only as a preparation for faith, or as a help towards the knowledge of God from his revelation."

In its section "On Holy Tradition and Holy Scripture" the introduction asks, "How is divine revelation spread among men and preserved in the true Church?" The answer: "By two channels—holy tradition and holy Scripture." The introduction also says, "The most ancient and original instrument for spreading divine revelation is holy tradition," but that Holy Scripture was given "to this end, that divine revelation might be preserved more exactly and unchangeably." Question 23 raises the issue of the relationship of the two: "Must we follow holy tradition even when we possess holy Scripture? We must follow that tradition which agrees with the divine revelation and with holy Scripture, as is taught us by holy Scripture itself . . . 2 Thess. ii.15" (Schaff, *CC*, 2.445–542; 2.275–449).

However, as Kallistos Ware says,

> The "Age of the Fathers" in eastern Christendom does not come to a close with the Council of Chalcedon in the fifth century, nor yet with the last meeting of the last Ecumenical Council in the eighth, but it extends uninterrupted until 1453; and even today—despite heavy borrowings from the Roman Catholic and Protestant west during the seventeenth and following centuries—Eastern Orthodoxy remains basically Patristic in outlook. ("CTE" in Drewery, *HCD*, 183–84.)

This is true of the Orthodox view of Scripture as well.

SUMMARY AND CONCLUSION

A survey of the history of the Christian church from the Reformation to recent times reveals that there is virtually unanimous consent that the Bible is the divinely inspired, infallible, and inerrant Word of God. This follows the basic view of the early church (see chapter 17), and deviations from this view were extremely rare before the late nineteenth century, when liberalism (see chapter 20) and neo-orthodoxy (see chapter 21) challenged the longstanding position of the Christian church, both East and West, Catholic and Protestant.

SOURCES

Burtchaell, James. *Catholic Theories of Inspiration Since 1810.*
Calvin, John. *Calvin's Commentaries.*
———. *Institutes of the Christian Religion.*
Clarke, Adam. *Miscellaneous Works.*
Dayton, Wilber T. "Infallibility, Wesley, and British Wesleyanism" in John Hannah, ed., *Inerrancy and the Church.*

Gonzalez, Justo L. *The History of Christian Thought*, volume 3 in *From the Protestant Reformation to the Twentieth Century.*

Hannah, John, ed. *Inerrancy and the Church.*

Henry, Carl F. H. *Revelation and Authority.*

Lumpkin, William L. *The Baptist Confessions of Faith.*

Luther, Martin. *Luther's Works.*

———. *Table Talks.*

McDonald, H. D. *Theories of Revelation: An Historical Study: 1700–1960.*

Neuner, J., and J. Dupuis. *The Christian Faith: Doctrinal Documents of the Catholic Church.*

Reu, M. *Luther and the Scriptures.*

Schaff, Philip. *The Creeds of Christendom.*

Urquhart, John. *Inspiration and Accuracy of the Holy Scriptures.*

Ware, Kallistos. "Christian Theology in the East: 600–1453" in Benjamin Drewery, *A History of Christian Doctrine: In Succession to the Earlier Word of G. P. Fisher* in the *International Theological Library Series.*

Watson, Richard. *Theological Institutes.*

Wesley, John. *The Works of John Wesley.*

[No author listed]. *The New Hampshire Declaration of Faith* in the Oklahoma *Baptist Messenger* 58, number 32 (April 1969).

CHAPTER NINETEEN

THE HISTORY OF DESTRUCTIVE BIBLICAL CRITICISM

Τhe word *criticism* simply means to exercise judgment, which is not only a legitimate but also a necessary thing for all rational beings to do. There are two basic kinds of biblical criticism: lower and higher. Lower criticism has to do with the *text* of Scripture, and higher criticism with the *source* of that text. The former takes the available manuscripts and attempts to reconstruct the original text; the latter asks what the actual source of the original text was. Evangelicals consider both of these to be legitimate disciplines.

Higher criticism can be divided into two categories: positive and negative, also called constructive and destructive. It is the latter, of course, that evangelicals oppose. Destructive criticism is based on presuppositions that are opposed to the Bible and to evangelical theology. One of the most persistent and unjustified presuppositions of negative biblical criticism is antisupernaturalism. The roots of this kind of criticism began in the early-to-mid–1600s.

THE PHILOSOPHICAL ROOTS OF DESTRUCTIVE BIBLICAL CRITICISM

Destructive biblical criticism is not the result of factual finds but of philosophical fallacies. It springs not from history but from philosophy—from philosophies that are alien to the realistic theism present in Scripture. The earliest of these ideologies began only a century after the Reformation.

Inductivism: Francis Bacon (1561–1626)

While Francis Bacon took his cue for scientific research from God's command to subdue the world in Genesis 1:28, he also set the stage for modern biblical criticism when he systematically expounded the notion that man's power to control nature rests in his own hands and can be achieved if he applies correct methods. In his *Novum Organum* (1620) Bacon claimed that all truth is discovered by induction and known experimentally. He argued that by making inductions from the simplest facts of experience man could reach forward to discover fundamental principles, which would issue forth in beneficial practical results—thus making truth and utility ("that which works") the very same things in the world of science. In addition, Bacon completely separated the realm of reason and science from the realm of faith and religion (see Geisler, *BEIPR*, chapter 1), thus setting the stage for later criticism of the Bible without touching matters of faith.

Materialism: Thomas Hobbes (1588–1679)

One of the first philosophers in the modern world to do subtle but destructive criticism on the Bible was the materialist Thomas Hobbes. From this vantage point Hobbes launched an attack on orthodox religion in the form of a defense of the English monarchy—a safe perspective from which to do so in his day.

Materialism

Hobbes wrote,

> Whatsoever we imagine is finite. Therefore there is no idea or conception of anything we call infinite. No man can have in his mind an image of infinite magnitude, infinite time, infinite force, or infinite power. When we say anything is infinite, we signify only that we are not able to conceive the ends and bounds of the thing named, having no conception of the thing, but our own inability. And therefore the name God is used . . . that we may honour Him. (*L*, 80.)

In view of his limited materialistic theory of knowing, Hobbes concluded,

> The world (I mean not the earth only . . . but the universe, that is, the whole mass of all things that are) is corporeal, that is to say, body; and hath the dimensions of magnitude, namely, length, breadth, and depth: also every part of the body is likewise body, and hath the like dimensions; and consequently every part of the universe is body, and that which is not body is no part of the universe: and because the universe is all, that which is no part of it is nothing, and consequently nowhere. (*L*, 269.)

Desupernaturalized View of the Gospels

On the basis of his materialistic understanding of the world, Hobbes engaged in some desupernaturalizing of the Gospel records more than three hundred years before Rudolph Bultmann (see page 343). Hobbes boldly proclaimed that "the Scriptures by the Spirit of God in man mean a man's spirit, inclined to godliness" (ibid., 70). As to the story of Jesus casting a demon out of a man, Hobbes said, "I see nothing at all in the Scripture that requireth a belief that demoniacs were any other thing but madmen" (ibid., 70–71). By implication the whole gospel record could be desupernaturalized. The miracles of the gospels were labeled parabolical or spiritual but not historical because

> Scripture was written to shew unto men the kingdom of God, and to prepare their minds to become his obedient subjects; leaving the world, and the philosophy thereof, to the disputations of men, for the exercising of their natural reason (ibid., 70).

Miracles Are Not Essential to Religion

For Hobbes, miracles are not necessary and probably not even helpful to religion. What is essential to religion is faith. Claiming that "natural reason" is the "undoubted word of God," Hobbes insists that in the religious realm we must live by "the will of obedience" to the lawfully imposed religion of the state. This means that "we so speak as, by lawful authority, we are commanded; and when we live accordingly; which, in sum, is trust and faith reposed in him that speaketh [the ruler], though the mind be incapable of any notion at all from the words spoken" (ibid., 165). In a word, faith and obedience are what is essential to religion, not reason; piety, not philosophy, is what God expects of believers. There is complete separation of faith and fact—hence, belief in objective factual miracles is not essential to true religious faith.

Hobbes's complete separation of divine revelation (for spiritual truth) from human reason (for cognitive truth) not only anticipates Søren Kierkegaard and Karl Barth, but it also goes beyond them in paving the way for a radical form of biblical criticism.

Antisupernaturalism: Benedict Spinoza (1632–1677)

As we have seen (see chapter 3), Benedict Spinoza was neither a theist nor a deist; rather, he was a Jewish pantheist, operating from a rationalistic and naturalistic framework of thought. Using a now outdated closed view of the universe and adhering to Euclidian geometric deductivism, Spinoza insisted on the universal, exceptionless nature of natural law, and from this he concluded that miracles are not possible.

Spinoza lived in an age increasingly impressed with the orderliness of a physical universe, an age in which it was believed that Newton's newly discovered law of gravitation was without exception. Because of this it seemed axiomatic to Spinoza that natural laws are immutable and, therefore, unbreakable.

Argument for Antisupernaturalism

In his highly influential *A Theologico-Political Treatise*, Spinoza declared,

> Nothing, then, comes to pass in nature in contravention to her universal laws, nay, everything agrees with them and follows from them, for ... she keeps a fixed and immutable order. [In fact,] a miracle, whether in contravention to, or beyond, nature, is a mere absurdity.

Spinoza was nothing short of dogmatic about the impossibility of miracles. He unashamedly proclaimed, "We may, then, be absolutely certain that every event which is truly described in Scripture necessarily happened, like everything else, according to natural laws" (*TPT*, 83, 87, 92).

As we observed in part 1, when Spinoza's argument against miracles is reduced to its basic premises, it goes something like this:

(1) Miracles are violations of natural laws.
(2) Natural laws are immutable.
(3) It is impossible to violate immutable laws.
(4) Therefore, miracles are impossible.

The second premise is the key to Spinoza's argument: Nature "keeps a fixed and *immutable* order"—everything "*necessarily* happened ... according to natural laws," and "nothing comes to pass in nature in contravention to her [nature's] universal laws." *If* this were true, then Spinoza would be right; to believe otherwise "*is* a mere absurdity."

Critics have noted serious problems with Spinoza's radical form of naturalism, including its basis in a now outmoded science; its unjustified deductivism; its fallacy of begging the question; its self-defeating determinism, and its philosophical pantheism (see chapter 2). From this unstable foundation, Spinoza launched the first systematic attack on the historic view of Scripture.

Negative Biblical Criticism

Over a century before biblical critic Johann Salomo Semler (1725–1791), and two centuries prior to Julius Wellhausen (1844–1918), Spinoza was engaged in systematic antisupernatural criticism of the Bible. *A Theologico-Political Treatise* was widely circulated in the late seventeenth century, and even though it took some two centuries to blossom, it was largely through the influence of this book that negative higher criticism began to undermine the traditional view of Scripture.

First, building on his naturalistic rationalism, Spinoza concluded that since "there are many passages in the Pentateuch that Moses could not have written, it follows that the belief that Moses was the author of the Pentateuch is ungrounded and even irrational" (ibid., 126). "Who wrote the first five books of the Old Testament? The same person," said Spinoza, "who wrote the rest of the Old Testament: Ezra the scribe, who lived around 400 B.C." (*TPT,* 129–30).

Second, Spinoza rejected the Resurrection accounts in the Gospels. Concerning Christianity he said that "the Apostles who came after Christ, preached it to all men as a universal religion *solely* in virtue of Christ's Passion" (ibid., 170, emphasis added). In other words, Spinoza reduced Christianity to a mystical, nonpropositional religion, a religion without foundations. The orthodox faith has held, since the apostle Paul (cf. 1 Cor. 15:1–14), that apart from the truth of the resurrection of Christ, Christianity is a religion without hope.

Third, for Spinoza, the Scripture merely *"contains* the word of God" (ibid., 165, emphasis added), a position characteristic of later liberal Christianity following Schleiermacher (see chapter 20). In Spinoza's view, it is false to say, as orthodox Christians have, that the Bible *is* the Word of God. For him the parts of the Bible that *contain* the word of God are known to be such because the morality in them conforms to a natural law known by human reason (ibid., 172, 196–97).

Fourth, Spinoza categorically denied all miracles in the Bible, commending "anyone who seeks for the true causes of miracles and strives to understand natural phenomena as an intelligent being" (*Ethics,* part 1, prop. XXXVI, appendix). Not only did he conclude that "every event . . . in Scripture necessarily happened, like everything else, according to natural laws" (*TPT,* 92), but also that Scripture itself "makes the general assertion in several passages that nature's course is *fixed and unchangeable*" (ibid., 96).

Fifth, Spinoza said that biblical authors did not speak from supernatural "revelation" and "the modes of expression and discourse adopted by the Apostles in the Epistles show very clearly that the latter were not written by revelation and divine command, but *merely by the natural powers* and judgment of the authors" (ibid., 159, emphasis added). When the Bible says the prophets spoke by "revelation," Spinoza understands this as the "extraordinary power . . . [of] the imagination of the prophets" (ibid., 24).

It is evident that Spinoza's antisupernaturalism led to a systematic and negative critique of Holy Scripture, denying the historicity of much of the text and changing the focus to the moral message of the Bible. This is the essence of liberalism—a view not to flower for two centuries after Spinoza (see chapter 20).

Skepticism: David Hume (1711–1776)

Skepticism did not originate with Scotland's David Hume, but it was seriously advanced in the modern world through his writings. Spurred by the revival of Greek skepticism in Western thought following the rediscovery and publication of the writings of Sextus Empiricus (flourished c. late second and early third centuries A.D.) in 1562, Hume's skeptical *Enquiry Concerning Human Understanding* (1748) became a classic of so-called Enlightenment thought. Between Spinoza and Kant, more than anyone else, Hume probably had the most adverse effect on views of biblical authority. His antisupernaturalism and his extreme emphasis on empiricism were the two most basic elements of Hume's attempt to undermine the traditional doctrine of Scripture.

Hume rejected the claim that Scripture is inspired or that the Bible is an authoritative revelation of God to humanity. He also denied the deity of Christ and rejected miracles as he sought to make theology the subject of empirical testing. He consigned the Bible and any other work speaking of metaphysical reality to the furnace in these famous words:

> When we run over libraries, persuaded of these principles, what havoc must we make? If we take in our hand any volume—of divinity or school metaphysics, for instance—let us ask, *Does it contain any abstract reasoning concerning quantity or number?* No. *Does it contain any experimental reasoning concerning matter of fact and existence?* No. Commit it then to the flames, for it can contain nothing but sophistry and illusion. (*ECHU*, 12.3.173.)

Recall, from part 1, Hume's antisupernaturalistic boast:

> I flatter myself that I have discovered an argument . . . which, if just, will, with the wise and learned, be an everlasting check to all kinds of superstitious delusion, and consequently will be useful as long as the world endures (ibid., 10.1.18).

Just what is this "final" argument against miracles? In Hume's own words:

> A miracle is a violation of the laws of nature; and . . . firm and unalterable experience has established these laws. . . . [Therefore,] the proof against a miracle, from the very nature of the fact, is as entire as any argument from experience can possibly be imagined (ibid., 10.1.122).

The reason for this is that "a uniform experience amounts to a proof, there is here a direct and full *proof,* from the nature of the fact, against the existence of any miracle" (ibid., 123). In summary, Hume wrote,

> There must, therefore, be a uniform experience against every mirac-

ulous event. Otherwise the event would not merit that appellation. [So] nothing is esteemed a miracle if it ever happened in the common course of nature (ibid., 122–23).

Agnosticism: Immanuel Kant (1724–1804)

Immanuel Kant is considered by many to be the crossroad thinker of modern philosophy. He synthesized the two dominant but conflicting modes of thought of the Enlightenment—empiricism and rationalism—into an intellectual whole. The result, unfortunately, was philosophical agnosticism (see chapter 3), though Kant remained a deist. In his creative synthesis (see *CPR*), Kant argued that the mind "knows" only *after* it constructs the data of experience, not before. Hence, we know only what *appears* (the *phenomenal*) to us, not that which really *is* (the *noumenal*). Further evidence for Kant that we cannot know the real world is that whenever one attempts to apply the categories of the mind (such as unity or causality) to the real world, hopeless contradictions and antinomies arise.

Another consequence of Kant's agnosticism is his fact/value dichotomy. For him, the "objective" world of fact is the phenomenal world of experience, while the "subjective" world of will cannot be known by pure reason. Instead, the subjective world is known by practical reason, or a morally postulated act of the will. Even though it is not possible to *think* that God exists, one must *live* as if God does exist. Thus Kant philosophically questioned the objectivity and rationality of divine revelation. He placed religion in the realm of the postulated rather than the known. This gave rise to the moral imperative that lies behind Kant's use of "moral reason" as the ground for determining what is essential to true religion.

Also from this Kant reasoned that miracles do not occur. Thus, like another deist, Thomas Jefferson, he was able to reject the Resurrection account at the close of the Gospels (Kant, *RWLRA*, 119). In making the moral imperative the criterion for true religion, Kant is the forerunner of Friedrich Schleiermacher (1768–1834). Following in the subjective footsteps of Kant and Schleiermacher, Rudolph Otto (1869–1937) used an irrational basis for his higher criticism of the Bible.

Romanticism (c. 1780–c. 1840)

Nothing seemed more characteristic of the late eighteenth century than the dominance of reason, as unemotional and intellectual questioning swept away ancient superstitions and abuses. Yet a strong opposition arose to that cold, one-sided approach, as the claims of feeling were reasserted. This movement emphasized great people and heroic movements of the past rather than ideas and institutions. The generic term "romanticism" is generally applied to this complex and elusive shift that radically challenged the older "rationalism." It had advocates in literature, music, painting, and philosophy throughout Europe before running its course in the late 1830s. Its most effective early proponent was Jean Jacques Rousseau (1712–1778), but it became most dominant in Germany, where its participants included Gotthold Lessing (1729–1781), Johan Wolfgang von Goethe (1749–1832), Johan Christoph Friedrich von Schiller (1759–1805), and Johann Christian Friedrich Hölderlin (1770–1843). Romanticism had a widespread negative influence on Christianity, especially through Friedrich Daniel Ernst Schleiermacher (1768–1834), the father of modern liberalism.

Deism (c. 1625–c. 1800)

Deism is theism minus miracles, or "theistic naturalism." It is the idea that God got the universe going, and it has run on its own natural steam since then; i.e., God is the universe's absentee Landlord. Some of the more prominent European deists were Herbert of Cherbury (1583–1648, the Father of English deism), John Toland (1670–1722), Anthony Collins (1676–1729), Thomas Woolston (c. 1670–1733), and Matthew Tindal (c. 1655–1733). Some of the more notable American deists were Benjamin Franklin (1706–1790), Thomas Jefferson (1743–1826), Stephen Hopkins (1707–1785), and Thomas Paine (1737–1809). Another well-known deist was the aforementioned Immanuel Kant, whose book *God Within the Limits of Reason Alone* is a deist classic.

Thomas Paine's Deistic View of God

"I believe in one God, and no more," wrote Paine, a belief he shared with theists. Also, like theists, he believed that the one God was all-powerful, all-knowing, all-good, infinite, merciful, just, and incomprehensible (see *CWTP*, 5, 26–27, 201). However, his God made the world but never intervened within it afterward. According to Paine, God created the world but never interacts with it.

Paine's Attack on the Bible

However, Paine rejected all forms of supernatural revelation, believing them to be unknowable. Paine also argued that supernatural revelation was impossible given the inadequacy of human language to convey it; God's revelation must be absolutely "unchangeable and universal" (ibid., 25). Given this, human language, which the Bible employs, could not be the means for its communication.

Paine's Contention That the Bible Is Not Verbally Inspired

Paine rejected all claims by any religious group to have received a verbal revelation from God. Instead he held that all such beliefs were "no other than human inventions, set up to terrify and enslave mankind, and monopolize power and profit" (ibid., 6). The "revealed religion" Paine had the most contempt for was Christianity. He wrote,

> Of all the systems of religion that ever were invented, there is none more derogatory to the Almighty, more unedifying to man, more repugnant to reason, and more contradictory in itself, than this thing called Christianity . . . [which is] too absurd for belief, too impossible to convince, and too inconsistent for practice; it renders the heart torpid, or produces only atheists and fanatics.

He added, "The only religion that has not been invented, and that has in it every evidence of divine originality, is pure and simple deism." In fact, deism "must have been the first, and will probably be the last that man believes" (ibid., 150).

Paine further argued,

> The continually progressive change to which the meaning of words is subject, the want of a universal language which renders translation necessary, the errors to which translations are again subject, the mistakes of copyists and printers, together with the possibility of willful alteration, are of themselves evidences that the human language, whether in speech or in print, cannot be the vehicle of the word of God (ibid., 19; cf. 55–56).

Early Critics of Deism

Deism's detractors included Thomas Sherlock (1678–1761), Joseph Butler (1692–1752), and William Paley (1743–1805), who attacked deism rationally, as well as John Wesley (1703–1791), George Whitefield (1714–1770), and Jonathan Edwards (1703–1758), who also added a theological and spiritual dimension to the defense of historical Christianity.

Transcendentalism: Georg Wilhelm Friedrich Hegel

G. W. F. Hegel (1770–1831) was born in Wurtenberg, Germany, to a Lutheran family. His main writings include: *Philosophy of History, Philosophy of Nature, Encyclopedia, Logic, Philosophy of Religion* (his major work), *Phenomena of Spirit,* and *Philosophy of Aesthetics.*

Hegel's Philosophical Roots

Like most other great figures, Hegel stood on the shoulders of many who had come before him. From *Plato* he learned that man's meaning is found in the state, that philosophy is the highest expression of reality, and that all determination is by negation. He accepted *Plotinus's* view that the world and consciousness are a manifestation of the Absolute—a form of pantheism. *Spinoza* taught him the inseparability of God and nature and, hence, antisupernaturalism. From *Kant*, Hegel concluded that we must begin with the phenomena of experience and use the transcendental method to arrive at truth. Of course, his *Judeo-Christian* training provided him with a linear view of history.

Hegel's So-Called Dialectic

Contrary to a widely held misunderstanding, Hegel did not believe in a Marxian kind of "dialectic" consisting of thesis/antithesis → synthesis. In fact, he never used the word *dialectic* in the body of any of his works. It appears once in the preface of his *Phenomenology of Mind*, where he claimed it came from Kant, and he rejected it, calling it "a lifeless schema" (Meuller, "HLTAS" in *JHI*, 412). The legend is based on Johann Gottlieb Fichte's (1762–1814) misinterpretation of Hegel and spread widely by Karl Marx's use of it in his dialectical materialism.

The Transcendental Argument

Following Kant, Hegel argued transcendentally, not dialectically (see Corduan, "TH" in Geisler, *BEIPR*). But unlike Kant, Hegel believed that both the content and form of all knowledge was transcendentally necessary to posit as a condition for knowing. Hence, he argued that partial (relative) knowledge is impossible because it presupposes knowledge of the whole (the absolute).

Hegel's Pantheistic View of God

Hegel's metaphysics is a kind of developmental pantheism (or panentheism—see chapter 2) worked out in the historical process. History is the footprints of God in the sands of time. Better, history is God's self-unfolding in the temporal world, the progressive overcoming of the world by Absolute Spirit.

Hegel's View of Christianity

Hegel viewed Christianity (Lutheranism) as the absolute religion, the highest manifestation of the Absolute to date. This is particularly manifest in the incarnation of God in Christ, by which God appeared on earth in a particular man at a particular time. Here the Infinite is identified with the finite.

The core of religion is the Incarnation. Absolute Spirit is where the God-man duality is overcome. This is done in three stages: art, religion, and philosophy, which are progressively more abstract. The highest manifestation of the Absolute, then, is in philosophy. It is the eternal Idea, the epitome, the fullest and most complete of all concepts. So, *while God becomes man in religion, man becomes God in philosophy.*

Hegel's View of the Bible

In an early attempt at a *Life of Jesus*, Hegel presented a desupernatural-ized view of Christ and formulated His teachings in terms of a Kantian ethic, something he had learned from Kant's famous *Religion Within the Limits of Reason Alone.* Here Jesus is depicted by Hegel as narrow-minded and obscurantist (as opposed to the open-minded Socrates). Further, Jesus is presented as not virgin-born, and all miracles mentioned are interpreted naturalistically. The prologue of John's gospel is reinterpreted to state: "Pure reason incapable of all limitations is the Deity itself."

Later, in *The Spirit of Christianity and its Fate,* Hegel contrasted the gos-pel ethic of love with the Jewish and Kantian ethics of law, but he never gave up either his antisupernaturalism or his moral-centered view of the Gospels. Hegel also reinterpreted the gospel stories of the redemptive death and resurrection of Christ in terms of Greek tragedy.

In *The Positivity of the Christian Religion,* Hegel affirms that in claiming to be the Messiah, Jesus was merely using the language of His listener, a form of the accommodation theory (see chapter 16). Instead of revering Him for His teaching about virtue, they revered His teaching about virtue because of the miracles He is supposed to have performed.

Hegel's Later Transcendental Pantheism

Even later, in his *Encyclopedia,* which is dominated by his transcendental idealism or developmental pantheism, Hegel was a radical revisionist of the literal, historical truth of the death and resurrection of Christ. The core of revealed religion is Christology: Jesus Christ is the God-man. As such, He died on the cross; thus both God and man died there. The Resurrection was neither of God nor man. Rather, in the Resurrection both God and man merge in Absolute Spirit. Therefore, in Hegel's developmental pan-theism is found the highest manifestation of Absolute Spirit.

Hegel's Influence on Modern Biblical Criticism

Of special interest to Christian apologetics is Hegel's significant influ-ence on negative biblical criticism. For example, following Hegel, F. C. Baur (1792–1860) and his Tubingen school claimed that the first-century tension between Peter's Judaistic form of Christianity opposed by Paul's anti-Judaistic form found its reconciliation in John's gospel in the second century, thus insisting on a late date of John's gospel. Also, David Strauss's desupernaturalized version of the life of Christ springs from Hegel's idea that spiritual reality is higher than the historical. Thus, as Rudolph Bultmann (1884–1976) was to affirm later, Christianity is myth. Likewise, Martin Heidegger's (1889–1976) mystical pantheism and hermeneutic, developed by Bultmann and Hans-Georg Gadamer (b. 1900), are rooted in Hegel's stress on spiritual interpretations of Scripture. This gave rise to the whole subjectivistic "new hermeneutic" (see chapter 10).

Scientism: Auguste Comte (1798–1857)

Naturalism has taken many forms in the modern and postmodern world, becoming a dominant view of its own, apart from its progenitors, in a view called positivism, and more descriptively known as scientism[1]. Auguste Comte is the forefather of this position, which, in his case, was also one of the early forms of secular humanism.

Comte's Life and Works

Auguste Comte was born in 1797 to a French rationalist Catholic family. He studied science and was secretary of Saint-Simone at *Ecole Polytechnique.* He said he "naturally ceased believing in God" at age fourteen.

Comte is known as the father of both positivism and sociology, which are terms he coined. He also developed a mystical (nontheistic) humanistic religious cult in which he installed himself as high priest. Comte's main works were *Cours, The Positive Philosophy of Auguste Comte* (1830–1842, trans. 1853) and *The Catechism of Positive Religion* (1852, trans. 1858). The latter included a humanistic religious calendar of secular "saints."

Scientism

With an epistemological starting point in Immanuel Kant's anti-metaphysical agnosticism and Hegel's historical developmentalism, Comte developed his law of growth. This included three stages of human development: *theological* (child)—ancient; *metaphysical* (youth)—medieval; and *positivistic* (adulthood)—modern. The first was the primitive belief in personal gods, later replaced by the Greek idea of impersonal law, only to be superseded by the modern (positivistic) belief in the methodological unity of science. These three stages represent the mythological (*mythos*), metaphysical (*logos*), and scientific (positivistic theories) stages of the human race. According to Comte, they move forward from the personal explanation of nature to impersonal law and finally to an objective method. They advance from the belief in supernatural beings to natural forces, and then to phenomenal (empirical) descriptions. Instead of animating spirits or impersonal powers, natural laws are posited. In this three-stage growth, spiritual and then rational causes are discarded for purely natural (positivistic) descriptions.

The religious stage has its own evolution whereby earlier polytheistic belief, which personified nature into gods, develops eventually into monotheistic faith, which consolidated them all into a godhead. The problem with the religious interpretation of nature is that it anthropomorphizes reality. The problem with the metaphysical stage is that it reifies (makes real) ideas rather than merely describing them and relating them as the positivistic stage does.

---

[1]The belief that science is the only valid form of knowledge.

Comte's goal was to find a general law by which all phenomena are related. Such a law, he believed, would be the ideal result of positivistic philosophy. However, the best likely result is a unity in the scientific method. True freedom lies in rational subjection to scientific laws. One law is that society must develop in the direction of scientism (positivism).

Religious Views

Comte disliked Protestantism, pronouncing it negative and productive of intellectual anarchy. As mentioned, he developed a humanistic (non-theistic) religion of his own in which he was the high priest of this cult of humanity; his mistress (Mme. Clothilde Vaux) was proclaimed the high priestess. Also, his humanistic religious calendar with "saints" included such persons as Frederick the Great, Dante, and Shakespeare.

In effect, Comte deified the scientific method, yet he protested that others had deified nature. Scientism was not just *a* method for discovering some truth, but *the* method for discovering truth. As such, it involved self-defeating beliefs in materialism, the denial of metaphysics, and the rejection of other absolute morality such as is taught in Scripture.

Evolutionism: Spencer and Darwin (1860f.)

Evolution existed as a philosophy before it existed as a science—even some ancient Greeks believed in evolution. However, it was not rooted in any testable scientific theory. Before Darwin's *On the Origin of Species* (1859), English philosopher Herbert Spencer "advocated a theory of evolution similar to that of Darwin's" (Edwards, *EOP*, Volume 7–8, 523).

Herbert Spencer (1820–1903)

Following in the line of the positivistic philosophy of Auguste Comte and John Stuart Mill (1806–1873), Herbert Spencer was the first to provide an overall philosophical framework for evolution; even Charles Darwin called him "our great philosopher Herbert Spencer." He published his first book, *Social Statistics*, in 1850, which was nine years before Darwin's *Origin* laid both an alleged scientific ground and philosophical model for evolution. This model he applied to all of science, and from 1860 to 1893 he developed his project: *First Principles* (1862), *Principles of Biology* (1864–1867), *Principles of Psychology* (1870–1872), *Principles of Sociology* (1876–1896), and *Principles of Ethics* (1879–1893). They are all an outworking of his synthetic view of evolution.

Despite the lack of any real scientific basis for his view, being grounded in the now disproved theory that inherited characteristics are genetically transmitted to one's offspring, Spencer's views gained wide recognition. Following Mill's empiricism, he was left with what he called the Unknowable. Pantheism was rejected along with theism, and Spencer was left with agnosticism as the only reasonable alternative in religion and metaphysics. Scientific (empirical) knowledge was regarded as the only valid form of knowledge about the physical universe, and it yields at best only general laws about its operation. Only philosophers deal with theories that hold for everything; nonetheless, Spencer believed that the Darwinian hypothesis could be used as the genuine core of an overall theory of evolution to explain everything in the physical universe.

Charles Darwin (1809–1882)

Charles Darwin accomplished what others before him (like Hume) had attempted but failed, namely, the supposed demise of the design argument by way of evolution. With the replacement of design by natural selection, there was finally no room left for a Designer (God); in the absence of any supernatural Creator, the rest of traditional supernatural Christianity would come crumbling down as well—at least as the dominant model in the intellectual world. This, of course, included the downfall of the traditional view of the divine inspiration of Scripture.

Darwin's View of Origins

What Darwin did for evolution was to give it, in the eyes of the scientific community, a plausible scientific basis in the mechanism of natural selection. This he did by convincingly combining the evidence for microevolution (small-scale changes *within* certain types of life) by natural selection with knowledge gained from Thomas Malthus's (1766–1834) population theory (as well as the alleged analogy of natural selection and artificial selection). From this Darwin concluded that macroevolution (large-scale changes *between* different types of life) is true. He knew this was a lead not justified by fossil evidence, and he considered it the weakest part of his theory (*OOS*, 152).

In spite of Darwin's admission, his conviction of the truth of evolution grew, and in his famous *On the Origin of Species* (1859) he set forth his hypothesis that all animal life evolved from one or a few simple forms of life. Later, in *The Descent of Man* (1871), Darwin ventured to argue that humankind too had evolved from lower forms of animal life. Since the evolution of Darwin's views on religion are a revelatory microcosm of the entire period, which experienced the overthrow of nearly two millennia of orthodox beliefs on God and the Bible, they will be treated biographically.

Darwin's Early Religious Training

Darwin was baptized in the Church of England and later, despite his rejection of Christianity, was buried in Westminster Abbey! Although christened an Anglican, Darwin was sent to a school conducted by a Unitarian minister (Moore, *PDC*, 315). He later entered the University of Cambridge in 1828, "where his father had decided that he should prepare for the ministry" (ibid.). Even at this early date, with the aid of Pearson's *Exposition of the Creed* and Bishop Sumner's *Evidence of Christianity Derived From Its Nature and Reception* (1824), "Darwin abandoned whatever were his scruples about professing belief in all the doctrines of the Church" (ibid.). Nonetheless, he read carefully and was deeply impressed with William Paley's books, *A View of the Evidences of Christianity* (1794) and *Natural Theology; or, Evidences of the Existence and Attributes of the Deity* (1802).

Darwin's Original Theistic Beliefs

Even as an adult, Darwin began his intellectual pilgrimage as a theist; he accepted, for example, Paley's design argument. In his *Autobiography* he referred to his journal entry about experiencing the wonder of creation standing in the midst of a Brazilian forest: "I remember my conviction that there is more in man than the mere breath of his body" (*ACD*, 91).

Darwin also spoke of "the extreme difficulty or rather impossibility of conceiving this immense and wonderful universe, including man with his capacity of looking far backward and far into futurity, as the result of blind chance or necessity." Thus, "when reflecting I feel compelled to look to a First Cause having an intelligent mind in some degree analogous to that of man; and I deserve to be called a Theist." He added, "This conclusion was strong in my mind about the time, as far as I can remember, when I wrote the *Origin of Species*; and it is since that time that it has very gradually become weaker" (*ACD*, 92–93).

Darwin's Rejection of Christianity

By 1835, before Darwin set sail on the *Beagle*, he was yet a creationist. Darwin describes his own religious descent in his *Autobiography*: "Whilst on board the *Beagle* [October 1836–January 1839] I was quite orthodox, and I remember being heartily laughed at by several of the officers (though themselves orthodox) for quoting the Bible as an unanswerable authority on some point of morality."

However, he did not believe the Bible was an unanswerable authority on science at this time. According to Ernst Mayr, Darwin had become an evolutionist some time between 1835 and 1837 ("Introduction" to Darwin's *Origin*, x): "By 1844, his views [on evolution] had reached considerable maturity, as shown by his manuscript 'Essay' " (ibid.).

Charles Darwin's son and biographer, Sir Francis Darwin, said that "although Darwin had nearly all the key ideas of *Origin* in mind as early as 1838, he deliberated for twenty years before committing himself publicly to evolution" (*LLCD*, 3.18). Only a decade later (1848) Darwin was fully convinced of evolution, defiantly declaring to J. D. Hooker: "I don't care what you say, my species theory is all gospel" (cited by Moore, *PDC*, 211).

Darwin's declining Christian beliefs began with an erosion of his belief in the trustworthiness of the Bible. As late as 1848 he read Harvard's Professor Andrew Norton (*The Evidence of the Genuineness of the Gospels*), who argued that the Gospels "remain essentially the same as they were originally composed" and that "they have been ascribed to their true authors" (*LLCD*, 212). However, Darwin's faith in the Old Testament had eroded some years before this.

The Acceptance of Negative Higher Criticism

> I had gradually come, by this time, to see that the Old Testament from its manifestly false history of the world, with its Tower of Babel, the rainbow as a sign, etc., etc., and from its attribution to God the feelings of a revengeful tyrant, was no more to be trusted than the sacred books of the Hindoos, or the beliefs of any barbarian. (*ACD*, 85.)

The Acceptance of Antisupernaturalism

Both Benedict Spinoza in 1670 and David Hume a century later had attacked the basis of supernatural intervention in the world. Darwin added,

> By further reflection that the clearest evidence would be requisite to make any sane man believe in miracles by which Christianity is supported—that the more we know of the fixed laws of nature the more incredible do miracles become—that the men of that time were ignorant and credulous to a degree almost incomprehensible by us—that the Gospels cannot be proved to have been written simultaneously with the events—that they differ in many important details, far too important as it seemed to me to be admitted as the usual inaccuracies of eyewitnesses—by such reflections as these . . . I gradually came to disbelieve in Christianity as a divine revelation (ibid., 86).

Nonetheless, Darwin continued,

> I was very unwilling to give up my belief . . . thus disbelief crept over me at a very slow rate, but was at last complete. The rate was so slow that I felt no distress, and have never since doubted even for a single second that my conclusion was correct (ibid., 87).

The "Damnable Doctrine" of Hell

Darwin notes the significance of the orthodox Christian belief in hell as a particular influence in his rejection of Christianity:

> I can indeed hardly see how anyone ought to wish Christianity to be true; for if so plain language of the text seems to show that the men who do not believe, and this would include my Father, Brother and almost all my best friends, will be everlastingly punished. And this is a damnable doctrine (ibid., 87).

The Death of Darwin's Daughter

Darwin's increased skepticism was heightened by the death of his beloved daughter, Anne, in 1851. James Moore notes that "two strong emotions, anger and grief, in the *Autobiography* mark off the years from 1848 to 1851 as the period when Darwin finally renounced his faith" (*PDC*, 209). This, of course, was just after his view in evolution had solidified (1844–1848) and before he wrote his famous *On the Origin of Species* (1859).

Darwin openly put himself outside the pale of Christianity. Referring to himself as a "horrid wretch" (one of the condemned), in May (1856) he warned a young entomologist: "I have heard Unitarianism called a feather bed to catch a falling Christian; and I think you are now on just such a feather bed, but I believe you will fall much lower and lower" (cited by Moore, *PDC*, 221). A month later, Darwin referred to himself as "the Devil's Chaplain," a satirical figure of speech of a confirmed unbeliever (ibid., 222).

Darwin's Descent to Deism

As late as 1841 Darwin reread William Paley's *Evidences* and was impressed by his "good" arguments. Yet Darwin gradually discarded theism for deism, leaving room only for the single act of divine intervention for the creation of the first form or forms of life. This was apparently his view at the time of *Origins* where, in the second edition, he wrote,

> There is grandeur in the view of life, with its several powers, having been originally breathed *by the Creator* into a few forms or into one; and that, whilst this planet has gone cycling on according to the fixed laws of gravity, from so simple a beginning endless forms most beautiful and most wonderful have been, and are being, evolved. (*OOS*, 490, second edition[2], emphasis added.)

Paley's Design Argument Rejected

Darwin had read and accepted William Paley's famous argument for design (found in nature) to a Designer (God) of nature. However, because of his growing belief in evolution he gradually discarded it. Although previously Darwin still clung to a deistic God who created the world but let it operate by "fixed natural laws," gradually he came to reject even the cogency of the design argument. He said he was "driven" to the conclusion:

> The old argument of design in nature, as given by Paley, which formerly seemed to me so conclusive, fails, now that the law of natural selection had been discovered. . . . There seems to be no more design in the variability of organic beings and in the action of natural selection

---

[2]The phrase "by the Creator" was not in the first edition.

than in the course which the wind blows. Everything in nature is the result of fixed laws. (*ACD*, 87.)

The only design involved, then, was that a Creator set up these fixed natural laws. Darwin wrote, "I am inclined to look at everything as resulting from designed laws, with the details, whether good or bad, left to the working out of what we may call chance" (F. Darwin, *LLCD*, 1.279; 2. 105).

In view of this Darwin even ventured so far as to refer to natural selection as "my deity." To believe in miraculous creations or in the "continued intervention of creative power," said Darwin, "is to make 'my deity Natural Selection' superfluous and to hold *the* Deity—if such there be—accountable for phenomena which are rightly attributed onto his magnificent laws" (cited by Moore, *PDC*, 322). By the phrase "if such there be," Darwin not only stated his deism but also signaled his growing agnosticism.

As early as 1871, in *Descent of Man*, Darwin denied a widely accepted basis for belief in an infinitely powerful God. He wrote, "*Belief in God— Religion*. There is no evidence that man was aboriginally endowed with the ennobling belief in the existence of an Omnipotent God" (3, 302). Here Darwin hints at finite godism (see chapter 2); be this as it may, it was short-lived, and Darwin definitely eventuated an agnostic.

Agnosticism

By 1879 Darwin was an agnostic, writing, "I think that generally (and more and more as I grow older), but not always, that an Agnostic would be the more correct description of my state of mind" (cited by Moore, *PDC*, 204). Eventually, he wrote, "The mystery of the beginning of all things is insoluble by us; and I for one must be content to remain an Agnostic" (ibid., 84).

His agnosticism notwithstanding, Darwin clearly denies ever being an atheist[3]: "In my most extreme fluctuations I have never been an atheist in denying the existence of God" (ibid., 204).

Most reputable scholars reject the stories of Darwin's deathbed conversion as apocryphal. Interestingly, as late as 1879, several years after *Descent of Man* (1871), Darwin declared, "It seems to me absurd to doubt that a man may be an ardent Theist and an evolutionist" (Letter 7, May 1879). However, Darwin himself was content to remain an agnostic.

It is difficult to overestimate the vast negative influence Darwin's view has had on the orthodox view of God and the Bible. Needless to say, it forms the turning point in the modern liberal view of Scripture. Before Darwin, unorthodox views of Scripture were never given a foothold in the nearly 1,900 years of the church's existence. Since the time of Darwin,

---

[3]An atheist claims to know that there is no God, while an agnostic claims not to know whether there is a God.

unorthodox views of God and Scripture have come against the church from all directions and have had tremendous effect.

Principial Atheism

Although Darwin, and many Darwinists, stoutly deny that Darwin's view is in principle atheistic, the charge has been laid very seriously at his door. Princeton scholar Charles Hodge, in a penetrating analysis, asked and answered his own question:

> What is Darwinism? It is Atheism. This does not mean that Mr. Darwin himself and all who adopt his views are atheists; but it means that his theory is atheistic, that the exclusion of design from nature is . . . tantamount to atheism. (*WID*, 177.)

Hodge's logic is challenging. Evolution excludes design, and if there is no design in nature there is no need for a Designer of nature. So regardless of protests to the contrary, evolution is in principle an atheistic theory.

Even many evolutionists acknowledge that Darwin's scenario of a "warm little pond" in which life first spontaneously generated excludes God entirely from the realm of biology. Darwin wrote, "It is often said that all the conditions for the first production of a living organism are now present which could ever have been present." Thus, spontaneous generation would be possible if "we could conceive in some warm little pond with all sorts of ammonia and phosphoric salts, light, heat, electricity present that a protein was formed ready to undergo still more complex changes" (cited by F. Darwin, *LLCD*, 3.18).

Francis Darwin admitted that his father "never claimed his theory could explain the origin of life, but the implication was there. *Thus, not only was God banished from the creation of species but from the entire realm of biology*" (ibid., 3.18). This being the case, there was no allowance for a Creator, at least not in the realm of biological science. All one needs to do is to posit what many long believed, that the material universe is eternal and there appears to be no place for a First Cause at all. And if there is no Creator, then the Bible, being a thoroughly theistic book, is completely undermined.

THE RELIGIOUS ROOTS OF
DESTRUCTIVE BIBLICAL CRITICISM

The philosophical roots of biblical criticism in various forms of naturalism were shadowed by certain religious movements that became fertile soil in which it could grow. These include pietism, liberalism, and existentialism.

Pietism (c. 1650–c. 1725)

Pietism arose in Germany under the leadership of Philipp Jakob Spener (1635–1705) and his close friend August Hermann Francke (1663–1727). Spener had published the influential *Pia Desideria* (1675) while serving as a pastor in Frankfurt. By 1694 they were settled at Halle, where they established charitable centers and founded a university. While pietists held to the traditional doctrine of the inspiration of Scripture, their stress on subjective personal experience eventually led to an undermining of the objective authority of Scripture. As Francke put it,

> We may safely assure those who read the word with devotion and simplicity, that they will derive more light and profit from such a practice, and from connecting meditation with it ... than can ever be acquired from drudging through an infinite variety of unimportant minutiae. (*AGRSHS*, 83.)

By stressing the primary importance of feeling, they hoped to avoid the cold orthodoxy of so-called Protestant scholasticism but inadvertently opened the door for the equally dangerous enemy known as subjective experimentalism. While first-generation pietists could recall and reflect on their grounding in Scripture while validly advocating the need for individual experience, the second generation focused on the need for individual experience and often neglected the sound basis for their experience in the authority of Scripture. Under the onslaught of naturalism, rationalism, and evolutionism, pietism soon gave way to deism, skepticism, and negative biblical criticism.

Liberalism: Friedrich Schleiermacher (1768–1834)

Friedrich Schleiermacher is the father of modern liberalism. He was a noted German theologian who was educated in Moravian (pietistic) institutions, ordained and preached in Berlin (1796), and later taught theology at Halle (1804) and Berlin (1810). His two major works are *On Religion* (1799), which is experiential in its orientation, and *The Christian Faith* (1821–22), which is doctrinal in its approach. He also wrote *Brief Outline on the Study of Theology* and a posthumously published book titled *Hermeneutics*.

Importance of Schleiermacher

Among Schleiermacher's more significant modern influences are pietism, which stressed the devotional over the doctrinal, romanticism (following Friedrich Schlegel, 1772–1829), which affirmed pantheism in contrast to theism, and agnosticism (following Kant), which emphasized the practical versus the theoretical.

Schleiermacher exerted a tremendous influence on his followers, including most major liberals after him: Albrecht Ritschl (1822–1889), who wrote *Critical History of the Christian Doctrine of Justification and Reconciliation* (1870–1874); Adolf von Harnack (1851–1930), who wrote *What Is Christianity*; and Julius Wellhausen (1844–1918), who wrote *Introduction to the History of Israel* (1878), in which he defended the famous JEPD hypothesis of the authorship of the Pentateuch (see chapter 15).

View of Religion

For Schleiermacher, the basis of religion is found in experience. In his famous work *On Religion* he argued that we must *have* it before we can *utter* it—the locus of religion is in the self; the inner is key to the outer. The object of religion is the All (which many call *God*), and the nature of religion is found in a feeling (sense) of absolute dependence, which is described as a sense of creaturehood, an awareness that one is dependent on the All, or a sense of existential contingency.

Schleiermacher distinguished religion from ethics and science in the following manner: Ethics is a way of living; science is a way of thinking; religion is a way of feeling (sensing). Whereas ethics is a way of acting and science a way of knowing, by contrast, religion is a way of being. Thus, ethics is practical, science is contemplative, and religion is attitudinal. Likewise, ethics is a matter of self-control, but religion involves self-surrender.

The relation of religion to doctrine is that of a sound to its echo or experience to its expression. Religion is found in feeling, and doctrine is only a form of the feeling. Religion is the "stuff," and doctrine is the structure. First one must sense it, and then he states it. Doctrine is not essential to religious experience and is scarcely necessary to the expression of it, since it can be expressed in symbol as well.

As to the universality of religion, Schleiermacher believed that all men have this religious feeling of dependence on the All; thus there are no real atheists. In this view Schleiermacher foreshadowed Paul Tillich (1886–1965), who believed everyone, even atheists, has an ultimate commitment to something.

Since religion is primarily a feeling, Schleiermacher believed it is primarily communicated by personal example—better caught than taught. Secondarily, religion can be communicated through symbols and doctrines, but doctrines are only accounts of religious feeling; they are statements about our feeling, not about God, His attributes, or His nature.

There are endless varieties of religious expressions, largely due to personality differences. The pantheistic expression results from those who delight in the obscure; theists by personal propensity are those who delight in the definite.

The liberalistic aim or goal of religion is the love of the All, the World-Spirit. This is achieved through loving other human beings; the result of religion is unity of life, and its influence is manifest in morals. Religion produces a wholeness of life, but it has no specific influence on individual acts—we act *with* religion but not *from* it.

Likewise, the influence of religion on science is not direct, as one cannot be scientific without piety. The feeling of dependence on the All removes presumption to knowledge, which is ignorance. The true goal of science cannot be realized without a vision arising from religion.

The Test for the Truth of a Doctrine

Schleiermacher believed religions are neither true nor false as such. Truth and falsity do not apply to religion, which is a feeling (sense) of absolute dependence. He held that truth and falsity apply to ideas, and the truth of an idea is determined by two sets of criteria: scientific and ecclesiastical.

Scientific criteria include clarity, consistency, coherence, and cohesion with other doctrines. The primary ecclesiastical criterion is the value a doctrine has for the life of the church. Indeed, the knowledge of God is mediated through the corporate experience of redemption rather than in a body of doctrine, and it is for this reason that Schleiermacher relegated his treatment of the Trinity to an appendix—he believed it was a speculation divorced from piety (see *CF*, appendix).

Schleiermacher's concept of salvation was less than orthodox. He understood redemption to be the impression made by Jesus; unclouded consciousness on the Christian community that replaced their own impoverished God-consciousness with that of Jesus. Schleiermacher's view of miracles and Providence was ambivalent, and his almost complete stress on God's immanence made him liable to the charge of pantheism.

Impact on Liberalism

Schleiermacher offers many notable insights into religion. Among them are: (1) his stress on the contingent and dependent nature of all creatures; (2) his emphasis on the importance of religious experience; (3) the helpfulness of many of his distinctions between religion, science, and ethics; (4) his belief that truth needs to be tested; (5) his stress on Christian community; and (6) his belief in systematic theology.

However, the negative influence of Schleiermacher's liberal views has been massive. Among these are: (1) his experimental form of pantheism; (2) his acceptance of a Kantian epistemology; (3) his disjunction of experience and doctrine; (4) his contention that truth does not apply to religion; (5) his reduction of theology to anthropology, and (6) his acceptance of negative (destructive) higher criticism of the Bible.

Schleiermacher's revision of Christian theology had its most radical impact on the issue of authority, because he argued that no external authority, whether it be Scripture, church, or historic creedal statement, takes precedence over the immediate experience of believers. He also contributed to a more critical approach to the Bible by questioning its inspiration and authority. Further, he rejected doctrines he believed were unrelated to the religious experience of redemption: for instance, the Virgin Birth, the Trinity, and the return of Christ. He felt such teachings implied a cognitive and indirect knowledge rather than immediate God-consciousness.

Schleiermacher greatly influenced Christianity through three major achievements. *First*, he made religion socially acceptable to those who no longer took the Bible and its doctrines seriously by showing its appeal to man's aesthetic tendencies. *Second*, he attracted to theology countless young men who were interested in religion primarily as an expression of man's imaginative spirit. And *third*, for a time he changed biblical criticism from historical to literary analysis. His influence, limited to Germany during his lifetime, was enormous on later Protestants because of Albrecht Ritschl (1822–1889), Adolf von Harnack (1851–1930), and Ernst Troeltsch (1865–1923).

Existentialism: Søren Kierkegaard (1813–1855)

The father of modern existentialism was not a twentieth-century French atheist (Sartre) but a nineteenth-century Danish Christian named Søren Kierkegaard, who was orthodox enough that he could have signed a statement subscribing to the historic fundamentals of the faith. He wrote, "On the whole, the doctrine as it is taught [in the church] is entirely sound."

Nonetheless, few have done more from within the evangelical fold to methodologically undermine historic orthodoxy than Kierkegaard. Indeed, it was his theological son, Karl Barth, who gave rise to neo-orthodoxy. Kierkegaard concluded that even if we assume that

> the defenders of Christianity have succeeded in proving about the Bible everything that any learned theologian in his happiest moment has ever wished to prove about the Bible, [namely,] that these books and no others belong in the canon; they are authentic; they are integral; their authors are trustworthy—one may well say, that it is as if every letter were inspired.

Kierkegaard then asked, "Has anyone who previously did not have faith been brought a single step nearer to its acquisition? No, not a single step" (*CUPPF*, 29–30).

Then Kierkegaard posed the opposite:

> [What if] the opponents have succeeded in proving what they desire about the Scriptures, with a certainty transcending the most ardent wish of the most passionate hostility—what then? Have the opponents

thereby abolished Christianity? By no means. Has the believer been harmed? By no means, not in the least (ibid., 31).

At the minimum, Kierkegaard's bifurcation of fact and value is axiologically misplaced.[4] In fact, it has been biblically disastrous, as Barth, Brunner, and Bultmann (and their followers) demonstrate. We need only mention these Kierkegaard-inspired beliefs: (1) Religious truth is located in personal encounter (subjectivity); (2) Propositional truth is not essential to the faith; (3) Higher criticism is not harmful to real Christianity; (4) God is "wholly other" and essentially unknowable, even through biblical revelation. These maxims give further significance to the Pauline warning to "beware of philosophy" (see Geisler, "BPWBE" in *JETS*).

THEOLOGICAL MANIFESTATIONS OF DESTRUCTIVE BIBLICAL CRITICISM

Theological manifestations of destructive biblical criticism shadow the destructive philosophies they imbibe both logically and historically. This is certainly true of the French scholar Richard Simon (1638–1712), "the father of biblical criticism," for his views were directly influenced by Spinoza. Likewise, David Strauss (1808–1874), who wrote the first desupernaturalized life of Christ, was influenced by the antisupernaturalism of David Hume, and so on.

Richard Simon (1638–1712)

After extensive studies in oriental language, Richard Simon published his *Histoire Critique du Vieux Testament (Historical Critique of the Old Testament)* in 1678 only a few years after Spinoza's *Tractatus* (1670). He later wrote *Histoire Critique du Texte du Nouveau Testament (Historical Critique of the Text of the New Testament)* (1683).

Although Simon believed he kept the interest of Roman Catholicism at heart, he denied that Moses wrote the Pentateuch. Contrary to Spinoza, however, he based his views on what he considered duplicate accounts of the same incident and a variation in style of writing.

Jean Astruc (1684–1766)

Jean Astruc was one of the first scholars to bring to prominence the notion that Genesis chapters 1 and 2 were written by two different authors. He published his *Conjectures* in 1753, in which he attempted to reconcile some of the difficulties he found in the Genesis record. As a result, he

---

[4]Axiology is the study of values.

emphasized the distinctions between such words as *Elohim, Yahweh Elohim* (or *Jehovah Elohim*), and *El-Elyon* in espousing a view that would later become popular among such German rationalists as Johann Gottfried Eichhorn (1752–1827), Karl H. Graf (1815–1869), Abraham Kuenen (1828–1891), Julius Wellhausen (1844–1918), and others.

Johann Salomo Semler (1729–1791)

Johann Semler is often referred to as the father of German rationalism because he was the first to advocate the so-called accommodation theory, which plays a crucial role in liberal theology. In this way he set the stage for the rise of the historical-critical method, of which Gerhard Maier says, "The general acceptance of Semler's basic concept that the Bible must be treated like any other book has plunged theology into an endless chain of perplexities and inner contradictions."[5]

Semler was reared in pietism before he adopted a more rationalistic approach.

> He distinguished between the permanent truths in Scripture and the elements due to the times in which the books were written. He denied the equal value of all parts of Scripture. Revelation, he taught, is in Scripture, but all Scripture is not revelation. The creeds of the church are a growth. Church history is a development. (Walker, *HCC*, 483.)

Gotthold Ephraim Lessing (1729–1781)

Gotthold Ephraim Lessing, the son of a pastor in Saxony, served as librarian to the Duke of Brunswick after 1770. Lessing published a series of *Fragments of an Unknown Writer,* popularly known as the *Wolfenbuttel Fragments* (1774–1778). This was actually a defense and restatement of skeptical deism by Hermann Samuel Reimarus (1694–1768), which included a fragment entitled *The Goal of Jesus and His Disciples.* Left unpublished during his own lifetime, this Reimarus fragment claimed to expose the Gospel accounts of Jesus as a piece of fraud because of their alleged unfulfilled eschatological predictions. It unreservedly rejected miracles and revelation and cast accusations of conscious fraud, innumerable contradictions, and fanaticism upon the biblical writers. Such a perspective raised a storm of controversy when it was published by Lessing, and it revolutionized the image of Jesus in modern theology. Indeed, it was the point of departure for Albert Schweitzer (1875–1965) in his *Quest for the Historical Jesus* (1906). Lessing himself wrote an essay in gospel criticism entitled *New*

---

[5]As we have seen (in chapter 17), the accommodation theory asserts that Christ accommodated His language to the current opinions of the Jews of His day regarding the Old Testament Scriptures.

Hypothesis on the Evangelists considered as merely human historical Writers (1788), which posited a single Hebrew or Aramaic source behind the Gospel narratives and portrayed Jesus as a merely human messiah.

Johann Gottfried Eichhorn (1752–1827)

Johann Gottfried Eichhorn was a German theologian who appears to have followed the views of Astruc and Presbyterian scholar Joseph Priestly (1733–1804) in preparing the way for the rise of the critical method. The term *higher criticism* was used as a synonym for historical criticism by Priestly, who regarded the historical method to be "one of the most satisfactory modes of argumentation" in the preface to his *History of the Corruptions of Christianity* (1782).

Eichhorn then used the term "higher criticism" in the preface to his three-volume *Einleitung in das Alte Testament* (1780–1783). He was one of the first commentators to make a scientific comparison between the biblical books and other Semitic writings; he also divided Genesis into "Jehovist" and "Elohist" sources and distinguished the priestly from the popular law code in the Pentateuch.

Although Eichorn's work was inaccurate, it was popular and did much to encourage biblical study and criticism. Later higher criticism came to be identified more particularly with literary criticism than with historical method.

Heinrich Eberhard Gottlob Paulus (1761–1851)

In his *Life of Jesus* (1828), Heinrich Paulus attempted to reconcile his belief in the substantial accuracy of the Gospel narrative with his personal disbelief in miracles and the supernatural. He attempted to turn miracles into ordinary facts and events that had been exaggerated or misconceived, and he treated the Gospel writers as sufferers of hallucinations who intentionally recorded such things as visions and miracles. Paulus applied Eichhorn's principles to the New Testament even though he believed himself to be championing the Bible's cause against rising skepticism. His influence waned in the face of the more radical skepticism of David Friedrich Strauss.

Wilhelm Martin Leberecht De Wette (1780–1849)

Wilhelm De Wette studied at one time under Heinrich Paulus before publishing his own works on biblical criticism from 1806 until 1813, when he turned to theological studies. He was a radical rationalist early in his career but became more conservative in later years. Although he was a nonsupernaturalist, he continually criticized the theories of Ferdinand

Christian Baur (1792–1860) and his disciples at the Tubingen School of New Testament Criticism.

De Wette also tried to reconcile the transcendent and finite. He was one of the most respected theologians of the nineteenth century, although he displeased rationalists with his condemnation of cold reason and offended pietists by doubting biblical miracles and by reducing the stories of the birth, resurrection, and ascension of Christ to myths. The employment of myths was De Wette's attempt to absolve the biblical writers from charges of lunacy and imbalance by contending that they prosaically turned metaphor and allegory into fact as they wrote.

David Friedrich Strauss (1808–1874)

Armed with antisupernatural bias in advance of looking at the evidence, liberal biblical scholars (as well as scientists) after Hume uniformly desupernaturalized God's revelation, whether general or special. David Hutton, a friend of Hume's, was one of the first to do it in science (geology), as was David Strauss in biblical studies.

Following Hume's lead, Strauss published his famous desupernaturalized *Life of Jesus* (two volumes, 1835–1836). He rejected all miracles, claiming they were an exercise in mythmaking, and also eventually denied God and the immortality of the soul. He threw out miracles, viewing the Gospels as unintentional myths created by the piety of the early second century, steeped in the messianic anticipation of the Old Testament and eager to prove that Jesus was the Messiah. Strauss was the first to apply this thesis consistently to every part of the New Testament.

In 1840–1841 Strauss published the *History of Christian Doctrine*, a polemical account of Christian doctrine from the New Testament to its dissolution in Hegel. In 1862 he wrote a work on Herman Samuel Reimarus, the noted biblical critic whose *Fragments* (published posthumously by Gotthold Lessing in 1778) gave rise to the first quest for the historical Jesus. In 1864 Strauss published a slightly more positive version of his first work, titled *The Life of Jesus for the German People*. In 1865 he penned *The Life of Christ and the History of Jesus*, which was an attack on Frederick Schleiermacher's attempt to combine the history of Jesus and the Christ of dogma. His last work, *The Old Faith and the New* (1872), is a call for a new religion of humanity that negates belief in theism and immortality in favor of scientific materialism. It is the first theological work to accept Darwinian evolutionism.

Karl Heinrich Graf, Abraham Kuenen, and Julius Wellhausen

Karl Graf (1815–1869), Abraham Kuenen (1828–1891), and Julius Wellhausen (1844–1918) picked up on the notion of Spinoza, who considered

Ezra to be the final composer of the Torah. Although Spinoza's view on this topic was largely ignored by his contemporaries, it was a remarkable anticipation of the final formulation of the documentary hypothesis (JEPD) by Graf, Kuenen, and Wellhausen in the latter half of the nineteenth century.

Although the documentary hypothesis had its beginning with Jean Astruc, it moved into its next stage of development with Eichhorn's *Einleitung* (1780–1783); and its third stage was reached with De Wette's *Dissertation* (1805) and *Beitrage zur Einleitung* (1806), with Hermann Hupfeld's epoch-making work *Die Quellen der Genesis* (*The Source of Genesis*) being published in 1853. Graf added to that work with his own efforts to show that the priestly code in the Pentateuch was distinct from and later than Deuteronomy itself (1866). Abraham Keunen refined Graf's work in *De Godsdienst van Israel* (*The Religion of Israel*) (1869). The stage was set for Wellhausen's important contributions, *Die Komposition des Hexateuchs* (*The Composition of the Hexateuch*) (1876), and *Prolegomena zur Geschichte Israel* (*Introduction to the History of Israel*) (1878).

Gleason Archer observes that although Wellhausen made no real innovations, he restated the documentary theory with great skill and persuasiveness, supporting the JEPD sequence upon an evolutionary basis. This was the age in which Charles Darwin's *On the Origin of Species* was capturing the allegiance of the scholarly and scientific world, and the theory of development from primitive animism to sophisticated monotheism as set forth by Wellhausen and his followers fit well with Darwinian evolutionism as well as with Hegelian dialecticism.

> The age was ripe for the documentary theory, and Wellhausen's name became attached to it as the classical exponent of it. The impact of his writings soon made itself felt throughout Germany . . . and found increasing acceptance in both Great Britain and America. (Archer, *SOTI*, 87.)

The Continuation of the Wellhausean Tradition

The publication of Wellhausen's *Introduction to the History of Israel* marks the beginning of the triumph of the *Religionsgeschichte* ("history of religions") approach to Old Testament studies over the next four decades. In England, William Robertson Smith (*The Old Testament and the Jewish Church*, 1881) introduced the Wellhausen view to the public, whereas Samuel R. Driver (1846–1914) (*Introduction to the Literature of the Old Testament*) gave the documentary hypothesis its classical English formulation. Sir George Adam Smith (1856–1942) applied the approach to the Old Testament prophets in his contribution to the *Expositor's Bible*, edited by W. R. Nicoll (1887f). In the United States the most notable advocates of the new school were Charles Augustus Briggs (1841–1913), who wrote *The*

Higher Criticism of the Hexateuch (1893), and his collaborator, Henry Preserved Smith (1847–1927).

During the twentieth century the general outlines of the Wellhausean theory continued to be taught in most nonconservative institutions, although some uncertainties were expressed concerning the comparative dating of the "documents" by W. O. E. Osterley and T. H. Robinson (*Introduction to the Books of the Old Testament*). In general, however, such advocates as Julius A. Bewer (*Literature of the Old Testament*) and Robert H. Pfeiffer (*Introduction to the Old Testament*) adhered to Wellhausen's theory.

No other systematic account of the origin and development of the Old Testament has commanded the general acceptance of the scholarly world. Nevertheless, vigorous reaction to the documentary hypothesis, which undermines the unity of the Old Testament, and additional developments in Old Testament studies have culminated in the provocative challenge to the documentary hypothesis by Isaac M. Kikawada and Arthur Quinn.

Ferdinand Christian Baur (1792–1860)

The rationalistic and naturalistic spirit invading New Testament studies also came from Germany through the writings of Schleiermacher, Eichhorn, and the more radical criticism of F. C. Baur. Following a so-called Hegelian dialectic of thesis, antithesis, and synthesis,[6] Baur postulated that the gospel of John must be a second-century synthesis between the thesis of Peter and antithesis of Paul in the first century. This, of course, is contrary to strong opposing historical evidence (see chapter 26) and is an example of how philosophical presuppositions have influenced the development of destructive biblical criticism.

Baur also reduced what he believed were the authentic Pauline Epistles to four (Romans, 1 and 2 Corinthians, and Galatians) and denied the genuineness of most other New Testament books. Although his critical opinions fell into disrepute with the rejection of his historical reconstruction and presuppositions, other critics began from equally tenuous assumptions.

Rudolph Bultmann (1884–1976)

Rudolph Bultmann developed an antisupernatural form of demythologizing the New Testament, contending that the New Testament world "is the scene of the supernatural activity of God and his angels on the one hand, and of Satan and his demons on the other. These supernatural forces intervene in the course of nature and in all that we think and will and do" (*KMTD*, 1).

---

[6]Once again, Hegel himself never held this kind of dialectic, but due to a popular misinterpretation by Fichte, it has commonly been attributed to him (see Winfried Corduan, "Transcendentalism: Hegel" in Norman Geisler, ed., *Biblical Errancy: Its Philosophical Roots*, 81–101).

Demythologizing the New Testament
According to Bultmann,

> The NT documents need to be stripped of this mythological struc-
> ture. For all this is the language of mythology and is incredible to mod-
> ern man, for he is convinced that the mythical view of the world is obso-
> lete.... All our thinking today is shaped for good or ill by modern
> science. [So] a blind acceptance of the New Testament ... would
> involve a sacrifice of the intellect.... It would mean accepting a view of
> the world in our faith and religion which we should deny in our every-
> day life (ibid., 3–4).

With unlimited confidence, then, Bultmann pronounced the biblical
picture of miracles to be impossible, for "man's knowledge and mastery of
the world have advanced to such an extent through science and technology
that it is no longer possible for anyone seriously to hold the NT view of the
world—in fact, there is hardly anyone who does." Therefore, the only honest way of reciting the creeds is to strip the mythological framework from
the truth they enshrine.

If the biblical picture is mythological, how then are we to understand
it? For Bultmann,

> The real purpose of myth is not to present an objective picture of
> the world as it is, but to express man's understanding of himself in the
> world in which he lives. [Therefore,] myth should be interpreted not
> cosmologically, but anthropologically, or better still, existentially. [That
> is,] myth speaks of the power or the powers which man supposes he
> experiences as the ground and limit of his world and of his own activity
> and suffering. [In other words,] the real purpose of myth is to speak of
> a transcendent power which controls the world and man, but that pur-
> pose is impeded and obscured by the terms in which it is expressed
> (ibid., 10–11).

Bultmann concluded confidently, "Obviously [the Resurrection] is not
an event of past history.... An historical fact which involves a resurrection
from the dead is utterly inconceivable" (ibid., 38–39). He offers several
reasons for this antisupernatural conclusion. *First,* there is "the incredibility
of a mythical event like the resuscitation of a corpse." *Second,* "there is the
difficulty of establishing the objective historicity of the resurrection no matter how many witnesses are cited." *Third,* "the resurrection is an article of
faith which, as such, cannot be a miraculous proof." *Fourth,* "such a miracle
is not otherwise unknown to mythology" (ibid., 39–40).

What, then, is the Resurrection if not an event of objective, space-time
history? For Bultmann, it is an event of subjective history; that is, it is an
event of faith in the hearts of the early disciples. As such, it is not subject to
objective historical verification or falsification, for it is not really an event

in the space-time world. Christ did not rise from Joseph's tomb; He arose by faith in the disciples' hearts.

Bultmann's reasoning goes like this:

(1) Myths are by nature more than objective truths—they are transcendent truths of faith.

(2) But what is not objective cannot be part of a verifiable space-time world.

(3) Therefore, miracles (myths) are not part of the objective space-time world.

An Evaluation of Bultmann's Demythological Naturalism

Several objections have been offered to this view, which, basically, is built on several unproven assumptions. It does not follow that because an event is *more* than historical it must be *less* than historical. Gospel miracles, to be sure, have a "moreness" or transcendent dimension; they cannot be reduced to mere historical events. For example, the Virgin Birth is more than biological; it points to the divine nature of Christ and to the spiritual purpose of His mission. It is not merely a matter of science; it is also presented as a "sign" (Isa. 7:14). The same is true of Christ's resurrection. Although it is at least that, it is portrayed as more than a mere resuscitation of a corpse. It has a divine dimension that entails spiritual truths as well (Rom. 4:25; 2 Tim. 1:10).

First, miracles can occur *in* the world without being *of* the world. A miracle can originate out of the supernatural world (its source) and yet it can occur in the natural world (its sphere). In this way the event can be objective and verifiable without being reducible to its purely factual dimensions. Thus one could verify directly by historical means whether or not the corpse of Jesus of Nazareth was raised and empirically observed (the objective dimensions of the miracle), without reducing the spiritual aspects of the event to mere scientific data. But in claiming that miracles such as the Resurrection cannot occur in space-time history, Bultmann is merely revealing an unjustified, dogmatic, naturalistic bias.

Second, it is clear that the basis of Bultmann's antisupernaturalism is not evidential, nor even open to real discussion; the dogmatism of his language is revealing. Antisupernaturalism is something he holds "no matter how many witnesses are cited" (ibid.). Miracles are "incredible," "irrational," "no longer possible," "meaningless," "utterly inconceivable," "simply impossible," and "intolerable." Hence, the "only honest way" for modern people is to hold that miracles are "nothing else than spiritual" and that the physical world is "immune from interference" in a supernatural way. This is not the language of one open to historical evidence for a miracle. It looks more like a mind that does not wish to be "confused" with the facts.

Third, Bultmann's mythological events are unverifiable. If miracles are not objective historical events, then they are unverifiable or unfalsifiable—there is no factual way to determine their truth or falsity. But if this is true, then they have been placed beyond the realm of objective truth and must be treated as purely subjective (see Flew, "TF" in *NEPT*, 98). To rephrase Flew's question for Bultmann, "If the corpse of Jesus of Nazareth had been discovered after the first Easter, would this falsify your belief in the Resurrection?" His answer, clearly, is no. By contrast the answer of the apostle Paul, clearly, is yes, for "if Christ has not been raised, your faith is futile; you are still in your sins" (1 Cor. 15:17). Therefore, it is obvious that Bultmann's understanding of miracles is contrary to that found in one of the earliest known Christian records of these events, the New Testament. First Corinthians is widely accepted, even by biblical critics, as the work of the apostle Paul from about A.D. 55 or 56.

Fourth, Bultmann's myths have no evidential value. If miracles are not historical events, then they have no power, and nothing can be proven by them, since they have value only for those who wish to believe them. However, the New Testament writers claim evidential value for miracles. They consider them "convincing proofs" (Acts 1:3) and not "cleverly devised myths" (2 Peter 1:16 RSV). Paul declared, "He [God] has given proof of this to all men, by raising him [Jesus] from the dead" (Acts 17:31).

Fifth, Bultmann's demythological view is unbiblical and is unjustified for several reasons. To begin with, it is contrary to the overwhelming evidence for the authenticity of the New Testament documents and the reliability of the witnesses. Also, it is contrary to the New Testament claim for itself not to be "cleverly invented stories" (2 Peter 1:16) but an eyewitness account (cf. John 21:24; 1 John 1:1–3). Finally, the New Testament is not the literary genre of mythology. As we saw in part 1, C. S. Lewis noted that "Dr. Bultmann never wrote a gospel." He asks, therefore,

> Has the experience of his learned . . . life really given him any power of seeing into the minds of those long dead [who have]? . . . The "assured results of modern scholarship," as to the way in which an old book was written, are "assured," we may conclude, only because the men who knew the facts are dead and can't blow the gaff.

In brief, Bultmannian biblical critiques are unfalsifiable because, as Lewis pointedly remarks, "St. Mark is dead. When they meet St. Peter there will be more pressing matters to discuss" (Lewis, *CR*, 161–63).

Post-Bultmannian Developments

In the 1960s two newer movements grew out of Bultmann's approach as they moved away from his historical skepticism. These "post-Bultmannians" went beyond his hermeneutic, particularly his adoption of existentialism, to criticize Bultmann's understanding of the way language functions in their pursuit of "new quest" and redaction criticism. Representatives of "new quest" seek to support some aspect of the historical as authentic without returning to the historical Jesus of the old liberal school. Among the leading "new quest" spokesmen are Ernst Käsemann, Gunther Bornkamm, and Ernst Fuchs. The diversity of theories proposed by these critics have little in common, and they do not instill confidence in their quest. Redaction criticism has arisen directly out of form criticism and focuses attention on the Evangelists as writers. Several German scholars, including Gunther Bornkamm, Willi Marxsen (who coined the term *redaktionsgeschichte*, "form history"), Hans Conzelmann, and Ernst Haenchen, have devoted attention to Matthew, Mark, Luke, and Acts respectively.

In recent times focus has ranged through source, form, redaction, and tradition criticism. Even more recently structuralism and then deconstructionism have been in vogue.[7] Other philosophical influences have infected evangelical scholarship, particularly New Testament studies. These include phenomenology, conventionalism, process theology, allegorism, and anthropological monism.[8] All have the same negative result—a denial of the historicity of the New Testament documents and with that an erosion of the very foundation of orthodox Christianity. These results have been popularized by the self-appointed radical group called the "Jesus Seminar," who deny the authenticity of some 82 percent of the sayings of Jesus recorded in the Gospels (see chapter 26).

THE RESULTS OF DESTRUCTIVE BIBLICAL CRITICISM

A couple of generations ago a popular apologist, Harry Rimmer, published a powerful image under the title: "The Assured Results of Higher Criticism"—a termite-eaten Bible.[9] In brief, the historicity and authenticity of the Bible have been seriously damaged by modern negative criticism. Along with that, divine authority has been completely undermined in the minds of those who accept these destructive critical forms. Many evangelical scholars who have bought into the philosophical presuppositions of negative higher criticism have been exposed in an excellent new work by Robert Thomas and others titled *The Jesus Crisis: The Inroads of Historical Criticism Into Evangelical Scholarship*. Former New Testament negative critic Eta Linnemann has the insight of an insider in her book *Is There a Synoptic Problem?* as well as an article called "Is There a Q?" (*Biblical Review*, Oct. 95), in which she attacks the very foundations of modern destructive criti-

---

[7]For an excellent treatment of recent trends and their impact on evangelicals, see Robert Thomas, et al., *The Jesus Crisis: The Inroads of Historical Criticism Into Evangelical Scholarship*.
[8]For a discussion of these see my presidential address to the Evangelical Theological Society: "Beware of Philosophy: A Warning to Biblical Exegetes" in *The Journal of the Evangelical Theological Society* (1999).
[9]Harry Rimmer, *Internal Evidence of Inspiration* (Grand Rapids, Mich.: Eerdmans, 1946), 4.

cism. More recently she has produced a scholarly tome titled *Biblical Criticism on Trial.*

CONCLUSION

Many forces converged to form liberalism and to mold its view of Scripture. The diversity of the attacking views may disguise the underlying unity. True, there were the inductivism of Bacon, the materialism of Hobbes, the rationalistic pantheism of Spinoza, the skepticism of Hume, the agnosticism of Kant, the romanticism of Rousseau, the pietism of Schleiermacher, the deism of Paine, the scientism of Comte and Mill, the evolutionism of Spencer and Darwin, or the more recent philosophies of phenomenology, conventionalism, and deconstructionism.[10] Unmistakably, however, is the commonality of a consistent and persistent antisupernaturalism that attacks orthodox Christianity at its core.

If miracles do not occur, then the Bible is unreliable and historic Christianity is not credible. On this unjustified premise (see chapter 3) modern liberalism is based. Its view of Scripture, then, is as faulty as its view of miracles. Of course, the Bible cannot be a supernatural revelation of God if there are no supernatural events. Some form of negative biblical criticism thus becomes necessary.

SOURCES

Archer, Gleason. *A Survey of Old Testament Introduction.*
Bacon, Francis. *Novum Organum.*
Bultmann, Rudolf. *Kerygma and Myth: A Theological Debate.*
Comte, Auguste. *The Catechism of Positive Religion.*
———. *Cours, The Positive Philosophy of Auguste Comte.* Hans Werner Comte, ed.
Corduan, W. "Transcendentalism: Hegel" in Norman Geisler, ed., *Biblical Errancy: Its Philosophical Roots.*
Darwin, Charles. *The Autobiography of Charles Darwin.*
———. *The Descent of Man.*
———. *On the Origin of Species.*
Darwin, Francis. *The Life and Letters of Charles Darwin* (vol. 3).
Edwards, Paul, ed. *The Encyclopedia of Philosophy.*
Flew, Antony. "Theology and Falsification," in *New Essays in Philosophical Theology.*
Geisler, Norman, "Beware of Philosophy: A Warning to Biblical Exegetes" in *The Journal of the Evangelical Theological Society* (1999).

---

[10]For a discussion of how recent philosophies have adversely affected contemporary evangelical thought, see my previously mentioned presidential address to the Evangelical Theological Society: "Beware of Philosophy: A Warning to Biblical Exegetes" in *The Journal of the Evangelical Theological Society* (1999).

———. *Miracles and the Modern Mind.*

———. *Philosophy of Religion.*

———, ed. *Biblical Errancy: Its Philosophical Roots.*

Hegel, G. W. F. *Early Theological Writings.*

———. *Encyclopedia.*

———. *Logic.*

———. *Phenomena of Spirit.*

———. *Philosophy of History.*

Hobbes, Thomas. *Leviathan.*

Hodge, Charles. *What Is Darwinism?*

Hume, David. *Enquiry Concerning Human Understanding.*

Kant, Immanuel. *The Critique of Pure Reason.*

———. *Religion Within the Limits of Reason Alone.*

Kierkegaard, Søren. *Concluding Unscientific Postscript to Philosophical Fragments.*

Lewis, C. S. *Christian Reflections.*

———. *Miracles.*

Linnemann, Eta. *Biblical Criticism on Trial.*

———. "Is There a Q?" in *Biblical Review* (October 1995).

———. *Is There a Synoptic Problem?*

Mayr, Ernst. "Introduction" to Darwin's *Origin* (1964 ed.).

Meuller, G. E. "The Hegel Legend of Thesis, Antithesis—Synthesis" in *Journal of History of Ideas*, 19:3 (June 1958).

Moore, James. *The Post-Darwinian Controversy.*

Paine, Thomas. *Complete Works of Thomas Paine.*

Schleiermacher, Friedrich. *The Christian Faith.*

———. *On Religion.*

Spinoza, Benedict. *Ethics.*

———. *A Theologico-Political Treatise.*

Walker, William. *A History of the Christian Church* (3rd ed., rev. by Robert T. Handy).

CHAPTER TWENTY

LIBERALISM ON THE BIBLE

The rise of modern antisupernaturalism (see chapters 3 and 19) undermined the historical orthodox view of Scripture. From it sprang the view called "liberalism," the roots of which, in regard to Scripture, go back as far as Thomas Hobbes and Benedict Spinoza (seventeenth century). These roots were embodied in many of the negative higher critical views of Scripture following the time of Darwin (1860f., see chapter 19). Their eventual manifestation in pulpits and denominations in the United States began in the early 1900s.

THE CLASSICAL LIBERAL VIEW OF SCRIPTURE

There are varying degrees of theological liberalism, from moderate to radical. As measured by the orthodox position, the liberal views can be classified under two headings: classical liberalism and neoclassical liberalism. Since there is a direct relationship between one's view of God and one's view of Scripture, the liberal views follow respectively from whether it embraces a more classical view of God or a more neoclassical view. Representatives of the former are Harold DeWolf and Harry Emerson Fosdick, and representatives of the latter are Schubert Ogden and John Cobb.

L. Harold DeWolf (1905–)

Well-known Methodist theologian Harold DeWolf expressed his perspective in two major works: *The Case for Theology in Liberal Perspective* and

A Theology of the Living Church. He believed that in view of modern thought it was necessary to revise the orthodox view of Scripture in a more naturalistic direction.

Antisupernatural Basis of the Liberal View of Scripture
DeWolf declared,

> The questions whether such miracles have actually happened and if so how they should be thought of in relation to the natural order are questions needing to be considered later. [But] just now we are concerned simply to point out that, in the light of our theistic evidences, if a miracle were to be properly called a special revelation it could not be so-called because of its being any more an act of God than are the ordinary processes of nature, but only because it was more revealingly meaningful to men. (*TLC*, 66.)

Cultural Accommodation Is Necessary
DeWolf held that "some degree of accommodation to culture seems inevitable unless Christian teaching is to become a mere irrelevant echoing of ancient creeds—which were themselves products of some accommodation to Hellenic [Greek] thought" (*CTLP*, 58).

The grounds of this cultural accommodation is the so-called "scientific" view of the world, but in reality it is a naturalistic and evolutionary view, which is made evident by DeWolf's insistence that there are scientific errors in the Bible:

> Plainly the narrator [of Gen. 30:35–43] simply accepted the false science prevalent in his day. Similarly, some or all Biblical writers assume the fixity of the earth[1], the actual movement of sun and moon from east to west, a space above the firmament reserved for God's dwelling and the demonological explanation of disease. Such views cannot be intelligently accepted as infallible teaching. (*TLC*, 71.)

Negative Criticism of Scripture
This compromise in favor of a naturalistic "scientific" view leads to the adoption of negative criticism of Scripture. DeWolf believed,

> The correcting of the text and the historical locating of the writing are but different aspects of one great task. The intimate and inseparable relation between textual and historical studies of the Bible seems not to be adequately appreciated by some conservative scholars.... [Thus,] textual and historical criticism are intricately interwoven with each

---

[1]Actually, the biblical writers made no statement about the fixity of the earth; they simply did what scientists (e.g., meteorologists) do every day—that is, they speak of things like "sunrise" and "sunset," meaning that they speak in everyday, observational language.

other and with non-Biblical archaeological, historical, and linguistic studies (ibid., 51–52).

What DeWolf said about natural theology

> serves to correct some of the errors produced by exclusively Biblical and traditional theology. [So,] God's word spoken to us through the Bible depends for the clarity and purity of its reception both upon our own open and understanding minds and also upon the reception and expression given his word by the ancient men who wrote the words of the Bible (ibid., 32).

He concluded,

> The insistence of some conservative Christians on a Biblical literalism that is rationally indefensible and an appeal based on the "proofs" of prophecy and miracles, in defiance of the natural sciences and the new historical understanding of Biblical times, needless derives from the Christian faith of intelligent young people who will not blind themselves to scientific and historical evidences (ibid., 43).

By what criterion does one judge what is of God in Scripture? DeWolf believes it is "the spirit of Christ." Thus he admonishes that "the untrained reader does well to read for the nurture of his spirit and not to become unduly concerned about passages that appear to contradict the spirit of Christ or the scientific knowledge of our times" (ibid., 48). Using a moral norm to determine what is truthful in the Bible follows the principles of Spinoza and Kant before him (see chapter 19).

Needless to say, a desupernaturalized Bible is also an errant Bible; a Bible that is wrong about the scientific world is not an inerrant Bible.

The Bible Is Not the Word of God
DeWolf wrote, "Strictly speaking, the Bible itself is not the pure Word of God. Although by figure of intimate association we may, on occasion, without impropriety, call the Bible the Word of God, we ought not to use this language in careful theological discourse" (*CTLP*, 17).

The Bible Is Fallible and Errant
The result of DeWolf's cultural "accommodation" to naturalism was that "to the intelligent student who is more concerned with seeking out and declaring the truth than with maintaining a dogma it must be apparent that the Bible is by no means infallible" (*TLC*, 68). According to DeWolf, "Jesus himself challenged some commands of the Old Testament (Matt. 5:21–48)" (*CTLP*, 48). He added, "But while we are treating the fallibility of the Scriptures we must note that Jesus unhesitatingly and repeatedly sets Old Testament teaching at naught" (*TLC*, 73).

In regard to many facts of minor importance there are obvious contradictions within the Bible. For example, in Exodus 37:1–9 we read that Bezalel made the Ark of the Covenant, while in Deuteronomy 10:1–5 Moses reports that God commanded him to make the Ark and he says, "So I made an ark of acacia wood. . . ." When Joab was ordered to take a census, 2 Samuel 24:1 tells us that it was by God's command while 1 Chronicles 21:1 says it was by Satan's command (ibid., 69).

The Origin of Scripture

What, then, is the origin of Scripture, if not God by divine inspiration? According to DeWolf, the time-honored designation of Scripture as the Word of God was no longer appropriate. His response:

> It is evident that the Bible is a collection of intensely human documents. These books were written by men who had their own characteristic education, interests, vocabularies and literary styles. [So] most of the events described are activities of obviously fallible human beings. Many passages contradict one another or well-established knowledge. Many of the moral and religious ideas, especially in the more ancient documents, are distinctly sub-Christian (ibid., 73).

In brief, while conservatives have long held that the Bible *is* the Word of God (see chapters 13–18), liberals insist that the Bible merely *contains* the Word of God. Inspiration is not supernatural; it is merely a divine elevation of natural powers.

The Meaning of "Inspiration"

According to DeWolf,

> This doctrine is that the writing of the Bible as a whole was accomplished by an extraordinary stimulation and elevation of the powers of men who devoutly yielded themselves to God's will and sought, often with success unparalleled elsewhere, to convey truth useful to the salvation of men and of nations. . . . This was possible mainly because they had truth of such extraordinary importance to convey. It is upon that truth that we must lay our principal stress (ibid., 76).

Indeed,

> The human fallibility of the Bible does not preclude the possibility of its divine inspiration nor of its unmatched moral and religious authority. . . . Although written by men with characteristic individual traits and typical human failings it may still have been written by men seized and impelled by the spirit of God (ibid., 75).

Sola Scriptura Rejected

Protestants have long held that the Bible is the only written and infallible authority for our faith. Roman Catholics added to this the teaching authority of the *church*; Protestant liberals like DeWolf mixed biblical authority with that of the *culture*. DeWolf held that "the authority of the Bible is not such as to be strengthened by isolation from all other authority." In fact,

> Throughout the history of Christendom, Christian scholars have organized total views of the world in which the sciences, philosophical inferences from the evidences of common human experience, and the teachings of the Bible have all been woven together in unity. (*CTLP*, 57.)

Harry Emerson Fosdick (1878–1969)

Popular American preacher Harry Emerson Fosdick promoted a more radical form of liberalism from his influential New York pulpit and in his many writings. Like his liberal predecessors and colleagues, Fosdick's foundational beliefs included antisupernaturalism, which was one of the two strong negative influences of his liberalism, both of which he acknowledged. The other was his evolutionism.

Antisupernatural Basis
Fosdick declared his disbelief in miracles:

> Multitudes of people, so far from being well-stabilized traditionalists, are all at sea in their religious thinking. . . . If ever they were drilled in older uses of the Bible they have rebelled against them. Get back to the nub of their difficulty and you find it in Biblical categories which they no longer believe—miracles, demons, fiat creation, apocalyptic hopes, eternal hell, or ethical conscience. (*GUB*, 5.)

Naturalistic Evolution
Like other liberals, Fosdick admitted the influence of evolutionism on his view of Scripture:

> As for the modern scene with its contemporary problems, the New Testament's idea of man faces immense difficulties in maintaining itself. [Thus] the vast enlargement of the physical cosmos, the evolutionary origin of man, materialistic theories which endeavor to explain him, brutality of social life involving low conceptions of him, the innumerable masses of men such that old cynicisms gain new force . . . tend in many minds to undo what the Hebrew-Christian development did (ibid., 97).

With fervent zeal, he confessed,

> On the one side we are paying for it in multitudes of churches waiting to be swamped by theological obscurantism, fanatical premillenni-

alists, antievolutionary propaganda, or any other kind of reactionary movement in religious thinking against which no intellectual dikes ever have been raised by thoroughgoing consistent teaching as to what our new knowledge really means to religion. . . . On the other side we are paying for it in the loss of our more intelligent young people (ibid., 61).

It is no surprise that with this naturalistic grid, Fosdick's view of Scripture would be seriously skewed. Since he believed the Bible was not the words of an infallible God, it is understandable that he believed it to be errant.

The Bible Is Fallible and Errant
Fosdick claimed,

> Any idea of inspiration which implies equal value in the teachings of Scripture, or inerrancy in its statements, or conclusive infallibility in its ideas, is irreconcilable with such facts as this book presents. The inspirations of God fortunately have not been thus stereotyped and mechanical (ibid., xiv).

He added, "The utmost cruelty was not only allowed but commanded by Yahweh against Israel's rivals, and in the presence of habitual conflict fine ideals of humaneness had their chance to develop only within the circle of blood-brotherhood" (ibid., 100).

> The fact that one biblical book is later in time than another is in itself not the slightest indication that it is superior in quality—Nahum is on a much lower spiritual level than Amos, and the Book of Revelation in the New Testament is morally inferior to the writings of the Great Isaiah in the Old Testament. . . . [Furthermore,] there is no smooth and even ascent in the Book. There are, instead, long detours, recrudescence of primitivism, lost ethical gains, and lapses in spiritual insight. There are even vehement denials of nascent truth, and high visions that go neglected for centuries (ibid., xiii).

The Bible Contains Contradictions
What is more, Fosdick held that the Bible was full of errors. He summarized:

> For one thing, we are saved by it [biblical criticism] from the old and impossible attempt to harmonize the Bible with itself, to make it speak with unanimous voice, to resolve its conflicts and contradictions into a strained and artificial unity. [So,] how could one suppose that such internal harmony ever could be achieved between writings so vital and real, springing hot out of the life of the generations that gave them being, and extending in their composition over at least twelve hundred years? (ibid., 24–25).

He went on:

> No straightforward dealing with these and other similar facts can resolve their incompatibility into even the semblance of consistent narrative. Moreover, underlying such disharmonies is the still more substantial conflict, which we earlier noted, between two ideas of Jesus' resurrected body, one altogether fleshly, the other so spiritualized as to escape the trammels of a material organism (ibid., 294).

The Bible Has Scientific Errors

Following logically from his uncritical acceptance of naturalistic evolution, Fosdick concluded that there were scientific errors in the Bible:

> It all was made in six days, each with a morning and an evening, a short and measurable time before. This is the world-view of the Bible. . . . [Moreover,] it remained the world-view of the Christian church for a long time. Augustine, with uncompromising strictness, stated the authority of Scripture in matters such as this: "Scripture, which proves the truth of its historical statements by the accomplishment of its prophecies, gives no false information." [Therefore,] those early fathers have been severely handled because they thus clung to a world-view which might have been outgrown long before it was, had not their literalism barred the way. In this insistence upon an old cosmology, however, they were but children of their age (ibid., 47).

Fosdick derided Martin Luther for his prescientific view of Scripture, saying, "Even Luther called Copernicus a fool for suggesting that the earth moved, and roundly capped his argument by calling to witness the Scripture which says that Joshua made the sun stand still and not the earth" (ibid., 50).

Negative Criticism of Scripture

Fosdick, like liberals before him, denied that Moses wrote the Pentateuch, adhering to the documentary hypothesis of Julius Wellhausen that there were at least four different authors: J, E, P, and D (see chapter 19). He wrote:

> This passage [Exodus 6:2–3] appears in the late Priestly document and all the more because of that the probabilities favor its truth. Without a solid basis in historic fact, such a delayed beginning of Yahweh's worship would not have been invented by succeeding generations. (ibid., 1).

The Nature of Biblical Inspiration

It is understandable that, given his antisupernaturalism and evolutionism, Fosdick's view of inspiration was severely truncated: "Our ideas of the method of inspiration have changed; verbal dictation, inerrant manuscripts, uniformity of doctrine between 1000 B.C. and A.D. 70—all such ideas have become incredible in the face of the facts" (ibid., 30–31).

Fosdick believed that the first results of critical research into the Bible seemed disruptive, tearing the once unified Book into many disparate and often contradictory documents. Even so, "The final result has turned out to be constructive, putting the Bible together again, not indeed on the old basis of a level, infallible inspiration, but on the factually demonstrable basis of a coherent development" (ibid., ix).

Immorality in the Old Testament

Fosdick commented,

> The Old Testament exhibits many attitudes indulged in by men and ascribed to God which represent early stages in a great development, and it is alike intellectually ruinous and morally debilitating to endeavor to harmonize those early ideals with the revelations of the great prophets and the Gospels. Rather, the method of Jesus is obviously applicable: "It was said to them of old time . . . but I say unto you" (ibid., 27).

The Bible's Theology Is Revised

For Fosdick,

> It is impossible that a Book written two to three thousand years ago should be used in the twentieth century A.D. without having some of its forms of thought and speech translated into modern categories. . . . [When, therefore,] a man says, I believe in the immortality of the soul but not in the resurrection of the flesh; I believe in the victory of God on earth but not in the physical return of Jesus; I believe in the reality of sin and evil but not in the visitation of demons; [and] I believe in the nearness and friendship of the divine Spirit but I do not think of that experience in terms of individual angels; only superficial dogmatism can deny that man believes the Bible (ibid., 29).

According to Fosdick,

> The Book is not a good forest to cut timber in for theistic dogmatism. Not only are its ideas of God in constant process of change, but it is everywhere conscious of depth beyond depth in the divine nature, uncomprehended and incomprehensible (ibid., 53).

Having forsaken an infallible guide to truth in the orthodox view of Scripture, Fosdick offered several other tests for truth. Among these were the Spirit of Christ, human reason, and human experience.

The Spirit of Christ

Fosdick declared that the Spirit of Christ was his test for what was true in Scripture. He wrote, "So long as a man knows the whole road and judges every step of it by the spirit of Christ, who is its climax, he can use it all'' (ibid., 30). It did not seem to occur to Fosdick that he could not be sure of the Spirit of Christ apart from the authenticity of Scripture. Indeed, he seemed oblivious to the circularity of his reasoning, since without a reliable Scripture he could not know what the Spirit of Christ is. To take this Spirit from the Bible and then use it to reject the Bible is inconsistent. Furthermore, his special pleading, whereby he took only part of the Spirit of Christ and rejected other parts (such as Jesus' statements on hell), reveal that his criteria were really extrabiblical, not biblical.

Human Reason

Fosdick believed,

> The man who ministers . . . must have an intelligible way of handling the Bible. He must have gone through the searching criticism to which the last few generations have subjected the Scriptures and be able to understand and enter into the negations that have resulted. Not blinking any of the facts, he must have come out with a positive, reasonable, fruitful attitude toward the Book. Only so can he be of service in resolving the doubts of multitudes of folk today (ibid., 5–6).

Human Experience

Fosdick confessed,

> The liberal emphasis rests upon experience; we regard that, rather than mental formulas, as the permanent continuum of the Gospel; we proclaim our freedom from bondage to the mental formulas of the past [and] often the total result is that our unformulated religious experience, refusing the discipline of older thinking and shirking the discipline of new thinking, lands in chaos. It is often much easier to discover what liberals do not think than to discover what they do think (ibid., 183).

A Fosdick Postscript

Fosdick had some serious second thoughts about his view of Scripture. Here is what he wrote a generation later:

> Today, however, looking back over forty years of ministry, I see an outstanding difference between then and now with regard to what is standard and who must do the adjusting. What man in his senses can now call our modern civilization standard? . . . It is not Christ's message that needs to be accommodated to this mad scene; it is this mad scene into which our civilization has collapsed that needs to be judged and saved by Christ's message.

And,

This is the most significant change distinguishing the beginning of my ministry from now. Then we were trying to accommodate Christ to our scientific civilization; now we face the desperate need of accommodating our scientific civilization to Christ. (*GTBA*, 201–02.)

THE NEOCLASSICAL LIBERAL VIEW OF SCRIPTURE

Like other forms of liberalism, there is a wide range in the neoclassical forms. What most of them share in common, however, is a neoclassical view of God, namely, process theology (panentheism, see chapter 2). In seeking to understand this view, we will examine the beliefs of Schubert Ogden.

Schubert Ogden (1928–)

Working out of the background of Alfred North Whitehead (1861–1947), Schubert Ogden represents the way many new liberal thinkers consider Scripture. As a process theologian, Ogden does not believe God is infinite, all-powerful, or all-knowing. Nor does he believe the Bible contains infallible predictions about the future. Another process theologian, Lewis Ford, observes,

> Divine providence cannot be understood as the unfolding of a predetermined course of events. Prophecy is not prediction, but the proclamation of divine intent, dependent for its realization upon the continued presence of those conditions which called forth that intent and upon the emergence of the means whereby that intent may be realized. [Thus] *God becomes the great improvisor and opportunist* seeking at every turn to elicit his purpose from every situation: if not by the hand of Sennacherib, then by the hand of Nebuchadnezzar. ("BRPP" in *I*, 206, emphasis added.)

"Revelation," then, is not supernatural but only a divine "lure," an attempt to persuade humankind. Indeed, as Ogden wrote, "What Christian revelation reveals to man is nothing new, since such truths as it makes explicit must already be known to him implicitly in every moment of existence" ("OR" in *OCHC*).

Not only does God not inform man in advance what will occur, God must be informed Himself. As John Rice frankly admits, "*God, as it were, has to wait with bated breath until the decision is made*, not simply to find out what the decision was, but perhaps even to have the situation clarified by virtue of the decision of that concrete occasion" (*OGBTB*, 49, emphasis added). So for neoliberals in the process tradition, like Schubert Ogden, the Bible has neither divine authority nor infallible predictions. It is a human document with only instrumental authority to bring about man's salvation.

Nature of Scripture

Ogden rejects the view that "what the Bible says, God says." He writes,

> In Protestant orthodoxy, then, the developed doctrine of the verbal
> inspiration of the canonical writings entailed the assertion of their uni-
> form authority, and thus made it possible to claim without qualification
> that "what Scripture says, God says." But, with the emergence of Prot-
> estant liberal theology and its commitment to the historical-critical
> method, as well as its insistence that Scripture neither is nor can be a
> sufficient authorization for the meaning and truth of theological asser-
> tions, this claim was abandoned, never again to be made by those who
> have led in the subsequent important developments in Protestant the-
> ology. ("AST.")

Negative Criticism

Given his acceptance of negative higher criticism, it is not surprising to
hear Ogden claim that "none of the New Testament writings, in its present
form, was authored by an apostle or one of his disciples" (ibid., 251).
Ogden believes the norm for the church is not the New Testament but,
rather, the apostolic witness: "This witness is, of course, found in the New
Testament, but it is not identical with the New Testament. In the strict sense
only the apostolic testimony to Jesus as the Divine revelation can be
described as canonical." In rejecting the divine authority of Scripture,
Ogden claims,

> We today must indeed recognize a higher theological authority than
> the canon of Scripture, and hence can no longer maintain that Scrip-
> ture is in some sense the sole primary authority for Christian theology.
> [Thus] the theological authority of Scripture, great as it may be, is
> nevertheless a limited authority, in that it could conceivably be greater
> than it is—namely, as great as that of the apostolic witness by which itself
> is and is to be authorized (ibid., 251–52).

For Ogden, the Bible has only a functional but not an essential authority
(ibid., 246); it is an authority insofar as it brings Christ to us. The Bible is
"perfect" only "with respect to the end of man's salvation, and so to wit-
nessing to all that is necessary to the attainment of that end" (ibid., 245).

Ogden's liberal theology is dependent on negative higher criticism.
Thus he believes that " 'the historic, apostolic Christ,' just like 'the historic
biblical Christ,' is every bit as historical as the so-called 'historical Jesus,'
and to this extent there is no escaping the dependence of theology on the
work of the historians." In fact, Ogden insists that "historical-critical
inquiry is theologically necessary and legitimate" (ibid., 256).

In his claim that the locus of the canon "cannot be the writings of the
New Testament as such but can only be the earliest traditions of Christian
witness accessible to us today by historical-critical analysis of those writings,"

Ogden rejects the New Testament as the canon. Rather, he believes that "the canon of the church, and hence also the highest authority for theology, must now be located in what form critics generally speak of as the earliest layer of the Synoptic tradition, or what Marxism in particular refers to as 'the Jesus-kerygma' " (ibid., 258).

AN EVALUATION OF LIBERAL VIEWS OF SCRIPTURE

For the sake of this evaluation, focus will generally be placed on the common elements in the various liberal views, and in an attempt to avoid reduplication, only brief reference will be made to points that are treated more fully elsewhere.

Some Positive Aspects of the Liberal Views

Liberal theologians have many positive things to offer in the search for a comprehensive and adequate view of Scripture. Indeed, without their extensive critique it is doubtful that evangelical scholars would have developed a full-orbed view of inspiration.

The Emphasis on the Human Element of Scripture
Some evangelicals and many fundamentalists, particularly those on the more conservative end of the spectrum, tend to downplay and at times even diminish the human side of Scripture (see chapter 15). However, the Bible is a 100 percent human book, as well as being a totally divine work. Liberals, then, do us the service of stressing the human dimension of Scripture, for like Christ, the Living Word of God, the Bible is theanthropic; both are fully human and fully divine, and to diminish the human nature of either is a serious error.

The Focus on Matters of Higher Criticism
Contrary to the belief of some extreme conservatives, biblical higher criticism is not a misdirected and essentially anti-Christian pursuit. Indeed, almost all conservative scholars engage in higher criticism; anyone who asks who wrote Genesis or Job or Esther or how they were written and under what circumstances and with what purpose, is engaging in a form of higher criticism. Likewise, so-called "lower" or textual criticism, which seeks to establish, by a study of the manuscripts, the content of the original text, is not an inherent enemy of the evangelical, and liberal scholars have long taken a leading role in both forms of biblical criticism.

An Understanding of the Need for Philosophy
The liberal emphasis on the understanding and use of philosophy for a proper understanding of inspiration is also a helpful element. Many

evangelicals fail to see that the basic issues behind biblical studies are of a philosophical nature, and without a proper understanding of philosophy, these issues cannot be resolved. Indeed, liberals correctly understand, as many evangelicals often do not, that one's philosophy will determine his bibliology. This too is a beneficial emphasis provided by a liberal approach to Scripture.

The Emphasis on the Need for Biblical Scholarship

All too often, and even more so in the past two generations, liberals have been in the forefront of biblical scholarship. Given evangelicalism's high view of Scripture, it seems ironic that we have failed to be leaders in this field. Liberals are to be commended for demonstrating in practice what so often evangelicals have only confessed in principle, namely, a high view of Scripture that warrants dedicating one's life to the pursuit of a better understanding of the biblical languages and text.

Some Negative Aspects of the Liberal Views

Of course, it does not follow from this that liberals have the correct understanding of the origin and nature of Scripture. Ironically, what it does demonstrate is that both liberals and evangelicals have been inconsistent with their own beliefs about Scripture. For example, why should liberals, who do not believe that the original language of the original text of Scripture is the verbally inspired Word of God, pursue with such dedication and scholarship a knowledge of the language and original text when they do not believe it expresses the very Word of God? And again, on the other hand, why have evangelicals, who do believe this, often lag behind in these disciplines?

Liberalism's Belief Is Contrary to the Claim of the Bible

Whatever else may be said in favor of a liberal view of Scripture, any fair and objective reading of the text reveals that this is not the Bible's view of itself. As has been demonstrated earlier (see chapters 13–16), the Bible claims that the very words of Scripture (cf. 2 Sam. 23:2; 2 Tim. 3:16) comprise the unbreakable (John 10:35), indestructible (Matt. 5:17–18), ultimately authoritative (Matt. 15:1–6), and absolutely true Word of God (John 17:17; cf. Heb. 6:18).

It Is Contrary to the Claim of Christ

Since liberal Christian scholars claim to be followers of Christ, it is inconsistent on their part to reject what Christ taught about the Bible. Since there is strong evidence, better than that for other books from antiquity, that the New Testament documents are historically reliable (see chapters 4 and 26), a careful examination of the Gospels reveals that Jesus taught that the Bible is the divinely inspired and authoritative Word of God (see chapters 13 and 27). But how can liberals be followers of the teachings of Jesus if they deny one of the essential teachings of Jesus, namely, that the Bible is God's Word?

It Is Contrary to the Historical Claim of the Church

What is more, the liberal view, of whatever stripe, is contrary to the historical confession of the Christian church. As was demonstrated earlier (see chapters 17–18), virtually every Father and major teacher in the Christian church from the time of the apostles to the present affirmed that the Bible is the divinely inspired, supremely authoritative, written Word of God. Once again, Augustine summed up the first four hundred years well when he wrote,

> I have learned to yield this respect and honour only to the canonical books of Scripture: of these alone do I most firmly believe that the authors were completely free from error. . . . If we are perplexed by any apparent contradiction in Scripture, it is not allowable to say, the author of this book is mistaken: but either the manuscript is faulty, or the translation is wrong, or you have misunderstood. (*AF*, 11.5.)

Later Thomas Aquinas summed up the first twelve hundred years of church history in these words: "The author of Holy Scripture is God" (*ST*, 1a. 1, 10), for "Holy Scripture looks at things in that they are divinely revealed" (ibid., 1a. 1, 3). So it is "in Holy Scripture, through which the divine will is declared to us" (ibid., 3a. 1, 3). Aquinas speaks of "Divinely inspired Scripture" (ibid., 1a. 1, 1), and after insisting that the biblical writers "so firmly asserted the truth that they left nothing to be doubted" and that anyone who rejects it should be "anathema," he added, "The reason for this is that *only the canonical Scriptures are normative for faith*" (*CJ*, 21.6, emphasis added).

Martin Luther then summarized the view in the time of the Reformation in these emphatic declarations: "The Scriptures, although they too are written by men, are neither of men nor from men but from God" (*LW*, 35:153). As we have seen, speaking of his opponents, Luther said,

> They do not believe they are God's words. *For if they believed they were God's words they would not call them poor, miserable words but would regard such words and titles as greater than the whole world and would fear and tremble before them as before God himself. For whoever despises a single word of God does not regard any as important.* (Reu, *LS*, 32, italics original.)

Luther added, "I have learned to ascribe this honor only to books which are termed canonical, so that I confidently believe that not one of their authors erred" (ibid., 17). Recall too the following citation:

My friend, God's Word is God's Word; this point does not require much haggling! When one blasphemously gives the lie to God in a single word, or says it is a minor matter if God is blasphemed or called a liar, one blasphemes the entire God and makes light of all blasphemy. Therefore it is true absolutely and without exception, *that everything is believed or nothing is believed.* The Holy Ghost does not suffer Himself to be separated or divided so that He should teach and cause to be believed one doctrine rightly and another falsely. (*LW*, 37:26, 33, italics original.)

In point of fact, right up to the time of Darwin (c. 1860) there was virtually no significant deviation on the absolute divine authority of Scripture (see H. D. McDonald, *TRHS*). Not until the rise of modern liberalism, with its rejection of miracles, was there a serious challenge inside the church for its nearly nineteen hundred years to the historical orthodox view on the divine inspiration of Scripture. Whatever else can be said for it, one thing is certain: The liberal view of Scripture is contrary to almost two millennia of confession by the Christian church.

It Is Based on a Wrong View of God

At the basis of the rejection of the divine inspiration of Holy Writ is a faulty view of God. Not until the influence of pantheism, deism, finite godism, and even agnosticism and atheism (see chapters 2 and 19) on the Christian church was there any significant deviation on its view of the nature of Scripture.[2] Logic demands that one's view of the *Word* of God can be no greater than his view of the *God* of this Word. Thus, it should come as no great surprise that naturalistic views of God, such as Spinoza's pantheism or Kant's deism or Mill's finite godism, would seriously undermine the orthodox view of Scripture, for if there is no God who can or does perform miracles, then the Bible's claim to authenticity must be seriously challenged, since it is filled with miracles. In point of fact, this is exactly how the denial of the historical orthodox view of Scripture came about.

Hence, it was the rejection of classical theism that led to the demise of the classical view of Scripture, but, as was demonstrated earlier (see chapter 2), there are solid reasons supporting classical theism that in turn argue for the traditional view of Scripture.

It Is Based on an Unjustified Antisupernaturalism

Furthermore, liberalism is grounded in antisupernaturalism, both logically and historically. If a theistic God exists, then miracles are possible (see chapter 3), for if there is a God who can perform special (i.e., super-

---

[2] In earlier times there was a pantheistic (neoplatonic) influence on the *interpretation* of Scripture via Origen, but there was no serious challenge by any otherwise orthodox Father on the origin and *nature* of Scripture.

natural) acts, such as creating the universe from nothing, then there can be special (supernatural) acts of God, and, if there can be supernatural acts, then the Gospel records cannot be summarily dismissed as inauthentic. But this is precisely what has occurred, for in the wake of David Hume's antisupernaturalism, there appeared the first desupernaturalized *Life of Jesus* (by David Strauss, 1835–1836), and from this to Rudolph Bultmann's demythologized New Testament (see *KM*), and then on to the "Jesus Seminar."[3] The history of liberalism reveals a continual rejection of the authenticity of the Gospel records based on an antisupernatural bias.

However, since it has been demonstrated that there are no valid philosophical grounds for ruling out miracles (see chapter 3), it follows that there are thereby no valid grounds for the antisupernaturalistic liberal view that denies the authenticity of the New Testament. Indeed, to the contrary, the historicity of the New Testament has been firmly established by both external and internal evidence (see chapter 26). Thus the liberal view of Scripture crumbles with the failure of antisupernaturalism.

It Is Inconsistent With Its Own Assumption

Finally, the classical liberal view of Scripture is circular, for it uses the Bible as an authentic basis for determining what the Spirit of Jesus is and then in turn uses the Spirit of Jesus to attack the authenticity of large parts of the Bible.

Nor does the attempt to avoid this succeed when it argues that the parts of the Gospels that contain miracles are to be rejected and the nonmiraculous narrations accepted. Jesus' strongest statements about Scripture are found in the nonmiraculous narrations (cf. Matt. 5:17–18; John 10:35), and to accept or reject parts of the Gospels on other grounds turns out to be arbitrary. Indeed, it is the case that one's view of what is authentic and what is not in the record becomes the ground for accepting or rejecting what is authentic and what is not.

SUMMARY AND CONCLUSION

Since liberal theologians differ in their view of God, ranging from modified theism through deism, finite godism, and into process theology, their views of Scripture cover a large spectrum as well. Nonetheless, they have many things in common. First and foremost is their rejection of the orthodox Christian view of Scripture, which entails a consistent antisupernaturalism, along with its concomitant acceptance of negative higher criticism.

Classical liberalism accepted partial inspiration of the Scriptures so that the Bible did at least *contain* the Word of God here and there amid the

---

[3]See Gregory Boyd, *Jesus Under Siege.*

many errors; hence, their theories of inspiration ranged from partial inspiration through divine illuminationism to mere human intuitionism. The neoclassical liberals, of course, with their process view of God, have a totally naturalistic view of Him. Thus, "inspiration" is allegedly no more than a natural resonance between the fallible human writers of Scripture and a finite process God who is trying to lure the writers into His process of self-perfection.

Whereas there are some positive features to the liberal approach to Scripture, such as the recognition of the Bible's humanness and the need for biblical scholarship, nonetheless, there are serious flaws in the liberal denial of the supernatural source, absolute authority, and complete historical reliability of the New Testament.

SOURCES

Augustine. *Against Faustus.*
———. *Commentary on John.*
Boyd, Gregory. *Jesus Under Siege.*
Bultmann, Rudolf. *Kerygma and Myth: A Theological Debate.*
DeWolf, Harold. *The Case for Theology in Liberal Perspective.*
———. *A Theology of the Living Church.*
Flew, Antony. "Theology and Falsification" in *New Essays in Philosophical Theology.*
Ford, Lewis. "The Authority of Scripture for Theology" in *Interpretation.*
———. "Biblical Recital and Process Philosophy" in *Interpretation.*
Fosdick, Harry Emerson. *Great Time to Be Alive.*
———. *A Guide to Understanding the Bible.*
Geisler, Norman, and William Nix. *A General Introduction to the Bible.*
Korysmeyer, Jerry. "A Resonance Model for Revelation."
Luther, Martin. *Luther's Works.*
McDonald, H. D. *Theories of Revelation: An Historical Study—1700–1960.*
Ogden, Schubert. "The Authority of Scripture for Theology."
———. "On Revelation" in *Our Common History as Christians: Essay in Honor of Albert C. Outler.*
Reu, M. *Luther on Scripture.*
Rice, John R. *Our God-Breathed Book—The Bible.*
Thomas Aquinas. *Commentary on John.*
———. *Summa Theologica.*

CHAPTER TWENTY-ONE

NEO-ORTHODOXY ON THE BIBLE

The neo-orthodox view of Scripture arises out of a reaction to dead orthodoxy (as in the reaction of Søren Kierkegaard—the grandfather of the movement) as well as out of a reaction to dead liberalism (as in the reaction of Karl Barth—the father of the movement). In Kierkegaard's case, he himself held an orthodox view of Scripture theologically, but axiologically he set the stage for its later denial by shifting the emphasis from doctrine to existential experience—something he did in attempting to counter the lifeless rigidity of the Scandinavian Lutheran Church.

In Barth's case, he was awakened from his liberal dogmatic slumber by the reality of the bankruptcy of optimistic liberalism in the face of the evil of World War I. Barth turned to the Bible (especially the book of Romans), to Martin Luther, and to Søren Kierkegaard, who helped him to take a step away from liberalism and toward orthodoxy.

THE FORERUNNER OF NEO-ORTHODOXY: SØREN KIERKEGAARD

Kierkegaard's Theological Orthodoxy

Søren Kierkegaard, a Danish literary figure and iconoclast[1] theologian, attempted to prod the Danish church back into a personal experience with Christ. Kierkegaard personally held to all the great fundamentals of the

---

[1]An iconoclast is one who speaks against the established tradition.

faith, including the Trinity, Christ's deity, the Virgin Birth, the Atonement, Christ's bodily resurrection, and the inspiration of the Bible. He wrote, "On the whole, the doctrine as it is taught [in the church] is entirely sound. Consequently that is not what I am contending for. My contention is that something should be done with it." (*SKJP*, 6:362.)

Kierkegaard's Axiological Unorthodoxy

Axiology is the study of values, and Kierkegaard succeeded in shifting the discussion from doctrine (which orthodoxy stressed) to values (which neo-orthodoxy would stress). Kierkegaard insisted that the confession of these orthodox beliefs was insufficient to save anyone; rather, he contended, these beliefs needed an existential encounter with the living Christ. This could be done by a "leap of faith" in order to move out of the lower aesthetic and ethical stages of life into personal relationship with Jesus. In his own words, Kierkegaard said,

> I am and was a religious author, that the whole of my work as an author is related to Christianity, to the problem "of becoming a Christian," with a direct or indirect polemic against the illusion that in such a land as ours all are Christians of a sort (*PVMWA*, 5–6).

In *Fear and Trembling* Kierkegaard reveals how the ethical transcends the religious. Abraham (Gen. 22), a man devoted to God's law, which declares "Thou shalt not kill," was asked by God nonetheless to take his son Isaac and offer him as a sacrifice. Unable to explain his action to anyone else or justify it before any human court, Abraham suspended the ethical and made a "leap of faith" to the religious. In so doing he dethroned the ethical but did not destroy it. It was only *temporarily* suspended, not permanently discarded, in order to show the transcendent value of the religious (experiential) over the ethical (moral).

Truth As Subjectivity

Søren Kierkegaard believed that religious truth is personal, not impersonal; i.e., it is something we are, not something we have—we must live it and not just know it. It is something that grips us, not just something we grip. Spiritual truth cannot be merely acknowledged; it must be appropriated; it is not correspondence but commitment. While there is objective truth (e.g., in science and history), according to Kierkegaard it is largely irrelevant to religious truth, which is found in a *subjective* encounter with God by the will, not by an *objective* understanding with the mind.

Kierkegaard's View of Faith and Reason

In his *Philosophical Fragments* Kierkegaard sets forth his view of the relation between faith and reason, the theme of which is an attack on man-centered philosophy at its best. He believed that, left to himself, man views the Christian God as a perplexing Unknown. This exercised a considerable influence on Karl Barth: If communication is to occur, God must initiate it. Two questions are raised:

(1) Is it possible to base eternal happiness on historical knowledge?
(2) How can the transcendent God communicate to us?

The Contrast of Revelation and Reason

The difference between God's revelation and human reason is illustrated by contrasting Socrates and Christ. Socrates' wisdom was a backward recollection, whereas Christ's was a forward expectation. The former aroused truth from within, but the latter gives truth from without. For Socrates truth was immanent, whereas for Christ truth is transcendent. According to the former truth is rational, but for the latter truth is paradoxical. Finally, in Socrates, truth comes from the wise man, whereas in Christ truth comes from the God-Man.

Christian truths are neither self-evident nor known from experience, because even if they are factually correct, such statements lack the certainty Christian claims have—they are paradoxical and can be accepted only by a leap of faith. There is a real transcendent God whom men gain only by choosing Him in His self-revelation; this God is meaningful and real, but also paradoxical. He is the Unknown limit to knowing who magnetically draws reason and causes passionate collision with man in the paradox.

Reason cannot penetrate God, nor can it avoid Him; the very zeal of the positivists[2] to eliminate God shows their preoccupation with Him. The supreme paradox of all thought is its attempt to discover something that thought cannot think. Herein thought attempts to commit suicide, that is, to run out of thinking.

Kierkegaard adds in *Concluding Unscientific Postscripts* that objective reason can never find real truth. Proofs can neither establish nor overthrow Christianity. To try to prove God is a shameless insult of ignoring Him, and to reduce Him to an objective probability would threaten Christianity, making it a treasure one could carelessly possess, like money in the bank.

Faith in religious facts, like the Incarnation or the Bible, is not true faith. True faith is the gift of God and is not something attainable by human effort. The Incarnation and the Bible are objective points of reference; however, they are not reasons, for they are unconvincing. True faith is a "leap" to God's revelations, but it does not rest on objectively rational or empirical evidence.[3] Reason, however, does have a negative role by

---

[2]Positivism, also called scientism, is a view (originating with the atheist Auguste Comte, 1798–1857) that insists only scientific propositions can be known to be true.
[3]In his *Journals* (page 581) Kierkegaard qualified this, disclaiming any senseless hurling of one's self into the realm of the holy. It is, nonetheless, a decision that is not based on evidence.

helping us distinguish nonsense from paradox. Kierkegaard wrote of the Christian, "Nonsense therefore he cannot believe against the understanding, for precisely the understanding will discern that it is nonsense and will prevent him from believing it" (*PF*, 504).

Kierkegaard's Orthodox View of the Bible

Kierkegaard believed the Bible was the inspired word of God. He wrote,

> To be alone with the Holy Scriptures! I dare not! When I turn up a passage in it, whatever comes to hand—it catches me instantly, it questions me (indeed it is as if it were God Himself that questioned me), "Hast thou done what thou readest there?"

He added, "My hearer, how highly dost thou esteem *God's Word?*" (*SE*, 51). He also believed the canon was closed and that God was not giving additional revelation today, severely criticizing someone who claimed he had received a new revelation.

Kierkegaard's Unorthodox View on the Historicity of the Bible

Nevertheless, Kierkegaard did not believe it was either necessary or important to defend the complete historicity or inerrancy of Scripture. This is evident from what he said about the relation of the eternal and temporal, as well as his comments about biblical criticism. According to Kierkegaard, the problem is, how can eternal salvation depend on historical (and thereby uncertain) documents? How can the historical give nonhistorical knowledge of God?

His answer is that insofar as the Bible gives empirical data it is an insufficient ground for religious belief. Only Spirit-inspired faith finds the eternal God in the temporal Christ. The biblical writers are not primarily certifying the historicity of Christ's deity but the deity of Christ in history; hence, biblical criticism is irrelevant. The important thing is not the historicity of Christ but His contemporaneity as a person who confronts men today by faith in the offense of the Gospel. The Jesus of history is a necessary presupposition, but history does not prove His messiahship. The only proof of His messiahship is our discipleship; the "proof" is not empirical but spiritual.

Faith is *centered* in an historical event but it is not *based* on it. No superficial contemporaneity can occasion faith; only spiritual contemporaneity can:

> If the contemporary generation had left nothing behind them but these words: "We have believed that in such and such a year God appeared among us in the humble form of a servant, that he lived and

taught in our community, and finally died," it would be more than enough (ibid., 130).

So, then, time is immaterial to faith. Non-eyewitnesses are at no disadvantage; there is no secondhand discipleship. Further, contemporaneity is not to be confused with like-mindedness through the centuries. Admiration of Jesus is not religious but aesthetic; allegiance is necessary.

Biblical Criticism Is Irrelevant to True Christianity

In a very clear passage, Kierkegaard addresses both the defender and critic of the Bible:

> Whoever defends the Bible in the interest of faith must have made it clear to himself whether, if he succeeds beyond expectations, there could from all his labor ensure anything at all with respect to faith. . . . [Likewise,] whoever attacks the Bible must also have sought a clear understanding of whether, if the attack succeeds beyond all measure, anything else would follow than the philological[4] result.

Thus, once again, even if we assume,

> [The defenders] have succeeded in proving about the Bible everything that any learned theologian in his happiest moment has ever wished to prove about the Bible, these books and no others belong in the canon; they are authentic; they are integral; their authors are trustworthy—one may well say that it is as if every letter were inspired.

So, asks Kierkegaard,

> Has anyone who previously did not have faith been brought a single step nearer to its acquisition? No, not a single step. Faith does not result simply from a scientific inquiry; it does not come directly at all. On the contrary, in this objectivity one tends to lose that infinite personal interestedness in passion, which is the condition of faith. (*CUP*, 29–30.)

Then, as we have seen, he theoretically assumes the opposite:

> If the opponents have succeeded in proving what they desire about the Scriptures, with a certainty transcending the most ardent wish of the most passionate hostility—what then? Have the opponents thereby abolished Christianity? By no means. Has the believer been harmed? By no means, not in the least, [for] if he had assumed it by virtue of any proof, he would have been on the verge of giving us his faith.

Indeed, Kierkegaard asks, "For whose sake is it that the proof is sought?

---

[4]Philology, literally "the love of learning," is also used of linguistics.

Faith does not need it; aye, it must even regard the proof as its enemy" (ibid., 31).

KARL BARTH: THE FATHER OF NEO-ORTHODOXY

Karl Barth was aroused from his liberal beliefs in the perfectibility of man by a strong dose of reality called the First World War. Though he had taught that the world was getting better, it was clearly getting worse. As he turned to the Bible, the Reformers, and Søren Kierkegaard, Barth moved from liberalism in the direction of orthodoxy, embracing Trinitarianism, the Virgin Birth, and Christ's deity and bodily resurrection. Unfortunately, however, he did not return to an orthodox view of Scripture, and he adopted an unorthodox view of salvation called universalism (see volume 3).

While orthodoxy proclaims that the Bible *is* the Word of God, and liberalism that at best the Bible merely *contains* the Word of God, neo-orthodoxy insists that the Bible is a fallible human witness to the Word of God (Christ) that only *becomes* the Word of God to us in an existential encounter with the Christ it conveys.

The Origin of Scripture

For Barth, God is the source of the Bible:

> Certainly it is not our faith that makes the Bible the Word of God. . . . That the Bible is the Word of God is not left to accident or to the course of history and to our self-will, but to the God of Abraham, Isaac and Jacob. (*CD*, 1:534.)

Even so, the Bible is not identical to the Word of God, for "the statement that the Bible is the Word of God cannot therefore say that the Word of God is tied to the Bible. On the contrary, what it must say is that the Bible is tied to the Word of God" (ibid., 1:513). The Bible merely conveys the Word of God: "It 'holdeth God's word,' is what Luther once said about the Bible. . . . It only 'holds,' encloses, limits and surrounds it: that is the indirectness of the identity of revelation and the Bible" (ibid., 1:492).

The Threefold Word of God

Barth said there are three levels to the Word of God. The first and primary level is Christ, the Living Word of God:[5]

---

[5] The Bible is the "Word of God" in a secondary sense, as a witness to God's primary revelation in Christ. Likewise, preaching from the Word of God is the "Word of God" in a tertiary (third) sense.

This is primarily because apart from Jesus Christ Himself there is still this other form of the Word of God, which Scripture needs to be the Word of God, just as it needs Scripture. Preaching and the sacrament of the Church do indeed need the basis and authority and authenticity of the original Word of God in Scripture to be the Word of God (ibid., 1:501).

The Purpose of the Bible

The Bible is not a revelation of God as such but merely the instrument through which God reveals His Word. "[The human words] are the instruments by which [the Bible] aims at becoming a Word which is apprehended by men and therefore a Word which justifies and sanctifies men, by which it aims at executing upon men the grace of God which is its content" (ibid., 1:223).

The Bible Is a Record of Revelation

The Bible is not itself a revelation from God; it is merely a record of God's revelation in Christ:

> In every age, therefore, the Evangelical decision will have to be a decision for Holy Scripture as such. As such, of course, it is only a sign. Indeed, it is the sign of a sign, i.e., of the prophetic-apostolic witness of revelation as the primary sign of Jesus Christ (ibid., 1:583).

God does not reveal Himself in words but in events:

> Among the signs of the objective reality of revelation we have to understand certain definite events and relations and orders within the world in which revelation is an objective reality, and therefore within the world which is also our world, the world of our nature and history. . . . [Hence,] to say "the Word of God" is to say the work of God. It is not to contemplate a state or fact but to watch an event, and an event which is relevant to us, an event which is an act of God, an act of God which rests on a free decision (ibid., 1:223, 1:527).

A Witness to the Word of God

The Bible is a human witness to God's revelation in Christ.

> "What stands there," in the pages of the Bible, is the witness to the Word of God, the Word of God in this testimony of the Bible. Just how far it stands there, however, is a fact that demands unceasing discovery, interpretation, and recognition. (*ET*, 36.)

Barth insisted,

In contrast to all kinds of similar literature these communities approved the canon as the original and faithful document of what the witnesses of the resurrection saw, heard, and proclaimed. They were the first to acknowledge this collection as genuine and authoritative testimony to the one Word of God, at the same time taking over, with a remarkable naturalness and ease, the Old Testament canon from the synagogue (ibid., 30).

The Bible Is Fallible and Errant

Barth believed that "there are obvious overlappings and contradictions—e.g., between the Law and the prophets, between John and the Synoptists, between Paul and James" (*CD*, 1:2.509). What is more, there are alleged cultural accommodations in the Scriptures: "Each [biblical author] in his own way and degree, they [sic] shared the culture of their age and environment." Instead of talking about the "errors" of the biblical authors in this sphere, if we want to go to the heart of things it is better to speak only about their "capacity for errors," for "in the last resort even in relation to the general view of the world and man the insight and knowledge of our age can be neither divine nor even Solomonic" (ibid., 1:2.508–9).

Scientifically, Barth held the Bible to be fallible:

> The post-Biblical theologian may, no doubt, possess a better astronomy, geography, zoology, psychology, physiology, and so on than these biblical witnesses possessed; but as for the Word of God, he is not justified in comporting himself in relationship to those witnesses as though he knew more about the Word than they. (*ET*, 31.)

Thus,

> [Higher criticism] migrates from the Old Testament to the New and returns again, from the Yahwist to the priestly codex, from the psalms of David to the proverbs of Solomon, from the Gospel of John to the synoptic gospels, from the Letter to the Galatians to the so-called "straw" epistle of James, and so on continually. Within all of these writings the pilgrimage leads from one level of tradition to another, taking into account every stage of tradition that may be present or surmised.
>
> The prophets and apostles as such . . . were real, historical men as we are, and therefore sinful in their action, and capable and actually guilty of error in their spoken and written word. . . . But the vulnerability of the Bible, i.e., its capacity for error, also extends to its religious or theological content. (*CD*, 1:2.529, 1:509.)

EMIL BRUNNER

Emil Brunner (1889–1966), another neo-orthodox theologian, was less conservative but clearer than Barth. Unlike Barth, Brunner gave more

validity to human reason, but like Barth he too rejected the historical orthodox doctrine of the divine inspiration of Scripture.

For Brunner the Bible is not the Word of God but the words of men
about God; revelation is not found in alleged words from God but in acts
of God for men.

The Bible Is Not the Word of God

According to Brunner, "There is a certain danger in this assumption
that the 'Word of God' can be equated with Holy Scripture." This view,
allegedly, arose from a twofold misunderstanding: first, from an academic
view of the nature of revelation, and second, from a Judaistic understanding of the Bible.

> The Bible itself does not give any occasion for this misunderstand-
> ing; by "revelation" it does not mean a supernaturally revealed doc-
> trine; nor does it equate "revelation" either with a collection of books
> or with one particular Book; in the Bible "revelation" means God's
> mighty acts for man's salvation. (*RR,* 118.)

Thus,

> The content of Scripture is true, not because as a whole it is to be
> regarded as God's word, but because and to the extent that God meets
> me there and speaks: He attests Himself to me as present and "decides
> me": that is why we call Scripture the Word of God. (*WGMM,* 32.)

The Bible Is the Word of Man

The Bible is intrinsically human: "The word of Scripture is not in itself
the word of God but of man, just as the historical appearance of the God-
man is in itself that of a man" (ibid.). Nonetheless, the Bible has divine
authority as an instrument God uses to convey His Word to us.

The nature of Scripture as a divine authority is instrumental—it is the
means by which God brings His Word (Christ) to us. As such, the Bible has
no formal authority, only an instrumental one:

> Scripture is not a formal authority which demands belief in all it
> contains from the outset, but it is an instrumental authority, in so far as
> it contains that element before which I must bow in the truth, which
> also itself awakens in men the certainty of truth. . . . This is what Luther
> means by the "Word of God," which therefore is not identical with the
> Word of Scripture, although it is only given to me through the Scrip-
> tures, and as the Word of the Scriptures. . . . [Therefore,] the content
> and the real authority of Scripture is Christ. (*CDG,* 110.)

The Bible Has Only a Derived Material Authority

From Brunner's perspective, the authority of the Bible is not formal but material; it is not intrinsic but derived.

> As in the case of the Reformers, we must express our first principle thus: the Scriptures have the authority of a norm, and the basis for this principle is this: the Scriptures possess this authority because they are the primary witness to the revelation of God in Jesus Christ (ibid., 45).

Therefore,

> We believe in Christ, not because Scripture, or the Apostles, teach us about Him in such and such a way, but we believe in the Scriptures because, and in so far as they teach Christ. The authority of Scripture is not formal but material: Christ [is] the revelation (ibid., 110).

The Bible Is a Subjective Authority

There is no objective divine authority in the text of Scripture; it *becomes* the Word of God in the hearts of believers: "The word in Scripture, Christ, becomes the same as the word in the heart, the Holy Spirit." (*GM*, 28.)

> Faith in Jesus Christ is not based upon a previous faith in the Bible, but it is based solely upon the witness of the Holy Spirit; this witness, [however,] does not come to us save through the witness of the Apostles—that apostolic testimony to which our relation is one of freedom, and, although it is true, it is fundamental for us, it is in no way dogmatically binding, in the sense of the theory of Verbal Inspiration (*CDG*, 34).

The Bible Is Fallible and Errant

Brunner believed,

> The orthodox view of the Bible . . . is an absolutely hopeless state of affairs. . . . God's revelation cannot be measured by the yardstick of theological doctrine. It has pleased God to make use of childlike and primitive ideas as an expression of His will. (*RR*, 291.)

Supposedly, contradictions are found in Scripture, even in the teachings of the apostles.

> At some points the variety of the Apostolic doctrine . . . is an irreconcilable contradiction. In spite of this, even the Epistle of James contributes something to our knowledge of Christ that we should not gain from Paul alone, and which acts as a corrective (ibid., 290).

Indeed,

> Literary criticism of the Bible brought to light the thousands of contradictions and human characteristics with which the Old and New Testaments abound. In this way the authority of the Bible was completely overthrown. (*GM*, 36.)

Brunner believed that there are also scientific inaccuracies in the Bible: "This truth is that the Holy Scriptures contain no divine oracles about all kinds of possible cosmological facts" (*RR*, 280). In fact,

> In so far as the Bible speaks about subjects of secular knowledge, it has no teaching authority. Neither its astronomical, cosmological picture of the world, nor its geographical view, nor its zoological, ethnographical or historical statements are binding upon us, whether they are in the Old Testament or in the New. Here, rather, free course should be given to rational scientific criticism. (*CDG*, 48.)

Brunner noted the similarity between his view and that of Karl Barth, saying,

> Fundamentally, Karl Barth's *Dogmatik* takes the same position: "The Bible is not a book of sacred oracles; it is not an organ of direct communication. It is real witness" (1, 2, 562). He says that we could not expect that the Apostles and Prophets, in addition to their encounter with the divine revelation, "should also have had imparted to them a compendium of . . . divine Wisdom concerning everything in the universe" (ibid., 113).

The Bible Is Only a Human Record of Revelation

According to Brunner, the Bible itself is not a revelation from God but only a human fallible record of divine revelation. He chides the historical view of Scripture:

> Orthodoxy, which understands revelation as revealed doctrine, finds it very easy to establish correct doctrine. All one has to do is to formulate the revealed doctrine—in a formal sense—for purposes of instruction, in a systematic or catechetical form. The doctrine is already there, in the revelation. We find it impossible to take this enviable short-cut; but we are also aware at what a price this short-cut was purchased, what terrible consequences sprang from it, and indeed, that these consequences are still bearing their own fruit (ibid., 28).

Further, "There is no such thing as revelation-in-itself, because revelation consists always of the fact that something is revealed to me. Revelation is . . . an act of God, an event involving two parties; it is a personal address" (*WGMM*, 32). More precisely, revelation is a Person.

Between us and the Old Testament, however, there stands a new form of revelation, the fulfillment of all that was only promised in the Old Testament, and the actual content of the divine revelation proclaimed by the Apostles and the Church: Jesus Christ Himself.

Thus, this "revelation" is not a "Word" but a Person—a human life fully visible within history, a human destiny so like, and so unlike, every other: Jesus of Nazareth (*CDG*, 23).

Truth Is Not Impersonal but Personal

[Jesus said:] "Therefore I am the Truth." This is not an impersonal, objective "it" truth, but a "Thou" truth. In this Event of revelation, in the Person of Christ the divine Thou addresses me, in love. God imparts Himself to me in the life of Him who alone was able to say [this]. (*RR*, 370.)

Truth, so the theory goes, is not found in an "it" but in an "I." Following the Jewish philosopher Martin Buber (1878–1965), Brunner believed that true revelation is found in an "I/Thou" experience with God, not in an "I/it" experience with a book. He even referred to the orthodox Protestant view of Scripture as belief in a "paper pope." Like Søren Kierkegaard, religious truth for Brunner was not objective but subjective.

There Is No Verbal Revelation

Further, verbal inspiration must be rejected, for "as a matter of fact . . . this doctrine of revelation [verbal inspiration] proved to be the death of faith, and the dogma of inspiration the very point on which orthodoxy quickly and finally came to an end" (*WGMM*, 36).

The doctrine of the verbal inspiration of Holy Scripture . . . cannot be regarded as an adequate formulation of the authority of the Bible. It is a product of . . . late Judaism, not of Christianity. The Apostolic writings never claim for themselves a verbal inspiration of this kind, with the infallibility that it implies. (*RR*, 127–28.)

Brunner believed it was fatal to regard the Bible as true. He wrote:

Once the fatal step is taken of regarding Scripture as true in itself, it is obvious that this quality applies equally to every single part of Scripture down to the smallest detail. . . . The dogma of verbal inspiration is involved not as the cause but as the consequence of the new unspiritual conception. The identity of the word of Scripture with the word of God has now changed from indirect to direct. (*WGMM*, 34.)

JOHN BAILLIE

John Baillie (1886–1960) was a prominent Scottish theologian. His influential book *The Idea of Revelation in Recent Thought* (1956) is a clear statement of the neo-orthodox view of Scripture from the British Isles.

The Bible Is Not Revelation

Baillie stated that "the weakness of Protestant orthodoxy has been that it could show no convincing reason for insisting on the plenary nature of the divine assistance to the Scriptural authors while as firmly denying it to the mind of the Church in later days" (*IRRT*, 112).

Baillie compared and summarized the positions of modern theologians about the impact of the doctrine of revelation in men's lives. In his work he stressed the existential nature of man's role in the revelatory process, opposed the notion of propositional revelation (which he confused with mechanical dictation), and suggested that revelation is essentially a personal encounter in the present moment. Also, he criticized the Roman Catholic and Protestant traditions for their "simple identification of divine revelation with Holy Scripture" (ibid., 36, 40).

The Need for Personal Encounter

Baillie asserted, "The propositions on the Scriptural page express the response of human witnesses to divine events, not a miraculous divine dictation" (ibid., 36). He also stated,

> The deepest difficulty felt about the equation of revelation with communicated truths is that it offers us something less than personal encounter and personal communion; and that difficulty is in no way relieved by the proposal to replace communicated truths by implanted images (ibid., 39).

True Knowledge of Scripture Is Determined by Man

Baillie held that "all true knowledge is knowledge that is determined not by the subject [God] but by the object [man]" (ibid., 20). Further,

> The intelligent reading of the Bible, in the Spirit but with the mind also, and the reading of it so as to understand how it *Christum treibt* [conveys Christ], depends entirely on our ability to distinguish what is central from what is peripheral; to distinguish its unchanging truth from its clothing in the particular cultural and cosmological preconceptions of the times and places in which it was written.

It further helps us

> to distinguish between its essential message and its numerous imperfections, historical inaccuracies, inaccurate or conflicting reports, misquotations or misapplied quotations from the Old Testament in the New, and such like; and withal to distinguish the successive levels of understanding both within the Old Testament and in the transition from that to the New (ibid., 120).

Even more candidly, when speaking of the inadequacy of the events portrayed in Scripture to reveal God, Baillie himself insisted,

> I could not know that God had revealed Himself to the prophets and apostles through these events, unless through His revelation of Himself to them He were now revealing Himself to me. . . . [Consequently,] I could know indeed that they claimed to have received such a revelation, but I can know that their claim is justified only if, as I read what they say, I too find myself in the presence of God (ibid., 105).

As Leon Morris rightly observes, for Baillie and others in his tradition, "The propositions laid down in Scripture are unimportant, even irrelevant. What matters is the encounter the man of faith has with God" (*IBR*, 113). The neo-orthodox view is hardly compatible with what the Bible has to say for itself (see chapters 13–16) and what has been taught by Christians throughout church history (see chapters 17–18).

To sum it up, the neo-orthodox view is that the Bible is a fallible human book. Nevertheless, it is the instrument of God's revelation to us, for it is a record of God's personal revelation in Christ. Revelation, however, is personal; the Bible is not a verbally inspired revelation from God—it is merely an errant human vehicle through which one can encounter the personal revelation, who is Christ. In itself it is not the Word of God: at best, the Bible only becomes the Word of God to the individual when he encounters Christ through it.

The Bible Has Errors

Finally, Baillie approves of the statement by C. H. Dodd, who quotes several passages from Isaiah and says,

> Any theory of inspiration of the Bible which suggests that we should recognize such utterances as authoritative for us stands self-condemned. They are relative to their age. But I think we should say more. They are false and they are wrong. (*AB*, 128.)

AN EVALUATION OF THE NEO-ORTHODOX VIEW OF SCRIPTURE

Like other unorthodox views of Scripture, the neo-orthodox view has many commendable features as well as some serious problems. First of all, several positive features of the neo-orthodox view will be set forth.

Among the commendable aspects of the neo-orthodox view of inspiration and revelation are its stress on the need for a personal, subjective encounter with God through Scripture and its appropriate critique of a form of bibliolatry that embraces mechanical dictation.

Rejection of Mechanical Dictation

Neo-orthodox adherents are to be commended for their uniform condemnation of the mechanical dictation theory that they attribute to a fundamentalist view of Scripture. The rejection of this form of biblical docetism, diminishing or denying the human side of Scripture, is contrary to both the claim and character of Scripture itself. The Bible claims to be and proves to be a completely human book in every proper sense of the word (see chapter 15). In this critique champions of neo-orthodoxy have rightly provided a corrective for overzealous conservative views of the Bible that are tacitly docetic, if not cultic, in their explanation of the role of human authors in the revelation process.

Emphasis on the Centrality of Christ

Another helpful emphasis of the neo-orthodox view is the stress on the centrality of Jesus Christ, God's Living Word. Overemphasis on the written Word, without stressing its purpose to convey the Living Word (Christ), has indeed led to some outlandish conservative views that make the Word of God the object of their study rather than the God of the Word. Jesus Himself warned against this error when He chided the Jews, saying, "You diligently study the Scriptures because you think that by them you possess eternal life. These are the Scriptures that testify about me, yet you refuse to come to me to have life" (John 5:39–40). Indeed, four other times Jesus said that He was the central theme of the Bible (Matt. 5:17–18; Luke 24:27; 24:44; Heb. 10:7). It is possible, as neo-orthodoxy rightly reminds us, to miss the person of the Living Word of God while stressing the propositions of the written Word of God.

Rejection of Bibliolatry

Neo-orthodoxy also sounds a proper alarm against bibliolatry: The Bible is not divine, and it should not be worshiped. It is the Word of God, but it is not God, and as such it should be treated with respect but not with the reverence due to God alone. Bibliology is a proper pursuit, but bibliolatry is not. Orthodoxy is right when it insists on being Bible-based but wrong when it becomes Bible-centered rather than Christ-centered.

Stress on the Need for Personal Encounter

The neo-orthodox view puts proper emphasis on the need for a personal, existential encounter with God. It tries to avoid abstract truth for a concrete relationship, and here again Jesus and the rest of the New Testament place a kindred stress. Our Lord condemned an impersonal, dispassionate, formal religion (cf. Matt. 6:1–7; Luke 18:1–8), and Paul spoke against "having a form of godliness but denying its power" (2 Tim. 3:5). Surely the aim of Scripture is not that we merely know more propositional truth but that we have an encounter with the person who is the Truth (John 14:6).

The Revelation of God in His Acts

Another neglected emphasis stressed by the neo-orthodox view of Scripture is that God reveals Himself in His works. Much of the Old Testament is an illustration of this truth: The God of the Bible is a God who performs mighty acts. The deliverance of His people Israel from Egypt displayed an awesome array of these mighty actions. The incarnation and life of Christ is an even more dramatic display of God's great acts in history, and the Bible declares that these actions were revelatory.

Indeed, the very common word for "do" (Heb: *asah*) in the Old Testament can and does often mean to reveal or to "show."[6] Likewise, the normal word for "reveal" (*galah*) in the Old Testament is associated with the mighty acts of God (see Isa. 53:1). God does not need to speak to reveal Himself; often, His actions speak louder than His words, as was the case, for instance, in the ten plagues on Egypt (cf. Ex. 7–12).

Focus on the Need for Illumination

Regardless of the term one uses to describe it, neo-orthodoxy is right in reminding us that the chain from God to us is not complete without an appropriation of God's truth to ourselves. Objective disclosure is not enough; there must be a subjective discovery of truth. Further, the Bible exhorts us: "Do not merely listen to the word, and so deceive yourselves. Do what it says" (James 1:22). Metaphorically put, the morocco leather of the Bible must be translated into the shoe leather of experience. In theological language, objective revelation is insufficient; we need subjective "illumination" (i.e., appropriation) of this revelation that effects a transformation in our lives.

Despite its many good emphases, the neo-orthodox view of Scripture

---

[6]*Asah* is so translated in a number of places (e.g., Ex. 9:16; 2 Sam. 2:6).

has many serious shortcomings. Among these are that it is unbiblical, contrary to the historical view of the Christian church, and inconsistent.

The Neo-Orthodox View of Scripture Is Biblically Unfounded

Whatever else may be said for it, the neo-orthodox view of the Bible is not biblical—it is contrary to what the Bible claims for itself, that it is the verbal, plenary Word of God (see chapters 13–14), composed of "writings" (Gr: *grapha*) that are God-breathed (2 Tim. 3:16). Indeed, the very words of Scripture came from God (2 Sam. 23:2; Matt. 4:4), who has revealed Himself in its words (1 Cor. 2:11–13). The prophets were told not to omit a single word God spoke to them (Jer. 26:2); in fact, the written Old Testament as a whole is referred to as the "Word of God" (John 10:34–35).

The Neo-Orthodox View of the Bible Is Historically Unsupported

One looks in vain to find support for the neo-orthodox contentions that the Bible is not to be identified with the Word of God or that it is fallible and errant (see chapters 13–16, 27). *The evidence in its entirety is to the contrary.* One must scrounge here and there to find a text—out of context—to provide even scant and superficial support for the view that the great Fathers of the church taught anything except the orthodox view that the Bible is the divinely inspired, infallible, and inerrant written Word of God. These feeble efforts fail in view of the multiple, repeated, and overwhelming support of the Fathers for the orthodox view of Scripture.

Some scholars, like Jack Rogers, have attempted to do this, but their attempts were in vain, for others have carefully and systematically answered them.[7] For example, in light of Martin Luther's repeated and emphatic declarations in favor of the inerrancy of Scripture, the futile effort to take his reference to the Bible as the lowly cradle of Christ (see chapter 18) in no way proves he disbelieved inerrancy. Likewise, his rejection of James as inconsistent with Paul is not a denial of inerrancy; rather, it is such a strong affirmation that the Bible cannot err that anything believed to be inconsistent with Scripture was to be rejected.

The Neo-Orthodox View of the Bible Is Philosophically Inconsistent

One of the interesting inconsistencies of neo-orthodoxy is its contention that God can *act* in human history but He cannot *speak* in human language. To this, one is inclined to extend the prophet's analogy and ask, "He who made the mouth, can He not speak?" Surely a God who created beings who

---

[7]See John Woodbridge's *Biblical Authority* and John Hannah's *Inerrancy and the Church.*

can communicate in language can Himself communicate in their language. Indeed, it is a denial of the principle of analogy (see chapter 9) to claim that God can give perfections He does not have. Can God share with others what He does not possess?

Neo-Orthodoxy Is Christologically Incoherent

For those, like Karl Barth, who accept the deity of Christ, the denial of the verbal nature of revelation is incoherent, for if Christ as God assumed a completely human nature in the Incarnation (John 1:14; 1 John 4:1–2), then it is inconsistent to affirm that this person (who is God), when He spoke while on earth, was not speaking the words of God. That is, since Christ was two natures in one person, then the words this one person spoke were both the words of God and the words of man. But if it is possible that one and the same words can be both divine and human as they came from the mouth of Jesus, then why can't this be true of the words of Scripture? In short, the orthodox view of the written Word and the orthodox view of the Living Word go hand-in-hand (see chapter 15).

The Neo-Orthodox View of Scripture Is Axiologically Misplaced

While it may be granted that the grandfather of neo-orthodoxy held an orthodox view of the *nature* of the historicity and inerrancy of Scripture, it is also true that Kierkegaard's view of the *value* of these facts was unorthodox, for the stance he took as to the relative unimportance of all but the bare historical facts of Jesus was axiologically unorthodox. His claim that events like the Resurrection, not being part of that bare historical core necessary for Christianity, weren't important, is contrary to the claim of the New Testament itself; Paul declared emphatically that "if Christ has not been raised, our preaching is useless and so is your faith. . . . And if Christ has not been raised, your faith is futile; you are still in your sins" (1 Cor. 15:14, 17).

Furthermore, by separating the realms of fact and value, existentialism, following Kierkegaard, succeeded in setting the stage for the later denial of the historicity of most of the Gospels, including the Resurrection, by other existentialists like Rudolph Bultmann (see chapter 19). But fact and value *cannot* always be separated. Paul made this clear in his statement about the Resurrection, and from the beginning God made it clear in his statement about murder: Murdering another human being is not just an attack on his/her facticity; it is an attack on the image of God (Gen. 9:6). Such action against a body (the factual) is also an attack on a person (the valuable). The two are inseparable in this world.

The Neo-Orthodox View Is Logically Fallacious

Much of the neo-orthodox rejection of the historical orthodox view is based on two logical fallacies. The false disjunction is a common one; for example,

(1) Either the Bible is a personal revelation, or it is a propositional revelation.
(2) Revelation is personal.
(3) Therefore, revelation cannot be propositional.

But even if one accepts the premise that "revelation is personal," the conclusion does not follow, for in an either/or form of reasoning (i.e., disjunctive syllogism), one of the two alternatives must be denied in order to get a valid conclusion. But the neo-orthodox reasoning affirms (rather than denies) one alternative, which is the fallacy of *affirming an alternate.* Why not both? Indeed, this is precisely what the orthodox view entails, namely, that God has given both a personal revelation (Christ) and a propositional revelation (Scripture), and it is the purpose of God's written Word (the Bible) to reveal God's Living Word (Christ).

Another common fallacy in neo-orthodox thought on the Bible is the Straw Man fallacy. The "paper pope" charge and the "mechanical dictation" allegation are cases in point. Few, if any, knowledgeable evangelical theologians in the history of the church held to mechanical dictation. To be sure, some used bad illustrations that, if taken to their logical conclusion, may have yielded that result. But none of them really did this, and all of them would have denied the charge of mechanical dictation.

For example, Augustine: "When they write that He has taught and said, it should not be asserted that he did not write it, since the members only put down what they had come to know at the dictation [*dictis*] of the Head. Therefore, whatever He wanted us to read concerning His words and deeds, He commanded His disciples, His hands, to write."

This may be an unfortunate illustration, but it does not prove Augustine held the mechanical dictation theory. We use the word "dictate" in the same nonmechanical sense today when we say that the laws we choose to obey came by the dictates of the legislature. Likewise, other earlier Fathers who spoke of the human authors of the Bible as flutes God played on did not mean that this be taken any more literally than Jesus intended when he said "I am the gate" (John 10:9).

The Neo-Orthodox View of Scripture Is Practically Unfruitful

While the neo-orthodox view sounds better than the liberal view, it reduces to the same fatal flaw: that the Bible is not the infallible Word of God but only the fallible words of men about God. How can one entrust his eternal destiny to fallible human teaching known to be riddled with errors?

The neo-orthodox illustration of the dog listening to his master's voice through a distorted record misses the point; it is a false analogy, for there is a big difference between a person listening to a recording of a true message from an actual long-lost loved one and listening to a false, scratchy message from an impostor. Unlike adherents to liberalism (see chapter 20) and neo-orthodoxy, evangelicals make an important distinction between *divine adaptation to finitude* (which involves some background noise on the record) and *divine accommodation to error* (which distorts the very message itself).

The doctrine of analogy (see chapter 9) demands that when an infinite God expresses truth to a finite mind, some form of *adaptation* is necessary, whether in negation, figures of speech, metaphors, similes, or anthropomorphism. However, the liberal and neo-orthodox views involve the position that the Bible teaches error, not just that there are "noises" on the record that gives us the truth. To be sure, too much noise could distort the truth, but this is precisely what the doctrine of analogy (see chapter 9) assures, namely, that finitude does not necessitate error. Or, in biblical terms, the "image of God" (Gen. 1:27), even in fallen man (Gen. 9:6), assures us that truth can be expressed in finite terms without distorting its truthfulness.

SUMMARY AND CONCLUSION

The neo-orthodox view of Scripture has much to commend it, including its rejection of mechanical dictation, its stress on the centrality of Christ, its rejection of bibliolatry, its emphasis on personal encounter with God, its focus on revelation as acts of God, and the need for illumination. Nonetheless, there are serious flaws in the view that cause it to fall far short of an adequate explanation of all the data. On careful examination, neo-orthodoxy has been found to be biblically unfounded, historically unsupported, philosophically inconsistent, Christologically incoherent, axiologically misplaced, logically fallacious, and practically unfruitful.

SOURCES

Baillie, John. *The Idea of Revelation in Recent Thought.*
Barth, Karl. *Church Dogmatics.*
———. *Evangelical Theology: An Introduction.*
Brunner, Emil. *The Christian Doctrine of God.*
———. *God and Man.*
———. *Revelation and Reason.*
———. *The Word of God and Modern Man.*

Dodd, C. H. *The Authority of the Bible.*
Geisler, Norman, and William Nix. *A General Introduction to the Bible.*
Geisler, Norman, ed. *Biblical Errancy.*
Kierkegaard, Søren. *Concluding Unscientific Postscripts.*
———. *Fear and Trembling.*
———. *My Point of View for My Work as an Author.*
———. *Philosophical Fragments.*
———. *Self-Examination . . .*
———. *Søren Kierkegaard's Journals and Papers.*
Linnemann, Eta. *Biblical Criticism on Trial.*
Morris, Leon. *I Believe in Revelation.*

CHAPTER TWENTY-TWO

NEO-EVANGELICALS ON THE BIBLE

T he new evangelical view is so named because it is a deviation from the longstanding evangelical teaching on Scripture (see chapters 13–18). It may also be called neo-Reformed, since it comes mainly from theologians in the Reformed tradition, but since other evangelicals have adopted similar views, it is appropriate to call it neo-evangelical. The most important proponent of this view is the Dutch theologian G. C. Berkouwer. His follower, American theologian Jack Rogers of Fuller Seminary, holds substantially the same position.

G. C. BERKOUWER (1903–1996)

The influence of European neo-orthodoxy made a marked effect on G. C. Berkouwer. While broadly remaining within the evangelical tradition, his subtle but significant alterations on the doctrine of Scripture have had a wide influence in the United States and elsewhere.

Berkouwer revealed a significant influence from the neo-orthodox view of Karl Barth in his handling of the question of whether the Bible is the Word of God. His answer is a dialectical yes and no.

Distinction Between the Word of God and the Words of Men

Berkouwer wrote,

> We have frequently come across the characterization of Scripture as the Word of God and the words of men. Reliability, of course, was always discussed in direct relationship to this, particularly in view of the truly human aspect of Scripture.

He continued,

> We do not merely have in mind the general consideration that error belongs to human nature. We have in mind above all the contrast noted frequently in Scripture between the Word of God and the words of men, between relying on God and relying on man. (*HS*, 240.)

Like Barth, Berkouwer believed that the voice of God could be heard within Scripture—a confession that falls short of the clear orthodox proclamation that the Bible *is* the Word of God. He declared,

> This "is" is not a postulate of our longings for certainty which cannot withstand the assaults of the human. Rather, it is truly a confession that continues to be filled with expectation in listening to the many voices within the one voice in this Scripture (ibid., 168).

The Bible Is Understood Non-Supernaturally

Berkouwer believed it is a misunderstanding to think of the Bible as a supernatural work of God. "This can be understood if one does not initially misunderstand the glory of God and does not wish to interpret the God-breathed character in an abstract supernaturalistic and 'miraculous' manner" (ibid., 170).

Leaning on his strong Calvinistic orientation, Berkouwer thought of Scripture more as a result of the sovereignty of God:

> In reading Scripture we encounter some of the questions aroused in men related to ... becoming bearers of God's Word. Moses does not deem himself "eloquent" (Ex. 4:10), and Isaiah exclaims "Woe is me" because he is a man of unclean lips (Isa. 6:5). ... [Thus] this divine taking-into-service has an aspect of triumph and sovereignty, yet it does not erase the weakness of the human word nor its limitations. Time and again we note a vivid awareness of God's using weak human "instruments" (ibid., 206).

Even prophecy was thought of nonsupernaturally, for "the speech of men in prophecy is the way of the reliable testimony of God" (ibid., 146).

Inspiration Is Organic, Not Verbal and Plenary

Contrary to the orthodox view, Berkouwer held that inspiration is organic[1] but not verbal and plenary:

> We are reminded, by way of background, of what is called—even in catechism books—the transition from a more "mechanical" to a more

---

[1] "Organic inspiration" is the idea that the Bible is inspired as a whole, but not necessarily in all its parts.

"organic" view of Scripture. It is clear that this too will determine the nature of one's account (ibid., 11).

Tracing his roots to his Dutch predecessor, Herman Bavinck (1854–1921), Berkouwer declared that "to Bavinck . . . organic inspiration [is] the unfolding and application of the central fact of revelation, the incarnation of the Word" (ibid., 199). He rejected the orthodox view:

> Every book of [the Bible], every chapter of it, every word of it, every syllable of it, every letter of it, is the direct utterance of the Most High, [claiming that] this statement . . . disregards all nuances of Scripture (consider the Psalms, Job, Ecclesiastes), as though it were a string of divine or supernaturally revealed statements, ignoring the fact that God's Word has passed through humanity and has incorporated its service (ibid., 23–24).

Inspiration Is Found in Intention

Embracing an intentionalist view of truth (see chapter 7), Berkouwer affirmed,

> At issue is whether and in what way faith is related to the gospel promised in Holy Scripture. Scripture is central because of its nature and intent. For this Scripture is only referred to because its sense and intent is the divine message of salvation (ibid., 147).

Like Herman Ridderbos, Berkouwer believed that "the evangelists did not intend to give 'a historical narrative of Jesus' words and works' but a portrayal of Jesus as the Christ. That is the character of our gospel, or, expressed in other terms, not report but witness" (ibid., 247). Thus the Bible is inspired only in what it intended to convey, and this, supposedly, did not always include matters of history and science.

Human Limitations of Scripture

Berkouwer implies that the limitations of the Bible seem to include error, like any other human writing:

> It is explicitly referred to in Bavinck's words: "Christ became flesh, a servant without form or comeliness, the most despised among men . . . and so also the Word, the revelation of God entered creation, in the life and history of men and people in every form of dream and vision, of research and meditation, even as far as the humanly weak and ignoble; the Word became Scripture and as *Scripture subjected itself to the fate of all writing*" (ibid., 199, emphasis added).

But the fate of all human writings is to contain error.

Indeed, Berkouwer chided fundamentalism[2] for not admitting the full humanity of Scripture.

> Fundamentalism greatly obscures the contexts in which God himself gave us Scripture. Back of fundamentalism lies something of an unconscious wish not to have God's Word enter the creaturely realm—or, to use Bavinck's words, "into the humanly weak and despised and base"—and the wish that Scripture should not subject itself "as writing to the fate of all writings" (ibid., 25).

He added,

> I believe that I am judging no one unfairly when I say that fundamentalism, in its eagerness to maintain Holy Scripture's divinity, does not fully realize the significance of Holy Scripture as a prophetic-apostolic, and consequently human, testimony (ibid., 22).

Since for Berkouwer the Bible is not equated with the Word of God but possesses limitations to the point of error, he must adopt a form of divine accommodationism to human error rather than the standard orthodox view of divine adaptation to human finitude without error. This is evident in a number of statements on the limitations and human errors in Scripture.

Cultural Accommodations

For example,

> Paul, in contrast, did not in the least render timeless propositions concerning womanhood. Rather, he wrote various testimonies and prescriptions applicable to particular—and to a certain degree transparent—situations against a background of specific morals and customs of that period. [Consequently,] this realization has increasingly penetrated even to areas where there has been no hesitation to affirm Scripture as the Word of God (ibid., 187).

Citing American theologian Bernard Ramm (1916–1992), who is noted for leaning in a neo-evangelical direction in his later years, Berkouwer said,

> Ramm wrote rightly . . . that the Holy Spirit "did not give to the writers the secrets of modern science." Various excessive examples (including even nuclear theories) are in his opinion "a misunderstanding of the nature of inspiration," for they do not take into account that Scripture came to us "in terms of the culture in which the writers wrote" (ibid., 189).

---

[2]Berkouwer, like many neo-evangelicals, regards the evangelical view of Scripture as "fundamentalist."

Scientific Accommodations

For Berkouwer,

The problem of the God-breathed character of Scripture and continuity gained renewed interest in its connection with the author's level of knowledge in a certain period (Ex. 20:4, Ps. 24:2, [3, Eng. text]; 2 Sam. 22:8; Ps. 136:6; Job 26:5; Ps. 46:3 [2, Eng. text]; Ps. 148:4). [Of course,] this does not mean a capitulation to science as an institution opposed to God's Word, with the additional conclusions that Scripture is unreliable and its witness untrustworthy. [Rather,] it means a greater degree of naturalness in speaking of Scripture, with a view to its nature and purpose. Corrections of various conceptions of the world—its composition and its place in the universe—are not at all needed then to guarantee the full and clear message of Scripture. [Thus,] formal problems of correctness (inerrancy alongside infallibility) disintegrate with such a naturalness (ibid., 182).

Historical Accommodations

According to Berkouwer,

He who demands that all conceptions occurring in Scripture be precisely correct on the basis of the God-breathed character of Scripture starts with the presupposition that the voice of God can only then be reliable and that the biblical authors cannot be witnesses and instruments of the God-breathed Scripture when they use certain time-bound conceptions in their writings. [Hence,] this notion of "inerrancy" can quickly lead to the idea that the "correctness" of all these conceptions anticipates later scientific discovery (ibid., 183).

Berkouwer denied the inerrancy of the Bible, claiming,

The concept of error in the sense of incorrectness is obviously being used on the same level as the concept of erring in the sense of sin and deception. The distinction is left rather vague.

As a consequence of this,

Limited historical perception within a certain cultural and scientific situation is, without further stipulation, put on a par with erring in the sense of lying, the opposite of truth. If erring is formalized in such a way, it cannot later be related to truth in a biblical sense, but it continues to function as a formal structure of exactness and correctness.

Thus,

We are quite far removed from the serious manner with which erring is dealt in Scripture. For there what is meant is not the result of a limited degree of knowledge, but it is a swerving from the truth and upsetting the faith (2 Tim. 2:18) (ibid., 181).

As to the Gospels, Berkouwer concluded,

> One will never solve the problem of the Gospels by indiscriminately operating with the concept of "historical reliability," precisely because then one leaves the impression that no further questions need to be answered. As a consequence, all further reflection on this point is subject to suspicion from the start (ibid., 251).

He added, "It was pointed out by many that it was impossible to write a 'biography' of Jesus based on the Gospels, not even by adding up the data from the Gospels so that one would complement another" (ibid., 247).

Worldview Limitations

In the paradigm of Berkouwer, the Bible is fallible even in the worldview it expresses:

> This is illustrated in Jan Ridderbos' words: "Moreover Scripture bears the marks of the period and of the milieu in which it was written and it shares in part these marks with the culture which in many ways was interrelated to that of Israel. This is true for writing, language, style, literary genre, ideas, conceptions, [and] world view (cf. the three-decker universe in Ex. 20:4)" (ibid., 182).

He also unconvincingly said, "It was pointed out that the authority of Scripture is in no way diminished because an ancient world view occurs in it; for it was not the purpose of Scripture to offer revealing information on that level" (ibid., 181).

Myths in Scripture

Berkouwer went so far as to claim there are myths in the Bible, arguing that we "cannot directly take up a position against Bultmann's theological concern with demythologizing by means of a text such as 2 Peter 1:15" [the retelling of Balaam being rebuked by the donkey, citing K. H. Schelke, *Die Petrusbriefe* (1961)] (ibid., 198):

> By "myth" Bultmann does not mean those myths that are rejected as fabrications and are opposed to the truth as *mythoi*. He means rather an imagery connected with a mythical world view. This world view is characterized by the presence of three levels—heaven, earth, and the underworld—so that earth is considered to be the "scene of the supernatural activity of God" [from Bultmann, "New Testament and Mythology" in *Kerygma and Myth*] (ibid., 254).

As to whether the Gospel writers were reporting or creating the words and events of Jesus, Berkouwer concluded, "If we are dealing with a penetration of story and interpretation, should we not accept a creativity of the evangelists from which 'fantasy' could be distinguished only with great difficulty?" (ibid., 248).

Biblical Criticism

Berkouwer believed that the Bible was not beyond critique:

> For various reasons students of Scripture began to wonder more and more whether Holy Scripture as God's Word was truly beyond all criticism as the indubitable *vox Dei*, as a book—however human—of indisputably divine signature.... Frequently, too little attention is paid to the possibility and legitimacy of biblical research. A supernaturalistic view of revelation would consider any human "research" puzzling and inconceivable (ibid., 13, 358).

JACK ROGERS (1934–)

As documented in Harold Lindsell's book *The Battle for the Bible,* Fuller Seminary has been a leader in the move to a neo-evangelical view of Scripture. The movement began in the 1960s when the faculty split over the inerrancy of the Bible, after the school eliminated it from its doctrinal position. Those who opposed this move left the seminary, including notable evangelicals such as Harold Lindsell, Carl Henry, Charles Woodbridge, Wilbur Smith, and Gleason Archer. The movement against inerrancy was championed by Daniel Fuller, George Ladd, Paul Jewett, and the president of the seminary, David Hubbard. The most significant work defending the neo-evangelical view was subsequently produced by faculty member Jack Rogers, titled *The Authority and Interpretation of the Bible.*

The Origin of Scripture

As to the origin of Scripture, Rogers holds that "evangelicals believe the Bible is the authoritative word of God" (*BA*, 17). Albeit, accommodation to human finitude and even error is involved in this process, for "in order to communicate effectively with human beings, God condescended, humbled, and accommodated himself to human categories of thought and speech" (*AIB*, 10).

Thus, following Berkouwer, the nature of inspiration is not verbal and plenary; rather, it is organic, meaning that the Bible is inspired as a whole, but not necessarily in all its parts.

Organic Inspiration

According to Rogers,

> The basic interpretative principle of the Reformation had been

stated in several ways: the analogy of faith, or Scripture as its own interpreter. The meaning of these phrases was that each part of the Bible was to be understood in relationship to the overall saving message of Scripture. . . . Bavinck attempted to express this relationship of the parts to the whole through the image of the human body. Bavinck's concept, which he called "organic inspiration," drew attention to the fact that there is a center and a periphery to Scripture (ibid., 391).

Unerring Only in Purpose

Rogers was willing to speak of the inerrancy of the Bible, but he redefined it in terms of his nontraditional view of truth (see chapter 7) as intentionality, not correspondence. That is to say, the Bible is without error in what it intends to accomplish, not in all it actually affirms.

> It is no doubt possible to define the meaning of biblical inerrancy according to the Bible's saving purpose and taking into account the human forms through which God condescended to reveal himself. (*BA*, 45.)

Factual Errors

This inerrancy-of-intent-but-not-fact view leaves the Bible with historical and scientific errors.

> It is historically irresponsible to claim that for two thousand years Christians have believed that the authority of the Bible entails a modern concept of inerrancy in scientific and historical details (ibid., 44).

Therefore, Rogers insists:

> To confuse "error" in the sense of technical accuracy with the biblical notion of error as willful deception diverts us from the serious intent of Scripture. The purpose of the Bible is not to substitute for human science. [Hence,] the purpose of the Bible is to warn against human sin and offer us God's salvation in Christ. Scripture infallibly achieves that purpose. We are called, not to argue Scripture's scientific accuracy, but to accept its saving message (ibid., 46).

The Purpose of Scripture

Once inerrancy was defined in terms of intention or purpose and not in terms of correspondence to fact, the neo-evangelical could speak of the saving purpose of Scripture being hermeneutically definitive in terms of what is meant by inspiration. Rogers writes in this connection:

Scripture could be interpreted by a regenerate mind in light of its purpose of bringing us to salvation in Christ. . . . Scripture was not to be used as a source of information in the sciences to refute what the scholars were discovering (ibid., 34).

Reinterpreting history in the light of his new definition of inspiration and inerrancy, Rogers claimed:

For the Westminster divines, the final judge in controversies of religion was not just the bare word of Scripture interpreted by human logic, but the Spirit of Christ leading us in Scripture to its central saving witness to him (ibid., 35).

That is to say, purpose determines meaning, and since the purpose of the Bible is judged to be unilaterally salvific (2 Tim. 3:15), one must overlook minor factual errors of history and science in favor of its central saving purpose.

Higher Criticism and the Bible

With the focus on purpose, not fact, Rogers is able to accommodate modern negative criticism of the Bible. In his words,

By distinguishing between the center and the periphery in Scripture, [Abraham] Kuyper and [Herman] Bavinck's tradition freed their followers from scholarship and for scholarship. The central saving message of Scripture could be received in faith without waiting for scholarly reasons. The supporting material of Scripture, the human forms of culture and language, were open to scholarly investigation. (*AIB*, 393.)

Rogers believes,

Biblical criticism became a problem, according to Bavinck, only when the critics lost sight of the purpose of Scripture. That purpose, goal, or "destination" of Scripture was "none other than that it should make us wise to salvation."

From Bavinck's perspective, Scripture was not meant to give us technically correct scientific information (*BA*, 43).

Rogers clearly rejected the traditional orthodox view of B. B. Warfield (1851–1921) on inerrancy—that the Bible is factually inerrant in the original manuscripts as an unprovable assumption: "Thus errorlessness was confined to the original (lost) manuscripts of the Bible. Since the original texts were not available, Warfield seemed to have an unassailable apologetic stance" (ibid., 39).

Rogers' Revision of Church History

Rejecting the orthodoxy of Charles Hodge (1797–1878), B. B. Warfield, and the Princetonian school, based as it was, he believed, on outmoded aristotelian logic, Rogers proceeded in his revisionist philosophy of church history to reinterpret the past in favor of his new evangelical view. He insisted,

> Augustine, Calvin, Rutherford, and Bavinck, for example, all specifically deny that the Bible should be looked to as an authority in matters of science. To claim them in support of a modern inerrancy theory is to trivialize their central concern that the Bible is our sole authority on salvation and the living of a Christian life (ibid., 44).

Rogers wrote, "It is equally irresponsible to claim that the old Princeton theology of Alexander, Hodge, and Warfield is the only legitimate evangelical, or Reformed, theological tradition in America" (ibid., 45).

In summary, the neo-evangelical view differentiates between the Word of God (divine content) and the words of the human authors (human form) of Scripture. The former is infallible, but the latter is not; hence, the Bible is not infallibly divine words but only reliable human words. Like adherents to neo-orthodoxy (see chapter 21), neo-evangelicals hold that the Bible is a human witness to divine revelation. The church confesses it as the Word of God, but the Bible does not express eternal truths about science, history, or even human relations (such as male/female roles).

Further, it sees the evangelical view of Scripture (which it calls "fundamentalism") as holding to mechanical dictation, and this caricature is rejected in favor of an "organic" inspiration, which maintains that there are myths and obsolete scientific views reflected in Scripture. The Bible, like all other human books, is subject to mistakes, and thus must be judged critically.

C. S. LEWIS

For those most familiar with C. S. Lewis's strong and eloquent defense of many of the basic tenets of historic Christianity, his view of Scripture comes as a great surprise. Indeed, his perspective almost defies categorization, since it combines seemingly contradictory elements of the orthodox, liberal, neo-orthodox, and neo-evangelical views. Some have called it "liberal evangelical." Since it is clearly neither an evangelical nor a liberal model, it is listed here with neo-evangelical views, though it has much in common with liberalism, particularly on the Old Testament.

Like those who maintain neo-orthodoxy, Lewis believed that the voice of God could be heard through the errant record of the Old Testament.

The origin of the message was divine, but the human pipeline by which it got here was often terribly polluted.

The Voice of God Through Human Distortion

Lewis wrote,

> Certainly it seems to me that from having had to reach what is really the Voice of God in the cursing Psalms through all the horrible distortions of the human medium, I have gained something I might not have gained from a flawless, ethical exposition. (*RP*, 114.)

He added, "Though hideously distorted by the human instrument, something of the Divine voice can be heard in these passages" (ibid., 32).

Divine Elevation of Human Genius

Lewis seemed to adopt a theistic evolutionary view of the origin of Scripture (see *CR*, 115), believing that the human body develops gradually and naturally until God infuses a human soul in it, thus stamping His image on it. Scripture was produced in a similar way:

> For we are taught that the Incarnation itself proceeded "not by the conversion of the godhead into flesh, but by taking of [the] manhood into God"; in it human life becomes the vehicle of Divine life. If the Scriptures proceed not by conversion of God's word into a literature but by taking up of a literature to be the vehicle of God's word, this is not anomalous. (*RP*, 116.)

This is true because

> If the Old Testament is a literature thus "taken up," made the vehicle of what is more than human, we can of course set no limit to the weight or multiplicity of meanings which may have been laid upon it. If any writer may say more than he knows and mean more than he meant, then these writers will be especially likely to do so. And not by accident (ibid., 117).

There was, according to Lewis, a constant divine/human conflict in the formation of Scripture, for "we read [about] the whole Jewish experience of God's gradual and graded self-revelation [so as] to feel the very contentions between the Word and the human material through which it works" (ibid., 114).

Divine Superintendence

For Lewis, Scripture resulted more from God's providence than from His supernatural intervention:

I take it that the whole Old Testament consists of the same sort of material as any other literature—chronicle (some of it obviously pretty accurate), poems, moral and political diatribes, romances, and what not; but all taken into the service of God's word. Not all, I suppose, in the same way.

Thus,

There are prophets who write with the clearest awareness that Divine compulsion is upon them. There are chroniclers whose intention may have been merely to record. There are poets like those in the Song of Songs who probably never dreamed of any but a secular and natural purpose in what they composed.

Also,

There is (and it is no less important) the work first of the Jewish and then of the Christian Church in preserving and canonizing just these books. There is the work of redactors and editors in modifying them. On all of these I suppose a Divine pressure; of which not by any means all need have been conscious (ibid., 111).

Lewis's belief in the divine authority of Scripture was severely modified by his acceptance of negative literary criticism of it. The result was that he concluded that there were many errors and contradictions in the Bible.

The Errant Nature of the Bible

Lewis believed,

Whatever view we hold of the divine authority of Scripture must make room for the following facts. (1) The distinction which St. Paul makes in 1 Cor. vii between [not I but the Lord] (v. 10) and [I speak, not the Lord] (v. 12). (2) The apparent inconsistencies between the genealogies in Matt. i and Luke iii; with the accounts of the death of Judas in Matt. xxvii. 5 and Acts i. 18–19. (3) St. Luke's own account of how he obtained his matter (i. 1–4). (4) The universally admitted un-historicity (I do not say, of course, falsity) of at least some narratives in Scripture (the parables), which may well extend also to Jonah and Job. (5) If every good and perfect gift comes from the Father of lights, then all true and edifying writings, whether in Scripture or not, must be in some sense inspired. (6) Inspiration may operate in a wicked man without his knowing it, and he can then utter the untruth he intends . . . as well as truth he does not intend (see John 11:49–52). (Cited by Christensen, *CSLS,* 98–99.)[3]

---

[3]See Norman Geisler and Thomas Howe, *When Critics Ask.*

Lewis said,

> Some people find the miraculous so hard to believe that they cannot imagine any reason for my acceptance of it other than a prior belief that every sentence of the Old Testament has historical or scientific truth. [But] this I do not hold, any more than St. Jerome did when he said that Moses described Creation "after the manner of a popular poet" (as we should say, mythically) or than Calvin did when he doubted whether the story of Job were history or fiction. (*RP*, 109.)

Myths in the Old Testament

Generally speaking, Lewis's view of the New Testament is more orthodox than that of the Old Testament, particularly his view of its historicity. This is due in part to his unique view of myths, namely, that God first reveals Himself in myth and then in history (*M*, 139).

Lewis found no difficulty in accepting the long-held liberal view that the story of Adam and Eve was mythological. He said, "I have therefore no difficulty in accepting, say, the view of those scholars who tell us that the account of Creation in Genesis is derived from earlier Semitic stories which were Pagan and mythical" (*RP*, 110).

> When a series of such re-telling turns a creation story which at first had almost no religious or metaphysical significance into a story which achieves the idea of true Creation and of a transcendent Creator (as Genesis does), then nothing will make me believe that some of the re-tellers, or some one of them, has not been guided by God. [Thus,] something originally merely natural—the kind of myth that is found among most nations—will have been raised by God above itself, qualified by Him and compelled by Him to serve purposes which of itself it would not have served (ibid., 110).

Likewise, wrote Lewis,

> The Book of Job appears to me unhistorical because it begins about a man quite unconnected with all history or even legend, with no genealogy, living in a country of which the Bible elsewhere has hardly anything to say; because ... the author quite obviously writes as a storyteller, not as a chronicler (ibid., 110).

Also,

> The question about Jonah and the great fish does not turn simply on intrinsic probability. The point is that the whole Book of Jonah has to me the air of being a moral romance, a quite different kind of thing from, say the account of King David or the New Testament narratives, not pegged like them into any historical situation. In what sense does

the Bible "present" the Jonah story "as historical"?

Lewis answers, "Of course, it doesn't say 'This is fiction,' but then neither does our Lord say that the Unjust Judge, Good Samaritan, or Prodigal Son are fiction. (I would put Esther in the same category as Jonah for the same reason)" (Christensen, *CSLS*, 96–97).

Historical Errors in the Bible

In like manner, Lewis had no difficulty accepting that there were historical errors in the Bible:

> It seems to me that 2 and 4 [see page 399, under "The Errant Nature of the Bible"] rule out the view that every statement in Scripture must be historical truth. And 1, 3, 5, and 6 rule out the view that inspiration is a single thing in the sense that, if present at all, it is always present in the same mode and the same degree.

Therefore,

> I think, rule out the view that any one passage taken in isolation can be assumed to be inerrant in exactly the same sense as any other: e.g., that the numbers of O.T. armies (which in view of the size of the country, if true, involve continuous miracle) are statistically correct. . . . That the overall operation of Scripture is to convey God's Word to the reader (he also needs his inspiration) who reads it in the right spirit, I fully believe. That it also gives true answers to all the questions (often religiously irrelevant) which he might ask, I don't. The very kind of truth we are often demanding was, in my opinion, not even envisaged by the ancients. (*RP*, 199.)

For Lewis,

> The human qualities of the raw materials show through. Naivety, error, contradiction, even (as in the cursing Psalms) wickedness are not removed. The total result is not "the Word of God" in the sense that every passage, in itself, gives impeccable science or history (ibid., 111–112).

Antireligious Portions of Scripture

Unlike many neo-evangelicals, Lewis did not limit the errancy of Scripture to nonreligious matters. He wrote,

> Nor would I (now) willingly spare from my Bible something in itself so anti-religious as the nihilism of Ecclesiastes. We get there a clear, cold picture of man's life without God. That statement is itself part of God's word (ibid., 115).

Likewise,

> We shall find in the Psalms expressions of a cruelty more vindictive and a self-righteousness more complete than anything in the classics. If we ignore such passages and read only a few selected favourite Psalms, we miss the point. [For] the point is precisely this: that these same fanatic and homicidal Hebrews, and not the more enlightened peoples, again and again—for brief moments—reach a Christian level of spirituality. (*CR*, 116.)

Some of the psalms Lewis believed were contemptible and even devilish:

> One way of dealing with these terrible or (dare we say?) contemptible Psalms is simply to leave them alone. But unfortunately the bad parts will not "come away clean"; they may, as we have noticed, be intertwined with the most exquisite things. (*RP*, 21–22.)

He added,

> It is monstrously simple-minded to read the cursings in the Psalms with no feeling except one of horror at the uncharity of the poets. They are indeed devilish. . . . Even more devilish in one verse is the otherwise beautiful 137, where a blessing is pronounced on anyone who will snatch up a Babylonian baby and beat its brains out against the pavement (ibid., 25, 20–21).

Orthodox View of Inspiration Rejected

C. S. Lewis clearly rejected the orthodox view of Scripture, saying,

> One can respect, and at moments envy, both the Fundamentalist's view of the Bible and the Roman Catholic's view of the Church. But there is one argument which we should beware of using for either position: God must have done what is best, this is best, therefore God has done this. For we are mortals and do not know what is best for us, and it is dangerous to prescribe what God must have done—especially when we cannot for the life of us see that He has after all done it (ibid., 112).

He went on,

> We are not fundamentalists. We think that different elements in this sort of theology have different degrees of strength. The nearer it sticks to mere textual criticism, of the old sort . . . the more we are disposed to believe in it (ibid., 163).

Negative Criticism of Scripture

Lewis rejected the traditional authorship of certain sections of the Old Testament, including the Psalms, even though doing so conflicted with his view of Christ (cf. Matt. 22:43–45). "How old the Psalms, as we now have them, really are is a question for the scholars. I am told there is one [Psalm 18] which might really have come down from the age of David himself; that is, from the tenth century B.C. Most of them," however, "are said to be 'post exilic' "; the book was put together "when the Hebrews, long exiled in Babylonia, were repatriated by that enlightened ruler, Cyrus of Persia. This would bring us down to the sixth century. How much earlier material the book took in is uncertain" (*CR*, 114).

Rejection of Old Testament Miracles

It comes as a great disappointment to those who know of Lewis's strong defense of supernaturalism in his otherwise excellent book on *Miracles* to hear him deny many Old Testament miracles: "A consideration of the Old Testament miracles is beyond the scope of this book and would require many kinds of knowledge which I do not possess." Nonetheless, he adds, "*My present view*—which is tentative and liable to any amount of correction[4]—would be that just as, on the factual side, a long preparation culminates in God's becoming incarnate as Man, so, on the documentary side, truth first appears in mythical form and then by a long process of condensing or focusing finally becomes incarnate as History." Of course,

> This involves the belief that Myth in general is not merely misunderstood history (as Euhemerus thought) nor diabolical illusion (as some of the Fathers thought) nor priestly lying (as the philosophers of the Enlightenment thought) but, at its best, a real though unfocused gleam of divine truth falling on human imagination. The Hebrews, like other people, had mythology: but as they were the chosen people so their mythology was the chosen mythology—the mythology chosen by God to be the vehicle of the earliest sacred truths, the first step in that process which ends in the New Testament where truth has become completely historical.

Lewis added,

> Whether we can ever say with certainty where, in this process of crystallization, any particular Old Testament story falls, is another matter. [Thus,] I take it that the memoirs of David's court come at one end of the scale and are scarcely less historical than St. Mark or Acts; and that the Book of Jonah is at the opposite end. (*M*, 139.)

Nevertheless, Lewis believed that "the resurrection of Christ is a historical and very important event, but the value of other events (e.g., the fate of Lot's wife) hardly matter at all. And the ones whose historicity matters

---

[4]Lewis is to be commended for allowing for the fact that his view may be erroneous.

are, as God's will, those where it is plain" (cited by Kilby, *CWCSL*, 153). Elsewhere Lewis explained,

> A theology which denies the historicity of nearly everything in the Gospels ... which either denies the miraculous altogether or, more strangely, after swallowing the camel of the Resurrection strains at such gnats as the feeding of the multitudes—if offered to the uneducated man can produce only one or the other of two effects. It will make him a Roman Catholic or an atheist. (*CR*, 153.)

Theistic Evolution Accepted

Although there is some evidence of later modification of his view, Lewis embraced theistic evolution in direct contradiction with a literal interpretation of the text (see volume 2, part 2): "For long centuries God perfected the animal form which was to become the vehicle of humanity and the image of Himself" (*RP*, 65):

> The creature may have existed for ages in this stage before it became man: it may even have been clever enough to make things which a modern archaeologist would accept as proof of its humanity. But it was only an animal because all its physical and psychical processes were directed to purely material and natural ends. [Then,] in the fullness of time, God caused to descend upon this organism, both on its psychology and physiology, a new kind of consciousness which could say "I" and "me," which could look upon itself as an object, which knew God, which could make judgments of truth, beauty, and goodness, and which was so far above time that it could perceive time flowing past (ibid).

AN EVALUATION OF THE NEO-EVANGELICAL VIEWS OF SCRIPTURE

With the exception of C. S. Lewis's more liberal and neo-orthodox thoughts on Scripture, which were critiqued under those titles (see chapters 20–21), the neo-evangelical view of Scripture is distinctive in contrast to the standard evangelical view from which it deviates:

Evangelical View of Bible	Neo-Evangelical View of Bible
True as whole and in all parts	True as whole but not in all parts
True spiritually and scientifically	True spiritually but not always scientifically
True in what it intends and affirms	True in what it intends, not in all it affirms
Truth is found in correspondence	Truth is found in intention

Like other deviant views of Scripture, the neo-evangelical position has both positive and negative dimensions. Some positive characteristics include the following:

It Emphasizes the Organic Whole of Scripture

Since God is the ultimate author of Scripture, it *is* an organic whole. Each part must be understood in the light of the whole, and our understanding of the whole is based on each part. To understand this systemic relationship between whole and part is crucial to a proper understanding of Scripture. In this sense, the stress on the organic wholeness of Scripture is a positive contribution of neo-evangelicalism.

Further, the flip side of this is the rejection of a mechanical view of verbal dictation, which is rightly disowned. Meaning, including the meaning of the Bible, is not found in atomistically revealed parts. Words have meaning as parts of sentences, and sentences as part of paragraphs, and paragraphs in the light of the broader literary unit of the book, and so on. No isolated parts are hermeneutical islands unto themselves (see chapter 6).

It Warns Against Alien Philosophical Views

While particular philosophical points of view can be disputed, there is no disagreement on the need to examine carefully the philosophical presuppositions brought to an understanding of the inspiration of the Bible, whether they spring from ancient philosophers or modern ones. Neo-evangelicals are correct in pointing out that one must be careful not to cast the doctrines of inspiration and inerrancy in the mold of philosophical perspectives that are alien to the teaching of Scripture.

It Takes Seriously the Human Nature of Scripture

Like two of its mentors, liberalism and neo-orthodoxy, neo-evangelicalism is right in stressing the human side of the Bible. Like Christ, the Bible is both divine and human, and a denial of either leads to substantial error. With regard to Scripture, a denial of its full humanity is a form of biblical docetism; here too neo-evangelicalism has rendered a worthwhile service.[5]

It Highlights the Need for Divine Adaptation

Neo-evangelicals are also to be commended for emphasizing the need for adaptation by God to the human situation in the communication of

---

[5]As we have established, the Bible has two natures—it is a theanthropic book, just as Christ is a theanthropic person. There is a significant similarity between God's Living Word and His written Word (see chapter 16).

truth in Scripture. After all, God is infinite, and the Bible is finite. In fact, everything about the Bible is finite, including the persons who wrote it, the languages it is written in, and the cultures through which it was expressed. Thus, whenever an infinite Mind wishes to communicate with finite minds, there must of necessity be an adaptation of the former to the latter. Hence, the doctrine of divine adaptation stressed by neo-evangelicals is crucial to any proper understanding of the inspiration of Scripture.

It Interacts With Contemporary Biblical Criticism

Since biblical criticism is a part of our culture, one must interact with it in order to give full recognition to the humanness of the Bible. To ignore facts brought forward in this discipline is to show disrespect for God's truth in general revelation in an attempt to preserve His truth in special revelation (see chapters 4 and 26). Facts are facts, and all must be accounted for in an adequate theory of inspiration. Therefore, evangelicals must interact with the data of biblical criticism, whether it is lower criticism (of the text) or higher criticism (of the source of the text). Again, the neo-evangelical emphasis is helpful.

All of this is not to say that there are no serious problems with the neo-evangelical view of Scripture; there are many. Some of the more significant ones will be briefly examined.

It Is Contrary to the Claims of Scripture

First and foremost, for anyone claiming legitimate use of the name "evangelical," his view is contrary to the very book claimed to be of divine authority. Since this point has already been supported by extensive biblical data (see chapters 13–16, 26), it will not be repeated here. It is sufficient to note the biblical claims:

(1) God cannot err in anything He affirms (cf. Heb. 6:18; Titus 1:2).
(2) The Bible is the Word of God.

So it follows necessarily (and contrary to neo-evangelicalism) that

(3) The Bible cannot err in anything it affirms (including history and science).

To claim otherwise is to deny either one or both of two well-established biblical teachings.

It Is Contrary to the Teachings of the Fathers and Reformers

Since this point also has been addressed extensively (see chapters 17–18), it will not be reemphasized. It is sufficient to give only the conclusion, which is that in the long history of the Christian church there is scarcely a single significant voice that denied the orthodox view that the Bible is the divinely inspired, absolutely authoritative, and factually inerrant written Word of God. This flatly contradicts the neo-evangelical position.

It Is Based on a Fallacious View of Truth

The neo-evangelical view of G. C. Berkouwer, Jack Rogers, and others is based on a mistaken view of truth, the position that truth is what is intended by the author. Although this has been completely refuted elsewhere (see chapter 19), it is important to note here its central errors.

First, it is contrary to the biblical use of the word "truth," which clearly implies the correspondence view (see chapter 7)—truth is what corresponds to its object (cf. Gen. 42:16; 1 Kings 22:16–22; Acts 5:1–4; 24:8–11).

Second, the biblical use of the word "err" does not support the intentionalist theory of truth, since it is also used of unintentional "errors" (cf. Lev. 4:2, 27, etc.). Certain acts were wrong (i.e., "errors"), whether the trespassers intended to commit them or not, and hence a guilt offering was called for to atone for their "error" (see chapter 7).

Third, if what is intended is true, then all statements ever made with good intentions were true, even those that were clearly false. This is absurd.

Fourth, even the intentionalist theory depends on the correspondence view of truth. The intentionalist theory claims something is true only if the accomplishments correspond to the intentions. Therefore, without correspondence of intentions and accomplished facts there is no truth.

Fifth, noncorrespondence views of truth are self-defeating, for all noncorrespondence views of truth imply a correspondence view of truth in their very attempt to deny the correspondence view. For instance, the claim that "the noncorrespondence view is true" implies that this view corresponds to reality. The noncorrespondence view cannot even express itself without using the correspondence view of truth.

It Undermines the Divine Authority of the Bible

Anti-inerrantist professor Paul Jewett is a case in point. In his book *Man as Male and Female* he argued that the apostle Paul affirmed that the man was the head of his wife, but then went on to claim that Paul was wrong! Regardless of what Paul was affirming, the point is the same, and it is this: If the Bible affirms anything, and the Bible is wrong, then the Bible is not the Word of God, since God cannot be wrong (cf. Rom. 3:4; Heb. 6:18; Titus 1:2). In other words, if what the author of Scripture affirms is not what God affirms, then nothing in the Bible has divine authority. In such a case, no matter what the author says is true, we do not know what God is affirming; we are forever locked out of any objective way to determine from the text what God is teaching. In this way, the neo-evangelical way undermines the divine authority of any teaching in Scripture by putting a wedge between what the author affirms is true and what God affirms is true. Thus, in this regard, the neo-evangelical view of the Bible is not better than the liberal view (see chapter 20); the neo-evangelical just makes it *seem* better.

SUMMARY AND CONCLUSION

Despite its claim to the name, the new evangelical view of the Bible is neither new nor evangelical. It is not new, since to the degree that it deviates from the historical evangelical view, it adopts older forms of liberalism or neo-orthodoxy. And it is not orthodox, since it denies the historical orthodox view that the Bible is the verbally inspired and factually inerrant Word of God. Furthermore, it is unbiblical and is based on a self-defeating view of truth. In short, the neo-evangelical view of Scripture is biblically ungrounded, theologically unsound, and philosophically incoherent.

SOURCES

Berkouwer, G. C. *Holy Scripture: Studies in Dogmatics.*
Christensen, M. J. *C. S. Lewis on Scripture.*
Geisler, Norman, and Thomas Howe. *When Critics Ask.*
Geisler, Norman, and William Nix. *A General Introduction to the Bible.*
Geisler, Norman, ed. *Inerrancy.*
Hannah, John, ed. *Inerrancy and the Church.*
Jewett, Paul. *Man as Male and Female.*
Kilby, Clyde. *The Christian World of C. S. Lewis.*
Lewis, C. S. *Christian Reflections.*
———. *Letters to Malcolm: Chiefly on Prayer.*
———. *Miracles.*
———. *Reflections on the Psalms.*
Rogers, Jack. *Biblical Authority.*
Rogers, Jack, and Donald McKim. *The Authority and Interpretation of the Bible.*
Woodbridge, John. *Biblical Authority.*

CHAPTER TWENTY-THREE

EVANGELICALS ON THE BIBLE

T he evangelical view of Scripture is a continuation of the historical orthodox view as expressed in the Bible (see chapters 13–16), the church Fathers (see chapter 17), and the Reformers and post-Reformers up to nearly the twentieth century (see chapters 18–19).

Even during the rise of liberalism and after, there was a continuously held orthodox position on Scripture from Jonathan Edwards through the Old Princetonians and on up to the International Conference on Biblical Inerrancy (ICBI) at the end of the twentieth century. This continues into the present century through the fast-growing cross-denominational Evangelical Theological Society (ETS).

It is clear from the evidence presented thus far (chapters 13–22) that the continuous, consistent, orthodox view on Scripture of the Christian church is continued by modern evangelicals who affirm the full inspiration and factual inerrancy of Holy Writ. In the United States, this was true from the very beginning.

FRANCIS TURRETIN

Reformed theologian Francis Turretin (1623–1687) was a professor at Geneva, and his great *Institutes of Elenctic Theology* is a classic of reformed scholasticism. In his section on Scripture he summarized and set forth the historical orthodox view on the nature and extent of Scripture in clear, concise, and categorical terms.

The Origin of Scripture

According to Turretin, "the authority of the Scriptures depends on their origin. Just because they are from God, they must be authentic and divine" (*IET*, 62). Thus "Christians should consider as an incontrovertible truth the fact that the Scriptures are inspired of God (*theopneuston*) as the primary foundation of faith" (ibid.).

The Nature of Scripture

Infallibility of the Bible

Turretin also held that the Bible is both infallible and inerrant: "The divine and infallible truth of these books (which have God as their author) is the foundation because he has the highest right to bind men to faith and duty" (ibid.).

Inerrancy of the Bible

Turretin asked, "Do real contradictions occur in Scripture? Or are there any inexplicable (*alyta*) passages which cannot be explained and made to harmonize?" His answer: "We deny" (ibid., 70). Why? Because "when the divinity of the Scriptures is proved, its infallibility necessarily follows" (ibid.).

There are not even small errors in the Bible.

> Some think that they can get rid of all difficulties by saying that the sacred writers could slip in memory or err in smaller things; [those such as] Socinus . . . Castellio . . . and others. But instead of being a defense against the atheists, this is a base abandonment of the cause (ibid).

"The contradictions (*antilogia*) found in Scripture are apparent, not real; they are to be understood only with respect to us who cannot comprehend and perceive the agreement everywhere, but not in the thing itself" (ibid., 72).

Turretin offered two basic reasons the Bible cannot err:

> (1) The Scriptures are inspired of God (*theopneustos*, 2 Tim. 3:16). The word of God cannot lie (Ps. 19:8–9; Heb. 6:18); cannot pass away and be destroyed (Matt. 5:18); shall endure forever (1 Peter 1:25); and is truth itself (John 17:17). For how could such things be predicated of it, if it contained dangerous contradictions, and if God suffered either the sacred writers to err and to slip in memory, or incurable blemishes to creep into it?
>
> (2) Unless unimpaired integrity characterize the Scriptures, they could not be regarded as the sole rule of faith and practice, and the door would be thrown wide open to atheists, libertarians, enthusiasts and other profane persons like them for destroying its authenticity and

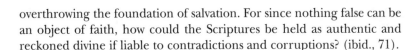

overthrowing the foundation of salvation. For since nothing false can be an object of faith, how could the Scriptures be held as authentic and reckoned divine if liable to contradictions and corruptions? (ibid., 71).

Only the Original Text Is Inerrant

The original Hebrew and Greek texts are without error.

> Whatever the men of God wrote, they wrote under the influence of the Holy Spirit (2 Peter 1:21), who, to keep them from error, dictated not only the matter but also the words, which cannot be said of any version. They [the Hebrew and Greek texts] are the standard and rule to which all the versions should be applied (ibid., 114).

The Exclusive Authority of Scripture (*Sola Scriptura*)

Not only are the Scriptures the final authority, they are the only written authority for believers: "Do the Scriptures so perfectly contain all things necessary to salvation that there is no need of unwritten (Gr: *agraphois*) traditions after it?" Turretin's response: "We affirm against the papists" (ibid., 134).

Again, as to

> whether the Scriptures (or God speaking in them) are the supreme and infallible judge of controversies and the interpreter of Scripture, or whether the church or the Roman pontiff is, we affirm the former and deny the latter against the papists (ibid., 154).

In brief, "The Scriptures alone are the supreme judge of controversy" (ibid., 155).

The Preservation of Scriptures

According to Turretin, God would not inspire what He did not preserve. So the copies, while not inerrant, are providentially preserved.

Providential Preservation of Scripture

Turretin wrote,

> Nor can we readily believe that God, who dictated and inspired each and every word to these inspired men, would not take care of their entire preservation, [for] if men use the utmost care diligently to preserve their words (especially if they are of any importance, as for example a testament or contract) in order that it may not be corrupted, how much more, [must we suppose,] would God take care of his word which he intended as a testament and seal of his covenant with us, so that it might not be corrupted; especially when he could easily foresee and

prevent such corruptions in order to establish the faith of his church? (ibid., 71).

The Copies Are Not Inspired

This does not mean that the copies are perfect:

> Although we give to the Scriptures absolute integrity, we do not therefore think that the copyist and printers were inspired (*theopneustous*), but only that the providence of God watched over the copying of the sacred books, so that although many errors might have crept in, it has not so happened (or they have not so crept into the manuscripts) but that they can be easily corrected by a collation of others (or with the Scriptures themselves) (ibid., 72–73).

Thus "it was not necessary therefore to render all the scribes infallible, but only so to direct them that the true reading may always be found out." Nevertheless, "this book far surpasses all others in purity" (ibid., 73).

However, the present Hebrew and Greek texts are authoritative:

> Is the present Hebrew text in things as well as words so authentic and inspired in such a sense that all the extant versions are to be referred to as a rule and, wherever they vary, to be corrected by it? . . . We affirm (ibid., 116).[1]

JONATHAN EDWARDS

Jonathan Edwards (1703–1758) stood out among the Puritan theologians and was a significant figure in the Great Awakening of the eighteenth century.

The Origin of Scripture

Edwards believed that the Bible was the very Word of God:

> Moses was so intimately conversant with God and so continually under the divine conduct, it can't be thought that when he wrote the history of the creation and fall of man, and the history of the church from the creation, that he should not be under the divine direction in such an affair. Doubtless he wrote by God's direction, as we are informed that he wrote the law and the history of the Israelitish Church. (*M*, 352.)

Indeed,

> that the prophets after they had once had intercourse with God by

---

[1]Turretin went so far as to deny that the Hebrew vowel points "were merely a human innovation made by the Masorites," at least with regard to their sound if not their shape (ibid., 169).

immediate revelation from God gained acquaintance with [him] so as afterwards to know him; as it were to know his voice or know what was indeed a revelation from God is confirmed by 1 Samuel 3:7. (*M*, 1144.)

In brief, for Edwards the Bible is God's Word:

> God may reveal things in Scripture, which way he pleases. If by what he there reveals the thing is any way clearly discovered to be the understanding or eye of the mind, it is our duty to receive it as his revelation. (*M*, 1426.)

So for Edwards as well as for Turretin, whatever the Bible says, God says.

Edwards believed that "ministers are not to preach those things which their own wisdom or reason suggest, but the things that are already dictated to them by the superior wisdom and knowledge of God" ("OMB," 27). He occasionally spoke of "dictation" and the biblical writers as "penmen" of the Holy Spirit. However, by this he did not believe in what is commonly called "mechanical dictation" of the Scriptures.

The Human Element in Scripture

Edwards believed that the Bible was also a human book. In reference to Solomon, for example, Edwards wrote,

> God's Spirit made use of his loving inclination, joined with his musing philosophical disposition, and so directed and conducted it in this train of imagination as to represent the love that there is between Christ and his spouse. God saw it very needful and exceedingly useful that there should be some representation of it. (*M*, 303.)

So the "dictation" mentioned by Edwards actually refers to the divinely authoritative product of inspiration and not to the human means by which it was produced.

THE OLD PRINCETONIANS (1812–1936)

George Whitefield (1714–1770) was also closely associated with the Great Awakening in the American colonies but was unable to assume his post at Princeton. There his successors would establish a conservative bastion when a general seminary for the denomination was established at Princeton in 1812. The first professor in the seminary was Archibald Alexander (1772–1851); he and Charles Hodge (1797–1878), his pupil and colleague, became founders of the Princeton theology and the architects of Reformed confessionalism at the seminary. Sidney Ahlstrom noted:

> The Princeton Seminary . . . shaped a new conservatism and created a fortress that held its ground for a century. Regarding the free-ranging

intellect of Edwards with suspicion and viewing revivalism as insubstantial, it chose biblical inerrancy and strict confessionalism as its means of defense. [So] to support this strategy Princeton marshaled great dialectical skill, massive theological efforts, and much impressive erudition. It provided shelter whither revivalists and Fundamentalists could flee when the ideas of Darwin or Wellhausen endangered their tents and tabernacles. [Thus] they taught theological responsibility to anti-intellectuals in many denominations where learning had been held in disrepute. (*TA*, 251.)

These men were succeeded in turn by the efforts of Archibald Alexander Hodge (1823–1886), Benjamin Breckinridge Warfield (1851–1921), and J. Gresham Machen (1881–1937), who "maintained the institution's reputation for unbending but erudite conservatism down to 1929–1936, when both the seminary and the denomination were disrupted by conservative secessions."

Charles Hodge (1797–1878)

Charles Hodge's thinking reflects the central Princetonian position on the inspiration and authority of Scripture. His view was expressed with clarity and conciseness.

The Origin of the Bible

In his discussion of "The Protestant Rule of Faith," Hodge argued that "all Protestants agree in teaching that 'the word of God, as contained in the Scriptures of the Old and New Testaments, is the only infallible rule of faith and practice'" (*ST*, 1:151). He cited with approval the *Smalcald Articles* and the *Form of Concord* of the Lutheran tradition and the various symbols of the Reformed churches that teach the same "doctrine" before drawing his conclusion, which asserts,

> From these statements it appears that Protestants hold (1) That the Scriptures of the Old and New Testaments are the Word of God, written under the inspiration of the Holy Spirit, and are therefore infallible, and of divine authority in all things pertaining to faith and practice, and consequently free from all error whether of doctrine, fact, or precept. (2) That they contain all the extant supernatural revelations of God designed to be a rule of faith and practice to his Church. (3) That they are sufficiently perspicuous to be understood by the people, in the use of ordinary means and by the aid of the Holy Spirit, in all things necessary to faith or practice, without the need of any infallible interpreter (ibid., 151–52).

The Nature of Scripture

Hodge affirmed that "the Scriptures are infallible, i.e., given by inspiration of God," where he states that "the infallibility and divine authority of the Scriptures are due to the fact that they are the word of God; and they are the word of God because they were given by inspiration of the Holy Ghost." He first discusses "The Nature of Inspiration—definition," which becomes the basis of his extended treatment of the whole subject. He wrote, "The nature of inspiration is to be learnt from the Scriptures; from their didactic statements, and from their phenomena. There are certain general facts or principles that underlie the Bible, which are assumed in all its teachings, and which therefore must be assumed in its interpretation." Hence, we must, for example, assume:

> (1) That God is not the unconscious ground of all things; nor an unintelligent force; nor a name for the moral order of the universe; nor mere causality; but a Spirit—a self-conscious, intelligent, voluntary agent, possessing all the attributes of our spirits without limitation, and to an infinite degree. [We must also assume:]
>
> (2) That He is the creator of the world, and extra-mundane, existing before, and independently of it; not its soul, life, or animating principle; but its maker, preserver, and ruler. [Further, we assume:]
>
> (3) That as a spirit He is everywhere present and everywhere active, preserving and governing all His creatures and all their actions. [Also, we assume:]
>
> (4) That while both in the external world and in the world of the mind He generally acts according to fixed laws and through secondary causes, He is free to act, and often does act immediately, or without the intervention of such causes, as in creation, regeneration, and miracles. [Too, we assume:]
>
> (5) That the Bible contains a divine, or supernatural, revelation. The present question is not whether the Bible is what it claims to be; but what does it teach as to the nature and effects of the influence under which it is written?

Hodge concluded,

> On this subject the common doctrine of the Church is, and ever has been, that inspiration was an influence of the Holy Spirit on the minds of certain select men, which rendered them the organs of God for the infallible communication of His mind and will. They were in such a sense the organs of God, and what they said God said (ibid., 153–54).

Opposition to Evolution

Hodge realized the impact Darwinian evolution would have on orthodoxy and wrote a penetrating book entitled *What Is Darwinism?* As we saw earlier, his answer was insightful and to the point:

> What is Darwinism? It is Atheism. This does not mean that Mr. Darwin himself and all who adopt his views are atheists; but it means that his theory is atheistic, that the exclusion of design from nature is . . . tantamount to atheism" (*WD*, 177).

As discussed previously (in chapter 19), the belief in naturalistic evolution was to have a devastating influence on the historicity and authority of the Bible. Hodge was trying to head it off at the pass.

Archibald Alexander Hodge and Benjamin Breckinridge Warfield

In the wake of Darwin's *On the Origin of Species* (1859) and the establishment of the higher critical theories following the lead of Karl H. Graf (1815–1869), Abraham Kuenen (1828–1891), and Julius Wellhausen (1844–1918), orthodox Christians found leaders for their cause in the son of Charles Hodge, A. A. Hodge (1823–1866), and in B. B. Warfield (1851–1921). Their document titled *Inspiration* became something of a normative statement for most conservative Christians since the time it was first published in 1881.

The Origin of the Bible

In contrast to those who were beginning to espouse the notion that the Bible *contains* the Word of God, Hodge and Warfield affirmed that the Bible *is* the Word of God, saying,

> The New Testament continually asserts of the Scriptures of the Old Testament, and of the several books which constitute it, that they ARE THE WORD OF GOD. What their writers said, God said. (*I*, 29, emphasis original.)

For Hodge and Warfield, it is not merely the thoughts but the very words of Scripture that are infallible:

> Every element of Scripture, whether doctrine or history, of which God has guaranteed the infallibility, must be infallible in its verbal expression. No matter how in other respects generated, the Scriptures are a product of human thought, and every process of human thought involves language. . . .

Besides this,

> The Scriptures are a record of divine revelations, and as such consist of words. . . . Infallible thought must be definite thought, and definite thought implies words. . . . Whatever discrepancies or other human limitations may attach to the sacred record, *the line* (of inspired or not inspired, of fallible or infallible) *can never rationally be drawn between the thoughts and the words of Scripture* (ibid., 21–23, parenthesis and emphasis original).

The Human Element in Scripture

Hodge and Warfield argued with regard to the Holy Scriptures:

> The result of the cooperation, in various ways, of the human agency, both in the histories out of which the Scriptures sprang, and their immediate composition and inscription, is everywhere apparent, and gives substance and form to the entire collection of writings (ibid., 12).

They go on to assert that they do not wish to

> deny an everywhere-present human element in the Scriptures. No mark of the effect of this human element, therefore, in style of thought or wording can be urged against inspiration unless it can be shown to result in untruth (ibid., 42).

The obvious humanness of Scripture eliminates any notion of a "mechanical" or "verbal dictation" view of inspiration, because

> each sacred writer was by God specially formed, endowed, educated, providentially conditioned, and then supplied with knowledge naturally, supernaturally or spiritually conveyed, so that he, and he alone, could, and freely would, produce his allotted part (ibid., 14–15).

The Nature of Scripture

For Hodge and Warfield, the nature of Scripture is not only one of full and complete verbal inspiration, but also of absolute errorlessness in all it affirms.

The Verbal Plenary Nature of Inspiration

According to Hodge and Warfield, what biblical writers produced by the inspiration of Scripture is a verbal, plenary, infallible, and inerrant book, the Bible. They indicate this in their definition of *plenary*, as they write, "the word simply means 'full,' 'complete,' perfectly adequate for the attainment of the end designed, whatever that might have been" (ibid., 18).

The Factual Inerrancy of Scripture

For Hodge and Warfield, "the expression *verbal inspiration* does not hold that what the sacred writers *do not affirm* is infallibly true, but only that what *they do affirm* is infallibly true" (ibid., 80). This is so because

> throughout the whole of his work the Holy Spirit was present, causing his energies to flow into the spontaneous exercises of the writer's faculties, elevating and directing where need be, and everywhere securing the errorless expression in language of the thought designed by God. This last element is what we call "Inspiration" (ibid., 16).

Not every copy of Scripture is inerrant, according to Hodge and Warfield; they say, for example, "We do not assert that the common text, but only that the original autographic text, was inspired" (ibid., 42).

In view of all the facts known to us, we affirm that a candid inspection of all the ascertained phenomena of the original text of Scripture will leave unmodified the ancient faith of the Church. In all their real affirmations these books are without error (ibid., 27).

A Response to Negative Biblical Criticism

In response to the rise of destructive higher criticism, ushered in by Graf, Kuenen, Wellhausen, and others, Hodge and Warfield declared that they

admit freely that the traditional belief as to the dates and origin of the several books may be brought into question without involving any doubt as to their inspiration, [yet they] confidently affirm that any theories of the origin or authorship of any book of either Testament which ascribe to them a purely naturalistic genesis, or dates or authors inconsistent with either their own natural claims or the assertions of other Scripture, are plainly inconsistent with the doctrine of inspiration taught by the Church (ibid., 39).

In addition to their joint work, B. B. Warfield produced several decisive tomes in defense of the full plenary inspiration and factual inerrancy of Scripture. Two are especially worthy of mention: *The Inspiration and Authority of the Bible* and *Limited Inspiration* (another term for inerrancy).

The position of Hodge and Warfield is consistent with the basic orthodox teaching about Scripture that had been held from the first century onward. It is also the position espoused by J. Gresham Machen and others into the present setting.

The International Council on Biblical Inerrancy (ICBI)

The position of Hodge and Warfield is essentially the same as that held by leading evangelicals in November 1978 as defined by the International Council on Biblical Inerrancy. That body drafted a short statement and a longer one. First, the short statement:

1. God, who is Himself Truth and speaks the truth only, has inspired Holy Scripture in order thereby to reveal Himself to lost mankind through Jesus Christ as Creator and Lord, Redeemer and Judge. Holy Scripture is God's witness to Himself.
2. Holy Scripture, being God's own Word, written by men prepared and superintended by His Spirit, is of infallible divine authority in all

matters upon which it touches: it is to be believed, as God's instruction, in all that it affirms; obeyed, as God's command, in all that it requires; embraced, as God's pledge, in all that it promises.

3. The Holy Spirit, Scripture's divine Author, both authenticates it to us by His inward witness and opens our minds to understand its meaning.

4. Being wholly and verbally God-given, Scripture is without error or fault in all its teaching, no less in what it states about God's acts in creation, about events of world history, and about its own literary origins under God, than in its witness to God's saving grace in individual lives.

5. The authority of Scripture is inescapably impaired if this total divine inerrancy is in any way limited or disregarded, or made relative to a view of truth contrary to the Bible's own; and such lapses bring serious loss to both the individual and the Church.

In the "Chicago Statement on Biblical Inerrancy" (1978), there are nineteen articles, all worth pondering. This longer statement has become a standard among evangelicals to this day:

ARTICLES OF AFFIRMATION AND DENIAL

Article I

We affirm that the Holy Scriptures are to be received as the authoritative Word of God.

We deny that the Scriptures receive their authority from the Church, tradition, or any other human source.

Article II

We affirm that the Scriptures are the supreme written norm by which God binds the conscience, and that the authority of the Church is subordinate to that of Scripture.

We deny that Church creeds, councils, or declarations have authority greater than or equal to the authority of the Bible.

Article III

We affirm that the written Word in its entirety is revelation given by God.

We deny that the Bible is merely a witness to revelation, or only becomes revelation in encounter, or depends on the responses of men for its validity.

Article IV

We affirm that God who made mankind in His image has used language as a means of revelation.

We deny that human language is so limited by our creatureliness that it is rendered inadequate as a vehicle for divine revelation. We further deny that the corruption of human culture and language through sin has thwarted God's work of inspiration.

Article V

We affirm that God's revelation in the Holy Scriptures was progressive.

We deny that later revelation, which may fulfill earlier revelation, ever corrects or contradicts it. We further deny that any normative revelation has been given since the completion of the New Testament writings.

Article VI

We affirm that the whole of Scripture and all its parts, down to the very words of the original, were given by divine inspiration.

We deny that the inspiration of Scripture can rightly be affirmed of the whole without the parts, or of some parts but not the whole.

Article VII

We affirm that inspiration was the work in which God by His Spirit, through human writers, gave us His Word. The origin of Scripture is divine. The mode of divine inspiration remains largely a mystery to us.

We deny that inspiration can be reduced to human insight, or to heightened states of consciousness of any kind.

Article VIII

We affirm that God in His Work of inspiration utilized the distinctive personalities and literary styles of the writers whom He had chosen and prepared.

We deny that God, in causing these writers to use the very words that He chose, overrode their personalities.

Article IX

We affirm that inspiration, though not conferring omniscience, guaranteed true and trustworthy utterance on all matters of which the Biblical authors were moved to speak and write.

We deny that the finitude or fallenness of these writers, by necessity or otherwise, introduced distortion or falsehood into God's Word.

Article X

We affirm that inspiration, strictly speaking, applies only to the autographic text of Scripture, which in the providence of God can be ascertained from available manuscripts with great accuracy. We further affirm that copies and translations of Scripture are the Word of God to the extent that they faithfully represent the original.

We deny that any essential element of the Christian faith is affected by the absence of the autographs. We further deny that this absence renders the assertion of Biblical inerrancy invalid or irrelevant.

Article XI

We affirm that Scripture, having been given by divine inspiration, is infallible, so that, far from misleading us, it is true and reliable in all the matters it addresses.

We deny that it is possible for the Bible to be at the same time infallible and errant in its assertions. Infallibility and inerrancy may be distinguished, but not separated.

Article XII

We affirm that Scripture in its entirety is inerrant, being free from all falsehood, fraud, or deceit.

We deny that Biblical infallibility and inerrancy are limited to spiritual, religious, or redemptive themes, exclusive of assertions in the fields of history and science. We further deny that scientific hypotheses about earth history may properly be used to overturn the teaching of Scripture on creation and the flood.

Article XIII

We affirm the propriety of using inerrancy as a theological term with reference to the complete truthfulness of Scripture.

We deny that it is proper to evaluate Scripture according to standards of truth and error that are alien to its usage or purpose. We further deny that inerrancy is negated by Biblical phenomena such as a lack of modern technical precision, irregularities of grammar or spelling, observational descriptions of nature, the reporting of falsehoods, the use of hyperbole and round numbers, the topical arrangement of material, variant selections of material in parallel accounts, or the use of free citations.

Article XIV

We affirm the unity and internal consistency of Scripture.

We deny that alleged errors and discrepancies that have not yet been resolved vitiate the truth claims of the Bible.

Article XV

We affirm that the doctrine of inerrancy is grounded in the teaching of the Bible about inspiration.

We deny that Jesus' teaching about Scripture may be dismissed by appeals to accommodation or to any natural limitation of His humanity.

Article XVI

We affirm that the doctrine of inerrancy has been integral to the Church's faith throughout its history.

We deny that inerrancy is a doctrine invented by Scholastic Protestantism, or is a reactionary position postulated in response to negative higher criticism.

Article XVII

We affirm that the Holy Spirit bears witness to the Scriptures, assuring believers of the truthfulness of God's written Word.

We deny that this witness of the Holy Spirit operates in isolation from or against Scripture.

Article XVIII

We affirm that the text of Scripture is to be interpreted by grammatico-historical exegesis; taking account of its literary forms and devices, and that Scripture is to interpret Scripture.

We deny the legitimacy of any treatment of the text or quest for sources lying behind it that leads to relativizing, dehistoricizing, or discounting its teaching, or rejecting its claims to authorship.

Article XIX

We affirm that a confession of the full authority, infallibility, and inerrancy of Scripture is vital to a sound understanding of the whole of the Christian faith. We further affirm that such confession should lead to increasing conformity to the image of Christ.

We deny that such confession is necessary for salvation. However, we further deny that inerrancy can be rejected without grave consequences, both to the individual and to the Church.

In addition to the long statement, the ICBI also produced a commentary on the nineteen articles so that there would be no misunderstanding as to their meaning.[2]

Thus, the orthodox doctrine that the Bible is the infallible, inerrant Word of God in its original manuscripts has maintained itself from the first century to the present. This position holds that the Bible is without error in everything that it affirms.

Indeed, according to the traditional teaching of the Christian church, what the Bible says, God Himself says. That includes all matters of history and science and any other element on which it touches. Any results of higher criticism that are contrary to this teaching are incompatible with the traditional doctrine of the inspiration and authority of Scripture as it has been held throughout church history.

The Evangelical Theological Society (1950–present)

One of the largest theological societies in the world is a cross-denominational group of conservative scholars founded on the statement that "the Bible alone and the Bible in its entirety, is the Word of God written, and therefore inerrant in the autographs." With this firm doctrinal commitment, the ETS has continued its growth to more than three thousand scholars. While the ETS has not officially defined inerrancy in great detail, an understanding of the view of its founding fathers, as well as the discipline it has exercised over deviations, leads to the firm conclusion that what the statement means is in direct line with that of the Hodge-Warfield and ICBI position which, in turn, is the consistent orthodox view of the Christian church from the very beginning.

AN EVALUATION OF THE EVANGELICAL
VIEW OF SCRIPTURE

The evangelical view of Scripture has been attacked by liberalism (see chapters 19–20), neo-orthodoxy (chapter 21), and neo-evangelicalism (chapter 22). Since these objections have already been addressed, it is

---

[2]See R. C. Sproul, *Explaining Inerrancy: A Commentary* (ICBI, 1980).

unnecessary to reply here. It is sufficient to say that without imbibing false antisupernatural and philosophical premises, there is no real foundation for these objections. The testimony of Scripture, the historical church, and good reasoning unite to defend the orthodox view of Scripture. Both the historicity (see chapters 25–26) and full inerrancy (see chapter 27) of Scripture are firmly supported.

There are two basic reasons the long-standing orthodox view of the full inspiration and factual inerrancy of Scripture have often been rejected in modern times: *First*, the unnecessary and unjustified acceptance of anti-supernaturalism; *second*, the uncritical and unsubstantiated acceptance of alien philosophical presuppositions.

Acceptance of Antisupernaturalism

Since the unfounded acceptance of antisupernaturalism has already been treated at length (see chapter 3), it will only be summarized here. There are two major points to make. *First*, philosophically, if one accepts theism, miracles are possible, for if the world was created from nothing (the biggest miracle of all), as the scientific and philosophical evidence shows (see chapter 2), then not only is there a supernatural Being who can intervene in the world, but it is a fact that He has already demonstrated that power by creating the world. In brief: if God, then miracles.

Second, historically, the rejection of the orthodox view of inspiration fell hard on the heels of the denial of supernatural intervention. The first negative critics, like Thomas Hobbes and Benedict Spinoza, make a direct connection between the two, as did many other critics to follow, from David Strauss to Rudolph Bultmann (see chapter 19). Hence, once the antisupernaturalism on which negative criticism was built is shown to be false, as it has been (see chapter 3), then this negative criticism crumbles with it.

To be sure, latter critics found literary and other grounds for rejecting the orthodox view of Scripture, but all of these are based, as we shall see, on unjustified philosophical premises.

Acceptance of Alien Philosophical Views

Ironically, during the same time period that destructive critical views of Scripture began to flourish, namely the late 1800s and early 1900s and following, the greatest factual evidence for the historicity of the biblical text was also emerging. It was during this time that archaeology as a science began to unearth thousands of finds that supported the general historicity of the Bible and in many cases even hundreds of minute details (see chapters 25–26).

Baseless Philosophical Premises

Former critic of Scripture and noted archaeologist William F. Albright (1891–1971) summed up his own journey from a more liberal to a more conservative view of the historicity of the Bible:

> "Authority of Scripture" is a valid theological principle, whereas the "School of Wellhausen" is only one of many ideological systems built on arbitrary philosophical postulates and baseless historical presuppositions. ("TMCV" in *CT*, [360] 4.)

The admonition of Paul the apostle is well taken: "See to it that no one takes you captive through hollow and deceptive philosophy, which depends on human tradition and the basic principles of this world rather than on Christ" (Col. 2:8). The failure to heed this admonition has led many astray from the historical evangelical view of Scripture. Since these were already discussed earlier (see chapter 19), they will only be briefly noted here.

Philosophical presuppositions lay at the root of the modern rejection of the historical orthodox view of Scripture. These include the antisupernaturalism of Spinoza and Hume, the inductivism of Bacon, the materialism of Hobbes, the rationalism of Spinoza, the skepticism of Hume, the agnosticism of Kant, the positivism of Comte and Mill, the romanticism of Rousseau, the pietism of Schleiermacher, the deism of Paine, and the evolutionism of Spencer and Darwin. In addition, one could add the conventionalism of Wittgenstein, the progressivism of Hegel, the existentialism of Kierkegaard, and the processism of Whitehead (see chapter 19 for discussion of these). Let's review a few examples of how these undermine a high view of Scripture.

Antisupernaturalism

Common to almost all forms of negative criticism, at least in their origin, is antisupernaturalism. The denial of miracles in the Bible began with Thomas Hobbes (1588–1679), was systematically treated by Benedict Spinoza (1632–1677), and was widely extended through David Hume (1711–1776). Once it became a generally accepted procedure for approaching Scripture, it was only a matter of time before it attacked the very foundations for an orthodox view of Scripture, for the very historicity of the documents became suspect when the numerous miracles they record could no longer be accepted.

Evolutionism

Any grammatical-historical analysis of Genesis, as well as hundreds of other verses on Creation (see Geisler, *KTAC*, 149–51), reveals that God created the cosmos, the first human beings, and all basic forms of life. However, if the Darwinian hypothesis is right, then Genesis must be wrong. Since Darwin's view was widely accepted beginning with 1860 and following, it is no surprise that, at the same time, the historicity of the Bible became more and more rejected, and thus the need to respond to the apostle's warning and beware of the philosophy of evolutionism.

The sad fact is that what Darwin called "the theory of evolution" is neither factually nor philosophically necessary. As Darwin himself said in the introduction to his *On the Origin of Species*:

> For I am well aware that scarcely a single point is discussed in this volume on which facts cannot be adduced, often apparently leading to conclusions directly opposite to those at which I have arrived.

He added, "A fair result can be obtained only by fully stating and balancing the facts and arguments on both sides of each question; and this is here impossible." Many other evolutionists have admitted that the general theory of macroevolution (large-scale change between species) is really a tautology—that is, an empty statement that cannot be falsified.

Again, one thing is certain: Macroevolution is neither philosophically nor factually necessary; an alternative view is logically possible. Indeed, as the current intelligent design movement has demonstrated, without the aid of a naturalistic philosophical presupposition that methodologically demands that all true scientific explanations be naturalistic, the so-called factual basis for macroevolution crumbles (see volume 2). At any rate, if there is no need to accept evolution, which is contrary to Genesis and the rest of Scripture, then there is no reason to reject the historicity of these passages because of the theory of evolution.

Progressivism

Much of modern biblical scholarship was sucked into the philosophy of historicism in the wake of the developmental pantheism of G. W. F. Hegel (1770–1831). In his massive work *The Phenomenology of Spirit* and his later *Encyclopedia of Philosophy*, Hegel spelled out his historical progressivism in what became known through the misinterpretation of Johann Gottlieb Fichte (1762–1814) as a dialectic of thesis, antithesis, and synthesis. Nonetheless, Hegel did affirm that history is the unfolding of Absolute Spirit in a developmental dialectic.

The results of this so-called "Hegelianism" for biblical scholarship were disastrous. F. C. Baur's (1792–1860) Tubingen School contended that the gospel of John must be viewed as second-century synthesis of the earlier thesis/antithesis conflict of Peter and Paul. This conclusion was arrived at with almost total disregard for the internal and external evidence for an earlier first-century date for John. The so-called "exegetical" conclusions, however massive and scholarly, were largely determined by a prevailing zeitgeist. Once again, the biblical exegete should have heeded the warning to "beware of philosophy."

Existentialism

The father of modern existentialism was not a twentieth-century French atheist (Jean-Paul Sartre) but a Danish Christian named Søren Kierkegaard (1813–1855) who believed that, on the whole, the doctrine as it is taught in the church was entirely sound. Nonetheless, few have done more undermining of the church from within; remember that it was his philosophical son, Karl Barth (1886–1968), who gave rise to neo-orthodoxy. Kierkegaard concluded that even if we assume that the defenders of Christianity have succeeded in proving about the Bible everything they could wish, no one has come to faith in that process.

Kierkegaard then argued that even if we assume that Christianity's opponents have proved what *they* desire to demonstrate about the Bible, the Christian faith has not been damaged in the slightest. Kierkegaard's assertion is not true, in either regard.

When considering damage, we need only mention the Kierkegaardian beliefs:

(1) Religious truth is located in personal encounter (subjectivity).
(2) Propositional truth is not essential to the faith.
(3) Destructive higher criticism is not harmful to Christianity.
(4) God is "wholly other" and essentially unknowable, even through biblical revelation.

These give further significance to the Pauline warning to "beware of philosophy."

There are many other philosophical positions which, wittingly or unwittingly, have been imbibed by modern biblical scholars to the detriment of their view of Scripture. They have been detailed and discussed elsewhere (see Geisler, "BPWBE" in *JETS*, 1999) and include aristotelianism, platonism, nominalism, agnosticism, and anthropological monism. The truth is that any philosophy alien to biblical theism will undermine our confidence in Scripture.

RESTATING A DEFENSE FOR THE EVANGELICAL VIEW

Biblical Defense

The biblical basis for the evangelical view of Scripture is sound (see chapters 13–16). Whatever one says about the truth or falsity of what the Bible teaches about itself, this seems inescapable; namely, it affirms that it is the God-breathed (2 Tim. 3:16), imperishable (Matt. 5:17–18), absolutely true (John 17:17), and unbreakable Word of God (John 10:35).

Historical Defense

The historical defense of the orthodox view of Scripture is also very strong. It has been shown to be the dominant, if not exclusive, view of every major Father and Reformer of the Christian church for nearly nineteen hundred years (see chapters 17–18). Deviations were considered unorthodox, and the major ones are late and philosophically unjustified (see chapters 19–22).

Philosophical Defense

Negatively, no philosophical premises that undermine the evangelical view of Scripture are necessary, and all are refutable. Positively, a realistic theism, for which there is good philosophical justification (see chapters 1–11), wards off all major attacks on the evangelical view of Scripture.

Practical Defense

If one believes, as both history and personal experience confirm, that ideas have consequences, then it is not difficult to defend the thesis that modern negative criticism of the Bible has left the non-evangelical segments of the church without an objective divine authority for faith and practice. The results of this are manifest in the life of the church on both a personal and social level. One need not recite the litany of moral decay we have experienced since (and logically, because of) the undermining of an objective divine authority. As the psalmist said, "When the foundations are being destroyed, what can the righteous do?" (Ps. 11:3).

SOURCES

Ahlstrom, Sidney E. *Theology in America: The Major Protestant Voices From Puritanism to Neo-Orthodoxy.*

Albright, William F. "William Albright: Toward a More Conservative View" in *Christianity Today* (January 18, 1963).

Bacon, Francis. *Novum Organum.*

Comte, Auguste. *The Catechism of Positive Religion.*

———. *Cours, The Positive Philosophy of Auguste Comte.*

Darwin, Charles. *On the Origin of Species.*

Edwards, Jonathan. *Miscellanies.*

———. "Ordination of Mr. Billing" (May 7, 1740), cited by John Gerstner in *The Nature of Inspiration.*

Edwards, Paul, ed. "Comte, Auguste" in *The Encyclopedia of Philosophy.*

Geisler, Norman. "Beware of Philosophy: A Warning to Biblical Exegetes" in *The Journal of the Evangelical Theological Society* (1999).

———. *Knowing the Truth About Creation.*

Geisler, Norman, and William Nix. *A General Introduction to the Bible.*

———, ed. *Errancy: Its Philosophical Roots.*

———, ed. *Inerrancy.*

Gerstner, John. "Jonathan Edwards and the Bible" in *Tenth: An Evangelical Quarterly.*

Hobbes, Thomas. *Leviathan.*

Hodge, A. A., and B. B. Warfield. *Inspiration.*

Hodge, Charles. *Systematic Theology.*

———. *What Is Darwinism?*

Kant, Immanuel. *God Within the Limits of Reason Alone.*

Lewis, C. S. *Miracles.*

Levy-Bruhl, Lucien. *The Philosophy of Auguste Comte.*

Mill, John Stuart. *Auguste Comte and Positivism.*

Paine, Thomas. *Complete Works of Thomas Paine.*

Spinoza, Benedict. *A Theologico-Political Treatise.*

Sproul, R. C. *Explaining Inerrancy: A Commentary.*

Turretin, Francis. *The Doctrine of Scripture.*

———. *Institutes of Elenctic Theology.*

Warfield, B. B. *The Inspiration and Authority of the Bible.*

———. *Limited Inspiration.*

CHAPTER TWENTY-FOUR

FUNDAMENTALISM ON THE BIBLE

T he term "fundamentalism" covers a wide variety of beliefs regarding inspiration. Many contemporary theologians who would call themselves fundamentalists accept the same view as expressed in the "evangelical" position (see chapter 23). Both groups, evangelical and fundamentalist, trace their roots back to Charles Hodge, A. A. Hodge, B. B. Warfield, and J. Gresham Machen, who were part of a group in the late nineteenth and early twentieth centuries called historic fundamentalists. Among the rest who call themselves fundamentalists there are at least two main views: the verbal dictation position and the Inspired-King-James-Version position.

Historic Fundamentalism

Historic fundamentalism, which arose out of the controversy between conservatives and liberals in the Presbyterian Church and their seminary at Princeton, held the standard orthodox view of Scripture, the view of the Fathers and Reformers of the church (see chapters 17–18). Their position is substantially the same as the one described as "evangelical" (in chapter 23): The Bible is the inspired, infallible, and inerrant written Word of God, and inspiration is both verbal and plenary. In brief, the Bible is both God's Word and man's words. Errors exist only in copies, not in the originals. Everything the Bible affirms, whether in theology or in science and history, is without error.

Contemporary Fundamentalism

Those who are currently called "fundamentalist" (by themselves or by evangelicals) do not hold a monolithic view of Scripture. They range in belief from the standard evangelical view to a verbal dictation position and even beyond to a "King-James-only" view.

THE VERBAL DICTATION VIEW

The typical charge by non-evangelicals against most forms of contemporary fundamentalism is not accurate. No knowledgeable proponent under the label "fundamentalist" confesses to believe in "mechanical dictation," which implies an Islam-like[1] view of God dictating word-for-word to biblical writers who served as mere secretaries and recorded precisely what they received. Even those few fundamentalists who are favorable to the term "*verbal* dictation" refuse to call it "*mechanical* dictation."

The Basis for the False Charge of Mechanical Dictation

The basis for this false charge springs from several non-evangelical misunderstandings, the *first* of which is a semantic issue. All fundamentalists and most evangelicals believe that the very words of the Bible are inspired: "All *scripture* [the writing] is God-breathed" (2 Tim. 3:16). Thus, each word (as part of a sentence and within its literary context) is the very word that God affirmed concurrently with the human author of Scripture (see chapters 13–15). That is to say, that each word is inspired of God *holistically*, insofar as it is a part of the literary unit of which it is a part. Unfortunately, the fundamentalist claim is often understood as each word being inspired *atomistically*—in and of itself. However, since words do not have meaning in and of themselves (see chapter 6) but are only a part of a sentence, which is the smallest unit of meaning, there are no such things as inspired words in the individual, atomistic sense. Words have potential meaning and can be put together into meaningful sentences, but individually and alone they do not have meaning.

Second, non-evangelicals often point to statements by the Fathers and Reformers (see chapters 17–18) that use the word *dictation* in regard to the Scriptures. However, their statements are often taken out of context: The Latin word *dictus*, translated "dictate" or "dictation," like the English word *dictates*, does not always mean a word-for-word dictation. To rephrase an earlier example, when we say that a given law comes to us at the dictates of the Congress, this does not necessarily mean that we possess the word-for-word rendition of it but simply that by the authority of Congress a law has

---

[1] For the Muslim view, see Norman Geisler and Abdul Saleeb, *Answering Islam*, chapters 5 and 9.

been established of which we have a summary.

Or, to put the matter another way, if evangelicals are to be charged with believing in verbal "dictation" in some sense of the term, then by the same token the Fathers and Reformers must be charged with the same view. But in this event, because of the clear testimony of the Fathers and Reformers, it is not a mechanical word-for-word kind of dictation that ignores the personality and vocabulary of the biblical authors (see chapter 15).

Third, the early Fathers of the church often used less-than-ideal illustrations of the biblical writers as used by the Holy Spirit to produce Scripture. By describing them as a musical instrument through which God brought the message, one can easily misunderstand it in the sense of a *mere* mechanical tool used by God to produce a word-for-word product. While the illustration may be unfortunate, its meaning is not to be construed as denying the human nature of Scripture. Like illustrations (parables) used by Jesus (cf. Luke 18), we should look for the main point being made and not try to make it walk on all fours.

The fact of the matter is that almost all fundamentalists deny the mechanical dictation view of Scripture, and very few even speak of any kind of verbal dictation. The famous American evangelist John R. Rice was an exception.

The Verbal Dictation View of John R. Rice

John R. Rice (1895–1980) is a key example of a fundamentalist who embraced a view he called "verbal dictation." " 'All Scripture is God-breathed,' that is, the Scripture itself is breathed out from God." And, he inquires, "if God gave all the words in the Bible, then is not that dictation?" (*OGBB*, 286).

However, Rice hastened to say that it was not *mechanical* dictation; it was simply *verbal* dictation. His response to identifying these two positions into one was to say,

> This charge of "mechanical dictation" against fundamental Bible believers is dishonest pretense. [After all,] a secretary is not ashamed to take dictation from a man. Why should a prophet be ashamed to take dictation from God? (ibid., 265, 287).

According to Rice, saying the Bible is verbally dictated does not mean it has no human dimension. "Certainly we admit gladly that there is a 'human side of the Bible in its style, language, composition, history and culture' " (ibid., 141). Just how did God get a word-for-word, verbal dictation recorded and yet use the different styles of the biblical writers?

> God planned all that so that each one was chosen before he was born and fitted to be the instrument God wanted to use. The varying

styles are all God's styles in the Bible. God made the men and made the styles, and used them according to plan (ibid., 206).

Rightly, then, "the Bible does not simply in some places 'contain the Word of God'; the Bible is the Word of God." This means the Bible is "absolutely correct when it speaks on matters of history or geography." Inerrancy does not extend to every copy of the Bible: "The original autographs of the Scriptures were infallibly correct" (ibid., 88). Thus Rice rejected all higher criticism of the Bible, saying, "Higher criticism tends to sit in judgment on the Bible and let poor, sinning, frail, ignorant, mortal men pass judgment on the Word of God" (ibid., 136). Instead of a fallible, mutilated divine message, Rice held to a verbally dictated, inerrant Book—the Bible.

THE INSPIRED-KING-JAMES-VERSION VIEW

Most fundamentalists were reared on the King James Version of the Bible. Indeed, after nearly seven hundred years it is still one of the most popular translations in the world, and this is no accident. In 1611, when it was translated, the English language was at its zenith. The King James translators used the beauty, rhythm, cadence, and descriptive power possible through this Elizabethan style to produce an enduring and endearing rendition of the Word of God. Those who have been accustomed to the King James Version understandably revere its majestic expression of God's truth.

The Inspired-King-James Claim

However, some have taken things too far by idolizing this aesthetically pleasing translation. In fact, they have frozen the truth of the original Hebrew and Greek texts of the Bible in this seventeenth-century book as time has passed them by. In so doing, they have lost the true meaning of God's Word as they cling to language that has lost much of its meaning to a twenty-first-century reader.

The most noted proponent of this position is Peter Ruckman, who has produced several works on the topic, including *The Christian's Handbook of Manuscript Evidence* and *Why I Believe the King James Version Is the Word of God.* The central thesis of this view is that "The King James Bible Alone = the Word of God Alone" (White, *KJOC*, 3).

Other popular books defending the KJV-only models and castigating other translations as demonic are Gail Riplinger's *New Age Bible Versions* and *Which Bible Is God's Word?* Few scholars, even among evangelicals, take these views seriously; James White has produced an excellent critique in *The King James Only Controversy.*

Peter Ruckman even goes so far as to affirm that the Greek text must be corrected by the King James Version (*CHME*, 115–38). Noteworthy is his statement that "mistakes in the A.V. 1611 [King James Version] are advanced revelation." Thus, he adds, "in exceptional cases, where the majority of Greek manuscripts stand against the A.V. 1611, put them in file 13"[2] (ibid., 126, 130). Ruckman appears to believe that the English text of the King James is an inerrant, "re-inspired" version. Armed with this presupposition, adherents of this view speak of other translations of the Bible as "perverted Bibles" and those who use them as "Bible haters."

A Critique of the Inspired-King-James-Version Claim

There are many reasons for rejecting the claims of the King-James-Version-only group. Among them the following are noteworthy.

First, the choice of versions is arbitrary. Why a Bible in English rather than one in German, French, Spanish, Russian, or Chinese? Further, why the King James Version when there are many other faithful English translations of the Bible? Some twelve hundred different versions of the Bible (in whole or in part) have been published in English (Geisler and Nix, *GIB*, 605–35).

Second, why choose only this English Bible as inspired? Certainly not because it is the most popular—the NIV is now more widely used. Nor because it has lasted longer, for the Greek text is older, and the Latin Vulgate has endured for longer than the King James Version, namely, for more than a thousand years.

Third, why a recent edition of the KJV? Why not the original one? The KJV has gone through numerous editorial changes; the original edition had innumerable errors. For example, in Matthew 26:36 the name "Judas" was used instead of "Jesus." In the second edition, twenty words are repeated in Exodus 14:10. Even the two editions issued in 1611 differ from each other (Lewis, *EB*, 37).

Later printings of the KJV produced the so-called "Wicked Bible," which left out the "not" in "Thou shalt not commit adultery" (Ex. 20:14). Intentional changes were made in the 1612 and 1613 editions (ibid., 38). In 1659 William Kilburne claimed to find *twenty thousand* errors that had crept into six different editions in the 1650s. In 1769 Benjamin Blayney changed spelling and punctuation. Words like Hierusalem, Marie, assone, Foorth, shalbe, et, creeple, fift, sixt, ioy, middes, and charet were no longer used. A study of all these changes was made by F. H. Scrivener in *The Authorized Edition of the English Bible* (1611).

Fourth, the original KJV had the apocryphal books in it. They were not taken out until a 1629 edition, but this did not become general until the nineteenth century (Lewis, *EB*, 38). If the original KJV was inspired, then why did it contain the Apocrypha? All fundamentalists reject these books as not being inspired.

---

[2]This is a figure of speech meaning "throw them in the trash."

Fifth, to hold to the KJV as an inspired translation is to confess that many things in it are meaningless and/or false. Many English words have not only lost their meaning since 1611, but some have even reversed in meaning.

"We do you to wit" (2 Cor. 8:1 KJV) is not commonly understood today—it means, "We want you to know." Also, "I trow not" (Luke 17:9 KJV) is senseless to modern readers; hence, it needs to be retranslated into today's English as "I think not" (NKJV).

In a classic example, one word has reversed its meaning since the seventeenth century. The King James Version says (in 2 Thess. 2:7), "He who now letteth, will let." At that time the word *let* meant to "hinder"; today it means to "permit." Another example is the word *prevent* (cf. 1 Thess. 4:15; Amos 9:10), which meant "precede" in 1611. Thus, those who cling to the King James have actually reversed the meaning of inspired Scripture in these cases and misconstrued it in many others.

It is one thing to embrace, as the author does, the beauty and majesty of the King James Version, but it is quite another to claim it is the inspired original against which all other translations should be measured. As Jack Lewis correctly noted, "Those who feel they can escape the problem of translations by retreating into the citadel of the KJV have a zeal for God that is not in accord with knowledge" (*EB*, 67).[2]

THE FAILURE OF EXTREME FUNDAMENTALISM'S VIEW OF SCRIPTURE

In general, fundamentalism's view of Scripture can be faulted on many levels, and two faults are prominent: It diminishes the human nature of Scripture, and it fails to engage the culture. While not all the following criticism applies to all who call themselves fundamentalists (since some of them hold an evangelical view of Scripture), many are subject to one or more of the following criticisms.

The Charge of Biblical Docetism—Diminishing Scripture's Humanity

One charge properly laid at the door of an extreme fundamentalist view of Scripture is that of biblical docetism. Docetism was an early heresy that, while affirming Christ's full deity, denied His full humanity—Christ was *truly* God, but only *apparently* human. So biblical docetism is an un-

---

[2]The debate as to whether the KJV is inspired should not be confused with that of whether the majority text behind the KJV is the superior one. Not all who have championed the majority-text view call themselves fundamentalists. Further, most scholars who hold the majority-text view do not hold that the KJV is an inspired version of the Bible. For a discussion of this, see D. A. Carson, *The King James Debate*.

orthodox view of Scripture, since it too diminishes the Bible's human side. Sometimes this is not done in principle but only in practice, yet it is done nonetheless (see chapter 15).

Diminishing the human side of the Bible is done in many ways, one of which is simply to neglect it. Another is to hold things inconsistent with it. In terms of specifics, as we saw in chapter 15, denying biblical humanity is a failure to recognize one or more of the following human characteristics of Scripture:

First, like all other human books, the Bible has human authors, some forty in all, including Moses, Isaiah, Jeremiah, Daniel, Matthew, Mark, Luke, John, Paul, and Peter.

Second, the Bible was written in human languages: Hebrew in the Old Testament (with some Aramaic) and Greek in the New Testament, the common trade language of the first century.

Third, the Bible also utilizes different literary styles, from the down-to-earth language of a farmer from southern Israel (Amos) to the exalted poetry of Isaiah and Luke's sophisticated training in the Greek culture.

Fourth, the Bible uses different human literary forms. These different human forms of speech include narrative (as in Samuel and Kings), poetry (as in Job and Psalms), parables (as in the Synoptic Gospels), some allegory (as in Galatians 4), and the use of symbols (as in the Revelation). Metaphors and similes abound in Scripture (cf. James 1–2), and even satire (Matt. 19:24) and hyperbole are found (Col. 1:23).

Fifth, the Bible reflects different human perspectives, from that of a shepherd (Psalm 23) to a prophet (Daniel) to a pastor (2 Tim.) to a chronicler (1 Chron.) to a historian (cf. Luke 1:1–4). Also, as we have seen, biblical writers speak from an observer's perspective, such as when writing of the sun rising or setting (Josh. 1:15; cf. 10:13), and even round numbers are used (Josh. 3:4; 4:13; 2 Chron. 4:2).

Sixth, the Bible reveals human thought patterns and processes, including human reasoning. Romans, for example, is a tightly knit logical treatise that has been used to demonstrate the principles and processes of rational thought (cf. Acts 17:2); Scripture even records a memory lapse (1 Cor. 1:14–16).

Seventh, the Bible reveals human emotions, including great sorrow (Rom. 9:2), anger (Gal. 3:1), and melancholy and loneliness (2 Tim. 4:9–16), along with joy (Phil. 1:4) and many others.

Eighth, the Bible manifests specific human interests. Luke had a medical interest, as indicated by his use of medical terms. Hosea had a rural interest, David a shepherd's viewpoint. The presentation of the material in each biblical book is colored by the experiences and interests of the author.

Ninth, as we have demonstrated, the Bible expresses human culture, basically Semitic. This included the common means of greeting by a kiss (1 Thess. 5:26). Likewise, a woman's veil as a sign of her respect for her husband is a manifestation of human culture (1 Cor. 11:5). Numerous other Near Eastern cultural practices are indicated, including washing feet upon entering a home (Luke 7:44; cf. John 13), shaking off the dust from one's feet as a sign of condemnation (Luke 10:11), and reclining (not sitting) at meals (John 13:23).

Tenth, the Bible utilizes other written human sources, including the Book of Jashar (Josh. 10:13), The Books of the Wars of the Lord (Num. 21:14), and the records of Samuel the seer . . . Nathan the prophet . . . Gad the seer (1 Chron. 29:29). It even quotes non-Christian poets three times (Acts 17:28; 1 Cor. 15:33; Titus 1:12), and Jude cited material from the non-canonical books of the Assumption of Moses and the Book of Enoch (Jude 9, 14).

The failure to take seriously these and other human traits in the Bible is a characteristic of many fundamentalists' views of Scripture. In addition to its divine source, the Bible comes to us through completely human instruments. To deny or neglect this is a docetic trait found in much of fundamentalism.

The Charge of Failing to Engage the Intellectual Culture

The extreme fundamentalist view of the Bible also tends to be anti-intellectual; it fails to study carefully and respond insightfully to the current culture. Out of fear of compromising, it moves toward the opposite extreme of isolating, which manifests itself in an ignorance of the opposing philosophies and ideologies set against Christianity in our intellectual milieu. Unlike the apostle Paul, who engaged with success the anti-Christian philosophers of his day (see Acts 17), many contemporary fundamentalists are content with a "Bible only" mentality that not only neglects God's general revelation but also believes wrongly that one can preach the Word effectively without understanding the world to whom they preach it. They focus on the message but neglect their surroundings. This often leads to a fortress mentality and increasing irrelevance in the eyes of the very people it needs to reach with the Gospel.

CONCLUSION

The more moderate fundamentalists have adopted an evangelical view of Scripture not unlike that of the historic fundamentalists from the turn of the twentieth century. However, more extreme fundamentalists have either adopted a verbal dictation view or else canonized the King James Version of the Bible. Their extreme separatism has led them to become more isolated from the culture and from intellectually engaging the ideologies that undermine their conservative view of Scripture. Further, they tend in the direction of a biblical docetism, downplaying the human elements of Scripture and stressing the divine side.

In summation, liberals claim that the Bible came by human intuition through natural processes, while liberal evangelicals insist that a divine elevation of human literature explains the source of Scripture. At the same time, adherents to neo-orthodoxy see Scripture as a fallible human record of revelational events, whereas neo-evangelicals see inspiration of only redemptive truth or purpose. Extreme fundamentalists go toward the opposite end of the spectrum, claiming that the Bible is verbally dictated. Between these extremes is the historic, orthodox, evangelical view that affirms both the full divinity and full humanity of Scripture in concurrence with the words of God and the words of the human authors He moved upon (2 Peter 1:20–21) to produce a God-breathed product (2 Tim. 3:16).

SOURCES

Carson, D. A. *The King James Debate.*
Geisler, Norman, and William Nix. *A General Introduction to the Bible.*
Geisler, Norman, and Abdul Saleeb. *Answering Islam.*
Geisler, Norman, ed. *Inerrancy.*
Hodge, A. A., and B. B. Warfield. *Inspiration.*
Lewis, Jack. *The English Bible: From KJV to NIV.*
Rice, John R. *Our God-Breathed Book—The Bible.*
Riplinger, Gail. *New Age Bible Versions.*
———. *Which Bible Is God's Word?*
Ruckman, Peter. *The Christian's Handbook of Manuscript Evidence.*
———. *Why I Believe the King James Version Is the Word of God.*
Scrivener, F. H. *The Authorized Edition of the English Bible* (1611).
White, James. *The King James Only Controversy.*

THEOLOGICAL

CHAPTER TWENTY-FIVE

THE HISTORICITY OF THE OLD TESTAMENT

C hristianity is a historical religion, and the main events on which it is based, such as Creation and the life, death, and resurrection of Jesus Christ, claim to be space-time events in the objective world. Also, the New Testament assumes the historicity of the Old; many of its most crucial teachings are based on it. Hence, the integrity of the two covenants is tied together.

Jesus referred to many of the most disputed passages of the Old Testament as historical, including the creation of Adam and Eve (Matt. 19:4–5), Jonah and the great fish (Matt. 12:40–41), and the Flood of Noah (Matt. 24:37–39). Indeed, He and the New Testament writers refer to persons or events from every chapter of Genesis 1–22 and many others in the rest of the Old Testament (see chapter 16).

The historicity of the Old Testament is based on two major factors: The reliability of the Old Testament text, and the reliability of those who put the text together.

THE RELIABILITY OF THE OLD TESTAMENT MANUSCRIPTS

The reliability of Old Testament manuscripts is based on three factors: the abundance of the manuscripts, the dating of the manuscripts, and the accuracy of the manuscripts. Accuracy is based in part on the reputation of the Jewish scribes for their meticulous work and for their ability to cross-check their work by internal and external means.[1]

The Abundance of Old Testament Manuscripts

Considering the paucity of manuscripts for other works of antiquity, even before modern discoveries there were a substantial number of Old Testament manuscripts. For example, most works from antiquity survive on a mere handful of manuscripts: There are only seven for Plato, eight for Thucydides, eight for Herodotus, ten of Caesar's *Gallic Wars*, and twenty for the works of Tacitus. Only Demosthenes' and Homer's works have numbers into the hundreds.[2] Yet as early as the late 1700s Benjamin Kennicott published 615 Old Testament manuscripts, and a few years later Giovanni de Rossi published 731 manuscripts (Geisler and Nix, *GIB*, 408).

Further, beginning around 1890 some ten thousand Old Testament manuscripts were found in the Cairo Geniza, and since 1947 caves by the Dead Sea at Qumran have produced over six hundred Old Testament manuscripts. The largest collection of manuscripts in the world, the Second Firkowitch Collection in Leningrad, contains 1,582 items of Bible and Masora[3] on parchment, plus twelve hundred Hebrew fragments (ibid., 257–58).

The Dating of the Old Testament Manuscripts

Not only the abundance but also the dating of these manuscripts vouches for their accuracy. Whereas conservatives place the last book of the Old Testament around 400 B.C. (and liberals put Daniel at c. 165 B.C.), some Old Testament manuscripts are even earlier than the liberal date. For example, certain Dead Sea Scrolls go back as far as the third century B.C., and the Nash Papyrus is dated between the second century B.C. and the first century A.D.[4]

While most Old Testament manuscripts are dated from A.D. 800–1100,

---

[1]Remember that every manuscript and fragment in possession is a copy. No originals (autographs) have been found.

[2]There are two hundred manuscripts for Demosthenes and 643 for Homer's *Iliad*.

[3]Masora were Jewish scribes of the fifth through ninth centuries who standardized the Hebrew text of Scripture (called the Masoretic Text).

[4]The significance of this is obvious: If extant *copies* are dated earlier than the liberal estimate, how much earlier, then, came the *originals?*

nonetheless, with the discovery of the Dead Sea Scrolls the overall accuracy of the later manuscripts has been attested. These Old Testament manuscripts include great documents like Oriental 4445 (of most of the Pentateuch), Codex Cairensis (most of the rest of the Old Testament), Codex Leningradensis (of the whole Old Testament), the Babylonian Codex (of the latter Prophets), the Reuchlin Codex (of the Prophets), the ten thousand manuscripts of the Cairo Geniza, and over six hundred in the Dead Sea Scrolls, which include parts of every Old Testament book except Esther (ibid., 358–65).

The Accuracy of the Old Testament Manuscripts

The accuracy of these multitudinous manuscripts is known from both internal and external evidence. The external evidence comes from the Dead Sea Scrolls, which provide a cross-check on how accurately manuscripts were copied during a thousand-year period, since the Dead Sea manuscripts were a millennium earlier than the previous (Masoretic) manuscripts (ibid., 380–82).

First, Jewish reverence for Scripture led to careful transmission of the Old Testament. The Talmud reveals the scrupulous rules Jewish scribes followed, including the counting of all the letters and lines to make sure they matched. Manuscripts that contained even one mistake were discarded (ibid., chapter 20).

Second, there are many duplicate passages in the Old Testament. Some Psalms occur twice (e.g., 14 and 53); much of Isaiah 36–39 is found in 2 Kings 18–20; Isaiah 2:2–4 and Micah 4:1–3 are almost identical; and Jeremiah 52 is a repeat of 2 Kings 25. An examination of these passages shows not only substantial agreement but an almost word-for-word identity, revealing how accurately they were copied down through the centuries.

Third, the Hebrew Old Testament was translated into Greek beginning about 250 B.C. This translation, known as the Septuagint (LXX, or "seventy"), is also a cross-check on the accuracy with which the Old Testament was transmitted. With the exception of minor variants that do not affect the overall message of the Old Testament, there is substantial agreement between the Hebrew and Greek translations of the Old Testament. Indeed, most of the New Testament citations of the Old Testament are from the Greek LXX.

Fourth, with regard to the Five Books of Moses, the Samaritan Pentateuch provides substantial support for the Hebrew Old Testament. While there are many minor variants, in chapter after chapter and verse after verse, the Samaritan Pentateuch is a confirmation of the general text of the Hebrew Old Testament.

Fifth, by far and away the most important cross-check on the accuracy of the transmission of the Hebrew Old Testament through the centuries is the

Dead Sea Scrolls, for they provide manuscripts that are one thousand years earlier than most that were used to establish the Hebrew text. Comparative studies have been made, and the results reveal a word-for-word identity in some 95 percent of the text; the minor variants consist mostly of slips of the pen or spelling.

To be specific, the Isaiah Scroll led the translators of the Old Testament in the Revised Standard Version originally to make only thirteen small changes in the whole book, eight of which were known from other ancient sources. On further, subsequent examination, these have collapsed down into only *three* (Kaiser, *OTDATR*, 46). Even more specifically, to use Isaiah 53 as an example, other than a few spelling and stylistic changes, there is only one word ("light" in v. 11) of difference in the entire text. In brief, *there were no changes in meaning after a thousand years of copying and relatively few changes in words!* (Geisler and Nix, *GIB*, 382).

Professor Walter Kaiser, citing Douglas Stuart, summarized it well:

> It is fair to say that the verses, chapters, and books of the Bible would read largely the same, and would leave the same impression with the reader, even if one adopted virtually every possible *alternative* reading to those now serving as the basis for current English translations. (*OTDATR*, 48.)

THE RELIABILITY OF THE OLD TESTAMENT AUTHORS

In addition to the reliability of the Old Testament manuscripts, there is strong evidence for the reliability of the Old Testament writers, and their historical accounts have found increasing acceptance by scholars.

The Historicity of Particular Sections of the Old Testament

As to the historicity of the Old Testament in general, world-renowned archaeologist William F. Albright (1891–1971) wrote, "There can be no doubt that archaeology has confirmed the substantial historicity of the Old Testament tradition" (*ARI*, 176). He added,

> As critical study of the Bible is more and more influenced by the rich new material from the ancient Near East we shall see a steady rise in respect for the historical significance of now neglected or despised passages and details in the Old and New Testaments. (*FSAC*, 81.)

Even usually liberal sources are now admitting the overall historical reliability of the Old Testament. Excerpting from his book *Is the Bible True?* Jeffery L. Sheler notes for *U.S. News & World Report*:

> In extraordinary ways, modern archaeology has affirmed the historical core of the Old Testament—corroborating key portions of the

stories of Israel's patriarchs, the Exodus, the Davidic monarchy, and the life and times of Jesus. (October 25, 1999, 52.)

The Historicity of Adam and Eve (Genesis 1–3)

Many critical scholars consider the first chapters of Genesis to be myth, not history. They point to the poetic nature of the text, the parallel between the early chapters of Genesis and ancient myths, the alleged contradiction of the text with science, and the late date for Adam in the Bible, which is opposed to scientific dating that places the first humans much earlier.

Evidence for the Historicity of Adam and Eve

However, the Bible presents Adam and Eve as literal people who had real children from whom the rest of the human race came (cf. Gen. 5:1f.). There are good reasons to believe that Adam and Eve were real historical persons.

First, Genesis 1–2 presents them as actual persons and even narrates the important events in their lives.

Second, they gave birth to literal children who did the same (Gen. 4:1, 25; 5:1f.).

Third, the phrase "this is the account of," used to record later history in Genesis (6:9; 10:1, 32; 11:10, 27; 25:12, 19, etc.), is used of the Creation account (2:4) and of Adam and Eve and their descendants (Gen. 5:1).

Fourth, later Old Testament chronology of historical persons places Adam at the top of the list (1 Chron. 1:1).

Fifth, the New Testament places Adam at the beginning of Jesus' literal ancestors (Luke 3:38).

Sixth, Jesus referred to Adam and Eve as the first actual "male and female," making their physical union the basis for His teaching on marriage (Matt. 19:4–5).

Seventh, the book of Romans declares that literal death was brought into the world by a literal "Adam" (Rom. 5:14).

Eighth, the comparison of Adam (the "first Adam") with Christ (the "last Adam") in 1 Corinthians 15:45 manifests that Adam was understood as being historical.

Ninth, Paul's declaration that "Adam was first formed, then Eve" (1 Tim. 2:13–14) reveals that he speaks of actual persons.

Tenth, logically there had to be a first real set of human beings, male and female, or the race would have had no way to get going. The Bible calls this literal couple "Adam and Eve," and there is no reason to doubt their true existence.

Answering Some Objections to Adam's Historicity

The objections to the historicity of Adam and Eve fall far short of the mark. Each one will be addressed in turn.

The Alleged Poetic Nature of Genesis 1

Many reasons can be given for rejecting the assertion that the Creation record of Genesis 1–2 is poetical:

First, even though there is some possible parallelism of ideas between the first three and last three days, Genesis 1 is not in the typical form of Hebrew poetry, which involves couplets set in parallel form. A comparison with Psalms or Proverbs readily shows the difference.

Second, Genesis 2 is part of the Creation record, and it has no poetic parallelism.

Third, the Creation account is a straightforward narration like any historical narration in the Old Testament.

Fourth, the Creation account is introduced like all the other historical accounts in Genesis—with the phrase "This is the account of . . ." (Gen. 2:4; 5:1).

Fifth, both Jesus and the New Testament writers refer to the Creation events as historical (cf. Matt. 19:4; Rom. 5:14; 1 Cor. 15:45; 1 Tim. 2:13–14).

Sixth, the Ebla tablets[5] have confirmed the Genesis account of a monotheistic *ex nihilo* creation. They read, "Lord of heaven and earth: the earth was not, you created it; the light of day was not, you created it; the morning light you had not [yet] made exist" (*Ebla Archives,* 259).

Seventh, by comparison with ancient myths, the Genesis account reveals it is the original, since it is simpler and unembellished. As noted Old Testament scholar Kenneth A. Kitchen observed:

> The common assumption that the Hebrew account is simply a purged and simplified version of the Babylonian legend is . . . fallacious on methodological grounds. In the ancient Near East, the rule is that simple accounts or traditions may give rise (by accretion and embellishment) to elaborate legends, but not vice versa. In the ancient Orient, legends were not simplified or turned into pseudo-history (historicized) as has been assumed for early Genesis. (*AOOT,* 89.)

The Alleged Contradiction with Science

The Genesis Creation account is contradictory to macroevolution in many ways (see volume 2, part 2).[6]

First, it speaks of the creation of Adam from the dust of the ground, not his evolution from other animals (Gen. 2:7).

Second, it speaks of direct immediate creation at God's command, not long natural processes (cf. Gen. 1:1, 3, 6, 9, 21, 27).

Third, according to Genesis, Eve was created from Adam; she did not evolve separately.

Fourth, Adam was an intelligent being who could speak a language,

---

[5]From Syria, depicting civilization from the mid-third millennium B.C. and before.
[6]See also Norman Geisler, "Science and the Bible" in *Baker Encyclopedia of Christian Apologetics.*

study and name animals, and engage in life-sustaining activity. He was not an ignorant, half ape-like creature.

However, granted that the Genesis record conflicts with macro-evolution, it begs the question to affirm Genesis is wrong and evolution is right. In fact, there is substantial scientific evidence to show that macro-evolution is wrong (see volume 2, part 2).

The Alleged Late Date for Adam's Creation

According to this objection, the supposed biblical date for the creation of Adam (c. 4000 B.C.) is much too late to fit the fossil evidence for early man, which ranges from tens of thousands to hundreds of thousands of years. Since the early date for humankind is based on scientific evidence, the historicity of the Genesis record, supposedly, must be rejected.

However, there are several false or challengeable assumptions in this objection.

First, it is assumed that one can simply add all the genealogical records of Genesis 5 and 11 and arrive at an approximate biblical date of 4000 B.C. for Adam's creation. But this is based on the false assumption that there are no gaps in these tables, which there are (see Geisler, "G, OC" in *BECA*). Three generations, for instance, are missing from Matthew 1:8–9 (cf. 1 Chron. 3:11–14), and at least one is missing from Genesis 11:12, since the name Canaan is not there (as it is in Luke 3:35–36).

Second, it is assumed that the dating method for early humanlike fossil finds is accurate; however, these dating methods are subject to many variables, including the change in atmospheric conditions, contamination of the sample, and changes of rates of decay.

Third, it is assumed that early (pre–10,000 B.C.) humanlike fossil finds were really human beings created in the image of God. But this also is a questionable assumption on several counts. For one thing, many of these finds are fragmentary and their reconstruction is highly speculative. The so-called "Nebraska Man" turned out to be an extinct pig's tooth, and "Piltdown Man" was proven to be a complete fraud. Again, identifying a creature from bones, especially a fragment of a bone, is extremely questionable (see Lubenow, *BC*). Ninety-nine percent of what is known about a creature comes through its soft biological tissue, which is not preserved in the rocks. Further, it is wrongly assumed that creatures that were morphologically similar to human beings must have been human beings created in the image of God. But bone structure cannot prove there was an immortal soul made in God's image inside the body. Also, it is incorrectly assumed that evidence for simple toolmaking proves the creature was human. Some animals (such as apes, seals, and birds) are known to use simple tools.

Fourth, it is assumed that the "days" of Genesis were twenty-four-hour solar days, rather than long periods of time. But this is not certain, since the word *day* in Genesis is used of all six days (cf. Gen. 1:1–2:3), and Day

Seven, on which God rested, is still going on many thousands of years later, since God is still in His Sabbath rest from Creation (cf. Heb. 4:4–10). In addition, there are other indications that the "days" of Genesis may be long periods of time (see volume 2, part 2).

In view of all these unproven, questionable, or false assumptions, it is impossible to affirm that Genesis is not historical. In fact, given the history of "scientific" misinterpretation of early humanlike fossils and the mistaken assumption that there are no gaps in the biblical genealogies of Genesis 5 and 11, the arguments against the historicity of Adam and Eve fail. What is more, there are substantial arguments that Genesis 1–11, like the rest of the Old Testament, is historical.

The Historicity of Noah and the Flood (Genesis 6–9)

The record of the Flood in Genesis 6–9 has raised several serious questions in the minds of Bible critics. Many of them have long believed the story is just a legend, but there is ample evidence to the contrary.

The Arguments for the Historicity of Noah's Flood

First, the account presents itself as historical, not mythological. It mentions viable names of people (Noah, Shem, Ham, and Japheth) and an identifiable location, Mt. Ararat (Gen. 8:4).

Second, it is part of a broader historical account, being linked by such literary connectives as "this is the account of Noah" (Gen. 6:9) and "this is the account of Shem, Ham and Japheth" (Gen. 10:1).

Third, it is immediately followed by a listing of nations and cities known to come from that area of the world, including Assyria, Nineveh, and Babylon (Gen. 10:9–12).

Fourth, Noah and his sons are listed in a later genealogical record in the historical book of 1 Chronicles (1:3–4).

Fifth, Isaiah the prophet referred to Noah and the Flood as historical (Isa. 54:9).

Sixth, during the time of Ezekiel the prophet, Noah was still considered one of the great figures in Jewish history (Ezek. 14:14, 20).

Seventh, Jesus affirmed that Noah, the Flood, and details surrounding the Flood were historical (Matt. 24:37–38).

Eighth, the writer of Hebrews places Noah in its great Hall of Faith, along with other historical figures like Abraham, Moses, and David (Heb. 11:7).

Ninth, the apostle Peter twice refers to Noah and the Flood as a literal person and event (1 Peter 3:20; 2 Peter 2:5), even comparing it with the literal destruction of the world by fire in the end times (2 Peter 3:5–13).

Tenth, there is abundant scientific evidence that water once covered the entire earth, including mountains and the poles, because of the remains of aquatic and nonpolar life that have been discovered all over the world.

Eleventh, the worldwide existence of Flood stories in diverse cultures and countries is also testimony to the historicity of Noah and the Flood.

Taking Genesis 6–9 historically has occasioned a number of criticisms. For one thing, how could this small ark hold hundreds of thousands of species? Further, how could a wooden ship survive such a violent storm? Also, how could Noah and all the animals survive so long in the ark?

The Problem of the Capacity of the Ark

The first problem deals with how such a small ark could hold all the animal species on earth. On the widely held belief that a cubit was about eighteen inches, Noah's ark was only forty-five feet high, seventy-five feet wide, and four hundred and fifty feet long (Gen. 6:15). Noah was told to take two of every kind of unclean animal and seven of every kind of clean animal (Gen. 6:19–21; 7:2–3), but scientists inform us that there are between one half billion and over a billion species of animals.

Biblical scholars have offered two solutions to this view. Some hold that the Flood was only local; if so, then Noah only had to take the main animals from that area for eating, for sacrificing, and for repopulating that local area when the Flood was over.

The Local Flood Theory. According to this view the Genesis Flood did not cover the whole earth; hence, Noah did not have to take all the species of the whole world into the ark. As evidence that the Flood was not universal the following arguments are offered.[7]

First, the universal language of Genesis 6–9 is used elsewhere of something less than the whole world. For example, the people on the Day of Pentecost were said to be "from every nation under heaven" (Acts 2:5), and yet it lists the nations, which do not include any from North or South America or Australia, or even China. Likewise, Paul said in Colossians 1:23, "This is the gospel that you heard and that has been proclaimed to *every creature under heaven"* when his trips in Acts show that he only went to the Mediterranean area (Acts 13–28).

Second, the silt deposits that a flood like Noah's would have left are found only in the Mesopotamian valley, not over the whole world.

Third, there would have been astronomical problems with the rotation of the earth had there been water deep enough to cover all the mountains. Yet this is what Genesis (7:20) seems to say happened.

The Universal Flood Theory. Many Old Testament scholars believe the Flood was universal, pointing to several things to support their view.

---

[7]See Arthur Custance, *The Flood: Local or Global?*

First, the language of Genesis is more intense than that of the citations used to support the local flood theory (cf Gen. 6:17; 7:23). Also, other parts of the Bible make it clear that the world was inundated and that only eight people were saved (cf. 2 Peter. 3:5–7).

Second, God's command to take animals of every kind does not make sense if the Flood was only local. Animals could have migrated in from other areas after a local flood. Further, if the Flood is recent, then the now commonly accepted view of continental drift could account for the disbursement of animals.

Third, since all the water of the Flood was already in the air (as a vapor canopy) or under the earth (in the "fountains of the deep"), there would have been no massive weight increase to cause an astronomical catastrophe.

Fourth, Genesis 10:32 declares that after the Flood the whole world was populated from the eight who were in Noah's ark. This would not have been true if there were others outside that local area who had not drowned. Peter confirms this fact (2 Peter 2:5).

Fifth, there is geological evidence to support a worldwide flood. Partial skeletons of recent animals are found in deep fissures in several parts of the world, and the Flood seems to be the best explanation for these. This would also explain how these fissures occur even in hills of considerable height—they extend from one hundred forty feet to three hundred feet. Since no skeleton is complete, it is safe to conclude that none of these animals (mammoths, bears, wolves, oxen, hyenas, rhinoceroses, aurochs, deer, and many smaller mammals) fell into these fissures alive, nor were they rolled there by streams. Because of the calcite cementing of these diverse bones together, they must have been deposited underwater. This is exactly the kind of evidence that a brief but violent episode like the Flood would be expected to show within the short span of one year.

Even assuming the Flood was universal, the solution as to how Noah could get all the animals in the ark is not as difficult as it may seem.

First, Noah's ark was the size of a modern ocean liner; furthermore, it had three stories (Gen. 6:13–16) and over 1.5 million cubic feet.

Second, the modern concept of "species" is not the same as a "kind" in the Bible. There may have been only several hundred different "kinds" of land animals, which the ark could easily have contained. The sea animals stayed in the sea, and many species could have survived in egg form.

Third, Noah could have taken younger or smaller varieties of some larger animals. Given all these factors, there would have been plenty of room for all the animals, food, and humans aboard.

The Problem of a Wooden Ark Surviving a Violent Flood

Since the ark was only made of wood and carried a heavy load of cargo, it would appear that a worldwide flood would have produced violent waters that would have broken it into pieces (cf. Gen 7:4, 11). In response, Bible scholars have made several points:

First, the Ark was made of a strong and flexible material (gopher wood) that "gives" without breaking.

Second, the heavy load was an advantage that gave stability to the ark.

Third, naval architects have established that a long floating boxcar, such as the ark was, is the most stable kind of craft in turbulent waters. Using the four basic standards for stability of naval architecture and the U.S. Coast Guard, a former naval architect concluded: "Noah's Ark was extremely stable; more stable in fact, than modern shipping."[8] Indeed, modern ocean liners follow the same basic dimensions or proportions of Noah's ark. However, their stability is lessened by the need to streamline for faster movement. So there is no reason Noah's ark could not have survived the tempestuous seas of a gigantic, even worldwide, flood.

The Problem of Surviving This Long Duration

There is some question as to just how long the Flood lasted. Genesis (7:24; 8:3) speaks of the Flood waters lasting for 150 days, but other verses seem to say it was only forty days (Gen. 7:4, 12, 17), and one verse indicates that it was over a year (Gen. 8:13–14; cf. Gen. 7:6). These are easily reconciled, since the numbers refer to different things.

Forty days refers to how long it *rained* (Gen. 7:12), and 150 days speaks of how long the floodwaters *prevailed* (Gen. 8:3 cf. 7:24). It was not until the fifth month after the rain began that the ark rested on Mount Ararat (Gen. 8:4), then about eleven months after the rain began the waters dried up (Gen. 8:13). Exactly one year and ten days after the Flood began, Noah and his family emerged on dry ground (Gen. 8:14).

But how could all these animals and humans last over one year coupled up on a boat? The answer is that living things can do almost anything they must to survive as long as they have enough food and water. Many animals could have gone into hibernation or semi-hibernation, and, as was just shown, Noah had plenty of room to store food in his million-and-a-half-cubic-foot floating zoo. As for water, Noah had more than he needed to tap into from forty days of abundant rain, to say nothing of the fresh water streams created by the rain and the "fountains of the deep" that existed on the outside.

The Issue of Ancient Mythology

Some critics claim the Flood story in Genesis 6–9 bears similarity to other ancient flood myths. This is used to suppose that it too is mythologi-

---

[8]See David Collins, "Was Noah's Ark Stable?" in *Creation Research Society Quarterly* (vol. 14: Sept. 1977), 86.

cal. However, there are not only strong differences between them, but the other flood stories also show evidence that they are mythological developments of the original Flood story recorded in Genesis.

As with the Creation accounts, the Flood narrative proves to be realistic and nonmythological as compared to the other ancient versions. The superficial similarities do not point toward plagiarism by Genesis but toward an historical core of events accurately recorded by Genesis and distorted by other ancient accounts. While the names may change (Noah is called Ziusudra by the Sumerians and Utnapishtim by the Babylonians), the basic story is similar: A man is told to build a ship to specific dimensions because God (or gods) is going to flood the world. He does it, rides out the storm, and offers sacrifice upon exiting the boat. The Deity (or deities) responds with remorse over the destruction of life and makes a covenant with the man. These core events point to the historical basis of the Genesis account.

Similar flood accounts are found all over the world. The Flood story is told by the Greeks, Hindus, Chinese, Mexicans, Algonquins, and Hawaiians. Also, one list of Sumerian kings treats the Flood as a real event—after naming eight kings who lived extraordinarily long lives (tens of thousands of years), this sentence interrupts the list: "[Then] the Flood swept over [the earth] and when kingship was lowered [again] from heaven, kingship was [first] in Kish" (Pritchard, *ANET*, 265).

There are good reasons to believe that Genesis gives the original story.

First, the other versions contain elaborations that display corruption.

Second, only in Genesis is the year of the Flood given, as well as dates for the whole chronology relative to Noah's life. In fact, Genesis reads almost like a diary or a ship's log of the events.

Third, the cubical Babylonian ship could not have saved anyone from the Flood. The raging waters would be constantly turning it over on every side. However, the biblical ark is rectangular—long, wide, and low (the same proportion as modern ocean liners)—so that it would ride the rough seas well.

Fourth, the duration of the rainfall in the pagan accounts (seven days) is not enough time for the devastation they describe. The waters would have to rise at least above most mountains, to a height of over 17,000 feet, and it is more reasonable to assume a longer rainfall to do this. The idea that all of the flood waters subsided in one day is equally absurd.

Fifth, another striking difference between Genesis and the other versions is that in the pagan accounts the hero is granted immortality and exalted, while in the Bible we see that Noah sinned. Only a version that seeks to tell the truth would include this realistic admission.

Sixth, the physical evidence (noted above) shows that there was indeed a universal flood.

In summation, if the Flood was local, there is no problem with taking it literally. And even if it was universal there are no insurmountable difficulties with the historicity of a worldwide flood as described in Genesis 6–9. In fact, taken as universal it fits with both the known historical and geological facts of the time, as well as with the rest of Scripture (cf. 2 Peter 3:5–7).

The Historicity of the Tower of Babel (Genesis 11)

Genesis 11:1–4 states,

> The whole world had one language and a common speech. . . . They said to each other, "Come, let's make bricks and bake them thoroughly." They used brick instead of stone, and tar for mortar. Then they said, "Come, let us build ourselves a city, with a tower that reaches to the heavens."

The Sumerian archaeological finds of this area support the historicity of this text. As for the Tower of Babel, archaeology has revealed that Ur-Nammu, King of Ur from about 2044 to 2007 B.C., supposedly received orders to build a great ziggurat (temple tower) as an act of worship to the moon god Nannat. A stele (monument) about five feet across and ten feet high reveals Ur-Nammu's activities. One panel has him setting out with a mortar basket to begin construction of the great tower, thus showing his allegiance to the gods by taking his place as a humble workman. Another clay tablet states that the erection of the tower offended the gods, so they threw down what the men had built, scattered them abroad, and made their speech strange. This is remarkably similar to the record in the Bible.[9]

The Problem of Writing in This Early Period

Early critical views held that there were no written languages in this period and, hence, no one could have written down these events. But it is now widely accepted that written languages go back as far as about 3500 B.C. As to who first recorded them and when, there are two possibilities.

The first is that God could have revealed them later directly to Moses, the author of Genesis. Just as God can reveal the future by prophetic revelation, He can reveal the past by retrospective revelation. The denial of this possibility is based on an unjustified rejection of theism and miracles (see chapters 2–3).

It is more likely, however, that Moses only compiled and edited earlier records of these events. This is not contrary to biblical practice; many scholars believe the author of Luke may have done the same in his gospel (Luke 1:1–4). Indeed, there are many other historical records referenced in the

---

[9]See Clifford Wilson, *Rocks, Relics, and Biblical Reliability*, 29.

Old Testament that may have been sources of information to the biblical writers.[10]

P. J. Wiseman has argued persuasively that the history of Genesis was originally written on clay tablets and passed on from one generation to the next with each "clan leader" being responsible for keeping them edited and up to date (*ARSG*, 74). The main biblical clue that Wiseman found for this is the periodic repetition of words and phrases, especially the phrase "This is the generation of . . ." (cf. Gen. 2:4; 6:9; 10:1; 11:10; etc.). Many ancient tablets were kept in order by making the first words of a new tablet a repetition of the last words of the previous stone. A literary evaluation of Genesis compared to other ancient literature indicates that it was compiled no later than the time of Moses, and it is quite possible that Genesis is a family history recorded by the patriarchs themselves and edited into its final form by Moses.

The Historicity of the Patriarchs (Genesis 12–50)

William F. Albright (1891–1971) wrote,

> Thanks to modern research we now recognize its [the Bible's] substantial historicity. The narratives of the patriarchs, of Moses and the exodus, of the conquest of Canaan, of the judges, the monarchy, exile and restoration, have all been confirmed and illustrated to an extent that I should have thought impossible forty years ago. (*CC*, 1329.)

Law codes have been found from the time of Abraham that show why the Patriarch would have been hesitant to throw Hagar out of his camp, for he was legally bound to support her. Only when a higher law came from God was Abraham willing to expel her.

The discovery of the Mari letters[11] reveals such names as Abam-ram (Abraham), Jacob-el, and Benjamites. Though these do not refer to the biblical people, they at least show that the names were in use.

These letters also support the record of a war in Genesis 14, where five kings fought against four kings. The names of these kings seem to fit with the prominent nations of the day; for example, Genesis 14:1 mentions an Amorite king Arioch; the Mari documents render the king's name Ariwwuk. All of this evidence leads to the conclusion that the source material of Genesis came from the firsthand accounts of someone who lived during Abraham's time.

---

[10]Once again, some examples of extrabiblical sources include The Book of Jashar (Josh. 10:13) and The Books of the Wars of the LORD (Num. 21:14). "The records of Samuel the seer . . . Nathan the prophet . . . and Gad the seer" may also fit in this category (1 Chron. 29:29). Paul quoted non-Christian poets three times (Acts 17:28, 1 Cor. 15:33: Titus 1:12); Jude cited material contained in The Assumption of Moses and the Book of Enoch (Jude 9, 14).

[11]Thousands of tablets discovered in Syria (1834f.) that depict life from about the time of the patriarchs in Genesis.

As to the patriarchal history, Albright said,

> Aside from a few die-hards among older scholars, there is scarcely a single biblical historian who has not been impressed by the rapid accumulation of data supporting the substantial historicity of patriarchal tradition. (Albright, *BP*, 1.)

In summation, Albright affirmed,

> Abraham, Isaac, and Jacob no longer seem isolated figures, much less reflections of later Israelite history; they now appear as true children of their age, bearing the same names, moving about over the same territory, visiting the same towns (especially Harran and Nahor), practicing the same customs as their contemporaries. [In other words,] the patriarchal narratives have a historical nucleus throughout, though it is likely that long oral transmission of the original poems and later prose sagas which underlie the present text of Genesis has considerably refracted the original events. (*AP*, 236.)

Walter Kaiser adds,

> The amount of epigraphic material for this period of history is staggering. Much of this material awaits further study and publication. Meanwhile, an increasingly high degree of probability and corroborating evidence continues to mount up from the external evidence to such a point that the case for the genuineness of the patriarchal stories is strong indeed. (*OTDATR*, 96.)

The Historicity of Sodom and Gomorrah (Genesis 18–19)

The destruction of Sodom and Gomorrah was thought to be spurious until evidence revealed that all five of the cities mentioned in the Bible were in fact centers of commerce in the area and were geographically situated as the Scriptures say. The biblical description of their demise seems to be no less accurate: Evidence suggests that there was earthquake activity and that the various layers of the earth were disrupted and hurled high into the air. Bitumen is plentiful there, and a good pictorial description would be to say that brimstone (bituminous pitch) was hurled down on those cities that had rejected God.

There is further evidence that the layers of sedimentary rock were molded together by intense heat; evidence of such burning has been found on the top of Jebel Usdum (Mount Sodom). This is permanent residue from the great conflagration that took place in the long-distant past, possibly when an oil basin beneath the Dead Sea ignited and erupted. Such an explanation in no way subtracts from the special providential quality of the event, for God is certainly in control of natural causes as well. The timing of the event, in the context of warnings and visitation by angels, reveals its overall divine origin.

THE HISTORICITY OF THE MOSAIC PERIOD
(EXODUS–DEUTERONOMY)

As for the critics' allegation that Moses could not have written the accounts attributed to him, William F. Albright contended,

> "Authority of Scripture" is a valid theological principle, whereas the "School of Wellhausen" is only one of many ideological systems built on arbitrary philosophical postulates and baseless historical presuppositions. (Albright, "WFATMCV" in *CT*, 36.)

He added,

> The contents of our Pentateuch are, in general, very much older than the date at which they were finally edited; new discoveries continue to confirm the historical accuracy or the literary antiquity of detail after detail in it. [Thus] even when it is necessary to assume later additions to the original nucleus of Mosaic tradition, these additions reflect the normal growth of ancient institutions and practices, or the effort made by later scribes to save as much as possible of extant traditions about Moses. [Accordingly,] it is . . . sheer hypercriticism to deny the substantially Mosaic character of the Pentateuchal tradition. (*AP*, 225.)

The Dating of the Exodus (Exodus 12)

While most scholars do not doubt that the nation of Israel came out of Egypt and into Palestine, many do not agree with the biblical statements as to when this happened. The generally accepted date for the entrance into Canaan is about 1230–1220 B.C.; the Scriptures, on the other hand, teach in four different places (Ex. 12:40; 1 Kings 6:1; Judg. 11:26; Acts 13:19–20) that the Exodus occurred in the 1400s B.C. and the entrance into Canaan forty years later. There are several ways that this conflict could be resolved; hence, there is no longer any necessity to accept the 1200s B.C. date as the correct one.

Confusion About Rameses

The first possibility is that the 1200s B.C. date is based on the faulty assumptions that "Rameses" in Exodus 1:11 was named after Rameses the Great, that there were no building projects in the Nile Delta before 1300, and that there was no great civilization in Canaan from the nineteenth century B.C. to the thirteenth. All of these, if true, would make the conditions described in Exodus impossible before 1300 B.C. However, the name

Rameses is not an uncommon name in Egyptian history and may have honored an earlier nobleman by that name. Since Rameses the Great is Rameses II, there must have been a Rameses I. Also, in Genesis 47:11, the name Rameses is used to describe the area of the Nile Delta where Jacob and his sons settled. This may be the name that Moses normally used to refer to the area.

Changing the Date of the Middle Bronze Period

Others have argued that moving the date of the Middle Bronze Age would show that the destruction done to the cities of Canaan was done by the Israelites, not the Egyptians. Evidence has come from recent digs that have shown that the last phase of the Middle Bronze period needs more time than originally thought, so that its end is closer to 1400 B.C. than 1550 B.C. The result would be that two events previously separated by centuries are brought together: The fall of Canaan's Second Middle Bronze Age cities becomes the archaeological evidence for the conquest. This would be an almost perfect match between the archaeological evidence and the biblical account.

Revising Traditional Egyptian Chronology

A third possible solution deals with a problem in the traditional view of Egyptian history. The chronology of the whole ancient world is based on the order and dates of the Egyptian kings, which generally was thought to have been fixed. However, Immanuel Velikovsky (1895–1979) and Donovan Courville assert that there are six hundred extra years in that chronology, which throw off the dates for events all around the Near East. Velikovsky's handling of this chronology discredited his theory, but Courville has shown that the lists of Egyptian kings should not be understood as completely consecutive. He argues that some of the "kings" listed were not pharaohs but local rulers or high officials. Historians had assumed that each dynasty followed after the one before it, when in actuality many dynasties list subrulers who lived at the same time as the preceding dynasty. Working out this new chronology places the Exodus at about 1440 B.C. and would make the other periods of Israelite history fall into line with the Egyptian kings mentioned.

The evidence is not generally considered to be definitively in favor of one of these views over the other. The important point is that there is no compelling reason to accept the late date for the Exodus and that resolution is possible in explaining the biblical date in the 1400s B.C.

Mosaic Authorship of Deuteronomy

The late date many critics assign to Deuteronomy (seventh century B.C.) has been thoroughly discredited by the excellent scholarship of Meredith

Kline in his landmark work on *The Treaty of the Great King*,[12] in which he demonstrated that Deuteronomy follows the typical suzerainty treaty of the Hittites in the second millennium century B.C.—the very time in which tradition informs us Moses wrote Deuteronomy.

Joshua and Jericho (Joshua 6)

Joshua 6 records the conquest and destruction of the city of Jericho. If the account of this monumental event is accurate, it would seem that modern archaeological excavations would have turned up evidence. However, critics insist that no such evidence from Joshua's time has been unearthed.

For many years the prevailing view of critical scholars has been that there was no city of Jericho at the time Joshua was supposed to have entered Canaan. Although earlier investigations by the notable British archaeologist Kathleen Kenyon confirmed the existence of the ancient city of Jericho, as well as its sudden destruction, her findings led her to conclude that the city could have existed no later than c. 1550 B.C., a date much too early for Joshua and the children of Israel to have been party to its demise.

However, recent reexamination of these earlier findings, and a closer look at current evidence, indicates that not only was there a city that fits the biblical chronology, but that its remains coincide with the biblical account of the destruction of this walled fortress. In an article published in *Biblical Archaeology Review* (Mar./Apr. 1990), Bryant G. Wood, visiting professor to the department of Near Eastern Studies at the University of Toronto, presented evidence that the biblical report is accurate. His detailed investigation yielded the following conclusions:

First, the city that once existed on this site was strongly fortified, corresponding to the biblical record in Joshua 2:5, 7, 15; 6:5, 20.

Second, the ruins give evidence that the city was attacked after harvest time in the spring, corresponding to Joshua 2:6; 3:15; 5:10.

Third, as reported in Joshua 6:1, the inhabitants did not have the opportunity to flee with their foodstuffs from the invading army.

Fourth, the siege was short, not allowing the inhabitants to consume the food that was stored in the city, as Joshua 6:15 indicates.

Fifth, the walls were leveled in such a way as to provide access into the city for the invaders, as Joshua 6:20 records.

Sixth, the city was *not* plundered[13] by the invaders, according to God's instructions in Joshua 6:17–18.

Seventh, the city was burned after the walls had been destroyed, just as Joshua 6:24 says.

---

[12]See also Gleason Archer, *SOTI*, 253–62.

[13]Meaning, they did not keep the goods for themselves but rather took them for the Lord's treasury.

Although some dispute that these clues are from the right time period, their strong similarity would argue that they are. Furthermore, the time periods are not set with absolute certainty and are subject to revision, which some scholars have suggested. At any rate, the possibility that this is indeed the remains of Joshua's Jericho has not been disproved, and no scientific disproof of the biblical story of Jericho has been established. What is more, even if there were no remaining evidence, it would not prove that the event did not occur. It is possible that the evidence was destroyed or that it is in another place. The argument that "no evidence has been found, therefore, there is none" is tenuous at best, involving the well-known fallacy of the argument from ignorance.

THE HISTORICITY OF THE MONARCHY OF ISRAEL (1 SAMUEL–2 CHRONICLES)

Saul became the first king of Israel, and his fortress at Gibeah has been excavated. One of the more noteworthy finds was that slingshots were one of the most important weapons of the day. This relates not only to David's victory over Goliath but also to the reference of Judges 20:16 that there were seven hundred expert slingers who "could sling a stone at a hair and not miss."

Upon Saul's death, Samuel tells us that Saul's armor was put in the temple of Ashtoreth (a Canaanite fertility goddess) at Beth Shan (1 Sam. 31:10), while Chronicles says that his head was put in the temple of Dagon, the Philistine corn god (1 Chron. 10:10). This was thought to be an error because it seemed unlikely that enemy peoples (Canaanites and Philistines) would have temples in the same place at the same time. However, excavations have found that there are two temples at this site that are separated by a hallway—one for Dagon, and the other for Ashtoreth. It appears that the Philistines had adopted the Canaanite goddess as their own.

One of the key accomplishments of David's reign was the capture of Jerusalem. This was problematic in that the Scriptures say the Israelites entered the city by way of a tunnel that led to the Pool of Siloam. That pool was thought to be *outside* the city walls at that time; however, in the 1960s excavations it was finally determined that the wall did indeed extend well past the pool.

Archaeological substantiation has now been found for King David. An inscription from the ninth century speaks of "the House of David," which lays to rest the skeptical contention that David was a legend invented during the Babylonian exile. What adds weight to the evidence is that this inscription was not written by Hebrew scribes but by the enemies of Israel a little more than a century after David's lifetime (Sheler, *IBT*, 50–51).

The psalms attributed to David are often said to have been written much later because their inscriptions suggest that there were musicians' guilds (e.g., the sons of Korah), which were not believed to have existed during his era. Such organization has led many to think that these hymns should be dated to about the time of the Maccabeans in the second century B.C. Following the excavations at Ras Shamra, and knowing now that there were such guilds in Syria and Palestine in David's time, it is unreasonable to attribute such psalms to another period.

The time of Solomon has no less corroboration from archaeology. The site of his temple cannot be excavated, because it is near the Muslim holy place, the Dome of the Rock. However, what is known about Philistine temples built in Solomon's time fits well with the design, decoration, and materials described in the Bible. The only piece of evidence from the temple itself is a small ornament, a pomegranate, that sat on the end of a rod and bears the inscription, "Belonging to the Temple of Yahweh." It was first seen in a shop in Jerusalem in 1979, verified in 1984, and was acquired by the Israel Museum in 1988.

The excavation of Gezer in 1969 ran across a massive layer of ash that covered most of the mound. Sifting through the ash yielded pieces of Hebrew, Egyptian, and Philistine artifacts. Apparently all three cultures had been there at the same time, which puzzled researchers greatly until they realized that the Bible told them exactly what they had found.

> Pharaoh king of Egypt had attacked and captured Gezer. He had set it on fire. He killed its Canaanite inhabitants and then gave it as a wedding gift to his daughter, Solomon's wife. (1 Kings 9:16)

The Historicity of the Assyrian Invasion (2 Kings 17)

A great deal is known about the Assyrians because of 26,000 tablets found in the palace of Ashurbanipal, the son of Esarhaddon, who had taken the northern kingdom of Israel into captivity in 722 B.C. These tablets tell of the many conquests of the Assyrian empire and record with honor the cruel and violent punishments that fell upon the conquered.

Several of these records confirm the Bible's accuracy; every reference in the Old Testament to an Assyrian king has proven correct. Even though Sargon was unknown for some time, when his palace was found and excavated, there was a wall painting of the battle mentioned in Isaiah 20. Also, the Black Obelisk of Shalmaneser adds to our knowledge of biblical figures by showing Jehu (or his emissary) bowing down to the king of Assyria.

Kaiser lists a detailed confirmation from this period with point-for-point comparison between archaeological finds and the biblical text. In conclusion he adds,

The facts, from whatever source, when fully known have consistently provided uncanny confirmation for the details of Old Testament persons, peoples and places by means of the artificial, stratigraphical and epigraphic remains evidence uncovered. (*OTDATR*, 108.)

Among the most interesting finds is Sennacherib's account of the siege of Jerusalem. Thousands of his men died and the rest scattered when he attempted to take the city and, as Isaiah had foretold, he was unable to conquer it. Since he could not boast about his great victory here, Sennacherib found a way to make himself sound good without admitting defeat:

> As to Hezekiah, the Jew, he did not submit to my yoke. I laid siege to 46 of his strong cities, walled forts, and to the countless small villages in their vicinity. . . . I drove out of them 200,150 people, young and old, male and female, horses, mules, donkeys, camels, big and small cattle beyond counting and considered (them) booty. Himself I made a prisoner in Jerusalem, his royal residence, like a bird in a cage. (Pritchard, *ANET*, 288.)

The Historicity of the Babylonian Captivity
(2 Kings 24–25; 2 Chronicles 36)

Various facets of the Old Testament history regarding the Captivity have been confirmed. Records found in Babylon's famous Hanging Gardens have shown that Jehoiachin and his five sons were given a monthly ration and a place to live and were treated well (2 Kings 25:27–30).

The name of Belshazzar (from Daniel 5) had caused problems, because there was not only no mention of him but also no room for him in the list of Babylonian kings. However, it was discovered that Nabodonius, his father, appointed Belshazzar to reign for a few years in his absence. Hence, Nabodonius was still king, but Belshazzar ruled in the capital.

Also, the edict of Cyrus as recorded by Ezra seemed to fit the picture of Isaiah's prophecies too well to be real, until a cylinder was found that confirmed the decree in all the important details.

In every period of Old Testament history, we find that there is good evidence from archaeology that the Scriptures speak the truth. In many instances, the Bible even reflects firsthand knowledge of the times and customs it describes. While many have doubted the accuracy of the Bible, time and continued research have consistently demonstrated that the Word of God is better informed than its critics.

THE HISTORICITY OF THE POST-CAPTIVITY PERIOD
(EZRA–NEHEMIAH)

The biblical books covering this period of time include Ezra, Nehemiah, Esther, Haggai, Zechariah, and Malachi. (The last three were prophets during the time of Ezra and Nehemiah.) The history of this period is well attested, since it overlaps with the height of the Medo-Persian empire; the kings and other figures of that period are well known to ancient historians, such as Cyrus (Ezra 1:2), Darius (Ezra 6:1), Artaxerses (Ezra 7:1), and Sanballat (Neh. 4:1).

Many archaeological finds support the biblical accounts, including the Elephantine Papyri, which mention Johanan the high priest and Sanballat the Samarian governor. Also, the palace at Susa (Shushan), the setting of the book of Esther and King Xerxes (Esther 1:1–2), has been unearthed.[14] The problems of the precise dating of Ezra and Nehemiah do not affect their historicity in this overall time period and have been adequately answered by noted Old Testament scholars like Gleason Archer[15] and John Whitcomb.[16]

CONCLUSION

Negative higher criticism of the Old Testament, based as it is on philosophical presuppositions and not factual data, has crumbled under the facts of archaeological discoveries. Again, as the dean of twentieth-century archaeologists has demonstrated, *"There can be no doubt that archaeology has confirmed the substantial historicity of the Old Testament tradition"* (Albright, *ARI*, 176).

Indeed, while literally thousands of finds have validated the picture presented in the Old Testament, none have refuted it. Noted biblical scholar Donald J. Wiseman affirmed,

> The geography of Bible lands and visible remains of antiquity were gradually recorded until today more than 25,000 sites within this region and dating to Old Testament times, in their broadest sense, have been located. ("ACOT" in *RB*, 301–02.)

Finally, Nelson Glueck has boldly asserted:

> As a matter of fact . . . it may be stated categorically that *no archaeological discovery has ever controverted a biblical reference.* Scores of archaeological findings have been made which confirm in clear outline or exact detail historical statements in the Bible. (*RD*, 31, emphasis added.)

SOURCES

Albright, William F. *Archaeology and Religion of Israel.*

———. *The Archaeology of Palestine.*

---

[14]See Gleason Archer, *A Survey of Old Testament Introduction*, 418–20.
[15]Ibid., 410f.
[16]See *Darius the Mede*.

———. *The Biblical Period.*

———. *From Stone Age to Christianity.*

———. "William F. Albright: Toward a More Conservative View" in *Christianity Today* (18 January 1963).

Archer, Gleason. *An Encyclopedia of Biblical Difficulties.*

———. *A Survey of Old Testament Introduction.*

Bimson, John, and David Livingston. "Redating the Exodus" in *Biblical Archeology Review* (Sept./Oct. 1987).

Blaiklock, E. M., and R. K. Harrison, eds. *The New International Dictionary of Biblical Archaeology.*

Christian Century (19 November 1958).

Collins, David. "Was Noah's Ark Stable?" in *Creation Research Society Quarterly* (Vol. 14, Sept. 1977).

Custance, Arthur. *The Flood: Local or Global?*

Fisher, E. "New Testament Documents Among the Dead Sea Scrolls?" in *The Bible Today.*

Geisler, Norman. "Genealogies, Open or Closed" in *Baker Encyclopedia of Christian Apologetics.*

———. "Science and the Bible" in *Baker Encyclopedia of Christian Apologetics.*

Geisler, Norman, and Thomas Howe. *When Critics Ask.*

Geisler, Norman, and William Nix. *A General Introduction to the Bible.*

Glueck, Nelson. *Rivers in the Desert.*

Kaiser, Walter. *The Old Testament Documents: Are They Reliable?*

Kitchen, Kenneth. *Ancient Orient and the Old Testament.*

Kline, Meredith. *The Treaty of the Great King.*

Lewis, Jack. *The English Bible.*

Lubenow, Marvin. *Bones of Contention.*

Pritchard, James, ed. *Ancient Near East Texts.*

Reiwinkel, Alfred. *The Flood.*

Sheler, Jeffery. *Is the Bible True?*

Vos, Howard H. "Albright, William Foxwell" in *The Dictionary of Evangelical Theology*, Walter Elwell, ed.

Whitcomb, John. *Darius the Mede.*

Whitcomb, John, and Henry Morris. *The Genesis Flood.*

Wilson, Clifford A. *Rocks, Relics, and Biblical Reliability.*

Wiseman, P. J. *Ancient Records and the Structure of Genesis.*

Woodmorappe, John. *Noah's Ark: A Feasibility Study.*

Yamauchi, Edwin. *The Stones and the Scriptures.*

Young, David A. *The Biblical Flood.*

CHAPTER TWENTY-SIX

THE HISTORICITY OF
THE NEW TESTAMENT

F ew scholars have denied the complete historicity of the New Testament.[1] Even Rudolph Bultmann (1884–1976), in his programmatic
demythologization of the New Testament, said, "By no means are we at the
mercy of those who doubt or deny that Jesus ever lived" ("SSG" in *FC*, 60).
The reason that so few historians or biblical scholars deny the New Testament's historicity will become clear as the mass of evidence is viewed.

The historicity of the New Testament is basically the historicity of the
Gospels, the book of Acts, and the early epistles of Paul, since those documents written after the end of Acts are of no consequence in establishing
the life, death, and resurrection of Christ, which is at the heart of the question regarding the historicity of the New Testament.

Most of the negative criticism of the Bible is pre-archaeological, based
on unproven philosophical presuppositions that have subsequently been
antiquated by archaeology. As with the Old Testament, the positive case for
the historical reliability of the New Testament is based on two main points:
the reliability of the New Testament manuscripts and the reliability of the
New Testament witnesses.

Of course, this whole discussion is predicated on the prior premise that
history is knowable, a premise that has come under increasing attack in the

---

[1]One rare exception is G. A. Wells, who suggests the possibility that Jesus never lived, though he
admits Jesus may have been an obscure man who perhaps lived centuries before Paul's time
(*Did Jesus Ever Exist?* chapter 5). Philosopher Michael Martin supports the view that we are
justified in questioning all but the barest data concerning the historical Jesus (see *The Case
Against Christianity*, chapter 2).

contemporary postmodern world. Since the objectivity of history is treated elsewhere (see chapter 11), it will not be discussed here.

THE RELIABILITY OF THE NEW TESTAMENT MANUSCRIPTS

There are several lines of evidence that support the reliability of the New Testament manuscripts. These include the number, dating, accuracy, and confirmation of the available manuscripts.

The Number of New Testament Manuscripts

Like the Old Testament, the number of New Testament manuscripts is overwhelming compared with the typical book from antiquity, which has only seven to ten manuscript copies. By contrast, the New Testament has almost 5,700 Greek manuscripts in existence—*this makes it the best textually supported book from antiquity*. As mentioned previously, the most for any other book is Homer's *Iliad*, with 643 manuscripts (see Geisler and Nix, *GIB*, chapter 22).

The Early Date of the New Testament Manuscripts

The earliest undisputed manuscript of a New Testament book is the John Rylands Papyri (P52, dated A.D. 117–138), which survives from within about a generation of the time most scholars believe it was composed (c. A.D. 95). Since it was written in Asia Minor and was found in Egypt, the demand for some circulation time would place the composition of John in the first century. Whole New Testament books (e.g., the Bodmer Papyri) are available from A.D. 200, and most of the New Testament, including all the Gospels, are available in the Chester Beatty Papyri from 150 years after the New Testament was finished (viz., c. A.D. 250).

Noted British manuscript scholar Sir Frederick Kenyon wrote:

> The interval then between the dates of original composition and the earliest extant evidence becomes so small as to be in fact negligible, and the last foundation for any doubt that the Scriptures have come down to us substantially as they were written has now been removed. [Thus] both the *authenticity* and the general *integrity* of the books of the New Testament may be regarded as finally established. (*BA*, 288f.)

No other book from the ancient world has as small a time gap (between composition and the earliest manuscript copies) as the New Testament.

The Accuracy of the New Testament Manuscripts

Additionally, not only are there more and earlier manuscripts of the New Testament but they are also more accurately copied than other books from the ancient world. New Testament scholar John A. T. Robinson (1919–1981) said,

> The wealth of manuscripts, and above all the narrow interval of time between the writing and the earliest extant, make it the best attested of any ancient writing in the world. (*CWTNT*, 36.)

Bruce Metzger, the great New Testament scholar and Princeton professor, made a comparison of the *Iliad* of Homer, the *Mahabarata* of Hinduism, and the New Testament. He found the text of the *Mahabarata* to represent 90 percent of the original (10 percent textual corruption), the text of the *Iliad* to be 95 percent pure, and the New Testament text to be only one half of one percent in question, or 99.5 percent intact (*CHNTTC*, 144f.). John A. T. Robinson estimated the general concern of textual criticism to be with only a "thousandth part of the entire text" (*ITCNT*, 14). *This would place the accuracy of the New Testament text at 99.9 percent— again, the best known for any book from the ancient world.*[2]

Further, significant portions of some ancient books are missing; for example, "107 of Livy's 142 books of Roman history have been lost. Of Tacitus's original Histories and Annals, only approximately half remain."[3] Yet *all* of the books of the New Testament have been preserved; no significant portion of any New Testament book is missing. Sir Frederick Kenyon noted,

> The number of manuscripts of the New Testament, of early translations from it, and of quotations from it in the oldest writers of the Church, is so large that it is practically certain that the true reading of every doubtful passage is preserved in some one or the other of these ancient authorities. *This can be said of no other ancient book in the world.* (*OBAM*, 55.)

The Confirmation of the New Testament Manuscripts by Early Church Fathers

Speaking of the four Gospels alone, there are some 19,368 citations of the Fathers from the late first century onward. This includes 268 by Justin Martyr, 1,038 by Irenaeus, 1,017 by Clement of Alexandria, 9,231 by Origen, 3,822 by Tertullian, 734 by Hippolytus, and 3,258 by Eusebius (Geisler and Nix, *GIB*, 431). Even before these men there were citations: Pseudo-Barnabas (A.D. 70–130) cited Matthew, Mark, and Luke; Clement of Rome

---

[2]Muslims claim the text of the Qur'an is perfect, but this is not contrary to our conclusion for two reasons: *First*, the Qur'an is not from the ancient world but from the medieval world (seventh century A.D.); *second*, there *are* textual imperfections in the Qur'an (see Geisler and Saleeb, *Answering Islam*, 191–92).

[3]See Gary Habermas, "Why I Believe the New Testament Is Historically Reliable" in Norman Geisler and Paul Hoffman, eds., *Why I Am a Christian*, 148.

(c. A.D. 95–97) cited Matthew, John, and 1 Corinthians; Ignatius (c. A.D. 110) referred to six of Paul's epistles; Polycarp (c. A.D. 110–150) quoted all four Gospels, Acts, and most of Paul's epistles; the Shepherd of Hermas (A.D. 115–140) cited Matthew, Mark, Acts, 1 Corinthians, and other books; the Didache (c. A.D. 120–150) referred to Matthew, Luke, 1 Corinthians, and other books; and Papias, companion of Polycarp, who was the disciple of the apostle John, quotes his gospel.

All of this argues powerfully that the Gospels were in existence before they were cited, which would place them well before the end of the first century while some eyewitnesses (like John) were still alive. Further, that some of these Fathers overlapped with the latest book of the New Testament, the gospel of John, which is widely believed to be dated around A.D. 95, virtually eliminates any time gap between the completion of the New Testament and the earliest citations of it.

THE RELIABILITY OF THE NEW TESTAMENT ACCOUNTS

Not only is there an extremely strong manuscript tradition supporting the conclusion that the present text of the New Testament is a highly accurate representation of the original, but there is also abundant evidence that the account of the life of Christ contained therein is also highly reliable history. Since the evidence for the historical reliability of the book of Acts is the strongest, we will begin there.

The Historicity of Acts

The date and authenticity of the book of Acts is crucial to the historicity of early Christianity and, thus, to apologetics in general. If Acts was written before A.D. 70 while the eyewitnesses were still alive, then it has great historical value in informing us of the earliest Christian beliefs. What is more, if Acts was written by Luke, the companion of the apostle Paul, it is placed in the apostolic circle of the earliest disciples of Jesus.

If Acts was written by A.D. 62 (the traditional date), then it was written by a contemporary of Jesus (who died in A.D. 33). And if Acts is shown to be accurate history, then it brings credibility to its reports about the most basic Christian beliefs in the miracles (Acts 2:22), death (Acts 2:23), resurrection (Acts 2:24, 29–32), and ascension of Christ (Acts 1:9–10). Further, if Luke wrote Acts, then his "former treatise" (Acts 1:1), the gospel of Luke, should be extended the same credibility manifested in the book of Acts.

Strong Evidence of an Early Date for Acts

Roman historian Colin Hemer numbers seventeen reasons for accepting the traditional early date of Acts (during the lifetime of the contemporaries of the events). These reasons strongly support the historicity of Acts and, indirectly, the historicity of the gospel of Luke (cf. Luke 1:1–4 and Acts 1:1).

The first five of Hemer's arguments are sufficient to show that Acts was penned by A.D. 62.

(1) There is no mention in Acts of the crucial historical event of the fall of Jerusalem in A.D. 70, which places Acts before that event.

(2) There is no hint of the outbreak of the Jewish War in 66 or of any serious or specific deterioration of relations between Romans and Jews, which implies Acts was written before that time.

(3) There is no hint of the more immediate deterioration of Christian relations with Rome involved in the Neronian persecution of the late 60s.

(4) There is no hint of the death of James at the hands of the Sanhedrin in c. 62, recorded by Josephus (*Antiquities*, 20.9.1.200).

(5) Since the apostle Paul was still alive (Acts 28), it must have been written before his death (c. A.D. 65).

Consider also some of the other arguments:

(1) Primitive formulation of Christian terminology is used in Acts, which reflects an earlier period. (Harnack lists a number of Christological titles: *Iesous* [Jesus] and *ho kurios* [the Lord] are used often, whereas *ho Christos* always designates "the Messiah," and not a proper name, and *Christos* is otherwise used only in formal combinations.)

(2) Rackham points to the optimistic tone of Acts, which would not have been there after Judaism had been destroyed and Christians martyred in the Neronian persecutions of the late 60s.

(3) The abrupt ending of the book of Acts is a factor. Surely, if Paul had died by then, for example, that would have been mentioned (cf. 2 Tim. 4:6–8).

(4) The "immediacy" of Acts 27–28 comes into play.

(5) The prevalence of insignificant details of a cultural milieu of an early, even Julio-Claudian, date shows evidence.

(6) There are areas of controversy within Acts that presuppose the relevance of an early Jewish setting while the Temple was still standing (see Colin Hemer, *The Book of Acts in the Setting of Hellenistic History* [Winona Lake, Ind.: Eisenbraun, 1990], 376–87.)

By comparison, claiming that Acts was written after A.D. 62 is like claiming that a book on the life of John F. Kennedy was written after 1963 (when he was assassinated) but never mentions his death; *if the event had already occurred, it was too important to omit.* In the same way, any book like Acts that was written after the death of the apostle Paul (c. A.D. 65) or the destruction of Jerusalem (A.D. 70) would surely have mentioned these momentous events.

Evidence That the Author of Acts was a First-Rate Historian

In addition to the arguments for an early date for Acts, Hemer demonstrates that the author was an historian of note. These points include:

(1) items of geographical detail and the like, which may be assumed to have been generally known;

(2) more specialized details, which may still have been widely known to those who possessed relevant experience: titles of governors, army units, major routes, etc., which may have been accessible to those who traveled or were involved in administration, but perhaps not to those without such backgrounds;

(3) specifics of local routes, boundaries, titles of city magistrates, and the like, which may not be closely controllable in date, but are unlikely to have been known except to a writer who had visited the districts;

(4) the correlation of the dates of known kings and governors with the ostensible chronology of the Acts framework;

(5) details appropriate to the date of Paul but not appropriate to the conditions of a date earlier or especially later;

(6) "undesigned coincidences" between Acts and the accepted Pauline Epistles;

(7) latent internal correlations within Acts;

(8) independently attested details that agree with the Alexandrian against the Western text (or the reverse), and may thus relate to stages in the textual tradition of Acts;

(9) matters of common geographical knowledge or the like, mentioned perhaps informally or allusively, with an unstudied accuracy that bespeaks familiarity;

(10) differences in formulation within Acts as a possible indication of different categories of sources;

(11) peculiarities in the selection of detail, such as the inclusion of details theologically unimportant, but explicable in other ways that may bear on the historical question;

(12) as a particular case of the preceding, details whose "immediacy" suggests the author's reproduction of recent experience and which are less readily explicable as the product of longer-term reflective editing and shaping;

(13) items reflecting culture or idiom that are suggestive of a first- rather than a second-century atmosphere;

(14) interrelated complexes in which two or more kinds of correlation are combined, or where related details each show separate corre-

lations, so that the possibility arises of building a larger fragment of historical reconstruction from a jigsaw of interlocking units;

(15) cases where the progress of discovery and knowledge simply provide new background information of use to the commentator of whatever viewpoint, while not bearing significantly on the issue of historicity;

(16) precise details that lie within the range of contemporary possibilities, but whose particular accuracy we have no means of verifying one way or the other. (*ASHH*, chapter 5.)

In addition to all this, the author of Acts demonstrates detailed knowledge of the historical names, places, persons, and events of the times.

Common Knowledge

The emperor's *title*, "Augustus," is rendered formally *Sebastos* in words attributed to a Roman official (Acts 25:21, 25), whereas "Augustus" as the *name* bestowed on the first emperor is transliterated *Augoustos* in Luke 2:1.

General facts of navigation and corn supply are exemplified by the voyage of an Alexandrian ship to the Italian port of Puteoli, following the institution of a state system of supply by Claudius, and allowing illustration at many levels.

The limits of the category may be illustrated by noting where Luke thinks it necessary or unnecessary to explain terms to his reader. Thus points of Judaean topography or Semitic nomenclature are glossed over or explained (Acts 1:12, 19, etc.), whereas basic Jewish institutions are not (Acts 1:12 again; 2:1; 4:1; etc.).

Specialized Knowledge

Acts 1:12, 19; 3:2, 11, etc., show knowledge of the topography of Jerusalem. In Acts 4:6 Annas is pictured as continuing to have great prestige and to bear the title "high priest" after his formal deposition by the Romans and the appointment of Caiaphas (cf. Luke 3:2; cf. Josephus, *A*, 18.2.2.34–35; 20.9.1.198).

In addition, Luke (in Acts 12:4) gives detail on the organization of a military guard (cf. Vegetius, *de Re Milit* [3.8]); in Acts 13:7 he correctly identifies Cyprus as a proconsular (senatorial) province at this time, with the proconsul resident at Paphos (v. 6); in Acts 16:8ff. he acknowledges the part played by Troas in the system of communication (cf. Section C, 112f. *ad* 16:11); in Acts 17:1 Amphipolis and Apollonia are known as stations (and presumably overnight stops) on the Egnatian Way from Philippi to Thessalonica. Chapters 27–28 contain many details in the geography and navigational details of the voyage to Rome, which will be noted more specifically under other headings.

Specific Local Knowledge

In addition, Luke manifests an incredible array of knowledge of local places, names, conditions, customs, and circumstances that befit only an eyewitness contemporary of the time and events. All of these have been confirmed by historical and archaeological research to be true of the persons, times, and places mentioned by Luke. This includes knowledge of:

(1) a natural crossing between correctly named ports (13:4–5);

(2) the proper port (Perga) along the direct destination of a ship crossing from Cyprus (13:13);

(3) the proper location of Lycaonia (14:6);

(4) the unusual but correct declension of the name Lystra (14:6);

(5) the correct language spoken in Lystra (Lycaonian, 14:11);

(6) two gods known to be so associated (Zeus and Hermes, 14:12);

(7) the proper port, Attalia, that returning travelers would use (14:25);

(8) the correct order of approach to Derbe, then Lystra, from Cilician Gates (16:1);

(9) the proper form of the name Troas (16:8);

(10) the place of a conspicuous sailor's landmark, Samothrace (16:11);

(11) the proper description of Philippi as a Roman colony (16:12);

(12) the right location for the river (Gangites) near Philippi (16:13);

(13) the proper association of Thyatira as a center of dyeing (16:14);

(14) the correct designations for the magistrates and of the colony (16:22);

(15) the proper location (Amphipolis and Apollonia) of where travelers would spend successive nights on this journey (17:1);

(16) the presence of a synagogue in Thessalonica (17:1);

(17) the proper title, "politarchs," used of the magistrates there (17:6);

(18) the correct implication that sea travel is the most convenient way of reaching Athens with favoring east winds of summer sailing (17:14);

(19) the abundant presence of images in Athens (17:16);

(20) the reference to a synagogue in Athens (17:17);

(21) the depiction of the Athenian life of philosophical debate in the Agora (17:17);

(22) the use of the correct Athenian slang word for Paul, *a spermologos* (17:18), as well as the court (*areios pagos*);

(23) the proper characterization of the Athenian character (17:21);

(24) an altar to an "unknown god" (17:23);

(25) the proper reaction of Greek philosophers who denied bodily resurrection (17:32);

(26) *areopagites* as the correct title for a member of the court (17:34);

(27) a Corinthian synagogue (18:4);

(28) the correct designation of Gallio as proconsul, resident in Corinth (18:12);

(29) the proper positioning of the *bema*, overlooking Corinth's *forum* (18:16f.);

(30) the name "Tyrannus" as attested from Ephesus in first-century inscriptions (19:9);

(31) the well-known shrines and images of Artemis (19:24);

(32) the reference to the well-attested "great goddess Artemis" (19:27);

(33) the Ephesian theater as the meeting-place of the city (19:29);

(34) the use of the correct title, *grammateus*, for the chief executive magistrate in Ephesus (19:35);

(35) the mention of the proper title of honor, *neokoros*, authorized by the Romans (19:35);

(36) the correct name to designate the goddess (19:37);

(37) the proper term used for those holding court (19:38);

(38) the use of plural, *anthupatoi*, which may be a remarkable reference to the fact that *two* men were conjointly exercising the functions of proconsul at this time (19:38);

(39) the "regular" assembly as the precise phrase is attested elsewhere (19:39);

(40) the use of precise ethnic designation, *beroiaios* (20:4);

(41) the employment of the ethnic term *Asianos* (20:4);

(42) the implied recognition of the strategic importance assigned to this city of Troas (20:7f);

(43) the danger of a coastal trip in this location (20:13);

(44) the correct knowledge of sequence of places (20:14–15);

(45) the correct name of the city as a neuter plural (Patara) (21:1);

(46) the appropriate route passing across the open sea south of Cyprus favored by persistent northwest winds (21:3);

(47) the suitable distance between these cities (21:7–8);

(48) this characteristically Jewish act of piety (21:24);

(49) the Jewish law regarding Gentile use of the Temple area (21:28);

(50) the permanent stationing of a Roman cohort at Antonia to suppress any disturbance at festival times (21:31);

(51) the flight of steps used by the guards (21:31, 35);

(52) the common way to obtain Roman citizenship at this time (22:28);

(53) the knowledge that the tribune is impressed with Roman rather than Tarsian citizenship (22:29);

(54) the fact that Ananias is high priest at the time (23:2);

(55) the fact that Felix is governor at this time (23:24);

(56) the natural stopping-point on the way to Caesarea (23:31);

(57) the fact of whose jurisdiction Cilicia was at the time (23:34);

(58) the provincial penal procedure of the time (24:1–9);

(59) the fact that the name "Porcius Festus" agrees precisely with that given by Josephus (24:27);

(60) the right of appeal for Roman citizens (25:11);

(61) the legal formula *de quibus cognoscere volebam* (25:18);

(62) the characteristic form of reference to the emperor at the time (25:26);

(63) the best shipping lanes at the time (27:4f.);

(64) the common bonding of Cilicia and Pamphylia (27:4);

(65) the principal port to find a ship sailing to Italy (27:5);

(66) the slow passage to Cnidus in the face of the typical northwest wind (27:7);

(67) the right route to sail in view of the winds (27:7);

(68) the locations of Fair Havens and the neighboring site of Lasea (27:8);

(69) the fact that Fair Havens was a poorly sheltered roadstead (27:12);

(70) a noted tendency of a south wind in these climes to back suddenly to a violent northeaster, the well-known *gregale* (27:13);

(71) the nature of a square-rigged ancient ship, having no option but to be driven before a gale (27:16–17);

(72) the precise place and name of this island (27:16);

(73) the appropriate maneuvers for the safety of the ship in its particular plight (27:16f.);

(74) the fourteenth night in a remarkable calculation, based inevitably on a compounding of estimates and probabilities, confirmed in the judgment of experienced Mediterranean navigators (27:27);

(75) the proper term of the time for the Adriatic (27:27);

(76) the precise term (*bolisantes*) to be used for taking soundings (27:28);

(77) the position that admirably was the probable line of approach of a ship now released again to run before an easterly wind (27:39);

(78) the severe liability on guards who permitted a prisoner to escape (27:42);

(79) the local people and superstitions of the day (28:4–6);

(80) the proper title *protos (tes nesou)* (28:7);

(81) Rhegium as a refuge to await a southerly wind to carry them through the strait (28:13);

(82) Appii Forum and Tres Tabernae as correctly placed stopping-places on the Appian Way (28:15);

(83) appropriate means of custody with Roman soldiers (28:16);

(84) the conditions of imprisonment, living "at his own expense" (28:30–31).

Conclusion

The historicity of the book of Acts is confirmed by overwhelming evidence. Nothing like this amount of detailed confirmation exists for any other book from antiquity. Acts is not only a direct confirmation of the earliest Christian belief in the death and resurrection of Christ, but also indirectly of the gospel record, for the same author (Luke) wrote a gospel as well (see below). Further, substantially the same basic events are recorded in two other gospels (Matthew and Mark), and for that matter the gospel of John provides the same picture of the most crucial events, namely, the death and resurrection of Christ. Thus, the historicity of the events most crucial to orthodox Christianity is thereby established.

Another noted Roman historian, A. N. Sherwin-White, calls the mythological view "unbelievable" (*RSRLNT*, 189). The reason for this is that the evidence for the book of Acts is much stronger than that for Roman history of that period.

The Historicity of the Gospel Accounts

Since Matthew and Mark provide the same basic data on the life, teaching, death, and resurrection of Christ, what argues for the authenticity of one also argues for the historicity of the other. Thus we will concentrate on Luke, since there are numerous arguments to support its historicity.

The Author of Luke Is Known to Be an Accurate Historian

Dr. Luke, travel companion of the apostle Paul, is widely believed to be the author of the book of Luke for many good reasons. *First,* the author of Acts

(1) was highly educated, judging by the good Greek he used (cf. Luke 1:1–4);
(2) was not one of the twelve apostles (Luke 1:2);
(3) was a participant in many events himself (Luke 1:3);
(4) was knowledgeable about the apostle Paul;
(5) knew and quoted the Old Testament in Greek;
(6) had a good knowledge of the political and social situation in the first century;
(7) was a traveler with the apostle Paul at times, as indicated by the "we" sections (Acts 16:10–17; 20:5–21:18; 27:1–28:16);
(8) was not Timothy, Sopater, Aristarchus, Secundus, Gaius, Tychicus, or Trophimus, who are excluded by Acts 20:4;
(9) had knowledge of medicine, as indicated by his use of medical

terms and references. The only companion of Paul known to fit all these characteristics was "Luke the beloved physician" (Col. 4:14 NKJV).[4]

However, it is not the question of who wrote the book that is important, but whether or not he was a reliable source. As R. T. France noted, "Authorship . . . is not a major factor in our assessment of the reliability of the Gospels" (*TEJ*, 124).

Second, the same person who wrote Acts also wrote the gospel of Luke, since

(1) both are written to "Theophilus" (cf. Luke 1:3 with Acts 1:1);
(2) both are written in excellent Greek;
(3) both show a medical interest;
(4) Acts refers to a "former account" the author had written about Jesus (Acts 1:1);
(5) there is an unbroken and virtually unchallenged tradition from the era of the early Christian church till modern times attributing it to Dr. Luke.

Third, the author of Acts is known to be a top-notch historian (see above), a fact established by both Sir William Ramsey in *St. Paul the Traveler and the Roman Citizen* and more recently by Colin Hemer in *The Book of Acts in the Setting of Hellenstic History*.[5] Another noted Roman historian strongly supports the historicity of the Gospels, saying,

> So it is astonishing that while Greco-Roman historians have been growing in confidence, the twentieth-century study of the gospel narratives, starting from no less promising material, have taken so gloomy a turn in the development of form-criticism . . . that the historical Christ is unknowable and the history of his mission cannot be written. This seems very curious. (Sherwin-White, *RSRNT*, 187.)

Thus the aforementioned belief that the idea that these accounts are legendary is simply "unbelievable" (ibid., 188–91).

The Gospel of Luke Was Written by About A.D. 60

From all of this information we can conclude that the gospel of Luke is also an excellent historical work written around A.D. 60. Since Matthew, Mark, and John present the same basic picture of Christ, they too are historically reliable.[6]

---

[4]The external evidence for Acts is also good, having been cited by the Didache, Tatian, Irenaeus, Tertullian, Clement of Alexandria, and Eusebius, and listed in the Muratorian Canon (see D. A. Carson, et al., *An Introduction to the New Testament*, 185–86).

[5]See Colin Hemer, ibid., and William Ramsey, *St. Paul the Traveler and the Roman Citizen*.

[6]For an explanation of the differences in John from the Synoptic Gospels, see Norman Geisler, "John, Gospel of" in *BECA*.

This conclusion is further supported by the fact that Luke states his historical interest in his prologue (Luke 1:1–4), claiming that

(1) he is aware of other earlier written accounts of Christ's life;
(2) the gospel of Luke is based on "eyewitness" testimony;
(3) he had "carefully investigated everything from the beginning."

Furthermore, Luke proves his historical interest by correlating his narration of the life of Christ with secular history and exact dates. He not only tells when Jesus was born (when "Caesar Augustus" was king, Luke 2:1) but also the exact year when Jesus began his ministry, namely, "In the fifteenth year of the reign of Tiberius Caesar—when Pontius Pilate was governor of Judea, Herod tetrarch of Galilee, his brother Philip tetrarch of Iturea and Traconitis, and Lysanias tetrarch of Abilene—during the high priesthood of Annas and Caiaphas, the word of God came to John son of Zechariah in the desert" (Luke 3:1–2). All of these check out with secular history of the time.

Also, Colin Hemer has provided strong arguments for Acts being written by A.D. 62 (see page 472), and since Luke was written before Acts (cf. Luke 1:3 with Acts 1:1), it follows that the gospel of Luke comes from around A.D. 60. But this is only twenty-seven years after Christ died and rose from the dead, which means that many of the generation of the eyewitnesses of Christ of which Luke speaks (Luke 1:2) were still alive when he wrote his gospel, a strong indication of its historical reliability.[7]

William F. Albright (1891–1971) on the Historicity of the Gospels

With a lifetime of research under his belt, the dean of twentieth-century archaeologists wrote:

> In short, thanks to the Qumran discoveries, the New Testament proves to be in fact what it was formerly believed to be: the teaching of Christ and his immediate followers between c. A.D. 25 and c. A.D. 80. (*FSAC*, 23.)

More specifically, Albright affirmed:

> I should answer that, in my opinion, *every book of the New Testament was written by a baptized Jew between the forties and the eighties of the first century* A.D. *(very probably sometime between about* A.D. *50 and 75).* ("WATMCV" in CT, 359, emphasis added.)

He even went so far as to say,

---

[7]This is a "strong indication of its historical reliability," because if Luke was written while eyewitnesses were still alive, it would have been refuted had it contained material that was false.

The evidence from the Qumran community shows that the concepts, terminology, and mindset of the gospel of John is probably early first century. (Davies and Daube, "RDPGSJ" in *BNTIE.*)

Albright also believed:

Biblical historical data are accurate to an extent far surpassing the ideas of any modern critical students, who have consistently tended to err on the side of hypercriticism. (*AP*, 229.)

Since Jesus died about A.D. 33, placing some books in the 50s and 60s would mean that *it was written within twenty to thirty years of the events—* while most of the eyewitnesses were still alive! That there are multiple records involved (eight or nine authors and twenty-seven books) provides a strong basis for the historicity of their writings.

Confirmation by a Liberal Critic of the New Testament

New Testament scholar John A. T. Robinson was noted for his role in spawning the "Death of God" movement in the twentieth century. Before he died and without recanting his negative views on Scripture, Bishop Robinson wrote a revealing book entitled *Redating the New Testament.* In it he places Matthew at c. A.D. 40–60+; Mark at c. A.D. 45–60; Luke at c. A.D. 57–60+; and John at c. A.D. 40–65+ (*RNT*, 352–354). This would mean that *some gospels could be as early as seven to twelve years after the time Jesus died!* Even by the outer limits they were all composed within the time frame of the eyewitnesses and contemporaries of the events. This is much too early to deny their basic historicity.

Possible Confirmations by Early Fragments of the Gospels

Jose O'Callahan, a Spanish paleographer, made headlines around the world in 1972 for his identification of a manuscript fragment from Qumran as the earliest known piece of the gospel of Mark. Fragments from cave seven had previously been dated between 50 B.C. and A.D. 50 and listed under "not identified" and classified as "Biblical Texts?" Using the accepted methods of papyrology and paleography, O'Callahan eventually identified several fragments from Qumran as follows:

Mark 4:28 7Q6? A.D. 50
Mark 6:48 7Q15 A.D. ?
Mark 6:52,53 7Q5 A.D. 50
Mark 12:17 7Q7 A.D. 50
Acts 27:38 7Q6? A.D. 60+[8]

---

[8]The number with "Q" indicates the cave at Qumran in which each fragment was found.

Both friends and critics acknowledge that, if valid, O'Callahan's conclusions would revolutionize current New Testament theories. The *New York Times* reported:

> If Father O'Callahan's theory is accepted it would prove that at least one of the gospels—that of St. Mark—was written only a few years after the death of Jesus.

The *UPI* noted that O'Callahan's findings indicated that "the people closest to the events—Jesus' original followers—found Mark's report accurate and trustworthy, not myth but true history" (Estrada and White, *FNT*, 137). *Time* magazine quoted scholars who claimed that if O'Callahan is correct, "They can make a bonfire of 70 tons of indigestible German scholarship" (ibid.).

The early dates (listed on page 474) are supported by the following lines of evidence:

(1) They were not dated by O'Callahan but by other scholars prior to his identification of them as New Testament texts.

(2) These dates have never been seriously called into question since that time.

(3) It fits with the dates determined for other manuscripts found in the same Qumran area.

(4) The archaeologists who discovered the cave (number seven) attested that it showed no signs of being opened since it was sealed in A.D. 70, and that its contents date from no later than A.D. 60.

(5) The style of writing (in Greek uncials) has been identified as early first century.

Of course, critics have raised objections, but many reasons are given in support of O'Callahan's identification of these texts with the New Testament, especially of the first two.

First, the criteria for identification of these fragments as New Testament are the normal, acceptable ones used by paleographers.

Second, the whole letters used (and most of the partial ones) were identified by other scholars before O'Callahan identified them.

Third, O'Callahan is a reputable paleographer who has made many successful identifications of ancient texts both before and after this time.

Fourth, his identification of the texts fits perfectly with these New Testament passages.

Fifth, no other viable identification of these fragments has been made with any other texts.

Sixth, the odds that these letter sequences represent some other text are incredibly high. Two scholars calculated the odds at 1 in 2.25 times 10^{65}!

If the identification of even some of these fragments is valid, then the implications for the historicity of the New Testament are enormous. First and foremost, it shows that the gospel of Mark and the book of Acts were written within the lifetime of the apostles and other contemporaries of the events. Also, this early date (before A.D. 50) leaves no time for mythological embellishment of the records; they must be accepted as historical. Furthermore, it argues against a late date for Mark, showing that it was one of the earlier gospels. Finally, since these manuscripts are not originals but copies, it reveals that the New Testament was "published," that is, copied and disseminated during the lifetime of the writers.

The Gospels Are Too Early to Be Mythological

Julius Muller challenged the scholars of his day (c. 1844) to produce even one example where in one generation a myth developed where the most prominent elements are myths (*TM*, 29). No one has ever met the challenge because none exist.

Sherwin-White observed:

> Herodotus enables us to test the tempo of myth-making, and the tests suggest that even two generations are too short a span to allow the mythical tendency to prevail over the hard historic core of the oral tradition. (*RSRLNT*, 190.)

Commenting on this, William Craig noted that this enables us to determine the rate at which legends develop: "The tests show that *even two generations is too short to allow legendary tendencies to wipe out the hard core of historical fact*" (*KTAR*, 101).

Archaeological Confirmation of the Gospels

Anyone familiar with first-century Jewish culture will recognize immediately that the gospel records breathe this same air. The mention of Pharisees, Sadducees, Jewish traditions, customs, and even the use of Aramaic words (cf. Matt. 27:46; Acts 9:36), along with the cities and topography of the land, are all very familiar to other documentation of first-century Judaism as recorded by Josephus and others.

In addition, the New Testament mentions historical figures like Caesar Augustus (Luke 2:1); Tiberius Caesar (Luke 3:1); Quirinius, governor of Syria (Luke 2:2); King Herod (Matt. 2:3); Pontius Pilate (Matt. 27:2); Annas and Caiaphas, the high priests (Luke 3:2); John the Baptist, and others. All of these are known to have existed and operated in the time and place to which the New Testament locates them.

Further, in addition to the overwhelming archaeological support for this overall time period (see above), there are references in the Gospels that are supported by specific archaeological finds, such as the Siloam pool, the pool of Bethesda, the synagogue in Capernaum, the foundation of Herod's temple, Pilate's pratorium, the vicinity of Golgotha, and the Garden Tomb. Likewise, the "Titulus Venetus" helps to illuminate Augustus's census (in Luke 2:1f). A Latin plaque mentions "Pontius Pilatus, Prefect of Judea." Even the bones of a first-century crucifixion victim, Yohanan, support the gruesome presentation of Christ's death. And the Nazareth Decree (found in 1878), perhaps circulated between A.D. 41 and 54, is curious in view of the Jewish claim that Jesus' body had been stolen rather than resurrected (cf. Matt. 28:12–13). Since all previous Roman indictments of this nature involved only a fine, why should such a strong penalty be leveled in Palestine just after Jesus died, was reported to have risen from the tomb, and with His disciples stirring up dissent in Palestine? (see Gary Habermas, *HJ*, 154).

Like the rest of Scripture, the life of Christ portrayed in the Gospels fits perfectly into the known facts unearthed by the archaeology of this period. Nothing has ever been found to contradict it, and numerous finds have supported it.

The Evidence for the Historicity of Paul's Early Epistles

Even liberal critics who reject the later epistles of Paul are in general agreement that Paul wrote 1 Corinthians and that it was composed around A.D. 55. D. A. Carson summarizes the evidence well:

> There is an inscription recording a rescript of the emperor Claudius to the people of Delphi that mentions Gallio as holding the office of proconsul in Achaia during the period of Claudius's twenty-sixth acclamation as *imperator*—a period known from other inscriptions to cover the first seven months of A.D. 52. . . . Paul's two-and-a-half-year stint in Ephesus would have taken him to the autumn of 55. (*INT*, 282–83.)

It was in Ephesus that Paul wrote 1 Corinthians some time before Pentecost (16:8). Because of a possible adjustment by one year of the beginning of Gallio's proconsulship, the date of 1 Corinthians may be A.D. 56.

First Corinthians presents the same basic information about Christ found in the Gospels but some five years earlier than Luke. *This places these documents founding the historicity of Christ's death and resurrection within twenty-two years of the time they happened!* Paul wrote,

> Now, brothers, I want to remind you of the gospel I preached to you, which you received and on which you have taken your stand. By this gospel you are saved, if you hold firmly to the word I preached to you. Otherwise, you have believed in vain. For what I received I passed on to you as of first importance: that Christ died for our sins according to the Scriptures, that he was buried, that he was raised on the third day

according to the Scriptures, and that he appeared to Peter, and then to the Twelve. After that, he appeared to more than five hundred of the brothers at the same time, most of whom are still living, though some have fallen asleep. (1 Cor. 15:1–6)

Several important facts emerge from this text.

First, the essence of the Christian message is the death and resurrection of Christ—the same thing stressed in all four gospels.

Second, Paul said that this message was "handed down" to him, implying that it had come from some time earlier. Some New Testament scholars posit the original message handed to Paul may have been in creedal form, from only a few years after the death of Christ. If so, then it places the central message of the Gospel beyond any reasonable historical doubt (see "Creeds," page 480).

Third, the evidence for the resurrection of Christ rested on over five hundred eyewitnesses, a fact that places it out of the category of reasonable doubt. Paul speaks of over two hundred and fifty eyewitnesses of the Resurrection that were still alive when he wrote (15:6), including "Cephas" (Peter), who was an apostle as one of the eyewitnesses (15:5), "the twelve" (apostles), and James, the brother of Jesus. And this is good evidence for the early date of 1 Corinthians.

Fourth, the readers of 1 Corinthians were contemporaries of the eyewitnesses of the Resurrection, and Paul gave them an implied challenge of checking out the eyewitnesses for themselves, since Paul added that "most of [them] are still living" (15:6).

Fifth, the internal evidence includes:

(1) the repeated claim of the book to be from Paul (1:1, 12–17; 3:4, 6, 22; 16:21);
(2) the many parallels with the book of Acts;
(3) the ring of authenticity from beginning to end;
(4) the mention of five hundred who had seen Christ, most of whom were still alive and could verify Paul's claims (15:6);
(5) the harmony of the contents with what was known about Corinth at the time.

Likewise, the external evidence is powerful from the first and second centuries on, including:

(1) Clement of Rome's epistle to the Corinthians (chapter 47);
(2) the epistle of Barnabas (chapter 4);
(3) the Didache (chapter 10);
(4) the Shepherd of Hermas (chapter 4). There are almost six hundred quotations of this in Irenaeus, Clement of Alexandria, and Tertullian alone, making it one of the best-attested books from its time period.

Sixth, 1 Corinthians, along with 2 Corinthians, Galatians, and Philippians (which are also well attested), not only reveals an historical interest in the events of Jesus' life, but it provides a vast array of details about it also found in the gospel records. Paul speaks of Jesus'

(1) Jewish ancestry (Gal. 3:16);
(2) Davidic descent (Rom. 1:3);
(3) virgin birth (Gal. 4:4);
(4) life under Jewish law (Gal. 4:4);
(5) brothers (1 Cor. 9:5);
(6) twelve disciples (1 Cor. 15:7),
(7) one of whom was named James (1 Cor. 15:7);
(8) that some had wives (1 Cor. 9:5),
(9) and that Paul knew Peter and James (Gal. 1:18–2:16);
(10) poverty (2 Cor. 8:9);
(11) humility (Phil 2:5–7);
(12) meekness and gentleness (2 Cor. 10:1);
(13) abuse by others (Rom. 15:3);
(14) teachings on divorce and remarriage (1 Cor. 7:10–11);
(15) on paying wages of ministers (1 Cor. 9:14);
(16) on paying taxes (Rom. 13:6–7);
(17) on the duty to love one's neighbors (Rom. 13:9);
(18) on Jewish ceremonial uncleanliness (Rom. 14:14);
(19) on His titles of deity (Rom. 1:3–4; 10:9);
(20) on vigilance in view of Jesus' second coming (1 Thess. 4:15),
(21) which would be like a thief in the night (1 Thess. 5:2–11);
(22) on the Lord's Supper (1 Cor. 11:23–25);
(23) sinless life (2 Cor. 5:21);
(24) death on the cross (Rom. 4:25; 5:8; Gal. 3:13; 1 Cor. 15:3),
(25) specifically by crucifixion (Rom. 6:6; Gal. 2:20),
(26) by Jewish instigation (1 Thess. 2:14–15);
(27) burial (1 Cor. 15:4);
(28) resurrection on the "third day" (1 Cor. 15:4);
(29) post-resurrection appearance to the apostles (1 Cor. 15:5–8),
(30) and to other eyewitnesses (1 Cor. 15:6); and
(31) position now at God's right hand (Rom. 8:34).

Such detail is strong support for the historicity of the Gospels, which present the same facts.

Seventh, Paul rests the very truth of Christianity on the historicity of the Resurrection (1 Cor. 15:12f.), and he gives historical details about Jesus' contemporaries, the apostles (1 Cor. 15:5–8), including his own private encounters with Peter and the others (Gal. 1:18f.; 2:1f.). What is more, he notes that more than two hundred and fifty eyewitnesses were still living when he wrote 1 Corinthians, leaving them with the implicit challenge to verify his claims (1 Cor. 15:6). One could scarcely ask for better evidence for the central historical truth of Christianity than is narrated in the four gospels with great detail.

Confirmation of the New Testament by Early "Creeds" or Traditions

A number of scholars point to evidence in the New Testament of earlier creeds or traditions that point to the historicity of the basic message in the Gospels. Since most people in the first century were illiterate, short memorizable statements about Christ were a good way to transmit truth. These "creeds" point to indicators such as rhythm and repetitive patterns, and even the authors note that it is a tradition. Possible examples are found in Luke 24:34; Acts 2:22–24, 30–32; 3:13–15; 4:10–12; 5:29–32; 10:39–41; 13:37–39; Rom. 1:3–4; 4:25; 10:9; 1 Cor. 11:23f.; 15:3–8; Phil. 2:6–11; 1 Tim. 2:6; 3:16; 6:13; 2 Tim. 2:8; 1 Peter 3:18; and 1 John 4:2.[9]

The most interesting of these is found in 1 Corinthians 15:3–8, which affirms:

> For what *I received* I passed on to you as of first importance: *that* Christ died for our sins according to the Scriptures, *that* he was buried, *that* he was raised on the third day according to the Scriptures, and *that* he appeared to Peter, and then to the Twelve. After that, he appeared to more than five hundred of the brothers at the same time, most of whom are still living, though some have fallen asleep. Then he appeared to James, then to all the apostles, and last of all he appeared to me also, as to one abnormally born. (emphasis added)

What is noteworthy here is that this is a teaching that Paul "received" from others—this implies it had been in existence for some time. Habermas notes that numerous critical scholars agree with a surprisingly early date: "Concerning a more exact time, it is very popular to date this creed in the A.D. mid-30s" (*HJ*, 154). Yet Paul is writing around A.D. 55–56. Again, *this would place the origin of this teaching about Jesus' death, burial, resurrection, and appearances to hundreds of persons by conservative estimates within a few short years of the time they happened.*

Confirmation for the New Testament From the Basic Facts Position

Professor Habermas argues from what can be called the basic facts position. Beginning with the truths that almost all critical scholars of the New

---

[9]This list is given by Habermas, ibid., 307, note 80. For a fuller treatment, see his *The Historical Jesus: Ancient Evidence for the Life of Christ*, chapter 7, where he lists forty-one such alleged early creeds.

Testament agree upon, he maintains that the best explanation is that Jesus lived, died, and rose from the dead—all of which is at the heart of the historicity of the New Testament. He lists "at least twelve separate facts [that] are agreed to be knowable history" by "practically all critical scholars" (*HJ*, 158). These include:

(1) Jesus died by crucifixion.
(2) Jesus was buried.
(3) His disciples despaired.
(4) The tomb was later found empty.
(5) The disciples believed they later saw literal appearances of Jesus.
(6) They were transformed from doubters to bold proclaimers of His resurrection.
(7) This message was the center of their early preaching.
(8) They preached this in Jerusalem shortly after it happened.
(9) The church was born and grew rapidly.
(10) Sunday was their primary day of worship.
(11) James was converted from skepticism to belief in the resurrection of Jesus.
(12) A few years later Paul was converted, proclaiming that he had seen the resurrected Christ.

On this basis it can be argued that no purely naturalistic theory explains all these facts and that the actual bodily resurrection of Jesus is the best explanation of all the facts.

Furthermore, taking even four of these facts that are accepted by virtually all critical scholars (1, 5, 6, and 12), the case can still be made that the literal resurrection of Christ is the best explanation for these four facts (*HJ*, 162–64). Habermas concludes,

> These core facts also provide the major positive evidence for Jesus' literal resurrection appearances. . . . Thus these core historical facts provide positive evidence which further verify the disciples' claims concerning Jesus' literal resurrection, especially in that these arguments have not been accounted for naturalistically. (ibid., 165.)

The Internal Evidence for the Historicity of the Gospels

In addition to the strong external evidence via early dating, archaeological finds, and multiple-eyewitness testimony, there are strong internal evidences for the authenticity of the gospel records. Once the books are dated within the lifetime of Jesus' immediate disciples, the question becomes moot as to who actually wrote them. In fact, there is no good reason not to accept the traditional authorship, well attested in early church history as Matthew, Mark, Luke, and John. Be that as it may, the documents were composed by first-century disciples of Jesus who were eyewitnesses and contemporaries of the events. This being the case, let's look at the internal evidence for their authenticity.

The Gospel Writers Made No Attempt to Harmonize Their Accounts

Eyewitnesses offering truthful accounts rarely tell the same story word-for-word. Overlaps in testimony on crucial points are expected, but exactness on details is rare. This is exactly what we have in the Gospels; there is unanimity on the central facts about the life, death, and resurrection of Christ, along with significant but reconcilable differences in the details.

Sometimes there is even apparent contradiction from one account to another. For instance, there was one angel at the tomb in Matthew (28:2–3), and two in John (20:12). Matthew 27:5 says Judas hanged himself, but Acts affirms that he fell down and his bowels burst out (Acts 1:18). Matthew (9:27) says Jesus healed two blind men, and yet Luke (18:35f.) says he cured one. Even something as simple as the inscription on the cross reads four different ways in the four gospels (cf. Matt. 27:37; Mark 15:26; Luke 23:38; John 19:19). Surely no writers in collusion would have allowed all these apparent contradictions in the record. While it has never been demonstrated that these are real contradictions,[10] this much is certain: the writers were not conspiring together to tell a story that was not true.

The Gospel Writers Included Passages That Placed Jesus in a Bad Light

Another internal evidence of authenticity is the fact that the gospel writers did not hesitate to put in the record things that placed Jesus, to whom they were devoted, in poor reflection. Among these are the facts that Jesus was called "a drunkard" (Matt. 11:19), a madman (John 10:20), demon-possessed (John 8:48), and that His brothers did not believe in Him (John 7:5). Surely no one trying to paint a perfect picture or tell a myth would have allowed this in the record of their great hero, to say nothing of the one whom they believed to be the Son of God.

The Gospel Writers Left Difficult Passages in Their Text

Even honest followers of Christ admit that it would be easier to defend Jesus' claims to be the Son of God had the text not contained some things Jesus said that are hard to explain. For example, if Jesus is really God, as the text records that He claimed to be (Mark 14:61–62; John 5:23; 8:58; 10:30; 17:5), then why did they leave in Jesus' statement "The Father is greater than I" (John 14:28), and "No one knows the time, not even the angels in heaven, nor the Son" (Matt. 24:36)? Also, why did He rebuke the

---

[10]For a defense of the fact that these conflicts are only apparent, rather than real, see Norman Geisler and Thomas Howe, *When Critics Ask.*

rich young ruler when he called Jesus "Good Master" and insist that only God was good (from whom He appeared to be disassociating Himself)?

Why also do they leave in the text those difficult passages that agnostics take to make Jesus look unwise, like cursing a fig tree for not having figs when it was not yet the season for figs (Matt. 21:18f.)? Why did they leave in the passages where Christ seems to say He was coming back to earth within a generation when He did not (Matt. 24:34), especially if one accepts, as most critics do, that this was not written until after the alleged prediction was already known to be false? The most plausible reason is that they were really reporting what He said and not what would make things look better, fit better, or make a better impression. In short, all these things argue for the truthfulness of the gospel writers.

The Gospel Writers Recorded Self-Incriminating Stories

Granted that one or more apostles wrote a gospel (say, Matthew and/or John), or even that they had a strong influence on a gospel writer (like Paul on Luke or Peter on Mark, their companions), then why did they leave self-incriminating things in the record, such as

(1) all the disciples falling asleep when Jesus asked them to pray (Mark 14:32–41);
(2) Peter being called "Satan" by Jesus (Matt. 16:23);
(3) Peter denying the Lord three times (Luke 22:34);
(4) the disciples fleeing when things got really tough (at the Crucifixion, Mark 14:50);
(5) Peter cutting off the ear of the servant of the high priest (Mark 14:47); or,
(6) in spite of repeated teaching that He would rise from the dead (John 2:18, 3:14–18; Matt. 12:39–41; 17:9, 22–23), the disciples being doubtful and disbelieving when they heard of Jesus' resurrection?

Again, the best explanation for these self-incriminating inclusions is that they really happened, and the gospel writers simply reported the truth.

The Gospel Writers Carefully Distinguished Jesus' Word From Their Own

Any literate young adult could take a black and white version of the Gospels and accurately add quotations marks around the words of Jesus, so carefully are they distinguished from the writers' own words. The fact that all red-letter editions of the Bible are virtually identical illustrates how clear this distinction is. But why should the gospel writers be so careful to distinguish Jesus' words from theirs if they were simply putting words in Jesus' mouth? This distinction demonstrates that, contrary to form and redaction criticism (see chapter 19), they were really reporting, not creating, the words of Jesus.

Likewise, Paul made the same careful distinction in his epistles and in the book of Acts:

> In everything I did, I showed you that by this kind of hard work we must help the weak, remembering the words the Lord Jesus himself said: "It is more blessed to give than to receive" (Acts 20:35).

And he said to the Corinthians: "To the married I give this command (*not I, but the Lord*)." Yet two verses later he wrote, "To the rest I say this (*I, not the Lord*)" (1 Cor. 7:10, 12, emphasis added).[11]

The Gospel Writers Did Not Deny Their Testimony Under Persecution or Threat of Death

One sure-fire way to determine whether a person is telling the truth is to persecute or threaten to kill him unless he changes his view. It is well known that the early Christians, among whom were the gospel writers, were put in this situation repeatedly; Acts 4, 5, 7, and 8 are notable examples of this in the early church. Paul tells of his incredible woes for Christ:

> Five times I received from the Jews the forty lashes minus one. Three times I was beaten with rods, once I was stoned, three times I was shipwrecked, I spent a night and a day in the open sea, I have been constantly on the move. I have been in danger from rivers, in danger from bandits, in danger from my own countrymen, in danger from Gentiles; in danger in the city, in danger in the country, in danger at sea; and in danger from false brothers. I have labored and toiled and have often gone without sleep; I have known hunger and thirst and have often gone without food; I have been cold and naked. Besides everything else, I face daily the pressure of my concern for all the churches. (2 Cor. 11:24–28)

It is a psychological fact that few, if any, persons would endure these experiences for what they knew to be a lie.

The Gospel Writers Claim They Based Their Record on Eyewitness Testimony

Surely if what the gospel writers said was a fraud, pious or not, someone would have cracked under this pressure and confessed that what they said was not true. But no one did. This in itself is a strong testimony to the truth of the gospel records.

---

[11]Of course, most scholars believe Jesus actually spoke in Aramaic; if this is true, since the New Testament is in Greek it is only a translation of Jesus' words. Also at times there appears to be a summary or abridgement of what Jesus said (observable by comparing one gospel to another), but here too the gospel writers give evidence that they are presenting the actual teachings of Jesus, not their own. Thus, while we do not claim to have the exact words (*ipsissima verba*) of Jesus (in Aramaic) in the Gospels, nonetheless, the gospel writers are providing the exact meaning (*ipsissima vox*).

First, there is the clear claim of the gospel of Luke to be historical. Luke 1:1–4 says,

> Many have undertaken to draw up an account of the things that have been fulfilled among us, just as they were handed down to us by those who from the first were eyewitnesses and servants of the word. Therefore, since I myself have carefully investigated everything from the beginning, it seemed good also to me to write an orderly account for you, most excellent Theophilus, so that you may know the certainty of the things you have been taught.

Furthermore, this is not a mere claim, since the author of Luke has been shown to be an excellent historian (see pages 471–72).

Second, the author of John claims he was witness to the events recorded there: "*This is the disciple who testifies to these things and who wrote them down.* We know that his testimony is true" (John 21:24, emphasis added). By the process of elimination, the author appears to be John the apostle, since the author was one of the inner circle of Jesus' disciples (John 13:23–25), which included Peter, James, and John (Matt. 17:1). James died much earlier (Acts 12:2), and Peter is distinguished from the writer by name (cf. 1:41–42; 13:6, 8; 21:20–24). Another New Testament book, written about the same time and in the same style and attributed to John the apostle from earliest times, claimed:

> That which was from the beginning, which *we have heard*, which *we have seen with our eyes*, which *we have looked at and our hands have touched*—this we proclaim concerning the Word of life. (1 John 1:1, emphasis added)

Third, the author of 2 Peter[12] claimed to be an eyewitness of Christ:

> *We did not follow cleverly invented stories* when we told you about the power and coming of our Lord Jesus Christ, but *we were eyewitnesses of his majesty.* (2 Peter 1:16, emphasis added)

Fourth, the entire New Testament record contains many indications of an eyewitness account, having a lively immediacy that bespeaks an eyewitness retelling, reflecting knowledge of first-century places, persons, customs, topography, and geography. There are references to verifiable cities like Bethlehem, Jerusalem, and many other cities of first-century Palestine, along with religious knowledge about Pharisees and Sadducees.

Non-Christian Sources Confirm the Gospel Record

In addition to the biblical data, there are non-Christian sources for the life of Christ, including Tacitus, Suetonius, Thallus, the Jewish Talmud, and

---

[12]The evidence that the apostle Peter wrote this book is substantial. See Donald Carson, Douglas Moo, and Leon Morris, *An Introduction to the New Testament*, 433–43.

Josephus. Citations from them are contained in the excellent work of noted English New Testament Scholar F. F. Bruce (*Jesus and Christian Origins Outside the New Testament*) and in Gary Habermas's *The Historical Jesus.*

Following Habermas, many important things can be ascertained from this text:

(1) Jesus was worshiped by Christians.
(2) Jesus introduced new teachings in the Holy Land.
(3) Jesus was crucified for His teachings. His teachings included
(4) the fellowship of all believers,
(5) the importance of conversion, and
(6) the importance of denying the gods of Greece. The Christians
(7) worshiped Jesus and
(8) lived according to His laws. Further, the followers of Jesus
(9) believed they were immortal and were characterized by
(10) contempt for death,
(11) voluntary self-devotion, and
(12) renunciation of material goods.

Habermas notes that the writings of the earliest non-Christian sources on Christ are approximately twenty to one hundred and fifty years after Jesus' death, which is quite early by the standards of ancient historiography. What is more, "at least seventeen non-Christian writings record more than fifty details concerning the life, teachings, death, and resurrection of Jesus, plus details concerning the earliest church" (*HJ*, 150). And if one includes the non-biblical Christian sources as well, then there are some one hundred and twenty-nine facts about the life of Christ listed outside the New Testament (ibid., 243–50). This is a powerful confirmation from early extra-biblical sources for the historicity of the New Testament.

OBJECTIONS TO THE HISTORICITY OF THE NEW TESTAMENT

In spite of the overwhelming evidence for the historicity of the New Testament, some continue to cast doubt on its reliability. The most frequently given reasons are two: the impossibility of knowing the past, and the unreliability of miraculous accounts.

Is History Knowable?

Some critical scholars have questioned whether history in general is knowable. This objection from the historical relativists has been answered earlier (see chapter 11).

Are Miraculous Accounts Unreliable?

Since the credibility of miracles has already been addressed (see chapter 3), it will only be addressed briefly here. *First*, no one has ever offered a definitive argument showing that miracles are impossible (again, see chapter 3). Every attempt simply begs the question by defining miracles as impossible. *Second*, if a theistic God exists, then miracles are possible, for a miracle is a special act of God, and if a theistic God exists who has performed the supernatural act of creating a world out of nothing, then other miracles are thereby made possible. *Third*, it follows, then, that the only way to disprove the possibility of miracles is to disprove the existence of God, and despite all attempts to cast doubt on the existence of God, no one has yet provided an absolute (or even convincing) disproof (see Geisler, "G, AD" in *BECA*).

Furthermore, there is an inconsistency in the critics' arguments. Ancient historians accept the reliability of other ancient accounts of events that contain miracle claims in them. As Habermas notes,

> Ancient histories regularly recounted supernatural reports of all sorts, including omens and portents, prophecies, healing miracles, various sorts of divine intervention, as well as demonic activity.

For example,

> In his widely recognized account of Alexander the Great, Plutarch begins by noting Alexander's likely descent from Hercules. Later Alexander talked with a priest who claimed to be the son of the god Ammon and then with Ammon himself. [Indeed,] near the end of his life, Alexander took almost every unusual event to be supernatural, surrounding himself with diviners and others who foretold the future. (*HJ*, 154.)

Inclusion of alleged miracles is also part of the reports of Tacitus and Suetonius, whose accounts are widely accepted by modern historians as containing reliable historical accounts.

Do Unusual Claims Demand Unusual Evidence?

A kindred criticism, though less obvious, is the oft-repeated claim that "Unusual claims demand unusual evidence." The New Testament makes unusual claims; hence, it demands unusual evidence. However, there are several serious flaws with this claim as it bears on the historicity of the New Testament.

First, the word *unusual* is ambiguous. Does it mean supernatural? If so, then it begs the question, for it amounts to saying, "A miraculous claim demands miraculous evidence." But if one provided miraculous evidence for that, then the objector would ask miraculous evidence for that, and so on to infinity. In this case, one could never verify anything by a miraculous claim.

Second, if "unusual" simply means merely more than normal, then the New Testament meets the challenge, since there are more manuscripts, earlier ones, more accurately copied ones, with more witnesses, and more corroborated by external evidence for the New Testament than any other book from antiquity.

Third, the word *unusual* is imprecise. How unusual does the evidence have to be? Who determines its meaning? What are the objective criteria for unusualness? Are these applied consistently with other unusual claims in history and other disciplines?

Fourth, many views in modern science that are very unusual have been accepted. The big bang theory is a case in point: By the standards operating in modern science, the explosion of the universe out of nothing was a highly unusual event.[13] Yet only normal scientific evidence has been required to believe it, such as the second law of thermodynamics, an expanding universe, etc. (see chapter 2).

Fifth, many purely natural events are highly unusual; for example, virtually everything in nature contracts as it gets colder, yet when water reaches 32° Fahrenheit, it expands. Scientists do not require highly unusual evidence that this is so—only the regular observation demanded to establish other natural events.

In short, the claim that "unusual events demand unusual evidence" is an unusual claim that needs unusual evidence as to why it should be accepted. Thus, it fails to undermine the historicity of the New Testament; there is more than ample evidence for the miraculous claims it contains.

Other objections such as "Is history knowable?" and "Do religious motives negate doing credible history?" have been treated elsewhere (see chapter 11). It is sufficient to mention here that all such objections either beg the question or are self-defeating.

Do We Have the Exact Words of Jesus?

Even granting the general reliability of the New Testament, some insist that we do not have the exact words of Jesus therein, and, in the minds of some, this weakens the case for the historical objectivity of the New Testament. The arguments for this view will be cited and evaluated.

Jesus' Aramaic Words Were Translated Into Greek

The first objection is that Jesus probably spoke in Aramaic, as is indicated by the fact that some words are preserved in that language (cf. Matt.

---

[13]See the account of the unusualness of the Big Bang theory and the unusual reaction by many scientists in Robert Jastrow's *God and the Astronomers*, chapter 6.

27:46). But the New Testament was written in Greek; therefore, it is already a translation of Jesus' words.

In response, several observations are in order.

First, even if Jesus spoke in Aramaic, it does not follow that the gospel writers did not faithfully translate His words.

Second, some scholars argue that since Jesus was at least bilingual, He may have spoken to His disciples in Greek (see Thomas, *JC*, 367f.), in which case no translation would be necessary.

Third, the fact that Jesus occasionally spoke in Aramaic, as He did a few words from the cross (Matt. 27:46), does not prove that He regularly spoke it in His discourses.

Fourth, even if Jesus gave His discourses in Aramaic, historical reliability does not depend on having those exact words (*ipsissima verba*), as long as the Greek translation preserves the exact meaning (*ipsissima vox*). And, contrary to speculations of the critics, which are based on questionable presuppositions, there is no factual evidence that the meaning of Jesus is not preserved in the gospel records.

Fifth, since the earliest copies of the gospel known are in Greek, and since it was the Greek-written original that was inspired (2 Tim. 3:16), it does not matter if He spoke the words originally in Aramaic. Since the Greek version is inspired, it was thereby preserved from all error (see chapter 27).

Parallel Gospel Accounts Do Not Contain the Exact Same Words

It is also noted by critics that Jesus' words spoken on the same occasion differ from gospel to gospel. Hence, it is argued that these cannot be the exact words He spoke.

In response, this objection also fails to prove its point for a number of reasons.

First, in most (if not all) cases, one account may simply be giving more of His exact words than the other. For example, in Peter's famous confession we may have Matthew recording more than Mark, and Luke less. Matthew recorded: "You are the Christ, the Son of the living God" (16:16); Mark's account gives only part of it, namely, "You are the Christ" (8:29); Luke wrote [You are] "the Christ of God" (9:20).

Second, other differences in the Gospel accounts can be explained by the reasonable assumptions that Jesus said:

(1) similar things on different occasions;

(2) more on a given occasion than what one or even all gospel writers recorded;

(3) the same thing more than one way on the same occasion (cf. Mark 10:23–24).

Third, in any event, the exact words are not necessary to give a historically reliable account, as long as the same meaning is conveyed.

Long Discourses Could Not Have Been Remembered Years Later

There are many long discourses of Jesus recorded in the Gospels, including the Sermon on the Mount (Matt. 5–7), the parables (e.g., Matt. 13), the denunciation of the Jewish leaders (Matt. 23), the Mount Olivet Discourse (Matt. 24–25), the Upper Room Discourse (John 14–17), and the high-priestly prayer (John 17). It is alleged to be very unlikely that these could have been remembered word-for-word a generation or more later, when they were recorded.

In response, the critics overlook some important facts.

First, their dates for the Gospels are too late (see page 474). Evidence places the writings closer to the events than previously thought, even within ten years, according to some (like liberal critic John A. T. Robinson).

Second, memories were more highly developed in this preliterary culture, making it feasible that all of this was memorized.

Third, even today many persons have memorized much more than this, even whole gospels.

Fourth, Matthew, who has most of the long discourses, was a record keeper by vocation. He may have kept records of Jesus' exact words that were then available for others, just as the early Christian writer Papias said he did (see Eusebius, *EH,* 3.24.6).

Fifth, even if these long discourses were summaries and paraphrases of Jesus' exact words, there is no evidence to indicate that they are not accurate. In fact, as we have seen above, all the evidence is to the contrary.

Sixth, Jesus promised supernatural activation of the disciples' memories, saying, "But the Counselor, *the Holy Spirit,* whom the Father will send in my name, will teach you all things and *will remind you of everything I have said to you"* (John 14:26).

John Records Jesus Saying Different Things

There is little doubt that the gospel of John records different sayings than the other gospels. Jesus' famous "I am" statements occur only in John (e.g., 4:26; 6:35; 8:12, 58; 10:9, 11; 11:25; 14:6). "Verily, verily" (or "truly, truly") occurs only in John (cf. 1:51; 3:3, 5, 11; 5:19, 24–25; 6:26, 32, 47, 53; 8:34, 51, 58; 10:1, 7; 12:24; 13:16, 20–21, 38; 14:12; 16:20, 23; 21:18). There is also great doubt that this in any way undermines the reliability of the gospel record (see Geisler, "J, GO" in *BECA,* 388f.).

There are solid reasons for the differences in John. His deviations from the Synoptic Gospels (Matthew, Mark, and Luke) can be explained largely by the location (Judean), date (early and later ministry), and nature (many private conversations) of Jesus' sayings. The "I am" claims can be understood as shorter, simpler statements Jesus made to those who did not at first understand Him. Indeed, the fact that John's account is so intimate, so fresh, and so detailed argues strongly for its authenticity.

The "verily, verily" statements have parallels in both Mark and Matthew, who say, "I tell you the truth" (Matt. 26:34; Mark 14:30); the doubling may have been for emphasis (see Blomberg, *HRG*, 159). Further, when John says Jesus used "verily, verily" he is reporting Jesus' statements on different occasions than events in the Synoptic Gospels. During His ministry Jesus avoided making explicit public claims to be the Messiah, yet He did not hesitate to do so in private to the woman at the well (John 4:25–26).

There are no instances where Jesus said only one "verily" in the Synoptics, and John doubled it as well. Indeed, John's is the only gospel that claims to be written by an eyewitness apostle (John 21:24–25). Carson's conclusion is correct:

> It is altogether plausible that Jesus sometimes spoke in nothing less than what we think of as "Johannine" style, and that John's style was to some degree influenced by Jesus himself. [Thus] when all the evidence is taken together, it is not hard to believe that when we listen to the voice of the Evangelist in his description of what Jesus said, we are listening to the voice of Jesus himself. (*GAJ*, 48.)

In summation, there is no good evidence that the Gospels do not convey to us the same truths that Jesus spoke, even if it could be shown that in some cases His exact words are not reported. What is certain is this: The gospel writers did not *create* the teachings and actions of Jesus but rather *reported* them. Even if some (or all) were originally spoken in Aramaic and then translated into Greek, they are translated accurately by eyewitnesses and contemporaries of the events whose lives and memories were dramatically impacted and changed by Him and whose memories were supernaturally activated by His Spirit. Further, the historicity of what they said is corroborated by multiple accounts, by archaeological discoveries, by early manuscript evidence, and by the morality and dedication of the writers. No such combination of evidence exists for any other book from the ancient world.

CONCLUSION

The historicity of the New Testament is based on more solid evidence than that for any other event of its era, for no other event is based on more manuscripts that are more accurately copied or that were written by more people who were eyewitnesses of the events and who wrote down the material within the lifetime of its contemporaries. Were it not for an ungrounded antisupernatural bias of the negative critics (see chapter 3), the gospel accounts would be unquestioned as to their historicity—which indeed they were among Bible scholars for some 1,800 years after the events (see chapters 15–18).

SOURCES

Albright, William F. *Archaeology and the Religion of Israel.*
———. *The Archaeology of Palestine.*
———. *From Stone Age to Christianity.*
———. "William Albright: Toward a More Conservative View" in *Christianity Today* (Jan. 18, 1963).
Archer, Gleason. *An Encyclopedia of Biblical Difficulties.*
Blaiklock, E. M., and R. K. Harrison, eds. *The New International Dictionary of Biblical Archaeology.*
Blomberg, Greg. *The Historical Reliability of the Gospels.*
Bultmann, Rudolf. *Kerygma and Myth: A Theological Debate.*
———. "A Study of the Synoptic Gospels" in *Form Criticism.*
Carson, D. A. *Gospel According to John.*
———, et al. *An Introduction to the New Testament.*
Craig, William. *Knowing the Truth About the Resurrection.*
Davies, W. D., and David Daube, "Recent Discoveries in Palestine and the Gospel of St. John" in *The Background of the New Testament and Its Eschatology.*
Estrada, David, and William White, Jr. *The First New Testament.*
Eusebius. *Ecclesiastical History.*
Fisher, E. "New Testament Documents Among the Dead Sea Scrolls?" in *The Bible Today.*
Flavius Josephus. *Antiquities.*
Garnet, P. "O'Callahan's Fragments: Our Earliest New Testament Texts?" in *Evangelical Quarterly* 45: 1972.
Geisler, Norman. *Baker Encyclopedia of Christian Apologetics.*
———. "God, Alleged Disproofs of" in *Baker Encyclopedia of Christian Apologetics.*
———. "John, Gospel of," in *Baker Encyclopedia of Christian Apologetics.*
Geisler, Norman, and Thomas Howe. *When Critics Ask.*
Geisler, Norman, and William Nix. *A General Introduction to the Bible.*
Geisler, Norman, and Abdul Saleeb. *Answering Islam.*
Habermas, Gary. "Why I Believe the New Testament Is Historically Reliable" in Norman Geisler and Paul Hoffman, eds. *Why I Am a Christian.*
———. *The Historical Jesus.*
Hemer, Colin J. *The Book of Acts in the Setting of Hellenistic History.*
Jastrow, Robert. *God and the Astronomers.*
Kenyon, Sir Frederick. *The Bible and Archaeology.*
———. *Our Bible and the Ancient Manuscripts.*
Linnemann, Eta. *Is There a Synoptic Problem?*
Martin, Michael. *The Case Against Christianity.*
Metzger, Bruce. *Chapters in the History of New Testament Textual Criticism.*
Meyerhoff, Hans, ed. *The Philosophy of History in Our Time: An Anthology.*

Muller, Julius. *The Theory of Myths, in Its Application to the Gospel History, Examined and Confuted.*

Orchard, B. "A Fragment of St. Mark's Gospel Dating From Before A.D. 50?" in *Biblical Apostolate*, Rome: 6, 1972.

Pickering, W. N. *The Identification of the New Testament Text.*

Ramsey, William. *St. Paul the Traveler and the Roman Citizen.*

Robinson, John A. T. *Can We Trust the New Testament?*

———. *An Introduction to the Textual Criticism of the New Testament.*

———. *Redating the New Testament.*

Sherwin-White, A. N. *Roman Society and Roman Law in the New Testament.*

Thomas, Robert, et al. *The Jesus Crisis.*

Vos, Howard H. "Albright, William Foxwell" in *The Dictionary of Evangelical Theology*, Walter Elwell, ed.

Wells, G. A. *Did Jesus Ever Exist?*

Wenham, John. *Redating Matthew, Mark, and Luke: A Fresh Assault on the Synoptic Problem.*

White, W., Jr. "O'Callahan's Identifications: Confirmation and Its Consequences" in *The Westminster Journal*, Philadelphia: 35, 1972.

Wilson, Clifford A. *Rocks, Relics, and Biblical Reliability.*

Yamauchi, Edwin. *The Stones and the Scriptures.*

Young, David A. *The Biblical Flood.*

CHAPTER TWENTY-SEVEN

THE INERRANCY OF THE BIBLE

The doctrine of inerrancy is not directly taught in Scripture, although it is logically implied. Two things, however, *are* directly taught:

(1) The Bible is the Word of God (see chapters 13–14).
(2) God cannot err (Heb. 6:18; Titus 1:2; Rom. 3:4).

The logically necessary result of these two premises is that (3) the Bible cannot err.

SOME IMPORTANT DEFINITIONS

The terms *inspiration, infallibility*, and *inerrancy* are all related. *Inspiration* means "breathed out by God," "what comes from God Himself" (see 2 Tim. 3:16–17). *Infallibility* means "what has divine authority," "what cannot be broken" (John 10:34–35). *Inerrancy* means "what is without error," "wholly true."

What is inspired is infallible, since *inspired* means to be breathed out by God, and what is God-breathed cannot be in error. Likewise, what is infallible, since it has divine authority, must also be inerrant—a divinely authoritative error is a contradiction in terms.

However, not everything inerrant is divinely authoritative. A phone book could be without error, but it would not thereby have divine authority. Hence, inerrancy is implied in a proper understanding of infallibility, but infallibility does not follow from inerrancy.

THE BIBLICAL BASIS FOR INERRANCY

The biblical basis for inerrancy is clearly taught in the Bible via the aforementioned two premises:

(1) The Bible is the Word of God.
(2) God cannot err.

The Bible Is the Word of God

That the Bible is the Word of God can be discerned from several biblical affirmations:

(1) that it is God-breathed;
(2) that it is a prophetic writing;
(3) that it has divine authority;
(4) that it is what God says;
(5) that it is called "the Word of God" or the like.

The Bible Is God-Breathed

Paul declared that "*All Scripture is God-breathed* and is useful for teaching, rebuking, correcting and training in righteousness" (2 Tim. 3:16).

This Word, often translated "inspired" (cf. KJV), means to be spirated—breathed—from God. A kindred idea is found in Jesus' words: "Man does not live on bread alone, but on *every word that comes from the mouth of God*" (Matt. 4:4).

The Nature of a Prophet

As previously elaborated, the Bible claims to be a prophetic writing (Heb. 1:1; 2 Peter 1:20–21); prophets, as mouthpieces of God, spoke only what God put in their mouths (Deut. 18:18; 2 Sam. 23:2; Isa. 59:21; cf. Deut. 4:2).

The Divine Authority of the Bible

That the Bible is the Word of God can also be determined from the fact that it has divine authority (Matt. 5:17–18); Jesus said it was exalted above all human authority (Matt. 15:3–6).

The Bible Is "What God Says"

Often the words of the authors of Scripture are equated with the words of God. For example, cross-reference Genesis 12:1–3 with Galatians 3:8, and Exodus 9:16 with Romans 9:17—it is verses like these (see chapter 13) that give rise to the statement "What the Bible says, God says."

The Bible Is Called "The Word of God"

This very phrase or its equivalent is used many times of the Bible in part or as a whole. Second Chronicles 34:14 speaks of "The book of the law of the LORD given by the hand of Moses"; Zechariah 7:12 refers to "The words that the LORD Almighty had sent by His Spirit through the earlier prophets." (See also Matthew 15:6, John 10:35, Romans 9:6, and Hebrews 4:12.)

God Cannot Err

There are two lines of evidence that God cannot err: general revelation and special revelation.

The Argument for God's Truthfulness From General Revelation

General revelation is written on human hearts (Romans 2:12–15), and the moral argument for God's existence is based on it (see chapter 2). It reasons:

(1) Every moral law has a Moral Lawgiver.
(2) There is an absolute moral law.
(3) Hence, there is an absolute Moral Lawgiver.

Even the standard argument against God from injustice in the world presupposes that there is a God, for one cannot know what is im-perfect (i.e., not-perfect) unless he knows what is perfect. Hence, an absolute standard of perfection must be posited as a basis for knowing what is imperfect. But all rational moral creatures know intuitively that lying as such is a moral imperfection. Hence, the perfect Moral Lawgiver cannot lie or give information He knows to be false.

Yet what if God does not know all things? Then the Bible could have false information in it. From a classical theistic point of view (see chapter 2) this is not possible, for God is omniscient (all-knowing), and an all-knowing God knows everything that is true and everything that is false. Since He is perfect, He would not share with anyone as true what is false.

The Argument for God's Truthfulness From Special Revelation

The Scriptures confirm what general revelation teaches about God's absolute truthfulness, declaring emphatically that "it is impossible for God to lie" (Heb. 6:18). Paul speaks of the "God who does not lie" (Titus 1:2), a God who, even "if we are faithless, he will remain faithful, for he cannot disown himself" (2 Tim. 2:13). God is truth (John 14:6), and so is His Word; Jesus said to the Father, "Your word is truth" (John 17:17). The psalmist exclaimed, "All your words are true" (Ps. 119:160; cf. Rom. 3:4).

Therefore, the Bible Cannot Err

Since the Bible is the Word of God and God cannot err, then it follows that the Bible cannot err. The only way to deny this conclusion is to deny

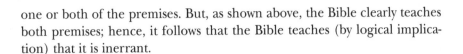

one or both of the premises. But, as shown above, the Bible clearly teaches both premises; hence, it follows that the Bible teaches (by logical implication) that it is inerrant.

Truth Is Correspondence With the Facts

It is important to remember that by "true" is meant that which corresponds with the facts (see chapter 7). Thus, when we speak about the inerrancy (or errorlessness) of the Bible we mean that it is actually and factually correct in whatever it affirms. There are no mistakes or incorrect statements in the Bible. That is to say, whatever the Bible says is true, is true; and whatever the Bible says is false, is false.

The Bible Has No Errors of Any Kind

Some have supposed to avoid the logic of inerrancy by claiming that the Bible is only inerrant in redemptive matters, not in matters such as science and history. But this is not so. First of all, whatever God affirms is true, is true no matter what the subject; He cannot err on any topic. Also, the Bible does make statements about history and the scientific world; thus, all these statements must be true, since God affirms whatever the Bible affirms.

Further, the Bible makes no such separation between redemptive and nonredemptive affirmations. Indeed, the redemptive and the scientific, as well as the redemptive and the historical, are often inseparable. "Christ died for ours sins" is redemptive, but the same passage says He was "buried" and "rose again on the third day," which are historical. Likewise, Jesus' virgin birth was a spiritual "sign" (Isa. 7:14; cf. Matt. 1:23), but it was also a biological fact, since Joseph "had no union with her [Mary, sexually] until she gave birth to a son" (Matt. 1:25). Also, Jesus' resurrection was a great redemptive event without which no one can be saved (Rom. 4:25; 10:9; 1 Cor. 15:14–19), yet the Resurrection was a literal event of history that left behind an empty tomb (Matt. 28:6; John 20:1–8), and Christ appeared in the same physical body, with nail scars and all (Luke 24:39–43; John 20: 27–28).

THEOLOGICAL DEFINITION OF
INSPIRATION AND INERRANCY

Many definitions of inspiration and inerrancy have been offered. B. B. Warfield said, "Inspiration is the supernatural influence exerted on the sacred writers by the Holy Spirit of God, by virtue of which their writings are given divine trustworthiness." In a fuller definition, Louis Gaussen (1790–1863) affirmed:

> Inspiration is that inexplicable power which the Divine Spirit put
> forth of old on the authors of Holy Scripture in order to give them

guidance even in the employment of the words they used, and to preserve them alike from all error and from all omission. (*T*)

The Essential Elements of a Definition

There appear to be at least six crucial elements in a complete definition of the inspiration and inerrancy of the Bible:

(1) its divine origin (from God);
(2) its human agency (through men);
(3) its written locus (in words);
(4) its original form (in the autographs or original text);
(5) its final authority, normative (for believers);
(6) its inerrant nature (without errors).

A Suggested Definition

Combining all these elements into one definition, *the inspiration of Scripture is the supernatural operation of the Holy Spirit who, through the different personalities and literary styles of the chosen human authors, invested the very words of the original books of Holy Scripture, alone and in their entirety, as the very Word of God without error in all that they teach (including history and science) and is thereby the infallible rule and final authority for the faith and practice of all believers.*

The Extent of Biblical Inerrancy

How far does the inerrancy of the Bible extend? Is it inerrant in every way and on every matter, or only in terms of theology and ethics? Some have suggested that Scripture can always be trusted on moral matters, but it is not always correct on historical matters; they rely on it in the spiritual domain, but not in the sphere of science. If true, however, this would render the Bible ineffective as a divine authority, since the spiritual is often inextricably interwoven with the historical and scientific.

A close examination of Scripture reveals that the scientific (factual) and spiritual truths of Scripture are often inseparable; for example, one cannot separate the spiritual truth of Christ's resurrection from the fact that His body permanently vacated the tomb and later physically appeared (Matt. 28:6; 1 Cor. 15:13–19). Likewise, if Jesus was not born of a biological virgin, then He is no different from the rest of the human race on whom the stigma of Adam's sin rests (Rom. 5:12). Also, the death of Christ for our sins cannot be detached from his shedding literal blood on the cross, for "without the shedding of blood there is no remission" (Heb. 9:22). And, Adam's existence and fall cannot be a myth, for if there were no literal

Adam and no actual fall, then the spiritual teachings about inherited sin and eventual or physical death are wrong (Rom. 5:12). Historical reality and the theological doctrine stand or fall together.

Also, the doctrine of the Incarnation is inseparable from the historical truth about Jesus of Nazareth (John 1:1, 14). Further, Jesus' moral teaching about marriage was based on His teaching about God's joining together of a literal Adam and Eve (Matt. 19:4–5). In each of these cases the moral or theological teaching is devoid of its meaning apart from the historical or factual event. If one denies that the literal space-time event occurred, then there is no basis for believing the scriptural doctrine built upon it.

Jesus often directly compared Old Testament events with important spiritual truths, such as His death and resurrection, which were related to Jonah and the great fish (Matt. 12:40), or His second coming, as compared to the days of Noah (Matt. 24:37–39). Both the occasion and the manner of comparison make it clear that Jesus was affirming the historicity of those Old Testament events. Indeed, Jesus questioned Nicodemus, "I have spoken to you of earthly things and you do not believe; how then will you believe if I speak of heavenly things?" (John 3:12). In short, if the Bible does not speak truthfully about the physical world, then it cannot be trusted when it speaks about the spiritual world.

Inspiration includes not only all that the Bible explicitly *teaches*, but also everything the Bible *touches*. Whatever the Bible declares is true, whether it is a major point or a minor point. The Bible is God's Word, and God does not deviate from the truth at any place in it. All the parts are as true as the whole they comprise.

ANSWERING SOME OBJECTIONS TO INERRANCY

Many objections have been leveled against the doctrine of inerrancy; the most important ones are addressed here.

The Objection That Inerrancy Is Not Taught in the Bible

Some critics argue that inerrancy is not taught in Scripture. There are two parts to this allegation.

First, some point out that the term "inerrancy" nowhere appears in the Bible. But this objection misses the point: The term "Trinity" nowhere appears in the Bible, nor does "substitutionary atonement." However, these doctrines are not to be rejected for lack of exact wording; it is not a question of whether the *term* inerrancy is used but whether the *truth* of inerrancy is taught. Even the word "Bible" does not appear in the Bible!

Second, it is implied that since the doctrine of inerrancy is not explicitly taught that it is not taught at all. It can be granted that inerrancy is not *formally* and *explicitly* taught in the Bible; however, this is not to say that inerrancy is not *logically* and *implicitly* taught. The Trinity isn't explicitly taught either, but it is the necessary logical deduction of what is taught, namely:

(1) There is only one God.
(2) There are three distinct persons (Father, Son, and Holy Spirit) who are God.

From these premises it necessarily follows that

(3) There are three persons in this one God.

Likewise, as shown, inerrancy logically follows from two premises that are clearly taught in Scripture, namely:

(1) God cannot err.
(2) The Bible is the Word of God.

So, like the Trinity, inerrancy is taught implicitly and logically, if not formally and explicitly.

The Objection That Inerrancy Is a Late Invention

Critics of inerrancy claim that it is a late nineteenth-century invention that the Old Princeton theologians (like Charles Hodge and B. B. Warfield) utilized for apologetic purposes to fight a growing liberalism in the orthodox church (see Rogers, *AIB*).

As a survey of the history of the doctrine of Scripture has shown (see chapters 17 and 18), this charge is without foundation. In fact, the infallibility and inerrancy of the Scripture has been virtually the unanimous teaching of all the great Fathers of the Christian church down through the centuries until modern times.

A few crucial examples long before the time of Warfield will illustrate the point.

Augustine (354–430)

In *The City of God* Augustine used such expressions as "Sacred Scripture" (9.5), "the words of God" (10.1), "Infallible Scripture" (11.6), "divine revelation" (13.2), and "Holy Scripture" (15.8). Elsewhere he referred to the Bible as the "oracles of God," "God's word," "divine oracles," and "divine Scripture." With his widespread influence throughout the centuries, such a testimony has stood as an outstanding witness to the high regard given to the Scriptures in the church.

Speaking of the gospel writers, Augustine said,

When they write that He has taught and said, it should not be asserted that He did not write it, since the members only put down what they had come to know at the dictation [dictis] of the Head. [Therefore,] whatever He wanted us to read concerning His words and deeds, He commanded His disciples, His hands, to write. Hence, one cannot but receive what he reads in the Gospels, though written by the disciples, as though it were written by the very hand of the Lord Himself. (*HG*, 1.35.54.)

Augustine added, "I have learned to yield this respect and honour only to the canonical books of Scripture: of these alone do I most firmly believe that the authors were completely free from error" (*L*, 82.1.3).

Thomas Aquinas (1225–1274)

Agreeing with Augustine, Aquinas confessed of Holy Scripture, "I firmly believe that none of their authors have erred in composing them" (*ST*, 1a.1, 8). In this same passage Aquinas referred to Scripture as "unfailing truth."

He went on, "That God is the author of holy Scripture should be acknowledged." Again, "The author of holy Scripture is God" (ibid., 1a.1, 10). God spoke through prophets: "Prophecy implies a certain vision of some supernatural truth beyond our reach" (ibid., 2a2ae. 174, 5). Therefore, "a true prophet is always inspired by the spirit of truth" (ibid., 2a2ae. 172, 6, ad 2); thus, his message is perfect. This is possible because of the perfection of the principal or primary Cause (God) working on the imperfect secondary cause.

In his commentary on *Job*, Aquinas declared, "It is heretical to say that any falsehood whatsoever is contained either in the gospels or in any canonical Scripture" (*CBJ*, 13, 1). Elsewhere he insisted that "a true prophet is always inspired by the spirit of truth in whom there is no trace of falsehood, and so he never utters untruths" (*ST*, 2a2ae. 172, 6, ad 2). He added, "Nothing false can underlie the literal sense of Scripture" (ibid., 1a.1, 10, ad 3). Consequently, "the truth of prophetic proclamations must needs be the same as that of divine knowledge. And falsity . . . cannot creep into prophecy" (ibid., 1a. 14, 3).

John Calvin (1509–1564)

John Calvin also affirmed inerrancy, declaring, "For our wisdom ought to consist in embracing with gentle docility, and without any exceptions, all that is delivered in the sacred Scriptures" (*ICR*, 1.18.4). Scripture is "the certain and unerring rule" (*CC*, Ps. 5:11).

Calvin asserted,

> For if we reflect how prone the human mind is to lapse into forgetfulness of God, how readily inclined to every kind of error, how bent every now and then on devising new and fictitious religions, it will be easy to understand how necessary it was to make such a depository of

doctrine as would secure it from either perishing by the neglect, vanishing away amid the errors, or being corrupted by the presumptuous audacity of men. (*ICR*, 1.6.3.)

So long as your mind entertains any misgivings as to the certainty of the word of God, its authority will be weak and dubious, or rather will have no authority at all. [Further,] nor is it sufficient to believe that God is true, and cannot lie or deceive, unless you feel firmly persuaded that every word which proceeds from him is sacred, inviolable truth (ibid., 3.2.6).

Martin Luther (1483–1546)

As we have seen, Martin Luther was even more emphatic on the inerrancy of Scripture, insisting,

When one blasphemously gives the lie to God in a single word, or says it is a minor matter if God is blasphemed or called a liar, one blasphemes the entire God and makes light of all blasphemy. (*WL*, 37:26.)

He added,

So the Holy Ghost has had to bear the blame of not being able to speak correctly but that like a drunkard or a fool He jumbles the whole and uses wild, strange words and phrases. [Thus] it cannot be otherwise, because the Holy Ghost is wise and also makes the prophets wise. But one who is wise must be able to speak correctly; that never fails. But because whoever does not hear well or does not know the language well may think he speaks ill because he hears or understands scarcely half the words. (Reu, *LS*, 44, italics original.)

Luther went so far as to say that inerrancy was an all-or-nothing matter:

And whoever is so bold that he ventures to accuse God of fraud and deception *in a single word* and does so willfully again and again after he has been warned and instructed once or twice will likewise certainly venture to accuse God of fraud and deception in all His words. [Therefore,] it is true absolutely and without exception, *that everything is believed or nothing is believed.* The Holy Ghost does not suffer Himself to be separated or divided so that He should teach and cause to be believed one doctrine rightly and another falsely (ibid., 33, italics original).

The clear, emphatic, and repeated affirmation of the inerrancy of Holy Scripture by the great Fathers and Reformers refutes the charge that inerrancy is a late nineteenth-century creation; this allegation is totally without foundation (see Woodbridge, *RMP*).

The Objection That Inerrancy Is Based on Non-Existent Originals

Some object to inerrancy because it affirms that only the original text is inerrant (there being admitted errors in the copies), and the originals are not extant. Hence, all the doctrine of inerrancy provides is a non-existent authority; supposedly, this isn't any different than having no Bible at all.

This allegation is unfounded. First of all, it is not true that we do not possess the original *text*. We do possess it in well-preserved copies; it is the original *manuscripts* we do not have. We do have an accurate copy of the original text represented in these manuscripts (see Geisler and Nix, *GIB*, chapter 11); the nearly 5,700 New Testament manuscripts we possess contain all or nearly all of the original text, and we can reconstruct the original text with over 99 percent accuracy.

Also, there is a difference between the *text* and the *truth* of the text. While the exact text of the original can only be reconstructed with 99 percent or so accuracy, nevertheless, 100 percent of the truth comes through. For example, recall that if you received notification that "Y#U HAVE WON 10 MILLION DOLLARS," you would have no problem understanding 100 percent of the message, even though the text is nearly 4 percent in error (1 letter out of 26).

To illustrate, were the original U.S. Constitution to be destroyed, we would not lose the constitutional authority for our country, even if all we had were copies with flaws in them. The original could be reconstructed with enough certainty to assure the continuance of our constitutional republic. The same is true of the Bible in our hands. Even though it is based on copies, they are accurate copies that convey to us 100 percent of all essential truths in the original.

In brief, the Bible in our hands is the infallible and inerrant Word of God insofar as it has been copied accurately. And it *has* been copied so accurately as to assure us that nothing in the essential message has been lost (see Geisler and Nix, *GIB*, chapters 22 and 26).

The Objection That Inerrancy Is Unnecessary

The answers to the previous objections lead to another: If errant copies of the original text are sufficient, then why did God have to inspire errorless originals? If a scratched record can convey the music of its master, then an errant Bible can convey to us the truth of the Master.

The response to this is simple. The reason the original text cannot err is that it was breathed out by God, and God cannot err. The copies, while demonstrated to have been providentially preserved from substantial error, are not breathed out by God. Hence, there can be errors in the copies.

To demonstrate, all human beings are imperfect copies of Adam, who was directly created by God. Nonetheless, as imperfect a copy as we may be, we are still 100 percent human. Adam was no more human than we are, yet there is a significant difference between Adam as He came fresh from the hand of the Creator, with absolutely no imperfections, and the imperfect copies of the original Adam that we are. We can no more conceive of God's breathing out an imperfect original text than we can of His breathing the breath of life into an imperfect Adam. What comes directly from the hand (or mouth) of the Creator must be perfect, and only later copies of it can be imperfect. To claim errors in the original Adam or Bible is to allege that there are flaws in the very nature of God.

The Objection That Inerrancy Is an Unfalsifiable View

Some critics insist that inerrantists have placed the bar so high for anyone to prove an error in the Bible that they have made the view unfalsifiable; that the standards for disproof are so high that there is no way to disprove it.

In response to this charge, we must point out several things.

First, the principle of falsifiability itself can be challenged. Is the principle itself falsifiable? If not, then it is self-defeating.

Second, even those who hold the principle often distinguish between what is falsifiable in principle and what is falsifiable in fact (see Flew, "M" in Edwards, *EP*). For instance, the claim that "there is no intelligent life in outer space" is falsifiable *in principle,* or it would be, if we could examine every nook and cranny of the cosmos. But since this is not presently possible, this statement is not falsifiable *in fact.*

Third, the doctrine of inerrancy *is* falsifiable in fact. All that is necessary is to either:

(1) find an actual error in an existing but accurate copy of Scripture;
(2) find an original manuscript with an error in it.

Incidentally, since earlier manuscripts (of other works) than the originals (of Scripture) have already been found, it is not beyond possibility to find an original.

Fourth, there is an even more decisive way to falsify evangelical Christianity—find the body of Jesus. If this could be done, according to the Bible itself, we would still be in our sins and our faith would be vain (1 Cor. 15:14–18). The truth is that it is not the evangelical view of Christianity that is unfalsifiable but the non-evangelical view, for according to non-evangelicals, finding the dead corpse of Jesus in the grave or even an original manuscript with an error would not be against their faith, since they do not believe either in the Resurrection of Christ or the inerrancy of Scripture. If one believes nothing, then nothing in his faith can be disproven.

The Objection That Inerrancy Is Not a Fundamental Doctrine

It has also been objected that the doctrine of inerrancy is not a fundamental truth of the Christian faith; hence, even if true, its importance is overestimated. Being a minor truth, supposedly, it should not be given major importance.

For one thing, by way of response, by almost any count of fundamentals of the faith, the infallibility and inerrancy of Scripture is to be included, as it is the foundation of all other doctrines. Every other fundamental of the Christian faith is based on the Scripture—if it does not have divine authority, then we have no divine authority for any doctrine to which we adhere. As the basis of all other doctrines, the inerrancy of the Bible is a fundamental of the Fundamentals, and if a fundamental of the Fundamentals is not fundamental, then what is fundamental? The answer is: fundamentally nothing.

In addition, the doctrine of inerrancy was not only affirmed by virtually all the great Fathers of the church (see chapters 16 and 17), it is also the foundation of all churches' creeds, councils, and confessions. Inasmuch as the teachings of the church were the basis for what we call orthodoxy, so must be the authority of Scripture, on which the Fathers of the church based their pronouncements.

The Objection That Inerrancy Should Not Be a Test for Orthodoxy

This objection follows from the one before it. If inerrancy is not a major doctrine, then it should not be a test for orthodoxy. However, as shown, it *is* a major teaching of Scripture, and, thus, it is a test of orthodoxy.

Of course, inerrancy is not a test of salvation—one can deny inerrancy and still be saved. Salvation depends on believing certain soteriological truths, such as the death and resurrection of Christ for our sins (see 1 Cor. 15:1–4; Rom. 10:9), and not on accepting all fundamental doctrines (e.g., the inspiration of Scripture and the second coming of Christ). One can be saved without believing in all doctrines essential to orthodoxy, but he cannot be a *consistent* evangelical without embracing all of them.

One other distinction is important here. A person can be evangelical or orthodox on all other fundamentals of the faith and still be unorthodox on this one, as inconsistent as it may be. For example, the neo-orthodox theologian Karl Barth affirmed the Virgin Birth, the Trinity, the deity of Christ, and Christ's bodily resurrection, yet he denied the inspiration and inerrancy of Scripture. Thus, he was orthodox on the rest of these fundamentals but unorthodox on his view of Scripture.

The Objection That Inerrancy Is a Divisive Doctrine

It is not uncommon to hear the charge that inerrancy is a divisive doctrine, unnecessarily dividing one believer from another against the Bible's call for the unity of all believers (Eph. 4:3–6).

Besides the emotional connotation of the word *divisive*, this allegation should also be rejected for several other reasons.

First, not everything that divides is divisive. A center aisle in a church divides one side from the other, but it is not thereby divisive. Marriage divides a person from all other individuals of the opposite sex, but it does not necessarily make one divisive toward them. Likewise, doctrine divides those who affirm it from those who deny it, but this does not mean it is a divisive doctrine.

Second, even if a doctrine were divisive simply because it divides, those who *affirm* the orthodox doctrine should not be considered divisive but rather those who *deny* it. For example, it should not be evangelicals who adhere to the deity of Christ who are called divisive, but the Jehovah's Witnesses, who reject it; likewise, it is not those who affirm the Trinity who are divisive but the Oneness Pentecostals (who hold that only Christ is God), who discard it. Let's put the shoe on the right foot.

Third, if taking a stand on a doctrine automatically makes it divisive and thereby wrong, then all stands for any doctrine would be wrong, for there is not an essential doctrine of the Christian faith that is not denied by some heresy somewhere.

Fourth, when push comes to shove, *it is better to be divided by truth than to be united by error.* All truth divides one from error; the real problem is not those who divide by standing for truth but those who divide by falling for error. The ancient dictum applies here: In essentials, unity; in nonessentials, liberty; and in all things, charity. But by any measure of consistency, the doctrines of the inspiration and inerrancy of Scripture are essential teachings of the Christian faith.

The Objection to the Term "Inerrancy"

Even some who believe in the errorlessness of the Bible object to the term because they believe it is either too negative or too technical. However, both reasons are misdirected.

First of all, while the term *inerrancy* can have a technical scientific connotation, it need not. Like most other words, there is a range of usage that must be determined by the context in which it is used.

This is not to say that no other terms are acceptable. One can also speak of the "errorlessness" of the Bible or that Scripture is "without error." The bottom line is not to insist on the *term* but on the *truth* of the matter.

Also, as to the term being negative (*not*-errant), two things are important to observe. For one, many of the Ten Commandments are negative; surely they should not be rejected for the same reason. Also, many terms for attributes of God are also negative, such as God is in-finite (not-finite) and im-mutable (not-changeable).

For another, negative terms are often more clear than positive ones. Try stating "You shall not commit adultery" in only positive terms. Take the two statements "The Bible is true" and "The Bible is without error." The latter is clearer than the former, since "true" can mean either wholly true or partly true, while "without error" must mean wholly true.

The Objection That Inerrancy Is Contrary to Fact

Finally, some insist that the doctrine of inerrancy is contrary to fact—that there are demonstrable errors in the Bible.

This view, however, makes errors of its own. The fact is that no one has ever demonstrated that there is an error in the original text of the Bible; rather, those who allege errors in the Bible have been found in error. Here is a list of the errors of those who claim to find errors in the Bible (Geisler and Howe, *WCA*, chapter 1):

Mistake 1: Assuming That the Unexplained Is Not Explainable
No scientist would assume that what is unexplained in nature is unexplainable; rather, they keep on doing research. Neither should any Bible critic assume that what is not yet explained in the Bible never will be explained. Both scientists and biblical scholars should keep looking for an answer.

Mistake 2: Presuming the Bible Guilty Until Proven Innocent
Like an American citizen charged with an offense, the Bible should be presumed innocent until it is proven guilty. This is not asking anything special for the Bible; it is the way we approach all human communication. If we did not, life would not be possible; for example, if we assumed road signs and traffic signals were not telling the truth, we would probably be dead before we could prove they were.

Mistake 3: Confusing Our Fallible Interpretations With God's Infallible Revelation
Human beings, whether scientists or biblical scholars, are finite, and finite beings make mistakes. That is why there are erasers on pencils, correcting fluid for typing, and a "delete" button on keyboards. And even though God's Word is perfect (Ps. 19:7), as long as imperfect human beings exist, there will be misinterpretations of God's Word and false views about His world. None of these prove errors in God's revelations but only errors in our interpretations of them.

Mistake 4: Failing to Understand the Context of the Passage

Perhaps the most common mistake of critics is to take a text out of its proper context. As the adage goes, "A text out of context is a pretext." One can prove anything from the Bible by this mistaken procedure. The Bible says, "There is no God" (Ps. 14:1). Of course, the context is that "The fool has said in his heart, 'There is no God.' "

Mistake 5: Neglecting to Interpret Difficult Passages in the Light of Clear Ones

Some passages of Scripture are hard to understand. Sometimes the difficulty is due to obscurity; at other times, it is due to the fact that passages appear to be teaching something contrary to what some other part of Scripture is clearly teaching. For example, James appears to be saying salvation is by works (James 2:14–26), whereas Paul taught clearly that it was by grace (Rom. 4:5; Titus 3:5–7; Eph. 2:8–9). In this case, James should *not* be construed so as to contradict Paul—Paul is speaking about justification *before God* (which is by faith alone), whereas James is referring to justification *before men* (who cannot see our faith, but only our works).

Mistake 6: Basing a Teaching on an Obscure Passage

Some passages in the Bible are difficult because their meaning is obscure, often because the context is not clear. This is true in 1 Corinthians 15:29, where Paul says, "Now if there is no resurrection, what will those do who are baptized for the dead? If the dead are not raised at all, why are people baptized for them?" Since the context is not clear, one cannot be certain that Paul is *recommending* this practice; he may only be *alluding* to what some were wrongly doing (cf. the use of "they" rather than "we"). At any rate, since the context is not clear, it is a mistake to assume that Paul is recommending a practice that is against other clear teachings of Scripture, such as salvation by grace alone through faith alone (Rom. 4:5; Eph. 2:8–9; Titus 3:5–7).

Mistake 7: Forgetting That the Bible Is a Human Book With Human Characteristics

In addition to having divine authorship, the Bible was written by human beings, each with their own style and idiosyncrasies. These *human authors*, about forty in all, sometimes used *human sources* for their material (Josh. 10:13; Acts 17:28; 1 Cor. 15:33; Titus 1:12). They manifest different *human literary styles*, from the mournful meter of Lamentations to the exalted poetry of Isaiah and the simple grammar of John. They also manifest *human perspectives*, whether a shepherd (David), a lawgiver (Moses), a prophet (Daniel), or a priest (Chronicles). They also reveal *human thought patterns*, including memory lapses (1 Cor. 1:14–16) and *emotions* (Gal. 4:14). The Bible discloses specific *human interests*, such as rural (Amos), medical (Luke), natural (James), or political (Kings).[1]

However, like Christ the Living Word, the written Word of God is completely human, yet without error. Forgetting the humanity of Scripture can lead to falsely impugning its integrity by expecting a level of expression higher than what is customary to a human document.

Mistake 8: Assuming That a Partial Report Is a False Report

The four gospels relate the same story in different ways to different groups of people and sometimes even quote the same saying with different words. For example, Matthew recorded Peter as saying, "You are the Christ, the Son of the living God" (16:16); Mark wrote, "You are the Christ" (8:29); and Luke said, "The Christ of God" (9:20). These are not contradictory but complementary; each gives part, but none the whole.

Mistake 9: Demanding That New Testament Citations of the Old Testament Always Be Exact Quotations

Critics sometimes mistakenly assume that every New Testament *citation* needs to be an exact *quotation*. Even today it is an accepted literary practice to quote the *essence* of a statement without using precisely the same *words*. The same *meaning* can be conveyed without using the same *verbal expressions*.

Sometimes the New Testament paraphrases or summarizes the Old Testament text (e.g., Matt. 2:6; cf. Mic. 5:2); others blend two texts into one (Matt. 27:9–10, cf. Jer. 32:6–9); occasionally a general truth is mentioned without citing a specific text (Matt. 2:23, cf. Zech. 11:12–13). There are also instances where the New Testament applies a text in a different way than the Old Testament did (Matt. 2:15, cf. Hos. 11:1), but in no case does the New Testament misinterpret or misapply the Old Testament (see Archer, *OTQNT*).

Mistake 10: Assuming That Divergent Accounts Are False Ones

Critics also err in assuming that because two or more accounts of the same event differ, they are mutually exclusive. For example, Matthew says there was one angel at the tomb after the Resurrection (28:5), whereas John informs us there were two (20:12). These are not contradictory reports. In fact, there is an infallible mathematical rule that easily explains this problem: Wherever there are two, there is always one—it never fails! Matthew did not say there was *only* one angel; one has to add the word

---

[1]The biblical authors include a lawgiver (Moses), a general (Joshua), prophets (Samuel, Isaiah, et al.), kings (David and Solomon), a musician (Asaph), a herdsman (Amos), a prince and statesman (Daniel), a priest (Ezra), a tax collector (Matthew), a physician (Luke), a scholar (Paul), and fishermen (Peter and John). With such a variety of occupations represented by biblical writers, it is only natural that their personal interests and differences should be reflected in their writings.

"only" to Matthew's account to make it contradict John's. If the critic comes to the Bible in order to show it errs, then the error is not in the Bible, but in the critic.

Mistake 11: Presuming That the Bible Approves of All It Records

It is a mistake to assume that everything recorded in the Bible is approved by the Bible. For example, it documents Satan's words (Gen. 3:4; cf. John 8:44) but does not affirm them; it gives a true record that he lied, but it does not imply that these lies are the truth. Likewise, the Bible records David's adultery (2 Sam. 12) and Solomon's polygamy (1 Kings 11), but it does not endorse them.

Mistake 12: Forgetting That the Bible Uses Non-Technical, Everyday Language

To be true, a source does not have to use scholarly, technical, or so-called "scientific" terminology. The Bible is written for the common person of every generation, and it therefore uses everyday language. The use of observational, nonscientific language is not *un*scientific, it is merely *pre*scientific. It is no more unscientific to speak of the sun "standing still" (Josh. 10:12) than to refer to the sun "rising" (Josh. 1:15). Contemporary meteorologists still speak daily of the time of "sunrise" and "sunset."

Mistake 13: Assuming That Round Numbers Are False

Another mistake sometimes made by Bible critics is claiming that round numbers are false. Not so. Like most ordinary speech, the Bible uses round numbers (1 Chron. 19:18; 21:5); for example, it refers to the diameter of something as being about one-third of the circumference of something (1 Kings 7:23). This may be imprecise from the standpoint of a contemporary technological society to speak of 3.14159265 . . . as 3, but it is not incorrect for an ancient, non-technological people. At any rate, 3.14 . . . rounds off to 3.

Mistake 14: Neglecting to Note That the Bible Uses Different Literary Devices

As a human book, the Bible uses various human literary devices. Several whole books are written in *poetic* style (e.g., Job, Psalms, Proverbs); the Synoptic Gospels are filled with *parables*; in Galatians 4, Paul utilizes an *allegory*; the New Testament abounds with *metaphors* (e.g., 2 Cor. 3:2–3; James 3:6) and *similes* (cf. Matt. 20:1; James 1:6); *hyperboles* may also be found (e.g., Col. 1:23; John 21:25; 2 Cor. 3:2), and possibly even *poetic figures* (Job 41:1); Jesus employed *satire* (Matt. 19:24 with 23:24); and *figures of speech* are common. It is incorrect to assume that all these should be taken literally, thus resulting in contradictions. All of the Bible is literally true, but not all the Bible is true literally (as opposed to figuratively).

Mistake 15: Forgetting That Only the Original Text, Not Every Copy of Scripture, Is Without Error

When critics do come upon a genuine error in a biblical manuscript copy, they make another mistake—they assume it was in the original inspired text of Scripture. They forget that God uttered only the original text of Scripture, not the imperfect copies. Inspiration does not guarantee that every copy of the original is without error, and, therefore, we are to expect that minor errors will be found in manuscript copies.

When we run into a so-called "error" in the Bible, we must assume one of two things: either the manuscript was not copied correctly, or we have not understood it rightly. What we may not assume is that God made an error in inspiring the original text.

Several things should be observed about these copyist errors.

First, they are errors in the copies, not the originals. No one has ever found an original manuscript with an error in it.

Second, they are minor errors (often in names or numbers) that do not affect any doctrine of the Christian faith.

Third, these copyist errors are relatively few in number.

Fourth, usually by the context, or by another Scripture, we know which one is in error.

Mistake 16: Confusing General Statements With Universal Ones

Critics often jump to the conclusion that unqualified statements admit no exceptions. For instance, proverbial sayings by their very nature offer only general guidance, not universal assurance. Proverbs 16:7 is a case in point—it affirms that "when a man's ways are pleasing to the LORD, he makes even his enemies live at peace with him." This obviously was not intended to be a universal truth, for Paul was pleasing to the Lord and his enemies stoned him (Acts 14:19), while Jesus was pleasing to the Lord and His enemies crucified Him. It is a mistake to take a general statement as a necessarily particular one.

Mistake 17: Forgetting That Later Revelation Supersedes Previous Revelation

Sometimes critics of Scripture forget the principle of progressive revelation. God does not reveal everything at once, nor does He always lay down the same conditions for every period of time. Therefore, some of His later revelation will supersede His former statements. But this is a change *of* revelation, not a change *in* revelation. Bible critics sometimes confuse a *change* in revelation with a *mistake.* For example, the fact that a parent allows a very small child to eat with his fingers only to tell him later to use a spoon, is not a contradiction. Nor is the parent contradicting himself to suggest later that the child should use a fork, not a spoon, to eat his vegetables. This is progressive revelation, each command suited to fit the particular circumstance in which the person finds himself.

There was a time when God tested the human race by forbidding them to eat of a specific tree in the Garden of Eden (Gen. 2:16–17). This command is no longer in effect, but the latter revelation does not contradict the former revelation—it simply supersedes it. Also, there was a period (under the Mosaic Law) when God commanded that animals be sacrificed for people's sins. However, since Christ offered the perfect sacrifice for sin (Heb. 10:11–14), this Old Testament command is no longer in effect. Here again, there is no contradiction between the former and the latter commands; there is simply a change of revelation, for new directions are given by which God's people are to live.

Don't forget Augustine's counsel about alleged errors in the Bible:

> If we are perplexed by any apparent contradiction in Scripture, it is not allowable to say, "The author of this book is mistaken"; but either the manuscript is faulty, or the translation is wrong, or you have not understood.[2]

The mistakes are not in the revelation of God, but are in the misinterpretations of man; the Bible is without mistake, the critics are not.

Mistake 18: The Allegation That Grammatical Irregularities Are Errors

Like most human books, the Bible has grammatically irregular construction. It is a mistake, however, to assume this is an error.

First, there is no absolute standard for grammar. There are regular and irregular usages, but no real grammatical errors.

Second, grammar as such does not deal with truth but is only the form through which verbal truth is expressed. So an error could be expressed in good (regular) grammar, and the truth could be expressed in bad (irregular) grammar.

Third, irregular grammar is often a more forceful expression of an idea, as slang reveals.

In summation, all the objections to inerrancy fail. The Bible is as flawless as the God who inspired it. As we have seen, it is not the Bible that errs but rather the Bible's critics.

CONCLUSION

The Bible by many lines of evidence (see chapter 29) contains all the earmarks of having divine origin: sanctity, divine authority, infallibility, indestructibility, indefatigability, infeasibility, and inerrancy. It is the only book of its kind and is still the world's all-time bestseller.

---

[2]Augustine, *Reply to Faustus the Manichaean* 11.5 in Philip Schaff, *A Select Library of the Nicene and Ante-Nicene Fathers of the Christian Church*, vol. 4.

SOURCES

Archer, Gleason. *The Old Testament Quoting the New Testament.*

Augustine. *Harmony of the Gospels.*

———. *Letters.*

———. *Reply to Faustus the Manichaean* in Philip Schaff, *A Select Library of the Nicene and Ante-Nicene Fathers of the Christian Church,* vol. 4.

Calvin, John. *Calvin's Commentaries.*

———. *Institutes of the Christian Religion.*

Clark, Gordon. *God's Hammer: The Bible and Its Critics.*

Flew, Antony. "Miracles" in Paul Edwards, ed., *The Encyclopedia of Philosophy.*

Gaussen, Louis. *Theopneustia.*

Geisler, Norman, and Thomas Howe. *When Critics Ask.*

Geisler, Norman, and William Nix. *A General Introduction to the Bible.*

Geisler, Norman, ed. *Inerrancy.*

Henry, Carl F. H., ed. *Revelation and the Bible.*

Hodge, Charles, and B. B. Warfield. *Inspiration.*

Johnson, S. Lewis. *The Old Testament In the New.*

Lindsell, Harold. *The Battle for the Bible.*

Luther, Martin. *The Works of Luther.*

Nash, Ronald. *The Word of God and the Mind of Man.*

Packer, J. I. *"Fundamentalism" and the Word of God.*

Pasche, Rene. *The Inspiration and Authority of Scripture.*

Reu, M. *Luther on the Scriptures.*

Rogers, Jack. *The Authority and Interpretation of the Bible.*

Thomas Aquinas. *Commentary on the Book of Job.*

———. *Summa Theologica.*

Turretin, Francis. *The Doctrine of Scripture.*

Warfield, B. B. *The Inspiration and Authority of the Bible.*

———. *Limited Inspiration.*

Woodbridge, John. *The Roger-McKim Proposal.*

CHAPTER TWENTY-EIGHT

THE CANONICITY OF
THE BIBLE

E vangelicals believe that not only is the original text of the Bible faithfully and accurately reproduced in the standard English translations,
but neither are there books missing from the original Bible. (This is true
of both Old and New Testaments.) Evangelicals also hold that the canon
(or normative collection) of Scripture, finished by the end of the first century, is closed; that is, we possess in the sixty-six books of the Bible all that
God intended to be there, from both Old and New Testament times. Further, we maintain that God never intended any more books to be added to
the Bible.

THE COMMON CANON

The word *canon* means rule or norm, and as used of the Bible it means
which books are the normative books for Christian faith and practice.
Those considered canonical are the ones held to be inspired of God
(2 Tim. 3:16); they were the books written by the prophets or the apostles
(2 Peter 1:20–21; Eph. 2:20; 2 Peter 3:15–17). Judaism, Catholicism, and
Protestantism agree over the common Old Testament (Jewish) canon,
which consists of thirty-nine books (numbered twenty-four in Jewish
Bibles). This can be called the *common canon*.

However, a crucial difference in Christendom emerges over eleven
pieces of Old Testament literature (seven books and four parts of books)
that the Roman Catholic Church "infallibly" pronounced to be part of the
Canon in A.D. 1546 at the Council of Trent. These books are known by
Protestants as the Apocrypha and by Catholics as the deutero-canonical (lit:

"second canon") books. After enumerating the books (see below), including the eleven apocryphal books, the Council of Trent stated,

> If anyone, however, should not accept the said books as sacred and canonical, entire with all their parts . . . and if both knowingly and deliberately he should condemn the aforesaid tradition let him be anathema [forever cursed]. (Denzinger, *SCD*, number 784.)

Vatican II repeats the same language affirming the Apocrypha to be part of the inspired Word of God.

THE DEBATE ABOUT THE APOCRYPHAL BOOKS

Since the time of the Reformation, there has been a serious debate about whether a collection of books known as the Apocrypha belongs in the Bible. Jews and Protestants unanimously reject them as noncanonical, and Roman Catholics pronounced them canonical at the Council of Trent (1546).

The Names of the Apocryphal Books

The Apocrypha includes eleven books.[1] These include all the fourteen (or fifteen) books in the Protestant Apocrypha, minus the Prayer of

	Revised Standard Version—**Apocrypha**	*New American Bible*
1.	The Wisdom of Solomon (c. 30 B.C.)	Book of Wisdom
2.	Ecclesiasticus (*Sirach*, 132 B.C.)	Sirach
3.	Tobit (c. 200 B.C.)	Tobit
4.	Judith (c. 150 B.C.)	Judith
5.	1 Esdras (c. 150–100 B.C.)	3 Esdras*
6.	1 Maccabees (c. 110 B.C.)	1 Maccabees
7.	2 Maccabees (c. 110–70 B.C.)	2 Maccabees
8.	Baruch (c. 150–50 B.C.)	Baruch 1–5
9.	Letter of Jeremiah (c. 300–100 B.C.)	Baruch 6
10.	2 Esdras (c. A.D. 100)	4 Esdras*
11.	Additions to Esther (140–130 B.C.)	Esther 10:4–16:24
12.	Prayer of Azariah (first century B.C.)	Daniel 3:24–90 (Song of Three Young Men)
13.	Susanna (second or first century B.C.)	Daniel 13
14.	Bel and the Dragon (c. 100 B.C.)	Daniel 14
15.	Prayer of Manasseh (2nd–1st century B.C.)	Prayer of Manasseh*

*These books were rejected by the Council of Trent.

---

[1]Or twelve books, depending on whether Baruch (1–6) is split into two books, consisting of Baruch 1–5 and the Letter of Jeremiah (Baruch 6).

Manasseh and 1 and 2 Esdras (called 3 and 4 Esdras by Roman Catholics, since the Protestant Ezra and Nehemiah are called 1 and 2 Esdras by Catholics).

Although the Roman Catholic canon has eleven more books than the Protestant Bible, only seven extra books appear in the table of contents of Roman Catholic Bibles (e.g., *The New American Bible*), making the total forty-six.[2] The four books or pieces of literature that do not appear in the table of contents are the Additions to Esther, added at the end of the book of Esther (Esther 10:4f.); the Prayer of Azariah, inserted between the Hebrew Daniel 3:23 and 24 (making it Daniel 3:24–90 in Roman Catholic Bibles); Susanna, placed at the end of the twelfth chapter in the Protestant and Jewish book of Daniel (as chapter 13); and Bel and the Dragon (chapter 14 of Daniel).

Reasons Advanced for Accepting the Apocrypha

The larger canon is sometimes referred to as the "Alexandrian canon," as opposed to the "Palestinian canon" (which does not contain the Apocrypha) because the extra books are alleged to have been a part of the Greek translation of the Old Testament (the Septuagint, or "Seventy" [LXX]), which originated in Alexandria, Egypt, beginning the third century B.C. The reasons generally advanced in favor of this broader Alexandrian list accepted by Roman Catholics, which includes the apocryphal books, are as follows:[3]

(1) The New Testament reflects the thought of the Apocrypha, and even refers to events contained in them (cf. Heb. 11:35 with 2 Macc. 7, 12).

(2) The New Testament quotes mostly from the Greek Old Testament (LXX), which contained the Apocrypha. This gives tacit approval of the whole text, including the Apocrypha.

(3) Some of the early church fathers quoted and used the Apocrypha as Scripture in public worship.

(4) Some of the early church fathers—for example, Irenaeus, Tertullian, and Clement of Alexandria—accepted all of the books of the Apocrypha as canonical.

(5) Early Christian catacomb scenes depict episodes from the Apocrypha, showing that they were part of the early Christian's religious life. If not for their *inspiration*, this at least reveals a *great regard* for the Apocrypha.

(6) The great Greek manuscripts interpose the Apocrypha among the

---

[2]The thirty-nine in the Protestant and Jewish Old Testament, plus seven more complete books.

[3]The discussion here follows that in Norman Geisler and William Nix, *A General Introduction to the Bible*, chapter 15.

Old Testament books. This reveals that they were part of the Jewish-Greek translation of the Old Testament (LXX).

(7) Several early church councils accepted the Apocrypha: for instance, the Council of Rome (A.D. 382), the Council of Hippo (393), and the Council of Carthage (397).

(8) The Eastern Orthodox Church accepts the Apocrypha, revealing that they are a common Christian belief, not simply a Catholic dogma.

(9) The Roman Catholic Church proclaimed the Apocrypha canonical at the Council of Trent (1546). This was in accord with pronouncements at early Councils (see point 7 above) as well as the Council of Florence not long before the Reformation (c. 1442).

(10) The apocryphal books continued in the Protestant Bible as late as the nineteenth century. This indicates that even Protestants accepted the Apocrypha until very recently.

(11) Some apocryphal books written in Hebrew have been found among canonical Old Testament books in the Dead Sea community at Qumran. This shows that they were originally part of the Hebrew Canon.

THE PROTESTANT VIEW OF THE APOCRYPHA

In response to the alleged support for considering the apocryphal books as canonical, we will do two things. *First,* we will respond to each of the Roman Catholic arguments in favor of the Apocrypha, showing that they fail to prove their point. *Second,* we will build a positive case in favor of the Jewish and Protestant canons, which exclude the apocryphal books.

A Response to Catholic Arguments in Favor of the Apocrypha

Our response will follow the order of the arguments given by Roman Catholics discussed above, corresponding point by point.

(1) There may be New Testament allusions to the Apocrypha, but there are no clear New Testament quotations from them—*not once* is there a definite quotation from any apocryphal book accepted by the Roman Catholic Church. There are, of course, allusions to pseudepigraphal[4] works that are rejected by Roman Catholics as well as Protestants, such as the Book of Enoch (Jude 14–15) and the Bodily Assumption of Moses (Jude 9). There are also citations from pagan poets and philosophers (Acts 17:28; Titus 1:12; 1 Cor. 15:33), but none of these are cited as Scripture. The New Testament simply refers to a truth contained in these books, which otherwise

---

[4]The "Pseudepigraphica" are "false writings." Neither Roman Catholics nor Protestants accept them as inspired.

may (and do) contain errors. *Roman Catholics agree.* Further, the New Testament never refers to any of the fourteen (or fifteen) apocryphal books as authoritative or canonical; for example, they are never cited with introductory phrases like "thus says the Lord" or "as it is written" or "the Scriptures say," such as are found when canonical books are quoted.

(2) The fact that the New Testament often quotes from the Greek Old Testament in no way proves that the apocryphal books contained in Greek manuscripts of the Old Testament are inspired. First of all, it is not certain that the Greek Old Testament (LXX) of the first century A.D. contained the Apocrypha; the earliest Greek manuscripts that include these books date from the fourth century A.D. Further, even if these books were in the LXX of the apostolic era, Jesus and the apostles never once quoted them, although they are supposed to have been included in the very version of the Old Testament (the LXX) that they usually cited. Finally, even the notes in the current Roman Catholic Bible (NAB) make the revealing admission that the Apocrypha are "religious books used by both Jews and Christians which were not included in the collection of inspired writings." Instead, they "were introduced rather late into the collection of the Bible. Catholics call them 'deutero-canonical' (second canon) books" (see *St. Joseph Edition of The New American Bible,* 413).

(3) Citations by the church fathers in support of the canonicity of the Apocrypha are selective and misleading. While some Fathers seemed to accept their inspiration, other Fathers used them only for devotional or homiletical (preaching) purposes but did not accept them as canonical. As a recent authority on the Apocrypha, Roger Beckwith observes,

> When one examines the passages in the early Fathers which are supposed to establish the canonicity of the Apocrypha, one finds that some of them are taken from the alternative Greek text of Ezra (1 Esdras) or from additions or appendices to Daniel, Jeremiah or some other canonical book, which . . . are not really relevant; that others of them are not quotations from the Apocrypha at all; and that, of those which are, many do not give any indication that the book is regarded as Scripture. (*OTCNTC,* 387.)

For instance,

> the *Epistle of Barnabas* 6.7 and Tertullian (see), *Against Marcion* 3.22.5, are not quoting Wisd. 2.12 but Isa. 3:10 LXX, and Tertullian, *On the Soul* 15, is not quoting Wisd. 1.6 but Ps. 139.23, as a comparison of the passages shows. Similarly, Justin Martyr (see), *Dialogue with Trypho* 129, is quite clearly not quoting Wisdom but Prov. 8.21–5 LXX. The fact that he calls Proverbs "Wisdom" is in accordance with the common nomenclature of the earlier Fathers (ibid., 427).

So the Roman Catholic appeal to the use of the Apocrypha is without basis. In many cases the Fathers were not claiming divine authority for one or more of the eleven books canonized by the Council of Trent; rather, they were either citing a book that *was* part of the Hebrew canon or they were not quoting the Apocryphal books as Scripture.[5]

(4) Although some individuals in the early church had a high esteem for the Apocrypha, there were many individuals who vehemently opposed it. For example, Athanasius, Cyril of Jerusalem, Origen, and the great Roman Catholic biblical scholar and translator of the Latin Vulgate, Jerome, all opposed the Apocrypha. Even the early Syrian church did not accept the Apocrypha; in the second century A.D. the Syrian Bible (Peshitta) did not contain it (Geisler and Nix, *GIB*, chapters 27–28).

(5) As even many Catholic scholars will admit, scenes from the catacombs do not prove the canonicity of the books whose events they depict. Such scenes indicate little more than the religious significance that the portrayed events had for early Christians; at best, they show only a respect for the books containing these events, not a recognition that they are inspired.

(6) None of the great Greek manuscripts contains all of the apocryphal books. In fact, only four—Tobit, Judith, Wisdom, and Sirach (Ecclesiasticus)—are found in all of them, and the oldest manuscripts totally exclude the books of the Maccabees. Yet Catholics appeal to these manuscripts for proof of their deutero-canonical books that include the Apocrypha. What is more, no Greek manuscript has the same list of apocryphal books accepted by the Council of Trent (Beckwith, *OTCNTC*, 194, 382–83).

(7) There are some important reasons why citing these church councils does not prove the Apocrypha belonged in the canon of the church.

First, these were only local councils, not binding on the whole church, and local councils have often erred in their decisions and have been later overruled by the universal church. Some Catholic apologists do argue that even though a council was not ecumenical, its results can be binding if confirmed by a pope; however, they acknowledge that there is no infallible way to know which statements by popes are infallible and which are not. Indeed, these apologists admit that other statements by popes were even heretical, such as the teaching of the monothelite heresy[6] by Pope Honorius I.

Second, these books were not part of the Christian (New Testament period) writings and, hence, they were not under the province of the Christian church to decide. They were the province of the Jewish community, which wrote them and which had centuries before rejected them as part of the Canon.

Third, the books accepted by these Christian councils may not have

[5]The Bible quotes many such works as well, but this does not claim they are God-breathed and thus canonical.
[6]The view that there was only one will in Christ, not both a divine will and a human will as Jesus manifested (cf. Matt. 26:39).

been the same ones in each case; hence, they cannot be used as proof of the exact canon later proclaimed by the Roman Catholic church (at Trent).

Fourth, the local councils of Hippo and Carthage in North Africa were influenced by Augustine, who is the most significant antiquated voice that accepted the same apocryphal books later canonized by the Council of Trent. However, Augustine's position is ill-founded for several reasons:

A. His contemporary, Jerome, a greater biblical authority than Augustine, rejected the Apocrypha (see page 526).

B. Augustine himself recognized that the Jews did not accept these books as part of their canon (*CG*, 19.36–38).

C. Augustine erroneously reasoned that these books should be in the Bible because of their mention "of extreme and wonderful suffering of certain martyrs" (ibid., 18.36). But on that ground *Foxe's Book of Martyrs* should also be in the Canon.

D. Augustine was inconsistent, since he rejected books not written by prophets, yet he accepted a book that appears to deny being prophetic (1 Mac. 9:27).

E. Augustine's mistaken acceptance of the Apocrypha seems to be connected with his mistaken belief in the inspiration of the Septuagint (LXX), whose later Greek manuscripts contained them. However, Augustine's later acknowledgment of the superiority of Jerome's Hebrew text over the Septuagint's Greek text should have led him to accept the superiority of Jerome's Hebrew canon as well, which did not have the Apocrypha.

The later Council of Rome (A.D. 382), which accepted apocryphal books, did not list the same books accepted by Hippo and Carthage; it does not list Baruch, thus listing only six, not seven, of the apocryphal books later pronounced canonical by the Roman Catholic Church. Even Trent lists Baruch as a separate book (Denzinger, *SCD*, number 84).

(8) The Greek Orthodox Church has not always accepted the Apocrypha, nor is its present position unequivocal. At the synods of Constantinople (A.D. 1638), Jaffa (1642), and Jerusalem (1672), these books were declared canonical. But even as late as 1839 their Larger Catechism expressly omitted the Apocrypha on the grounds that its books did not exist in the Hebrew Bible.

(9) At the Council of Trent the infallible proclamation was made accepting the Apocrypha as part of the inspired Word of God. Some Catholic scholars claim that the earlier Council of Florence (1442) made the same pronouncement; however, this was not infallible and it does not have any real basis in Jewish history, the New Testament, or in early Christian history. Unfortunately, the "infallible" decision at Trent came a millennium and a half after the books were written and in an obvious polemic against Protestantism and the Reformation. Even before Martin Luther, the Council of Florence had proclaimed the Apocrypha inspired, which helped to bolster the doctrine of purgatory that had already blossomed in Cathol-

icism. However, the manifestations of this belief in the sale of indulgences came to full bloom in Luther's day, and Trent's proclamation of the Apocrypha was a clear reaction against Luther's teaching. Furthermore, the official addition of books that support prayers for the dead is highly suspect, coming as it did only a few years after Luther protested against this very doctrine. The decision of the Council of Trent has all the appearance of an attempt to provide infallible support for Roman Catholic doctrines that lack any real biblical basis.

(10) Apocryphal books appeared in Protestant Bibles prior to the Council of Trent, and they were generally placed in a separate section because they were not considered of equal authority. While Anglicans and some other non-Roman Catholic groups had a high regard for the inspirational and historical value of the Apocrypha, they did not consider it inspired and of equal authority with Scripture. Even Roman Catholic scholars through the Reformation period made the distinction between the Apocrypha and the Canon. Cardinal Ximenes made this distinction in his *Complutensian Polyglot* (A.D. 1514–1517) on the very eve of the Reformation; Cardinal Cajetan, who later opposed Luther at Augsburg in 1518, published a *Commentary on All the Authentic Historical Books of the Old Testament* (1532) many years after the Reformation began. Neither did this contain the Apocrypha. Luther spoke against the Apocrypha in 1543, placing its books at the back of his Bible (Metzger, *IA*, 181f.).

(11) The discovery of the Dead Sea Scrolls at Qumran included not only the community's Bible (the Old Testament) but also their library, with fragments of hundreds of different books. Among these were some Old Testament apocryphal books, but the fact that no commentaries were found on an apocryphal book and that only canonical books, not the Apocrypha, were found in the special parchment and script, indicates that the apocryphal books were not viewed as canonical by the Qumran community. Menahem Mansoor lists the following fragments of the Apocrypha and Pseudepigrapha: Tobit, in Hebrew and Aramaic; Enoch, in Aramaic; Jubilees, in Hebrew; The Testament of Levi and Naphtali, in Aramaic; apocryphal Daniel literature, in Hebrew and Aramaic; and the Psalms of Joshua (*DSS*, 203). Millar Burrows, noted scholar on the Dead Sea Scrolls, concluded, "There is no reason to think that any of these works were venerated as Sacred Scripture" (*MLDSS*, 178).

At best, all that the arguments urged in favor of the canonicity of the apocryphal books prove is that various apocryphal books were given varied degrees of esteem by different persons within the Christian church, usually falling short of a statement of canonicity. Only after Augustine and the local councils he dominated mistakenly pronounced them inspired, did they gain wider usage and eventual "infallible" acceptance by the Roman Catholic Church at Trent. This falls far short of the kind of initial, continual, and full recognition of the canonical books of the Protestant Old

Testament and Jewish Torah (which exclude the Apocrypha) by the Christian church.

This is but another example of how the teaching Magisterium of the Roman Catholic Church proclaims infallible one tradition to the neglect of strong evidence in favor of an opposing tradition because it supports a doctrine that lacks any substantial support in the canonical books. The real (*proto*) canonical books were received *immediately* by the people of God into the growing canon of Scripture (Geisler and Nix, *GIB*, chapter 13). The *subsequent* debate was by those who were not in a position, as was the immediate audience, to know whether they were from an accredited apostle or prophet. Hence, this subsequent debate over the antilegomena[7] was directly over its *authenticity*, not canonicity. These books were *already* in the Canon; what some individuals in subsequent generations questioned was whether they rightfully belonged there. Eventually, all of the antilegomena were retained in the Canon, which is not true of the Apocrypha, for Protestants reject all of the apocryphal works, and even Roman Catholics reject some (e.g., 3 & 4 Esdras and The Prayer of Manasseh).

Arguments in Favor of the Jewish/Protestant Old Testament Canon

The evidence indicates that the Jewish/Protestant canon, consisting of thirty-nine books identical to the Hebrew Bible (Protestant Old Testament) and excluding the Apocrypha, is the true Canon.[8] The Palestinian Jews represented Jewish orthodoxy; therefore, their canon was recognized as the orthodox one. It was the canon of Jesus (Geisler and Nix, *GIB*, chapter 5), Josephus, and Jerome, and for that matter it was the canon of many of the early church Fathers, including Origen, Cyril of Jerusalem, and Athanasius. The arguments in support of the Protestant canon can be divided into two categories: historical and doctrinal.

The True Test of Canonicity

Contrary to the Roman Catholic argument from Christian usage, the true test of canonicity is propheticity. That is, propheticity determines canonicity: God determined which books would be in the Bible by giving their message to a prophet. So only books written by a prophet or an accredited spokesperson for God are inspired and belong in the canon of Scripture.

Of course, while God *determined* canonicity by propheticity, the people

---

[7]Gk., meaning "to speak against"; viz. the books challenged by some for a time but eventually accepted by all.

[8]In the Jewish Bible, the numbering of thirty-nine books is reduced to twenty-four by combining the following two books into one each: 1–2 Samuel, 1–2 Kings, 1–2 Chronicles, Ezra-Nehemiah (thus reducing the number by four), and counting the twelve Minor Prophets as one book (thus reducing the number by eleven). Thus the total of fifteen (four plus eleven) from thirty-nine leaves twenty-four.

of God had to *discover* which of these books were prophetic. This was done immediately by the people of God to whom the prophet wrote, not centuries later by those who had no access to him or any way to verify his prophetic credentials. For example, Moses' books were accepted immediately and stored in a holy place (Deut. 31:26); likewise, Joshua's books were immediately accepted and preserved along with Moses' law (Josh. 24:26). Samuel wrote a book and added it to the collection (1 Sam. 10:25); Daniel already had a copy of his prophetic contemporary Jeremiah (Dan. 9:2, 11, 13); Paul encouraged the churches to circulate his inspired epistles (Col. 4:16); and Peter had a collection of Paul's writings, calling them "Scripture" along with the Old Testament (2 Peter 3:15–16).

There were a number of ways for immediate contemporaries to confirm whether someone was a prophet of God; among these were supernatural confirmations (cf. Ex. 3:1f; Acts 2:22; Heb. 2:3–4; 2 Cor. 12:12). Sometimes this came in the form of feats of nature, and other times in terms of predictive prophecy. Indeed, false prophets were weeded out if their predictions did not come true (Deut. 18:22). Of course, alleged revelations that contradicted previously revealed truths were rejected as well (Deut. 13:1–3).

The evidence that there was a growing canon of books accepted immediately by contemporaries who could confirm its prophetic authenticity is that succeeding books cited preceding ones. Moses' writings are cited through the Old Testament beginning with his immediate successor, Joshua (Josh. 1:7; 1 Kings 2:3; 2 Kings 14:6; 2 Chron. 17:9; Jer. 8:8; Ezra 6:18; Neh. 13:1; Mal. 4:4). Likewise, later prophets cited earlier ones (e.g., Jer. 26:18; Ezek. 14:14, 20; Dan. 9:2; Jonah 2:2–9; Mic. 4:1–3). In the New Testament Paul cites Luke (1 Tim. 5:18); Peter recognizes Paul's epistles (2 Peter 3:15–16), and Jude (4–12) cites 2 Peter. And the book of Revelation is filled with images and ideas taken from previous Scripture, especially Daniel (cf. Rev. 13).

In fact, the entire Jewish Bible/Protestant Old Testament was considered prophetic. Moses, who wrote the first five books, was a prophet (Deut. 18:15), and the rest of the Old Testament books were known as "the Prophets" (Matt. 5:17; Luke 24:27). "The Prophets" were later divided into Prophets and Writings. The reasons are not clear, but some believe this division was based on whether the author was a prophet by office or only by gift, while others claim it was for topical use at Jewish festivals. Some say they were arranged chronologically in descending order of size (Geisler and Nix, *GIB*, 244–45), but whatever the reason, it is clear that the original (cf. Zech. 7:12; Dan. 9:2) and continual way to refer to the entire Old Testament up to the time of Christ was the twofold division of the "Law and Prophets." In the same way, the "apostles and prophets" (Eph. 2:20; cf. 3:5) composed the entire New Testament; hence, the whole Bible is a prophetic book, including the last book (cf. Rev. 22:7, 9–10, 19). But, as we will see, this cannot be said for the apocryphal books.

There is strong evidence that the apocryphal books are not prophetic. Since propheticity is the test for canonicity, this would eliminate them from the Canon.

First, no apocryphal book claims to be written by a prophet. Indeed, as already noted, one apocryphal book even disclaims being prophetic (1 Mac. 9:27).

Second, there is no supernatural confirmation of any of the writers of the apocryphal books, as there is for the prophets who wrote canonical books.

Third, there is no predictive prophecy (see "P, PB" in *BECA*) in the Apocrypha, such as we have in the canonical books (e.g., Isa. 53; Dan. 9; Mic. 5:2), which is a clear indication of their propheticity.

Fourth, there is no new messianic truth in the Apocrypha; thus, it adds nothing to the messianic truths of the Old Testament.

Fifth, even the Jewish community, whose books they were, acknowledged that the prophetic gifts had ceased in Israel before the Apocrypha was written.

Sixth, the apocryphal books were never listed in the Jewish Bible along with the "Prophets," or any other section for that matter.

Seventh, never once is any apocryphal book cited authoritatively by a prophetic book written after it. Taken together, this provides overwhelming evidence that the Apocrypha was not prophetic and, therefore, should not be part of the canon of Scripture.

The Continuous Testimony From Antiquity

In addition to the evidence for the propheticity of only the books of the Jewish Bible/Protestant Old Testament (which exclude the Apocrypha), there is a virtually unbroken line of support from ancient to modern times for rejecting the Apocrypha as part of the Canon. This is true both for Jewish rabbis and for Christian Fathers.

(1) Philo (20 B.C.–A.D. 40), an Alexandrian Jewish teacher, quoted the Old Testament prolifically from virtually every canonical book. However, he never once quoted from the Apocrypha as inspired.

(2) Josephus (A.D. 30–100), a Jewish historian, explicitly excludes the Apocrypha, numbering the Old Testament as twenty-two books (the thirty-nine books of the Protestant Old Testament). Neither does Josephus ever quote apocryphal books as Scripture, though he was familiar with them. In "Against Apion" (1.8) he wrote,

> For we have not an innumerable multitude of books among us, dis-agreeing from and contradicting one another [as the Greeks have,] but *only twenty-two books, which are justly believed to be divine; and of them, five belong to Moses, which contain his law, and the traditions* of the origin of mankind till his death. This interval of time was little short of three thousand years; but as to the time from the death of Moses till the reign

of Artaxerxes king of Persia, who reigned as Xerxes, *the prophets*, who were after Moses, wrote down what was done in their times in *thirteen books*. The remaining *four books contain hymns to God*, and precepts for the conduct of human life. (emphasis added)

These correspond exactly to the present Jewish and Protestant Old Testament.

(3) The Jewish teachers acknowledged that their prophetic line ended in the fourth century B.C. Yet, as even Catholics acknowledge, the apocryphal books were written after this time. Josephus wrote,

From Artaxeres until our time everything has been recorded, but has not been deemed worthy of like credit with what preceded, because the exact succession of the prophets ceased (ibid).

Additional rabbinical statements on the cessation of prophecy support these (see Beckwith, *OTCNTC*, 370). Seder Olam Rabbah 30 declares,

Until then [the coming of Alexander the Great] the prophets prophesied through the Holy Spirit. From then on, "Incline thine ear and hear the words of the wise."

Baba Bathra 12b asserts,

Since the day when the Temple was destroyed, prophecy has been taken from the prophets and given to the wise.

Rabbi Samuel bar Inia said,

The Second Temple lacked five things which the First Temple possessed, namely, the fire, the ark, the Urim and Thummin, the oil of anointing and the Holy Spirit [of prophecy].

Thus, the Jewish fathers (rabbis) acknowledged that the time period during which the Apocrypha was written was not a time when God was giving inspired writings.

(4) Jesus and the New Testament writers never once quoted the Apocrypha as Scripture, even though they were aware of them and alluded to them at times (e.g., Heb. 11:35 may allude to 2 Mac. 7, 12, though this may be a reference to the canonical book of Kings—see 1 Kings 17:22). Yet the New Testament writers have *hundreds* of citations from all but a few canonical books in the Old Testament, and the manner in which they are cited with authority indicates that they believed them to be part of the "Law and Prophets" [i.e., whole Old Testament], which was believed to be the inspired and infallible Word of God (Matt. 5:17–18; cf. John 10:35). In fact, Jesus specifically quoted books from each of the parts of the Old Testament—"Law and Prophets," which He called "all the Scriptures" (Luke 24:27). There was also a threefold division of the Old Testament into Law,

Prophets, and Writings, but this simply divided the "prophets" into two sections called "prophets and writings" (Geisler and Nix, *GIB*, chapter 14).

(5) The Jewish Scholars at Jamnia (c. A.D. 90) did not accept the Apocrypha as part of the divinely inspired Jewish canon (see Beckwith, *OTCNTC*, 276–277). Since the New Testament explicitly states that Israel was entrusted with the oracles of God and was the recipient of the covenants and the law (Rom. 3:2), the Jews should be considered the custodians of the limits of their own canon. And they have *always* rejected the Apocrypha.

(6) No canonical list or council of the Christian church accepted the Apocrypha as inspired for nearly the first four centuries. This is especially significant since all of the lists available and most of the Fathers of this period rejected the Apocrypha. The first councils to accept the Apocrypha were local ones without ecumenical[9] force. The Catholic contention that the Council of Rome (A.D. 382), though not an ecumenical council, was all-inclusive because Pope Damasus (c. 305–384) ratified it, is without grounds.

First, this begs the question, making the assumption that Damasus was a pope with infallible authority.

Second, even Catholics acknowledge this council was not an ecumenical one.

Third, not all Catholics agree that statements like this by popes are infallible. There are no infallible lists of infallible statements by popes, nor are there any universally agreed-upon criteria that yield conclusions on issues like this that even all Catholics confirm.

Fourth, appealing to a pope to make infallible a statement by a local council is a double-edged sword. Catholic scholars admit that some popes taught error and were even heretical at times (see Geisler and McKenzie, *RCE,* chapter 11).

(7) Many of the early Fathers of the Christian church spoke out against the Apocrypha. This included Origen, Cyril of Jerusalem, Athanasius, and the great Roman Catholic Bible translator Jerome.

(8) Jerome (340–420), the greatest biblical scholar of the early medieval period and the translator of the Latin Vulgate, explicitly rejected the Apocrypha as not part of the Canon. He said the church reads them "for example and instruction of manners" but does not "apply them to establish any doctrine" (Beckwith, *OTCNTC,* 343, citing Jerome's preface to his Vulgate version of the Book of Solomon). In fact, he disputed Augustine's unjustified acceptance of these books. At first, Jerome even refused to translate the Apocrypha into Latin but later made a hurried translation of a few books. After listing the exact books of the Jewish and Protestant Old Testament (which excludes the Apocrypha), Jerome concluded,

---

[9]Meaning, the inclusion of all segments of orthodox Christianity.

> And thus altogether there come to be 22 books of the old Law [according to the letters of the Jewish alphabet], that is, five of Moses, eight of the Prophets, and nine of the Hagiographa [holy writings]. Although some set down . . . Ruth and Kinoth among the Hagiographa, and think that these books ought to be counted (separately) in their computation, and that there are thus 24 books of the old Law; which the Apocalypse of John represents as adoring the Lamb in the number of the 24 elders.

He added,

> This prologue can fitly serve as a Helmed (i.e. equipped with a helmet, against assailants) *introduction to all the biblical books*, which have been translated from Hebrew into Latin, so that we may know that *whatever is not included in these is to be placed among the Apocrypha* (ibid).

In his preface to Daniel, Jerome clearly rejected the apocryphal additions to Daniel (Bel and the Dragon, and Susanna) and argued only for the canonicity of those books found in the Hebrew Bible:

> The stories of Susanna and of Bel and the Dragon are not contained in the Hebrew. . . . For this same reason when I was translating Daniel many years ago, I noted these visions with a critical symbol, showing that they were not included in the Hebrew. . . . After all, both Origen, Eusebius and Appolinarius, and other outstanding churchmen and teachers of Greece acknowledge that, as I have said, these visions are not found amongst the Hebrews, *and therefore they are not obliged to answer to Porphyry for these portions which exhibit no authority as Holy Scripture* (ibid).

The suggestion that Jerome really favored the apocryphal books but was only arguing that the Jews rejected them is groundless. For one thing, he said clearly in the above quotation, "*these portions which exhibit no authority as Holy Scripture.*" In addition, he never retracted his rejection of the Apocrypha; further, he stated (in *Against Rufinius*, 33) that he had "followed the judgment of the churches" on this matter, and his statement "I was not following my own personal views" appears to refer to "the remarks that they [the enemies of Christianity] are wont to make against us." In any event, he nowhere retracted his many statements against the Apocrypha.

Finally, the fact that Jerome cited apocryphal books is no proof that he accepted them, for this was a common practice by many church fathers. What is important is that he never retracted his statement that the church reads them "for example and instruction of manners" but does not "apply them to establish any doctrine."

(9) The Apocrypha was even rejected by noted Roman Catholic scholars during the Reformation period, such as Cardinal Cajetan, who opposed Martin Luther. As already noted, Cajetan wrote *Commentary on All the Authentic Historical Books of the Old Testament* (1532), which excluded the

Apocrypha. If he believed they were authentic, they certainly would have been included in a book on "all the authentic" books of the Old Testament.

(10) Martin Luther, John Calvin, and the other Reformers rejected the canonicity of the Apocrypha. Lutherans and Anglicans used it only for ethical/devotional matters but did not consider it authoritative in matters of faith. Reformed churches followed *The Westminster Confession of Faith* (1647), which states,

> The Books commonly called Apocrypha, not being of divine inspiration, are not part of the canon of the Scriptures; and therefore are of no authority in the Church of God, nor to be any otherwise approved, or made use of, than any other human writings.

In short, the universal Christian church has not accepted the apocryphal books as part of the Canon to this date. The church rejects the Apocrypha because it lacks the primary determining factor of canonicity, which is propheticity; that is, the apocryphal books lack evidence that they were written by accredited prophets of God. Further evidence is found in the fact that the apocryphal books are never cited as authoritative in Scripture in the New Testament; the Apocrypha was never part of the Jewish canon, whose books they are, and the early church never accepted the Apocrypha as inspired.

The Mistake of the Council of Trent

The "infallible" pronouncement by the Council of Trent that the apocryphal books are part of the inspired Word of God is unjustified for many reasons. This statement actually reveals how fallible an allegedly infallible statement can be, since it is historically unfounded, being a polemical overreaction and an arbitrary decision that involved a dogmatic exclusion.

Prophetically Unverified

Again, the true test of canonicity is propheticity, and, as just observed, there is no evidence that the apocryphal books were prophetic. They lack prophetic authorship, prophetic content, and prophetic confirmation.

Historically Unfounded

As also noted, the pronouncement at Trent went against a continuous line of teaching from ancient to modern times, including both noted Jewish and Christian Fathers such as Philo, Josephus, Cyril of Jerusalem, Athanasius, and Jerome.

A Polemical Overreaction

The occasion of Trent's pronouncement on the Apocrypha was part of a polemical action against Luther, supporting teaching he had attacked (such as prayers for the dead—cf. 2 Mac. 12:45–46, which reads, "Thus he made atonement for the dead that they might be freed from his sin").

An Arbitrary Decision

Not all of the Apocrypha was accepted by Rome at Trent. In fact, the Council arbitrarily accepted a book favoring its belief in prayers for the dead (2 Mac.) and rejected one opposed to prayers for the dead (2 [or 4] Esdras; cf. 7:105).[10] There were fourteen books, and yet they selected only eleven for their canon.

A Dogmatic Exclusion

In fact, the very history of this section of 2 (4) Esdras reveals the arbitrariness of the Trent decision. Second (4) Esdras was written in Aramaic by an unknown Jewish author (c. A.D. 100) and circulated in Old Latin versions (c. A.D. 200). The Latin Vulgate printed it as an appendix to the New Testament (c. A.D. 400), and it disappeared from Bibles until Protestants, beginning with Johann Haug (1726–1742), began to print it in the Apocrypha based on Aramaic texts, since it was not in Latin manuscripts of the time. However, in 1874 a long section in Latin (seventy verses of chapter 7) was found by Robert Bently in a library in Amiens, France. Bruce Metzger notes,

> It is probable that the lost section was deliberately cut out of an ancestor of most extant Latin Manuscripts, because of dogmatic reasons, for the passage contains an emphatic denial of the value of prayers for the dead. (*IA*.)

Some Catholics argue that this non-selection was not arbitrary because

(1) Second (4) Esdras was not part of earlier deutero-canonical lists.
(2) It was written after the time of Christ.
(3) It was relegated to an inferior position in the Vulgate.
(4) It was only included among the Apocrypha by Protestants in the eighteenth century.

This argument is unconvincing.

First, 2 (4) Esdras was part of earlier lists of books not considered fully canonical, as even Catholics acknowledge.

Second, according to the Catholic criterion the date of the book has nothing to do with whether it should be in the Jewish Apocrypha but whether it was used by early Christians. And it *was* used, just as the other apocryphal books were.

---

[10]As we have seen, Protestants call this book 2 Esdras and Catholics 4 Esdras. Since Catholics call the books of Ezra and Nehemiah by the names of 1 and 2 Esdras, they then call 1 and 2 Esdras, 3 and 4 Esdras, respectively.

Third, 2 (4) Esdras should not have been rejected simply because it was reduced to an inferior position in the Vulgate. Otherwise, Catholics would have to reject all the Apocrypha, since Jerome, who translated the Vulgate, relegated all the Apocrypha to an inferior position.

Fourth, the reason it did not reappear in Latin until the eighteenth century is apparently that early on some Catholic monk cut out the section against praying for the dead.

In spite of the testimony of antiquity against them, in A.D. 1546, just twenty-nine years after Luther posted his *Ninety-five Theses*, in an attempt to counteract his attack on the sale of indulgences, which eventually led to a rejection of prayers for the dead and purgatory, the Roman Catholic Church proclaimed that these apocryphal books were on the same level as Scripture, declaring,

> The Synod . . . receives and venerates . . . all the books [including the Apocrypha] both of the Old and the New Testaments—seeing that one God is the Author of both . . . as having been dictated, either by Christ's own word of mouth or by the Holy Ghost . . . if anyone receives not as sacred and canonical the said books entire with all their parts, as they have been used to be read in the Catholic Church . . . let him be anathema. (Schaff, *CC*, 2:81.)

The Wrong Test for Canonicity

When all is said and done, the Roman Catholic Church uses the wrong test for canonicity. The correct test of what determines canonicity can be contrasted with the incorrect as follows (see Geisler and Nix, *GIB*, 221):

Incorrect View of Canon	Correct View of Canon
Church Determines Canon	Church Discovers Canon
Church Is Mother of Canon	Church Is Child of Canon
Church Is Magistrate of Canon	Church Is Minister of Canon
Church Regulates Canon	Church Recognizes Canon
Church Is Judge of Canon	Church Is Witness of Canon
Church Is Master of Canon	Church Is Servant of Canon

In spite of the fact that Catholic sources can be cited supporting what looks very much like the "correct view" above, Catholic apologists often equivocate on this issue. Peter Kreeft, for example, argues that the church must be infallible if the Bible is, since the effect cannot be greater than the cause and since the church caused the Canon. But if the church is regulated by the Canon, not ruler over it, then the church is not the cause of the Canon.

Other defenders of Catholicism make the same mistake, giving lip service on the one hand to the fact that the church only discovers the Canon, yet on the other hand constructing an argument that makes the church the determiner of the Canon. They neglect the fact that it is God who caused (by inspiration) the canonical Scriptures, not the church.

This misunderstanding is sometimes evident in the equivocal use of the word *witness*. When we speak of the church as being a witness to the Canon (after the time it was written) we do not mean in the sense of being an eyewitness (i.e., firsthand evidence itself). Only the people of God contemporary to the events were firsthand witnesses. Rather, the later church is a witness *to* the evidence in the sense that it has reviewed the historical evidence for the authenticity of the canonical books as coming from prophets and apostles. The church is not evidence itself; it merely reviews the evidence. Yet when Roman Catholics speak of the role of the church in determining the Canon, they endow it with an evidential role it does not have. Several points will help clarify the proper role of the Christian church in discovering which books belong in the Canon.

First, only the people of God contemporary to the writing of the biblical books could be actual eyewitnesses to the evidence. They alone were witnesses to the Canon as it was developing, and only they can testify to the evidence of the propheticity of the biblical books, which is the determinative factor of canonicity.

Second, the later church is not an evidential witness for the Canon; it does not create or constitute evidence for the Canon. It is only a discoverer and observer of the evidence that remains for the original confirmation of the propheticity of the canonical books. Assuming that the church is evidence in and of itself is the mistake behind the Roman Catholic view favoring the canonicity of the Apocrypha.

Third, neither the earlier nor later church is the judge of the Canon. The church is not, as judges are, the final authority for the criteria of what will be admitted as evidence; that is, it does not determine the rules of canonicity. Since the Bible is the Word of God, only God can determine the criteria for our discovery of what is His Word. Or, to put it another way, what is of God will have His fingerprints on it, and only God is the determiner of what His fingerprints are like.

Fourth, both the earlier and later church is more like a jury than a judge. The role of a jury is to

(1) listen to the evidence, not create it or try to be it;
(2) weigh the evidence, not make it or constitute it, and
(3) render a verdict in accordance with the evidence.

This, as we have shown, is precisely what the Christian church has done in rendering its verdict that the Apocrypha is not part of Sacred Scripture. The contemporary (first-century) church looked at the firsthand evidence for the *propheticity* (miracles, etc.), and the historical church has reviewed the evidence for the *authenticity* of these books, which were directly confirmed by God when they were written.

There is, of course, a certain sense in which the church is a "judge" of the Canon, namely, it is called upon, as all juries are, to engage in an active use of its mind in sifting and weighing the evidence and in rendering a verdict. But this is a far cry from what Roman Catholics believe, in practice, if not in theory, that the church plays a magisterial role in determining the Canon. After all, this is what is meant by the "teaching magisterium" of the church. The Roman Catholic hierarchy is not merely ministerial; it is magisterial—it has a judicial role, not only an administrative one. It is not only a jury looking at evidence; it is a judge determining what counts as evidence and what does not. And therein is the problem.

In exercising its magisterial role, the Roman Catholic Church chose the wrong course in rendering its decision about the Apocrypha, thus showing its fallibility.

First, it chose to follow the wrong criterion: Christian usage rather than propheticity.

Second, it used secondhand evidence of later writers rather than the only firsthand evidence for canonicity (divine confirmation of the author's propheticity).

Third, it did not use immediate confirmation by contemporaries of the events but later statements by people often separated from the events by generations or centuries.

All of these mistakes arose out of a misconception of the very role of the church as judge rather than jury, as magistrate rather than minister, a sovereign *over* rather than servant *of* the canon. By contrast, the Protestant rejection of the Apocrypha was based on a proper understanding of the role of the contemporary eyewitness to the evidence of propheticity and the succeeding church as being possessor of historical evidence for the authenticity of these prophetic books.

Differences over the Apocrypha are crucial to the doctrinal differences of Roman Catholics and Protestants, such as purgatory and prayers for the dead. In answering questions regarding these differences, as shown above, there is no evidence that the apocryphal books are inspired and, therefore, should be part of the canon of inspired Scripture. They do not claim to be inspired, nor does the Jewish community that produced them claim this. Indeed, they are never quoted as Scripture in the New Testament, and many early Fathers, including the great Roman Catholic biblical scholar Jerome, categorically rejected them. Adding them to the Bible in an infallible decree at the Council of Trent has all the air of a polemical pronouncement, calculated to bolster support for doctrines for which there is no clear support in any of the sixty-six canonical books.

In view of the strong evidence against the Apocrypha, the decision by the Roman Catholic Church to pronounce them canonical is both unfounded and rejected by orthodox Protestants. Further, it is a serious error to admit nonrevelational material into the written Word of God, since it corrupts the revelation of God and thereby undermines the divine authority of Scripture (see Ramm, *PRA*, 65).

THE NEW TESTAMENT CANON IS COMPLETE

The New Testament was written between about A.D. 50 and 90, and all major branches of Christianity accept its twenty-seven books as inspired and canonical. There are several lines of evidence that support the evangelical belief that the New Testament canon is closed. Primarily, Jesus promised a closed canon by limiting teaching authority to the apostles, who all died before the end of the first century.

The Evidence for the Completeness of the New Testament Canon

The reasons for believing that the twenty-seven books of the current New Testament, and those alone, belong in the Christian canon are very strong. The evidence includes the promise of Jesus, the providence of God, the preservation by the people of God, and the proclamation of the church.

The Promise of Jesus

There are clear indications in the New Testament that the Spirit of Christ's revelation to the apostles would complete the biblical revelation.

First, Jesus was the full and complete revelation of the Old Testament (Matt. 5:17). Indeed, Hebrews teaches that Jesus is the full and final revelation of God in "the last days" (Heb. 1:1–2). Further, it refers to Christ as "better than" the angels (Heb. 1:4), "better than" the law (Heb. 7:19), and "better than" the Old Testament law and priesthood (Heb. 9:23). Indeed, His revelation and redemption is said to be "eternal" (Heb. 5:9; 9:12, 15) and "once for all" (9:28; 10:12–14). So Jesus was the full and final revelation of God to humankind; He alone could say, "He who has seen me has seen the Father" (John 14:9), and of Him alone could it be said that "in Christ all the fullness of the Deity lives in bodily form" (Col. 2:9).

Second, Jesus chose, commissioned, and credentialed twelve apostles (cf. Heb. 2:3–4) to teach this full and final revelation that He gave them (Matt. 10:1f.), and before He left this world He promised these apostles to guide them into all truth, saying, "the Holy Spirit . . . will teach you all things and will remind you of *everything I have said to you*" (John 14:26). And, "When he, the Spirit of truth, comes, he will guide you into *all truth*" (John 16:13). This is why it is said the church is "built on the foundation of the apostles and prophets" (Eph. 2:20) and the earliest church "continued steadfastly in the apostles' doctrine" (Acts 2:42 NKJV). If the apostles of Jesus did not teach this completed revelation of God, then Jesus was wrong. But as the Son of God He could not be wrong in what He taught; therefore, the full and final revelation of God in Christ was given by the apostles.

Third, the apostles of Christ lived and died in the first century; consequently, the record of this full and final revelation of Christ to the apostles was completed in the first century. Indeed, one of the qualifications of an apostle was that he was an eyewitness of the resurrection of Christ, which occurred in the first century (Acts 1:22). When Paul's credentials as an apostle were challenged, he replied, "Am I not an apostle? Have I not seen Jesus our Lord?" (1 Cor. 9:1). Indeed, he is listed with the other apostles as the "last" to have "seen" the resurrected Christ (1 Cor. 15:6–8).

Fourth, so that there would be no doubt as to who was authorized to teach this full and final revelation of God in Christ, God gave special supernatural powers to the apostles (who in turn gave them to their associates— Acts 6:6; 8:15–18; 2 Tim. 1:6). That these powers were unique to the apostles is clear from the fact that they were called "the signs of an apostle" (2 Cor. 12:12) and that certain things could only occur through the "laying on of the apostles' hands" (Acts 8:18; cf. 19:6). Further, this "power" was promised to the apostles (Acts 1:1, 8), and after Jesus' ministry (cf. John 14:12) they exercised special apostolic functions and powers, including striking people dead who lied to the Holy Spirit (cf. Acts 5:9–11) and performing special signs and wonders (Acts 5:12; Heb. 2:4; 2 Cor. 12:12), which included even raising the dead on command (Matt. 10:8; Acts 20:7–12).

Fifth, there is only one authentic record of apostolic teaching in existence, and that is the twenty-seven books of the New Testament. All other books that claim inspiration come from the second century or later; these are known as the New Testament Apocrypha and are clearly not written by apostles, since the apostles all died before the end of the first century. Since we know the New Testament books have been copied accurately from the very beginning (see chapter 26), the only remaining question is whether all of the apostolic writings from the first century have been preserved. If they have, then these twenty-seven books complete the canon of Scripture, and anything written after them cannot be a revelation of God to the church.

There are two lines of evidence that all the inspired writings of the apostles and their associates were preserved and are found in the twenty-seven books of the New Testament. The first reason is based on the character of God and the second on the care and the testimony of the church.

The Providence of God

Since the God of the Bible is all-knowing (Ps. 139:1–6; 147:5), all-loving (Matt. 5:48; 1 John 4:16), and all-powerful (Gen. 1:1; Matt. 19:26), it follows that He would not inspire books for the faith and practice of believers down through the centuries that He did not preserve. Lost inspired books would be a lapse in God's providence. The God who cares for the sparrows will certainly care for His Scriptures, and the God who has preserved His general revelation in nature (Rom. 1:19–20) will certainly not fail to preserve His special revelation in Scripture (Rom. 3:2). In short, if God inspired them (2 Tim. 3:16), God will preserve them.

The Preservation by the Church

Not only does the providence of God promise the preservation of all inspired books, but the preservation of these books by the church confirms it. This preservation is manifest in a number of ways.

First, a collection of these books was made from the earliest times; even within the New Testament itself this preservation process was put into action. Luke refers to other written records of the life of Christ (Luke 1:1–4), possibly Matthew and Mark. In Paul's epistle of 1 Timothy (5:18) the gospel of Luke (10:7) is quoted. Peter refers to a collection of Paul's epistles (2 Peter 3:15–16). Paul charged that his epistle of 1 Thessalonians "be read to all the brethren" (1 Thess. 5:27), and he commanded the church at Colosse: "After this letter has been read to you, see that it is also read in the church of the Laodiceans" (Col. 4:16). Jude (6–7, 17) apparently had access to 2 Peter (2 Peter 2:4–6), and John's book of Revelation was circulated to the churches of Asia Minor (Rev. 1:4). So the apostolic church itself was involved by divine imperative in the preservation of the apostolic writings.

Second, the contemporaries of the apostles show a concerned awareness of their mentors' writings, quoting from them prolifically (see chapter 17). Following them the Fathers of the second to fourth centuries made some 36,289 citations from the New Testament, including all verses except eleven! This includes 19,368 citations from the Gospels, 1,352 from Acts, 14,035 from Paul's epistles, 870 from the General Epistles, and 664 from Revelation (see Geisler and Nix, *GIB,* chapter 24). The Fathers of the second century alone cited from every book of the New Testament except one (3 John), which they simply may have had no occasion to cite. This reveals not only their great respect for the writings of the apostles but also their ardent desire to preserve their written words.

Third, when challenged by heretical teaching, such as that of Marcion the Gnostic (c. 85–c. 160), who rejected all but part of Luke and ten of Paul's epistles (all but the Pastoral Epistles—1 and 2 Timothy and Titus), the church responded by officially defining the extent of the Canon. Lists of apostolic books and collections of their writings were made from early times, beginning with the second century. These include the Muratorian canon (A.D. 170), Apostolic canon (c. 300), Cheltenham canon (c. 360), and Athanasian canon (c. 367), as well as the Old Latin translation (c. 200). This process culminated in the late fourth and early fifth centuries at the Councils of Hippo (393) and Carthage (410), which listed the twenty-seven books of the New Testament as the complete Canon. Every major section of Christendom has accepted this as the permanent verdict of the church. Evangelical Protestants agree that the Canon is closed.

The Proclamation of the Church

While there was some debate about the books that had initially been accepted into the New Testament church, eventually the universal Christian church came to pronounce unanimously on the twenty-seven books of the present New Testament canon. There has been no significant debate on this since around A.D. 400.

THE DEBATE ABOUT THE NEW TESTAMENT CANON

Unlike the Old Testament, additional books have never been accepted into the New Testament canon long after they were written. Furthermore, there have never been any serious long-term debates over the books that were accepted into the Canon. Nonetheless, there were some questions about some books for some time; these books will be called the New Testament Apocrypha.

The List of New Testament Apocrypha

The New Testament Apocrypha includes the Epistle of Pseudo-Barnabas (c. A.D. 70–79); the Epistle to the Corinthians (c. 96); The Gospel According to the Hebrews (65–100); the Epistle of Polycarp to the Philippians (c. 108); the Didache, or Teaching of the Twelve (c. 100–120); The seven Epistles of Ignatius (c. 110); the Ancient Homily, or the Second Epistle of Clement (c. 120–140); the Shepherd of Hermas (c. 115–140); the Apocalypse of Peter (c. 150); and the Epistle to the Laodiceans (fourth century?).

Sometimes a number of books known as the New Testament Pseudepigrapha (lit: "false writings") are sometimes also called apocryphal. These books have been and are universally rejected by the Christian church. They include second-century books like the Gospel of Thomas (a Gnostic work), the Gospel of Peter (containing Docetic heresies), the Protevangelium of James (containing early devotion to Mary), the Gospel of the Hebrews, and the Gospel of the Egyptians, as well as others (see Geisler and Nix, GIB, chapter 17).

Reasons for Rejecting the New Testament Apocrypha

There are several reasons for rejecting these books as noncanonical.

First, none of them experienced any more than a local or temporary acceptance.

Second, most of them had at best a quasi-canonical status, being merely appended to various manuscripts or listed in tables of contents.

Third, no major canon or church council accepted them as part of the inspired Word of God (see "B, IO" in *BECA*).

Fourth, their limited and temporal acceptance is explainable on the grounds that they were believed wrongly (1) to have been written by an apostle, or (2) to have been referred to in an inspired book (e.g., Col. 4:16). Once this was known to be false they were completely and permanently rejected by the Christian church.

THE COMPLETENESS OF THE BIBLICAL CANON

There is no evidence that any inspired book has been lost. This is confirmed by

(1) the providence of God,
(2) the immediate and careful preservation of the church, and
(3) the absence of any evidence of any other prophetic or apostolic book.

Alleged contrary examples are easily explained as either

(4) uninspired works to which the biblical author made reference, or
(5) inspired works contained in the sixty-six inspired books but with another name.

The list on the next page illustrates the point.

The Confirmation of the Canon

Unlike other holy books, including the Qur'an (see Geisler and Saleeb, *AI,* chapter 9) and the *Book of Mormon* (see Geisler, *CGM*), the Bible alone has been supernaturally confirmed to be the Word of God. Only the Scriptures were written by prophets who were supernaturally confirmed by signs and wonders. When Moses questioned how his message would be accepted, God performed miracles through him "that they may believe that the LORD, the God of their fathers—the God of Abraham, the God of Isaac and the God of Jacob—has appeared to you" (Ex. 4:5). Later when Korah rose up to challenge Moses, God again miraculously intervened to vindicate His prophet (Num. 16). Likewise, Elijah was verified to be a prophet of God by supernatural intervention on Mount Carmel (1 Kings 18).

The New Testament Canon During the First Four Centuries A.D.

Legend: **X** = Citation or allusion **O** = Named as authentic **?** = Named as disputed

Source groupings (left to right in original): COUNCILS, TRANSLATIONS, CANONS, INDIVIDUALS

Source (date)	Matthew	Mark	Luke	John	Acts	Romans	I Cor	II Cor	Galatians	Ephesians	Philippians	Colossians	I Thess	II Thess	I Tim	II Tim	Titus	Philemon	Hebrews	James	I Peter	II Peter	I John	II John	III John	Jude	Revelation
CARTHAGE (c. 419)	O	O	O	O	O	O	O	O	O	O	O	O	O	O	O	O	O	O	O	O	O	O	O	O	O	O	O
CARTHAGE (c. 397)	O	O	O	O	O	O	O	O	O	O	O	O	O	O	O	O	O	O	O	O	O	O	O	O	O	O	O
HIPPO (c. 393)	O	O	O	O	O	O	O	O	O	O	O	O	O	O	O	O	O	O	O	O	O	O	O	O	O	O	O
NICEA (c. 325–40)	O	O	O	O	O	O	O	O	O	O	O	O	O	O	O	O	O	O	O	O	O	?	O	?	?	?	O
OLD SYRIAC (c. 400)	O	O	O	O	O	O	O	O	O	O	O	O	O	O	O	O	O	O	O	O	O		O				
OLD LATIN (c. 200)	O	O	O	O	O	O	O	O	O	O	O	O	O	O	O	O	O	O			O	O	O	O	O		O
TATIAN DIATESSARON (c. 170)	O	O	O	O																							
ATHANASIUS (c. 367)	O	O	O	O	O	O	O	O	O	O	O	O	O	O	O	O	O	O	O	O	O	O	O	O	O	O	O
CHELTENHAM (c. 360)	O	O	O	O	O	O	O	O	O	O	O	O	O	O	O	O	O	O	O	O	O	?	O	?	?		O
APOSTOLIC (c. 300)	O	O	O	O	O	O	O	O	O	O	O	O	O	O	O	O	O	O	O	O	O	O	O	O	O	O	
MURATORIAN (c. 170)	O	O	O	O	O	O	O	O	O	O	O	O	O	O	O	O	O	O					O	O	O	O	O
MARCION (c. 140)			O			O	O	O	O	O	O	O	O	O				O									
AUGUSTINE (c. 400)	O	O	O	O	O	O	O	O	O	O	O	O	O	O	O	O	O	O	O	O	O	O	O	O	O	O	O
JEROME (c. 340–420)	O	O	O	O	O	O	O	O	O	O	O	O	O	O	O	O	O	O	O	O	O	O	O	O	O	O	O
EUSEBIUS (c. 325–40)	O	O	O	O	O	O	O	O	O	O	O	O	O	O	O	O	O	O	O	O	O	?	O	?	?	?	O
CYRIL OF JERUSALEM (c. 315–86)	O	O	O	O	O	O	O	O	O	O	O	O	O	O	O	O	O	O	O	O	O	O	O	O	O	O	
ORIGEN (c. 185–254)	X	X	X	X	X	X	X	X	X	X	X	X	X	X	X	X	X		?		O	?	O		?	?	O
TERTULLIAN (c. 150–220)	X	X	X	X	X	X	X	X	X	X	X	X	X	X	X	X	X		X		O		O			X	X
CLEMENT OF ALEXANDRIA (c. 150–215)	X	X	X	X	X	O	O	O	O	X	O	O	O	X	O		O		O		O		O			O	O
JUSTIN MARTYR (c. 150–55)	X	X	X	O	X	X	X		X	X		X	X	X							X						X
DIOGNETUS (c. 150)							X	X				X				X											
IRENAEUS (c. 130–202)	O	O	O	O	O	O	O	O	O	O	O	O	O	O	X	X	X		X		O		O	X		X	O
PAPIAS (c. 130–40)				X																							O
DIDACHE (c. 120–50)	X						X						X		X											X	X
HERMAS (c. 115–40)	X	X		X	X	X	X			X		X	X		X	X			X	X	X		X				X
POLYCARP (c. 110–50)	X	X	X	X	X	X	X	X	X	X	X	X	X	X	X	X					X		X	X			
IGNATIUS (c. 110)	X	X	X	X	X	X	X			X	X	X	X	X	X			X									
CLEMENT OF ROME (c. 95–97)	X							X		X	X	X	X	X			X		X								
PSEUDO-BARNABAS (c. 70–130)	X	X		X		X	O		X						X	X			X	X	X	X	X				X

Used by permission from GIB, 294

In the Gospels, even the Jewish teacher Nicodemus said to Jesus, "Rabbi, we know that you are a teacher who has come from God. For no one could perform the miraculous signs you are doing if God were not with him" (John 3:2; cf. Luke 7:22). Luke recorded, "Jesus of Nazareth was a man accredited by God to you by miracles, wonders and signs, which God did among you through him" (Acts 2:22). Hebrews affirms that "God also testified to it by signs, wonders and various miracles, and gifts of the Holy Spirit distributed according to his will" (Heb. 2:3–4). And the apostle Paul proved his apostleship by affirming that "the things that mark an apostle—signs, wonders and miracles—were done among you with great perseverance" (2 Cor. 12:12).

No other book in the world has authors who were confirmed in this miraculous manner. Of all the world's religious leaders, not Confucius, not Buddha, not Muhammad, and not Joseph Smith were endorsed by miracles that were verified by contemporary and credible witnesses.[11] *The Bible alone proves to be the Word of God written by prophets and apostles of God who were confirmed by special acts (miracles) of God* (see chapter 29).

CONCLUSION

The Bible is the only infallible written revelation of God to man. It is complete, since both Old and New Testaments contain all the books God inspired for the faith and practice of future generations. This is confirmed by the promise of Christ, the providence of God, the preservation by the people of God, and the proclamation of the early church. Further, the Bible is sufficient for faith and practice; nothing more is needed; the spiritual guide to life needs no new chapters. The Author inspired a complete manual from the beginning and has preserved all of it, intact.

SOURCES

Andrews, Herbert. *An Introduction to the Apocryphal Books of the Old and New Testaments.*

Augustine. *The City of God.*

Beckwith, Roger. *The Old Testament Canon of the New Testament Church and Its Background in Early Judaism.*

Burrows, Millar. *More Light on the Dead Sea Scrolls.*

Denzinger, Henry. *The Sources of Catholic Dogma.*

Foxe, John. *Acts and Monuments of Matters Happening in the Church* (1563).

Geisler, Norman. "Bible, Inspiration of" in *Baker Encyclopedia of Christian Apologetics.*

———. "Prophecy, as Proof of the Bible" in *Baker Encyclopedia of Christian Apologetics.*

---

[11]See Geisler and Saleeb, *AI,* chapter 8.

Geisler, Norman, and Ralph McKenzie. *Roman Catholics and Evangelicals.*

Geisler, Norman, and William Nix. *A General Introduction to the Bible.*

Geisler, Norman, and Abdul Saleeb. *Answering Islam.*

Geisler, Norman, et al. *The Counterfeit Gospel of Mormonism.*

Harris, Laird. *The Inspiration and Canonicity of the Bible.*

Jerome. *Against Rufinius.*

———. "Preface" to *Jerome's Commentary on Daniel,* trans. Gleason Archer.

Josephus, Flavius. "Against Apion" in *Antiquities* (1.8).

Mansoor, Menahem. *The Dead Sea Scrolls.*

Metzger, Bruce. *An Introduction to the Apocrypha.*

Ramm, Bernard. *The Pattern of Religious Authority.*

Schaff, Philip. *The Creeds of Christendom.*

Souter, Alexander. *The Text and Canon of the New Testament.*

Westcott, Brooke Foss. *Documents of Vatican II.*

———. *A General Survey of the Canon of the New Testament.*

———. *New Catholic Encyclopedia.*

———. *St. Joseph Edition of the New American Bible.*

CHAPTER TWENTY-NINE

SUMMARY OF THE EVIDENCE FOR THE BIBLE

The foundation for apologetics is prolegomena (see part 1). The Bible cannot be the Word of God unless there is a God (see chapter 2), nor can the Bible be supernaturally confirmed to be the Word of God unless there are special acts of God, such as miracles (see chapter 3). Nonetheless, within this context there are many lines of supporting evidence that the Bible is the Word of God.

As was shown earlier (see chapter 2), science has demonstrated that there is a supernatural, super-intelligent Creator of the universe, just as the book of Genesis declares (1:1, 27; 2:4). In addition, the Bible foresaw many things that have only been known by science centuries later.

SCIENTIFIC EVIDENCE FOR A SUPERNATURAL CAUSE OF THE UNIVERSE

Based on the intuitively obvious truth that every thing that comes into existence has a cause, modern science has shown that the universe must have had a Cause, since the material universe came into existence. All the evidence for the universe having a beginning supports this conclusion, including the second law of thermodynamics, the expanding universe, the radiation echo, the discovery by the Hubble Space Telescope of the large mass of energy predicted by the Big Bang theory, Einstein's general theory of relativity, and the impossibility of an infinite number of moments before today.[1]

---

[1]See Fred Heeren, *Show Me God: What the Message From Space Is Telling Us About God.*

As we saw earlier, in the light of the overwhelming scientific evidence, agnostic astronomer Robert Jastrow wrote, *"That there are what I or anyone would call supernatural forces at work is now, I think, a scientifically proven fact"* ("SCBTF" in *CT* 15, 18, emphasis added). The British physicist Edmund Whittaker added, "It is simpler to postulate creation ex nihilo— divine will constituting nature from nothingness" (*GA*, 111).[2]

SCIENTIFIC EVIDENCE FOR A SUPER-INTELLIGENT CAUSE OF THE UNIVERSE

There are two powerful arguments for a super-intelligent Cause of the universe and all living things. The first is from astronomy and the second from microbiology.

The Anthropic Principle—Astronomy

The anthropic (Gk: *anthropos*, "human being") principle states that the universe was fitted from the very first moment of its existence for the emergence of life in general and for human life in particular. As Robert Jastrow noted, the universe is amazingly preadapted to the eventual appearance of humanity, for if there were even the slightest variation at the moment of the Big Bang, the conditions for human life would not have been possible. If conditions in our universe were different, even in the smallest degree, no life of any kind would exist. In order for life to be present today an incredibly restrictive set of demands must have been present in the early universe—and they were ("SCBTF" in *CT*, all).

Theistic Implications of the Anthropic Principle
The incredible balance of multitudinous factors in the universe that make life possible on earth (and so far as we know, nowhere else) bespeak of fine-tuning by an intelligent Being. As even agnostic scientists have noted, the conditions that give rise to the anthropic principle are such that would lead one to believe that the universe was "providentially crafted" for our benefit. It is, as Robert Jastrow put it, a "theistic" principle. Nothing known to human beings, other than an intelligent Creator, is capable of pre-tuning the conditions of the universe to make life possible. Or, to put it another way, the kind of specificity and order in the universe that makes life possible on earth is just the kind of effect that is known to come from an intelligent Cause.

Famous astronomer Alan Sandage remarked,

---

[2]See chapter 2 for more evidence.

As I said before, the world is too complicated in all of its parts to be due to chance alone. I am convinced that the existence of life with all its order in each of its organisms is simply too well put together. Each part of a living thing depends on all its other parts to function. . . . How does each part know? How is each part specified at conception? The more one learns of biochemistry the more unbelievable it becomes unless there is some kind of organizing principle—an architect for believers. ("SRRB" in *T*, 54.)

Robert Jastrow summarized:

The anthropic principle is the most interesting development next to the proof of the creation, and it is even more interesting because it seems to say that *science itself has proven, as a hard fact, that this universe was made, was designed, for man to live in. It is a very theistic result.* ("SCBTF" in *CT*, 17.)

Intelligent Design Explains the Origin of Complex Life— Microbiology

Contrary to the claims of modern evolutionists, the Bible declared centuries in advance that life does not arise from purely non-intelligent natural laws. The only cause known to scientists that can produce incredible complexity, even the simplest one-celled life, is super-intelligence. Former atheist Sir Fred Hoyle (1915–2001) affirmed,

Biochemical systems are exceedingly complex, so much so that the chance of their being formed through random shufflings of simple organic molecules is exceedingly minute, to a point indeed where it is insensibly different from zero. . . . [Thus, the existence of] an intelligence, which designed the biochemicals and gave rise to the origin of carbonaceous life. (*EFS*, 3, 143.)

Microbiology has demonstrated,

(1) The genetic code of life is mathematically identical to that of a human language.
(2) The specified complexity of a *one-celled animal* is equal to thirty volumes of the *Encyclopedia Britannica*.

Some of the same naturalistic scientists who reject the fact that this one-celled life had a super-intelligent Creator inconsistently believe, nevertheless, that one small message to us from outer space would prove the existence of intelligent life there. Astronomer Carl Sagan (1934–1996), for example, believed that "the receipt of a single message from space would show that it is possible to live through such technological adolescence" (*BB*, 275). Yet Sagan noted elsewhere that the genetic information in the human brain expressed in bits is probably comparable to the total number of connections among neurons—about a hundred trillion, 10^{14} bits. If written out in English, this information would fill some twenty million volumes, as many as in the world's largest libraries. "The equivalent of twenty million books is inside the heads of every one of us. The brain is a very big place in a very small space." Sagan goes on to note that "the neurochemistry of the brain is astonishingly busy, the circuitry of a machine more wonderful than any devised by humans" (*C*, 278). But if this is so, then why does the human brain not need an intelligent Creator just like those wonderful machines (such as computers) devised by humans?

Michael Behe's excellent book *Darwin's Black Box* provides strong evidence from the nature of a living cell that life could not have originated or evolved by anything but intelligent design. The cell represents irreducible complexity that cannot be accounted for by small incremental changes called for by evolution. As we have seen, Charles Darwin admitted,

> If it could be demonstrated that any complex organ existed which could not possibly have been formed by numerous, successive, slight modifications, my theory would absolutely break down. (*OOS*, 6th ed., 154.)

Even evolutionist Richard Dawkins agrees:

> Evolution is very possibly not, in actual fact, always gradual. But it must be gradual when it is being used to explain the coming into existence of complicated, apparently designed objects, like eyes. For if it is not gradual in these cases, it ceases to have any explanatory power at all. Without gradualness in these cases, we are back to miracle, which is a synonym for the total absence of [naturalistic] explanation. (*BW*, 83.)

But Behe provides numerous examples of irreducible complexity that cannot evolve in small steps. He concludes,

> No one at Harvard University, no one at the National Institutes of Health, no member of the National Academy of Sciences, no Nobel Prize winner—no one at all can give a detailed account of how the cilium, or vision, or blood clotting, or any complex biochemical process might have developed in a Darwinian fashion. But we are here. All these things got here somehow; if not in a Darwinian fashion, then how? (*DBB*, 187.)

Also,

> Other examples of irreducible complexity abound, including aspects of DNA reduplication, electron transport, telomere synthesis, photosynthesis, transcription regulation, and more. [Hence,] life on earth at its most fundamental level, in its most critical components, is the product

of intelligent activity (ibid., 160, 193).

Behe adds,

> The conclusion of intelligent design flows naturally from the data itself—not from sacred books or sectarian beliefs. Inferring that biochemical systems were designed by an intelligent agent is a humdrum process that requires no new principles of logic or science (ibid.).

Thus,

> The result of these cumulative efforts to investigate the cell—to investigate life at the molecular level—is a loud, clear, piercing cry of "design!" The result is so unambiguous and so significant that it must be ranked as one of the greatest achievements in the history of science. The discovery rivals those of Newton and Einstein (ibid., 232–33).

ADVANCED SCIENTIFIC KNOWLEDGE IN THE BIBLE

The Exact Order of Events Known by Modern Science

In addition, in a day when the ancient polytheistic myths of origin prevailed, the author of Genesis declared that the universe came into being out of nothing by the act of a theistic God in the exact order that modern science discovered a millennium and a half later. The universe came first (Gen. 1:1a), then the earth (1:1b), then the land and sea (1:10). After this came life in the sea (1:21), then land animals (1:24–25), and finally, last of all, human beings (1:27). This too supports the view that the author of Genesis had access to some intelligence as to how the Creator made the universe.

Everything Reproduces After Its Kind

Further, the first chapter of Genesis informs us that everything reproduces "after its kind," a scientific fact contrary to many ancient and even earlier modern "hopeful monster views" that in effect a reptile laid an egg and a chicken hatched from it. Both repeated observation and the fossil record demonstrate that each type of life produces its own kind. Indeed, even noted evolutionist Stephen J. Gould declared,

> Most species exhibit no directional change during their tenure on earth. They appear in the fossil record looking much the same as when they disappear; morphological change is usually limited and directionless. [Further,] in any local area, a species does not arise gradually by the steady transformation of its ancestors: it appears all at once and "fully formed" ("EEP" in *NH*, 13–14).

Human Bodies Were Made From the Earth

Many ancient polytheistic beliefs claim that humans came from the gods or that they evolved from lower animals. Modern naturalistic science concurs with the latter, though the means of evolving has changed. Other religious books claim equally unscientific views. The Qur'an, for example, teaches that human beings were created from a "blood clot" (Sura 23:14).

By contrast, the Bible declares, "The LORD God formed the man from the dust of the ground and breathed into his nostrils the breath of life, and the man became a living being" (Gen. 2:7). Solomon added that at death, "The dust returns to the ground it came from, and the spirit returns to God who gave it" (Eccl. 12:7). Modern science confirms the biblical record, showing that, in addition to being largely water, the human body is made of the very same elements found in the earth.

Rain Water Returns to Its Source

The process we know of as evaporation, condensation, and precipitation was described in the Bible in these terms centuries before scientists knew how it worked: "All streams flow into the sea, yet the sea is never full. To the place the streams come from, there they return again" (Eccl. 1:7). Before it rained in the Garden of Eden, it says,

> But streams came up from the earth and watered the whole surface of the ground—the LORD God formed the man from the dust of the ground and breathed into his nostrils the breath of life, and the man became a living being. (Gen. 2:6–7)

Here again, the biblical author's description, perhaps without being aware of the modern technicalities, is in perfect accord with what the Bible declared centuries in advance.

The Earth Is Round and Hangs in Space

Unlike the ancient belief that the world was square, the Bible declares that the earth is round. Isaiah wrote, "He sits enthroned above the circle of the earth, and its people are like grasshoppers. He stretches out the heavens like a canopy, and spreads them out like a tent to live in" (Isa. 40:22).

One of the oldest books in the Bible, whose story goes back to around four thousand years ago, declared that the earth was hung in space. While other myths in the ancient world held that the earth rested on the back of Hercules or rested on pillars, Job said of God, "He spreads out the northern skies over empty space; he suspends the earth over nothing" (Job 26:7).

Life Is in the Blood

Another secret of modern science, hidden for centuries, was announced over three thousand years ago in the Bible. Moses wrote in Leviticus (17:11): "For the life of a creature is in the blood, and I have given it to you to make atonement for yourselves on the altar; it is the blood that makes atonement for one's life." It is likewise known by modern science that life is in the blood, a fact attested to by a loss of blood bringing death.

The Sea Has Paths and Boundaries

The Bible also states well in advance of modern science that the sea has paths. Psalm 8:8 wrote of "the birds of the air, and the fish of the sea, all that swim the paths of the seas." Proverbs 8:29 adds, "He gave the sea its boundary so the waters would not overstep his command, and . . . he marked out the foundations of the earth." The continental shelf that makes this possible is a fairly recent discovery of modern science.

The Laws of Sanitation

The book of Leviticus, long before there was any knowledge of bacteria and germs, set forth laws of sanitation and cleansing that presuppose a knowledge that diseases spread by germs invisible to the naked eye (cf. Lev. 12–15). Cleansing of hands, dishes, and clothes, as well as laws for disposing of human waste all reveal a source in touch with knowledge known by the Creator.

While modern science has demonstrated that there is a supernatural, super-intelligent Creator of the universe, the writer of Genesis had access to this information thousands of years in advance (see, McMillen, *NTD*).

THE TESTIMONY OF THE SCROLLS

As has been demonstrated in chapters 24 and 25, no book from the ancient world has more manuscript support than does the Bible. While the original manuscripts are not available, the copies are highly reliable in that we possess more, earlier, and better copied manuscripts than for any other book from the ancient world.

The New Testament Manuscripts Are More Numerous

Many great classics from antiquity survive in only a handful of manuscript copies. According to the great Manchester scholar F. F. Bruce (1910–1991), we have nine or ten good copies of Caesar's *Gallic Wars*, twenty copies of Livy's *Roman History*, two copies of Tacitus's *Annals*, and eight manuscripts of Thucydides' *History* (*NTD*, 16). Once again, the most documented secular work from the ancient world is Homer's *Iliad*, surviving in some six hundred and forty-three manuscript copies. By contrast, there are now thousands of Greek manuscripts of the New Testament. *The New Testament is far and away the most highly documented book from the ancient world.*

The New Testament Manuscripts Are Earlier

Generally the older the better, since the closer to the time of original composition, the less likely it is that the text has been corrupted. Most books from the ancient world survive not only in a mere handful of manuscripts but also in manuscripts that were made around *one thousand years* after they were originally composed. The oldest manuscript for the *Gallic Wars* is some *nine hundred years* later than Caesar's day. The two manuscripts of Tacitus are *eight* and *ten centuries* later, respectively, than the original. In the case of Thucydides and Herodotus, the earliest manuscript is some *thirteen hundred years* after their autographs. But with the New Testament it is altogether different (Bruce, *NTD*, 16–20). In addition to complete manuscripts from only three hundred years later, most of the New Testament is preserved in manuscripts less than *two hundred years* from the original (P[45], P[46], P[47]), some books of the New Testament dating from little over *one hundred years* after their composition (P[66]), and one fragment (P[52]) coming within *a generation* of the first century.

For other sources it is rare to have, as the *Odyssey* does, one manuscript copied only *five hundred years* after the original. The New Testament, by contrast, survives in complete books from a little over a hundred years after the New Testament was completed. As mentioned, the John Rylands Papyri (P[52]) is dated A.D. 117–138 and survives from within about a generation of the time it was composed. Whole books (the Bodmer Papyri) are available from A.D. 200, and most of the New Testament, including all the Gospels, are available in the Chester Beatty Papyri from 150 years after the New Testament was finished (viz., c. A.D. 250).

Beginning in A.D. 350 the great New Testament manuscripts known as Vaticanus and Sinaiaticus provide us with virtually the entire New Testament. *No other book from the ancient world has as small a time gap (between composition and earliest manuscript copies) as the New Testament.*[3]

The New Testament Manuscripts Are More Accurately Copied

The New Testament (first century) is the most accurately copied book from the ancient world. The famous textual scholars Westcott and Hort

---

[3]As previously stated, the Qur'an has a smaller gap than most early books, yet it is not from the ancient world but rather from the medieval world, nearly seven hundred years after the New Testament was composed.

estimated that only one-sixtieth of its variants rise above "trivialities," which would leave the text 98.33 percent pure. The great scholar John A. T. Robertson said that the real concern is only with a "thousandth part of the entire text" (*ITCNT*, 22), which would make the New Testament 99.9 percent free of variants. The noted historian Philip Schaff calculated that of the 150,000 variants known in his day, only four hundred affected the meaning of a passage, only fifty were of any significance, and *not even one* affected "an article of faith or a precept of duty which is not abundantly sustained by other and undoubted passages, or by the whole tenor of Scripture teaching" (*CGTEV*, 177).

One hundred percent of the message of the New Testament has been preserved in its manuscripts! Sir Frederick Kenyon, an authority on the subject, concluded,

> The number of manuscripts of the New Testament, of early translations from it, and of quotations from it in the oldest writers of the Church, is so large that it is practically certain that the true reading of every doubtful passage is preserved in some one or other of these ancient authorities.... *This can be said of no other ancient book in the world.* (*OBAM*, 55.)

The New Testament Manuscripts Were Written by Contemporaries and Eyewitnesses

Not only were the copies of the manuscripts more, earlier, and better, but they were so early as to vouch for the fact they were composed by eyewitnesses and contemporaries.

The New Testament itself claims to come from eyewitness testimony. Read again what Luke wrote:

> Many have undertaken to draw up an account of the things that have been fulfilled among us, just as they were handed down to us by those who from the first were eyewitnesses and servants of the word. Therefore, since I myself have carefully investigated everything from the beginning, it seemed good also to me to write an orderly account for you, most excellent Theophilus, so that you may know the certainty of the things you have been taught. (Luke 1:1–4)

Indeed, Colin Hemer (*ASHH*, all) has shown that Luke must have composed his gospel by around A.D. 60, just before he wrote Acts (cf. Acts 1:1 and Luke 1:1). Since Jesus died around A.D. 33, this would place Luke only twenty-seven years after the events, while most eyewitnesses were still alive.

Paul speaks of over five hundred eyewitnesses of the results of the Resurrection when he wrote 1 Corinthians, which even critics date by A.D. 55–56. This is only twenty-two or twenty-three years after the events mentioned therein (1 Cor. 15:6). John the apostle also claims to be an eyewitness in his writings:

> That which was from the beginning, which we have heard, which we have seen with our eyes, which we have looked at and our hands have touched—this we proclaim concerning the Word of life. . . . (1 John 1:1–2; cf. John 21:22–25)

Peter added,

> We did not follow cleverly invented stories when we told you about the power and coming of our Lord Jesus Christ, but we were eyewitnesses of his majesty. (2 Peter 1:16)

Many noted scholars, including critical ones, have argued convincingly that the New Testament books were written during the time of the eyewitnesses. Former liberal archaeologist William F. Albright (1891–1971) wrote,

> Every book of the New Testament was written by a baptized Jew between the forties and the eighties of the first century A.D. (very probably sometime between about A.D. 50 and 75). ("WA" in *CT*, 359.)

Famous for his role in launching the "Death of God" movement, Bishop John Robertson wrote a revolutionary book entitled *Redating the New Testament* in which he posited revised dates for the New Testament that place it earlier than even most conservative scholars have held. Remember that he placed Matthew at c. A.D. 40–60+; Mark at c. 45–60; Luke at 57–60+; and John at c. 40–65+ (*RNT*, 352–354). This would mean that some gospels could be as early as seven years after the time Jesus died and would put the reliability of the New Testament documents beyond reasonable doubt.

THE TESTIMONY OF THE SCRIBES

Another strong line of evidence that the Bible is of divine origin is the testimony of the authors. These men not only taught but also lived and died by the highest standard of morality and truthfulness known to humanity. In spite of persecution and death (Heb. 11:32–38), they insisted that their message came from God.

The Nature of a Prophet as a Mouthpiece of God

A biblical prophet is described in these vivid terms: "The Sovereign LORD has spoken—who can but prophesy" (Amos 3:8). He is one who speaks "all the words which the LORD [has] spoken" (Ex. 4:30 NKJV). God said to Moses of a prophet: "I will put my words in his mouth, and he will tell them everything I command him" (Deut. 18:18). He added, "Do not add to what I command you and do not subtract from it" (Deut. 4:2). Jeremiah was ordered, "This is what the LORD says: Stand in the courtyard of the Lord's house and speak to all the people. . . . Tell them everything I command you; do not omit a word" (Jer. 26:2). In brief, a prophet was someone who said what God told him to say, no more and no less.

Prophets Claimed to Be Moved by the Spirit of God

Throughout the Sacred Scriptures, the authors claimed to be under the direction of the Holy Spirit (2 Sam. 23:2; 2 Peter 1:21), but not all prophets were known by the name of prophet. Some were kings, like David, yet he was a mouthpiece of God, nonetheless.[4] Others were lawgivers, like Moses, but he too was a prophet or spokesman for God (Deut. 18:18). Some biblical writers even disclaimed the term *prophet* (Amos 7:14–15), meaning they were not professional prophets, like Samuel and his school of the prophets (1 Sam. 19:20). Nonetheless, even if Amos was not a prophet by office, he was certainly a prophet by gift (cf. Amos 7:14–15). That is, prophets were being used as mouthpieces of God.

"Thus Saith the Lord"

Nor did all who were prophets always speak in the first-person style of an explicit "Thus *saith* the LORD." Phrases like this (Isa. 1:11, 18; Jer. 2:3, 5, etc. KJV), "God said" (Gen. 1:3, 6, etc.), "the Word of the Lord came to me" (Jer. 32:6; Ezek. 30:1, etc.), or the like are found hundreds of times in Scripture. These reveal beyond question that the writers were claiming to give the very Word of God.

Those who wrote historical books, as did the prophet Jeremiah (Kings), spoke in an implied "Thus *did* the Lord." Theirs was a message more about the *acts* of God on behalf of His people than the *words* of God to His people. Nonetheless, all the biblical writers were vessels through whom God conveyed His message to humankind.

The Scriptures Claim to Be Breathed Out by God

Writing about the entire Old Testament canon, the apostle Paul declared, "All Scripture is *God-breathed* and is useful for teaching, rebuking, correcting and training in righteousness, so that the man of God may be thoroughly equipped for every good work" (2 Tim. 3:16–17). Jesus described the Scriptures as the very "word that comes *from the mouth of*

---

[4]Even so, David *is* called a "prophet" (Acts 2:29–39).

God" (Matt. 4:4). They were written *by* men who spoke *from* God. Paul said his writings were "*words taught by the Spirit*" (1 Cor. 2:13).

What the Bible Says, God Says

As we have established, another way the Bible claims to be the Word of God is expressed in the formula "What the Bible says, God says." This is manifested in the fact that often an Old Testament passage will claim God said it, yet when this same text is cited in the New Testament it asserts that "the Scriptures" said it. And sometimes the reverse is true, namely, in the Old Testament it is the Bible that records it, but the New Testament declares that it was God who said it (cf. Genesis 12:3 and Gal. 3:8; Gen. 2:24 and Matt. 19:4–5).

The Bible Claims to Be the "Word of God"

Many times the Bible claims to be "the word of God" in these very terms (Matt. 15:6). Paul speaks of the Scriptures as "*the oracles of God*" (Rom. 3:2 NKJV), and Peter declares, "For you have been born again, not of perishable seed, but of imperishable, through *the living and enduring word of God*" (1 Peter 1:23; see also Heb. 4:12, emphasis added in all).

Since there is every evidence that the biblical authors were men of the truth (they not only taught the highest ethic, but they lived it and were willing to die for it), when they declared the Bible was of divine, not human, origin, there is good reason to believe what they said. Indeed, the truth of their writings is verified for further supporting evidence both from miracles (the supernatural) and archaeology (the stones).

THE TESTIMONY OF THE SUPERNATURAL

The Bible is a supernatural book, making supernatural predictions and containing supernatural confirmations.

Supernatural Predictions in the Bible

The Bible contains nearly three hundred predictions concerning Christ. Even critics agree that the latest of these come from some two hundred years before His time; many come hundreds of years earlier. Every one has come to pass as predicted, and they are often clear and specific. They include that Jesus would be:

(1) born of a woman (Gen. 3:15; cf. Gal. 4:4);
(2) born of a virgin (Isa. 7:14; cf. Matt. 1:21f);
(3) "cut off" (killed) 483 years after the declaration to reconstruct the

temple in 444 B.C. (Dan. 9:24f). (This was fulfilled to the very year [Hoehner, *CALC*, 115–38].);

(4) of the seed of Abraham (Gen. 12:1–3 and 22:18; cf. Matt. 1:1 and Gal. 3:16);

(5) of the tribe of Judah (Gen. 49:10; cf. Luke 3:23, 34 and Heb. 7:14);

(6) of the house of David (2 Sam. 7:12f; cf. Matt. 1:1);

(7) born in Bethlehem (Micah 5:2; cf. Matt. 2:1 and Luke 2:4–7);

(8) anointed by the Holy Spirit (Isa. 11:2; cf. Matt. 3:16–17);

(9) heralded by the messenger of the Lord (Isa. 40:3 and Mal. 3:1; cf. Matt. 3:1–2);

(10) a performer of miracles (Isa. 35:5–6; cf. Matt. 9:35);

(11) a cleanser of the Temple (Mal. 3:1–3; cf. Matt. 21:12f.);

(12) rejected by the Jews (Ps. 118:22; cf. 1 Peter 2:7);

(13) the sufferer of a humiliating death (Ps. 22 and Isa. 53; cf. Matt. 27:31f.), involving:

    A. rejection by His own people (Isa. 53:3; cf. John 1:10–11; 7:5, 48);

    B. silence before His accusers (Isa. 53:7; cf Matt. 7:12–19);

    C. being mocked (Ps. 22);

    D. piercing His hands and feet (Ps. 22:16; cf. Luke 23:33);

    E. being crucified with sinners (Isa. 53:12; cf. Mark 15:27–28 and Matt. 27:38);

    F. praying for His persecutors (Isa. 53:12; cf. Luke 23:34);

    G. piercing His side (Zech. 12:10; cf. John 19:34);

    H. burial in a rich man's tomb (Isa. 53:9; cf. Matt. 27:57–60);

    I. casting lots for His garments (Ps. 22:18; cf. Luke 23:24 and John 19:23–24);

(14) raised from the dead (Ps. 2:7; 16:10; cf. Acts 2:31 and Mark 16:6);

(15) ascended into heaven (Ps. 68:18; cf. Acts 1:9); and

(16) seated at the right hand of God (Ps. 110:1; cf. Heb. 1:3).

Unlike psychic predictions, which are generally not short-term, are often general, and are usually wrong (see Geisler, "PAPB" in *BECA*), these biblical predictions were often specific, always long-term, and never wrong. A study made of top psychics (*The People's Almanac*, 1976) revealed that they were wrong 92 percent of the time. Jeanne Dixon, for example, was usually wrong, and her biographer, Ruth Montgomery, admits that she made false prophecies. Dixon "predicted that Red China would plunge the world into war over Quemoy and Matsu in October of 1958; she thought labor leader Walter Reuther would actively seek the presidency in 1964." On October 19, 1968, she assured us that Jacqueline Kennedy was not considering marriage; the next day, Mrs. Kennedy wed Aristotle Onassis. She also said that World War III would begin in 1954, the Vietnam War would end in 1966, and Castro would be banished from Cuba in 1970.

A study of prophecies made by psychics in 1975 and observed until 1981, including Jeanne Dixon's projections, showed that of seventy-two predictions, only six were fulfilled in any way. Two of these were vague and two others were hardly surprising—the U.S. and Russia would remain leading powers and there would be no world wars (see Geisler, "PAPB" in *BECA*). With only an 8 percent accuracy rate, how seriously can we take these claims? Such a percentage could easily be explained by chance and general knowledge of circumstances.

Even Jeanne Dixon's prophecy of John Kennedy's death is vague, wrong in some aspects (she says that the 1960 election would be dominated by labor, which it was not), and contradicted by her other prophecies—she said Nixon was supposed to win and he didn't. Certainly, there was nothing miraculous about it.

First, Dixon never named "Kennedy," while the Bible, by contrast, named King Cyrus a century and a half before he was born and told what he would do (see Isa. 45:1).

Second, Dixon gave no specificity as to how, where, or when Kennedy would be killed (cf. the specificity in the biblical predictions as to where, when, and how Christ would be born and die).

Third, Dixon's prediction was general. All she divined was that a Democratic president would die in office. Since there was about 50/50 chance that a Democratic president would be elected and a reasonable chance that he would be shot at during an expected two-term time period, there was nothing altogether unusual about this. Furthermore, there was about a century-old cycle going in which nearly every twenty years or so a president was shot. Even Ronald Reagan was later almost killed in office.

Likewise, the highly reputed "predictions" of Nostradamus are not amazing. Contrary to popular belief, he was often wrong when specific, he was usually vague, and he never predicted some of the things attributed to him (see Geisler, "N" in *BECA*). For example, he never predicted either the place or the year of a great California earthquake, and the date later added did not come to pass. Further, most of his "famous" predictions, such as the rise of Hitler, are completely misplaced. He mentioned "hister" (a place), not Hitler (a person).

It is the Bible that makes long-range, specific predictions, which were fulfilled as predicted. This is further evidence of the Bible's divine origin.

Supernatural Confirmations in the Bible

In addition to the supernatural predictions in the Bible, there are numerous supernatural confirmations in it. When there was need, prophets of God were given special divine confirmation.

Moses was given miracle-working ability (Ex. 4:1f.), including creating life from dust (Ex. 8:16–17) and dividing the waters of the Red Sea (Ex.

14). Elijah was confirmed as a prophet of God by bringing fire down from heaven (1 Kings 18), and Elisha performed many miracles to prove he was a prophet, including raising a boy from the dead (2 Kings 4:8–37).

The New Testament informs us that "Jesus of Nazareth was a man accredited by God to you by miracles, wonders and signs, which God did among you through him, as you yourselves know" (Acts 2:22). Indeed, the unbelieving Jewish leader Nicodemus said to Jesus, "Rabbi, we know you are a teacher who has come from God. For no one could perform the miraculous signs you are doing if God were not with him" (John 3:2). Paul said he had the miraculous signs of an apostle (2 Cor. 12:12). The writer of Hebrews affirmed:

> How shall we escape if we ignore such a great salvation? This salvation, which was first announced by the Lord, was confirmed to us by those who heard him. God also testified to it by signs, wonders and various miracles, and gifts of the Holy Spirit distributed according to his will. (Heb. 2:3–4)

Even the Qur'an acknowledges that Jesus was confirmed as a prophet by miracles, including raising a person from the dead (Sura 5:113). Muhammad himself refused to do miracles like the prophets before him (Sura 6:37). The truth is that there is no other book in the world other than the Bible whose truths are confirmed by historically credible supernatural events.

THE TESTIMONY OF THE STRUCTURE (OF THE BIBLE)

One of the supporting lines of evidence for the Bible's divine origin is its amazing unity amid its vast diversity. That is, even though the Bible was composed by many persons of diverse background and in different periods, nonetheless, it manifests astounding evidence that there is one Mind behind it.

Consider first the awesome diversity of the Bible.

First, it was written over *a period of some fifteen hundred years* or more (from at least 1400 B.C. to nearly A.D. 100).

Second, it is composed of *sixty-six different books.*

Third, these books were written by some *forty different authors.*

Fourth, it was composed in *three languages*—Hebrew, Greek, and some Aramaic.

Fifth, it contains *hundreds of different topics.*

Sixth, it was written in a *variety of different literary styles,* including history, poetry, didactic, parable, allegory, apocalyptic, and epic.

Seventh, it was composed by *authors of many different occupations.*

Yet in spite of all this vast diversity, the Bible reveals an astounding unity.

First, it is a continuous, unfolding drama of redemption, from Genesis to Revelation, from Paradise lost to Paradise regained; from the creation of all things to the consummation of all things (Sauer, *DWR* and *TC*, all).

Second, the Bible has one central theme: the person of Jesus Christ (Luke 24:27, 44). In the Old Testament Christ is seen by way of anticipation; in the New Testament by way of realization. In the Old Testament He is predicted, and in the New Testament He is present (Matt. 5:17–18). The Old Testament expectation came to a historic realization in the New Testament.

Third, the Bible has one unified message: Humankind's problem is sin, and the solution is salvation through Christ (Luke 19:10; Mark 10:45). Such incredible unity amid such great diversity is best accounted for by Deity. The very Mind the writers of Scripture claimed inspired them appears to have superintended them, weaving each of their pieces into one overall mosaic of truth.

Critics claim that this is not so amazing considering that succeeding authors were aware of preceding ones and, hence, could build upon the foundation without contradicting it. Or, later generations only accepted their book into the growing canon of Scripture because it seemed to fit with the others. However, these objections overlook several important facts.

First, not all biblical authors possessed all the other books when they wrote theirs. Some wrote in exile (Ezekiel). Others wrote from foreign lands (Esther). Some were written in the East (Hebrews), while others came from Asia Minor (John) or Rome (2 Timothy).

Second, not all writers of biblical books were aware of the fact that their book would be used in the Canon in the way it has been (e.g., Song of Solomon or Proverbs). Hence, they could not have slanted in the way in which it would best fit.

Third, the books were not accepted into the Canon hundreds of years later by people who were looking for books that would fit. Though some later generations raised legitimate questions as to how a book came to be in the Canon, there is evidence that the books were accepted immediately by the contemporaries as they were written. For example, when Moses wrote, his books were placed by the ark of the covenant (Deut. 31:26). Later, when Joshua wrote, his book was placed there along with Moses' books. Likewise, Daniel possessed a copy of Moses and the prophets before him, including a contemporary named Jeremiah (Dan. 9:2). In the New Testament Paul cites Luke (1 Tim. 5:18; cf. Luke 10:7), and Peter possessed Paul's epistles (2 Peter 3:15–16). While not every Christian everywhere possessed every book immediately, those to whom it was written accepted it immediately and others eventually as it was confirmed to them as authentic.

Fourth, even if every author of Scripture possessed every other book before he wrote his own, there is still a unity of Scripture that transcends normal human ability. Indeed, one would have to assume (contrary to fact) that every author of Scripture was an incredible literary genius who saw both the broader unity and "plan" of Scripture and just how his piece was to play a part in it so that the unforeseen end would come out even though he could not foresee it himself. It is simply easier to posit a single, superintending Mind behind the whole thing, who devised the plot and the plan and how it would unfold and eventuate from the beginning (Isa. 46:10).

To illustrate the incredible unity of the Bible, suppose, for example, that a family medical advisor was composed by forty doctors over 1,500 years, in different languages, on hundreds of different medical topics, etc. What kind of unity would it have, even if all the succeeding authors knew what the preceding one had written? One chapter would say all disease is caused by demons that need to be exorcised. Another would claim that disease is in the blood, which needs to be drained out (hence the red in the barber pole), while still another would claim disease is psychosomatic, a matter of mind over matter. Such a book would consistently lack unity and continuity, and no one would seriously consider it a definitive source to answer what is the cause and cure of disease. Yet the Bible, with even greater diversity, is the world's number one bestseller, still sought out by countless millions as the solution to humankind's spiritual maladies. It alone, of all books known to humankind, needs Deity to account for its amazing unity in the midst of its beautiful diversity. And since there is evidence that such a Deity exists (see chapter 2), the unity of the Bible provides evidence that it is His Book.

THE TESTIMONY OF THE STONES

The rocks cry out in support of the historicity and authenticity of the Bible. No archaeological find has ever refuted a biblical claim, and thousands of finds have confirmed in general and in detail the biblical picture. As we read previously, noted archaeologist Nelson Glueck has boldly asserted,

> As a matter of fact . . . it may be stated categorically that no archaeological discovery has ever controverted a biblical reference. Scores of archaeological findings have been made which confirm in clear outline or exact detail historical statements in the Bible. (*RD*, 31.)

William F. Albright concluded, "There can be no doubt that archaeology has confirmed the substantial historicity of the Old Testament tradition" (*ARI*, 176). Further,

> As critical study of the Bible is more and more influenced by the rich new material from the ancient Near East, we shall see a steady rise in respect for the historical significance of now neglected or despised passages and details in the Old and New Testaments. (*FSAC*, 81.)

For the Old Testament, archaeological confirmations have spanned the Creation record (Gen. 1–2) in the Ebla Tablets[5], including Noah's Flood (Gen. 7–9), the Tower of Babel (Gen. 11), patriarchal history (Gen. 12–50), Sodom and Gomorrah (Gen. 18–19), the fall of Jericho (Josh. 6), King David (2 Sam.), and the Assyrian Captivity (Isa. 20).

In the New Testament book of Acts alone there are literally hundreds of archaeological confirmations of innumerable details of the narration. Noted Roman historian A. N. Sherwin-White said of Luke's writings:

> For Acts the confirmation of historicity is overwhelming.... Any attempt to reject its basic historicity even in matters of detail must now appear absurd. Roman historians have long taken it for granted. (*RSRL*, 189.)

Indeed, during decades of research in the area, Sir William Ramsay wrote,

> I found myself often brought into contact with the book of Acts as an authority for the topography, antiquities, and society of Asia Minor. It was gradually borne in upon me that in various details the narrative showed marvelous truth. (*SPTRC*, 8.)

Colin Hemer has detailed these in his volume *The Book of Acts in the Setting of Hellenistic History*. This includes common knowledge, specialized knowledge, and even detailed local knowledge of topography (see chapter 26).

In addition, Luke manifests an incredible array of knowledge of local places, names, conditions, customs, and circumstances that befit only an eyewitness contemporary of the time and events—all without a single mistake. And all of this is to say nothing of the numerous other biblical places, names, and events that have been confirmed by archaeology (see Yamauchi, *SS*, 115–19).

THE TESTIMONY OF THE SAVIOR

Jesus claimed to be the Son of God (John 8:58; Matt. 16:16–18; 26:63–64) and was confirmed by acts of God (John 3:2; Acts 2:22). But Jesus said the Bible is the Word of God (see chapter 16); hence, either the Bible is the Word of God or else Jesus is not the Son of God. If Jesus is the Son of God that He was supernaturally confirmed to be, then the Bible is the Word of God.

---

[5]The Ebla Tablets affirm creation from nothing, declaring, "Lord of heaven and earth: the earth was not, you created it, the light of day was not, you created it, the morning light you had not [yet] made exist" (*Ebla Archives*, 259, cited by Eugene Merrill, "Ebla and Biblical Historical Inerrancy" in *Bibliotheca Sacra* [Oct./Dec. 1983]).

Jesus Confirmed the Old Testament to Be the Word of God

Jesus declared that the Old Testament was *divinely authoritative* (Matt. 4:4, 7, 10); *imperishable* (Matt. 5:17–18); *infallible* (John 10:35); *inerrant* (Matt. 22:29; John 17:17); historically reliable (Matt. 12:40; 24:37–38); scientifically accurate (Matt. 19:4–5; John 3:12); and ultimately supreme (Matt. 15:3, 6). Indeed, many things Bible critics deny, Jesus personally affirmed as true, including:

(1) Daniel was a prophet, not a mere historian (Matt. 24:15).
(2) God created a literal Adam and Eve (Matt. 19:4).
(3) Jonah was literally swallowed by a great fish (Matt. 12:40).
(4) The world was actually destroyed by a flood (Matt. 24:39).
(5) There was one prophet Isaiah (not two or three) who wrote all of Isaiah (1–39 and 40–66: see Luke 4:17–20 and Mark 7:6).

Jesus Promised the New Testament Would Be the Word of God

Jesus not only confirmed the Old Testament as the Word of God but He also promised the New Testament would be God's Word as well. He declared that the Holy Spirit would teach the apostles "all things" and lead them into "all truth" (John 14:26; 16:13). The apostles claimed this divine authority for their words (John 20:31; 1 John 1:1; 4:1, 5–6)—the apostle Peter acknowledged Paul's writings as "Scripture" (2 Peter 3:15–16). Since the New Testament is the only authentic infallible record of apostolic teaching, it must be the "all truth" Jesus promised through the apostles. Thus Jesus taught that both the Old Testament and the New Testament are the Word of God (see chapter 28).

THE TESTIMONY OF THE SPIRIT

No amount of evidence apart from the work of the Holy Spirit will convince anyone of the significance of the fact that the Bible is God's Word. The Bible informs us: "The Spirit himself testifies with our spirit that we are God's children" (Rom. 8:16). This, of course, is based on the testimony of the Word of God, for "faith comes from hearing the message, and the message is heard through the word of Christ" (Rom. 10:17). John added, "I write these things to you who believe in the name of the Son of God so that you may know that you have eternal life" (1 John 5:13).

God not only bears witness to the believer that Christ is the Son of God, but also that the Bible is the Word of God. John wrote,

We accept man's testimony, but God's testimony is greater because it is the testimony of God, which he has given about his Son. Anyone who believes in the Son of God has this testimony in his heart. Anyone who does not believe God has made him out to be a liar, because he has not believed the testimony God has given about his Son. (1 John 5:9–10)

The record, of course, is the Bible. John went on, "I write these things to you who believe in the name of the Son of God so that you may know that you have eternal life" (1 John 5:13). Indeed, "These are written that you may believe that Jesus is the Christ, the Son of God, and that by believing you may have life in his name" (John 20:31). So the Spirit of God bears witness that the Bible is the Word of God and that the Christ revealed in it is the Son of God.

God's witness, however, is through the Word, not apart from it. He provides the subjective assurance through the objective Word and the objective evidence for it. God does not bypass the head on the way to the heart. He said, "Come now, let us reason together . . . though your sins are like scarlet, they shall be as white as snow; though they are red as crimson, they shall be like wool" (Isa. 1:18).

THE TESTIMONY OF THE SAVED

The life-transforming power of the Bible is widely known. Blasphemers, murderers, prostitutes, adulterers, derelicts, drug addicts, and sinners of every stripe have been transformed by its message. One chief example was Saul of Tarsus, hater and persecutor of Christ and Christians, whose miraculous conversion is recorded in Acts 9. He later wrote, "I am not ashamed of the gospel, because it is the power of God for the salvation of everyone who believes: first for the Jew, then for the Gentile" (Rom. 1:16).

Literally millions of people worldwide, from stone-age pagans to modern-age scientists, have testified to the power of the Word of God to make them children of God. Many social organizations, such as the Salvation Army and Inner City Ministries, can attest to the fact that "the word of God is living and active. Sharper than any double-edged sword, it penetrates even to dividing soul and spirit, joints and marrow; it judges the thoughts and attitudes of the heart" (Heb. 4:12). The apostle Peter added, "For you have been born again, not of perishable seed, but of imperishable, through the living and enduring word of God" (1 Peter 1:23).

While early Islam experienced its greatest growth under the military sword, early Christianity grew by "the sword of the Spirit, which is the word of God" (Eph. 6:17). Christianity took over the old Roman Empire not by military might (it had none) but by the might of the Spirit of God working through the Word of God (Zech. 4:6).

The great Christian apologist William Paley (1743–1805) summarized the difference between the growth of Christianity and Islam in this vivid comparison:

For what are we comparing? A Galilean peasant (Jesus) accompanied by a few fishermen, with a conqueror at the head of his army (Muhammad). We compare Jesus, without force, without power, without support, without one external circumstance of attraction or influence, prevailing against the prejudices, the learning, the hierarchy, of his country, against the ancient religious opinions, the pompous religious rites, the philosophy, the wisdom, the authority, of the Roman empire, in the most polished and enlightened period of its existence—with [Muhammad] making his way among Arabs; collecting followers in the midst of conquests and triumphs, in the darkest ages and countries of the world, and when success in arms not only operated by that command of men's wills and persons which attend prosperous undertakings, but was considered as a sure testimony of Divine approbation. That multitudes, persuaded by this argument, should join the train of a victorious chief; that still greater multitudes should, without any argument, bow down before irresistible power—is a conduct in which we cannot see much to surprise us; in which we can see nothing that resembles the causes by which the establishment of Christianity was effected (*EC,* 257).[6]

SUMMARY AND CONCLUSION

The Bible is the only known book in the world that both claims to be and proves to be the Word of God.[7] The evidence supporting this claim has been summarized in this chapter: The testimony of science that demonstrates it, of the scrolls that transmit it, the scribes who wrote it, the supernatural that confirms it, the structure that manifests it, the stones that support it, the Savior who verified it, the Spirit that witnesses to it, and the saved who have been transformed by it. These combined testimonies confirm that the Bible is what it claims to be—the divinely inspired, infallible, and inerrant Word of God (see chapters 13–14, 27).

SOURCES

Albright, William F. *Archaeology and the Religion of Israel.*
———. *Archaeology of Palestine.*
———. *From Stone Age to Christianity.*
———. "William Albright: Toward a More Conservative View" in *Christianity Today* (Jan. 18, 1963).
Behe, Michael J. *Darwin's Black Box.*

---

[6]Many Muslim critics argue that the spread of Christianity in many lands was certainly not always due to peaceable evangelism but also through the use of wars. While this may be true of some later periods, such as the Crusades, it certainly was not true of early Christianity (first to third centuries) when it grew from 120 (Acts 1–2) to the dominant spiritual force in the Roman world before Constantine was converted in A.D. 313.
[7]The Bible's claim has been set forth in great detail in chapters 13–16.

Bruce, F. F. *The New Testament Documents, Are They Reliable?*

Darwin, Charles. *On the Origin of Species.*

Dawkins, Richard. *The Blind Watchmaker.*

Denton, Michael. *Evolution: A Theory in Crisis.*

Einstein, Albert. *Ideas and Opinions—The World as I See It.*

Geisler, Norman. "Nostradamus" in *Baker Encyclopedia of Christian Apologetics.*

———. "Prophecy, As Proof of the Bible" in *Baker Encyclopedia of Christian Apologetics.*

Geisler, Norman, and William Nix. *A General Introduction to the Bible.*

Geisler, Norman, and Abdul Saleeb. *Answering Islam: The Crescent in the Light of the Cross.*

Glueck, Nelson. *Rivers in the Desert.*

Gould, Stephen. "Evolution's Erratic Pace" in *Natural History.*

Hawking, Stephen. *A Brief History of Time.*

Heeren, Fred. *Show Me God.*

Hemer, Colin. *The Book of Acts in the Setting of Hellenistic History.*

Hoehner, Harold. *Chronological Aspects of the Life of Christ.*

Hoyle, Sir Fred. *Evolution From Space.*

———. *The Intelligent Universe.*

Hume, David. *An Enquiry Concerning Human Understanding.*

Jastrow, Robert. *God and the Astronomers.*

———. "A Scientist Caught Between Two Faiths: Interview with Robert Jastrow" in *Christianity Today* (Aug. 6, 1982).

Kenyon, Sir Frederick. *The Bible and Archaeology.*

———. *Our Bible and the Ancient Manuscripts.*

Kitchen, Kenneth. *Ancient Orient and Old Testament.*

McMillen, S. I. *None of These Diseases.*

Merrill, Eugene. "Ebla and Biblical Historical Inerrancy" in *Bibliotheca Sacra* (Oct.–Dec., 1983).

Metzger, Bruce. *Chapters in the History of New Testament Textual Criticism.*

———. *Manuscripts of the Greek Bible.*

———. *Text of the New Testament.*

Orgel, Leslie. *The Origin of Life.*

Paley, William. *Evidences of Christianity.*

Polanyi, Michael. "Life Transcending Physics and Chemistry" in *Chemical Engineering News.*

Pritchard, James B., ed. *Ancient Near East Texts.*

Ramsay, Sir William. *St. Paul the Traveler and the Roman Citizen.*

Robertson, John A. T. *An Introduction to the Textual Criticism of the New Testament.*

———. *Redating the New Testament.*

Ross, Hugh. *The Fingerprints of God.*

Sagan, Carl. *Broca's Brain.*

———. *Cosmos.*

Sandage, Alan. "A Scientist Reflects on Religious Belief" in *Truth* (1985).

Sauer, Eric. *The Dawn of World Redemption.*

———. *The Triumph of the Crucified.*

Schaff, Philip. *Companion to the Greek Testament and English Version.*
Sherwin-White, A. N. *Roman Society and Roman Law in the New Testament.*
Thaxton, Charles, et al. *The Mystery of Life's Origin.*
Warfield, Benjamin B. *The Inspiration and Authority of the Bible.*
Weinberg, Steven. *Dreams of a Final Theory—The Search for the Fundamental Laws of Nature.*
Wilson, Clifford. *Rocks, Relics, and Reliability.*
Yamauchi, Edwin. *The Stones and the Scriptures.*
Yockey, Hubert P. "Self-Organization, Origin of Life Scenarios, and Information Theory" in *Journal of Theoretical Biology*, 1981.

APPENDIX ONE

OBJECTIONS AGAINST THEISTIC ARGUMENTS

I n chapter 2 the traditional theistic arguments were set forth. Since the time of David Hume (1711–1776) and Immanuel Kant (1724–1804) many objections have been leveled against these arguments. Most of them are without merit, and none are telling; nonetheless, each will be addressed briefly.

Objection One: Maybe God Once Existed, But No Longer Exists

The kalam (horizontal) cosmological argument (see Craig, *KCA*) posits a First Cause to explain how a universe that had a beginning got started. In response, some have objected that, at best, this only shows a need for a Cause at the beginning of the universe; it does not prove that this Cause (God) now exists.

Response to Objection One

First of all, at best this objection only applies to the kalam (horizontal) form of the cosmological argument, not the vertical form of Aquinas (*ST*, 1.2.3), for the latter argues from the existence of a present contingent (or changing) being to a present Necessary Being.

Further, even the kalam argument can be expanded by adding (like the vertical cosmological argument) that the First Cause must be a Necessary Being, since that is the only kind of Cause that can produce a contingent being, such as the universe is. A Necessary Being cannot cease to exist; hence, it must exist now.

Objection Two: Finite Beings Need Only a Finite Cause

Following David Hume (see *DCNR*), some object that only a finite cause is necessary to account for a finite effect, such as the universe. Positing an infinite Cause is unnecessary, representing a kind of metaphysical overkill.

Response to Objection Two

In response, it is noted that, according to the principle of causality, *every* finite (limited) being or effect is caused to exist. Thus, this Cause of all finite beings cannot be finite. It is the Unlimited Limiter of every limited thing that exists; thus, this First Cause cannot be finite or limited, because if it were limited (i.e., caused) it would need a cause beyond it to ground its limited existence. So, if there is a limited existence, then Something must be limiting it that is itself Unlimited.

Objection Three: If Everything Needs a Cause, Then So Does God

Bertrand Russell (1872–1970) claimed that if everything needs a cause, then so does God. If everything does *not* need a cause, then neither does the world. So, in either case there is no need for God (see *WIANC*).

Response to Objection Three

However, this dilemma is based on a misunderstanding of the principle of causality, which does not state that "everything needs a cause" but only that "every *finite* (or contingent) thing needs a cause." A being that is not finite (viz., is infinite) does not need a cause, nor does one that is not contingent (viz., is necessary). Since the physical universe is finite, it does need a cause.

Likewise, not everything that is eternal needs a cause (e.g., God) but everything that has a beginning does need a cause. Since the physical universe had a beginning, it must have had a Cause.

Objection Four: The Universe as a Whole Does Not Need a Cause

Some anti-theists claim that the universe as a whole needs no cause; only its parts do, for to claim otherwise, allegedly, is the fallacy of composition, assuming that the whole must have the characteristics of the parts.

Response to Objection Four

This is not the case, as was demonstrated previously (see chapter 2 on the vertical cosmological argument).

Objection Five: Chance Can Explain the Origin of All Things

Following Hume, many appeal to chance as an explanation of the apparent design in the world. Improbable events do happen, just like an improbable roll of the dice does, and given an eternal universe, sooner or later any improbable combination of events will occur.

Response to Objection Five

First, insofar as it is directed at the need for an intelligent cause, this argument violates a fundamental law of thought. An effect cannot be greater than its cause; the Cause of intelligent beings must be intelligent, for it cannot give perfections it does not have to give.

Second, chance has no causal power—it is merely the intersection of lines of causality. There are natural causes and intelligent causes, but there are no chance causes.

Third, the evidence does not support a chance cause of the universe. No scientist would claim that the presidential faces on Mount Rushmore were the result of chance; only intelligent intervention adequately explains these results. Likewise, there is more information in DNA, the simplest form of life, than in either the skeptics' words or Mount Rushmore. Only an intelligent Creator is adequate to account for this vast complexity of information in the code of life.

Fourth, the agnostic would not agree that the very words he used to express his view were a purely chance product rather than an expression of an intelligent being. If he did claim this, then his words have no meaning and, hence, no truth value to refute theism.

Objection Six: The Principle of Causality Is Unprovable

Since all forms of the cosmological argument depend on the principle of causality, the cosmological argument would fail if the principle of causality were not sound. David Hume insisted that either it is based on experience (which could be otherwise), or it is a mere tautology (empty statement) that is true only by definition.

Response to Objection Six

First of all, Hume's argument is based on his epistemological atomism—that all empirical (experiential) impressions are "entirely loose and separate" (see *ECHU*), which is self-defeating, for if all events were entirely loose and separate, there would be no way to know it.

Further, the cosmological argument is not based on merely empirical observation but on metaphysical necessity. For example, a contingent being is one that of necessity can *not* be, and a Necessary Being is of necessity One that can *not* not be.

It is impossible that something could arise from nothing; the principle of causality is that "every limited being has a cause for its existence." This principle is not based in any mere conceptional or definitional necessity but in the fundamental reality that nonexistence cannot cause existence.

What is more, Hume himself emphatically denied that things do not have a cause for their existence (*LDH*, 1:187).

Finally, the reason that all finite, contingent beings need a cause is that "contingent" means "what could not be," and if all contingent beings could not be, then there could be nothing at all. However, there is something; hence, a state of total nothingness is not actually possible. There must be a noncontingent (i.e., necessary) Cause of all contingent beings.

Objection Seven: The Cosmological Argument Commits the Post Hoc Fallacy

David Hume argued that we cannot be sure which effects have which causes, since the post hoc fallacy is always possible; that is, it does not follow logically that something happens *because* of something else simply because it always happens *after* that something else. Therefore, we cannot infer that the universe follows from an intelligent supernatural Cause.

Response to Objection Seven

It is true that it is sometimes difficult empirically, if not practically, to determine which cause is responsible for which effect. Nonetheless, this a-theistic conclusion does not follow from this for many reasons.

First, the cosmological argument does not infer a specific (i.e., finite) cause from a specific effect. It infers an infinite Cause for all finite effects.

Second, even on Hume's empirical grounds he was willing to admit that some things occur so regularly in connection with others that we have a practical "proof" (*ECHU*, VI) that they are connected. We know that only intelligent causes regularly and repeatedly produce specified complexity; consequently, the incredible complexity in the universe points to an intelligent Cause.

Third, as noted above, Hume never denied that there was a causal connection, i.e., that events need causes. He simply questioned the grounds on which some people argue for this. But again, even he admitted that some things are so regularly connected as to call the connection a "proof."

Fourth, even though we cannot always know which finite cause produces which effect, this does not apply to an infinite Cause, for there can only be one infinite Being. There cannot be two Alls, nor can there be two absolutely perfect Beings, because to be two they would have to differ, yet if one lacked some perfection the other had, then one would not be absolutely perfect.

Fifth, if we could not know which kind of cause is behind which kind of effect, then we could not validly infer that there was an atheist's mind behind the atheist's thoughts in the very objection he presents. Further, even the atheist assumes that there is a real theist's mind (cause) behind the theist's writings (effects).

Objection Eight: An Infinite Series of Causes Is Possible

Critics often object that the First Cause is invalid because there could be an endless series of causes, each cause being caused by another before it.

Response to Objection Eight

As is well known in mathematics, infinite numbers are possible; however, several very important considerations invalidate this criticism.

First of all, mathematical infinites are abstract, not concrete. As has been demonstrated, there are an infinite number of points between A and B, but one cannot get an infinite number of sheets of paper between them, no matter how thin the sheets are.

Likewise, an infinite number of moments is not possible before today (see chapter 2), otherwise today would never have come. So a temporal series of infinite causes going backward is not possible either.

Further, in the vertical form of Thomas Aquinas's cosmological argument, the very first cause outside of a finite, contingent, changing being must be infinite and uncaused. This is so because *every* finite being needs a cause; hence, one finite being cannot cause the existence of another. So there cannot be even *one* intermediate efficient causal link between the Creator and His creatures. The very first efficient cause outside of beings whose existence is actualized (caused) by another must be the Actualizer of all other beings.

In addition, an infinite series of simultaneous and existentially dependent causes is not possible. There must be a here-and-now ground for a simultaneous series of causes, none of which would otherwise have a ground for its existence. An ungrounded infinite regress is tantamount to affirming that the existence in the series arises from nonexistence, since no cause in the series has a real ground for its existence. Or, if one cause in the series grounds the existence of the others, then it must be a First Cause (and hence the series is not infinite). Otherwise it turns out to be a cause that causes its own existence (which is impossible), while it is causing the existence of everything else in the series.

Objection Nine: The Concept of an Uncaused Being Is Meaningless

It is urged by some critics that there is no meaning to terms like an "Uncaused" or "Necessary" Being, since we have nothing in our experience to which they correspond.

Response to Objection Nine

This is not a valid objection for many reasons. For one thing, if an uncaused God is meaningless, then so is an uncaused universe, which many atheists posit. Since nothing cannot produce something, then ultimately something must be uncaused—either the universe or its Cause. But, as demonstrated, the universe cannot be eternal since it is running down.

In addition, the very sentence "A Necessary Being has no meaning" would be meaningless unless there were some meaning to the words "necessary being." In short, the atheist assumes the phrase has meaning, otherwise his claim that it is meaningless is self-defeating.

Further, there is nothing incoherent about the term, since it is not contradictory. We know what "contingent being" means (viz., what exists but *can* not exist), and necessary is the opposite of contingent (viz., what cannot not exist).

Finally, the meaning of these terms is derived from their relationship to what is dependent upon them, and this meaning is twofold: *First*, terms like *necessary* or *infinite* are negative terms; they describe what God is not. God is not limited (unlimited) and not contingent (necessary). *Second*, we know what these limitations mean from experience, and so, by contrast, we know that God does not have any of these limitations.

It is important to mention that a negative term does not denote a negative attribute. It is not the affirmation of nothing; rather, it is the negation of all contingency and limitation in the First Cause. The positive content of what God is derives from the causal principle; He is Actuality because He causes all actuality; He is Being since He is the Cause of all being. However, as the Cause of all being His being cannot be caused; as the ground of all contingent beings, He cannot be a contingent being.

Objection Ten: It Is Possible That Nothing Ever Existed, Including God

Anti-theists rightly insist that if there is a Necessary Being, it is impossible for it not to exist. However, it is supposedly not necessary for a Necessary Being to exist; even though something now exists, it is logically possible that nothing ever existed, including God. In short, the ontological argument—that it is logically necessary that a Necessary Being exists—is invalid.

Response to Objection Ten

In response, we acknowledge that this is true and that it is a valid criticism of the ontological argument. However, this reasoning does not work against the cosmological argument, which begins with something that actually exists, namely, a contingent being. And if even one contingent (dependent) being exists, then there must be a Necessary Being on which it depends for its existence.

Furthermore, if a Necessary Being exists, then it is not possible that it not exist, for the only way a Necessary Being could exist is to exist necessarily. In like manner, there need not be any triangular shaped things in existence, but if there are, then they must have three sides. Hence, the atheist's objection to the concept of a Necessary Being applies only to a logically necessary being, not to an actually Necessary Being, which must exist to account for the actual contingent being(s) that exist.

Objection Eleven: The Cosmological Argument Depends on the Invalid Ontological Argument

Following Kant, many critics of theism believe that there is an ontological sleight-of-hand by importing the existence of a Necessary Being into every cosmological argument, which is an illegitimate move from experience to logical necessity.

Response to Objection Eleven

However, this criticism is not applicable to the metaphysical form of the cosmological argument. First of all, the ontological argument need not assume that existence is a perfection or predicate that adds to the concept of the subject. Existence does not have to be a predicate; one can simply say that everything that exists must be predicated according to one or more modes of existence (for example, contingently, necessarily, or impossibly).

For another thing, since the cosmological argument begins with existence, rather than thought, it does not have to smuggle in existence. The first premise is "Something exists," not the idea of a Necessary Being—with which Anselm (see *BW*, 2f.) began his ontological argument.

Furthermore, the cosmological argument proceeds with principles that are grounded in reality, not in mere thought; that is, they are ontologically grounded principles and not simply rationally inescapable ideas. The cosmological argument is based on the metaphysical truth that "Nothing cannot cause something," rather than the rational assertion that "Everything must have a sufficient reason."

Finally, the cosmological argument concludes with an Actual Ground of all finite beings, as opposed only to a logically Necessary Being; that is, it ends with Pure Actuality as the cause of existence for all limited existence, as opposed to a Being that logically cannot not be. In other words, the cosmological argument is not based on the invalid ontological argument.

Objection Twelve: Necessity Does Not Apply to Existence But Only to Concepts

According to this objection, a Necessary Being is a misapplication of the term "necessary," for necessity applies only to concepts or ideas, never to actual reality.

Response to Objection Twelve

This argument fails for two basic reasons.

First, something does not have to be necessarily true in order to be true. There are different degrees of certainty about true propositions. Most theists (except those who defend the ontological argument) agree that the existence of God is not known with logical inescapability. Some, however, believe that it can be demonstrated with actual undeniability.

Further, the objection is self-defeating, for either the statement "Necessity does not apply to existence" is itself a statement about existence, or else it is not. If it is a statement about existence, then it is self-defeating, for it claims to be both necessary and about reality, while it is saying no necessary statements can be made about reality. On the other hand, if it is merely a meta-statement, or statement about statements (and not really a statement about reality), then it cannot mandate what kind of statements may or may not be made about reality. In brief, the only way to deny existentially necessary statements as possible is to make (or imply) one in the very denial, which is self-falsifying.

Second, this criticism begs the question: How do these critics know that necessity does not apply to being? Because there is no Necessary Being? There is no valid way in advance of looking at the argument for God's existence to know if a Necessary Being exists. The concept is not contradictory; it simply means not-contingent, which is a coherent idea. But if there is no prior way to know that a Necessary Being cannot exist, then it is possible that necessity may apply to being, namely, if a Necessary Being does in fact exist.

Objection Thirteen: Theistic Arguments Lead to Metaphysical Contradictions

Immanuel Kant offered several alleged contradictions, or antinomies, that he thought resulted from applying cosmological argumentation to reality. At least three of these antinomies apply to the cosmological argument.

Response to Objection Thirteen

The Antinomy About Time

If we assume that time applies to reality, then a contradiction seems to result that the world is *both* temporal and eternal.

Thesis: The world must have begun in time, or else an infinity of moments elapsed before it began, and this is impossible (since an infinity of moments can never be completed).

Antithesis: The world could not have begun in time, for this implies that there was a time before time began, and this is contradictory.

In response, we note that Kant's thesis is correct; an infinite number of moments is not possible before today. However, Kant's antithesis is mistaken, since it does not follow that there was time before time, if the world had a beginning. The only thing prior to time is the Eternal (i.e., God). In other words, it could have been a creation *of* time, not a creation *in* time.

The Antinomy About Causality

This antinomy argues that it must be true that the world both has a First Cause and does not have a First Cause.

Thesis: Not every cause has a cause, or else a series of causes would not begin to cause, as they in fact do.

Antithesis: A series of causes cannot have a beginning, since everything demands a cause. Hence, the series must go on infinitely.

Again, the "antithesis" of this alleged dilemma is incorrect in stating that *every* cause needs a cause. According to the principle of causality, every cause does not need a cause; only *finite* things need causes. Thus, the series does not need to go on infinitely—there can be an Uncaused Cause of all other things.

The Antinomy About Contingency

Kant insisted that everything must be both contingent and not contingent, if we assume that these concepts apply to reality.

Thesis: Not everything is contingent, or else there would be no condition for contingency. In other words, the dependent must be depending on something that is not dependent.

Antithesis: Everything must be contingent, for necessity applies only to concepts and not to things.

This objection fails, for as noted above there is no way to deny that necessity can apply to reality without making a necessary statement about reality. Only an ontological disproof could possibly establish Kant's point, and ontological disproofs fail, since they make necessary statements about existence.

Further, the cosmological argument concludes that something necessarily exists, which is a refutation of Kant's contention that necessity does not apply to existence.

Objection Fourteen: There Is No Need for a Here-and-Now Cause of the Universe

Some critics argue that even if God is the *originating* Cause of the universe, He is not the *sustaining* Cause of it. God brought the world into existence, but He is not needed to keep it in existence.

Response to Objection Fourteen

First, it was shown above that God could not have caused the universe and then subsequently ceased to exist Himself. Such is not possible because the theistic God is a Necessary Being, and a Necessary Being cannot cease to be—if it exists, it must by its very nature exist necessarily. A Necessary Being cannot exist in a contingent mode any more than a square can exist without four sides.

Second, a Necessary Being must be causing a contingent being at all times, for a contingent being must always be contingent as long as it exists, since it is impossible to become a Necessary Being (which, by its very nature, cannot come to be or cease to be). Other than going out of existence, this is the only other alternative for a contingent being, but if a contingent being is always contingent, then it always needs a Necessary Being on which it can depend for its existence. Since no contingent being holds itself in existence, it must have a Necessary Being to hold it from going into nonexistence—at all times.

Third, it is important to note that the hidden assumption of this objection is that simultaneous causality does not make sense. But there is no contradiction in saying that an effect is being effected at the very instant it is being caused. This is clearly the case with the relation between the premises (cause) and the conclusion (effect) of a syllogism. Cause and effect are simultaneous, for the instant one takes away the premise(s), at that very instant the conclusion does not follow. Likewise, the causal relation between one's face and the image in the mirror is simultaneous.

Many who misunderstand the simultaneous nature of causality confuse an *effect* with an *after-effect*. For example, when the ball is thrown, it continues to move after the thrower is no longer throwing it, just as the clock continues to run after it is wound. However, in each of these and like examples the after-effect is being directly and simultaneously effected by some cause, after the original cause is no longer causing it. For instance, the force of inertia keeps the ball moving after the pitcher throws it, and the forces of tension and reaction keep the spring of a clock moving after the person winds it. But if any of these forces should go out of existence, at that very instant the after-effect would stop dead. For example, if inertia ceased the very instant after the ball left the pitcher's hand, the ball would instantly stop in midair; in the same way, the clock would stop ticking the instant the physical laws "effecting" it were not operative. Every so-called after-effect is only an effect of some other cause(s).

There are no existential after-effects: Whatever is existing, exists here-and-now, and whatever is being caused to exist right now must have something causing it to exist right now. A basic distinction will help illustrate the point. The artist is not the cause of the *being* of a painting; he is only the cause of the *becoming* (or coming to be) of the painting. The painting continues to be after the artist takes his hands off of it. In like manner, the mother does not cause the being of her son but only his becoming, for when the mother dies the son continues to live.

Now, it is necessary that finite beings have a cause not only of their becoming but also of their here-and-now being, for at every moment of their existence they are dependent for their existence on another. They never cease to be limited, finite, contingent beings, and as such they demand a cause for their existence.

Every finite being is caused; therefore, it does not matter at what moment (m^1, m^2, m^3, etc.) of his existence—he is still receiving his existence from something beyond him. Changing the moment of his dependent existence does not make him a nondependent existent.

Part of the problem would be removed if we did not talk of exist-*ence* (as though it were a whole package received at once) but of exist-*ing* (which is a moment-by-moment process). The word "being" is even more misleading in this regard. No one receives his whole being at once, not even the next instant of it. Each creature has a present "be-ing," and at each moment of a dependent be-ing there must be some independent Being on which he is depending for that moment.

In this respect, the distinction between the Latin *esse* (to be) and *ens* (a being, a thing) is helpful. God is pure *Esse*, and our present *esse* (to-be-ness) is dependent on Him. Pure Existence must existentialize our continuing existence; otherwise, we would not continue to exist. God as Pure Actuality is actualizing everything that is actual; hence, it is the present actuality of all that is actual, of all that demands a causal ground.

Objection Fifteen: Act/Potency or Necessary/Contingent Models Are Arbitrary

This objection states that the act/potency or necessary/contingent models used to conclude the existence of a theistic God are arbitrary. Reality can be conceived in other ways that do not lead to God.

Response to Objection Fifteen

In response, theists point out that the necessity/contingency model is not arbitrary but is logically exhaustive. Either there is only a Necessary Being, or else there is a contingent being(s) as well as a Necessary Being. But there cannot be merely contingent beings, for contingent beings do not account for their own existence, since they are, but they can *not* be.

Likewise, either everything is one pure undifferentiated Actuality, or pure potentiality, or a combination of actuality and potentiality. *No other possibility exists.* Yet there cannot be two Pure Acts, since act as such is unlimited and unique; there cannot be two Ultimates or two Infinite Beings, so whatever else exists must be a combination of actuality and potentiality. Since no potentiality can actualize itself, then whatever beings there are that are composed of actuality and potentiality must be actualized by Pure Actuality. Thus, there is nothing arbitrary whatsoever about these models; they are logically exhaustive.

Objection Sixteen: The Cosmological Argument Commits Modal Fallacies

Modal logic is based on the distinction between what is possible and what is necessary. This form of reasoning has developed its own list of fallacies; for instance, some modal logicians argue that it does not follow from the fact that it is possible for all the parts of my car to break down at one time or another that it is necessary that all the parts will break down at one time. Thus, though all contingent beings possibly do not-exist, they do not necessarily not-exist at one time and thus would need no universal cause of their existence.

Response to Objection Sixteen

In response, two points are important:

First, modal logic has certain presuppositions that one need not accept. For example, it assumes that "no world at all" is not a possible world. Hence, it comes to the ungrounded conclusion via an ontological argument that a Necessary Being must exist.

Second, even granting modal logic, this objection would only cast doubt on some forms of the argument from contingency. This objection does not apply to the cosmological argument from contingency used above, since it is not concerned with showing that all things that could not-exist needed a Cause to produce their existence, but that *all things that do exist* (though possibly could not-exist) *need a cause for their present existence*, both individually and *en toto*.

Another possible charge of committing a modal fallacy is that it is illegitimate to infer from the fact that the world necessarily needs a being as First Cause that the world needs a Necessary Being as First Cause. Again, this charge would be correct in some forms of the argument, but not the one (following Aquinas) used above, for in it God is not considered a Necessary Being because the argument demonstrates His being necessarily— He is called a Necessary Being because ontologically He cannot not be. We learn of His Necessary Being not from the rigor of our premises, but because the Cause of all contingent being cannot be a contingent being— He must be necessary.

The mistake of many theists, especially since the time of Gottfried Wilhelm Leibniz (1646–1716), is to cast the cosmological argument in a context of *logical necessity* based on the principle of *sufficient reason*. This ultimately leads to contradictions and an invalidating of the argument. In contrast to this procedure, other theists (like Aquinas) used the principle of existential causality to infer the existence of unlimited Cause or Actualizer of all existence. This conclusion is not rationally inescapable, but it is actually undeniable. In brief, if any contingent being exists, then a Necessary Being exists; if any being with the potentiality not to exist does exist, then a Being with no potentiality not to exist must exist.

Objection Seventeen: An Imperfect World Does Not Need a Perfect Cause

Following David Hume (*DCNR*), it is also objected that if there is a cause of the universe, it need not be perfect, since the world is imperfect. If a cause resembles its effects, then it would seem that the world must be caused by an imperfect, finite, male and female group of gods, for this is what we know as the causes of similar imperfect things in our experience.

Response to Objection Seventeen

First, the Ultimate Cause cannot be im-perfect (not-perfect), since the not-perfect can only be known if there is a Perfect by which it is known to be not perfect.

Second, the cause does not have to be equal to its effect. The cause cannot be less than the effect (since no effect can be greater than its cause), but it can be more than its effect.

Third, the Cause of finite beings cannot be imperfect, since it is Being itself or Pure Actuality; only Pure Actuality can actualize a potency (potentiality) for existence, and no potency for existence can actualize itself, for if it could, then nothing could produce something. Hence, the Cause of being must be perfect in its Being, since it has not potency, limitations, or privation that can constitute an imperfection.

Objection Eighteen: What Is Logically Necessary Does Not Necessarily Exist

Some anti-theists argue that it is logically necessary for a triangle to have three sides, but it is not necessary for any three-sided thing to exist. Therefore, even if it were logically necessary for God to exist it would not mean that He actually does exist.

Response to Objection Eighteen

At best, this is only an objection to the ontological argument, not to the cosmological and teleological arguments (see chapter 2). Further, theists need not, and most theists do not, conceive of God as a *logically* Necessary Being but as an *actually* Necessary Being. That is, it is logically possible that God does not exist, but if He does exist, then it is actually necessary that He exists, just as it is logically possible that no triangle exists, but if one does, then it is actually necessary that it have three sides. Likewise, it is logically possible that there is no Necessary Being, but if a Necessary Being does exist, then it is actually necessary for it to exist, for if it is a Necessary Being, then by its very nature it must exist necessarily.

Objection Nineteen: Real Causes Cannot Be Inferred From Observed Effects

Immanuel Kant (*CPR*) argued that we cannot validly infer a real cause from effects that we experience. There is an unsurpassable gulf between the thing-to-me (*phenomena*, or perceived) and the thing-in-itself (*noumena*, or real). We cannot know the latter; we know things as they appear to us but not as they really are.

Response to Objection Nineteen

First, this objection either begs the question or is self-defeating. It begs the question if it supposes that our senses do not provide us information about the real world, wrongly assuming that we sense only sensation rather than sense reality through sensations. Or to put it another way, this argument mistakenly believes that we know only our ideas rather than knowing reality through our ideas.

Second, if this objection claims that we cannot know reality, the agnostic is making a statement about reality, claiming that he knows enough about reality that he is sure that he cannot know anything about reality. But this is a self-defeating claim. Put in terms of the principle of causality, how can Kant know that reality is causing our experiences unless there is a valid causal connection between the real (*noumenal*) world of the cause and the apparent (*phenomenal*) world of our experience? Further, one could not even know his own ideas and words were the result of his mind unless there were a real connection between cause (his mind) and effect (his ideas). Nor would he write books, as agnostics do, assuming that readers would look at the phenomenal effects (words) and be able to know something about the noumenal (real) cause (his mind).

Objection Twenty: It Is Impossible for an All-Powerful God to Exist

Theists claim God is all-powerful, but many non-theists insist this is impossible. The logic of their argument can be outlined as follows:

(1) If God were all-powerful, then He could do anything.
(2) If God could do anything, then He could make a rock so big that He couldn't move it.
(3) But if God could not move this rock, then He could not do everything.
(4) An all-powerful God that can do anything cannot make a rock too heavy for Him to lift. Hence, the theistic God (who is all-powerful) cannot exist.

Response to Objection Twenty

Put in this form, the theist rejects the first premise, since it is an improper definition of omnipotence. God cannot literally do everything; He can only do anything that is *possible* to do. There are many things God cannot do: He cannot cease being God; He cannot contradict His own nature; He cannot do what is logically impossible; He cannot do what is actually impossible (like force someone to freely love Him). Likewise, God cannot make a rock so heavy that He cannot lift it for the simple reason that *anything He can make is finite*, and anything that is finite He can move by His infinite power. If He can make it, He can move it.

Objection Twenty-One: If God Is Infinite, Then He Is Contradictory Things

If God is infinite, then He is everything, including opposites, but this is impossible, for then an infinite God would be both good and evil, both perfect and imperfect, both being and nonbeing. These are opposites, and God cannot be opposites. Further, the theist cannot admit that God is evil or nonexistent. Therefore, no theistic God exists.

Response to Objection Twenty-One

The theist responds by rejecting the premise that God is everything; He is only what He is—an absolutely perfect Being. God is not what He is not—an imperfect being; God is Pure and Necessary existence; thus, He cannot be non-existent.

When we say that God is unlimited or infinite, we do not mean that He is everything. God is not a creature, for instance—He made all but is not all. We do not mean, for example, that God is both limited and infinite; the unlimited cannot be limited, and the uncreated Creator cannot be a created creature. Nor do we mean that God is imperfect—as an unlimited Being, God cannot be limited in His perfection, and evil is not a perfection; it is an imperfection. The standard of all good cannot be evil; the Perfect cannot be imperfect.

Objection Twenty-Two: God Is Nothing But a Projection of Our Imagination

Ludwig Feuerbach (1804–1872) argued that man made God in his image (*EC*), that God is only a projection of what we think of ourselves, nothing more. All our ideas of God come from our ideas of human beings; hence, God is only a projection of these ideas and does not exist beyond them. The essence of Feuerbach's argument can be stated this way:

(1) God exists in human consciousness.
(2) But humans cannot go beyond their own consciousness.
(3) Therefore, God does not exist beyond our consciousness.

Response to Objection Twenty-Two

For one thing, this objection fails because God is not a mere projection of human imagination. As the theistic arguments show (see chapter 2), the existence of God is supported by cogent rational explanations.

Furthermore, the problem with this argument is the second premise—that we cannot go beyond our consciousness does not mean nothing exists beyond our consciousness. I cannot go beyond my mind, but I know there are other minds beyond mine with whom I can communicate. Further, if we cannot go beyond our consciousness, then even Feuerbach could not make the statement: "There is no God beyond our consciousness." How does he know there is no God out there, unless his knowledge can go beyond his consciousness? To put the criticism another way, to make "nothing but" statements (such as, "God is nothing but a projection of our imagination") is to imply "more-than" knowledge. How could one possibly know God is nothing but a projection of his imagination unless he knew more than his imagination?

Finally, that we do not go beyond our own consciousness does not mean that our consciousness is not of things that are beyond us. Of course, we cannot *get out of* ourselves, but we can *reach out of* ourselves. And this is precisely what knowledge does. Consciousness is not simply consciousness of itself; we are also conscious of others. When we read a book we are not simply conscious of our own ideas; we are conscious of another mind who wrote the words from which we got those ideas.

Objection Twenty-Three: God Is Only an Illusion

Sigmund Freud (1856–1939) insisted that God is an illusion—someone we wish to be true but having no basis beyond our wishes. God is a child-hood neurosis we never outgrew, the result of a desire for a Cosmic Comforter, a kind of Heavenly Linus Blanket. But the fact that we wish for a pot of gold at the end of a rainbow does not mean there is one there. Likewise, the desire for a heavenly Father to comfort us in the woes of life is illusory (*FI*).

Response to Objection Twenty-Three

There are many ways to respond to Freud's objection to God. For one thing, it is very difficult to put this into any kind of argument that has premises that cannot be easily challenged. Perhaps the following is what is meant:

(1) An illusion is something based only in wish but not in reality.
(2) Belief in God has the characteristics of an illusion.
(3) Therefore, belief in God is a wish not based in reality.

Of course, in this form the theist challenges the minor premise on many grounds. First of all, not all who believe in God do so simply because they wish for a Cosmic Comforter. Some find God because they thirst for reality, and many find God because they are interested in truth, not simply because they are concerned about feeling good.

Further, there are numerous discomforting dimensions to the Christian belief in God. God is not only a Father who provides; He is also a Judge who punishes. Christians believe in hell, and yet no one really wishes this to be true.

In addition, Freud may have it backwards. Maybe our images of earthly fathers are patterned after God rather than the reverse. Perhaps this is because God has created us in His image rather than the opposite.

Also, the mere human desire for God is not the only basis for believing that God exists. Freud's argument would, at best, only apply to those who had no other basis than their own wish that God exists.

What is more, God may exist even if many (even all) people had the wrong reason (their own wish) for believing that He did. That one wishes he will win the lottery does not mean that he will not win it—some do. That many wish for a better way of life does not mean it is unobtainable—many attain it.

Furthermore, Freud confuses *wish* and *need*. What if, as even many atheists admit, there is a *real need* for God in the human heart? One may want prime rib and wine, but he only needs bread and water. Children want candy, but what they need is real food. If the desire for God is a need, not merely a want, then Freud's analysis of religious experience is inadequate.

Finally, it may be that Freud's belief that there is no God is itself an illusion. After all, if one does not wish to follow and obey God, is it not much easier to believe that no God exists? Indeed, for anyone living in sin and rebellion against God, it is very comforting to believe that neither He nor hell is real (cf. Ps. 14:1; Rom. 1:18f.). It is at least as likely, if not more so, that the atheist has killed the Father as that the theist has created Him.

Objection Twenty-Four: Theistic Arguments Are Not Persuasive

Some object that theistic arguments are persuasive only to those who already believe, and they do not need them. Thus, they are useless.

Response to Objection Twenty-Four

This objection fails for several reasons. Whether anyone is convinced by it will depend on several factors. For one thing, even if the argument is sound, persuasiveness will depend in part on whether the argument is understood.

Further, once the mind understands the argument, it is a matter of the will whether one assents to it. No one is ever forced to believe in God simply because his mind understands *that* there is a God; there may be other personal factors beyond the analysis here that lead a man to remain uncommitted to belief *in* God. Theistic arguments do not automatically convert unbelievers, but persons of good will who understand the arguments ought to accept them as true. If they do not, it does not prove that the arguments are wrong; it simply shows that they are unwilling to accept them.

Objection Twenty-Five: If God Knows Everything, Then Man Is Not Free

According to theism, God's knowledge is infinite, but if God knows everything, including the future, then we are not free, for whatever an omniscient (all-knowing) God knows must come to pass (is determined).

Response to Objection Twenty-Five

First of all, knowing what men *will* do with their freedom is not the same as preordaining what they *must* do. God's knowledge is not incompatible with free will; there is no contraction in God's knowing in advance what we will do with our freedom. God is responsible for the *fact* of freedom, but men are responsible for the *acts* of freedom.

In addition, God in His foreknowledge might even persuade men to make a certain decision, but there is no reason to suppose that He coerces any decision so as to destroy freedom. He works persuasively but not coercively.

Further, one and the same act can be determined from the standpoint of God's knowledge and yet free from the standpoint of our choice. God can know for sure (is determined) what we will freely do (is free).

What is more, as an eternal Being God does not really *fore*-know anything. He is eternal and, as such, He simply *knows* in one eternal Now everything there is to know. God sees all of time—past, present, and future—from His lofty perch of eternity; whereas human beings looking through the tunnel vision of time can see only the present.

If God does not *fore*-know (but simply *knows* all of time in His eternal present), then our free choices are not determined in advance; He is simply seeing them in His present.

Finally, as the First Cause of all things, God does not have to wait to see them, for the effect preexists in its cause. Hence, God knows the future by knowing it in Himself as its Cause.

CONCLUSION

Many objections have been proposed against proofs for the existence of God. Most of them are straw-man arguments or are based on a misunderstanding of the proof for God's existence, and none of them succeed in diminishing the classical proofs for God. These venerable arguments remain firm, having stood the test of time.

SOURCES

Anselm. *Basic Writings.*
Craig, William. *The Kalam Cosmological Argument.*
Eslick, L. J. "The Real Distinction" in *Modern Schoolman 38* (Jan. 1961).
Feuerbach, Ludwig. *The Essence of Christianity.*
Findlay, J. N. "Can God's Existence Be Disproved?" in the *Ontological Argument*, Alvin Plantinga, ed.
Flint, Robert. *Agnosticism.*
Freud, Sigmund. *The Future of an Illusion.*
Garrigou-LaGrange, Reginald. *God: His Existence and His Nature.*

Geisler, Norman. *Baker Encyclopedia of Christian Apologetics.*
Geisler, Norman, and W. Corduan. *Philosophy of Religion.*
Hoyle, Sir Fred, et al. *Evolution From Space.*
Hume, David. *Dialogues Concerning Natural Religion.*
———. *An Enquiry Concerning Human Understanding.*
———. *The Letters of David Hume.*
Jastrow, Robert. *God and the Astronomers.*
———. "A Scientist Caught Between Two Faiths: Interview With Robert Jastrow" in *Christianity Today* (Aug. 6, 1982).
Kant, Immanuel. *A Critique of Pure Reason.*
Kenny, Anthony. *Five Ways.*
Parmenides. *Proem.*
Plato. *Parmenides.*
———. *Sophists.*
Russell, Bertrand. *Why I Am Not a Christian.*
Sproul, R. C. *Not a Chance: The Myth of Chance in Modern Science and Cosmology.*
Teske, R. J. "Platos's Later Dialectic" in *Modern Schoolman 38* (Mar. 1961).
Thomas Aquinas. *On Being and Essence.*
———. *Summa Theologica.*

DO HISTORICAL FACTS SPEAK FOR THEMSELVES?

D o the facts of history speak for themselves, or must they be interpreted? If the latter, is there more than one way to interpret them?
What role does one's worldview play in the interpretation of facts? Is there
any way to adjudicate between one worldview and another?

If facts do not speak for themselves, then how can we argue from biological facts, like irreducible complexity, to a Creator? Or from the fact of
the origin of the universe to a Creator? (see chapter 2). Is it not inconsistent to argue from the fact of the second law of thermodynamics or from
specified complexity to a theistic God, and yet reject the view that the facts
of history also reveal a theistic God? More specifically, if one can argue
from the singularity of the origin of the universe to a Creator, then why
can't one argue from the singularity of the resurrection of Christ to a God?

Several possible answers present themselves. Most of these are incompatible with the view that the historical facts speak for themselves; this
view begs the question.

THE FIRST POSSIBLE ANSWER

Some claim that facts do not need an overall interpretive framework
(like theism) for one to see that they lead to an intelligent Creator. Even
an unbeliever can see that irreducible complexity, such as is in the human
eye, demands a Creator.

Problems With the First Response

There are several difficulties with this answer.

First, few unbelievers would admit this. Darwin acknowledged that the eye was difficult to explain, but he concluded it was not necessary to posit a Creator to explain it (see *OOS*). If unbelievers were to hold that it is necessary to posit an intelligent Cause of the eye, then they would not be unbelievers in God. Unbeliever Richard Dawkins posits a "blind watchmaker," that is, natural law to account for the eye and all other specified complexity in nature (*BW*).

Second, suppose all reasonable persons either do or should accept the conclusion that the irreducible complexity in a human eye or the incredible specified complexity in a single-celled animal calls for an intelligent cause. Even so, this cause does not have to be beyond the universe (as in theism); it could be within the universe (as in panentheism or pantheism). Hence, even in this case, these facts do not lead to a theistic view.

Third, it is highly doubtful by the nature of the case that any fact or facts within the universe logically demand an intelligent Cause beyond the universe. This seems to be true for two reasons. For one thing, a worldview (such as theism) is an interpretation of the whole universe. But no one fact within the universe, which gets its meaning from being part of the whole, can be used without begging the question to interpret the whole of which it is a part.

Also, there are other possible ways to interpret these facts within the universe without appealing to a theistic God (e.g., as naturally caused or as anomalies). As long as some other interpretation is logically possible, then a theistic explanation is not logically necessary. For instance, as to the claim that Christ's rising from the dead demands a theistic God as an explanation, the unbeliever responds by questioning

(1) whether He really died;
(2) whether He really rose;
(3) whether resurrection demands a supernatural Cause as opposed to
    (a) a yet unknown natural cause or
    (b) a cause within the universe.

Unless all these alternatives can be shown to be impossible, then the so-called "facts" of the Resurrection do not speak for themselves.

ANOTHER POSSIBLE ANSWER

Others argue that facts must speak for themselves, otherwise it would not be possible to argue from facts in this world to God, which proponents of the cosmological, teleological, and moral arguments believe is possible.

For example, proponents of the kalam cosmological argument claim that a great deal of scientific evidence points to a beginning of the universe, and since nothing can arise without a cause, there must be a Cause of the entire universe. But any Cause that existed before and beyond the whole natural world is by definition a supernatural Cause. Hence, beginning with scientific facts (like the second law of thermodynamics) can lead to a theistic conclusion.

A Response to the Second Posed Solution

It would seem on the surface that this position has demonstrated that one can begin with facts and argue back to theism. However, on closer examination there is an equivocation on the term *facts*. The facts that *do not* logically lead to theism are facts that are within the universe. They are a part of the whole, but not the whole. The facts that *do* lead to a theistic conclusion are facts that are the facts of the whole universe, not just part of it.

For example, in the valid form of the cosmological argument the facts are the condition of the *whole universe* coming into existence, not just part of it. Likewise, isolating an eye or a one-celled animal and pointing to its design does not thereby prove a Designer beyond the universe. However, if one could demonstrate that the entire universe manifests design (as the anthropic principle is employed to do), then this would point to a theistic Designer beyond the universe.

In brief, there are two reasons why facts within the universe, no matter how much they may point to a Cause, cannot be used as such to demonstrate that a theistic God exists.

First, the Cause may be within the universe, not beyond it.

Second, a Cause is needed to explain only part of but not the whole universe, whereas in a theistic universe a Cause is needed to explain the whole universe. Indeed, the cause needed to explain just part of the universe may be the whole universe, but no theist would agree that the whole natural universe is God.

A THIRD POSSIBLE ANSWER

Of course, one may simply *presuppose*, without any reason or argument, that the theistic view is correct and that no fact within the universe speaks for itself. In this case, no facts in the world speak for themselves, for all bare facts carry no meaning, and all interpreted facts must be interpreted from the presupposed worldview framework (such as theism).

The problem with this view is not with the claim that facts do not speak for themselves but with the claim that there is no way to adjudicate conflicts between worldviews. In this case, no fact or argument, historical or otherwise, can be used to defend one worldview over another; everyone is speaking about the same facts with entirely different meaning grids. There is no real communication between different worldviews, no common ground on which to stand, and no way to establish one worldview over another. But in this event, either all worldviews are true—even opposing ones, which is impossible—or no worldview is true, which is unreasonable, since at least one viewpoint must correspond to reality (be true). Every view cannot be false (see chapter 8).

ANOTHER ALTERNATIVE: THE FACTS SPEAK FOR THEMSELVES APART FROM A WORLDVIEW

Finally, one may argue, as some historical apologists do, that the facts speak for themselves apart from presupposing (or proving) one worldview over another. One argument proposed in favor of this view goes as follows: It is self-defeating to affirm that there are any facts without meaning, since the very affirmation about the allegedly meaningless fact is a meaningful statement about the facts. Therefore, all facts are meaningful; there are no so-called bare facts.

However, this argument does not really prove that facts speak for themselves; rather, it merely shows that facts can and do bear meaning. But what the argument must prove (and fails to do so) is that facts are capable of only one meaning and that they manifest it evidently. Nevertheless, it is evident that meaningful statements about facts can be made without attributing some meaning to the facts themselves, and this does not prove that the meaning is inherent in the facts. It is possible that the meaning was assigned to the facts by the one making the meaningful statement about them. Indeed, only "mean-ers" (i.e., minds) can give meaning.

Further, it is not at all clear in what sense an objective fact can mean anything in and of itself. It is a subject (e.g., a mind) that utters meaning about objects (or about other subjects), but objects as such are not subjects that are emitting meaning. This is true unless we assume that all objective facts are really little transmitters of meaning or thought from some Mind that communicated this meaning through them. But to assume this would be to invoke one particular worldview over another in order to prove that "facts speak for themselves." And even then it could be argued that the facts are not speaking for themselves but for the Mind (God) who is speaking through them.

It seems best to conclude, then, that objective and isolated facts as such do not speak for themselves. Finite minds may give differing interpretations of them or an infinite Mind may give an absolute interpretation of them, but the facts as such do not emanate any meaning of and from themselves. Of course, if there is an absolute Mind from whose vantage point the facts are given absolute or ultimate meaning, then there is an objective interpretation of the facts that all finite minds should concur is the ultimate meaning. If this is the correct worldview, then there is an objective meaning to all facts in the world. All facts are theistic facts, and no non-theistic way of interpreting them is objective or true. Hence, objectivity in history is possible since in a theistic world, history would be His-story. Objectivity, then, is possible only from within an established theistic worldview.

Furthermore, as we have seen (see chapter 2), there are some general facts about the universe as a whole from which one can reasonably infer a theistic worldview. For instance: (1) Its coming into being; (2) its contingency; and (3) its anthropic nature from conception. Once this theistic context is established, the particular and isolated facts, which have no meaning in themselves, get their meaning from this overall theistic framework.

CONCLUSION

The sum of the matter as it relates to history is that history is objectively knowable, even if one must posit a worldview framework to interpret the facts. Either the facts of history "speak for themselves" and, hence, are objectively knowable, or else they do not. If not, there is a rational way to establish the correct worldview framework by which they should be interpreted. However, theism is grounded in sound reasons (see chapter 2), and it provides the proper way to understand and interrelate the facts of history and thus avoid pure historical subjectivism.

SOURCES

Darwin, Charles. *On the Origin of Species.*
Dawkins, Richard. *The Blind Watchmaker.*
Geisler, Norman, and William Watkins. *Worlds Apart.*

BIBLIOGRAPHY

Ahlstrom, Sydney E. *Theology in America: The Major Protestant Voices From Puritanism to Neo-Orthodoxy.* Indianapolis: Bobbs-Merrill Co., 1967.

Albright, William F. *Archaeology and the Religion of Israel.* Baltimore: The Johns Hopkins Press, 1953.

———. *The Archaeology of Palestine.* Baltimore: Penguin, 1949.

———. In *Christian Century* (November 19, 1958).

———. *From Stone Age to Christianity.* Garden City, N.Y.: Doubleday (Anchor), 1957.

———. *Recent Discoveries in Bible Lands.* New York: Funk & Wagnalls, 1956.

———. "Toward a More Conservative View" in *Christianity Today* (January 18, 1963).

Ambrose. "Letters" in *Early Latin Theology; Selections From Tertullian, Cyprian, Ambrose, and Jerome.* Edited by S.L. Greenslade. Philadelphia: Westminster Press, 1956.

Andrews, Herbert T. *An Introduction to the Apocryphal Books of the Old and New Testaments.* Revised and edited by Charles F. Pfeiffer. Grand Rapids: Baker, 1964.

Anselm. *Basic Writings: Proslogium, Monologium, Gaunilon's: On Behalf of the Fool, Cur Deus Homo.* 2nd edition. Translated by S. W. Deane. LaSalle, Ill.: Open Court, 1962.

———. *Truth, Freedom, and Evil: Three Philosophical Dialogues.* Edited and translated by Jasper Hopkins and Herbert Richardson. New York: Harper & Row, 1967.

Aquinas, Thomas. *Commentary on the Gospel of John: Part II.* Translated by Fabian R. Larcher. Petersham, Miss.: St. Bede's Publications, 1985.

———. *The Literal Exposition on Job: A Scriptural Commentary Concerning Providence.* Translated by Anthony Damico. Atlanta: Scholar's Press, 1989.

———. *On Being and Essence.* Translated by Armand Maurer; 2nd edition. Toronto: The Pontifical Institute of Mediaeval Studies, 1968.

———. *On the Power of God.* 3 volumes. Edited and translated by Lawrence Shapcote. London: Burns, Oates, and Washbourne, 1932.

———. *On Truth.* Translated by J. V. McGlynn. Chicago: H. Regnery, 1952–54.

———. *Summa Contra Gentiles.* In *On the Truth of the Catholic Faith: Book One: God.* Translated by Anton C. Pegis. New York: Image, 1955.

———. *Summa Theologica.* 60 volumes. Edited by O. P. Gilby. New York: McGraw-Hill, 1966.

Archer, Gleason L., Jr. *Encyclopedia of Biblical Difficulties.* Grand Rapids: Zondervan, 1982.

———. *Old Testament Quotations in the New Testament.* Chicago: Moody Press, 1983.

———. *A Survey of Old Testament Introduction.* Revised edition. Chicago: Moody, 1974.

Aristotle. *Metaphysics.* Edited and translated by John Warrington. New York: Denton, 1966.

———. *Posterior Analytics.* 2nd edition. Edited by Jonathan Barnes. Oxford: Oxford University Press, 1994.

———. *Prior Analytics.* Translated by Robin Smith. Indianapolis: Hackett Publishing Company, 1997.

———. *Topics.* Edited by Robin Smith. New York: Oxford University Press, 1996.

Augustine. *Against the Academicians: The Teacher.* Translated by Peter King. Indianapolis: Hackett, 1995.

———. "City of God." In *Nicene and Post-Nicene Fathers.* 14 volumes. 1st series (1886–1894). Edited by Philip Schaff. Reprint, Grand Rapids: Eerdmans, 1952.

———. *The Greatness of the Soul and the Teacher.* Translated by Joseph M. Colleran. Westminster, Md.: Newman, 1950.

———. "Letters" 82.3. In *The Nicene and Post-Nicene Fathers of the Christian Church.* 1st series. Volumes 1–7 (1886–1888). Edited by Philip Schaff. Reprint, Grand Rapids: Eerdmans, 1979.

———. "On the Gospel of John." In *The Nicene and Post-Nicene Fathers* (ibid.).

———. "On the Trinity." In *The Nicene and Post-Nicene Fathers* (ibid.).

———. *Principii Della Dialettica.* Como: Gruppo Amici del Liceo Volta, 1985.

———. "Reply to Faustus the Manichaean." 11.5 in Philip Schaff. *A Select Library of the Nicene and Ante-Nicene Fathers of the Christian Church.* Volume 4. (Grand Rapids: Eerdmans, 1956). In *The Nicene and Post-Nicene Fathers* (op. cit.).

Bacon, Francis. *The New Organon and Related*

Writings. Edited by Fulton H. Anderson. New York: Bobbs-Merrill, 1960.

Baillie, John. *The Idea of Revelation in Recent Thought.* New York: Columbia University Press, 1956.

Barr, James. *The Semantics of Biblical Language.* London: Oxford University Press, 1961.

Barrow, John D. *The Anthropic Cosmological Principle.* New York: Oxford University Press, 1986.

Barth, Karl. *Church Dogmatics.* Introduction by Helmut Gollwitzer. Translated and edited by G. W. Bromiley. New York: Harper Torchbooks, 1961.

———. *Evangelical Theology: An Introduction.* New York: Holt, Rinehart, and Winston, 1965.

Beckwith, Roger. *The Old Testament Canon of the New Testament Church and Its Background in Early Judaism.* Grand Rapids: Eerdmans, 1986.

Behe, Michael J. *Darwin's Black Box.* New York: The Free Press, 1996.

Berkouwer, G. C. *Holy Scripture.* Translated by Jack Rogers. Grand Rapids: Eerdmans, 1975.

Bimson, John, and David Livingston. "Redating the Exodus" in *Biblical Archeology Review* (September-October 1987).

Blackstone, Sir William. *Commentaries on the Laws of England.* London: Strahan, 1809.

Blaiklock, E. M., and R. K. Harrison, eds. *The New International Dictionary of Biblical Archaeology.* Grand Rapids: Zondervan, 1983.

Blomberg, Craig. *The Historical Reliability of the Gospels.* Downers Grove, Ill.: InterVarsity, 1987.

Boyd, Gregory A. *Jesus Under Siege.* Wheaton, Ill.: Victor, 1995.

Bromiley, Geoffry, ed. "Accommodation" in *International Encyclopedia of Bible and Ethics.* Revised edition. Grand Rapids: Eerdmans, 1979.

Bruce, F. F. *The New Testament Documents, Are They Reliable?* Downers Grove, Ill.: InterVarsity, 1960.

Brunner, Emil. *The Christian Doctrine of God.* Volume 1 (*Dogmatics*). Translated by Olive Wyon. London: Lutterworth, 1949.

———. *God and Man. Four Essays on the Nature of Personality.* Translated by David Cairns. London: Student Christian Movement, 1936.

———. *Revelation and Reason.* Philadelphia: Westminster, 1946.

———. *The Word of God and Modern Man.* Translated by David Cairns. Richmond, Va.: John Knox, 1964.

Buber, Martin. *I and Thou.* 2nd edition. Translated by Ronald Gregor Smith. New York: Charles Scribner's Sons, 1958.

Bultmann, Rudolph. "Aleithia" in *Theological Dictionary of the New Testament.* Edited by Gerhard Kittel and Gerhard Friedrich. Grand Rapids: Eerdmans, 1994.

———. *Kerygma and Myth: A Theological Debate.* Edited by Hans Werner Bartsch. Translated by Reginald H. Fuller. London: Billing & Sons, 1954.

Burrell, David B. *Analogy and Philosophical Language.* New Haven, Conn.: Yale University Press, 1973.

Burrows, Millar. *More Light on the Dead Sea Scrolls.* New York: Viking, 1958.

Burtchaelle, James Tustead. *Catholic Theories of Inspiration Since 1810.* Cambridge: Cambridge University Press, 1960.

Butler, Joseph. *The Analogy of Religion Natural and Revealed to the Constitution and Course of Nature.* 3rd edition. First published 1872. London: George Routledge and Sons, 1887.

Calvin, John. *Calvin's Commentaries.* 22 volumes. Edited by David W. Torrance and Thomas F. Torrance. Grand Rapids: Eerdmans, 1972.

———. *Institutes of the Christian Religion.* 2 volumes. Edited by John T. McNeill. Translated by Ford Lewis Battles. In *Library of Christian Classics.* Volumes 20–21, edited by John Baillie, John T. McNeill, and Henry P. Van Dusen. Philadelphia: Westminster, 1960.

Carnell, Edward John. *An Introduction to Christian Apologetics: A Philosophic Defense of the Trinitarian-theistic Faith.* 5th edition. Grand Rapids: Eerdmans, 1956.

Carson, D. A. *The Gagging of God.* Grand Rapids: Zondervan, 1996.

———. *The King James Version Debate: A Plea for Realism.* Grand Rapids: Baker, 1979.

Caven, William B. "The Testimony of Christ to the Old Testament" in *The Fundamentals.* Grand Rapids: Baker, 1972.

Childs, Brevard S. *Introduction to the Old Testament as Scripture.* London: SCM, 1983.

Christiansen, Michael J. *C. S. Lewis on Scripture: His Thoughts on the Nature of Biblical Inspiration, the Role of Revelation, and the Question of Inerrancy.* Waco, Tex.: Word, 1979.

Clark, David, and Norman Geisler. *Apologetics in the New Age.* Grand Rapids: Baker, 1990.

Clark, Gordon. *A Christian View of Men and Things.* Grand Rapids: Eerdmans, 1952.

———. *God's Hammer: The Bible and Its Critics.* Jefferson, Md.: Trinity Foundation, 1982.

Clarke, Adam. *Discourses on Various Subjects Relative to the Being and Attributes of God, and His Works in Creation, Providence, and Grace.* London: William Tegg, 1868.

Clarke, Andrew D., and Bruce Hunter, eds. *One God, One Lord: Christianity in a World of Religious Pluralism.* Wheaton, Ill.: Tyndale, 1991.

Collins, David. "Was Noah's Ark Stable?" in *Creation Research Society Quarterly,* Volume 14 (1997).

Comte, Auguste. *The Catechism of Positive Religion.* 3rd edition. Translated by Richard Congreve. London: Kegan Paul, Trench, Trubner, 1858.

———. *Cours: The Positive Philosophy of Auguste Comte.* New York: D. Appleton, 1853.

Copan, Paul. *True for You, But Not for Me.*

Minneapolis: Bethany House, 1998.

Corduan, Winfried. "Transcendentalism: Hegel" in *Biblical Errancy: An Analysis of Its Philosophical Roots*. Edited by Norman L. Geisler. (81–101). Grand Rapids: Zondervan, 1981.

Craig, William. *The Kalam Cosmological Argument*. London: Macmillan, 1979.

———. *Knowing the Truth About the Resurrection*. Revised edition. Ann Arbor, Mich.: Servant, 1981.

Cross, F. L. *The Oxford Dictionary of the Christian Church*. 2nd edition. London: Oxford University Press, 1974.

Custance, Arthur. *The Flood: Local or Global?* Grand Rapids: Zondervan, 1979.

Darwin, Charles. *The Autobiography of Charles Darwin* (original omissions restored). Edited by Nora Darwin Barlow. New York: W. W. Norton, 1993.

———. *The Descent of Man and Selection in Relation to Sex*. New York: D. Appleton, 1896.

———. *On the Origin of Species* (1859). New York: New American Library, 1958.

Darwin, Francis. *The Life and Letters of Charles Darwin*. Volume 3. London: John Murray, 1888.

Dawkins, Richard. *The Blind Watchmaker: Why the Evidence of Evolution Reveals a Universe Without Design*. New York: W. W. Norton, 1996.

Dayton, Wilbur. "Infallibility, Wesley, and British Wesleyanism" in *Inerrancy and the Church*. Edited by John Hannah. Chicago: Moody Press, 1984.

Deissman, Adolph. *Light From the Ancient East*. Translated by L. R. M. Strachan. New York: Harper, 1923.

Demarest, Bruce A. *General Revelation: Historical Views and Contemporary Issues*. Grand Rapids: Zondervan, 1983.

Denton, Michael. *Evolution: A Theory in Crisis*. Bethesda, Md.: Adler & Adler, 1985.

Denzinger, Henry. *The Documents of Vatican II*. Edited by Walter M. Abbot. New York: Guild Press, 1966.

———. *The Sources of Catholic Dogma*. Translated by Roy J. Deferrari. London: B. Herder, 1957.

Derrida, Jacque. *Of Grammatology*. Baltimore: John Hopkins University Press, 1976.

———. *Limited, Inc*. Evanston, Ill.: Northwestern University Press, 1988.

———. *Speech and Phenomena*. Evanston, Ill.: Northwestern University Press, 1973.

———. *Writing and Differance*. Chicago: University of Chicago Press, 1978.

Descartes, René. *Discourse on Method*. Indianapolis: Hackett, 1980.

———. *Meditations*. Translated by L. Lafleur. New York: Liberal Arts, 1951.

Dewey, John. *A Common Faith*. London: Yale University Press, 1934.

———. *Logic: The Theory of Inquiry*. New York:

Henry Holt and Company, 1938.

DeWolf, L. Harold. *The Case for Theology in Liberal Perspective*. Philadelphia: Westminster, 1959.

———. *A Theology of the Living Church*. New York: Harper & Brothers, 1960.

Dodd, C. H. *The Authority of the Bible*. London: n.p., 1928.

Dooyeweerd, Herman. *A New Critique of Theoretical Thought*. 4 volumes. Ontario: Paideia, 1984.

Edwards, Jonathan. "Miscellanies" in *The Works of Jonathan Edwards*. 2 volumes. Carlisle, Pa.: Banner of Truth, 1974.

———. "Ordination of Mr. Billing," cited by John Gerstner in *The Nature of Inspiration*, 27.

Edwards, Paul, ed. "Comte, Auguste" in *Encyclopedia of Philosophy*. 8 volumes. New York: Macmillan and The Free Press, 1967.

Einstein, Albert. *Ideas and Opinions—The World As I See It*. 3rd edition. New York: Crown, 1982.

Eslick, Leonard J. "The Real Distinction: Reply to Professor Resse" in *Modern Schoolman*. Volume 38 (January, 1961), 149–60.

Estrada, David, and William White, Jr. *The First New Testament*. Nashville: Thomas Nelson, 1978.

Eusebius. *The Ecclesiastical History*. Grand Rapids: Baker, 1990.

Evans, C. Stephen, and Merold Westphal, eds. *Christian Perspectives on Religious Knowledge*. Grand Rapids: Eerdmans, 1993.

Ferre, Frederick. "Analogy" in *Encyclopedia of Philosophy*. Volume 1. Edited by Paul Edwards. New York: Macmillan and The Free Press, 1967.

Feuerbach, Ludwig. *The Essence of Christianity*. Translated by George Eliot. New York: Harper Torchbooks, 1957.

Findlay, J. N. "Can God's Existence Be Disproved?" in *The Ontological Argument*. Edited by Alvin Plantinga. Garden City, N.Y.: Doubleday, 1965.

Fisher, E. "New Testament Documents Among the Dead Sea Scrolls?" in *The Bible Today*. Collegeville, Minn.: 1972.

Flew, Antony. "Miracles" in *Encyclopedia of Philosophy*. Volume 5. New York: Macmillan and The Free Press, 1967.

———. "Theology and Falsification" in the *New Essays in Philosophical Theology*. London: SCM, 1963.

Flint, Robert. *Agnosticism*. New York: Charles Scribner's Sons, 1903.

Ford, Lewis. "Biblical Recital and Process Philosophy" in *Interpretation*. Volume 26 (1972).

Fosdick, Harry Emerson. *A Great Time to Be Alive*. New York: Harper & Brothers, 1944.

———. *A Guide to Understanding the Bible*. New York: Harper & Brothers, 1938.

Foxe, John. *Acts and Monuments of Matters Most Special and Memorable, Happening in the*

Church. 4th edition. London: John Daye, 1583.

Frazer, James G. *The Golden Bough.* London: Macmillan, 1890. One-volume abridged edition. New York: Crown, 1981.

Frege, Gottlob. *Uber Sinn und Bedeutung* in *Translations From the Philosophical Writings of Gottlob Frege.* Edited by Peter Geach and Max Black. Oxford: Blackwell, 1980.

Freud, Sigmund. *The Future of an Illusion.* Translated by W. D. Robson-Scott. New York: Doubleday, 1957.

Garnet, P. "O'Callahan's Fragments: Our Earliest New Testament Texts?" in *Evangelical Quarterly* 45 (1972).

Garrigou-LaGrange, Reginald. *God: His Existence and His Nature.* 2 volumes. St. Louis: B. Herder, 1934–36.

Gaussen, S. R. L. *Theopnuestia: The Bible, Its Divine Origin and Inspiration, Deduced from Internal Evidence and the Testimonies of Nature, History, and Science.* Revised edition. New York: Jennings & Pye, 1867.

Geisler, Norman L. "The Anthropic Principle" in *BECA.*

———. *Baker Encyclopedia of Christian Apologetics (BECA).* Grand Rapids: Baker, 1999.

———. "Beware of Philosophy." *Christian Apologetics Journal* 2 (Spring 1999), 15–30.

———. "Bible, Inspiration of" in *BECA.*

———. "The Bible, Jesus' View of" in *BECA.*

———, ed. *Biblical Errancy: An Analysis of Its Philosophical Roots.* Grand Rapids: Zondervan, 1981.

———. "Christ, Deity of" in *BECA.*

———. *Christian Apologetics.* Grand Rapids: Baker, 1976.

———. *Decide for Yourself: How History Views the Bible.* Grand Rapids: Zondervan, 1982.

———. "The Extent of The Old Testament Canon" in *Current Issues in Biblical and Patristic Interpretation.* Edited by Gerald F. Hawthorne. Grand Rapids: Eerdmans, 1975.

———. "Geneaologies, Open or Closed" in *BECA.*

———. "God, Alleged Disproofs of" in *BECA.*

———. "God, Evidence for" in *BECA.*

———. "God's Revelation in Scripture and Nature" in *The Opening of the American Mind.* Edited by David Beck. Grand Rapids: Baker, 1991.

———. "John, Gospel of" in *BECA.*

———. "Kant" in *BECA.*

———. *Knowing the Truth About Creation: How It Happened and What It Means to Us.* Ann Arbor, Mich.: Servant, 1989.

———. *Miracles and the Modern Mind.* Grand Rapids: Baker, 1992.

———. "Prophecy, as Proof of the Bible" in *BECA.*

———. *Thomas Aquinas: An Evangelical Appraisal.* Grand Rapids: Baker, 1991.

———. "Truth, Nature of" in *BECA.*

Geisler, Norman L., and J. Kerby Anderson. *Origin Science: A Proposal for the Creation-Evolution Controversy.* Grand Rapids: Baker, 1987.

Geisler, Norman L., and Ronald M. Brooks. *Come Let Us Reason: An Introduction to Logical Thinking.* Grand Rapids: Baker, 1990.

Geisler, Norman L., and Winfried Corduan. *Philosophy of Religion.* 2nd edition. Grand Rapids: Baker, 1988.

Geisler, Norman L., and Thomas Howe. *When Critics Ask.* Wheaton, Ill.: Victor, 1992.

Geisler, Norman L., and Ralph MacKenzie. *Roman Catholics and Evangelicals: Agreements and Differences.* Grand Rapids: Baker, 1995.

Geisler, Norman L., and William E. Nix. *A General Introduction to the Bible.* Revised edition. Chicago: Moody, 1986.

Geisler, Norman L., and Abdul Saleeb. *Answering Islam: The Crescent in the Light of the Cross.* Grand Rapids: Baker, 1993.

Geisler, Norman L., and William D. Watkins. *Worlds Apart: A Handbook on World Views.* Grand Rapids: Baker, 1989.

Geisler, Norman L., et al. *The Counterfeit Gospel of Mormonism.* Edited by Dennis L. Okholm and Timothy R. Phillips. Eugene, Ore.: Harvest House, 1988.

Geisler, Norman L., ed. *Inerrancy.* Grand Rapids: Zondervan, 1979.

Geivett, Douglas R., et al. *Four Views on Salvation in a Pluralistic World.* Edited by Dennis L. Okholm and Timothy R. Phillips. Grand Rapids: Zondervan, 1996.

Geivett, Douglas R., and Gary Habermas, eds. *In Defense of Miracles: A Comprehensive Case for God's Action in History.* Downers Grove, Ill.: InterVarsity, 1997.

Gerstner, John H. "Jonathan Edwards and the Bible" in *Inerrancy and the Church.* Edited by John Hannah. Chicago: Moody Press, 1984.

Gilson, Étienne. *Linguistics and Philosophy.* South Bend, Ind.: University of Notre Dame Press, 1988.

———. *The Unity of Philosophical Experience.* New York: Charles Scribner's Sons, 1937.

Glueck, Nelson. *Rivers in the Desert: A History of the Negev.* New York: Farrar, Strauss & Cudahy, 1959.

Gnanakan, Ken. *The Pluralistic Predicament.* Bangalore, India: Theological Book Trust, 1992.

Gonzalez, Justo L. *A History of Christian Thought.* Volume 3: *From the Reformation to the Twentieth Century.* Nashville: Abingdon, 1975.

Gould, Stephen J. "Evolution's Erratic Pace" in *Natural History* 86 (1977).

Greenleaf, Simon. *The Testimony of the Evangelists* (1874). Grand Rapids: Baker, 1984.

Gregory the Great. "The Commentary on Job" in *The Library of Christian Classics.* (n.p., n.d.).

Habermas, Gary. *The Historical Jesus: Ancient*

Evidence for the Life of Christ. Joplin, Mo.: College Press, 1996.

———. "Why I Believe the New Testament Is Historically Reliable" in Norman Geisler and Paul Hoffman, eds. *Why I Am a Christian.* Grand Rapids: Baker, 2001.

Hackett, Stuart. *The Resurrection of Theism.* Chicago: Moody, 1957.

Hannah, John, ed. *Inerrancy and the Church.* Chicago: Moody, 1984.

Hawking, Stephen. *A Brief History of Time: From the Big Bang to Black Holes.* New York: Bantam, 1988.

Heeren, Fred. *Show Me God: What the Message From Space Is Telling Us About God.* Wheeling, Ill.: Search Light, 1995.

Hegel, G. W. F. *Early Theological Writing.* Philadelphia: University of Pennsylvania Press, 1988.

———. *Encyclopedia of Philosophy.* New York: Philosophical Library, 1959.

———. *Logic.* Oxford: Clarendon, 1975.

———. *Phenomenology of Spirit.* University Park: Pennsylvania State University, 1994.

———. *Philosophy of History.* New York: Wiley, 1944.

Hemer, Colin J. *The Book of Acts in the Setting of Hellenistic History.* Winona Lake, Ind.: Eisenbrauns, 1990.

Henry, Carl F. H. *God, Revelation, and Authority.* Volume 2: *God Who Speaks and Shows: Fifteen Theses, Part One.* Waco, Tex.: Word, 1976.

———. *God, Revelation, and Authority.* Volume 3: *God Who Speaks and Shows: Fifteen Theses, Part Two.* Waco, Tex.: Word, 1979.

———. *God, Revelation, and Authority.* Volume 4: *God Who Speaks and Shows: Fifteen Theses, Part Three.* Waco, Tex.: Word, 1979.

———. *Revelation and the Bible.* Grand Rapids: Baker, 1958.

Hick, John. *An Interpretation of Religion: Human Responses to the Transcendent.* London: Macmillan, 1989.

———. *The Metaphor of God Incarnate: Christology in a Pluralistic Age.* Louisville: Westminster/John Knox, 1993.

———. "A Pluralist's View" in *More Than One Way? Four Views on Salvation in a Pluralistic World.* Edited by Dennis L. Okholm and Timothy R. Phillips. Grand Rapids: Zondervan, 1995.

Hobbes, Thomas. *Leviathan* in *Great Books of the Western World.* Volume 23. Edited by Robert M. Hutchins. Chicago: Encyclopaedia Britannica, 1952.

Hodge, Archibald A., and Benjamin B. Warfield. *Inspiration.* Philadelphia: Presbyterian Board of Publication, 1881. Reprint, Grand Rapids: Baker, 1979.

Hodge, Charles. *Systematic Theology.* 3 volumes. New York: Scribner's, 1872. Grand Rapids: Eerdmans, 1940.

———. *What Is Darwinism?* Edited by Mark A. Noll and David N. Livingstone. Grand Rapids: Baker, 1994.

Hoehner, Harold. *Chronological Aspects of the Life of Christ.* Grand Rapids: Zondervan, 1978.

Hooker, Richard. *Of the Laws of Ecclesiastical Polity.* Edited by G. Edelen. Cambridge, Mass.: Harvard University Press, 1977.

Howe, Thomas. "Objectivity in Hermeneutics: A Study of the Nature and of the Role of Presuppositions in Evangelical Hermeneutical Methodology and Their Impact on the Possibility of Objectivity in Biblical Interpretation." Ph.D. dissertation, Southeastern Baptist Theological Seminary, 1998.

Hoyle, Fred. *The Intelligent Universe.* London: Joseph, 1985.

Hoyle, Fred, and N. C. Wickramasinghe. *Evolution From Space.* London: J. M. Dent & Sons, 1981.

Hume, David. *Dialogues Concerning Natural Religion.* Indianapolis: Bobbs-Merrill, 1962.

———. *Enquiry Concerning Human Understanding.* Edited by Chas. W. Hendel. New York: Liberal Arts, 1955.

———. *The Letters of David Hume.* 2 volumes. Edited by J. Y. T. Greig. Oxford: Clarendon, 1932.

Irenaeus. "Against Heresies" in *The Ante-Nicene Fathers.* Edited by Alexander Roberts and James Donaldson. Grand Rapids: Eerdmans, 1885.

Jaki, Stanley L. *Miracles and Physics.* Front Royal, Va.: Christendom, 1989.

James, William. *Pragmaticism. A New Name for Some Old Ways of Thinking: Popular Lectures on Philosophy.* New York: Longmans, Green and Co., 1907.

Jastrow, Robert. *God and the Astronomers.* New York: W. W. Norton, 1978.

———. "A Scientist Caught Between Two Faiths: Interview With Robert Jastrow" in *Christianity Today* (August 6, 1982).

Jefferson, Thomas. *Declaration of Independence.* New York: Harmony Books, 1976.

Jerome. "Preface" to *Jerome's Commentary on Daniel.* Translated by Gleason L. Archer. Grand Rapids: Baker, 1958.

———. *St. Jerome: Select Letters* in the *Loeb Classical Library.* Translated by F. A. Wright. New Haven, Conn.: Harvard University Press, 1992.

Jewett, Paul K. *Man as Male and Female.* Grand Rapids: Eerdmans, 1975.

Johnson, S. Lewis. *Old Testament in the New: An Argument for Biblical Inspiration?* Grand Rapids: Zondervan, 1980.

Josephus, Flavius. "Against Apion" in *The Antiquities of the Jews.* New York: Ward, Lock and Bowden, 1900.

———. *The Antiquities of the Jews.* Translated by William Whiston. London: George Routledge and Sons, 1920.

Kaiser, Walter C., Jr. *The Old Testament Docu-*

ments: Are They Reliable & Relevant? Downers Grove, Ill.: InterVarsity, 2001.

Kant, Immanuel. *Critique of Pure Reason.* Translated by Norman Kemp Smith. New York: St. Martin's, 1965.

———. *Religion Within the Limits of Reason Alone.* New York: Harper & Row, 1960.

Kelly, J. N. D. *Early Christian Doctrines.* New York: Harper & Row, 1960.

Kenny, Anthony. *The Five Ways: St. Thomas Aquinas' Proof of God's Existence.* New York: Schocken, 1969.

Kenyon, Frederick. *The Bible and Archaeology.* New York: Harper, 1940.

———. *Our Bible and the Ancient Manuscripts.* 4th edition. Revised by A. W. Adams. New York: Harper, 1958.

Kierkegaard, Søren. *Concluding Unscientific Postscript 1: Kierkegaard's Writings Volume 12.1.* Edited by Edna H. Hong and Howard V. Hong. Princeton, N.J.: Princeton University Press, 1992.

———. *Fear and Trembling and the Sickness Unto Death.* Translated, with introduction and notes, by Walter Lowrie. New York: Doubleday, 1954.

———. *For Self-Examination and Judge for Yourselves and Three Discourses.* Translated by Walter Lowrie. Princeton, N.J.: Princeton University Press, 1941.

———. *Philosophical Fragments/Johannes Climacus: Kierkegaard's Writings, Volume 7.* Edited by Edna H. Hong. Princeton, N.J.: Princeton University Press, 1985.

———. *The Point of View for My Work as an Author; a Report to History and Related Writings.* Translated by Walter Lowrie. New York: Harper, 1962.

———. *Søren Kierkegaard's Journals and Papers.* Translated by Howard V. Hong and Edna H. Hong. Bloomington, Ind.: Indiana University Press, 1967.

Kilby, Clyde S. *The Christian World of C. S. Lewis.* Grand Rapids: Eerdmans, 1964.

Kitchen, K. A. *Ancient Orient and the Old Testament.* Downers Grove, Ill.: InterVarsity, 1966.

Kline, Meredith G. *Treaty of the Great King: The Covenant Structure of Deuteronomy—Studies and Commentary.* Grand Rapids: Eerdmans, 1963.

Levy-Bruhl, Lucien. *The Philosophy of Auguste Comte.* London: S. Sonnenschein, 1903.

Lewis, C. S. *The Abolition of Man.* New York: Macmillan, 1947.

———. *Christian Reflections.* Edited by Walter Hooper. Grand Rapids: Eerdmans, 1967.

———. *Letters to Malcolm: Chiefly on Prayer.* New York: Harcourt, Brace & World, 1964.

———. *Miracles.* New York: Macmillan, 1947.

———. *Reflections on the Psalms.* New York: Harcourt & Brace, 1958.

Lewis, Jack P. *The English Bible From KJV to NIV: A History and Evaluation.* Grand Rapids: Baker, 1982.

Lightner, Robert. *The Savior and the Scriptures.* Philadelphia: Presbyterian & Reformed, 1966.

Lindsell, Harold. *The Battle for the Bible.* Grand Rapids: Zondervan, 1976.

Linnemann, Eta. *Biblical Criticsm on Trial.* Grand Rapids: Kregel, 2001.

———. "Is There a Q?" in *Biblical Review* (11: October 1995).

———. *Is There a Synoptic Problem? Rethinking the Literary Dependence of the First Three Gospels.* Grand Rapids: Baker, 1990.

Locke, John. *The Reasonableness of Christianity With a Discourse of Miracles and Part of a Third Letter Concerning Toleration.* Stanford: Stanford University Press, 1974.

———. *The Second Treatise of Civil Government and a Letter Concerning Toleration.* Edited by J. W. Gough. Oxford: B. Blackwell, 1948.

Lubenow, Marvin. *Bones of Contention: A Creationist Assessment of the Human Fossils.* Grand Rapids: Baker, 1992.

Lumpkin, William. *Baptist Confessions of Faith.* Chicago: Judson Press, 1959.

Lundin, Roger. *The Culture of Interpretation.* Grand Rapids, Eerdmans, 1993.

Luther, Martin. *Bondage of the Will.* Translated by Henry Cole. Grand Rapids: Baker, 1976.

———. *Works of Martin Luther.* Philadelphia: Muhlenberg Press, 1943.

Lyotard, Jean-Francois. *The Postmodern Condition: A Report on Knowledge.* Minneapolis: University of Minnesota Press, 1984.

MacLaine, Shirley. *Out on a Limb.* New York: Bantam Doubleday Dell, 1983.

Madison, Gary B. *Working Through Derrida.* Evanston, Ill.: Northwestern University, 1993.

Mansoor, Menahem. "The Dead Sea Scrolls" in *New Catholic Encyclopedia,* 2:390. Washington, D.C.: Catholic University Press of America, 1967, 1974, 1979.

———. *New Catholic Encyclopedia.* Washington, D.C.: Catholic University Press of America, 1967, 1974, 1979.

Martin, Michael. *The Case Against Christianity.* Philadelphia: Temple University Press, 1991.

Maurer, Armand. "St. Thomas and the Analogy of Genus" in *New Scholasticism* (29: April 1955).

Mayr, Ernst. "Introduction" in Darwin's *On the Origin of Species.* Cambridge, Mass.: Harvard University Press, 1964.

McCallum, Dennis, ed. *The Death of Truth.* Minneapolis: Bethany House, 1996.

McDonald, H. D. *Theories of Revelation: An Historical Study 1700–1960.* 2 volumes. Twin Books Series. Grand Rapids: Baker, 1979.

McGrath, Alister. "The Challenge of Pluralism for the Contemporary Christian Church" in *Journal of the Evangelical Theological Society* (September 1992).

McInerny, Ralph. *The Logic of Analogy.* The Hague: Nijhoff, 1961.

McMillen, S. I. *None of These Diseases.* Grand

Rapids: Baker, 1984, revised 2000.

Merrill, Eugene. "Ebla and Biblical Historical Inerrancy" in *Bibliotheca Sacra* (140: October-December 1983).

Metzger, Bruce. *Chapters in the History of New Testament Textual Criticism.* Grand Rapids: Eerdmans, 1963.

———. *An Introduction to the Apocrypha.* New York: Oxford University Press, 1957.

———. *Manuscripts of the Greek Bible: An Introduction to Greek Paleography.* New York: Oxford University Press, 1981.

———. *The Text of the New Testament.* New York: Oxford University Press, 1964.

Meuller, G. E. "The Hegel Legend of Thesis, Antithesis-Synthesis" in *Journal of History of Ideas* (19.3: 1958).

Meyerhoff, Hans, ed. *The Philosophy of History in Our Time: An Anthology.* New York: Garland, 1985.

Mibiti, J. S. *African Religion and Philosophy.* London: Heinemann, 1992.

Mill, John Stuart. *Auguste Comte and Positivism.* Bristol, England: Thoemmes, 1993.

———. *A System of Logic: Ratiocinative and Inductive.* 8th edition. New York: Harper, 1874.

———. *Three Essays on Religion: Nature, Utility of Religion, and Theism.* London: Longmans & Green, 1885.

Mondin, Battista. *The Principle of Analogy in Protestant and Catholic Theology.* The Hague: Nijhoff, 1963.

Moore, James R. *The Post-Darwinian Controversies.* New York: Cambridge University Press, 1979.

Morris, Leon. *I Believe in Revelation.* Grand Rapids: Eerdmans, 1976.

Mossner, E. C. *Bishop Butler and the Age of Reason.* New York: Macmillan, 1936.

Muller, Julius. *The Theory of Myths, in Its Application to the Gospel History, Examined and Confuted.* London: John Chapman, 1844.

Nash, Ronald. *Is Jesus the Only Savior?* Grand Rapids: Zondervan, 1994.

———. *The Word of God and the Mind of Man.* Phillipsburg, N.J.: Presbyterian & Reformed, 1992.

Netland, Harold. *Dissonant Voices: Religious Pluralism and the Question of Truth.* Grand Rapids: Eerdmans, 1991.

Neuner, S. J., and J. Dupuis. *The Christian Faith: Doctrinal Documents of the Catholic Church.* 5th revised edition. New York: Alba House, 1990.

Nielsen, Niels C., Jr., "Analogy and the Knowledge of God: An Ecumenical Appraisal" in *Rice University Studies* (60: 1974).

Ogden, Schubert M. "The Authority of Scripture for Theology" in *Interpretation* (30: July 1976).

———. "On Revelation" in *Our Common History as Christians: Essays in Honor of Albert C. Outler.* 1975: 261–92.

Orchard, B. "A Fragment of St. Mark's Gospel Dating From Before A.D. 50?" in *Biblical Apostolate* (6: 1972).

Orgel, Leslie. *The Origins of Life.* New York: Wiley, 1973.

Pache, Rene. *The Inspiration and Authority of Scripture.* Translated by Helen I. Needham. Chicago: Moody, 1969.

Packer, J. I. *"Fundamentalism" and the Word of God.* Grand Rapids: Eerdmans, 1958.

Paine, Thomas. *Complete Works of Thomas Paine.* Edited by Calvin Blanchard. Chicago: Belford, 1885.

Paley, William. *Natural Theology.* Houston: St. Thomas Press, 1972.

Parmenides. "Proem." in G. S. Kirk, et al., *The Presocratic Philosophers.* Cambridge: Cambridge University Press, 1964.

Philips, Timothy R., and Dennis L. Okholm, eds. *Christian Apologetics in the Postmodern World.* Downers Grove, Ill.: InterVarsity, 1995.

Pickering, Wilbur N. *The Identity of the New Testament Text.* Nashville: Thomas Nelson, 1977.

Pierce, Charles Sanders. In *Popular Science Monthly* (1878).

Pinnock, Clark. *A Wideness in God's Mercy.* Grand Rapids: Zondervan, 1992.

Plato. *Cratylus.* Translated by C. D. C. Reeve. Indianapolis: Hackett, 1998.

———. *Meno.* n.p., n.d.

———. "Parmenides" in *The Collected Dialogues of Plato.* Edited by Edith Hamilton and Huntington Cairns. New York: Pantheon, 1964.

———. "Sophist" in *The Collected Dialogues of Plato.* Edited by Edith Hamilton and Huntington Cairns. New York: Pantheon, 1964.

———. "Timaeus" in *The Collected Dialogues of Plato.* Edited by Edith Hamilton and Huntington Cairns. New York: Pantheon, 1964.

Polanyi, Michael. "Life Transcending Physics and Chemistry" in *Chemical Engineering News* (August 21, 1967).

Pritchard, James B., ed. *The Ancient Near East.* Volume 2 of *A New Anthology of Texts and Pictures.* Princeton, N.J.: Princeton University Press, 1975.

Ramm, Bernard. *The Pattern of Religious Authority.* Grand Rapids: Eerdmans, 1959.

———. *Protestant Biblical Interpretation: A Textbook of Hermeneutics for Conservative Protestants.* Boston: W. A. Wilde, 1950.

Ramsay, William. *Luke the Physician.* Grand Rapids: Baker, 1956.

———. *St. Paul the Traveler and the Roman Citizen.* New York: G. P. Putnam's Sons, 1896.

Ramsey, Ian. *Models and Mystery.* London: Oxford University Press, 1964.

Rehwinkel, Alfred. *The Flood.* St. Louis: Concordia, 1951.

Renan, Ernest. *The Life of Jesus.* New York: A. L. Burt, 1897.

Reu, M. *Luther and the Scriptures.* Columbus, Ohio: Wartburg, 1944. Reissued with correction to notes in *The Springfielder.* Springfield, Ill.: Concordia Theological Seminary, August 1960.

Rice, John R. *Our God-Breathed Book—The Bible.* Murfreesboro, Tenn.: Sword of the Lord, 1969.

Riplinger, Gail. *New Age Bible Versions.* Ararat: A.V. Publications, 1995.

———. *Which Bible Is God's Word?* Oklahoma City: Hearthstone, 1994.

Robertson, A. T. *An Introduction to the Textual Criticism of the New Testament.* Nashville: Broadman, 1925.

Robinson, John A. T. *Redating the New Testament.* Philadelphia: Westminster, 1976.

Rogers, Jack B., and Donald K. McKim. *The Authority and Interpretation of the Bible: An Historical Approach.* San Francisco: Harper & Row, 1979.

Rogers, Jack B., ed. *Biblical Authority.* Waco, Tex.: Word, 1978.

Ross, Hugh. *The Fingerprint of God: Recent Scientific Discoveries Reveal the Unmistakable Identity of the Creator.* Orange, Calif.: Promise, 1989.

Ruckman, Peter. *The Christian's Handbook of Manuscript Evidence.* Pensacola, Fla.: Pensacola Bible Press, 1976.

———. *Why I Believe the King James Version Is the Word of God.* Pensacola, Fla.: Bible Baptist Bookstore, 1988.

Rurak, James. "Butler's Analogy: A Still Interesting Synthesis of Reason and Revelation" in *Anglican Theological Review* (62: October 1980).

Russell, Bertrand. *Why I Am Not a Christian.* New York: Simon & Schuster, 1957.

Sagan, Carl. *Broca's Brain.* New York: Random House, 1979.

———. *Cosmos.* New York: Random House, 1980.

Sandage, Alan. "A Scientist Reflects on Religious Belief" in *Truth.* Volume 1. Dallas: Truth Incorporated, 1985.

Saphir, Adolph. *Christ and the Scriptures.* Kilmarnock, Scotland: Ritchie, n.d.

Sauer, Erich. *The Dawn of World Redemption.* Translated by G. H. Lang. London: Paternoster, 1951.

———. *The Triumph of the Crucified.* Translated by G. H. Lang. London: Paternoster, 1951.

Saussure, Ferdinand. *Cours de Linguistique Generale* [*Course in General Linguistics*]. London: Fontana/Collins, 1974.

Schaff, Philip. *A Companion to the Greek Testament and English Version.* 3rd edition. New York: Harper, 1883.

———. *The Creeds of Christendom.* 3 volumes. 6th revised edition. New York: Harper, 1919.

Schaff, Philip, ed. *Nicene and Post-Nicene Fathers of the Christian Church.* 14 volumes. 1st series (1886–94). Grand Rapids: Eerdmans, 1952.

Schleiermacher, Friedrich. *The Christian Faith.* Philadelphia: Fortress, 1976.

———. *On Religion.* New York: Cambridge University Press, 1996.

Schmidt, W. *High Gods in North America.* Oxford: Clarendon, 1933.

Scotus, John Duns. *Philosophical Writings.* Translated, with an introduction, by Allan Wolter. Indianapolis: Bobbs-Merrill, 1962.

Scrivener, F. H. *The Authorized Edition of the English Bible* (1611). Cambridge, England: The University Press, 1884.

Shedd, W. G. T. *Dogmatic Theology.* Volume 1. New York: Charles Scribner's Sons, 1868–94.

Sheler, Jeffery. *Is the Bible True?* San Francisco: Harper & Row, 1999.

Sherwin-White, A. N. *Roman Society and Roman Law in the New Testament.* Oxford: Clarendon, 1963.

Souter, Alexander. *The Text and Canon of the New Testament.* London: Duckworth, 1913. Reprint. Edited by C. S. C. Williams. Naperville, Ill.: Allenson, 1954.

Spinoza, Benedict. *Ethics.* Translated by A. Boyle. New York: Dutton, 1910.

———. *A Theologico-Political Treatise and a Political Treatise.* Translated, with introduction, by R. H. M. Elwes. New York: Dover, 1951.

Sproul, R. C. *Explaining Inerrancy: A Commentary.* Oakland, Calif.: International Council on Biblical Inerrancy, 1980.

———. *Not a Chance: The Myth of Chance in Modern Science and Cosmology.* Grand Rapids: Baker, 1994.

Stokes, George. *International Standard Bible Encyclopedia.* Chicago: The Howard-Severance Company, 1915.

Suzuki, D. T. *An Introduction to Zen Buddhism.* New York: Grove, 1964.

Swinburne, Richard. *Miracles.* New York: Macmillan, 1989.

Tanner, Gerald and Sandra. *The Changing World of Mormonism.* Chicago: Moody, 1981.

Tenney, Merrill Chapin. *The Bible: The Living Word of Revelation, With Essays by John H. Gerstner [and others].* Grand Rapids: Zondervan, 1968.

Tertullian. *On Exhortation to Chastity* in *The Nicene and Post-Nicene Fathers.* 14 volumes. 1st series (1886–94). Edited by Philip Schaff. Grand Rapids: Eerdmans, 1952.

Teske, R. J. "Plato's Later Dialectic" in *The Modern Schoolman* (38: March 1961).

Thaxton, Charles B., Walter L. Bradley, and Roger Olsen. *The Mystery of Life's Origin: Reassessing Current Theories.* New York: Philosophical Library, 1984.

———. "The New Hampshire Declaration of Faith" in E. Y. Mullins, *Baptist Beliefs.* Louisville: Baptist World Publishing Company, 1912.

Thomas, Robert, et al. *The Jesus Crisis.* Grand Rapids: Kregel, 1998.

Trueblood, D. Elton. *Philosophy of Religion.* New York: Harper & Brothers, 1957.

Turretin, Francis. *The Doctrine of Scripture.* Grand Rapids: Baker, 1981.

———. *Institutes of Elenctic Theology.* Phillipsburg, N.J.: Presbyterian and Reformed, 1992.

Urquhart, John. *Inspiration and Accuracy of the Holy Scriptures.* London: Marshall Brothers, n.d.

Van Til, Cornelius. *The Defense of the Faith.* Philadelphia: Presbyterian & Reformed, 1955.

Vos, Howard H. "Albright, William Foxwell" in *Evangelical Dictionary of Theology.* Grand Rapids: Baker, 1984.

Walker, Williston. *A History of the Christian Church.* 3rd edition. Revised by Robert T. Handy. New York: Charles Scribner's Sons, 1970.

Ware, Kallistos. "Christian Theology in the East: 600–1453" in Hubert Cauliffe-Jones, ed., *A History in Christian Doctrine.* Philadelphia: Fortress, 1980.

Warfield, B. B. *The Inspiration and Authority of the Bible.* Philadelphia: Presbyterian & Reformed, 1948.

———. *Limited Inspiration.* Grand Rapids: Baker, 1991.

Watson, Richard. *Theological Institutes.* New York: T. Mason and G. Lane, 1936.

Weinberg, Steven. *Dreams of a Final Theory— The Search for the Fundamental Laws of Nature.* New York: Pantheon, 1992.

Wells, David F. *No Place for Truth.* Grand Rapids: Eerdmans, 1993.

Wenham, John. *Christ and the Bible.* Downers Grove, Ill.: InterVarsity, 1972.

———. "Christ's View of Scripture" in *Inerrancy.* Edited by Norman Geisler. Grand Rapids: Zondervan, 1979.

———. *Redating Matthew, Mark, and Luke: A Fresh Assault on the Synoptic Problem.* Downers Grove, Ill.: InterVarsity, 1992.

Wesley, John. *The Works of John Wesley.* Grand Rapids: Baker, 1996.

Westcott, Brooke Foss. *A General Survey of the History of the Canon of the New Testament.* 6th edition. New York: Macmillan, 1889. Reprint. Grand Rapids: Baker, 1980.

———. *An Introduction to the Study of the Gospels.* 7th edition. London: Macmillan, 1888.

———. *New Catholic Encyclopedia.* No publication data.

———. *St. Joseph Edition of The New American Bible.* No publication data.

Whateley, Richard. *Historic Doubts Concerning the Existence of Napoleon Bonaparte in Famous Pamphlets.* Grand Rapids: Eerdmans, 1954.

Whitcomb, John. *Darius the Mede.* Grand Rapids: Presbyterian and Reformed, 1975.

Whitcomb, John, and Henry Morris. *The Genesis Flood: The Biblical Record and Its Scientific Implications.* Philadelphia: Presbyterian and Reformed, 1961.

White, James R. *The King James Only Controversy.* Minneapolis: Bethany House, 1995.

White, W., Jr. "O'Callahan's Identifications: Confirmation and Its Consequences" in *The Westminster Journal* (35: 1972).

Whitehead, Alfred North, and Bertrand Russell. *Principia Mathematica.* New York: Cambridge University Press, 1964.

Wiles, M. F. "Theodore of Mopsuestia as Representative of the Antiochene School" in *The Cambridge History of the Bible.* Edited by P. R. Ackroyd and C. F. Evans. New York: Cambridge University Press, 1978.

Wilson, Clifford A. *Rocks, Relics, and Biblical Reliability.* Grand Rapids: Zondervan, 1977.

Wiseman, P. J. *Ancient Records and the Structure of Genesis.* Nashville: Thomas Nelson, 1985.

Wittgenstein, Ludwig. *Philosophical Investigations.* New York: Macmillan, 1953.

Wolterstorff, Nicholas. *Divine Discourse.* New York: Cambridge University Press, 1995.

Woodbridge, John D. *Biblical Authority: A Critique of the Roger/McKim Proposal.* Grand Rapids: Zondervan, 1982.

Woodmorappe, John. *Noah's Ark: A Feasibility Study* in *Impact* (March 1996).

Yamauchi, Edwin. "Easter—Myth, Hallucination, or History" (2 parts) in *Christianity Today* (March 29, 1974; April 15, 1974).

———. *The Stones and the Scriptures.* Philadelphia: J. B. Lippincott, 1972.

Yockey, Herbert P. "Self-Organization, Origin of Life Scenarios and Information Theory" in *The Journal of Theoretical Biology* (91: 1981).

Young, David A. *The Biblical Flood: A Case Study of the Church's Response to Extrabiblical Evidence.* Grand Rapids: Eerdmans, 1995.

SCRIPTURE INDEX

SUBJECT INDEX